Communications in Computer and Information Science 739

Commenced Publication in 2007
Founding and Former Series Editors:
Alfredo Cuzzocrea, Orhun Kara, Dominik Ślęzak, and Xiaokang Yang

More information about this series at http://www.springer.com/series/7899

Gennaro Costagliola · James Uhomoibhi
Susan Zvacek · Bruce M. McLaren (Eds.)

Computers Supported Education

8th International Conference, CSEDU 2016
Rome, Italy, April 21–23, 2016
Revised Selected Papers

Springer

Editors
Gennaro Costagliola
University of Salerno
Fisciano
Italy

Susan Zvacek
University of Denver
Denver, CO
USA

James Uhomoibhi
Ulster University
Belfast
UK

Bruce M. McLaren
Carnegie Mellon University
Pittsburgh, PA
USA

ISSN 1865-0929 ISSN 1865-0937 (electronic)
Communications in Computer and Information Science
ISBN 978-3-319-63183-7 ISBN 978-3-319-63184-4 (eBook)
DOI 10.1007/978-3-319-63184-4

Library of Congress Control Number: 2017945736

Printed on acid-free paper

This Springer imprint is published by Springer Nature
The registered company is Springer International Publishing AG
The registered company address is: Gewerbestrasse 11, 6330 Cham, Switzerland

Preface

This book includes extended and revised versions of selected papers from the 8th International Conference on Computer-Supported Education (CSEDU 2016), which was held in Rome, Italy, during April 21–23, 2016.

CSEDU 2016 received 164 paper submissions from 49 countries, of which 15% were deemed academically deserving of inclusion in this volume. The papers in this book were selected by the event chairs, based on a number of criteria including the comments of Program Committee members, the session chairs' assessment, and the program chairs' assessments. The authors of the selected papers were then invited to submit revised and extended versions of their papers with at least 30% new material.

CSEDU is an annual meeting held in a different European venue each year. Past locations have been: Lisbon, Valencia, Noordwijkerhout, Oporto, Aachen, Barcelona, and Rome. The conference provides an opportunity for researchers and practitioners to present and discuss new educational environments, best practices, and case studies of innovative technology-based learning strategies, and institutional policies on computer-supported education including open and distance education. CSEDU 2016 covered state-of-the-art instructional technologies, as well as emerging trends. The conference also promoted lively discussion about the pedagogical potential of new learning and instructional technologies in academic and corporate environments.

The papers selected for this book contribute to the understanding of trends in current research on computer-supported education, including games-based learning, collaborative learning, intelligent tutoring systems, MOOCs, and online learning. Additionally, topics related to healthy aging and e-health are represented by papers that explore the use of digital games among senior populations and how gaming may influence quality of life, attitudes, and learning.

We would like to thank all of the authors for their contributions, as well as the reviewers who helped to ensure the high quality of this publication.

February 2017

Gennaro Costagliola
James Uhomoibhi
Susan Zvacek
Bruce M. McLaren

Organization

Conference Chair

Bruce M. McLaren	Carnegie Mellon University, USA

Program Co-chairs

Susan Zvacek	University of Denver, USA
James Uhomoibhi	University of Ulster, UK
Gennaro Costagliola	Università di Salerno, Italy

Program Committee

Mehdi Adda	Université du Québec à Rimouski, Canada
Carlos Alario-Hoyos	Universdad Carlos III, Spain
Peter Albion	University of Southern Queensland, Australia
Nelma Albuquerque	Concepts and Insights, The Netherlands
Efthimios Alepis	University of Piraeus, Greece
George Anastassakis	University of Piraeus, Greece
Galia Angelova	Institute of Information and Communication Technologies, Bulgarian Academy of Sciences, Bulgaria
Inmaculada Arnedillo-Sanchez	Trinity College Dublin, Ireland
Juan Ignacio Asensio	University of Valladolid, Spain
Anders Avdic	Dalarna University, Sweden
Breno Fabrício Terra Azevedo	Instituto Federal de Educação, Ciência e Tecnologia Fluminense, Brazil
Adriano Baratè	Università degli Studi di Milano, Italy
Jorge Barbosa	UNISINOS, Brazil
Clemens Bechter	TBS, Thailand
Patricia Alejandra Behar	Universidade Federal do Rio Grande do Sul, Brazil
Lilia Cheniti Belcadhi	University of Sousse, Tunisia
Kay Berkling	Cooperative State University Baden Württemberg, Karlsruhe, Germany
Marlies Bitter-Rijpkema	Open University, The Netherlands
Lars Bollen	Universiteit Twente, The Netherlands
Andreas Bollin	Klagenfurt University, Austria
Elmar-Laurent Borgmann	Hochschule Koblenz, University of Applied Sciences, Germany
Ivana Bosnic	University of Zagreb, Croatia
Federico Botella	Miguel Hernandez University of Elche, Spain

Mikuláš Gangur	University of West Bohemia, Czech Republic
Sébastien George	Université du Maine, France
Ramon Fabregat Gesa	Universitat de Girona, Spain
Biswadip Ghosh	Metropolitan State University of Denver, USA
David Gibson	Curtin University, Australia
Henrique Gil	Escola Superior de Educação do Instituto Politécnico de Castelo Branco, Portugal
Manuel Castro Gil	National University for Distance Education, Spain
Blandine Ginon	University of Birmingham, France
Mercè Gisbert	Universitat Rovira i Virgili, Spain
Anabela Gomes	Polytechnic Institute of Coimbra, Portugal
Cristina Azevedo Gomes	Instituto Politécnico de Viseu, Portugal
Maria João Gomes	Universidade do Minho, Portugal
Nuno Pina Gonçalves	Polythecnical Institute of Setúbal, Portugal
Anandha Gopalan	Imperial College London, UK
Angela Guercio	Kent State University, USA
Christian Guetl	Graz University of Technology, Austria
Nathalie Guin	Université Claude Bernard Lyon 1, France
David Guralnick	Kaleidoscope Learning, USA
Leontios Hadjileontiadis	Aristotle University of Thessaloniki, Greece
Ibrahim A. Hameed	Norwegian University of Science and Technology (NTNU), Ålesund, Norway
Yasunari Harada	Waseda University, Japan
Roger Hartley	University of Leeds, UK
George Hloupis	Technological Educational Institute of Athens, Greece
Kin-chuen Hui	Chinese University of Hong Kong, Hong Kong, SAR China
Marc Jansen	University of Applied Sciences Ruhr West, Germany
Stéphanie Jean-Daubias	Université Claude Bernard Lyon 1/LIRIS, France
Jelena Jovanovic	University of Belgrade, Serbia
Michail Kalogiannakis	University of Crete, Greece
Achilles Kameas	Hellenic Open University, Greece
Atis Kapenieks	Riga Technical University, Latvia
Charalampos Karagiannidis	University of Thessaly, Greece
Ilias Karasavvidis	University of Thessaly, Greece
Göran Karlsson	KTH Stockholm, Sweden
Jalal Kawash	University of Calgary, Canada
Samer Khasawneh	The College of Wooster, USA
Maria Kordaki	University of the Aegean, Greece
Miroslav Kulich	Czech Technical University in Prague, Czech Republic
Jean-Marc Labat	Université Pierre et Marie Curie, France
Timo Lainema	Turku School of Economics and Business Administration, Finland
Elicia Lanham	Deakin University, Australia

George Palaigeorgiou	University of Western Macedonia, Greece
José Palma	Escola Superior de Tecnologia de Setúbal, Portugal
Viktoria Pammer	Know-Center, Austria
Kyparisia A. Papanikolaou	School of Pedagogical and Technological Education, Greece
Iraklis Paraskakis	South East European Research Centre, Greece
Francisco García Peñalvo	Salamanca University, Spain
Emanuel Peres	University of Trás-os-Montes e Alto Douro/Inesc-Tec, Portugal
Donatella Persico	Consiglio Nazionale Ricerche (CNR), Italian National Research Council, Italy
Antonio Ramón Bartolomé Pina	Universitat de Barcelona, Spain
Niels Pinkwart	Humboldt University, Germany
Elvira Popescu	University of Craiova, Romania
Petra Poulová	University of Hradec Králové, Czech Republic
Philippos Pouyioutas	University of Nicosia, Cyprus
Khalid Rabayah	Arab American University, Palestinian Territory, Occupied
Eliseo Reategui	Universidade Federal do Rio Grande do Sul, Brazil
Petrea Redmond	University of Southern Queensland, Australia
Manuel José Cabral Dos Santos Reis	University of Trás-os-montes e Alto Douro, Portugal
Martin Reisslein	Arizona State University, USA
Manuela Repetto	INDIRE, Italy
Fernando Reinaldo Ribeiro	Instituto Politécnico de Castelo Branco, Portugal
Alessia Rosa	INDIRE, Italy
Razvan Rughinis	University Politehnica of Bucharest, Romania
Rebecca Rutherfoord	Kennesaw State University, USA
Libuse Samkova	University of South Bohemia, Czech Republic
Demetrios Sampson	Curtin University, Australia
Ian Sanders	University of South Africa, South Africa
Eileen Scanlon	Open University, UK
Georg J. Schneider	University of Applied Sciences Trier, Germany
Ulrik Schroeder	RWTH Aachen University, Germany
Edgar Seemann	Furtwangen University, Germany
María Luisa Sein-Echaluce	Universidad de Zaragoza, Spain
Abhishek Shukla	R.D. Engineering College, India
Pei Hwa Siew	Universiti Tunku Abdul Rahman, Malaysia
Juarez Bento da Silva	Universidade Federal de Santa Catarina, Brazil
Ole Smørdal	University of Oslo, Norway
Zacharoula Smyrnaiou	University of Athens, Greece
Filomena Soares	Algoritmi Research Centre, UM, Portugal
Michael Sonntag	Johannes Kepler University, Austria
J. Michael Spector	University of North Texas, USA
Karl Steffens	University of Cologne, Germany

Craig Stewart	Indiana University, USA
Masanori Sugimoto	Hokkaido University, Japan
Wayne Summers	Columbus State University, USA
Katsuaki Suzuki	Kumamoto University, Japan
Ekaterina Talalakina	NRU HSE, Russian Federation
Bénédicte Talon	ULCO, Université Lille Nord de France, France
Brendan Tangney	Trinity College Dublin, The University of Dublin, Ireland
Marco Temperini	Sapienza University of Rome, Italy
Uwe Terton	University of the Sunshine Coast, Australia
Neena Thota	University of Saint Joseph, Macau
Stephan Trahasch	University of Applied Sciences Offenburg, Germany
Stefan Trausan-Matu	University Politehnica of Bucharest, Romania
James Uhomoibhi	University of Ulster, UK
Andreas Veglis	Aristotle University of Thessaloniki, Greece
Ioanna Vekiri	Independent Researcher, Greece
Harald Vranken	Open Universiteit, The Netherlands
Charalambos Vrasidas	CARDET, Cyprus
Pieter de Vries	Delft University of Technology, The Netherlands
Alf Inge Wang	Norwegian University of Science and Technology, Norway
Edgar Weippl	SBA Research, Austria
Martin Wessner	Darmstadt University of Applied Sciences, Germany
David Whittinghill	Purdue University, USA
Leandro Krug Wives	Universidade Federal do Rio Grande do Sul, Brazil
Jie Chi Yang	National Central University, Taiwan
Katarina Zakova	Slovak University of Technology in Bratislava, Slovak Republic
Diego Zapata-Rivera	Educational Testing Service, USA
Iveta Zolotova	Technical University in Kosice, Slovak Republic
Amal Zouaq	University of Ottawa, Canada
Javier García Zubía	Universidad de Deusto, Spain
Susan Zvacek	University of Denver, USA

Additional Reviewers

Odette auzende	LIP6, France
Anke Berns	Universidad de Cádiz, Spain
Lorena Gutierrez-Madronal	University of Cadiz, Spain
Juan Antonio Caballero Hernández	UCA, Spain
Iza Marfisi	LIUM Computer Science Lab, Université du Maine, France
Lisa Palathingal	University of Nevada, Reno, USA
Giorgio Presti	Università degli studi di Milano, Italy
Stelios Sergis	University of Piraeus, Greece

Rui Wu	University of Nevada, Reno, USA
Panagiotis Zervas	Centre for Research and Technology Hellas, Greece

Invited Speakers

Alison Clark-Wilson	University College London, UK
Francisco Arcega	Universidad de Zaragoza, Spain
Leon Rothkrantz	Delft University of Technology, The Netherlands
Margaret Ross	Southampton Solent University, UK
Maria Amata Garito	Representative of ICDE ON MEDSE, Italy

Contents

Invited Papers

The Complex Process of Scaling the Integration of Technology Enhanced Learning in Mainstream Classrooms

Alison Clark-Wilson(✉)

UCL Knowledge Lab, University College London,
23-29 Emerald Street, London, WC1N 3QS, UK
a.clark-wilson@ucl.ac.uk

Abstract. The early optimism for how technology might transform teaching and learning practices in mainstream school classrooms has long faded in many countries around the world. Whilst early research findings suggested that this was due to obvious barriers such as access to the technology itself, more recent attempts to scale student-access have illuminated other factors and provided a more sound theoretical foundation for us to understanding the processes and products of scaling educational technology innovations. This keynote will use findings from key projects and initiatives to highlight what is being learned – and how this might inform future endeavours to realise a more 21st century curriculum.

1 Introduction and Overview

This paper summarises the keynote presentation given at CSEDU 2016 in Rome that aimed to highlight the complexity of the processes of integration of educational technology in mainstream classroom. What follows is a brief overview of the talk.

There are many interpretations of how digital technologies impact upon learners' educational experiences in the broadest sense. I begin by drawing on the ideas of two early visionaries, Burrhus Skinner and Seymour Papert, in order to contrast their very different perspectives on children's learning experiences during school education. I then use the example of a current large-scale longitudinal research study in England to highlight the processes and products of scaling that is providing substantial research evidence to enable us to characterise features of successful widespread implementations. I conclude by highlighting the implications of these findings and suggest questions for future research and further consideration by the educational technology design and research communities.

2 Early Optimism – The Visionaries in Education

Technology is not a new idea in education. There have been significant attempts at technology integration in education since the early 1900s. For example, the introduction of paper and pencil caused much anxiety for teachers who had developed confident

G. Costagliola et al. (Eds.): CSEDU 2016, CCIS 739, pp. 3–13, 2017.
DOI: 10.1007/978-3-319-63184-4_1

practices in their classrooms with the traditional classroom slate, based on teacher exposition and rote learning. Teachers questioned why they should opt for a new technology that threatened aspects of their existing pedagogic approaches, such as the requirement to mark students' written work and hand it back to them. Worries about the spiraling costs of widespread implementation of paper and pencils were expressed - alongside concerns about the need for new pedagogies and classroom management techniques. The arrival of moving film in the 1910s promised another educational revolution - with pioneers such as Thomas Edison predicting widespread use of what we now call video in the future. The radio broadcasts of the 1920s prompted similar predictions. In my own primary school education in England during the 1960s we had radios on the walls of all classrooms and it was a commonly used media as the class sat to listen to stories and plays. Similarly for television in the 1950s and, with the arrival of computers to mainstream education in the 1970s, again came an early optimism and the promise of yet another educational technology revolution.

However, there were very different views on how all of these technologies might impact on the students' learning experiences. I contrast the perspectives of two early visionaries to highlight this point.

The psychologist and social philosopher B.F. Skinner, conceived an early mechanical *teaching machine*. In Skinner's vision of the classroom students worked individually and in silence as they responded to exercises that were administered and 'assessed' by the learning machine. See Fig. 1.

Fig. 1. A boy working on a teaching machine (c1950).

Skinner claimed that use of the teaching machine would lead to the "formation of correct behaviours – the student quickly learns to be right" by giving immediate feedback to students and, by doing so, students would be "free of uncertainty or anxiety about success or failure – his work is pleasurable" [1].

By contrast, the mathematician Seymour Papert, who was the father of constructionism, believed that computers could be an expressive medium for students' own mathematical ideas and creations saying "the idea is simple, let a child learn mathematics by speaking in mathematics about things that really matter to him" [2]. With colleagues at MIT, he developed the LOGO programming language and its most influential peripheral device, the floor turtle. See Fig. 2.

Fig. 2. Young children working with a LOGO floor turtle (c1980).

Furthermore, Papert believed that expressive mathematical media such as the LOGO computing language provided an opportunity to affect the nature of mathematical knowledge itself, leading to new computational approaches and insights into topics such as recursion and fractal geometry.

If we move to the present day, the internet abounds with millions of digital exercises in the spirit of Skinner's vision, and, even though the nature of the interactions and the opportunity for more nuanced and intelligent feedback are now possible, these resources are predominantly designed to provide fast and efficient ways to assess particular educational content that has already been taught. This prompts the question, what about the digital design of educational content that aims to *introduce students to significant knowledge* in the first place?

Within the mathematics education community, technology has been a topic of interest since the early 1980s. The International Commission on Mathematics Instruction (ICMI) held its very first topic study conference on *The Influence of Computers and Informatics on Mathematics and its Teaching* in 1985. During this conference mathematicians and mathematics educators explored the way the computer was influencing mathematics itself and the way in which mathematicians worked, its likely influences on the curriculum of high-school and undergraduate students, and the way in which the computer might be used to improve mathematics teaching and learning [3].

The topic was revisited by the community in 2008 within the 17th ICMI Study on *Mathematics Education and Technology - Rethinking the Terrain* that focused on "cultural diversity and how this diversity impinges on the use of digital technologies in mathematics teaching and learning. Within this focus, themes such as mathematics and mathematical practices; learning and assessing mathematics with and through digital technologies; teachers and teaching; design of learning environments and curricula; implementation of curricula and classroom practice; access, equity and socio-cultural issues; and connectivity and virtual networks for learning, serve to organize the study and bring it coherence" [4]. In the opening editorial, Hoyles and Lagrange highlight a common concern within the mathematics education community that, despite early optimism for the potential for technology to transform school, college and university education, very little seemed to have changed in the intervening twenty years with respect to students' mathematical experiences as learners in classrooms. Mathematics education research concerning technology use has now shifted to focus more explicitly on the role of the teacher within technology mediated classrooms [5, 6]. Researchers have begun to articulate the complexity of the teacher's role, which combines:

- Selecting appropriate technologies for teaching mathematical topics.
- Designing tasks that are mediated by chosen technologies.
- Supporting students to become familiar and confident users of the technology within the mathematical context (the processes of *instrumentation* and *instrumentalisation* [7]).
- Developing new pedagogies to employ productive use of the technology in whole-class, small group and individualised teaching.
- Adapting assessment practices to take account of students' digital work and productions.

3 Two Important Definitions

In the examples that follow, which are taken from mathematics education, there are two key terms that warrant deeper explanation: *transformative mathematics technology* and *landmark activities.*

3.1 Transformative Mathematics Technology

The earlier illustrative examples from Skinner and Papert demonstrate how the underlying affordances of the technological tool can shape and be shaped by the associated epistemology (and the potential pedagogies). It is possible to take the same tool and use it in very different ways within educational settings - the technology itself does not necessarily define its subsequent use. Artigue, referring to secondary mathematics teachers' uses of computer algebra software, commented on "an explosion of techniques which remain relatively ad hoc, and pose a didactic obstacle to the progressive building of mathematical activity instrumented in an efficient way" [8]. Consequently, my colleagues and I have defined the term transformative mathematics technology as a class of 'computational tools through which students and teachers (re-)express their mathematical understandings' [9, 10]. For teachers, these new mathematical understandings concern both the content matter and the related pedagogies. So when I begin to discuss the scaling of technology, I am referring to the scaling of this particular class of technologies, an example of which will be provided later.

3.2 Landmark Activities

When considering both the design and evaluation of technology enhanced learning *at scale*, we use the notion of a *landmark activity* as one that is mediated by a disruptive but carefully designed task that prompts a cognitive breakdown, or a "situation of non-obviousness" [11]. These landmark activities serve two purposes:

- As focusing tasks for teachers during professional development. Teachers work through the landmark activities for themselves before working collaboratively with

colleagues to plan and reflect upon how they intend to support their students through the planned moments of cognitive conflict within their particular classroom settings. This approach offers focused support for teachers as they begin to think how they will respond to a diversity of learner responses, supporting them to develop contingent knowledge.
- As a research methodology to support the evaluation of teachers' classroom implementations. i.e. during observations of the landmark activities being taught in the classroom, judgments can be made concerning the implementation fidelity of the intervention in relation to the design principles (For more on this theme, see [12]).

4 The Current Picture Around the World

Many countries are now grappling with issues that relate to the scaling of educational technology in mathematics classrooms. This is partly due to the more ubiquitous nature of technology - even in developing countries – but also due to the immense financial and human investments that have been made to this end.

Around the world, recent research highlights some common and recurring issues irrespective of the level of mathematics teaching. For example, it is common that teachers' early pedagogies with technology tend to emulate their traditional teaching approaches. Trigueros, Lozano and Sandoval concluded from their study in Mexican primary schools that "teachers, who have only received training on the general use of the software, without a hint of how to introduce them into specific lessons, often develop teaching strategies where technology is used as replacement or amplification" [13]. Many researchers also comment on the influence of teacher's confidence to teach using technology on their resulting practices. In New Zealand, Thomas and Palmer's study highlighted the "strong correlation between confidence in using technology in the mathematics classroom and pedagogical technological knowledge" [14] in a secondary school setting. Concerning teachers' motivations to use technology in their teaching, the research within undergraduate mathematics teaching in Canada by Buteau and Muller concludes that "overall it seems that the great majority of tutors who integrate technology into their mathematics teaching do so by their own volition" [15]. We know much about the issues and barriers that mitigate against teachers' take-up of technology in their mathematics teaching – but far less about the conditions that might lead to successful implementations on a regional or national scale.

In England, which provides the setting for the research that follows, the situation is:

- Most secondary mathematics students do not use transformational mathematics technology in lessons [16].
- Most English secondary schools are very well equipped with technology with ratios of computers to students in the region of 1:3 [17].
- Most secondary mathematics teachers have had limited training to use technology in lessons. There are no subject-level standards for technology competency within teacher training, nor is it mandated that technology should be used within the National Curriculum and its associated assessments.

5 The Cornerstone Maths Project in England

The Cornerstone Maths project built on the foundations of the *SimCalc* project in the US, which had demonstrated students' learning gains in the key mathematical topic linear functions in a series of studies [18]. The key features of Cornerstone Maths are:

- Replacement curriculum units that use mathematical representational technologies to enhance the teaching and learning of 'big ideas in mathematics' that are 'hard to teach'.
- Teacher professional development materials, time for professional learning alongside school-based support.
- A phased research project that is 'scaling up' across the country.

5.1 Linear Functions – A Landmark Activity, 'Shakey the Robot'

To give a sense of the particular transformative mathematical technology developed within the Cornerstone Maths project, a landmark activity from the curriculum unit on linear functions is described.

The curriculum unit is set within a 'realistic' context within which students become developers of games for mobile phones for a fictitious IT design company in which their role is to advise the programmers on the mathematics that will make the game characters move in particular ways – the students use mathematics to analyse and create simulated motion games.

The design of the (web-based) software and the related tasks for students are based on the following principles:

- Multiple mathematical representations show a dynamic simulation with linked representations: animation; Cartesian graph of position-time; table of values; and mathematical function.
- Edit functionality enables the simulation to be controlled via the animation, the graph or function.
- Representations can be shown and hidden, as required and/or necessitated.

Figure 3 shows the software for the landmark activity 'Shakey the Robot'.

In a traditional introduction to this mathematical content students would be given the mathematical function, $y = f(x)$ and, by substituting values of x into the function, generate a value of y to produce co-ordinate pairs that are then plotted on a Cartesian graph plane. The Cornerstone Maths environment supports a more experiential approach whereby the students observe the effect of a particular function on the position-time relationship for the character and, by editing different features arrive at a more meaningful understanding of, in this case, linear functions. In particular, the resulting mathematical knowledge includes:

- coordinating algebraic, graphical, and tabular representations;
- $y = mx + c$ as a model of constant velocity motion – the meaning of m and c in the motion context.

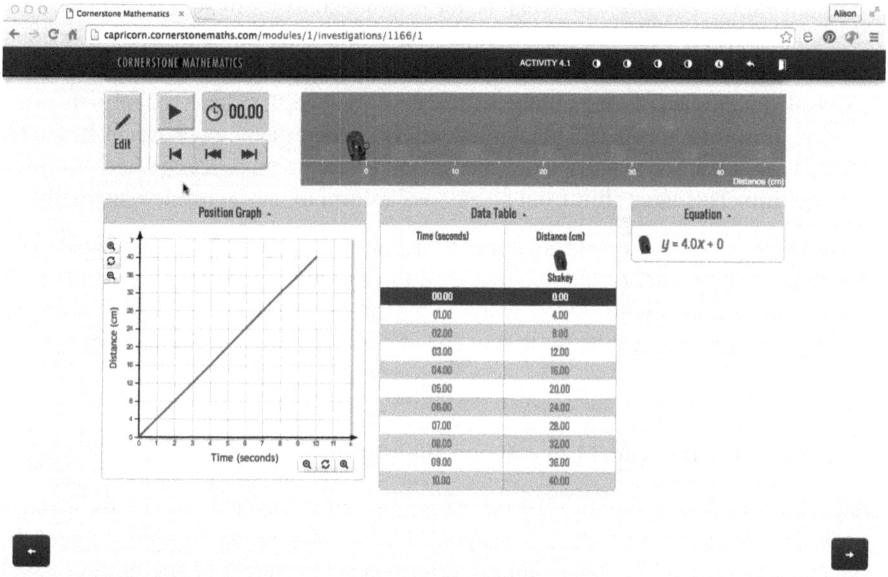

Fig. 3. Shakey the Robot.

Within the landmark activity, students are directed to edit Shakey's graph to produce a faster and slower animation and, in doing so, make sense of how speed, position and time are represented in each of the graph, table and function. For teachers, the pedagogical challenges arise as they develop ways to mediate the students' learning in partnership with the technology.

To date, we have worked with over 300 teachers from over 100 diverse schools in England, involving nearly 8000 students aged 11–14 years. Teachers are reporting positive outcomes – both in terms of their students' mathematical learning - and their motivation and attitudes towards learning mathematics. However, how do we decide whether or not we have 'scaled' our innovation?

6 Conceptualising Scaling in Education

6.1 Scaling Educational Innovations

Cordingley and Bell carried out an extensive literature review that resulted in a framework to support how 'scaling' might be conceptualised within the context of educational reform - drawing heavily on the work of Coburn [19], who had conceived four interrelated and overlapping dimensions:

- Depth: Going beyond surface structures and practices to alter beliefs, norms of social interaction and pedagogical principles.

- Sustainability: The innovation can better respond consistently to new demands and changing contexts - requires support mechanisms including a supportive professional community of colleagues within a school.
- Spread: not only increasing numbers (of schools/teachers/students) but also the ways in which reform norms and principles influence identifiable operational structures such as policies, procedures and professional development processes and priorities.
- Ownership: This must shift from an external reform to one controlled internally.

Cordingley and Bell added fifth dimension, *purpose or aim*, whereby the goal of the innovation must be understood and connected to the starting point [20]. Whilst technology is not specifically excluded, Cordingley and Bell's review did not focus on, nor draw any conclusions in relation to any specific aspects of educational technological innovations.

6.2 Scaling Technological Educational Innovations

Hung, Lim and Huang theorised about the scaling of maths and science technology-based educational innovations in Singapore, leading to a *product-process* model. By products, they refer to the deliverables (performance indicators) of successful scaling, which are commonly defined according to strict numeric outcomes (e.g. the number of teachers, the number of schools, the number of school clusters, etc.). They define innovation-scaling as a set of processes "not to be replicated, but instead to be re-created/re-instantiated/re-enacted" [21]. In our Cornerstone Maths research we have applied and

Table 1. Scaling Cornerstone Maths: products and processes.

Theme	Products	Processes
1. Geographical reach	(a) Number of schools involved	(a) Development of web-based curriculum activity system (b) Development of teacher community
	(b) Number of local hubs involved	(c) Development and maintenance of regional hub-based offer of professional support (d) Development of school clusters, supported by project team leading to development of local hubs with local CM project lead
2. School buy-in	(c) Improved student attainment	(e) School-devised methods to evaluate students' outcomes
	(d) Number of whole departments involved	(f) Development of school-based PD (g) Support to embed CM within local of schemes of work
	(e) Wider use of the materials	(h) Teacher use of the materials beyond their original project commitment (e.g. with older classes or revision classes)
3. Penetration in mathematics department	(f) Number of participating teachers in each school	(i) Development of a lead practitioner (who may be the subject leader) (j) Development of peer-support for participating teachers

expanded Hung et al.'s construct to give the themed set of products and processes as shown in Table 1.

Our earlier phases of work, funded by Li Ka Shing Foundation, focused on extending the geographical reach of Cornerstone Maths, which resulted in the refinement of the web-based curriculum activity system, support for the teacher community and the regional/local professional support through school clusters. However, as the number of schools has increased and our evaluation research has indicated wide variation of outcomes related to Theme 2, the school 'buy-in' of the innovation, our attention has moved to research successful features of 'within-school' scaling that in turn lead to Theme 3, 'penetration within departments'.

7 Implications for Further Research

The current phase of Nuffield Foundation-funded research is responding to the following research questions:

- What is the impact on teachers' mathematical knowledge for teaching of their engagement with cycles of professional development and associated teaching of the difficult mathematical concepts; algebraic generalisation, geometric similarity, and linear functions?
- What mathematical knowledge for teaching and mathematical pedagogic practices are desirable for teachers to integrate dynamic visual technologies in their teaching of these concepts?
- What are the design features of professional development activities for lower secondary mathematics teachers that support them to use dynamic, visual technology in ways that become embedded for both the teachers and their pupils and lead to effective learning?

Our methodology involves design-based research cycles of co-development of web-based resources to support 'within school' scaling of Cornerstone Maths working in collaboration with project schools and teachers. We conjecture that, by articulating the specific mathematical knowledge for teaching and associated mathematical pedagogic practices with [Cornerstone] Maths landmark activities, we can produce research-informed professional development resources that better meet teachers' needs. Alongside this, we aim to illuminate the processes of 'within-school' scaling through longitudinal (3 year) case studies in a sample of project schools.

In closing, I would like to highlight for wider consideration three tensions that exist within the educational design community.

1. Do we design technology-enhanced learning **for** teachers/lecturers that aim to solve epistemological or pedagogical issues that neither recognise? ***OR*** do we **work with** teachers/lecturers to design TEL that <u>takes account of</u> prevailing epistemologies/pedagogies?
2. Do we design 21st century technology-enhanced learning to provide access to 21st century curricula ***OR*** do we design 21st century technology-enhanced learning to support 19th century curricula?

3. Do we design technology-enhanced learning solution 'because we can' ***OR*** do we design and implement technology-enhanced learning to develop 21st century skills/ knowledge/practices?

There are no simple answers to these questions, however, whatever you conclude, without a clear understand about how any technology-enhanced learning might scale, the efforts and resources might never realize that early optimism!

Acknowledgements. The particular research on scaling reported in this paper was funded by the Nuffield Foundation (Award reference 91909) and it involved my close colleagues Celia Hoyles and Richard Noss. In addition, we gratefully acknowledge funding by the Li Ka Shing Foundation for the prior research that took place between 2010–13, which was an intensive collaboration between teams at the London Knowledge Lab, UCL Institute of Education and at the Center for Technology in Learning, SRI International, Menlo Park, USA.

References

1. Skinner, B.F.: Teaching machine and programmed learning (1955). https://www.youtube.com/watch?v=jTH3ob1IRFo
2. Papert, S.: LOGO Programming language (1972). https://www.youtube.com/watch?v=5dZMgdqy7zY
3. Churchhouse, R.F., Cornu, B., Howson, A.G., Kahane, J.-P., van Lint, J.H., Pluvinage, F., Pluvinage, F., Ralston, A., Yamaguti, M.: The Influence of Computers and Informatics on Mathematics and its Teaching. ICMI Study, vol. 1. Cambridge University Press, Cambridge (1986)
4. Hoyles, C., Lagrange, J.B. (eds.): Mathematics Education and Technology - Rethinking the Terrain: The 17th ICMI Study. New ICMI Study Series, vol. 13. Springer, Berlin (2009). doi: 10.1007/978-1-4419-0146-0
5. Clark-Wilson, A., Robutti, O., Sinclair, N.: The Mathematics Teacher in the Digital Era: An International Perspective on Technology Focused Professional Development. Mathematics Education in the Digital Era, vol. 2. Springer, Dordrecht (2014). doi:10.1007/978-94-007-4638-1
6. Clark-Wilson, A., Aldon, G., Cusi, A., Goos, M., Haspekian, M., Robutti, O., Thomas, M.O.J.: The challenges of teaching mathematics with digital technologies - the evolving role of the teacher. In: Liljedahl, P., Nichol, C., Oesterle, S., Allan, D. (eds.) Proceedings of the Joint Meeting of PME 38 and PME-NA 36, Vancouver, Canada, 2014, vol. 1, pp. 87–116. University of British Columbia (2014)
7. Guin, D., Trouche, L.: The complex process of converting tools into mathematical instruments: the case of calculators. Int. J. Comput. Math. Learn. **3**(3), 195–227 (1999)
8. Artigue, M.: Learning mathematics in a CAS environment: the genesis of a reflection about instrumentation and the dialectics between technical and conceptual work. Int. J. Comput. Math. Learn. **7**(3), 245–274 (2002). doi:10.1023/A:1022103903080
9. Clark-Wilson, A., Hoyles, C., Noss, R., Vahey, P., Roschelle, J.: Scaling a technology-based innovation: windows on the evolution of mathematics teachers' practices. ZDM Math. Educ. **47**(1) (2015). doi:10.1007/s11858-014-0635-6
10. Hoyles, C., Noss, R.: What can digital technologies take from and bring to research in mathematics education? In: Bishop, A., Clements, M., Keitel, C., Kilpatrick, J., Leung, F. (eds.) Second International Handbook of Mathematics Education. Kluwer Academic, Dordrecht (2003)

11. Winograd, T., Flores, F.: Understanding Computers and Cognition: A New Foundation for Design. Ablex Publishing Corp., Norwood (1986)
12. Clark-Wilson, A., Hoyles, C., Noss, R.: Conceptualising the scaling of mathematics teachers' professional development concerning technology. In: Krainer, K., Vondrová, N. (eds.) Proceedings of the Ninth Congress of the European Society for Research in Mathematics Education, Prague, Czech Republic, pp. 2333–2339 (2015)
13. Trigueros, M., Lozano, M.-D., Sandoval, I.: Integrating technology in the primary school mathematics classroom: the role of the teacher. In: Clark-Wilson, A., Robutti, O., Sinclair, N. (eds.) The Mathematics Teacher in the Digital Era: An International Perspective on Technology Focused Professional Development. MEDE, vol. 2, pp. 111–138. Springer, Dordrecht (2014). doi:10.1007/978-94-007-4638-1_6
14. Thomas, M.O.J., Palmer, J.M.: Teaching with digital technology: obstacles and opportunities. In: Clark-Wilson, A., Robutti, O., Sinclair, N. (eds.) The Mathematics Teacher in the Digital Era: An International Perspective on Technology Focused Professional Development. MEDE, vol. 2, pp. 71–89. Springer, Dordrecht (2014). doi:10.1007/978-94-007-4638-1_4
15. Buteau, C., Muller, E.: Teaching roles in a technology intensive core undergraduate mathematics course. In: Clark-Wilson, A., Robutti, O., Sinclair, N. (eds.) The Mathematics Teacher in the Digital Era: An International Perspective on Technology Focused Professional Development. MEDE, vol. 2, pp. 163–185. Springer, Dordrecht (2014). doi: 10.1007/978-94-007-4638-1_8
16. Office for Standards in Education: Mathematics: made to measure. Department for Children, Schools and Families, London (2012)
17. OECD: Students, Computers and Learning: Making the Connection. PISA, OECD Publishing, Paris (2015)
18. Hegedus, S.J., Roschelle, J.: The SimCalc Vision and Contributions. Advances in Mathematics Education. Springer, Dordrecht (2013). doi:10.1007/978-94-007-5696-0
19. Coburn, C.: Rethinking scale: moving beyond numbers to deep and lasting change. Educ. Res. **32**(6), 3–12 (2003)
20. Cordingley, P., Bell, M.: Transferring learning and taking innovation to scale. The Innovation Unit, London (2007)
21. Hung, D., Lim, K., Huang, D.: Extending and scaling technology-based innovations through research: the case of Singapore. In: Organisation for Economic Co-operation and Development (ed.) Inspired by Technology, Driven by Pedagogy: A Systemic Approach to Technology-Based School Innovations, pp. 89–102. OECD Publishing, Paris (2010)

Quality and Evaluation in Higher Education

Francisco J. Arcega(✉)

Department of Electrical Engineering, University of Zaragoza,
C/María de Luna 3, 50018 Saragossa, Spain
arcegafj@unizar.es

Abstract. Quality is important in industrial production and all kinds of services. In particular, education is one very important service for our society. Since the Bologna process, European universities try to do their best using the resources the society has given them to satisfy the needs of the European citizens.

Quality is very important but it has no value without a well-established system of continuous improvement based on measurement and knowledge of our capabilities and the needs of the society. The best way to measure the results of a service is by the way of the evaluation. Evaluation always needs to consider two inputs: self-evaluation and external evaluation, but it is particularly interesting when evaluation is considered for improving, not when evaluation is considered as inspection.

During this paper, a review and comparative analysis between quality and evaluation in industry and in universities, based on the author´s own experience, will be done. The experience of industries and other services implemented in our world is a source of knowledge for improvement, so the main part of this paper will be addressed to the review of what is done in industries and how to translate it into the European Higher Education Area. Finally, some proposals for daily activity in university education will be presented, based on the experience of the research group EduQTech.

Keywords: Evaluation · Accreditation · Quality evaluation

1 Introduction

Quality is a property of products and services very important in our life. It started in production of products, initially for the automotive industry because of the large amount of spear parts to be included in cars. Later, it was extended to other parts of the fabrication world. Industries are interested in produce their products with quality as a commercial way to sell more against the other companies. One of the meanings of Quality is doing things well. Therefore, Quality is important in Engineering.

Finally, service industries were included in the Quality philosophy as banks and other service companies are interested in using Quality as a tool for competitiveness. In parallel, the continuous improvement philosophy was extended as a way to do things as good as possible and better and better.

At the beginning, production companies were interested only in production and the Quality was only for controlling that the products maintain a level of quality in the

G. Costagliola et al. (Eds.): CSEDU 2016, CCIS 739, pp. 14–24, 2017.
DOI: 10.1007/978-3-319-63184-4_2

characteristics. All activities related with the quality were limited to inspection. No matter the product, the aim of the system was control the quality for assuring that the level of the product was the same nevertheless the quality were poor.

Later the companies changed to the assurance of quality in the way that they try to maintain a minimum of quality, not only a level but also a minimum level to guaranty this quality.

Finally, around the 90ties the evolution was for the continuous improvement. Companies must produce products with a minimum level of quality but they need to improve the product in a continuous way for reaching the excellence. This system is working today and the most popular method to do that is the PDCA process or Deming cycle (Plan, Do, Check and Act-Correct if needed) as it is shown in the Fig. 1.

Fig. 1. Typical Deming cycle.

The new version of the standard ISO 9001:2015 has updated the role of management to the more modern thought process of leadership. This change puts new responsibilities on the senior management, who must demonstrate commitment and take responsibility for the effectiveness of the quality system, while enhancing customer satisfaction. The new orientation of the standard and as well the way of doing Quality is that management's role has changed from focusing on things to focusing on people, and from doing things right to doing the right things. Also, instead of planning, doing and directing, the role of management has moved to inspiring, influencing and motivating. This part is very important because people must be motivated and the labor of the direction for companies or of the university managers is to motivate people to do the right things.

Education is one service more to the Society but is one of the most important services because the future of our Society depends on Education. Therefore, this philosophy of Quality has been introduced as well in our universities and in Colleges. Engineering has been related with Quality since the beginning because of the production of goods and services and in Higher Education Institutions (HEI) related with engineering, is where most strong the implementation of this Quality and continuous improvement philosophy is. United Sates was the first country to introduce this Quality system in their Engineering faculties for controlling the quality of the students [1]. Different programs were established and with the evolution in the time, we know very well one of the most important accreditation system of the engineering. The Accreditation Board for Engineering and Technology (ABET) is probably the most prestigious accreditation board of the world.

For the Society and the European countries, we must to do as best as possible with the resources we have received. Not the excellence. Excellence is a must. A product is manufactured in the factory and can be checked and tested relatively fast, but the product in university education is the technological knowledge transferred to the student and the abilities and skills obtained at the university. So, how to measure the quality? By the evaluation, but this is not an absolute measurement but a level that must be overpassed. Ranking is not the objective of a good quality system in higher education.

Quality in companies is measured by the method described in the standard ISO 9001 [2] or by other documents like the ones related with Total Quality Management (TQM) [3]. In higher education, quality is measured by Criteria described in documents belonging to institutions, for instance: Accreditation Board for Engineering and Technology (ABET) [1] mainly in United States or European Standard Guidelines (ESG) [4] in Europe.

Similar to the introduction of Quality (ISO 9001) in companies in the 80 –ties, that the accreditation of the fabrication process was before the certification of the product, now all degrees are accredited but in a short future only degrees/universities working with continuous improvement will survive.

Engineers are working all over the world and it is important that all Engineering Schools reach a level of quality understandable for all companies in Europe and in the World. In Europe, all the quality system is based in the Bologna declaration [5] but the model is quite similar to the models based in international criteria and used in different countries in the World. The skills and competencies are oriented to the enterprise (customer).

The objectives of the Bologna process are [5]:

- Mobility, students must be able to work in different countries
- Transparency, the knowledge reached by students must be clear to employer and to the Society
- Employability, the knowledge must be oriented to the needs of the companies
- Competitiveness of the students, they must be able to develop their career in a competitive world

Finally, the Bologna declaration looks for improving the quality of the European Higher Education Area (EHEA).

The main advantages of implementing a Quality Systems in Education are that:

- There is more control and repeatability of the teaching actions
- The academic work is measurable
- It is easier to stablish an horizontal and vertical coordination
- The education is oriented to the results, not to the knowledge per se.

2 What Is Accreditation?

Accreditation is a certification (of a school, college, diploma, or the like) as meeting all formal official requirements of academic, curriculum, facilities, etc. So a certification of his quality Accreditation is based on three legs: Personnel, Facilities and Procedures.

The accreditation can be granted by an independent organisation as third party, in general, with some dependence of the Administration and following rules or international standards.

Evaluation is the verification process where the accreditation body confirms the quality of the diploma by means of an internal evaluation done by the team of the diploma and an external evaluation by an external team that study the documentation, visit the university and the facilities where the diploma is given and interview the different actors of the diploma: academic, other personnel and students. Finally, the team reports about the diploma and this report is evaluated by a committee of the independent organization that accredits or not the diploma.

In other European countries, there are agencies of accreditation like:

- ASIIN [6] in Germany.
- CTI [7] for engineering or HCERES [8] (Haute Conseil pour l´Evaluation de la Recherche et l´Education Supérieure) in France.

Fig. 2. Spanish regional accreditation agencies [11].

The coordination of the European accreditation of diplomas is carried out by ENQA [9] (European Association for Quality Assurance in Higher Education). The list of accredited or recognized agencies is controlled by EQAR [10] (European Quality Assurance Register). All the European accreditation is based in the European Standard Guidelines (ESG), last edition of 2015 [4].

In Spain, there are regional agencies responsible for the accreditation of the HE diplomas and one national agency (ANECA) [11]. Some Regional agencies are: ACPUA (Aragón) [12], ACSUG (Galicia) [13], AQU (Cataluña) [14], Madri+D (Madrid) [15], between others. Some agencies develop other activities moreover the accreditation activity. In the Fig. 2, it can be seen several regional agencies. All the accreditation activity, developed by the agencies, is coordinated by the network of regional agencies (REACU) [16] in a similar way as in Europe there is a coordination by EQAR.

3 Accreditation Requirements

Accreditation in Spain is compulsory. All higher institution diplomas must be accredited before the start of the teaching activity (Verifica Program: Verification at the beginning) [17] and renewed after 4 years of activity if it is a master and 6 years if it is a degree (Accredita Program) [18]. The accreditation is based in 7 criteria. In Spain, this process has started in 2014 for masters and, in 2015; degrees started the process of accreditation. As six years is a long period, there is an intermediate program to check the follow up of the accreditation called Monitor Program [19]. This program checks in a documentary way that the diploma is working properly in accordance with the conditions given in the Verifica program at the beginning.

This process of accreditation needs, like a stable chair, three legs: personnel, installations and procedures. For good procedures, the best is to have a Quality System implemented in the University or in the Faculty. More and more Spanish universities have an Internal Quality System implemented and the same organization that checks the Quality of the programs check the quality of the management system (Audit Program) [20] and, as well the quality of the academic personnel (Docentia Program) [21]. In a short future, universities with a certified Audit Program will not need to accredit all the diplomas, only a part of them, or all of them with a reduced accreditation evaluation.

The seven criteria for the Spanish compulsory accreditation program are [18]:

- Organization & curriculum implementation. The curricula is actualized and has been implemented in accordance with the conditions accorded at the beginning when the implementation.
- Public information & transparency. The university has the mechanisms for communicating effectively to all the stakeholders the characteristics and the processes to guaranty the Quality.
- SGIC, The Institution has an Internal Quality System well established and implemented that guaranties the continuous improvement of the diploma.
- Academic staff is in accordance with the characteristics and the number of students of the diploma.

- Support staff, resources and services. The Institution has the support staff, resources and services to fulfill the needs of the diploma in order to assure the skills and abilities to be obtained by the students.
- Learning outcomes. By the time of graduation, graduates have the knowledge and skills defined in the verification process at the beginning when they started the diploma.
- Satisfaction and performance indicators. The results are adequate to the needs of the Society and the satisfaction of the stakeholders is clear in all the sectors: staff, students and employers.

A part from this compulsory accreditation, there is another volunteer accreditation, that it is named EUR-ACE for Engineering [22] or EUR-INF for Informatics [23]. This accreditation is based in 9 criteria, the 7 criteria for compulsory accreditation plus two more criteria that for engineering are related with the engineering character and the institutional support for the program.

In a similar way, in the United States there is ABET Accreditation that is volunteer and is based in 10 criteria. For the accreditation, the diploma must be running and has to have several promotions of graduates.

The ten criteria for the ABET volunteer accreditation program are nine general and one particular to the family of degree accredited [1].

- **Students** - Student progress must be monitored to foster success in attaining student outcomes, thereby enabling graduates to attain program educational objectives. Students must be advised regarding curriculum and career matters.
  The program must have and enforce policies for accepting both new and transfer students, awarding appropriate academic credit for courses taken at other institutions, and awarding appropriate academic credit for work in lieu of courses taken at the institution.
- **Program Educational Objectives** - Program educational objectives (POE) are broad statements that describe what graduates are expected to attain within a few years of graduation. Program educational objectives are based on the needs of the program's constituencies.
- **Student Outcomes** - The program must have documented student outcomes that prepare graduates to attain the program educational objectives. There must be a documented and effective process for the periodic review and revision of these student outcomes.
- **Continuous Improvement** - The program must regularly use appropriate, documented processes for assessing and evaluating the extent to which the student outcomes are being attained. The results of these evaluations must be systematically utilized as input for the continuous improvement of the program. Other available information may also be used to assist in the continuous improvement of the program.
- **Curriculum** - The curriculum must effectively develop the following subject areas in support of student outcomes and program educational objectives
  - Mathematics
  - Physics
  - Technical content

- **Faculty** - Each faculty member teaching in the program must have expertise and educational background consistent with the contributions to the program expected from the faculty member. The competence of faculty members must be demonstrated by such factors as education, professional credentials and certifications, professional experience, ongoing professional development, contributions to the discipline, teaching effectiveness, and communication skills.
- **Facilities** - Classrooms, offices, laboratories, and associated equipment must be adequate to support attainment of the student outcomes and to provide an atmosphere conducive to learning. Modern tools, equipment, computing resources, and laboratories appropriate to the program must be available, accessible, and systematically maintained and upgraded to enable students to attain the student outcomes and to support program needs.
- **Institutional Support** - Institutional support and leadership must be adequate to ensure the quality and continuity of the program.

Both programs ABET and European are quite similar but focus is stronger in students and in institutional support in ABET. Institutional support is only taken into account in volunteer EUR-ACE and EUR- INF.

ABET focus on POE´s, results and knowledge of the students several years after finishing the diploma. In European system, only the results at the end of the studies are considered.

EUR ACE program is more similar to ABET including more focus on institutional support and in engineering and technology and both are volunteer.

The panel composition depends on each system. In Spain, the chair of the panel is always academic. There are several academic members (1 or 2) depending on the number of diplomas to evaluate and one student, plus the Secretary that represents and belongs to the agency of accreditation. In EUR-ACE or EUR-INF there is one more member, representing the Engineering professionals.

The panel composition in ABET is as follow: The president is a member representing the agency and there are so many members as diplomas to evaluate. Each member evaluates his diploma, but there is coordination between all the team. Members can be academics or professionals.

Students take part in the evaluation panels (teams) for the accreditation in Europe, but not in the ABET system

In ABET panels, the Team chair is the link with the Agency in Spain panels, the link is the Secretary of the panel.

Team members in Spain evaluate all diplomas assigned to the panel. In ABET only one diploma by each team member.

4 My Experience

4.1 In Accreditation

In my experience, evaluation and assessment of quality system in industry and in university follow the same pattern. The speed and the needs in both places is different but, as universities are delayed with respect to the industries, looking at the experience in industries, it can be introduced faster and better in universities.

The three main aspects to be taken into account in the accreditation of diplomas are: The continuous improvement, stablish good procedures or documented processes and obtain good information through surveys to students, staff and mainly employers.

Sometimes it is difficult to change some things because there is some inertia in the staff and even in students. For instance, names of some activities, and their significance, are difficult to modify (modify final year project to final year work) and the need to measure the time devoted by the student to this work and how to measure the skills obtained by the students.

Introduction of Quality concepts in Higher Education is very difficult and it takes a lot of time and explanation to the staff [24]. Some teachers are not involved in the quality aspects neither procedures of the Faculty. Some staff is not well used to work with skills, abilities, and the way to measure them, so they are not happy with the system. As well, students are not involved in the committees for improving; they are only interested in passing the exams and not in the quality of the education that they are receiving.

Support staff is not involved in the quality system. They are reactive to change. There is some feeling between staff that quality means bureaucracy.

Changes and modifications from one curriculum to another is very difficult and they are limited by the Administration. In the contrary, the change from teaching to learning has been very fast, in particular for teachers that have modified the content and adapted it to the new situation with some facility. An important number of staff have found interesting the changes for introduce the innovation activities in Higher Education.

Not the same for students that they continue with the former system of studying before the exams and they do not like to work during all the academic year.

To have good quality it is important to have a good institutional support but a good management can improve the budget and optimise it. The problem in Spanish system is that employers are not involved in Committees in the diplomas and only a small amount of them takes part in the definition of skills and abilities to be reached by the students. As the ISO 9001 standard has incorporated in his last version, motivation is very important in the process and it must be incorporated in the management. In this way, in universities the participation of the different stake holders is very important and for that they need to be motivated and they need to know the importance of all of them in a good diploma and the best results in the students and in the Society.

The activities to be done by academic staff for a good quality system are:

- Coordination with other peers to assure that no duplication is in the content of the curricula and which activities need to do in each subject in order that at the end all students reach the same skills and abilities.
- Take different data every day and store them in the appropriate place for a good information for the manager of the diploma

4.2 Our Activities

In our research group, EduQTech [25], we are working in two big areas: Software for the management of the daily activity [26–29] and the measurement of the time of study [30].

With the management software, we try to give the teachers tools for facilitating his academic and management work in the quality system. For that, we have designed and implemented several processes based on accreditation criteria and in quality standards. This software is applicable to all kind of subjects of degrees or masters or even to all other subjects of other kind of courses demanded by the industries. These processes are based on quality criteria and are a very good guide for applying quality concepts in the academic activity.

Three kinds of processes have been designed: Basic, Strategic and Support Processes. The Table 1 shows the main groups of processes developed and implemented.

Table 1. Some processes implemented.

Basic processes	Strategic processes	Support processes
Planification	Management	Resources
Teaching	Planification	Documentation
Evaluation, exams	Improvement	Problem solving
End of the academic year	...	Quality
...		...

With the time of study we try to measure the time that one average student devotes to learning one subject. The main basic research has been a survey done to all the students of the Engineering School during the three academic years from 2005 to 2008. Every week during the two semesters a survey through internet, in a special web page, has been launched, allowing the access only to registered students. The software had a system for self-detection of errors like too much hours of study in a day.

The survey collects all kind of activity in the classroom and at home. A 20% of all registered students had good and full answers during all the period surveyed.

Some general comments about the results obtained in the survey were [30]:

- The duration of the work in the laboratory is lower than expected. The students finish before of the two hours expected.
- They use only an average of half an hour for reading the notes and theoretical information.
- The time for writing the intermediate reports of the laboratory work is about 1 h per report
- The time for writing the final report is about 7.5 h

The big amount of information obtained with the survey, allowed each teacher to analyze his subject and adjust it to a more realistic situation in accordance with the effort done by students for learning the subject.

This work has allowed obtaining information of the time devoted by the average student to learn a subject, but as well other information has been obtained about when the activities are done or the links between different activities and the influence in the results. It has been possible to check the evolution of the effort of the students in every subject in function of the number of the week. The correspondence of the time devoted by the students with reports that student need to fill and present to the teacher it has been clearly seen. The correlation between time of study and difficulty for passing an exam has been shown too.

5 Conclusions

The application of the Quality in Higher Education follows the Industrial experience. As products are global, engineers and degree holders must travel and work into a global market, so their skills and abilities must be global and well known by the employers.

Universities are changing, but there are some questions that need to move faster in the process of the introduction of a quality system:

- Introduction of Quality concepts to all levels of partners in the teaching and learning process.
- Orientation to the needs of the Society (Companies and Industries in the case of Engineers)

The application of the quality system in Higher Education in different countries follows a similar process to the convergence and finally, as it has been in industry; multilateral agreement will arrive between different countries to recognize the different academic diplomas and skills of students.

References

1. ABET. http://www.abet.org. Accessed Apr 2016
2. ISO 9001:2015. Quality management systems – Requirements
3. TQM. https://www.isixsigma.com/methodology/total-quality-management-tqm/introduction-and-implementation-total-quality-management-tqm/. Accessed July 2016
4. ESG: Standards and Guidelines for Quality Assurance in the European Higher Education Area (2015). http://www.enqa.eu/wp-content/uploads/2013/06/ESG_3edition-2.pdf. Accessed July 2016
5. Bologna declaration (1999). http://www.magna-charta.org/resources/files/text-of-the-bologna-declaration. Accessed July 2016
6. ASIIN. http://www.asiin.de. Accessed Apr 2016
7. CTI. http://www.commission-cti.fr/. Accessed Apr 2016
8. HCERES. www.hceres.fr. Accessed Apr 2016
9. ENQA. www.enqa.eu. Accessed Apr 2016
10. EQAR. www.eqar.eu. Accessed Apr 2016
11. ANECA. www.aneca.es. Accessed Apr 2016
12. ACPUA. http://www.aragon.es/DepartamentosOrganismosPublicos/Organismos/ACPUA. Accessed Apr 2016
13. ACSUG. http://www.acsug.es/es. Accessed Apr 2016
14. AQU. http://www.aqu.cat/. Accessed Apr 2016
15. Madri+D, http://www.madrimasd.org/. Accessed Apr 2016

16. REACU. http://www.acsucyl.es/acsucyl/opencms/noticiasantiguas/noticias/noticia_0004.html. Accessed Apr 2016
17. VERIFICA. http://www.aneca.es/Programas/VERIFICA. Accessed Apr 2016
18. ACREDITA. http://www.aneca.es/Programas/ACREDITA. Accessed Apr 2016
19. MONITOR. http://www.aneca.es/Programas/MONITOR. Accessed Apr 2016
20. AUDIT. http://www.aneca.es/Programas/AUDIT. Accessed Apr 2016
21. DOCENTIA. http://www.aneca.es/Programas/DOCENTIA. Accessed Apr 2016
22. EURACE. http://www.enaee.eu/eur-ace-system/. Accessed July 2016
23. EURINF. http://www.eqanie.eu/pages/quality-label.php. Access July 2016
24. Plaza, I., Ibáñez, F., Igual, R., Arcega, F.J.: The use of quality standards as element of innovation in higher education. In: Iberic Conference on Systems and Information Technology (CISTI), pp. 567–572 (2009)
25. EduçQTech. http://eduqtech.unizar.es/. Accessed Apr 2016
26. Plaza, I., Ibáñez, F., Igual, R., Arcega, F.: Use of quality standards as element of innovation in higher education. In: The 4th Iberian Conference on Information Systems and Technologies, Povoa de Varzim, Portugal, pp. 567–572 (2009)
27. Igual, R., Plaza, I., Ibañez, F., Medrano, C., Arcega, F.: Quality and innovation. Web-based code of good teaching practice. In: The 3rd Workshop on Interaction Design in Educational Environments, Albacete, España, 9 Junio 2014
28. Plaza, I., Marcuello, J.J., Igual R., Arcega, F.: Proposal of a quality model for educational software. In: En XX EAEEIE Annual Conference (Innovation in Education for Electrical and Information Engineering), Valencia, España (2009)
29. González, R., Torres, F., Yoldi, V., Plaza, I., Arcega, F.: Integration of quality, labor risks prevention, environment and ethical management. Model Appl. R&D&I Manufact. Process. Organ. Key Engin. Mater. **502**, 85–90 (2012)
30. Arcega, F., et al.: Measurement of the time of study evaluation of the ECTS really devoted to study. In: FINTDI Conference (2011)

Dropout Rates of Regular Courses and MOOCs

Léon Rothkrantz[1,2(✉)]

[1] Delft University of Technology, Mekelweg 4, Delft, The Netherlands
L.J.M.Rothkrantz@tudelft.nl
[2] Technical University in Prague, Konviktska Street 20, Prague, Czech Republic

Abstract. Recently we observe an enormous grow of Massive Open Online Courses (MOOCs). But it proves that the dropout rates of MOOCs are very high. One of the main causes are missing of necessary capabilities of students, inability of students to manage their study and a missing appropriate didactic model. In this paper we compare the dropout rates of MOOCs, regular courses and courses using new didactical approaches as blended learning and flip the classroom. We introduce a new teaching learning model to explain high dropout rates of students in distant learning courses. Finally we discuss possible ways how to teach 21st century skills as cooperative working, learning, creativity, networking and how to solve real life problems in a context sensitive approach. Our research findings are based on educational experiments at Delft University of Technology (DUT).

Keywords: Dropout rates · MOOCs · Learning models · Flip the classroom · Didactical models · Blended learning

1 Introduction

In a complex, globalizing, unpredictable world full of networks, worldwide communications and social media we have to train students in acquisition of typical 21st century skills such as critical reflection, cooperating, networking, creativity, ability to handle big data, ability to solve real life problems, ability for life-long learning. We have to educate students which are able to face and contribute to the future world [1]. The question is whether and how educational innovations as "blended learning" and MOOCs enable students to acquire such skills. It is not enough to offer courses as MOOCs but it is also necessary to develop didactic models to challenge students to take this courses and complete them successfully [2]. At this moment many courses are focused on individual learning. To enable individual learning it is necessary to design MOOCs as self-paced courses. But we will show in this paper that this contributes to the high dropout rate of students

The process of teaching and learning has an impact in three domains [1]:

- Qualification, this is about the role of teaching in acquisition of knowledge, abilities, competencies, and attitudes such that after graduation students are qualified to perform their job or play their role in society.
- Socialisation, this is the way how we teach students the social processes in a job environments or culture and democracy in general.

G. Costagliola et al. (Eds.): CSEDU 2016, CCIS 739, pp. 25–46, 2017.
DOI: 10.1007/978-3-319-63184-4_3

- Personal development, the impact of teaching on the process of individualisation and subjectivity.

The question is how to realise these goals with a student population of increasing diversity, differences in cultural background, interest, abilities, learning style, speed/pacing. Most regular courses are focussed on realisation of the qualification goal. By introducing MOOCs and blended learning courses the hope was that they support socialisation and personal development. But as we will show in common used didactic models it is assumed that students master already 21st century skills. But in most secondary schools these skills have not been trained, so they have to be learned at University. From a recent study in the Netherlands [1], it proves that the teaching process at Universities is still focussed on knowledge transfer and qualifications of students and not on socialisation and personal development. The concept Bildung introduced by Humboldt in the 19th century focussed on the development of all human abilities and not only some cognitive abilities and knowledge acquisition is a relevant item.

To realise such educational goals there is a request of smaller learning communities with intense interaction students and teacher. But in MOOCs the direct interaction with a teacher is minimised and is embedded in the teaching material in a non-direct way. We observe also a trend of creating honours programmes challenging and enabling students to compose their individual self-paced programmes. Concepts as freedom, responsibility, societal relevance and innovation, are very appealing to students. But we can observe that only a minority is able to implement such programmes successfully.

Many students don't know what they really want, are not aware of requirements of individual studies and of the required capabilities. MOOCs have a high dropout rate because students don't have the required capabilities, attitudes and ability to control their own study behaviour. Student are used to take precooked programmes and a teacher taking the supervision on their study. Self-paced studies require a new study behaviour which has to be learned.

In the next chapter we discuss related works. We show that researchers studied the problem of study success and failure already for many years. In many studies, researchers try to find the characteristics of students and teaching learning environment to predict study success. For many years psychological assessment of students was used to predict high dropout rate. In Sect. 3 we present the main causes of the high dropout rates. We developed a special teaching-learning model to understand the process of attachment of students with their study and university. At the end of the chapter we discuss the emotional components in the teaching learning process. In Sect. 4 we discuss the results of a psychological assessment at TUDelft. First years students were tested using the Big Five personality test to assess if students have the abilities to learn 21st century skills [2]. Then we will discuss the results of a huge experiment performed at TUDelft from 1953–1957 [3]. Students were tested using personality tests, (cognitive) ability tests, completed with interviews of student counsellors and surveys on assessment of features in the teaching-learning environment. The goal of this experiment was to research if psychological assessment could provide additional information next to the results of final examination at secondary schools to predict study-success or–failure. In 2014 an experiment has been started using new teaching learning models in mathematical courses for first years students at Delft University of Technology. Again we will report the study performance of students compared to traditional ways of teaching mathematics. To summarize the goals of this paper are:

- Identification of factors/reasons explaining the high dropout rate of MOOCs.
- Comparison of factors underlying different teaching-learning models varying from classroom teaching up to MOOCs, with respect to study-success or–failure.

Our research findings are based on results of experiments performed at Delft University of Technology.

2 Literature Survey

In [4] the authors researched MOOC dropout rates from different perspectives. They listed a number of reasons for dropout based on literature search. Next they researched data from a specific MOOC provided by the University of Warwick. Their results indicate that many participants who may be classified as dropouts are still participating in the course in their own preferred way, either with a slower pace or with selective engagement.

In [5] the author explores students dropout behaviour in MOOCs. As a case study they took a special class. He developed a survival model that allows to measure the influence of factors extracted from that data on student dropout rate. His study shows that specific social factors as interaction between students, emergent sub community structure affect dropout behaviour

In [6] the author researched the underlying interaction mechanisms which govern students' influence on each other in Massive Open Online Courses (MOOCs. Specifically, they outlined different ways in which students can be negatively exposed to their peers on MOOC forums and discuss a simple formulation of learning network diffusion, which formalizes the essence of how such an influence spreads and can potentially lead to student attrition over time.

In [7] researchers extended traditional features for MOOC analysis with richer and higher granularity information to make more accurate predictions of dropout and performance. The results show that finer-grained temporal information increases the predictive power in the early phases of the Pattern-Oriented Software Architectures (POSA) tested on a MOOC offered in summer 2013 by Vanderbilt University.

Prediction of study success is a popular research topic over the years [8]. Wilbrink, wrote a literature survey of assessment in historical perspective with more than 200 reviewed papers.

In [9] a theoretical longitudinal model has been introduced by Tinto, demonstrating how different personality characteristics and characteristics of the University have their impact on the interaction process student-University. Such a process resulted in delay, dropout or study success. In fact Tinto describes the interaction process between three systems, the individual student, the academic system and the social system. According to Tinto the individual student will enter the University with a specific social background, personality education and training. He will have a special binding with the University and goal of the study. This binding will be expressed in motivation and expectations. The binding will change over time, caused by the influence of the academic and social systems and the interaction of both and will eventually result in dropout.

A similar study has been performed in Belgium at the Universities of Ghent and Leuven. Researcher Lacante and Janssen were involved in research on prediction of study-success for a long time [10]. They developed special surveys to predict the academic performance at Universities. From 1968 Janssen [11] was involved in research on teaching and learning in higher education. In his whole research, the student with his study and exam experience and perception of teaching behaviour is the focus of attention. Janssen perceives studying as "deep level learning" and teaching as facilitating studying. Together with Goethem and Lacante [11] Janssen researched study experiences of students. They developed a questionnaire of more than 100 items and surveyed first years students at the University of Leuven. After analyzing the responses of students using factor analysis they discovered three underlying components intrinsically motivation, self-confidence and activity. These components are similar to the Osgood dimensions evaluation, potency and activity [12]. In 1990 we performed similar research at Delft University of Technology.

In [13] Kalogiannakis states that effective communication between the learners and the tutor-counsellor has been proved to significantly promote the positive emotions, reduce the negative ones and reinforce the learners' participation in a distance learning program. He investigates the emotions experienced by the learners of the Hellenic Open University (HOU) and how these emotions may vary through interaction with the tutor-counsellor. The research findings confirms the dominant place occupied by emotions in the learning process, a place that has been until recently entirely attributed to reason, while highlighting the communicative and supportive role to be taken by the tutor-counsellor in distance learning programs.

In [14–18] Rothkrantz states that in a face-to-face learning environment emotions can be expressed by (non-)verbal behavior as way of speaking, facial expressions or words with an emotional loading. In experiments using different ways of distant learning, the emotional state of learners was assessed using special tools to analyse video recordings captured via Skype.

The didactic Adagio of the famous Dutch mathematician and didactic specialist in mathematics Freudenthal [19] was "You can learn mathematics only by doing and discover mathematics in the real world". For him was teaching mathematics an educational task and it should be context sensitive and application oriented. Students should be able to design mathematical models and translate real world problems formulated in natural language in a mathematical language. It is very important to give students opportunities to reflect on and clarify their thinking about mathematical ideas. Most of current didactic models fits in the discovery learning tradition developed around 1960. Piaget, Dewey, Vygotsky and Freire and many others support constructivist learning. Up to then drill and practice was one of the favourite pedagogical principles in mathematics. Now the focus is on learning based on personal and societal experience. Our developed didactic model FETCH 2.0 is based on similar ideas [2]. The question is of course how to implement this didactic model in the developed MOOC. The oldest, and still the most powerful, teaching tactic for fostering critical thinking is Socratic teaching.

In Socratic teaching we focus on giving students questions, not answers. The next step is that students themselves learn to generate questions around a learning text [20].

Mathematicians are trained to ask (critical) questions reading a scientific journal. These questions are stimulated by the learning material but also by the surrounding environment and context. Developing a critical attitude by students is not limited to mathematics. Freudenthal writes about "Mathematics as an educational task". Many mathematicians use the inquiry based methods also during reading or reviewing a paper, or documents or listening to a presentation. It proves that inquiry based method is an efficient way to keep the reader/listener alert and is a first step to processing the presented information.

3 Dropout

3.1 Description of Possible Reasons for Dropout

MOOCs are in principle open for everybody. No entrance exam has been required. But some knowledge and capabilities are required to finish a MOOC successfully. This is stressed in information about the course but some students missing the required knowledge and abilities still believe they can do it. Similar experiences we have with regular students at DUT. No entrance exam is required to enter DUT. The first year of study should be used for selection, orientation and adaptation. It proves that low grades for mathematics and physics at secondary school are good predictors for dropout. Over the years the failure rate of regular academic courses has been studied. We will report about a study at Delft University of Technology with a psychological assessment of all freshmen. It proves that results of students at their secondary school predict about 40% of the study success or failure in the first year. Psychological assessments ads about 10%.

To complete a MOOC successfully a student should have a strong motivation, based on the expected outcomes, interest in science and increase of knowledge and competences. Next a student should be able to manage his time and plan a study. In current MOOCs a global time schedule of video lectures, simulations, exercises and exams is presented. To enable communication and cooperation between students all students are part of one group taking the course together. In more individual based schedule students will lack support of fellow students. Many students reported that they prefer to manage their own course without cooperation. This violates of course the goal to realize 21st century skills. Individually based studies are offered for many years by the open University. But they also offer meetings for participants to create a community. Given a strong motivation and ability to plan their study, students should be able to come to activities. Viewing video lectures and simulations don't require active participation of students. It may give them the feeling that they have everything under control. They are confronted with reality if they have to make assignments or exams. Inadequate time management, un-ability to set themselves into action and missing of other study skills, results in many cases to dropout.

An adapted didactic model for MOOCs is needed. Recorded web lectures of gifted teachers or successful lectures are no guarantee of high study success of MOOCs. In many cases the didactic model of regular courses in lecture halls is copied. A teacher explains the theory, gives some examples during the course and students are supposed to study the learning material and to make exercises. But making homework is a great problem. The gap between lectures and making exercises is (too) big and most students are not able to manage their time and set themselves into action.

It can be observed at Delft University of Technology that a week before the exams students start to visit libraries, study-halls etc. to start their preparation for exams. Observing this study behaviour of fellow students triggers other students to start similar behaviour. It is difficult to implement similar triggers in the MOOC community. But we have to realise that used didactic models assuming regular study behaviour of students in general don't work for MOOCs. In regular courses students are creative in finding alternatives, observing peers, similar models are still under development in the MOOC community.

Personal, intensive study guidance results in better study results. A good binding with the study and study community is an essential prerequisite for successful study. Unfortunately the massive character of MOOCs makes individual tutoring by teachers impossible. One of the assumptions of creating a study community via social media is that students will support each other. But it proves from surveys at DUT that creating study communities is far from trivial. One of the outcomes of the surveys is that many students don't like networking and cooperation and prefer to study in their own individual way. Students get stronger involvement with the study and study community.

To be a member of a learning community has a great impact on the motivation, emotions and study results/achievement. [21]. It is important to give students the feeling that it is exceptional to take these courses and that they should be involved in learning communities. In case of MOOCs it cannot be expected that there is much individual support or supervision of teachers. Fellow students can take the role of a teacher and the community of fellow students should support and stimulate the members of the community.

Many students following MOOCs don't live in a student environment. Via social media they can be involved in learning environments. Participation in such an environment is important to develop 21st century abilities. MOOCs offer the opportunity for internationalisation, integration of research in the learning environment. In research based education students are involved in common research activities and in research tutored education students perform research activities themselves.

Students following MOOCs have to take the responsibility for their own learning process. It is definitely true that part of the students are able to manage their study. But most students need group pressure, supervision of teachers, counsellors, fellow students to complete a MOOC successfully. Nevertheless many educators prefer self-paced instruction so that every student is able to define his individual study path. This enables students to accomplish their study at their own speed. But it creates problems to give support from the community. In the Netherlands some PhD students have to follow MOOCs instead of common courses at some University. This is highly appreciated by PhD students and the success rate is high. After completion of a course PhD students are supposed to do an exam at the home University.

3.2 Dropout Model Regular Courses

In many studies on dropout and study-delay researchers try to explain the phenomena of dropout by a description of personal characteristics of (non-) successful students and characteristics of educational Institutes. In 1975 Tinto [9] introduced a theoretical longitudinal model showing how personal characteristics and characteristics of educational institutes have their impact on the interaction process students-institute. In fact he describes the interaction process of three systems: the individual students, the academic and social system. According to Tinto an individual student will enter the institute with some social background, personality characteristics and secondary school education. Based on that he builds up a binding with the Institute and goal of the study. Such a binding is measurable by motivations and expectations. The academic and social system and the interaction of both systems have their impact on the binding. A reduction of the strength of the binding can result in the decision of the student to stop his study. In Fig. 1 we present a didactic model inspired by Tinto and system theory.

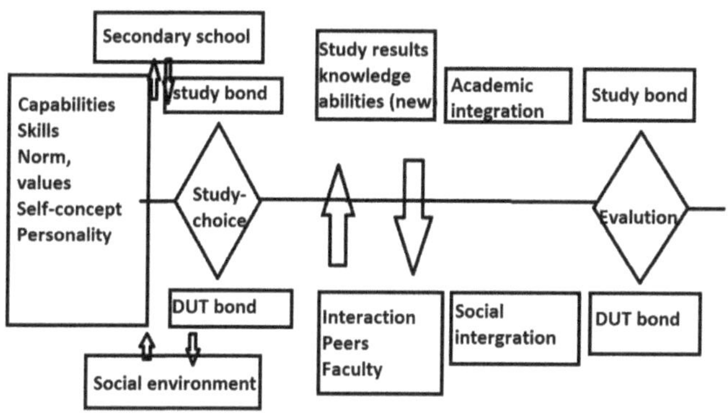

Fig. 1. Didactic model teaching learning on macro-meso level, based on the interation student with teaching learning environment.

To validate the model we developed a questionnaire composed of 130 item distributed over the following topics:

Choice of study, motivation, study environment, education, tutoring, study problem, study-methods, personal problem, study-skills. A second part of the questionnaire was only for students having a significant delay after half a year of study. In 30 items (131–161) possible reasons of delay were described and students have to indicate on a three point scale which reasons play a significant role in their personal situation. The data of delayed students were analyzed principal component analysis. We were able to detect 4 underlying factors and in Table 1 we describe the underlying factors: study commitment, choice of study, skills/abilities, impersonal teaching and we list the items with corresponding factor loadings.

Table 1. Four factors describing study delay.

		Factor loading			
Factor	Items	F1	F2	F3	F4
Commitment	Insufficient preparation exams	.55	.26	−.05	.05
	Insufficient time spend to the study	.77	−.11	.05	.15
	Delay in the first weeks of study	.61	.18	.12	.05
	Too much time spend to social activities	.52	.01	.03	.14
	Too tired to study in the evening	.52	.12	.20	−.22
	Insufficient time spend to homework	.76	−.08	.14	.19
	Wrong study approach	.57	.07	.02	.11
Study-choice	Chosen study was second choice	−.09	.43	.12	03
	Atmosphere at Faculty	.12	.80	.21	.19
	Personalities of fellow students	.10	.73	.02	.29
Skills/capabilities	Study different from expectations	.08	.19	.62	−.04
	Study-delay in first weeks of study demotivating	.25	.21	.50	−.06
	Some courses to complex/difficult	−.01	.06	.69	.08
	Limited capabilities, Missing background- knowledge	.03	.02	.62	.13
(in-)personal teaching	Less social contacts with teachers	.16	.31	−.16	.69
	No time for tutoring	.11	.26	.05	.62
	Academic freedom	.32	−.05	.13	.53
	Way of teaching less appreciated	.11	.08	.18	.63

3.3 Dropout Model MOOCs

In the last section we discussed a dropout model for regular courses. In this section we discuss an additional model for MOOCs. The dropout model for regular courses was describes the interaction process of individual students, the academic and social system. In case of a MOOC at start we can consider the same model. But as soon a student starts his course the interaction student, learning material is dominant. In Fig. 1 we visualize the interaction student-learning material as a melting pot filled with boiling study-liquid. At the bottom there is a leakage of study liquid by two pro-cesses distraction and physiological condition of the students. New input of study liquid is provided by three components Attraction, Capability and Activity. These components correspond to the well-known Osgood dimensions Evaluation, Potency and Activity [12]. Janssen, Goethem and Lacante [10, 11] researched study experiences of students found similar results. Before a student starts a study activity he first evaluates the effects of that behavior. Next he researched if he has the required capabilities and finally he set himself into action. We discuss the components of our interaction model in more detail:

Attraction: An important component in the interaction student learning material is interest of students. As long as the learning material is interesting a student keeps on board. But as soon the learning material gets boring, student lose their interest and the dropout process has been started. In case of regular courses there is a lot of pressure of peers, institute, teaching schemas to follow lectures the other day. New topics provide opportunities for a new start. Usually this is missing in case of MOOCs. By the huge amount of students individual tutoring is difficult to realize. A special didactic approach is needed. The span of attention control is very short, only some minutes. A varied way of presentation of learning material is needed by showing movies, video lectures, simulations and interesting applied assignments for students.

Capabilities: A student assumes at start he has sufficient capabilities to complete the course successfully. But when he interacts with the learning material and it proves that it is far beyond his capabilities, the dropout process has been started. In regular face to face courses a student is usually not allowed to leave the teaching hall. In case many students lose their interest an experienced teacher starts a summary, a clarifying example to get students back in the teaching-learning process. In regular courses there is support of peers during the breaks or after the lectures. In MOOCs social support of peers is wanted but usual less developed. There is a trend to develop MOOCs as self-paced courses for individual students. That makes these students vulnerable for negative interactions.

Activity: Attractive learning material and sufficient required capabilities are prerequisite of a positive interaction process of a student with his learning material. Next a student is assumed to play an active role in this process. Many students read the description of the offered courses, they even enroll in the courses but the next step is to start study activity. Most MOOCs are not designed for passive students, a lot of activity is required varying from posing and answering questions, making assignments and involvement in project activities.

Distraction: Interest and sufficient capabilities are the positive drives of interaction students with the learning material. But there are also two negative drives. Distraction is the first negative drive. In case of MOOCs students usually study in a stimulus rich environment. The computer used for taking the course offers a lot of alternatives for distraction especially in case the MOOC material gets boring or is beyond the capabilities of students.

Physiology: A second negative drive is the physiological state of the students. If a student gets hungry, sleepy he can start a break. A lot of discipline is needed for a restart and to keep the length of the break under control. In case of regular courses there are social rules, institutional rules regulating breaks.

In Fig. 2 we display the dropout process of MOOCs on a micro-level. The model has been validated by some exit interviews of students. Drop-off students usually receive a questionnaire to research the causality of a drop-off. But the response of such questionnaire is usually very low. So additional research is needed.

Success of study is not only dependent of students characteristics as capabilities, knowledge, used study methods, but is the result of a complex interaction process. This is also the basic idea underlying our didactic model presented in this section. Most didactic models describe the teaching-learning process over a longer period of time. But as we pointed in MOOCs a strong focus is on the direct interaction student-learning material. Emotions play an important role in this interaction process. In the next section we research the impact of emotions as driving forces of the teaching-learning process.

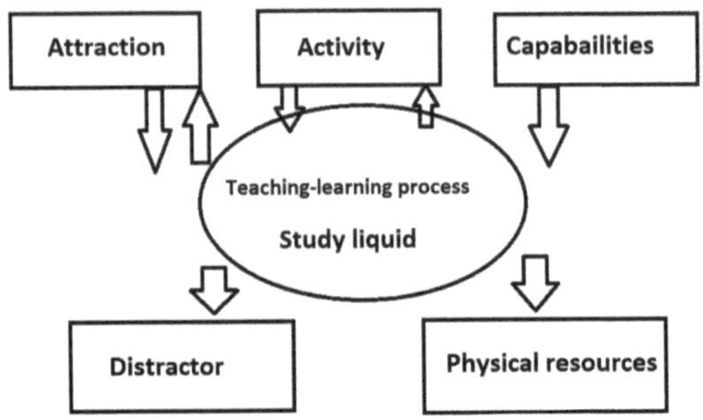

Fig. 2. Didactic model teaching-learning on micro level.

3.4 Emotional Aspects

It is commonly agreed that emotions have a strong impact on our behavior. Students with well-developed abilities and trained skills show the expected behavior if they get motivated and activated by internal or external emotional triggers. Happiness has a positive effect on the learning behavior. Students who are able to understand the learning material and to solve the corresponding assignments successfully get a motivational boost. But from the other site students who are not able to master the learning material successfully lose their self-confident and self-worth and their motivation to learn.

Distance learning is usual a lonely process. Only chatting with study-friends in the social network can provide some support. By collaborative learning students are able to share their responsibilities, share their planning and mutual control. In full isolation there is a risk of upcoming negative emotion and moods. Strong negative emotions as fear and anxiety can block the learning behaviour.

Recently we observe some attempts to design a digital tutor. But one of the requirements of digital tutoring is assessment of the emotional state of the student online. Usually assessment of emotions is done by questionnaires. But for instantaneous assessment of emotions questionnaires cannot be used. In [14, 15] Rothkrantz et al. describe some experiments to asses emotions of students via analysis of facial expressions and sound recordings. It is required that the teaching learning environment is equipped with a multimodal camera. But it proves that many students don't like supervision by a camera. More succesfull were the experiments using Skype. In that case students were aware of the fact that they are monitored all the time.

After Darwin, Ekman spent a lot of research on the automatic recognition of facial expressions. He claimed that 6 emotions are universal namely happiness, sadness, disgust, anger, fear and surprise. Many systems have been developed to recognize the six basic emotions in speech and recordings of facial expressions. But in daily life most emotions are not pure but blended and of varying intensity. And even the six basic emotions can be displayed in many ways. This can also be expected in an e-learning environment.

Russell [22] analyzed qualitative values of emotion words based on humans' social value and depicted them in a 2D space of pleasureness and activation. These two dimensions correspond with the dimensions attraction and action in our didactic model. The dimension can categorize emotions in a comprehensible way; however, the approach is not yet sufficient to differentiate between emotions, e.g. anger and fear fall close together on the 2D map. We used the results of the experiment above and selected the stem of 140 emotion labels and words. The distance between words was based on Whissell's Dictionary of Affect in Language [23].

In [24] Fitrianie et al. researched the relation between text and emotions. We created a talking face as model of a tutor. In this study we researched the relation between facial expressions and words with an emotional meaning. By the introduction of serious gaming in distant learning the interest for the impact of emotion on learning has been increased (see Fig. 3).

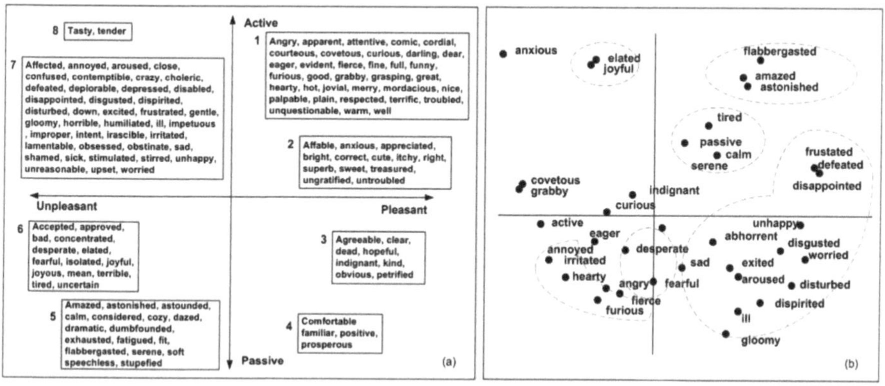

Fig. 3. Display of emotional words on the dimensions activity and attraction.

4 Psychological Assessment

4.1 Big Five Personality Test

One of the research goals of this paper was to investigate how to teach students 21st century skills as networking, cooperation, creativity etc. Traditionally teaching mathematics is rather individually oriented. A lecturer introduces students in lecture halls into new topics. Students listen and make notes. Parallel to the lectures are usually lab hours during which time students are supposed to make exercises alone or together. Especially during the lectures students are passive consuming knowledge, instead of exploring new topics and discovering new knowledge and even more important it is an individual process. It takes students less energy to listen to lecturers and see how he discovers new knowledge. But the challenge is to take students out of their comfort zone and challenge them to actively search for knowledge and problem solving.

Changing the didactic approach may change the learning attitude of students. It can be expected that there will be resistance leaving the comfort zone. A second question is if students have the right personality characteristics to learn the 21st skills. If students are not able to cooperate, socializing and networking they are not well prepared for the future. To research that problem a group of first years students in mathematics and computer science were tested using the Big Five Personality test in September 2015 at start of the academic year. Students were supposed to fill in a questionnaire of 4 × 5 questions. Then the score on 5 factors E, A, C, N, O listed below were computed. Students with high scores on the factors A and O are supposed to be open for learning the 21st century skills. But it proves that students score significant lower on A and higher on O. This supports the hypothesis that students in technology or exact courses have the tendency to work individually and are open for new knowledge. The factors underlying the Big Five Personality test can be described as follows:

- Extroversion (E) is the personality trait of seeking fulfilment from sources outside the self or in community. High scorers tend to be very social while low scorers prefer to work on their projects alone.
- Agreeableness (A) reflects much individuals adjust their behavior to suit others. High scorers are typically polite and like people. Low scorers tend to 'tell it like it is'.
- Conscientiousness (C) is the personality trait of being honest and hardworking. High scorers tend to follow rules and prefer clean homes. Low scorers may be messy and cheat others.
- Neuroticism (N) is the personality trait of being emotional.
- Openness to Experience (O) is the personality trait of seeking new experience and intellectual pursuits. High scores may day dream a lot. Low scorers may be very down to earth.

From Table 2 it can be observed that students mathematics and computer science have the same average score on the factor Extroversions indicating that in principle they are open/not open for social contacts and open/not open for networking.

Table 2. Average values of the five factors of the Big Five test E, A, C, N, O for a cohort of TUD students computer science and mathematics and a general cohort.

Number of respondents	10189	179
Extroversion	3.05	3.05
Agreeableness	3.84	3.69
Conscientiousness	3.38	3.06
Neuroticism	2.98	3.39
Openness	4.05	3.71

The students in the DUT cohort score lower on the factor Openness and less open for new experience and intellectual pursuits. But we may conclude that students in exact/technical sciences are in principle open for learning 21st century skills.

4.2 Psychological Assessment Procedure at TUDelft 1953–1957

For most academic studies at Universities in the Netherlands there is no entrance exam. Only a limited studies with capacity problems have a special admission procedure. Students with low grades at the final exam at their secondary school have a lesser chance to pass this special entrance procedure than students with higher grades. As a consequence many students start a study with insufficient intellectual capabilities. The assumption is that Universities have the opportunities to select the students for the higher years based on their academic performance in the first year. It is a well-known saying that students with limited intellectual capabilities can compensate this shortage by hard working. To research the impact of personality characteristics, motivation, social environment on academic performance and study-success or –failure a huge assessment procedure was performed in 1953 at Delft University of Technology. All students in the first, second and third year got a psychological assessment. They were supposed to fill in questionnaires corresponding with test assessing cognitive abilities and personality. Next all students were interviewed by student counsellors.

The outcomes of all these assessments were correlated with the results of exams of students and results of students at their secondary school. It proves that there was a significant correlation between academic performance at the university and final results at secondary school for the subjects mathematics and physics. Not a big surprise taking into account that the subjects mathematics and physics play an important role in technical studies at Delft University of Technology. From Table 2 we can see that students with lower grades for the subjects mathematics and physics have a low study progress in the first year and students with high grades have a high chance of study success. For the middle group of about 50% it was difficult to predict study success or –failure. A disappointing result was the fact that the outcome of psychological assessment has a very limited added value to the prediction of study-success or –failure. Apparently the impact of personality, social environment were already included in the performance at secondary school.

From Tables 3 and 4 can be observed that the dropout rate in the first two years is 31%. In total the dropout rate was 43%. About half of the dropouts started another study at TUD or at a Polytechnic School. The function of the first year was orientation and selection. But still 10% of the students started a second year and dropout during that year and additionally 12% of the students drop out later in the study. At this moment the university spend a lot of time and effort to stimulate students to take their decision of dropout as soon as possible. It is in general not possible to start the second year before completing the first year. There are special programs and even a special MOOC enabling student to get a better orientation of the study.

A special problem with presented tables is that some students enrolled in the study but never show up. In the early days even no-show students could get a student loan for the whole year. So no-show behaviour has financial consequences. A similar problem can be observed in the cohort of MOOCs students. In the past the group of slow starters made a successful start in the second year. The phenomena of restarting students is not observed in the cohort of MOOCs students. One of our recommendations for MOOCs designers is to take care of slow starters, students who need a longer adaptation time or to apply the spiral principle of in increasing difficulties.

Students with a low respectively high average score on the subjects mathematics/physics have a low chance/high chance to complete the study successfully. But students with modal scores are rather unpredictable. The hope was that psychological personal improved prediction of study-success or failure for the middle group. Unfortunately this was not the case.

From Table 4 can be observed that dropouts miss more than half of the exams already in the first session. Some students with bad results in the first year give themselves a second start but have again bad results in the next exam session. The phenomena of restarting students is not observed at MOOCs.

Table 3. Study-progress/delay/dropouts in percentages crossed with average score mathematics/physics grades at school, after two years of study, Cohort 1953.

Study progress ≥ 150%	0%	4%	11%	15%	7%
Study progress ≤ 150%	0%	8%	13%	4%	0%
Delayed students with Incomplete first year	2%	2%	1%	1%	0%
Dropouts during second year	2%	6%	2%	0%	0%
Dropouts during first year	2%	9%	9%	1%	0%
Average math/physics grades at school exam	5–6	6–7	7–8	8–9	9–10

Table 4. Study-progress/delay/dropouts crossed with number of passed exams in the first exam-session.

Studyprogress ≥ 150%	0%	1%	7%	14%	16%
Studyprogress ≤ 150%	3%	8%	8%	4%	3%
Delayed students with Incomplete first year	2%	1%	1%	0%	0%
Dropouts during second year	2%	6%	1%	1%	0%
Dropouts during first year	6%	9%	5%	0%	0%
Numbers of exams passed successfully in first period	0	1	2	3	4

5 Experiments

In this section we discuss possible causalities of the high drop off rate of MOOCs. DUT launched more than 20 MOOCs, accessible via edX platform. In this section we focus on the MOOC Pre-Un Calculus, visited by more than 26.000 students. Via interviews and questionnaires experiences of students and teachers were assessed and reported in by Vos [25]. Most (early) dropouts from the course didn't take part in the assessment procedure, so we realize that the results are biased.

5.1 Pre-university Calculus July–September 2015

TUDelft designed a special MOOC called Pre University calculus (see Figs. 4, 5 and 6). The goal of the MOOC was to refresh mathematical knowledge of students before they start their academic study at the University and to teach students missing topics of the mathematics at secondary schools. The teaching material was composed of small, 10 min video fragment with a lot of simulations, video lectures, gaming etc. The focus was on applications of mathematics.

Fig. 4. Screenshot of the Pre-Un. Calculus MOOC (source DUT).

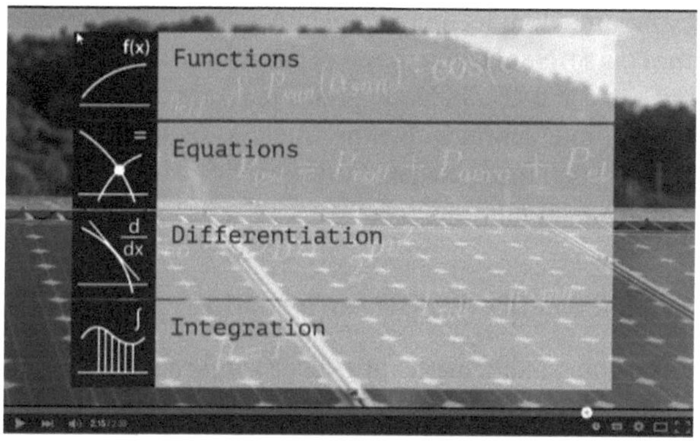

Fig. 5. Topics of the Pre-Un. Calculus MOOC (source DUT).

Students were stimulated to cooperate by interacting via special blogs. Students were supposed to define questions stimulated by the lectures and the learning material. Fellow students in the network are invited to answer the questions and commenting solutions in the course forum. This is common practice in mathematics learning.

In 2015 more than 26.000 students worldwide followed the course and via data analytics the performance of students was analysed. We will report some main findings from participating students, first students from TUD and after that students from all over the world. Aspirant students from TUD were stimulated to take part in the special MOOC. Usually lectures were offered during the summer holidays after the school exam and just before the start of the academic year. The MOOC was supposed to attract more students because there was no need to come to the University and also no need for teachers to lecture to lecture during the summer holidays.

In total 794 TUD students enrolled in the course, 420 (53%) of them attempted an exercise and 40 (5%) attempted all exercises. Only 46 students passed the final exam successfully. From the interviews it proves that most students had the feeling that they master the topics already. Just before the start of the academic year, other activities got a higher priority as finding housing in Delft, increasing the income by performing a job or just taking holidays after passing the school exam successfully. Students didn't feel the need to participate in the MOOC.

From Table 4 it can be observed or computed that there is no significant difference in mathematics grades between students that enrolled and students that did not enrol.

In total 27.186 students enrolled in the course, 4.150 students attempted to make an exercise and only 273 attempted all exercises.

All students were requested to fill out some questionnaires. We report the results from students who showed some activity in the course. About 59% of the students took part in the course from begin to the end, 18% browsed through the topics and videos and 4% mainly watched the videos, 7% mainly did the exercises.

Students on average stated they rarely participated in study groups, connected to other students, posted a comment or a question, or looked at the forum. They also rated their perceived support from either other students or staff rather low.

However, they reported that feelings of loneliness or missing interaction negatively affected them in the course. Neither did they feel that lack of feedback negatively affected them. Rather, they rated the feedback as good. It seems, students in general neither expect nor need a lot of interaction with either students or staff. We stress that this only holds for students taking part in the course. From students who didn't take part or dropout in an early stage we have no information.

5.2 Experiment Mathematics at TUD During 2015

It was decided that teaching mathematics at TUDelft will change dramatically from 2015 on. The dropout rate had to be reduced. There should be more focus on applications of mathematics, self-discovery, teaching 21st century skills such as networking, cooperation via social media etc. In a first experiment 370 students studying Civil Engineering got mathematical courses new style. First the didactical principle "flip the class room" was applied. For many years students got their lectures mathematics in big lecture halls followed by making exercises in small classrooms. Now the order has been changed. Students are supposed to study video lectures and make exercises before they meet the teachers and fellow students in small classrooms to discuss problems and outcomes of the exercises. In the video lectures there was a focus on applications of mathematics, self-discovery activities of students. They are stimulated to cooperate in study groups. The MOOC Pre-Un Calculus was integrated in video lectures. Many new videos were added especially on simulation and applications of mathematics.

From [25] we take some of the results from surveys and interviews. It proves that on average only 20% of the students viewed the video lectures before the classroom meeting. So the assumption that students activate the right pre-knowledge was not correct. That poses a didactical problem for the teacher. Repeating or summarising the homework is boring for students making their homework and will not stimulate viewing

Table 5. Distribution of students who enrolled and didn't enrol in the MOOC.

Grade math at school exam						
	5	6	7	8	9	10
# of students that did not enroll	101	764	1017	703	332	52
Number of students that enrolled	32	173	200	166	63	10

video lectures in the future. One of the critical comments of students was that the video lectures are interesting but are not direct integrated with the learning material/book. Viewing the video lectures maybe will result in a better understanding of mathematics in general but it is not necessary to pass the exam successfully. One of the goals of the new mathematics teaching was to focus on real applications. Then the applications should be part of the exam and not additional. In the compulsory homework assignments it is possible to make links with some topics discussed in the video lectures (Table 5).

At start about 80% of the students visited the classroom meeting and at the end it was about 65%. The classroom meetings were highly appreciated. Especially the moments the teacher was lecturing or explaining difficult topics. It proves that teachers were better in raising questions or pointing to typical problems. Individual or group wise making assignments during the classroom lectures was highly appreciated. Because there was a meeting place for the students in the classroom there was no need to cooperate via social media. Teachers were asked if and how many times during a lecture they provide opportunities for students to discuss topics or cooperate. In Table 6 we summarize the results.

Table 6. Overview of opportunities teachers offered for discussion or cooperation.

Opportunities for discussion or cooperation	Never	1 time	2–3 times	4 or more times
	11%	22%	34%	33%

Teachers like to teach and play a central role during the lessons. Many students come to the lessons and expect that the teacher lectures. Parallel to the classroom meetings there was a digital Lab room (My.MathLab). Students were supposed to make assignments and got feedback in an automated way. It proves that many students joined their effort and meet each other to make assignments

An interesting option for students was to provide feedback during the lectures using their smart phones or laptop. One of the start-up companies from DUT, FeedBackFruits developed a tool for mobile devices which enables students to ask questions during a lecture. The questions are visualised on a display in front of the teacher. It proves that students consider the tool as an interesting option. But defining questions takes some time and usual the lecture is going on. It is up to the teacher if he introduces breaks to allow and discuss questions. Some questions can be used by the teacher to summarize a topic. If there are many questions about the same topic the teacher has the option to explain the topic in an different way or to come up with some examples. To support the didactical approach "flip the classroom", the start-up company FeedBackFruits was requested to generate a plugin to make the "questioning tool" available via edX, one of the MOOCs consortia. A layer of new functionalities was developed over the edX platform. This enables students to make specific notes online and make digital notes out of it. The plug-in also allows users to add new content to the course and share a message information board way questions of the students can be considered as an online feedback system for the teacher.

6 Recent Developments

In many surveys it has been shown that students spend less time than expected to their study. Students in social sciences spend about 24 h weekly to their study and students in exact studies about 32 h. This is significant less than the expected 40 h pro week. It also proves that over the year the time spend to the study is not equally distributed. When exams are approaching there is an increase in time spend to the study. Students spend a significant amount of study time in social activities, jobs and doing nothing. The Ministry of Education in cooperation with the Universities were brainstorming for many years about measures to increase the flow rate of students. Everybody agrees that the freedom of students to spend their time in an individual way should be limited. This conflicts ideas of self-management of students and personal development. The focus should be on development of cognitive skills and improvement of results of exams.

Recent years Universities in the Netherlands took the following measures to improve the flow rate of students

- Study advice at the end of the first year. All students get an advice at the end of the first year of study. In case of a negative advice students have to stop their study but may switch to another study or university. We observe that students having a huge study delay after half a year of study and expect a negative advice at the end of the first year stop their study and switch before the end of the academic year
- Hard cut at the end of the bachelor (Since 2012). Student have to finish their bachelor program before they can start their master program. In the past it could happen that students finish their master program but still miss some courses from the bachelor program. Students who are forced to stop focus on the remaining bachelor courses, take a part time job or even stop the study. But in general more students do their best to finish their Bachelor in time or after 4 years of study.
- Performance agreements Universities and Ministry of Education. In 2012 Universities promised to increase the quality of the teachers, to increase the number of teaching hours and to reduce the dropout rate of students. From the financial budget 7% will be re-distributed depending of the outcomes of the educational improvements.

Interesting to note that the flow rate of female students is much higher compared to male students (see Figs. 6 and 7).

Recent years Universities took some measures to increase the quality and motivation of starting students. Delft University of Technology offers online courses (premaster calculus) in the summer holidays before the start of the study. The idea is to refresh and improve the knowledge of mathematics taught at secondary school.

TUD offers also online courses for starting students in their study of preference. Interesting topics from the study are lectured by the best teachers. The idea is that students reconsider their choice of their study, get more familiar with the study and are able to see if they have the right ability and motivation to complete the chosen study successfully.

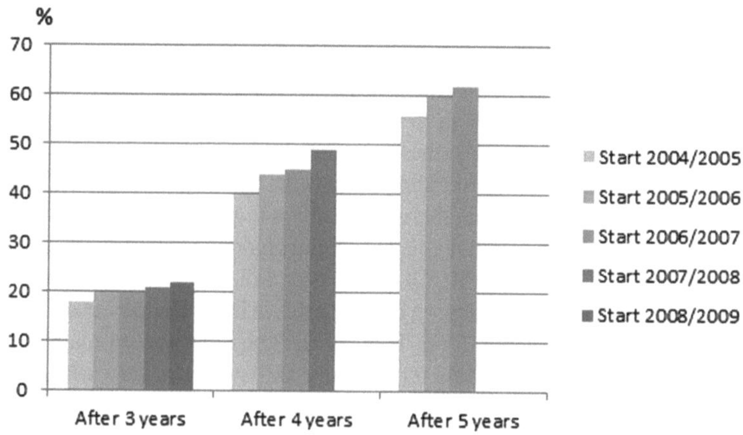

Fig. 6. Percentage of students completing an academic study successfully in the Netherlands (data from CBS).

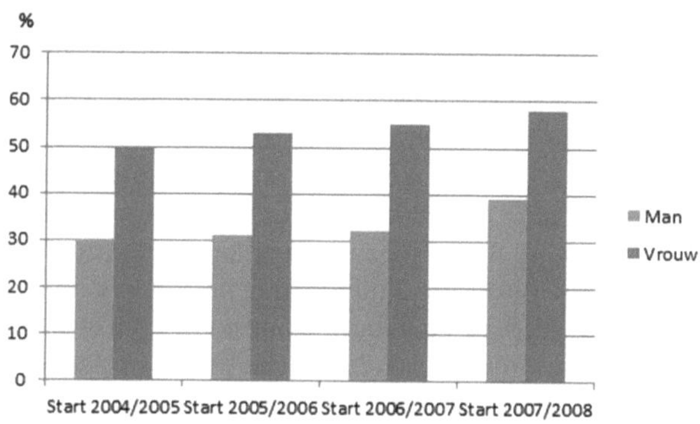

Fig. 7. Percentage of male and female students completing an academic study in the Netherlands (data CBS).

7 Conclusions

The main goals of this paper was to study the high drop off of MOOCs, to find possible causes and to develop new didactical models. Secondly we want to invest in how far if it is possible to teach students 21st century skills. We used the data from two experiments at Delft University of Technology. The current version of the paper is an extended version of the paper [25].

In the first experiment, Delft University of Technology designed a special MOOC called Pre University Calculus. The goal of the MOOC was to refresh mathematical knowledge of students before they start their academic study and to teach students missing topics of the mathematics taught at secondary schools. The teaching material was composed of small, 10 min video fragment with a lot of simulations, video lectures, gaming etc. The focus was on applications of mathematics. Students were stimulated to cooperate by interacting via special blogs. In 2015 more than 26.000 worldwide followed the course and via data analytics the performance of students was analysed. Only a minority of 5% of the students completed the course successfully. These students stated in surveys and interviews that they prefer to work individually and not in groups or in a digital community. Unfortunately the early dropouts were not surveyed. From the questionnaires and interviews we found many reasons for dropout behaviour. From the available data can be concluded that there were only a few network activities and cooperation between students via social media. Teaching students 21st century skills will not take place automatically by using MOOCs but special didactic models are needed.

Secondly it was decided that teaching mathematics at Delft University of Technology will change dramatically from 2015 on. There should be more focus on applications of mathematics, self-discovery, teaching 21st century skills such as networking, cooperation via social media etc. In a first experiment students studying Civil Engineering got mathematical courses new style. First the didactical principle flip the class room was applied. For many years students got their math lectures in big lecture rooms followed by making exercises in small classrooms. Now the order has been changed. Students are supposed to study video lectures and make exercises before they meet the teachers and fellow students in small classrooms to discuss problems and outcomes of the exercises. In the video lectures there was a focus on applications of mathematics, self-discovery activities of students. They are stimulated to cooperate in study groups. It proves that less than 20% prepared the lessons by viewing the video lectures in advance. Most students reported that lack of time and motivation was the main reason. And they expect that the teacher will summarise the main topics in the lessons so that they are able to follow the lessons. Following the lessons is important for the students because they expect the teacher will provide essential information needed to pass the exam successfully. Students cooperated via the digital Lab making homework together. In the lessons there was less cooperation also because the teachers didn't provide the opportunity. During the lessons and video lectures students were able to give comment or asking questions. This provides essential feedback for the teacher and information for the evaluation of the course. Again we to conclude that blended courses don't guarantee that students learn 21st century skills.

Students mathematics and computer science got a psychological assessment using the Big Five personality test. From the results it proves that students have the abilities to learn the 21st century skills but this will not happen automatically. A special didactic model is needed. We developed a special didactic model based on the model of Tinto and system theory. This models holds for regular classroom lectures and distant learning and is able to explain dropout behavior on global level of teaching and learning. We also developed a didactic model for short time process of teaching and learning. Emotions play an important role in this model. In recent years researchers stress the important role of emotions in the teaching learning process and dropout behavior.

We also described some measurements of Universities in the Netherlands restricting the study freedom of students. It proved that many students are not able to manage their study time and external pressure is needed to increase the study flow.

A comparison was made between a huge assessment study at Delft University of Technology during 1953–1957 and recent experiments at Delft University of Technology. It proves that over the years 40% of the students dropout. We reported many causes based on surveying and interviewing students.

As a final conclusion we state that also regular courses have high dropout rates varying around 40%. MOOCs show even higher dropout rates and we conclude from the outcomes of surveys and interviews that lack of cooperation in networking, lack of social control of peer students inability to manage the study and decreasing or lacking motivation were the main causes of high dropout rates.

Acknowledgements. We thank Ingrid Vos providing me with the results of evaluation of the experiments at TUDelft. We thanks the colleagues of the FETCH project for their valuable help.

References

1. Bussemaker, J.: Strategische Agenda Hoger Onderwijs en Onderzoek 2015–20125 (Dutch), Ministerie van Onderwijs Cultuur en Wetenschappen (2015)
2. Rothkrantz, L.J.M.: How social media facilitate learning communities and peer groups around MOOCS. Int. J. Hum. Cap. Inf. Technol. Prof. **6**(1), 1–13 (2015). IGI
3. Bottema, O., Bakker, H.T.: Mislukking en vertraging van de studie. Verslag van een onderzoek verricht aan de Technische Hogeschool te Delft 1953–1957 (Dutch). Technische Hogeschool, Delft, vol. 106, p. 32 (1959)
4. Onah, D.F., Sinclair, J., Boyatt, R.: Dropout rates of massive open online courses, behavioural patterns. In: 6th Annual International Conference on Education and New Learning Technologies, Edulearn 14, Barcelona. IATED (2014)
5. Yang, D., Sinha, T., Adamson, D., Rosé, C.P.: Turn on, tune in, drop out: anticipating student dropouts in massive open online courses. In: Proceedings of the 2013 NIPS Data-Driven Education Workshop, NIPS (2013)
6. Sinha, T.: Who negatively influences me? Formalizing diffusion dynamics of negative exposure leading to student attrition in MOOCs. In: LTI Student Research Symposium, Carnegy Mellon (2014)
7. Ye, C., Biswas, G.: Early prediction of student dropout and performance in MOOCs using higher granularity temporal information. J. Learn. Anal. **1**(3), 169–172 (2014). UTS e-Press
8. Wilbrink, B.: Assessment in historical perspective. Stud. Educ. Eval. **23**, 31–48 (1997). Elsevier
9. Tinto, V.: Dropout from higher education: a theoretical synthesis of recent research. Rev. Educ. Res. **45**, 89–125 (1975). Sage Publications
10. Lacante, M.: Van intelligentie, persoonlijkheid, studiestrategie en studeergedrag naar studieresultaat. Pedagogische Studie **60**, 289–299 (1983)
11. Janssen, P., de Neve, H.: Studeren en doceren aan het Hoger Onderwijs, Uitgevery Acco (1988)

12. Osgood, C., Succi, G.J., Tannenbaum, P.H.: The Measurement of Meaning. University of Illenois Press, Urban (1961)
13. Kalogiannakis, M.: Emotions experienced by learners and their development through communication with the tutor-counsellor. Eur. J. Open Distance E-Learn. **18**, 36–48 (2015)
14. Rothkrantz, L., Datcu, D., Chiriacescu, I., Chitu, A.: Assessment of the emotional states of students during e-Learning. In: Proceedings of The International Conference on E-Learning and The Knowledge Society, Conference, Ruse (2009)
15. Datcu, D., Rothkrantz, L.J.M.: Assessment of emotion states during e-learning. Commun. Cogn. **43**(1–2), 81–92 (2010). University of Ghent
16. Rothkrantz, L.J.M.: E-learning in virtual communities. Commun. Cogn. **42**(1), 37–52 (2009). Nr 1&2. University of Ghent
17. Rothkrantz, L.J.M.: A training tool for non-verbal communication. In: Proceedings of the International Conference on E-Learning and The Knowledge Society, pp. 88–93. University of Ruse (2010)
18. Datcu, D., Rothkrantz, L.J.M.: Multimodal web based system for human emotion recognition. In: Proceedings ISC 2007, pp. 91–98. Eurosis-Eti (2007)
19. Freudenthal, H.: Mathematics as an Educational Task. Springer Science & Business Media, New York (1973)
20. Rothkrantz, L.J.M.: Inquiry based learning as didactic model in distant learning. Int. J. Inf. Technol. Secur. **7**(4), 1–10 (2015). Dobi Press Food
21. Furrer, C., Skinner, E.A.: Sense of relatedness as a factor in children's academic engagement and performance. J. Educ. Psychol. **95**, 148–162 (2003)
22. Russell, J.A.: A circumplex model of affect. J. Pers. Soc. Psychol. **39**(6), 1161–1178 (1980)
23. Whissell, C.: Whissell's dictionary of affect in language. Measur. Emot. **4**, 113–131 (1989)
24. Fitrianie, S., Rothkrantz, L.: Constructing knowledge for automated text-based emotion expressions. In: CompSysTech (2009)
25. Vos, I.: Evaluation pre university calculus MOOC, TUDelft Press (2015)
26. Rothkrantz, L.: Dropout rates of regular courses and MOOCs. In: Proceedings of the 8th International Conference on Computer Supported Education (CSEDU), Rome, pp. 9–18 (2016)

Papers

Hybrid Matrix Factorization Update for Progress Modeling in Intelligent Tutoring Systems

Carlotta Schatten(✉) and Lars Schmidt-Thieme

Information Systems and Machine Learning Lab,
University of Hildesheim, Hildesheim, Germany
{schatten,schmidt-thieme}@ismll.uni-hildesheim.de
http://www.ismll.uni-hildesheim.de

Abstract. Intelligent Tutoring Systems often profit of intelligent components, which allow to personalize the proposed contents' characteristics and sequence. Adaptive sequencing, in particular, requires either a detrimental data collection for users or extensive domain information provided by experts of the educational area. In this paper we propose an efficient domain independent method to model student progress that can be later used to sequence tasks in large commercial systems. The developed method is based on the integration of domain independent Matrix Factorization Performance Prediction with Kalman Filters state modeling abilities. Our solution not only reduces the prediction error, but also possesses a more computationally efficient model update. Finally, we give hints about a potential interpretability of student's state computed by Matrix Factorization, that, because of its implicit modeling, did not allow human experts, to monitor user's knowledge acquisition.

Keywords: Progress modeling · Kalman filerts · Matrix factorization · Performance prediction · Sequencing

1 Introduction

Intelligent Tutoring Systems often profit of intelligent components, which allow to personalize the proposed contents' characteristics and sequence. Adaptive sequencing, in particular, requires either a detrimental data collection for users or extensive domain information provided by experts of the educational area. In this paper we propose an efficient domain independent method to model student progress that can be later used to sequence tasks in large commercial systems. In this paper we want to extend domain independent performance prediction to progress modeling. In order to keep track of the learning progress of a student

G. Costagliola et al. (Eds.): CSEDU 2016, CCIS 739, pp. 49–70, 2017.
DOI: 10.1007/978-3-319-63184-4_4

it is not sufficient to estimate current/next state of the user, the students' state has also to evolve in a meaningful, plausible and therefore interpretable way over time. In this scenario three problems arise:

1. Domain information, like tagging involved skills in tasks, necessitates experts and thus is a time-consuming, costly, and, subjective. For large commercial ITS it is even unfeasible.
2. Progress modeling requires to be able to interpret the model, i.e. to be able to associate the value of the model parameters with a specific user state.
3. The continuously changing student's state and the necessity of new data requires online updating algorithms, that refine their prediction after each interaction.

Problem (1) involves domain dependent performance prediction algorithms: Bayesian Knowledge Tracing (BKT) [2] and Performance Factors Analysis (PFA) [14]. Therefore, [26] proposed Matrix Factorization (MF) as domain agnostic alternative. As such, MF does not require skills' tagging [18] and can be easily integrated in larger systems [22]. By using domain independent performance prediction and a score-based policy inspired by Vygotsky's concept of Zone of Proximal Development [29], the so-called Vygotsky Policy Sequencer (VPS) sequenced tasks with similar results with state of the art rule based sequencers without using rich experts' knowledge [20]. [10] stresses the fact that intelligent components' too high requirements often prevent them to be used in commercial environments. Therefore, domain independence and lightweight integrability are desirable properties as large ITS often do not possess the skills involved in the tasks and cannot invest large efforts either in tagging all their contents or in changing their systems'structure.

If MF algorithms represent a good solution to Problem (1), they unfortunately suffer from Problem (2) since the parameters of the model cannot be used to interpret the state of the user and its progress over time. Finally, Problem (3) arise for MF applications in ITS. Item Recommendation is affected by time differently than task recommendation, since voting movies in different permuted orders will not affect the user's ratings unless a long time passes between ratings. For this reason it is possible to model user evolution and item characteristics in aggregated time slices, where more subsequent ratings are considered as generated from the same static model. In ITS, instead, the students learn something according to their learning rate after each exercise. If exercises are shown in order or in reverse order of difficulty not only scores will change, but also in the acquired knowledge will be different. Therefore the usage of an online updating model is mandatory for an accurate prediction. Best way to do so, would be to refine the prediction after each action to allow in the future also hints and feedback recommendation.

We present in this paper how we developed domain independent progress modeling by integrating the MF algorithms with Kalman Filters, one of the most famous state modeling techniques of control theory. This is achieved by exploiting equations of a student simulator, which mimics the learning process of a student.

As a result, the model: has reduced computational requirements, remains domain independent, has a reduced prediction error, is less sensitive to the lack of user data, and is made interpretable. In this paper, we first present related works about students' performance prediction (Sect. 2). Then, in Sect. 3 the algorithms of MF and its online update are explained. After a brief introduction of Kalman Filters in Sect. 4, we combine the latter with MF and the equations of a student simulator to obtain a student progress modeler. Finally, in the Experiment Section (Sect. 5), we analyze the novel algorithm under different perspectives, which involves prediction error and progress modeling.

2 State of the Art

MF has many applications like, for instance, dimensionality reduction, clustering and also classification [1], but its most famous application is for Recommender Systems [8], where the algorithm recommends items to a user by predicting the ratings (s)he would give to them. Recently the algorithm was extended to time modeling. In papers predicting movie ratings or doing item recommendations, such as [9,32] the time is modeled with time slices, so that the user's model needs to be updated at each time slice. Because of that, no forecasting can be done for time slices after the current and last one, for which data are available. More similar to our approach is the online method proposed in [16,27] that we explain in detail in Sect. 3.2. There, for each new sample available the model of the user is accordingly updated. Unfortunately, the algorithm requires for each update the entire student's history. Therefore, computational requirements for systems that work in real time performances, such as ITS, becomes too restrictive. As reported by [18] 6 s were required for an update, whereas real time performances should stay under the 0.1 s threshold [11].

As we explained in the introduction, when the aforementioned algorithms are applied in a new domain other problems arise. The first time that MF was applied to ITS, [24–26] associated users with students, items with tasks, and ratings to the probability of a correct answer at first attempt. Alternatively, as in [17] and [28], ratings could be associated to the percentage of correctly answered questions. Also other Machine Learning techniques have been used to model the students' state. Bayesian Knowledge Tracing (BKT) is built on a given prior knowledge of the students and a data set of binary students' performances. It is assumed that there is a hidden state representing the knowledge of a student and an observed state given by the recorded performances. The model learned is composed by slip, guess, learning and not learning probability, which are then used to compute the predicted performances [2]. In the BKT extensions difficulty, multiple skill levels and personalization are taken into account separately [3,12, 13,30], whereas in our framework those aspects are considered at the same time. MF most famous advantage in comparison to BKT is the reduced authoring effort, since experts are not requested to insert the required skills to solve a task or use a hint. However, MF computed parameters cannot be associated to the student's knowledge as BKT modeled skills [13].

In this paper we want to develop a progress modeling algorithm based on MF online-updating performance prediction that can work with fast performances to schedule the recommendation of tasks, hints and feedbacks. Usual approaches for sequencing are Reinforcement Learning techniques, which are applicable in ITS with strong restrictions [19], since the collection of an exploratory corpus implies frustrating users with either too easy and too difficult tasks or random hints and feedbacks. Therefore, we started from the implementation of [18], where MF was used successfully combined with a simple policy to schedule tasks with particular attention to the computational requirements defined in [22]. An additional reason for choosing [18] is the possible extension to multi-modal data analysis as presented in [4–6], or hint sequencing as suggested by [19].

3 Online Matrix Factorization

We define our problem as a tuple $(S, C, \hat{y}, \tau)$ where, given a set S of students, $s_i \in \{1, \ldots S\}$ is the i–th student modeled as a vector $\varphi^t \in \mathbb{S} := \mathbb{R}^K$, where K is the number of skills involved and $\mathbb{S}$ is the student's space. C is a set of tasks, where $c_j \in \{1, \ldots C\}$ is the j–th task, defined with a vector $\psi_j \in \mathbb{C} := \mathbb{R}^K$ representing the K skills required to solve a task defined in the tasks' space $\mathbb{C}$. In this context we want to find a suitable prediction function able to compute the predicted performance $\hat{y}(\varphi_i, \psi_j)$ of a student s_i on a task c_j considering all his past interactions. In order to do so we need also to find $\tau : \mathbb{S} \times \mathbb{C} \rightarrow \mathbb{S}$ a function defining the follow-up state φ^{t+1} of a student s_i after interacting with task c_j. We explain hereafter how this is done with pure MF techniques.

3.1 Static Matrix Factorization

Generally, in Recommender Systems MF predicts which are the future user ratings on a specific item based on its previous ratings and the previous ratings of other users [8]. The concept has been extended to student performance prediction, where a student's next performance, or score is predicted. The matrix $Y \in \mathbb{R}^{n_s \times n_c}$ can be seen as a table of n_c total tasks and n_s students used to train the system, where for some tasks and students performance measures are given. MF decomposes the matrix Y in two other ones $\Psi \in \mathbb{R}^{n_c \times K}$ and $\Phi \in \mathbb{R}^{n_s \times K}$, so that $Y \approx \hat{Y} = \Psi \Phi^T$. Ψ and Φ are matrices of latent features, where each task c_j, and each student s_i, is represented, i.e. modeled, with a vector of K latent features (ψ and φ respectively). Although these latent features cannot be mapped to an exact meaning as done in BKT technology, in [26] those values were associated with the skills involved in the tasks and the skills of the students. The latent features learned with stochastic gradient descent from the given performances allow computing the missing elements of Y for each student i in each task j of a dataset D (Fig. 1) without manually tagging the skills of the domain. For this reason this approach has been called domain independent in [20]. The optimization function of MF is represented by:

$$\min_{\psi_j, \varphi_i} \sum_{i,j \in D} (y_{ij} - \hat{y}_{ij})^2 + \lambda(\|\Psi\|^2 + \|\Phi\|^2) \tag{1}$$

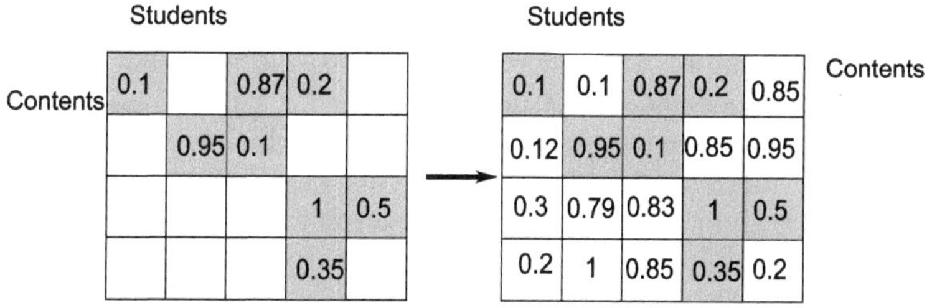

Fig. 1. Table of scores given for each student on tasks (or interacting with generic tasks) (left), completed table by the MF algorithm with predicted scores (right).

where one wants to minimize the regularized Root Mean Squared Error (RMSE) on the set of known scores. The prediction function is represented by:

$$\hat{y}_{ij} = \sum_{k=0}^{K} \varphi_{ik} \psi_{jk}, \tag{2}$$

3.2 Online Update

One of the criticized problems of MF is that it does not deal with time, i.e. the latent features are constant after the first training. In order to keep the model up to date, [18] implemented, in a large commercial ITS, the online update proposed in [16]. The update, that we will call hereafter UpMF, consists in solving again the minimization problem of Eq. (1) optimizing only φ with stochastic

Algorithm 1. UpMF Rendle et al. (2008), where β is the learning rate, λ is the regularization parameter, Ψ are the tasks' latent features, $iter_{Max}$ is the number of algorithm's iterations, $History_i$ are all the tasks IDs j the student i interacted with with performance y.

Input: $History_i$, λ,Ψ, β, K, $iter_{Max}$
Output: φ^t
$\varphi^t \sim N(0, \sigma^2)$
$iter_{Max}$= $History_i.length * iter_{Max}$;
for $iter = 1$ *to* $iter_{Max}$ **do**
  Select j randomly from $History_i$;
  $err = y - \left(\sum_{k=0}^{K} \varphi_{ik}\psi_{jk}\right)$;
  for $k = 1$ *to* K **do**
    $\frac{\partial err}{\partial \varphi_{ik}} + = \beta(err * \psi_{jk} - \lambda\varphi_{ik})$;
    update φ_{ik};
  end
end

gradient descent algorithm. This means the student's model is learned at each interaction from scratch. [18] coherently with [16] noticed that after approximately 20 interactions the model update's error for UpMF was degenerating. [18] overcame the problem by retraining the model each night, assuming students would see approximately 10 tasks per day. This was of course imposing strong requirements on the machine where the application ran since the training is more demanding computationally in comparison to the prediction phase. According to the pseudo-code Algorithm 1 reported, there are two main limitations of this algorithm. The first one is the dependency between the history length and the number of algorithm's iterations required to converge to a solution. The more student's interactions are available, the more iterations are needed by UpMF to converge (see Algorithm 1). As a consequence the time required to update the model increases over time. To keep the update time constant one should select meaningful samples out of the given history. Unfortunately, we are not aware of previous work analyzing this aspect in detail. The second issue is related to the invariance to the samples sequence, i.e. when a sample is selected out of the ones available old and new ones are considered equally. This means that the sequence has no influence in the model computation.

4 Kalman State Estimation for MF (KSEMF)

In this Section we present a novel update method that overcomes the main issues of the current state of the art. Kalman Filters are one of the most used state estimation algorithms in operations research [7] and therefore constitute a valid approach to our progress modeling problem.

4.1 Kalman Filter Theory

Before explaining the Kalman's equations into detail, we briefly introduce the Kalman approach in modeling state evolution. As shown in Fig. 2 the Kalman algorithm can be described as a two-steps cycle, where the alternating phases are called "predict phase" and "correct phase". During the predict phase the state and error estimation are projected, i.e. one tries to predict what influence a certain input would have on the state's evolution. The input can be seen as the set of actions that could be performed. With a more actual state estimate we can try to predict the next observed measurement, where the measurement is what we can observe from the surrounding environment. When a new measurement is finally observed, the algorithm uses the information to correct its estimates. At this point, the cycle starts from the beginning. In order to implement the cycle equations, it is required to identify in the problem under analysis the state, input and observable measurement of the system as shown in Fig. 2 with the step "[A] System information". How this was done for student progress modeling is one of the key contributions of this paper. It is important to note also how the sequentiality both of state evolution and measurements plays a major role. Moreover, the Kalman Filter cycle is often referred to as recursive

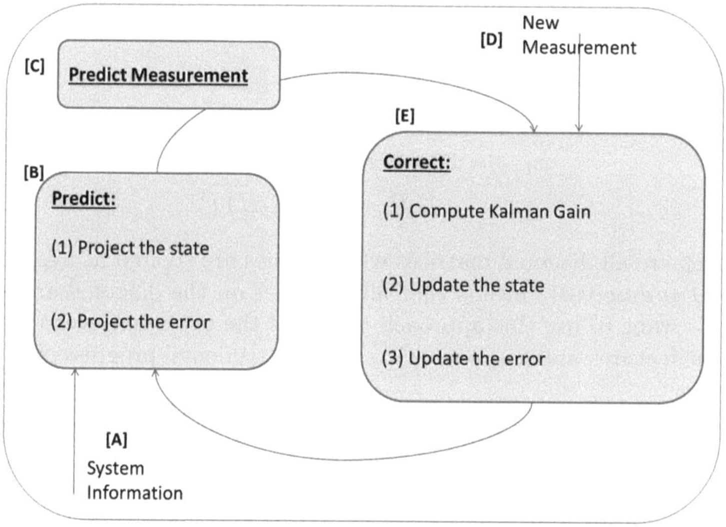

Fig. 2. Kalman cycle.

as to reconstruct the entire state evolution it does not require the load of the entire student's history but uses only the last estimate in an iterative fashion, so that the update time is constant.

The state $\boldsymbol{x}$ at time t is modeled as a linear combination of the state at time $t-1$ and a control input $\boldsymbol{u}$ at time $t-1$ with additive Gaussian noise $\mathbf{w}$ (Eq. (3)), where A and B are matrices of coefficients multiplying the state and control variables respectively (Fig. 2[B]).

$$\boldsymbol{x}_{t+1} = A\boldsymbol{x}_t + B\boldsymbol{u}_t + w_t \tag{3}$$

In Eq. 4 the measurements of the environment are predicted adding the current state estimation multiplied by a coefficient matrix H to Gaussian noise $\mathbf{v}$.

$$y_{t+1} = H\boldsymbol{x}_t + v_t \tag{4}$$

Kalman Filters predict the current state $\hat{\boldsymbol{x}}_t^-$ and the error covariance matrix P_t^- by means of Eq. (5) (Fig. 2[B]), where Q is the state noise covariance matrix derived from the Gaussian noise variance $\mathbf{w}$ of the state variables.

$$\begin{aligned} \hat{\boldsymbol{x}}_{t+1}^- &= A\hat{\boldsymbol{x}}_t + B\boldsymbol{u}_t \\ P_{t+1}^- &= AP_tA^T + Q \end{aligned} \tag{5}$$

Then, with a new measurement $\boldsymbol{y_t}$ (Fig. 2[D]), state estimation $\hat{\boldsymbol{x}}_t$ and error covariance matrix P_t are corrected with Eqs. 6 (Fig. 2[E]), where K_t is the so-called Kalman Gain and R the measurement noise covariance matrix derived from the variance of the measurement noise $\boldsymbol{v_t}$.

$$\begin{aligned} K_t &= P_{t+1}^{-} H^T \left(H P_{t+1}^{-} H^T + R \right)^{-1} \\ \hat{\boldsymbol{x}}_{t+1} &= \hat{\boldsymbol{x}}_{t+1}^{-} + K_t \left(y_t - H \hat{\boldsymbol{x}}_{t+1}^{-} \right) \\ P_k &= \left(I - K_t H \right) P_t^{-} \end{aligned} \tag{6}$$

R, Q and P_0 are all diagonal matrices whose values are treated as hyperparameters, e.g. $Q = diag(0.01)$ means that all Q values on the diagonal are assigned to 0.01. We want to use this approach to model the evolution over time of the MF's latent features and consequently show the students' progress over time.

4.2 Kalman State Estimation for Matrix Factorization (KSEMF)

In this Section we present our novel method for progress modeling: the Kalman State Estimation for Matrix Factorization (KSEMF). In order to integrate the Kalman Filter and MF we first need to identify the state and the control of the system. As aforementioned, at each time step $\boldsymbol{\varphi}^t$ of student s_i, i.e. the student's MF latent features, needs to be updated to $\boldsymbol{\varphi}^{t+1}$ with a function τ. Under this interpretation, $\boldsymbol{\varphi}_i^t$ should be the evolving state. The control over the system are the tasks' latent features $\boldsymbol{\psi}_j$ presented to the student, whereas the score y_t represents the measurement and its prediction $\hat{y}_t$ at time t (Eq. (7)). Since this algorithm is modeling the state and the interaction with the environment explicitly, a working Kalman Filter does not only show that the approach is valid for performance prediction, but also that (1) the students' latent features can be interpreted as the students' state and that (2) the tasks' latent features can be interpreted as the tasks' characteristics.

$$\begin{aligned} \begin{bmatrix} \varphi_1 \\ \vdots \\ \varphi_k \end{bmatrix}_{t+1} &= A \begin{bmatrix} \varphi_1 \\ \vdots \\ \varphi_k \end{bmatrix}_t + B \begin{bmatrix} \psi_1 \\ \vdots \\ \psi_k \end{bmatrix}_t + \mathbf{w}_t \\ \hat{y}_{t+1} &= H \begin{bmatrix} \varphi_1 \\ \vdots \\ \varphi_k \end{bmatrix}_t + \mathbf{v}_t \end{aligned} \tag{7}$$

In order to integrate the prediction function of MF (Eq. (2)) we formalized the relationship between state $\boldsymbol{\varphi}_i^t$ and predicted measurement $\hat{y}_t$ as in (8), having then $H = \boldsymbol{\psi}^T$.

$$\hat{y}_t = \begin{bmatrix} \psi_1 \\ \vdots \\ \psi_k \end{bmatrix}_{t-1}^T \begin{bmatrix} \varphi_1 \\ \vdots \\ \varphi_k \end{bmatrix}_{t-1} + \mathbf{v}_{t-1} \tag{8}$$

Still missing is Eq. (3), i.e. the function τ mapping the state $\boldsymbol{\varphi_i}^t$ with the state at time $t+1$.

4.3 Skill Deficiency Aware KSEMF(KSEMF_SD)

In order to make KSEMF aware of the student's skills deficiency, we will model the update function τ, which represents the learning from one task interaction, in a specific way. We started from the simulated student developed in [20] that was able to simulate a learning process with continuous knowledge and score representation and tasks with multiple difficulty levels. Nevertheless, we do not exclude the possibility to use also other equations to model the relationship between $\boldsymbol{\varphi}^{\boldsymbol{t}}$ and $\boldsymbol{\varphi}^{\boldsymbol{t+1}}$. The simulator models a learning process defined by the Zone of Proximal Development (ZPD) [29], i.e. a student can learn from a task only if it is of the correct difficulty level. This is defined in the simulated environment as the difference $\boldsymbol{\alpha}^{\boldsymbol{i,j}}$ between the skills of the student $\boldsymbol{\varphi}_{\boldsymbol{i}}^{\boldsymbol{t}}$ and those required to solve the task $\boldsymbol{\psi}_{\boldsymbol{j}}$. As a consequence $\boldsymbol{\alpha}^{\boldsymbol{i,j}}$ represents the skill deficiency of the student.

$$\begin{aligned} \tilde{y}(\varphi_i, \psi_j) &= \max(1 - \frac{||\boldsymbol{\alpha}^{\boldsymbol{i,j}}||}{||\boldsymbol{\varphi_i}||}, 0) \\ \tau(\varphi_i, \psi_j)_k &= \tilde{y}(\varphi_{ik}, \psi_{jk})\alpha_k^{i,j} \\ \alpha_k^{i,j} &= \max(\psi_{jk} - \varphi_{ik}, 0) \end{aligned} \tag{9}$$

In Eq. (9) $\tilde{y}$ represents the simulated score of the student and the skills are positively definite. Therefore $\boldsymbol{\varphi_{ik}} > \boldsymbol{\varphi_{i2k}}$ means student i is more knowledgeable than student $i2$ and $\boldsymbol{\psi_{jk}} > \boldsymbol{\psi_{j2k}}$ means task j is more difficult than task $j2$. Finally $\psi_{jk} < \varphi_{ik}$ means a task j is too easy for student i and (s)he cannot learn from it [20]. To develop the Skill Deficiency aware Kalman State Estimation for Matrix Factorization (KSEMF_SD) we interpreted the simulator modeled skills ψ_{jk} and φ_{ik}, for all i, j, and k as the from MF computed latent features. We then reformulated the equations modeling the process, Eq. (9), to fit Eq. (3) and work also with negative latent features. Therefore, we slightly modified Eq. (9) to Eq. (10). These changes allowed also negative latent features, but kept the ZPD properties of the simulator, i.e. a student cannot learn from too easy tasks and learns from a task proportionally to his knowledge and the skills required to solve the task. The equations were changed as shown in Eq. 10.

$$\begin{aligned} \tilde{y}(\varphi_i, \psi_j) &= \max(1 - \frac{||\boldsymbol{\alpha}^{\boldsymbol{i,j}}||}{||\boldsymbol{\varphi_i}||}, 0) \\ \tau(\varphi_i, \psi_j)_k &= \tilde{y}(\varphi_{ik}, \psi_{jk})\gamma\delta(\alpha_k^{i,j} > 0)\psi_{jk} \\ \alpha_k^{i,j} &= \psi_{jk} \max(1 - \varphi_{ik}/\psi_{jk}, 0), \end{aligned} \tag{10}$$

where γ is a weight and δ is a Kronecker δ that is equal to 1 when its condition $\alpha_k^{i,j} > 0$ is verified and 0 elsewhere. $\alpha_k^{i,j} > 0$ for $\max(\psi_{jk} - \varphi_{ik}, 0)$ when $\psi_k > 0$ and for $\min(\psi_{jk} - \varphi_{ik}, 0)$ for $\psi_k < 0$. Under the interpretation $\varphi_{i,k} = 0$ means student i does not possess skill k and $|\varphi_{i,k}| > 0$ now means having some ability in skill k. The mathematical properties of the equations did not change much from the previous version and are:

1. The simulated performance $\tilde{y}$ of a student on a task decreases proportionally to his skill deficiencies w.r.t. the required skills.
2. The student will improve all the required skills of a task proportionally to his simulated performance $\tilde{y}$, his learning rate γ up to the skill level a task requires.
3. As a consequence it is not possible to learn from a content more than γ times the required skills.
4. A further property of this model is that tasks requiring twice the skills level a student has, i.e. $\|\boldsymbol{\psi}_j\| \geq 2\,\|\boldsymbol{\varphi}_i\|$, are beyond the reach of a student.

Given Eq. (10) we obtained $\varphi_{ik}^{(t)} = \varphi_{ik}^{(t-1)} + (\tilde{y}(\varphi_{ik}, \psi_{jk})\gamma\delta(|\varphi_{ik}| < |\psi_{jk}|))\psi_{jk}$, i.e.

$$A = \; diag(1)$$

and

$$B = \; diag(\tilde{y}(\varphi_{ik}, \psi_{jk})\delta(|\varphi_{ik}| < |\psi_{jk}|)\gamma). \tag{11}$$

5 Experiment Section

In this Section we analyze different aspects of the algorithm. First, we describe the dataset used for the experiments; then, we analyze the hyperparameters' selection and the model initialization. Afterwards, we discuss the ability of the algorithm to model the student progress. This is done from different perspectives, which involve the personalization of the state and the update rate. sensitiveness of the algorithm to the lack of data.

5.1 Dataset Characteristics

To test the presented algorithm and model the progress of the students we use the dataset collected with an ITS with 20 topics about maths for children aged from 6 to 14, who can practice with over 2000 tasks at school or at home.

An example of questions proposed to the students can be found in Fig. 3. From these questions proposed in sets, that we call interactions or tasks, we do not know which ones precisely were answered correctly since the ITS aggregates the information in a single score. For these multiple-skills interactions we do not possess the skills involved, therefore, in this context, we cannot use classic BKT and PFA approaches. The score, as in [20], is represented in a continuous interval which goes from 0 to 1. The topics and new skills to be acquired are introduced following the curriculum of the country. The tasks are presented with a rule-based sequencer, which increases the difficulty of the tasks once the student completed and passed all the tasks of the difficulty level. If the tasks are not passed the student gets a regression exercise or can try again to solve the task. Of the large dataset of the commercial ITS we selected two subsets described in Table 1 in order to minimize the noise due to the lack of data and monitor the progress of the error and latent features over time. Consequently, we selected only the students i with at least $N_i > 10$ interactions, where one interaction correspond to a student solving a set of 10 questions aggregated in a single score. The available students are then divided in two groups. The group of those with $10 < N_i < 100$ is used to initialize the latent features of all algorithms (D_{Train}, Table 1), whereas the others with $N_i > 100$ are used to test online updates UpMF and KSEMF_SD (D_{Test} Table 1).

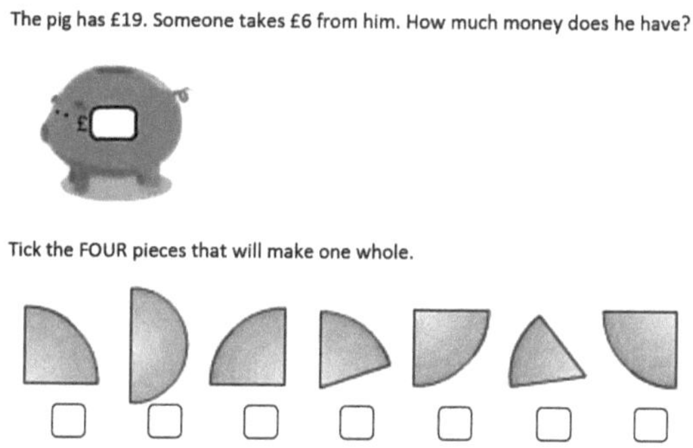

Fig. 3. Two questions of the commercial ITS.

5.2 Hyperparameters' Selection

All the model hyperparameters of MF, UpMF and KSEMF_SD were selected with a full Grid Search, i.e. the influence on the model error of different combinations of hyperparameters is analyzed in a brute force manner. First MF ones were evaluated considering the RSME obtained with a further split of D_{Train}. 66% of D_{Train} was used to train the MF model and its 34% was used to test the model with the different hyperparameters. UpMF and KSEMF_SD best hyperparameters are then selected in the ranges presented in Table 2 according to the performances in D_{Test} in particular we used the value $Total\_RMSE$ computed as in Algorithm 2 to evaluate the performances of the algorithm.

Algorithm 2. Experiments' Framework.

Input: D_{Train}, D_{Test}, Q, R, P_0
Use D_{Train} and Eq. (1) to obtain $\Phi^{(t=0)}$ and Ψ;
for ***each*** s_i c_j *interactions in* D_{test} N **do**
  $A = diag(1)$, $H = {\psi_j}^T$;
  Compute B using Eq. (11);
  $\hat{y}$=Predict, Eq. (5);
  Correct, Eq. (6);
  Err$+= (y - \hat{y})^2$;
end
Total_RMSE=$\sqrt{Err/N}$;

Table 1. Dataset Statistics.

	D_{Train}	D_{Test}
Number of Tasks	2035	2035
Number of Students	24288	713
Total Student-Task Interactions, N	751109	102038

UpMF and MF hyperparameters are λ, β, $iter_{Max}$ and K. In addition to these, KSEMF_SD possesses four more hyperparameters: Q, R, γ, and P_0. The empirical approach is to model Q, R, and P_0 as diagonal matrices and test their diagonal values with a logarithmic scale. The selected hyperparameters are reported in Table 2.

Table 2. Hyperarameters' ranges tested and selected values for UpMF and KSEMF_SD.

Parameters	Range	Step	UpMF	KSEMF_SD
Learning rate β	0.01–0.1	0.01	0.01	0.01
Latent features K	2–120	20	102	62
Regularization λ	0.01–0.1	0.01		
	0.001–0.01	0.001	0.01	0.01
Number of iterations $Iter_{Max}$	10–200	10	100	25
State noise cov. Q	0.00001–1	Logarithmic	-	0.00001
Error noise cov. P_0	0.00001–1	Logarithmic	-	1
Measurement noise cov. R	0.00001–1	Logarithmic	-	0.001
Weight γ	0.00001–1	Logarithmic	-	0.001

In the future more efficient approaches to hyperparameters' selection could be used as the ones suggested by [23,31].

5.3 State Variables Initialization

The next question to answer was how to initialize the latent features of UpMF and KSEMF_SD. Since both algorithms are fully personalized they both suffers from the so called cold-start problem, which occurs when no information is available about the students or the tasks. Therefore, a random initialization of the latent features would lead to very bad performances [28]. Usual approach to solve the problem is to train a model with the classic MF algorithm and use the computed tasks' latent features to initialize KSEMF_SD and UpMF. These are then kept constant while applying Algorithm 2 or Algorithm 1. Since D_{Train} and D_{Test} have no overlapping students, the D_{Test} students' cold-start problem is solved by including in D_{Train} data of their first interactions with the ITS, so that their latent features can be learned in a full training. The samples necessary to avoid the cold start problem, both for students and tasks, are generally 0. This amount was empirically defined by [15]. Since these 10 interactions are not always available, we show also results when just one interaction is included in D_{Train}. The by MF computed students' and tasks' latent features are then used to initialize respectively $\boldsymbol{\Phi}^{(t=0)}$ and $\boldsymbol{\Psi}$ of UpMF and KSEMF_SD. The MF results shown in all the subsequent figures are the ones of the MF used to initialize KSEMF_SD, so that it is possible to see the lift obtained by the KSEMF_SD update.

In Fig. 4 we can see how the Total_RMSE, computed as in Algorithm 2, evolves over time. Models marked with the "Cold" label are initialized with only 1 sample whereas the others are initialized with 10. MF Cold behaved like a random predictor with an error around 0.5 and is not shown in Fig. 4. As it is possible to see, the 10 samples substantially improved the error. Nevertheless, we believe this is still not an optimal initialization for KSEMF_SD, since for the first interactions KSEMF_SD is outperformed by UpMF and MF with 10 samples initialization. KSEMF_SD, initialized with 10 samples, has a similar behavior as MF because it inherits the error of MF tasks' latent features whereas KSEMF_SD error amelioration is due to the better students' latent features modeling.

If these 10 interactions are not available, KSEMF_SD Cold converges faster to smaller errors than UpMF Cold. In [28] it was discussed how the cold start problem limits the usage of MF in small ITS or for short experiments with new students. Therefore, a faster converging error is an appealing property, that could further reduce the requirements of MF.

Despite a better performance in the first interactions UpMF error increases over time. The problem was reported also by [18], who, to avoid this issue, retrained the model each night. This is however a quite demanding computational requirement and, as we will see in Sect. 5.5, can affect the progress modeling approach we want to use. Moreover, UpMF requires the entire history of one student as input parameter for Algorithm 1 that in case of DB implementation will not only slow down the performances but also increase the complexity of the system. KSEMF_SD does not require demanding DB accesses to extract the entire student's history since it uses only information of the current time step to predict the next one.

Finally, in this experiment we also provide the first proof that KSEMF_SD is able to predict the student performances, meaning that it is possible to interpret the student's latent features as their state.

5.4 RMSE Evaluation

In this Section we evaluate the overall algorithm performances by computing the $Total\_RMSE$, as in Algorithm 2. For MF, UpMF and KSEMF_SD we analyze the sensitiveness to the number of latent features. Moreover, we repeated the experiment five times to be able to exclude the variance influence due to the random initialization of the MF. As shown in Fig. 5 the algorithm is able to outperform our reference baselines in all tried latent features configurations.

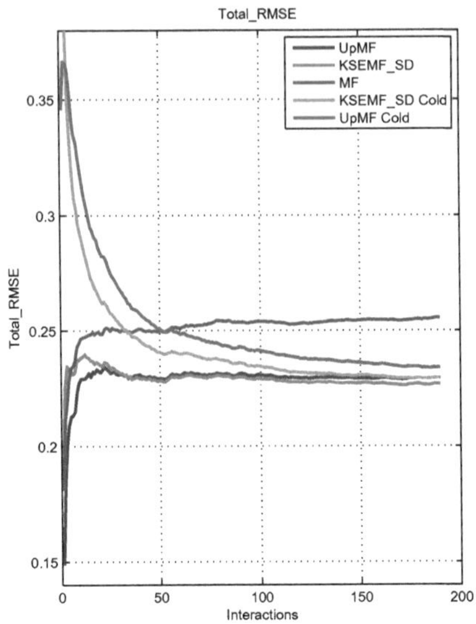

Fig. 4. D_{Test} **Total_RMSE behavior over time:** Models marked with "Cold" label are initialized with only 1 interaction in D_{Train} whereas the others with 10.

5.5 Modeling Student Progress

In order to use the developed algorithm to model student progress, it is important to be able to use the performance predictor as model for the user state and take decisions accordingly. One of the claimed disadvantages of MF approaches

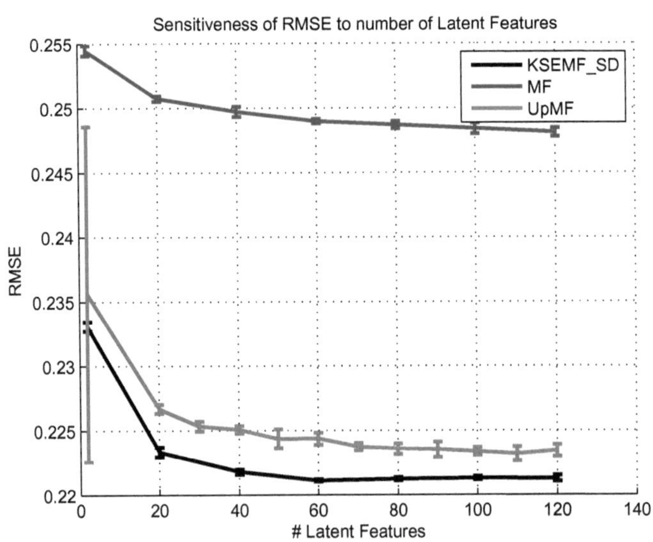

Fig. 5. RMSE sensitiveness analysis to latent features.

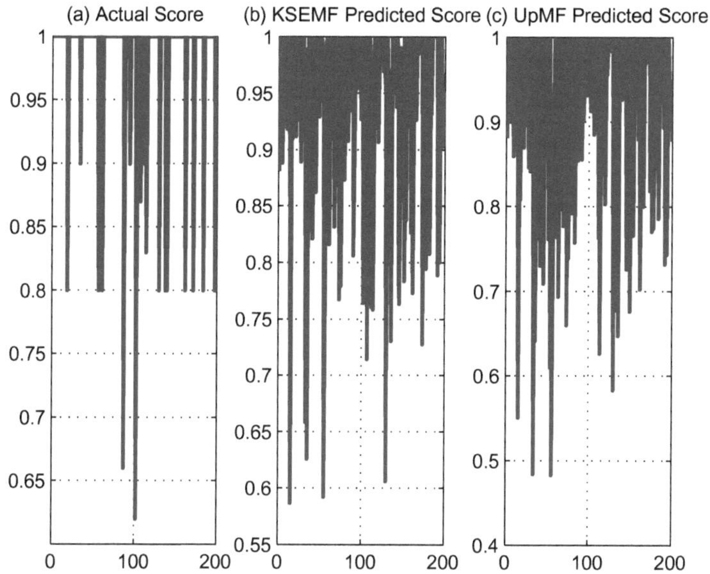

Fig. 6. Actual score (left), KSEMF_SD predicted score (center), UpMF predicted score (left).

in comparison to BKT and PFA is that the amount of knowledge of the student cannot be extracted directly from the latent features computed by the algorithms. For this reason [20] proposed a sequencer which uses only the information coming from the predicted score. In Fig. 7 it is shown (a) how the latent features evolve according to KSEMF_SD algorithm in a scenario with 62 latent features and (b) how the latent features evolve according to UpMF algorithm in a scenario with 102 latent features. Figure 7(f) shows the actual score of the student (blue) and the predicted performance of the student by KSEMF_SD (green) and MF (red). This figure can be enlarged in Fig. 6. There, one can see how the actual score curve cannot be used to interpret the student progress. This can be more easily understood if one considers that the 200 interactions involve a period of one year, where the student could have increased its knowledge in each of the 22 topics of several difficulty levels. Since both UpMF and KSEMF_SD mimic the actual score behavior, the same interpretability problem occurs. However, the predicting ability of KSEMF_SD let us suppose that the latent feature have indeed a state meaning for the algorithm and consequently an evolution according to the student's performance should be monitored. Therefore, to monitor a meaningful trend, we aggregated the features computing the norm 1 normalized for the number of latent features as in Eq. (12) and depicted the results in Fig. 7(c) for KSEMF_SD and (d) for UpMF.

$$kn = \frac{1}{K}\sum_{k=0}^{K}|\varphi_k| \tag{12}$$

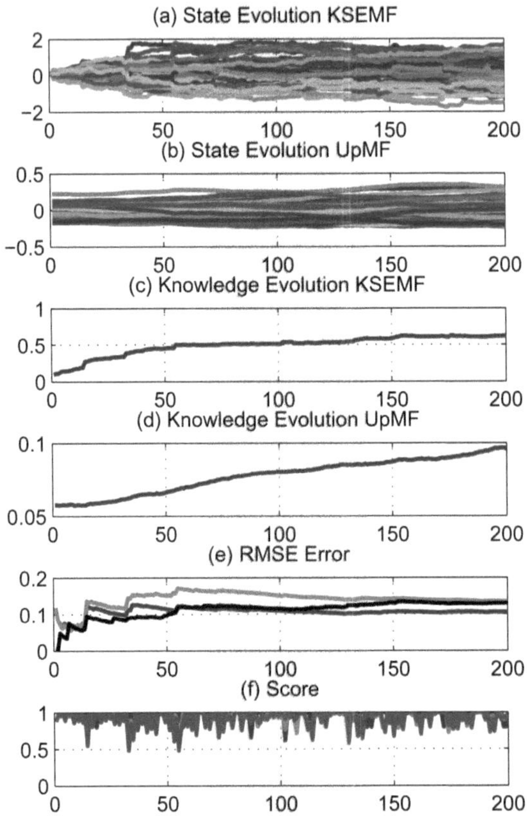

Fig. 7. x-Axis: Number of tasks seen by the student or interactions. **y-Axis:** *(a)* state evolution according to KSEMF_SD with K = 62. *(b)* state evolution according to UpMF with K = 102. *(c) and (d):* knowledge evolution for KSEMF_SD and UpMF computed as in Eq. (12). *(e)* Total_RMSE of KSEMF_SD (blue), MF (green) and UpMF (black). *(f)* Actual performance of the student (blue), predicted performance by KSEMF_SD (green), MF (red). (Color figure online)

Under the interpretation that $\varphi_{i,k} = 0$ means student i does not possess skill k, whereas $|\varphi_{i,k}| > 0$ means having some ability in skill k, variable kn could be understood as the personalized knowledge evolution or the learning curve of the user. Although UpMF latent features are learned from scratch after each interaction one can notice in the figures an evolution trend, which is as plausible as the one of KSEMF_SD. This also confirms that the latent features in MF approaches represents the state of the user and their value could be used to retrieve the students knowledge amount. We believe this works because the tasks' latent feature are kept constant. Therefore, in order to keep track of the current state of the students one cannot do a full retrain of the UpMF model, as done by [18], since this would reset the values of the tasks' latent features, that allow reconstructing at each interaction the state of the student by means of the student's history.

5.6 Personalization

One important aspect of progress modeling is personalization. MF creates an individualized model as well for tasks as for students. In order to do so also for KSEMF_SD, each student has his/her own KSEMF_SD equations updating according to his/her modeled state and performances. Since the simulator equations are based on the state variable, in this context, also the B matrix is personalized and change at each interaction. Therefore, the update equations of KSEMF_SD model personalization in two different ways. The B matrix represents the influence of the student on the update, i.e. what is his/her learning rate and its skills' deficiency. The control u, i.e. the tasks' latent features ψ,

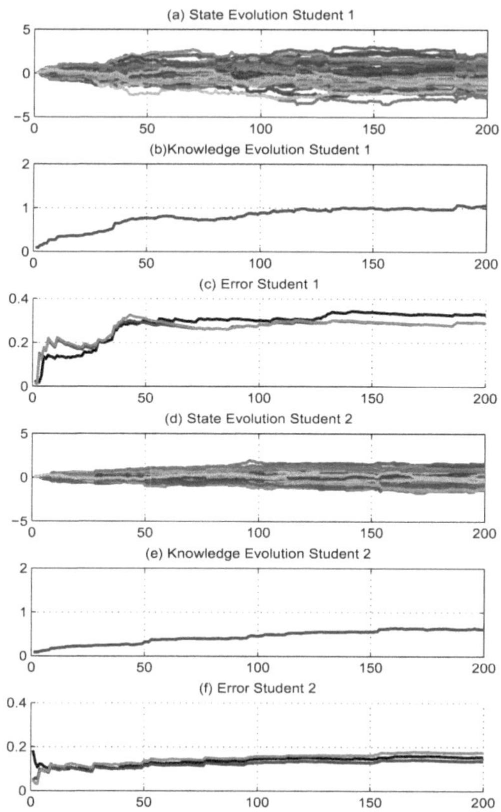

Fig. 8. x-Axis: Number of tasks seen by the student or interactions. **y-Axis:** *(a) and (d):* KSEMF_SD state evolution of two different students, K=62. *(b) and (e):* kn of KSEMF_SD latent features computed as in Eq. 12. *(c) and (f):* Total_RMSE of KSEMF_SD (blue), MF (green) and UpMF (black) of two different students.

represents the influence of the task on the knowledge acquisition of the student. Hereafter, we will see how the state as well as the update evolve over time in a personalized way.

Personalized State Evolution. See Fig. 8(b) and (d) to see the personalized latent features' trends of KSEMF_SD. In Fig. 5(c) and (f) and in Fig. 7(e) we can see the Total_RMSEs of the models for three specific students. These are overall coherent with the results presented in Fig. 4. This information could be used in several ways, e.g. by later establishing the mapping between the computed kn trend and the actual knowledge acquisition of the users, we could design novel

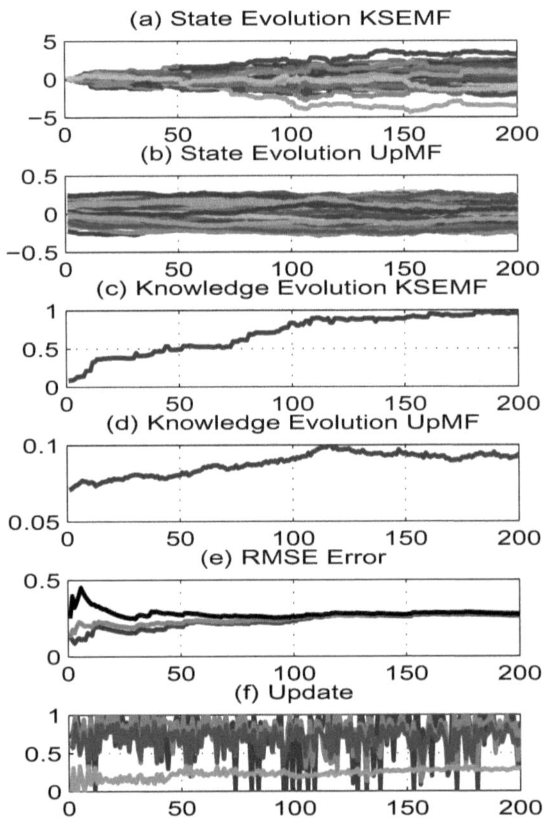

Fig. 9. **x-Axis:** Number of tasks seen by the student or interactions. **y-Axis:** *(a)* how the state evolves according to KSEMF_SD with K = 62. *(b)* shows how the state evolves according to UpMF algorithm with K = 102. *(c)* and *(d)* show the knowledge evolution, computed as in Eq. (12). *(e)* RMSE of KSEMF_SD (blue), RMSE of MF (green) and UpMF (black). *(f)* Actual Performance of the student (blue), predicted performance of the student by the KSEMF_SD (green), predicted performance by MF (red) and $\tilde{y}$ (turquoise). (Color figure online)

policies for sequencing tasks, feedbacks and hints. In addition, the relationship between kn and the model error should be further analyzed. This will allow also to monitor the performances of the performance predictor over time.

Personalized Update Evolution. In this Section we discuss the plausibility of the personalized update trend derived through Eqs. (10). For simplicity we considered $\tilde{y}$, which represents the update of the state, since it is later multiplied with constant γ to obtain B (See Eq. 3). In Fig. 9(f) we show, for a student, how $\tilde{y}$ evolves over time. An almost constant update is plausible, since it mimics the learning rate of the student, which is related to his/her learning ability. However, its adaptive computation through the state is of advantage, since it allows the model to faster adjust to the students' states changes. In Fig. 10 we see that the average update for all students evolves over time converging only in the last interactions to a constant value. This is explicable with the previously seen behavior of KSEMF_SD in the first interactions (see Fig. 4) and should be seen as another indicator that the initialization of the algorithm is not optimal.

Although we were not interested in keeping the simulation properties of the simulator from which we derived our equations, we briefly discuss why $\hat{y}$ is smaller than the actual performance. Since the variables of φ and ψ are not clipped between 0 and 1 as in [20] $\left\|\alpha_k^{i,j}\right\|$ is consequently bigger on average and $\tilde{y}$ smaller than the actual performance. In conclusion, given the ameliorated results of KSEMF_SD over UpMF, reported in both Figs. 4 and 5, we overall showed that the designed equations for KSEMF_SD are suitable to update the students' latent features.

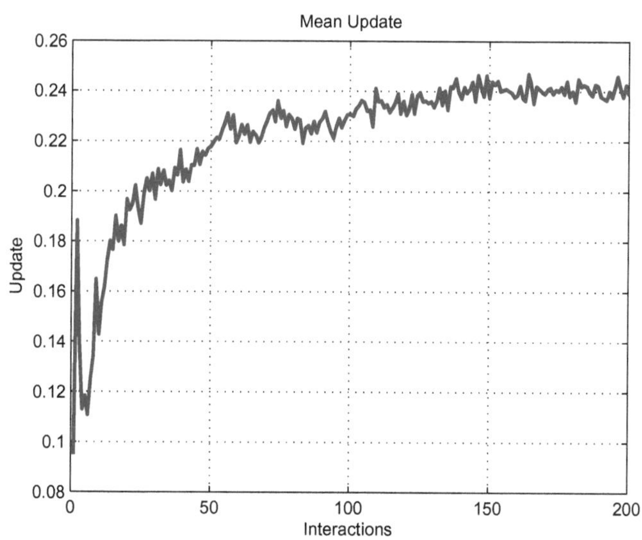

Fig. 10. Mean Update Over Time Update behavior at each interaction on average for all students.

6 Conclusions

In this paper we presented KSEMF_SD a novel method for student progress modeling based on online updating MF performance prediction and skills' deficiency aware Kalman Filters. Progress modeling is proposed, as amelioration of domain independent performance prediction, it allows showing the evolution of the students over time in a plausible way. We showed that it is possible to give a specific interpretation to latent features which represents the state of the student and the characteristics of a task. In future work, the relationship between the computed kn could be mapped with the real knowledge evolution with the final goal to deliver an effortless analysis tool to teachers and developers. In order to do so, an idea could be to apply the same approach to the contents' latent features associating the normed sum of the latent features with the estimated difficulty level of a task. With a laboratory experiment it would be easier to map the from the algorithms retrieved curve to the available tasks' domain information, rather than trying to map predicted and real students' knowledge.

KSEMF_SD also showed appealing properties in comparison to other potential domain independent progress modeler. First, the algorithm requires less resources as the entire student's history is not necessary to compute the updated latent features. Then, the algorithm is still domain independent because the tagged skills of the tasks are not used to deliver a score prediction. Finally, KSEMF_SD reduced the prediction error and is less sensitive to the lack of data. In future work we believe to further be able to reduce the error by developing a better initialization of the students' latent features. In conclusion, in this paper we showed that Recommender Systems and Kalman Filters can be successfully combined. We are then looking forward in testing such approach with other user modeling applications.

Acknowledgement. This research has been co-funded by the Seventh Framework Programme of the European Commission, through project iTalk2Learn (#318051). www.iTalk2Learn.eu. This paper is an extended version of [21] presented at the 8th International Conference on Computer Supported Education.

References

1. Cichocki, A., Zdunek, R., Phan, A.H., Amari, S.: Nonnegative Matrix and Tensor Factorizations: Applications to Exploratory Multi-way Data Analysis and Blind Source Separation. Wiley.com, Chichester (2009). Wiley.com
2. Corbett, A., Anderson, J.: Knowledge tracing: modeling the acquisition of procedural knowledge. UMAI **4**, 253–278 (1994)
3. Baker, R.S.J., Corbett, A.T., Aleven, V.: More accurate student modeling through contextual estimation of slip and guess probabilities in Bayesian knowledge tracing. In: Woolf, B.P., Aïmeur, E., Nkambou, R., Lajoie, S. (eds.) ITS 2008. LNCS, vol. 5091, pp. 406–415. Springer, Heidelberg (2008). doi:10.1007/978-3-540-69132-7_44
4. Janning, R., Schatten, C., Lars, S.-T.: Feature analysis for affect recognition supporting task sequencing. In: ECTEL (2014)

5. Janning, R., Schatten, C., Schmidt-Thieme, L.: Multimodal affect recognition for adaptive intelligent tutoring systems. In: FFMI EDM (2014)
6. Janning, R., Schatten, C., Schmidt-Thieme, L.: Perceived task-difficulty recognition from log-file information for the use in adaptive intelligent tutoring systems. Int. J. Artif. Intell. Educ. **26**, 855–876 (2016)
7. Kalman, R.E.: A new approach to linear filtering and prediction problems. J. Fluids Eng. **82**(1), 35–45 (1960)
8. Koren, Y., Bell, R., Volinsky, C.: Matrix factorization techniques for recommender systems. Computer **42**(8), 30–37 (2009)
9. Li, B., Zhu, X., Li, R., Zhang, C., Xue, X., Wu, X.: Cross-domain collaborative filtering over time. In: Proceedings of the Twenty-Second International Joint Conference on Artificial Intelligence, vol. 3, pp. 2293–2298. AAAI Press (2011)
10. Manouselis, N., Drachsler, H., Vuorikari, R., Hummel, H., Koper, R.: Recommender systems in technology enhanced learning. In: Ricci, F., Rokach, L., Shapira, B., Kantor, P.B. (eds.) Recommender Systems Handbook, pp. 387–415. Springer, New York (2011). doi:10.1007/978-0-387-85820-3_12
11. Nielsen, J.: Usability Engineering. Elsevier, San Diego (1994)
12. Pardos, Z.A., Heffernan, N.T.: Modeling individualization in a Bayesian networks implementation of knowledge tracing. In: Bra, P., Kobsa, A., Chin, D. (eds.) UMAP 2010. LNCS, vol. 6075, pp. 255–266. Springer, Heidelberg (2010). doi:10.1007/978-3-642-13470-8_24
13. Pardos, Z.A., Heffernan, N.T.: KT-IDEM: introducing item difficulty to the knowledge tracing model. In: Konstan, J.A., Conejo, R., Marzo, J.L., Oliver, N. (eds.) UMAP 2011. LNCS, vol. 6787, pp. 243–254. Springer, Heidelberg (2011). doi:10.1007/978-3-642-22362-4_21
14. Pavlik, P., Cen, H., Koedinger, K.: Performance factors analysis-a new alternative to knowledge tracing. In: AIED (2009)
15. Pilászy, I., Tikk, D.: Recommending new movies: even a few ratings are more valuable than metadata. In: RecSys (2009)
16. Rendle, S., Schmidt-Thieme, L.: Online-updating regularized kernel matrix factorization models for large-scale recommender systems. In: Proceedings of the 2008 ACM Conference on Recommender Systems, pp. 251–258. ACM (2008)
17. Schatten, C., Janning, R., Schmidt-Thieme, L.: Vygotsky based sequencing without domain information: a matrix factorization approach. In: Zvacek, S., Restivo, M.T., Uhomoibhi, J., Helfert, M. (eds.) CSEDU 2014. CCIS, vol. 510, pp. 35–51. Springer, Cham (2015). doi:10.1007/978-3-319-25768-6_3
18. Schatten, C., Janning, R., Schmidt-Thieme, L.: Integration and evaluation of a machine learning sequencer in large commercial ITS. In: AAAI 2015. Springer (2015)
19. Schatten, C., Mavrikis, M., Janning, R., Schmidt-Thieme, L.: Matrix factorization feasibility for sequencing and adaptive support in ITS. In: EDM (2014)
20. Schatten, C., Schmidt-Thieme, L.: Adaptive content sequencing without domain information. In: CSEDU (2014)
21. Schatten, C., Schmidt-Thieme, L.: Student progress modeling with skills deficiency aware Kalman filters. In: CSEDU (2016)
22. Schatten, C., Wistuba, M., Schmidt-Thieme, L., Gutirrez-Santos, S.: Minimal invasive integration of learning analytics services in ITS. In: ICALT (2014)
23. Schilling, N., Wistuba, M., Drumond, L., Schmidt-Thieme, L.: Joint model choice and hyperparameter optimization with factorized multilayer perceptrons. In: 2015 IEEE 27th International Conference on Tools with Artificial Intelligence (ICTAI), pp. 72–79. IEEE (2015)

24. Thai-Nghe, N., Drumond, L., Horvath, T., Krohn-Grimberghe, A., Nanopoulos, A., Schmidt-Thieme, L.: Factorization techniques for predicting student performance. In: Educational Recommender Systems and Technologies: Practices and Challenges. IGI Global (2011)
25. Thai-Nghe, N., Drumond, L., Horvath, T., Schmidt-Thieme, L.: Using factorization machines for student modeling. In: UMAP Workshops (2012)
26. Thai-Nghe, N., Drumond, L., Krohn-Grimberghe, A., Schmidt-Thieme, L.: Recommender system for predicting student performance. Procedia Comput. Sci. **1**(2), 2811–2819 (2010)
27. Vinagre, J., Jorge, A.M., Gama, J.: Fast incremental matrix factorization for recommendation with positive-only feedback. In: Dimitrova, V., Kuflik, T., Chin, D., Ricci, F., Dolog, P., Houben, G.-J. (eds.) UMAP 2014. LNCS, vol. 8538, pp. 459–470. Springer, Cham (2014). doi:10.1007/978-3-319-08786-3_41
28. Voss, L., Schatten, C., Schmidt-Thieme, L.: A transfer learning approach for applying matrix factorization to small its datasets. In: EDM 2015 (2015)
29. Vygotsky, L.S.: Mind in Society: The Development of Higher Psychological Processes. HUP, Cambridge (1978)
30. Wang, Y., Heffernan, N.T.: The student skill model. In: Cerri, S.A., Clancey, W.J., Papadourakis, G., Panourgia, K. (eds.) ITS 2012. LNCS, vol. 7315, pp. 399–404. Springer, Heidelberg (2012). doi:10.1007/978-3-642-30950-2_51
31. Wistuba, M., Schilling, N., Schmidt-Thieme, L.: Sequential model-free hyperparameter tuning. In: 2015 IEEE International Conference on Data Mining (ICDM), pp. 1033–1038. IEEE (2015)
32. Xiong, L., Chen, X., Huang, T.-K., Schneider, J.G., Carbonell, J.G.: Temporal collaborative filtering with Bayesian probabilistic tensor factorization. In: SDM, vol. 10, pp. 211–222. SIAM (2010)

Co-presence in the Real and the Virtual Space: Interactions Through Orientation

Athanasios Christopoulos(✉), Marc Conrad, and Mitul Shukla

Department of Computer Science and Technology,
University of Bedfordshire, Park Square, Luton, UK
{athanasios.christopoulos,marc.conrad,mitul.shukla}@beds.ac.uk

Abstract. The global aim of this research is to identify, map, and form a taxonomy of the ways, the elements, and the factors that affect learner engagement with virtual worlds when Hybrid Virtual Learning models are used. Thereafter, the more specific objective of the research is to provide clear guidance to educators who are already utilising or are planning to embed this learning model in their educational agenda. For the examination of this topic, a quanti-qualitative research approach is used, as this allows to investigate the subject both from the students' and the instructional designer's point of view. The sample of this study consists of both undergraduate and postgraduate university students. Participants are requested to fill in two different questionnaires, one before using the virtual world and one after completing their assignment. That way it is possible not only to fully mirror their thoughts, preconceptions, and opinions towards the use of virtual worlds in Higher Education, but also the impact that the instructional designer's choices have on enhancing the opportunities for interactions. In addition, a focus group is being observed – both in the physical classroom and in the virtual world – during the course of the assignment. The focus of this experiment was on the impact that the orientation/induction process has on learner engagement. The findings suggest that students' interactions with the content of the virtual world, and the in-class student-to-student interactions, have stronger impact on student engagement. This is because students' simultaneous co-existence in both environments eliminated the drawbacks of each educational approach, and broadened the network of interactions.

Keywords: Virtual world · Virtual learning · Interactions · OpenSimulator · Orientation · Induction · Engagement

1 Introduction

Computer supported education can be classified in four different ways (see Table 1). Virtual reality and virtual worlds, which were first introduced to the public in the 1980s and have continued to develop ever since, are cornerstones of 'learning in technology' [26].

In the literature [19], virtual worlds are defined as 2D or 3D computer generated environments that either depict parts of the physical world or imaginary sceneries. In these worlds, users are able to perform a wide range of interactions with the content of the world and other users [17], such as: (i) object creation [14], (ii) object manipulation

G. Costagliola et al. (Eds.): CSEDU 2016, CCIS 739, pp. 71–99, 2017.
DOI: 10.1007/978-3-319-63184-4_5

[3], (iii) terrain editing [1], (iv) navigation around the world [20], (v) synchronous or asynchronous communication, either orally or via chat, and vi) use of avatar gestures and other forms of in-world visual interactions [5].

Table 1. The framework of Schrader [26].

Relations of technology with education	
Learning about technology	Learning with technology
Technology as a topic	Technology as a tool
Learning from Technology	Learning in technology
Technology as a delivery mechanism	Technology as the context

These kinds of interactions are performed through the use of avatars [21], that is users' artificial figures [13]. Virtual worlds provide not only the necessary context for all the aforementioned interactions, but they are also increasingly providing more complex interactions. Both these facts have led educators to use them extensively, taking into account all their educational potentials [26]. Content creation activities, exploratory, problem-based, collaborative, blended, and synchronous or asynchronous distance learning are only some of the in-world educational paradigms that have been extensively used and studied from many different perspectives [17, 30].

Despite some differentiations in recent researchers' foci [25, 30], all of them have acknowledged Vygotsky's Social Constructivist Learning Theory [31] to have great practical application on learning within virtual worlds. According to the Social Constructivist Learning Theory [31], students construct their cognitive structures through interactions and engagement with any kind of activity that motivates them to learn. Thus, interacting within virtual worlds can be very beneficial for learners [14]. Jones [22] underlines that it is the learners' ability to affect, alter, and enhance – according to their needs – the content of the virtual world in which they learn, that enables them to construct their cognitive schemes and engage with the phenomena they study. Consequently, learning becomes more self-directed and student-centered [2], whilst the educator gets the role of the designer, instructor, and supporter of activities that aim to engage students in learning [2].

The historic context of these studies derives from the plethora of research activities into Second Life since 2003 – including research at the University of Bedfordshire such as Shukla and Conrad [28], or Christopoulos and Conrad [9] – and subsequent research on OpenSim in view of the similarities and differences identified [9]. It is fully acknowledged that other interfaces such as textual virtual environments exist; however, they do not fall within the focus of this study.

Several frameworks have been developed to aid educators define and conceptualise their new role and the potential utilisation of virtual worlds in educational contexts [18]. Most of them focus on the interactivity of the worlds or the interactions that can be developed in order to cover students' learning needs. Camilleri et al. [4] studied in-world interactions in detail aiming to explain how students learn in-world, yet disregarded the perspective of learning in the physical classroom, focusing on the viewpoint of distance-learning.

Furthermore, de Freitas et al. [15], investigating the use of virtual worlds for distance learning, suggested a four-dimensional framework for the evaluation of students' learning experiences. Those dimensions (see Table 2) are the learner's dimension, the pedagogic dimension, the representational dimension, and the contextual dimension. Even though in-world interactions were part of their study, the focus was not exclusively on that aspect, since they aimed to give a more holistic view of the affordances of distance education in virtual worlds.

Table 2. The framework of de Freitas et al. [15].

Four-dimensional framework	
Learner specifics	*Pedagogy*
Profile	Associative
Role	Cognitive
Competencies	Social/Situative
Representation	*Context*
Fidelity	Environment
Interactivity	Access to learning
Immersion	Supporting resources

At this point, a question arose regarding the way in-world interactions are being developed, in cases where learners are simultaneously co-present in the physical classroom and in the virtual world.

Another interesting point of de Freitas et al. framework [15] is that it takes into consideration a 'learner's dimension'. Thus, the answer that will be provided through this study will supplement the aforementioned framework. It will also analyse how engagement occurs as a synergy or component between the learner's personal choices and preconceptions, on the one hand, and the instructional designer's plans, on the other.

Childs [7], who investigated the skills students acquire when they start using virtual worlds, formed a taxonomy of interactions related to the use of virtual words (see Table 3). He divided interactions into four categories: interacting with the world, interacting with others, interacting with the avatar, and, finally, finding and searching.

Table 3. Child's [8] taxonomy of interactions.

Interacting with the world	Interacting with others
Motion Manoeuvring Way-finding Changing camera positions Mouselook (first-person)	Using local (public) chat Using private chat Using the minimap to find people and move to them
Interacting with the avatar	Finding & searching
Changing avatar appearance Creating folders to save appearances Animating the avatar	Creating a landmark Finding a landmark in the inventory Teleporting to a new location and back again

Chafer and Childs [6] identified the elements that affect a world's interactivity, that is manipulability, reciprocation, and responsiveness. Addressing the same topic from a different angle, Steuer [29] noted three alternative factors when examining interactivity: speed, range, and mapping of interactions. These two different frameworks can be helpful tools for educators who need to measure how interactive their existing virtual environments are. One of the few researchers looking at the educational use of virtual worlds both from the inside and from the outside, both in-world and in-class, is that of Levesque and Lelievre [23]. Specifically, they presented the outcome of their experiment on applying a hybrid approach, where students were simultaneously present in-class and in-world. They pointed out that students' virtual and physical co-location led to the development of a complex network of interactions both in-world and in-class; both among students, and between students and the virtual environment. Although Levesque and Lelievre [23] studied interactions quite extensively, they did not identify how interactions are linked to engagement. This is another issue that this study aims to investigate.

However, this taxonomy did not include the interactions between students and the content of the virtual world, nor the building and scripting skills students usually need to acquire, since this subject was out of the scope of Child's [7] study. This issue is intended to be covered in this study.

De Freitas et al. [16] underline the need for further investigation of the potential and the affordances of hybrid spaces with simultaneous student physical and virtual presence. In addition, Elliott et al. [18] point out a lack of a detailed taxonomy of all the interactions related to the use of virtual worlds in an educational context.

To sum up, this study aims to fill the gaps highlighted in the literature, and provide educators, who aim to include the use of virtual worlds in their educational agenda, with instructions on how to design and develop engaging and interactive learning activities. Even though learner's choices and preconceptions regarding the use of virtual worlds have been extensively investigated in the literature, the impact of the synergy between the learner's personal choices and the instructional designer's plans is blurred. Furthermore, the existing literature is mostly focusing on the in-world interactions aiming to create effective e-learning models. However, it lacks detailed frameworks that explore the relationship between the interactions in hybrid-learning models and learner engagement with the learning material, on the one hand, and the educational activities, on the other.

2 Materials and Methods

Primarily two research methods were used, observations and surveys. This was thought to be the most appropriate way to examine the subject under investigation, since it would give a more thorough view of the phenomena, aid validity and diversity, and allow for the triangulation of the primary data. In other words, observations would allow to record students' actions and behaviour both in the physical classroom and in the virtual world, whilst surveys would provide the opportunity to record students' preferences.

2.1 Observation

Research through observation may have several strengths [11]. Three were the main aspects that indicated observation as the most suitable method for this study. Firstly, as described in Cohen, Manion, and Morrison [11] that led to the emergence of unique primary data, the most essential advantage of observation is considered to be the principles of 'immediate awareness' and 'direct cognition' — i.e. the opportunity given to a researcher to have a 'direct look' at the actions that take place without having to rely on second-hand accounts. Secondly, observation is a very flexible form of data collection that allows researchers to alter their focus, depending on the observed actions and behaviours. Finally, the method of observation allows the researcher to gather any necessary data, while the participants unimpededly follow their own agenda and priorities.

Nevertheless, when conducting observation research, there are unavoidably – as with most methods – certain disadvantages in the data collection process [24, 32]. Even though a great effort was made to eliminate them as much as possible, they cannot be disregarded. The main challenge, when collecting primary data through observation, is the 'selective attention of the observer'. When two or more observers are observing the same sample, different outcomes are likely to be reached, due to the very unique way the human brain perceives what one sees, feels, and hears. To eliminate the negative impact of this issue, it was attempted to explicitly log students' actions the way they were taking place in real time.

In addition, the 'reactivity' of the sample can also run the risk of bias. According to Shaughnessy et al. [27], human behaviour may alter when someone is being observed. In terms of the observations in question, students may feel stressed or anxious during the observation and this can affect their overall behaviour, e.g. working harder, or performing worse, or even behaving in ways that they feel will have a positive impact on the researcher's work. This is why the lab observer maintained an overall low profile, roaming almost silently around the lab, while keeping a 'safe distance' from the students so as to not make his presence distracting for them.

Finally, observations are recording only what happens in a given period of time or what can be seen in a given interface. This is eventually the 'problem of inference' and the suggested solution is the triangulation of the primary data. This was, eventually, the main reason why surveys were also used in conjunction with the observations in this study [12].

2.2 Experiment Structure and Sample

This research was conducted in a university-based environment with a cohort of postgraduate students who volunteered to be part of this study during their weekly practical session (see Table 4). A university-hosted virtual world, based on the OpenSimulator architecture, was used to allow students to explore and familiarise themselves with the Linden Scripting Language — an event-driven programming paradigm — and also with 3D modelling concepts.

Table 4. Sample's identity.

Observation week	1	2	3	4	5	6
Male	10	8	9	5	8	6
Female	7	7	7	6	5	4

The aforementioned cohort of students utilised the virtual world as an innovative tool to deal with, in the context of working and collaborating in groups with task division, similar to circumstances taking place in companies. Each group had to choose an emerging technology subject, research that subject, create a virtual showcase for its promotion, and document all the aspects of their work. For more information about the assignment setup the reader is directed to Christopoulos, Conrad, and Shukla [11] (Table 5).

Table 5. Students' prior experience with virtual worlds like Second Life/OpenSimulator.

None	7
Up to a week	5
Up to a month	2
More than six months but less than a year	1
More than one year	2

2.3 Experiment's Overview and Setup

Many new users are either simply unable to acquire the navigation and operation mechanisms of virtual worlds, or refuse to do so because they consider this practice as a waste of time and effortt with no practical value [7]. When a virtual world is to be used for educational purposes, it is essential that time be devoted to the students' familiarisation with the world. This is necessary in order to enable them to form their avatar – and, by extension, their virtual identity – and also learn to interact fundamentally with the virtual environment, as reported by Childs [7] and De Freitas et al. [15]. Additionally, De Freitas et al. [15] note that the realisation of these procedures, which on the whole they call 'orientation', requires that specific actions be undertaken under the supervision and assistance of the educator in charge.

Therefore, in this experiment the focus was on the impact that the orientation (induction) process has on learners' actions, interactions, and engagement with the virtual world and the learning material (Fig. 1).

While designing the experiment, various setups were considered in order to examine the effectiveness of the virtual world, in general, and of the orientation process, in particular, on learner engagement. The initial idea was to have a cross-over design, in which half of the students would have access to the virtual world first, and the other half would not; it should be noted that the roles would have been switched in a predefined period of time. In the meantime, there would theoretically be the possibility to observe students' performance, and notice the difference between their performance and the learning outcomes. Nevertheless, as the use of the virtual world was an integral component of students' assignment – not to mention that the assignment brief had specific

Fig. 1. Avatars' appearance editing room.

deadlines and time plan for all the tasks – giving 'early access' to some students could have been considered as an advantage over to others, and, therefore, this idea had to be disregarded. It is worth mentioning that even though having different control groups (e.g. a cohort of students that would go through the orientation process, whereas the second group would not) would be desirable, it was not feasible to establish this, due to students' perceiving they might be disadvantaged as to their learning experience.

3 Results

A semi-structured observational checklist [11] was used for the collection of primary data. This checklist included: sixteen (16) focus points regarding the interactions taking place in the physical classroom when a virtual world is used; seventeen (17) focus points regarding the interactions taking place in-world, not only among students but between the students and the virtual world as well; and, finally, six (6) focus points regarding students' willingness to remain in the virtual world, and, by extension, in the physical classroom.

The focus points of the checklist were carefully chosen to cover all the potential interactions that students could have both with the content of the virtual world and with each other. Tables 6 and 7 illustrate the rationale based on which the observation checklist was developed, and the spectrum of interactions were mapped.

Any remarkable detail of each observation was noted in the open-ended part of the checklist. Observations were taking place on a weekly basis and lasted six (6) weeks. Students were simultaneously co-present both in the physical (university) classroom and in the virtual world, whilst each practical session was lasting for 2 h (12 h in total). In order to observe all the participants for an equal amount of time, students' actions were observed in rotation for approximately 30 s until the completion of the practical session.

Table 6. Student interactions with others.

	In-world	In-class
Student-to-student/teacher interactions	Student chats with his/her classmate about the project or the virtual world	Student talks to classmate about the project or the virtual world
	Student chats with student about something irrelevant to the project or the virtual world	Student talks to classmate about something irrelevant to the project or the virtual world
	Student uses in chat phrases/words revealing enjoyment (e.g. 'that's funny', 'cool', etc.)	Student talks to tutor/demonstrator about the project or the virtual world
	Student uses in chat words/phrases revealing exclamation (e.g. 'that's fantastic')	Student talks to tutor/demonstrator about something irrelevant to the project or the virtual world
	Student uses in chat words/phrases often used is social networks (e.g. 'lol')	Student makes positive comments about the technology of the virtual world
	Student refers to avatar in the first person/identifies with avatar (avatar as 'I')	Student makes negative comment about the technology of the virtual world
	Student refers to avatar in the second person/addresses avatar directly (avatar as 'you')	Student makes a positive comment about the emotional experience of the virtual world
	Student refers to avatar in the third person (avatar as 'him or her')	Student makes a negative comment about the emotional experience of the virtual world
	Student refers to avatar as object (avatar as 'it')	Student refers to avatar in the first person/identifies with avatar (avatar as 'I')
	Student makes a negative comment about the technology of the virtual world	Student refers to avatar in the second person/addresses avatar directly (avatar as 'you')
	Student makes a negative comment about the emotional experience of the virtual world	Student refers to avatar in the third person (avatar as 'him' or 'her')
	Student uses emoticons	Student refers to avatar as an object (avatar as 'it')

Table 7. Student interactions with the worlds.

	In-world	In-class
student-to-world interactions	Student works on his/her project (building/scripting)	Student seems focused on his/her project
	Student performs actions irrelevant to the project (e.g. dancing, flying, visiting places, etc.)	Student seems to enjoy the project
	Student modifies his/her avatar's appearance	Student seems 'absent-minded'
	Student uses avatar gestures	Student seems displeased using the virtual world
	Student explores his/her classmates' virtual artifacts	Student 'logs-in' before the beginning of the practical session
	Student uses his/her own virtual creations	Student 'logs-in' at the beginning of the practical session
	Student uses the in-world tools	Student 'logs-in' later than the beginning of the practical session
		Student 'logs-out' before the end of the practical session
		Student 'logs-out' right after the end of the practical session
		Student stays in-world after the end of the practical session

3.1 Actions and Interactions in the Physical Classroom

The focus points for the first fundamental category are grouped in three sub-categories (see Sects. 3.1.1–3.1.3).

3.1.1 Students' in-Class Talking and Making Comments About the Virtual World

While being in-class, students were often observed talking and making comments about the virtual world. This activity can be summarised as follows:

- They were considerably talkative in-class during the practical sessions.
- They were mostly discussing with their classmates about matters related to the virtual world and their project.
- Their discussions with the teaching team regarded mostly the virtual world and the assignment.
- Students' discussions were not always relevant but also irrelevant to the project or the virtual world.
- Students' comments about the technology and the emotional experience of the virtual world were usually positive (Table 8).

Table 8. Students' in-class talking and making comments about the virtual world.

Week	Student talks to classmate about the project or the virtual world	Student talks to classmate about something irrelevant to the project or the virtual world	Student talks to tutor/ demonstrator about the project or the virtual world	Student talks to tutor/ demonstrator about something irrelevant to the project or the virtual world	Student makes a positive comment about the technology of the virtual world	Student makes a negative comment about the technology of the virtual world	Student makes a positive comment about the emotional experience of the virtual world	Student makes a negative comment about the emotional experience of the virtual world	Sum
1	154	27	14	15	8	0	14	3	***235***
2	103	17	96	0	0	0	31	0	***247***
3	87	43	105	7	4	0	4	9	***259***
4	91	26	71	26	0	4	0	0	***218***
5	78	17	93	11	0	0	0	6	***205***
6	41	35	43	27	5	0	3	0	***154***
Sum	***554***	***165***	***422***	***86***	***17***	***4***	***52***	***18***	***1318***

Observation Week 1. During the first minutes of the session, students' communication was taking place mainly in-class. Students were discussing about the orientation building (which was where they were first logged-in and the first part of the content they came in contact with), the avatars, the instructions they were given, and their in-world task. As soon as they started the modifications of their avatars' appearance, several comments about that were heard in the classroom. At a point when a student used gestures imitating punching, two students expressed their idea of embedding a health system in-world in order to create a game where they would beat their project manager, obviously referring to an avatar fighting in a joking manner. Approaching the end of the session, several students opted to fly around the world. That was when they pointed out that the virtual world was empty and that they would have preferred it if there had been some former students' artefacts or showcases available for them to see. Other students preferred to stay in the orientation building until the end of the session, having their avatars sit on the couches and chairs available. They were calling their classmates to join them saying 'come sit with us', 'would you like some coffee? We have coffee here', 'I'd prefer some tea, please'. In a sense, that was a role-play game taking place partially in-world and partially in-class. Finally, close to the end of the session five students noted that the virtual world seemed empty and that they would have preferred it if there had been former students' artefacts available for them to explore.

In general, students were enjoying their time in-world and they were making positive comments about their experience. Their communication in-class was very extensive, sharing ideas about anything related with the virtual world, from the look of the avatars to the content of the virtual world, which (the latter) was limited.

Observation Week 2. Students' communication took place mainly in the physical classroom. The session started with students discussing about their project and the setup of the virtual showcase, and until the end of the session almost all conversations were focused on that topic. Students were expressing their thoughts and their plans regarding their in-world development to the demonstrator, asking for their feedback and advice, and also clarifying questions. An interesting point is that, even though each group worked with task division, several students that were not responsible for the in-world development were willing to work on it, and, thus, they asked for the demonstrator's permission to do so. That was encouraged by the teaching team, but what was pointed out was that the developers of the team had the responsibility for the final outcome. Generally, students seemed very keen to collaborate and help each other, either that was a teammate or any other classmate. Finally, students asked for further information, tutorials, guides, and relevant online sources to broaden their knowledge about the virtual world.

Observation Week 3. During this practical session, all the team members that had the role of developing the virtual showcase decided to sit next to each other, separated from the rest of their team members that were working on a different aspect of the assignment. Those (latter) students were exchanging ideas about their projects and helping each other in a form of spontaneous peer-tutoring process. They were very frequently asking for the demonstrator's help and guidance on how to proceed with their task, as well as feedback about their ideas and progress until that point. A student, after having explored the virtual world, asked the reason why it was rather empty, while other students also seemed a bit disappointed by the fact that the content of the world was limited. At some point around the middle of the session, a student was persuaded by his teammates to enter the virtual world for the first time, after being told that it was an action worthy to take, since he would fully understand the affordances of the virtual world, he would be more productive and more able to have spot-on ideas, and, in any case, he would enjoy the process (Fig. 2).

Observation Week 4. The practical session started with students discussing about the progress of their work and their future plans. Several questions were addressed to the demonstrator regarding the same issues. A group of students asked for permission to build their virtual objects on a third-party program, and import them into the virtual world when they would be ready. They claimed that their experience on building using the virtual world tools was minimal, and that this would obstruct them from having the desired results. However, they were experienced users of the aforementioned third-party software, and, thus, they were given the permission. Other students expressed some queries concerning the basic in-world object creation mechanisms. They were referred to the posters placed in the sandbox, and then they were encouraged to come back for further questions, if necessary. Students continued discussing and brainstorming ideas about the setup of their showcases until the end of the session.

An interesting observation was that of a student saying that she did not like flying with her avatar, when her classmate asked her the reason why she opted to walk instead of flying around.

Observation Week 5. Initially, the students that were responsible for the in-world development presented to their teammates the artefacts that had been created in the intermediate period since the previous week's session. Afterwards, the teams' conversations were focused on the in-world development and the refinement of the existing

Fig. 2. Meeting room with information about the communication.

artefacts that needed to be done until the end of the course of the sessions. Members of two teams complained to the demonstrator that their ideas were stolen by other teams that had created showcases closely resembling theirs. From that point on, those students started discussing ways to conceal their showcases and the artefacts placed in them from the rest of the teams, asking for the demonstrator's assistance on that, too. Other teams asked for the demonstrator's help on scripting, claiming that it was difficult for them to understand the logic behind the programming language of the virtual world.

Observation Week 6. Students were talking most of the time about scripting and the potential ways of making their showcases more interactive. They took the orientation building as an exemplar of the way their showcases should be in terms of interactivity, and they claimed that a showcase without interactivity would be incomplete and not interesting. The conversations with the demonstrator concerned the same topic and several queries regarding it were formed. Students were discussing more about poseballs and the ways these can animate the bodies of the avatars.

3.1.2 Students' Attitude Towards the Use of the Virtual World

Students' attitude towards the use of the virtual world includes four (4) focus points. Their frequencies are illustrated in Table 9, whilst the findings can be summarised as follows:

- Most of the time students were working focused on their projects.
- More often than not they seemed to enjoy the use of the virtual world.
- Rarely did students seem absent-minded.
- A few times students seemed displeased using the virtual world, mostly when they were struggling with its technology and tools.

Table 9. Students' attitude towards the use of the virtual world.

Week	Student seems focused on his/her project	Student seems to enjoy the project	Student seems 'absent-minded'	Student seems displeased using the virtual world	Sum
1	17	29	0	29	*75*
2	147	68	0	17	*232*
3	113	49	9	3	*174*
4	154	57	0	27	*238*
5	126	39	0	41	*206*
6	136	57	0	19	*212*
Sum	*693*	*299*	*9*	*136*	*1137*

Observation Week 1. All students seemed focused on their task which, in that specific session, was to familiarise themselves with the virtual world, its tools, and its navigation system, while the whole process took place in a pleasant atmosphere. Apart from some moments when students seemed confused about what to do and how to use the tools of the world, students seemed to enjoy the use of the virtual world. Very often they were observed laughing with the unexpected results of their actions, or the look of other avatars, or the gestures used by some students, or the comments they were making in-class about anything taking place in-world, or jokes shared with IMs.

Nevertheless, some students seemed disappointed when they realised that even though there was much free space on the virtual land, they were restricted to create their showcases inside specific buildings that were designed with a plan of being formed as an expo. In any case, that was part of the instructional design, and students, according to their assignment brief, had to adjust their work to anything they would find in-world as a workspace area.

Observation Week 2. All students were working focused on their projects most of the time. They seemed to enjoy the process and the fact that they were given the opportunity to be creative and productive. In the few cases when students were not working on their project they were still active in-world, creating objects not related to their showcase, or using the existing in-world objects. But even in those cases when students were taking breaks from their work, they were enjoying and familiarising themselves with the features of the virtual world.

Observation Week 3. All students were observed working focused on their projects throughout the whole duration of the practical session. They enjoyed the use of the virtual world, and, even in cases when they were facing difficulties, they seemed intrigued to look for further information on the use of the virtual world and its tools. At some point close to the end of the session, one student seemed absent-minded and completely detached from what was going on in the virtual world and the physical classroom (Figs. 3 and 4).

Fig. 3. Student project A.

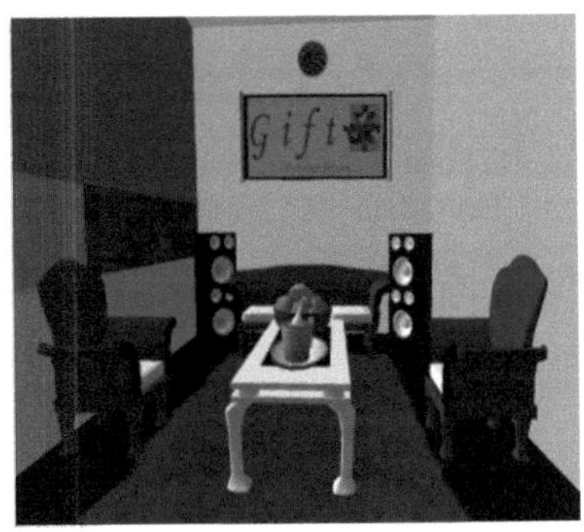

Fig. 4. Student project B.

Observation Week 4. Students were working focused on their projects for as long as the practical session lasted. A group of students seemed to have difficulties in using the virtual world, but as soon as these difficulties were overcome, they seemed pleased with the progress and the results of their work.

Observation Week 5. All teams seemed to be working focused on their projects. The members of the teams who had made a satisfying for them progress on their project seemed to enjoy the use of the virtual world and the results of their work. On the other hand, other teams seemed to be struggling to understand the world's mechanism; that deprived them from the enjoyment of achieving good results and from using the tools of the virtual world in a creative way.

Observation Week 6. Students seemed to work very focused on their projects. Their enthusiasm was obvious when they could see their showcases taking their final form. They were also enjoying seeing the functionality of their scripts.

3.1.3 Student Identity and Avatar Identity

The way students referred to their avatars while being in the physical classroom included four (4) focus points and their frequencies are illustrated in Table 10. Generally, the findings can be summarised as follows:

- References to the avatars were few during the first 4 sessions.
- No reference to avatars was made during the last two sessions.
- Students referred to their avatars mostly in the first person.
- Students referred to their avatars in the second and third person very few times.
- No student referred to their avatar as an object.

Table 10. Student identity and avatar identity.

Week	Student refers to avatar in the first person/identifies with avatar (avatar as 'I')	Student refers to avatar in the second person/addresses avatar directly (avatar as 'you')	Student refers to avatar in the third person (avatar as 'him' or 'her')	Student refers to avatar as an object (avatar as 'it')	Sum
1	9	0	4	0	*13*
2	6	3	0	0	*9*
3	4	2	2	0	*8*
4	2	0	0	0	*2*
5–6	0	0	0	0	*0*
Sum	*21*	*5*	*6*	*0*	*32*

Observation Week 1. Students spent a considerable amount of time editing and re-editing their avatars' appearance, and comments about the look of the avatars were heard during that time. Since many students were trying to give their avatars their own physical look, they kept asking 'do I look like him/her?' or 'does he look like me?'. Other students were trying to make their avatars have the 'ideal' for them look, and they kept asking for their classmates' feedback ('Do I look nice?', 'She is pretty, isn't she?'). A student was very disappointed with his avatar's look, complaining that it looked too female no matter what he did. Eventually, one of his classmates helped him make the necessary modifications. Many comments were also heard about a naked avatar with all its features stretched to the limits (too short, too fat, too big nose etc.), such as ‘oh, this is ugly’, ‘who is that ugly thing?’, ‘shame on you! Go get dressed’. Another student that had removed all the avatar’s clothes by mistake shouted in the classroom ‘Help me! I don’t have any clothes on. I can’t find them’. Another student, in a role-play mood, pretended to be Adam and he was calling for Eve. Generally, students either identified with their avatars, or they were referring to them as a third person.

Observation Week 2. Students referred to their avatars in very few cases. There was a case of one student that was entering the virtual world for the first time; his teammates helped him modify his avatar’s appearance, while their discussions were focused around this topic for a few minutes (~10). Students were referring to their avatars either in the first person (e.g. ‘look at me’, ‘do you like my t-shirt?’) or in the third (e.g. ‘He looks strong’). Moreover, a student, disapproving of her classmate’s avatar appearance, which she thought to be too revealing for a university student, said ‘shame on you’ to her and that led the latter to change the clothes of her avatar.

Observation Week 3. A few comments about an avatar were heard in-class when the firstly-introduced-to-the-virtual world student was modifying his avatar’s appearance. Students were referring to the ‘newbie’ avatar in the third person (e.g. ‘you can change his clothes’, ‘he is a bit short’, ‘he looks like a woman, how can I make him more masculine?’). They referred to their own avatars in the third person too, though these references were very limited.

Observation Week 4. The only reference made to an avatar was that of a student who asked her classmate ‘why don’t you fly instead of walking?’ to get as answer ‘I can’t. I find flying difficult’. However, one might say that this was not a direct reference to the avatar, but to the student herself.

Observation Weeks 5–6. None of the students was observed making reference to avatars at any time of this observation.

3.2 Actions and Interactions in the Virtual World

The aforementioned focus points for the second fundamental category concerning students’ actions and interactions in the virtual world are grouped in four sub-categories (see Sects. 3.2.1–3.2.4).

3.2.1 Students' in-World Talking and Making Comments About the Virtual World

Students' communication in the virtual world includes seven (7) focus points and their frequencies are illustrated in Table 11. The term 'chat' mentioned below refers exclusively to typewritten communication. Summarising the observation findings it can be noted that:

- Students used the chat tool only during the first and the second practical sessions.
- Their typewritten communication mostly concerned the virtual world and the utilisation of its tools.
- Students' comments in chat about the virtual world and their in-world experience were mostly positive.

Observation Week 1. A few minutes after the students' first log in, one of them spontaneously encouraged the rest to use the chat tool saying 'hi, can someone talk to me?', and the rest instantly responded with greetings, such as 'greetings', 'hi', 'hello', 'hi guys' etc. Later, when most of the students were editing their avatars' appearance, one of the students, who apparently had not noticed that there were posters giving him all the information needed, used the chat to ask his classmates 'how to change my style?'. However, he got no reply, since the student sitting next to him showed him the way. Apart from that, students used the chat in several cases to comment about the actions or the appearance of the avatars, using phrases revealing enjoyment, such as 'haha that's hilarious', or exclamation, such as 'wow great', and even to exchange ideas and thoughts with the students located in the next classroom. The most extensive use of the chat took place when a student, who had prior experience in this virtual world, used several gestures, and students, who were located in different rooms, were praising his actions asking how these gestures could be used. Finally, the most interesting case was that of two students who, despite the fact that they were seated next to each other, they opted to use IMs in their mother-tongue to communicate with each other. Even though the content of their conversation is unknown, both of them were laughing and they seemed to be enjoying their in-world communication.

Observation Week 2. Some students greeted each other when they first logged in. Later on, the use of the chat was limited. It took place especially when students made their first building attempts in their showcase area, and other students, physically located in different rooms, were asking each other information about building, in general, or about the showcases, in particular.

Observations Weeks 3–6. No use of the chat tool was observed.

Table 11. Students' in-world talking and making comments about the virtual world.

Week	Student chats with classmate about the project or the virtual world	Student chats with student about something irrelevant to the project or the virtual world	Student uses in chat phrases/ words revealing enjoyment	Student uses in chat words/ phrases revealing exclamation	Student uses in chat words/ phrases often used is social networks	Student makes a negative comment about the technology of the virtual world	Student makes a negative comment about the emotional experience of the virtual world	Sum
1	28	14	9	11	7	0	0	***69***
2	7	2	0	0	0	0	0	***9***
3–6	0	0	0	0	0	0	0	0
Sum	***35***	***16***	***9***	***11***	*7*	***0***	***0***	*78*

3.2.2 Student Identity and Avatar Identity

With regard to student engagement and avatar identity as expressed by students in-world, their actions were observed based on five (5) focus points, the frequencies of which are illustrated in Table 12. The findings can be generally summarised as follows:

- Students modified their avatars' appearance extensively during the first practical session and less in the second and third.
- Some students spent time between sessions to modify their avatar appearance.
- No avatar modifications were observed during the last three sessions.
- Avatar references in chat were very rare.

Table 12. In-world nonverbal communication.

Week	Student modifies avatar appearance	Student refers to avatar in the first person/identifies with avatar	Student refers to avatar in the second person/ addresses avatar directly	Student refers to avatar in the third person	Student refers to avatar as an object	Sum
1	98	1	1	0	0	***100***
2	16	0	0	0	0	***16***
3	12	0	0	0	0	***12***
4–6	0	0	0	0	0	***0***
Sum	***126***	***1***	***1***	***0***	***0***	***128***

Observation Week 1. The avatar modifications were very extensive during the first observation. Some of the students with prior experience started editing their avatars' appearance with ease, immediately after their log-in. The rest of the students followed their lead, and in several minutes the avatar modifications were massive. Some students were paying attention to every detail of their avatars' appearance, trying to make them look like their physical self, whilst others used their imagination to form their virtual selves. One of the students opted to form a completely white avatar, pretending to be a ghost. Another student that had prior experience in the use of this virtual world created an avatar with all its features stretched to the limits (i.e. too short, too fat, too long hair, too big eyes, too big feet, etc.). There was also another who created a short, fat, female, naked avatar. It should be noted that both of them were using their avatars to tease their classmates. Later on, one of the students removed all the avatar's clothes by mistake and that made him feel shocked and embarrassed, while two of his friends did the same thing wishing to tease him. Then, another student who saw that incident removed all the avatar's clothes, and put a palm tree texture on his avatar pretending to be Adam looking for Eve. Finally, despite the fact that all students were aware of the existence of ready-to-use outfits in the 'edit your appearance' section of the orientation building, only one of the students used one of those outfits, whilst the rest preferred to create their own.

Initially, most of the students were modifying their avatars' appearance in front of the corresponding poster in the orientation area. Later on, when they became familiar with the mechanism, they did so anywhere and anytime. Interestingly, some students preferred to change the outfit of their avatars behind a folding screen to give a more real-life feeling to the process. Another student had his avatar sitting on a chair in the 'edit your appearance' section, pretending to be judging his friend's appearance and helping him pick the best outfit.

Aside from the above, very interesting was the case of a student who had formed her avatar based on her physical look. However, she then preferred to use the default look again, since 'the default one is way better, because it does not wear glasses' unlike herself, or an imitation of herself.

As regards students' in-world references to their avatars, they were very few. A student, who had not noticed the related posters in the orientation building, asked through chat 'how can I change my look?' and his friend gave him instructions on how to do that.

Observation Week 2. One student, who was entering the virtual world for the first time, was observed modifying his avatar's appearance for approximately 10 min, after having read the corresponding posters in-world, and after following his teammates' example and guidelines. Interestingly, another student opted to change her avatar's appearance after her friend had disapproved of it.

Observation Week 3. Solely the newly introduced to the virtual world student spent approximately 15 min to change his avatar appearance, trying to imitate his physical look.

Observation Weeks 4–6. No avatar modification or reference to the avatars through the chat tool was observed.

3.2.3 In-World Nonverbal Communication

One of the alternative ways of communication that virtual worlds offer is nonverbal communication, through avatar gestures and emoticons. Table 13 presents their frequencies and the observations can be summarised as follows:

- Students used random avatar gestures only during the first practical session.
- Emoticons were never observed being used.

Table 13. In-world nonverbal communication.

Week	Student uses avatar gestures	Student uses emoticons	Sum
1	34	0	***34***
2–6	0	0	***0***
Sum	***34***	***0***	***34***

Observation Week 1. A student with prior experience in this virtual world was the first who used gestures, mainly to present to his classmates one more feature of the virtual world which he deemed to be enjoyable. Initially, he used some of the built-in gestures of the virtual world (waving, jumping on a jumping ball, bodybuilder posing, punching), but later on he created his own 'dance' combining the aforementioned gestures. He even used the punching gestures to 'punch' the demonstrator's avatar and that made everyone in the room laugh. Several students tried to imitate him and started experimenting with the available gestures, whilst others used the poseballs available in the orientation building in order to animate their avatars.

Observation Weeks 2–6. No student was observed using avatar gestures or emoticons.

3.2.4 Interactions with the World

Even though the main reason for using a virtual world was for teaching and learning purposes, the fact that students' attention can be distracted by other stimuli could not be disregarded. Therefore, this category consisted of four (4) focus points, including the various types of interactions that students had while being in the virtual world; the frequencies of which are illustrated in Table 14. These findings can be summarised as follows:

- Students spent most of their time in-world building and scripting.
- Most of student-to-world interactions were relevant to their project.
- Students often visited their classmates' workspaces to observe their work.
- Students were using their own virtual creations very often, mostly to check the functionality of their scripts.

Table 14. Interactions with the world.

Week	Student works on project	Student performs actions irrelevant to the project	Student explores classmates' virtual artefacts	Student uses own virtual creations	Sum
1	0	107	21	66	***194***
2	35	82	17	57	***191***
3	76	46	13	73	***208***
4	107	19	8	61	***195***
5	126	4	3	86	***219***
6	73	0	7	39	***119***
Sum	***417***	***258***	***69***	***382***	***1126***

Observation Week 1. From the very first minute of students' presence in-world, they used the orientation building to the maximum extent, exploiting all the artefacts available in it. Initially, they read the posters and followed the given instructions in order to familiarise themselves with the mechanisms of the virtual world. As soon as students had completed, or paused for a while, the avatar modification process, almost all of them used (at least once) one of the objects existing in the orientation building. Students were usually using more than 2 or 3 objects for multiple times, since they were experimenting with the mechanisms of the world, trying to understand them. In addition, students used the given poseballs to sit on chairs and armchairs, but later on they tried to sit on any available object, ending up sitting on the tables, on the walls, on the lights, etc.

Subsequently, most of the students sporadically moved to the sandbox, where posters containing information about building were available. The sandbox fully served its goal, since students were reading the posters and experimenting with building in it, creating from very simple primitives to very complex ones, even combining some of them to create an artefact. Some students, though a minority, started building objects without visiting the sandbox first where the corresponding posters were placed. Most of them visited that spot later on and read the information about building. Very few students never visited the sandbox, whilst even those with prior experience in such environments read all the posters, even at a glance, mostly motivated by their curiosity. By the end of the session, all students had created at least one object in the virtual world, either in the sandbox or elsewhere, either big (someone created a house) or small, either complex or simple. Moreover, several students flew around the world in order to explore it, and visited the workspaces where they would build their showcases in the following sessions. Interestingly, about 10 min before the end of the session, all the avatars of a group were sitting at a meeting table inside the virtual world, while their physical selves were simultaneously sitting in similar positions in-class in order to (orally) discuss about their project.

At this point, though not directly related to the actual interactions students had with the world, it should also be noted that the majority of students sent friend requests to their friends and even to their other classmates, and then used the 'offer teleport' and 'teleport to friend' functions.

Observation Week 2. The student that was entering the virtual world for the first time went through the whole orientation process guided by his classmates, read all the available posters, and used the majority of the existing objects, while familiarising himself with the mechanisms of the virtual world. The rest of the students were reading the posters regarding building, and were trying to create some objects inside the sandbox. The objects students were creating were mostly not related to their project, though some students were observed creating objects that would serve the needs of their showcase. Other students were observed having their avatars sitting on chairs or armchairs or at the meeting table inside the orientation building, while they were having their meeting in the physical classroom. By the end of the practical session, all the teams had started modifying their workspaces according to their needs, and they had created some objects with only very basic modifications. Interestingly, one of the groups had already started working on their project since the previous week, and, thus, their work progress was one step further than the rest of the groups by the time this observation took place. However, they made no further building during this session.

Observation Week 3. Several students opted to spend some time in the orientation area again, using the virtual objects available there. One student went through the whole orientation process for about 30 min in order to familiarise himself with the virtual world, since that was the first time he was using it. As soon as he felt satisfied with his orientation, he had his avatar sitting on a chair in the orientation building, and then went on working on another task completely detached from the virtual world. Other students stayed in the orientation building for several minutes trying to make copies of the available objects, but got disappointed when they realised that all the objects were locked – since content creation was the main task students had to perform in-world. Others were searching the web for further information regarding building and scripting. From that point on, students started their actual in-world development, working either in the sandbox – in order to keep their showcase clean and tidy – or in their workspaces – in order to have immediate awareness of the progression of their work and the look of their showcases. Students were working with such dedication taking care of every detail, that they even created labels outside their showcases with the logos of their teams. A worthwhile observation is that during this session students' need for more content became clear. Some of them explored the virtual world once again and even tried to fly across the sea looking for unexplored lands with more content.

Observation Week 4. The teams' in-world progress since the previous week was obvious, as students had created new objects in their showcases. Their in-world interactions with the virtual world during the practical session were mostly limited to building and scripting, according to the needs of their showcases. Sometimes they were observed being in the sandbox looking over the posters for information on building. Some avatars were observed being in-world without performing any actions, while students were working in the physical classroom.

Observation Week 5. Students seemed to have created the greatest part of their in-world infrastructure, having created more artefacts with more attention to detail and fitting the purposes of their projects, since the previous week. They continued working on their showcases during this practical session, refining their existing artefacts and implementing their teammates' ideas. They were also using their virtual objects, in order to check the functionality of the scripts they had written, and correcting their mistakes, in order to give the desired functionality to their objects. However, they seemed to focus more on the object creation rather than on the script writing, as they seemed to be more interested in giving their showcase the desired look, rather than making interactive the objects they had created. Moreover, the students were also visiting other teams' showcases to view their classmates' artefacts and get ideas about their further progress. That was when some students felt uncomfortable with their classmates' observing their work; thus, they decided to conceal their showcases with additional walls, and then continued working isolated.

Observation Week 6. Very few students were working in-world. Their focus was on scripting, since they had completed most of the building they had planned to do, and they were aiming to make their objects more interactive at this point. They used scripts on some objects and even created poseballs, which they placed on chairs, armchairs, sofas, etc. As soon as they had created their scripts, they started using them to test their functionality.

3.3 Students' Willingness to Remain in-World

The final sub-category, consisting of five (5) focus points, concerns students' willingness to use the virtual world for additional time, while being physically located in the physical classroom. Table 15 illustrates their frequencies.

As a general note it can be said that:

- Students usually entered the virtual world at the beginning of the practical session.
- Students usually exited the virtual world right after the end of the practical session.
- In few cases student remained in-world after the end of the session.

Observation Week 1. Apart from 9 students, who were all members of the same group and did not log in at all during the whole practical session, all the rest of the students actively used the virtual world for at least as long as the practical session lasted. One student was observed online 10 min prior to the beginning of the session, whilst 5 students stayed in-world for approximately 15 min after the end of it.

Observation Week 2. At least one member of one of the groups seemed to have logged in since the previous week, as modifications had been made in their workspace. Even though none of the students was observed logging in earlier than the beginning of the practical session and most of them logged out as soon as the session ended, 4 students opted to stay in-world for approximately 15 more minutes to finalise their work in progress.

Observation Week 3. At least one member of each group seemed to have logged in since the previous week, as modifications had been made in all workspaces. During this practical session, mainly the developers of each team were online, whilst there were several other avatars online that remained non-active throughout the whole session. All students logged out as soon as the practical session was over.

Observation Week 4. At least one member of each group seemed to have logged in since the previous week, as modifications had been made in all workspaces. Three students remained in-world for 10 min after the end of the practical session in order to complete the task in progress.

Observation Week 5. At least one member of each group seemed to have logged in since the previous week, as modifications had been made in all workspaces. All students that logged in did so at the beginning of the session and logged out as soon as the practical session was over.

Observation Week 6. At least one member of each group seemed to have logged in since the previous week, as modifications had been made in all workspaces. All students that logged in did so at the beginning of the session. A few students stayed in-world for 20 more minutes than expected in order to finalise their work, given that this was the last practical session of the course and some final help from the demonstrator was still offered.

Table 15. Students' willingness to remain in-world longer than expected.

Week	Student 'logs-in' before the beginning of the practical session	Student 'logs-in' at the beginning of the practical session	Student 'logs-in' later than the beginning of the practical session	Student 'logs-out' before the end of the practical session	Student 'logs-out' right after the end of the practical session	Student stays in-world after the end of the practical session	Sum
1	1	16	0	0	12	5	***34***
2	0	15	0	0	11	4	***30***
3	0	9	7	0	16	0	***32***
4	0	11	0	0	8	3	***22***
5	0	13	0	0	13	0	***26***
6	0	10	0	0	6	4	***20***
Sum	***1***	***74***	*7*	***0***	***66***	***16***	***164***

4 Discussion

The impact that the orientation process had on learners' engagement – while using a hybrid virtual learning approach – was clearly positive, as it also enhanced the opportunities for interaction between the students and the virtual world. Those who went through the orientation process were keener to interact both with their fellow students and with the virtual world. The same students used the in-world tools more intensively. They also found the whole process more enjoyable, constructive, and rewarding. Likewise, students that followed the instructions regarding the avatar modification process – though with some exceptions – were usually having considerably more intense modifications on their avatars compared to others. On the other hand, those students that disregarded partially or even completely the existence of the orientation area, were almost constantly struggling to deal with the virtual world, and, by extension, with their assignment (even though this can be attributed to the lack of information regarding the programming process).

Nevertheless, the references made to avatars were overall limited, most likely because of the fact that they did not consider them as a special feature of the virtual world, but rather as a tool to work on their project. The opportunity given to students to simultaneously be co-present both in the virtual world and in the physical classroom, resulted in a limited use of the chat tool or of any other nonverbal communication method in the virtual world, since this need was primarily covered in the physical classroom. Furthermore, most of the students were working on their task without being distracted or struggling, due to the fact that they had all the necessary knowledge base to deal with the tools of the virtual world, and, by extension, with their project. Finally, students' willingness to stay in the virtual world and the physical classroom for extra time, for the whole course of the practical session or even longer than expected, is also an important indication that confirms their engagement with the virtual world and their project.

Considering the above, there is a clear indication that the orientation process can play a crucial role in learner engagement, something that is also reinforced by the findings attained from the students who decided not to go through this process. These finding are also confirmed by the Virtual Games industry, which introduced the idea of the orientation process long time ago aiming to 'teach' gamers (learner level) how to use certain controls or functions of the game in order to increase the levels of engagement.

Aside from this, considering the clear increase of interactions between the students and the virtual world, it can be hypothesised that an – at least basic – understanding of the 3D tools is required on any commercial attempt as part of the digital learning process. Thus, the following suggestions are given to stakeholders who have different interests in and responsibilities towards the use of virtual worlds:

Instructional designers should always ensure that a proper induction process will be provided to learners in order to help them understand quickly and deeply the mechanisms of the virtual world, as this is the key to increase the chances of having successful learning activities and the desired outcomes.

Educators should provide learners with enough time to undertake the orientation process for a proper induction and familiarisation with the virtual world and its tools. Students should be encouraged to use and engage with this process, as this will help them achieve better results – in terms of their assignment – and also work within the virtual world effortlessly.

Future researchers should focus on designing different setups of induction processes that will fit the personalities of different learners (in terms of their learning style) and their perspectives, as well as the levels of education considering that this experiment was conducted with university-level students.

As seen from all the theoretical background reviewed and presented above, interacting within the physical classroom does have advantages but certain disadvantages that cannot be disregarded, as well. The same applies when students interact in the virtual world and use its tools. However, when these two educational approaches are combined and students simultaneously co-exist in both environments, the drawbacks of each are eliminated. This is exactly where the most significant contribution of this research lies; students' network of interactions is broadened and educationally enriched when working within both the physical and the virtual world.

5 Conclusions

The orientation process helped most of the students to have a smooth induction to the virtual world and its tools, and also enhanced the opportunities for interaction. Thus, students should be given enough time to orient themselves into the virtual world, familiarise with its tools, and explore its potentials. Nevertheless, the learners' choices might be opposed to the instructional designer's, and, therefore, clear instructions and information should be given to learners. In addition, educators should encourage their students to use the in-world infrastructure. As regards the hybrid virtual learning approach, the findings suggest that the co-presence in both environments definitely contributed to the enhancement of the engagement with the virtual world and the educational material.

References

1. Allison, C., Campbell, A., Davies, C.J., et al.: Growing the use of virtual worlds in education: an OpenSim perspective. In: Gardner, M., Garnier, F., Kloos, C.D. (eds.) Proceedings of the 2nd European Immersive Education Summit (EiED 2012), pp. 1–13, Departamento de Ingeniería Telemática, Universidad Carlos III de Madrid, Paris, France (2012)
2. Anasol, P.R., Callaghan, V., Gardner, M., Alhaddad, M.J.: End-user programming and deconstrutionalism for co-creative laboratory activities in a collaborative mixed-reality environment. In: Gardner, M., Garnier, F., Kloos, C.D. (eds.) Proceedings of the 2nd European Immersive Education Summit (EiED 2012), pp. 171–182, Departamento de Ingeniería Telemática, Universidad Carlos III de Madrid, Madrid, Spain (2012)
3. Bredl, K., Groß, A., Hünniger, J., Fleischer, J.: The avatar as a knowledge worker? How immersive 3D virtual environments may foster knowledge acquisition. Electron. J. Knowl. Manage. **10**(1), 15–25 (2012)

4. Camilleri, V., de Freitas, S., Montebello, M., McDonagh-Smith, P.: A case study inside virtual worlds: use of analytics for immersive spaces. In: Proceedings of the 3rd International Conference on Learning Analytics and Knowledge (LAK 2013), pp. 230–234, Leuven, Belgium (2013)
5. Carter, B.: Virtual harlem: an innovative past, an evolving present and an exciting future. In: Gardner, M., Garnier, F., Kloos, C.D. (eds.) Proceedings of the 2nd European Immersive Education Summit (EiED 2012), pp. 1–13, Universidad Carlos III de Madrid, Departamento de Ingeniería Telemática, Paris, France (2012)
6. Chafer, J., Childs, M.: The impact of the characteristics of a virtual environment on performance: concepts, constraints and complications. In: Proceedings of the Researching Learning in Virtual Environments (ReLIVE 2008), pp. 94–105, Open University, Milton Keynes, UK (2008)
7. Childs, M.: Learners' experience of presence in virtual worlds. Ph.D thesis, University of Warwick (2010)
8. Childs, M., Peachey, A. (eds.): Understanding Learning in Virtual Worlds. Human–Computer Interaction Series, pp. 1–20. Springer, London
9. Christopulos, A., Conrad, M.: Views of educators on immersion in virtual worlds from second life to OpenSim. In: Gardner, M., Garnier, F., Kloos, C.D. (eds.) Proceedings of the 2nd European Immersive Education Summit (EiED 2012), pp. 48–59, Universidad Carlos III de Madrid, Departamento de Ingeniería Telemática, Paris, France (2012)
10. Christopoulos, A., Conrad, M.: Maintaining context in a Changing (Virtual) world: educators' perspectives for OpenSim and second life. In: Proceedings of 5th International Conference on Computer Supported Education (CSEDU 2013). Aachen, Germany (2013)
11. Christopoulos, A., Conrad, M., Shukla, M.: Objects, worlds, and students: virtual interaction in education. Educ. Res. Int. **2014** (2014). 20 pages, doi:10.1155/2014/318317
12. Cohen, L., Manion, L., Morrison, K.: Research Methods in Education, 7th edn. Routledge Taylor & Francis, London (2011)
13. Conrad, M., Neale, J., Charles, A.: Of mice or men? The avatar in the virtualscape. In: Proceedings of the International Conference on Information Society (i-society 2010), pp. 242–247, London, UK (2010)
14. Dalgarno, B., Lee, M.J.W.: What are the learning affordances of 3-D virtual environments? Br. J. Educ. Technol. **41**(1), 10–32 (2010)
15. de Freitas, S., Rebolledo-Mendez, G., Liarokapis, F., Magoulas, G., Poulovassilis, A.: Developing an evaluation methodology for immersive learning experiences in a virtual world. In: Proceedings of the Conference in Games and Virtual Worlds for Serious Applications (VS-GAMES 2009), pp. 43–50, Coventry, UK (2009)
16. de Freitas, S., Rebolledo-Mendez, G., Liarokapis, F., Magoulas, G., Poulovassilis, A.: Learning as immersive experiences: using the four-dimensional framework for designing and evaluating immersive learning experiences in a virtual world. Br. J. Educ. Technol. **41**(1), 69–85 (2010)
17. Dickey, M.D.: Brave new (interactive) worlds: a review of the design affordances and constraints of two 3D virtual worlds as interactive learning environments. Interact. Learn. Environ. **13**(1–2), 121–137 (2005)
18. Elliott, J.B., Gardner, M., Alrashidi, M.: Towards a framework for the design of mixed reality immersive education spaces. In: Gardner, M., Garnier, F., Kloos, C.D. (eds.) Proceedings of the 2nd European Immersive Education Summit (EiED 2012), pp. 63–76, Universidad Carlos III de Madrid, Departamento de Ingeniería Telemática, Paris, France (2012)

19. Frutos-Perez, M.: Practice, context, dialogue: using automated conversational agents to extend the reach and depth of learning activities in immersive worlds. In: Proceedings of the World Conference on Educational Multimedia, Hypermedia and Telecommunications, pp. 70–77, Open University Press, Milton Keynes, UK (2011)
20. Hockey, A., Esmail, F., Jimenez-Bescos, C., Freer, P.: Built environment education in the era of virtual learning. In: Proceedings of the W089 Special Track — 18th CIB World Building Congress, pp. 200–217, Salford, UK (2010)
21. Johnson, C.M., Vorderstrasse, A.A., Shaw, R.: Virtual worlds in health care higher education. J. Virtual Worlds Res. **2**(2), 3–12 (2009)
22. Jones, D.: An alternative (to) reality. In: Proceedings of the Researching Learning in Virtual Environments (ReLIVE 2008), pp. 113–121, Open University, Milton Keynes, UK (2013)
23. Levesque, J., Lelievre, E.: Creation and communication in virtual worlds: experimentations with OpenSim. In: Richir, S., Shirai, A. (eds.) Proceedings of the Virtual Reality International Conference (VRIC 2011), pp. 22–24, Laval, France (2011)
24. Moyles, J.: Observation as a research tool. In: Coleman, M., Briggs, A.J. (eds.) Research Methods in Education with SPSS. Sage, London (2002)
25. Padrós, A., Romero, M., Usart, M.: Measuring the knowledge convergence process in the collaborative game metavals. Procedia Comput. Sci. **15**, 193–202 (2012)
26. Schrader, P.G.: Learning in technology: reconceptualizing immersive environments. Assoc. Adv. Comput. Educ. J. **16**(4), 457–475 (2008)
27. Shaughnessy, J.J., Zechmeister, E.B., Zechmeister, J.S.: Research Methods in Psychology, 6th edn. McGraw-Hill, New York (2003)
28. Shukla, M., Conrad, M.: Second life is not an Island. In: Proceedings of the IADIS International Conference on e-Society, Avila, Spain (2011)
29. Steuer, J.: Defining virtual reality: dimensions determining telepresence. J. Commun. **42**(2), 73–93 (1992)
30. Veletsianos, G.: The impact and implications of virtual character expressiveness on learning and agent-learner interactions. J. Comput. Assist. Learn. **25**(4), 345–357 (2009)
31. Vosinakis, S., Anastassakis G., Koutsabasis, P.: A platform for teaching logic programming using virtual worlds. In: IEEE International Conference on Advanced Learning Technologies, ICALT 2014 (2014)
32. Vygotsky, L.S.: Mind Society: The Development of Higher Mental Processes. Harvard University Press, Cambridge (1978)
33. Wilkinson, J.: Direct Observation. In: Breakwell, G.M., Hammond, S., Fife-Shaw, C. (eds.) Research Methods in Psychology, 2nd edn. Sage, London (2000)
34. Zhao, H., Sun, B., Wu, H., Hu, X.: Study on building a 3D interactive virtual learning environment based on OpenSim platform. In: Proceedings of the International Conference on Audio, Language and Image Processing (ICALIP 2010), pp. 1407–1411, Shanghai, China (2010)

Evaluation of Adaptive Teamwork System Based upon Individual Differences in Culture Dimension (Individualism - Collectivism)

Wesam Shishah(✉)

School of Computer Science, University of Nottingham, Nottingham, NG8 1BB, UK
psxws@nottingham.ac.uk

Abstract. Although there are various personalised and adaptive eLearning systems developed, a culture factor has been not sufficiently considered in adaptive and personalised learning environments. This paper presents a personalised and adaptive system based on individual differences in cultural backgrounds (individualism and collectivism). A culturally adaptive teamwork system called IdeasRoom is used to implement cultural additions. The IdeasRoom system has adaptations to its interface to include two different versions of design: individualist version (IND) and collectivist version (COL). The paper summarises an initial evaluation of the proposed system. This evaluation of the proposed IdeasRoom system relates to the responses of the participants of the study that involved 52 postgraduate students, so that the version that was not personalised to participants' cultural backgrounds is compared with the version that was personalised to participants' cultural backgrounds in terms of their perceptions of usability their preferences of design. The findings show that the participants had perceptions of usability that are shown to be at a higher level when teamwork learning systems are personalised to participants' cultural backgrounds, which suggests that these results based on identifying users' cultural backgrounds are of significant importance. Also, this evaluation concludes that participants' preferences for experiencing a system are matched to their cultural inclinations.

Keywords: Culture · Group work · Teamwork · Higher education · Design · HCI · CSCW · Personalisation · Adaptation

1 Introduction

Societies worldwide are rapidly becoming culturally diverse, and specifically in Western Europe. Universities are increasingly embracing multiculturalism, which is demonstrated by diversity in cultural traditions and religion [43]. The increasingly multicultural profile of students entering higher education leads to the requirement for designers of online course materials to recognise the role of culture within higher education. Educators use group work activities more within coursework, which is in line with current thinking that teamwork is an essential skill for students to understand [11]. One of the main challenges faced by educators within higher education and designers in the field of computer support cooperative work (CSCW) is working within multicultural teams.

G. Costagliola et al. (Eds.): CSEDU 2016, CCIS 739, pp. 100–117, 2017.
DOI: 10.1007/978-3-319-63184-4_6

The 'one size fits all' approach in current user interfaces is a critical limitation in teamwork technology, since it ignores cultural differences in design. In addition, cross-cultural cognition is shown to be complex, but the content of some teaching and learning technologies appear to be insensitive to this critically important issue. Although technology sometimes offers localised versions of content, such localisations tend to be related solely to date/time formats and language adaptions. This research challenges this view and suggests that user interfaces should adapt their presentation to a user's culture cognitive factor, which can best accommodate their personal preferences.

This research proposes a novel approach in the design adaptive system that supports teamwork in higher education. The adaptation is based on differences between individualists' and collectivists' perceptions, beliefs and preferences through group work. The paper is structured as follows. Section 2 discusses the scope of culture in this research. Adaptive eLearning and related works are discussed in Sect. 3. Section 4 discusses teamwork in education. Section 5 examines a set of culture-related design strategies called R.I.N.G that are proposed and used as adaptive rules for the proposed system. Section 6 evaluates how a culturally adaptive teamwork system called IdeasRoom is used to implement cultural additions (individualism and collectivism). IdeasRoom is a novel teamwork tool, which has the facility to adapt its interface to the users' cultural cognitive style. The IdeasRoom system has adaptations to its interface to include two different versions of design: individualist version (IND) or collectivist version (COL) based upon users' culture cognitive type (individualism or collectivism). In Sect. 7, the evaluation of the usability and preference of the design are discussed, and Sect. 8 offers conclusions for this research study.

2 Cultural Dimensions

In this study there is a focus on two common societal dimensions of culture: individualism and collectivism, and are defined as follows:

- Societies described as individualist tend to be mainly associated with their close families and often live independently, so that they are expected to look after themselves; therefore, there are loose ties between individuals. People living in individualist societies tend to be motivated by loss of self-respect and guilt, and are often perceived to be goal-oriented and self-motivated, so that group interests are less important than individual interests [19, 21]. People living in individualist societies tend to demonstrate a personal identity rather than an identity of specific groups, so that they often seek benefit from their duties and activities, and have a more consistent behaviour and attitude approach to life than those from collectivist societies [45].
- These findings are contrasted with societies described as collectivist, where people tend to form groups that are cohesive and strong throughout life, so that the welfare of individuals becomes the concern of the group associated with them, and anxiety can result when individuals are separated from their group. Unquestioning loyalty is shown to individuals in collectivist societies, as the groups they are associated with, and often known as 'in-groups', give them protection when needed. Generally, people in collectivist societies attempt to maintain tradition, adopt virtues and skills that are

needed to demonstrate that they are good members of their group, and attempt to maintain social harmony, so individual interests are less important than group interests. Therefore, people living in collectivist societies tend to be motivated by loss of face and shame [19, 21]. The identities of individuals in collectivist societies are usually associated strongly with the values of their group, so that they generally support what is acceptable in their group [45].

The main focus of individualism and collectivism is how individuals are integrated within groups. Therefore, this research focuses on peer group interaction with individuals from different cultures, within a group-learning environment. Although this categorisation of societies is widely supported in the literature review, the definition of cultural identity involves greater complexity than factors discussed above, as individuals in all societies are likely to demonstrate various cultural identities at different times and in different circumstances. This study presents only one perspective on how to examine culture and there are others that could be drawn upon. However, to form a concept of different groups in terms of their behaviour patterns and general belief, the individualism-collectivism dimension proposed in previous research studies provides a very useful and important initial categorisation on which to ground future work.

Many sociologists, such as Hofstede and Triandis, have worked on classifying individualism and collectivism at two levels - namely, the nationality and individual level. Hofstede's research applies the classification of individualism and collectivism to the nationality level, while Triandis' research applies it at the individual level. Hofstede's work has often been criticised, because of his classification that reduces culture to nationality. It also ignores the on going changes that a person or a group who share cultural values undergo [29]. This research relies on the individual level of classification of individualism and collectivism.

3 Adaptive eLearning

Advanced technology enables software designers to ensure that learning tasks and materials are appropriate and relevant to the characteristics of individual users, instead of providing all users with the same content of materials and tasks. Therefore, software designers need to understand the preferences, requirements and needs of individual learners better, so that they can adapt learning tasks and materials, and learning experiences become more dynamic and effective, rather than providing learning tasks and materials without recognising that learners are different [7]. This insufficient recognition that eLearning strategies need to be personalised to individual learners exposes significant problems and limitations for many platforms of learning described as eLearning [18].

The on-going process of learning for individuals needs consideration of their preferences and needs, because the process of learning is adaptive and personal [5]. Effective learning could be prevented for some learners if software designers fail to understand factors that could influence their specific requirements, such as personal interests, learning styles, skills, prior knowledge and previous experience. This suggests that information is processed and learned in ways that are different for each individual, because individuals are different [23].

Therefore, learning programs need to ensure that presentation styles, sequences of resources and content selection are personalised and adapted based on data available from the profile of the learner, so that different techniques are used to enable the software system to adapt these appropriately for individual users. This approach should ensure that requirements, interests, needs and preferences of individual users are recognised to design a learning experience that is personalised for users.

Various systems have been developed to design eLearning systems that are adaptive, such as Internet-based educational fields, adaptive hypermedia educational fields and intelligent tutoring systems (ITS) [32]. These adaptive strategies are often developed to combine learner knowledge and learning style in eLearning systems, but can also only focus on one of these factors [1, 13, 18]. Limited studies consider culture factors in adaptation techniques [22, 35, 42], but none focus on the context of teamwork learning activities.

4 Teamwork in Education

According to Smith and Bath [40], the most effective approach to ensure students acquire knowledge and enhance their communication skills at educational institutions is teamwork, as this provides significant advantages to supervisors and teachers to reduce the quantity of their marking, give students opportunities to work collaboratively, enhance the challenge and complexity of tasks given to students to improve their experience of working, and to engage students more effectively [17]. When compared with face-to-face collaboration for group work projects, the performance of students collaborating online can be significantly better, because the interactions with other members of the group are more meaningful and frequent for students collaborating online, when compared with students involved in learning activities on a face-to-face basis [48]. Online learning tasks for teamwork is perceived more negatively by Smith et al. [41], who report that resolving logistical problems is easier for students seated physically together in one room, when compared to students learning in online classes. Personal factors can influence the perceptions of teamwork by students, so that how they perform within group activities is affected by these perceptions.

Perceptions of group work by students might also be affected by their communication and personality traits [31], but this is challenged by findings from other research, which suggests that the previous experience of students working in groups could change their perceptions of teamwork through online channels. In a study by Powell, Piccoli and Ives [34], the findings report that when students had wider experience of working with other students online and were involved in more online courses, their perceptions of teamwork through online channels were increased positively. This was related to the students spending more time online, and using this time to adapt to (and benefit from) the technology and online teamwork activities.

Research studies evaluating behaviour and teamwork preferences for employees and students suggest that the cultural dimensions of individualism and collectivism developed by Hofstede are an important factor in terms of profiling such groups and a useful way of assessing group behaviours [4]. When students work collaboratively in groups, their working processes are likely to be different, due to differing approaches that are likely to be taken by students from primarily individualist versus primarily collectivist cultures [15].

5 A Set of Culture-Related Design Strategies

To design group-based technologies that are meaningful and effective for their target audiences, designers should reference – or at least allow for – the audiences' cultures in their approaches. This section summarises the findings of the interviews carried out with lecturers and university students who have experienced group work, to establish how students incorporate culture as a factor from their current practice [38]. This section also presents a set of culturally relevant group-based technology design strategies based on insights from the interviews, as well as findings from cross-cultural psychology literature on behavioural tendencies of individualists and collectivists. These strategies have resulted from our work in a previous study [38]. A set of four main culturally relevant design strategies is presented and each strategy involves two sub strategies. One is aimed at use in tools developed for collectivist users and the other is aimed at use in tools for individualist users. Each strategy is presented with the following information: **Description**, which attempts to explain the strategy presented, **Antecedents**, which highlight the factors based on the review of the literature that lead to the strategy, **Real World Parallels**, which demonstrate the strategy in real world situations, and **The Two Sub-Strategies** produced from each main strategy. The two sub strategies are presented with a description and target audience, which suggests whether the audience would likely to be collectivist or individualist. This way of describing the strategies is intended to help designers include appropriate strategies in systems that are relevant for target audiences where cultural backgrounds could be a significant factor. It is anticipated that designers could find the discussions, descriptions and antecedents helpful in understanding the strategies, why they were developed and how they could be applied.

5.1 Strategy 1: In-Group Relationships

Description: The difference between collectivist users and individualist users forms the basis of this overall strategy to define relationships between members of a group.

Antecedents: In studies of education theory, findings suggest that individuals from individualist cultures often display less cooperative behaviour in groups than those from collectivist cultures, which supports the views discussed above [10]. Collectivists often highly value group solidarity and interpersonal harmony, prefer cooperation to competition, value group success rather than individual success, and tend to avoid individual recognition. This contrasts with individualists who often demonstrate additional effort to attain individual goals, and are generally motivated by individual recognition and competition [10, 26, 44].

Real World Parallels: The study investigated communication in the USA (individualist culture) and in Syria (collectivist culture), and reported that Syrian respondents preferred strategies that were ritualistic, indirect and cooperative, but American respondents preferred strategies that were hostile, direct and competitive [30].

The Sub-Strategies: This strategy contributes to the competitive strategy and the harmony strategy.

- ***The Competitive Strategy:*** A sense of competition between members of a group could be promoted with the competitive strategy. ***Target audience***: Individuals in individualist cultures.
- ***The Harmony Strategy:*** When the level of cooperation between group members is increased, a sense of harmony relationship is promoted by the harmony strategy. ***Target audience:*** Individuals in collectivist cultures.

5.2 Strategy 2: Identity

Description: The differences between collectivist users and individualist users in the views about the self are described by the strategy.

Antecedents: How individual people understand themselves in relating to other people explains the concept of the self, and Erez and Earley [12] suggest that people represent their social roles, social identity and personality as the self. People in individualist cultures often perceive themselves as separate from the social context, and independently follow their own projects and interests. People in collectivist cultures often perceive themselves as connected to social contexts with relationships with other people that are interdependent [28]. Therefore, people living in individualist cultures often perceive themselves as unique [39, 44], but people living in collectivist cultures tend to feel they fit into or belong to society, and do not feel isolated [44, 46].

Real World Parallels: An example of parents in an individualist culture, such as the USA, would encourage their children when reluctant to eat the meal prepared for them by telling them that children in other countries have very little food, and that they should be pleased that they are fortunate. An example of parents in a collectivist culture, such as Japan, would encourage their children when reluctant to eat the meal prepared for them by telling them that the farmer that had grown the rice had wasted his time, so he would feel bad if the children did not eat the rice, so they are encouraged to think more about the producer of the food rather than themselves. The example of the Japanese family suggests the importance of interdependence with others and fitting in and being concerned about others. The example of the USA family suggests the importance of promoting the self, noticing the differences with others and focusing on the self [28].

The Sub-Strategies: This strategy contributes to Individual-identity strategy and Group-identity strategy.

- ***Individual-identity Strategy:*** This strategy aims to promote uniqueness, independence, and an independent view of self in cooperation. ***Target audience:*** Individuals in individualist cultures.
- ***Group-identity Strategy:*** This strategy aims to promote belonging, fitting in and an interdependent view of self in cooperation. ***Target audience***: Individuals in collectivist cultures.

5.3 Strategy 3: Assessment Norm

Description: The differences between collectivist users and individualist users form the basis for the strategy in terms of the perceptions of compensation or rewards for an individual within a group.

Antecedents: The review of literature into reward allocation preferences indicates cross cultural differences, so that individuals from an individualist culture tend to prefer equity based allocation of rewards, but individuals from a collectivist culture tend to prefer equality based allocation of rewards [14, 46]. Therefore, values of collectivist cultures emphasise affiliation and cooperation, but values of individualist cultures emphasise achievement and competition, so that individualist values are more compatible with equity norms and identify individual performance for career progression and reward systems, as well as pay for performance systems [16].

Real World Parallels: In a study that compared distribution of rewards in a group and decision rules, Japanese respondents described as collectivist and Australian respondents described as individualist, were involved in a game of decisions for classroom administration. Australian respondents had a tendency to follow self-interest rules in this game, and Japanese respondents had a tendency to follow equal-say rules [27].

The Sub-Strategies: This strategy contributes to Equity strategy and Equality strategy:

- ***The Equity Strategy:*** The equity strategy proposes that persons who allocate rewards or compensation within a group distribute them in proportion to each member's contributions. ***Target audience***: Individuals in individualist cultures.
- ***The Equality Strategy:*** The equality strategy proposes that persons who allocate rewards or compensation within a group distribute them for a group of users for the actions of an individual user. ***Target audience***: Individuals in collectivist cultures.

5.4 Strategy 4: Superordinate Goals

Description: The differences between collectivist users and individualist users in goals, interests and motivations described by the strategy.

Antecedents: In societies defined as having an individualist culture, group interests are less important than individual interests, so that individuals in this type of culture are often motivated by potential loss of self-respect and feelings of personal guilt, so that they tend to be goal orientated and self-motivated. This contrasts with societies defined as having a collectivist culture, as individuals tend to maintain traditions by being good members of groups by adapting their virtues and skills, and in a collectivist culture typical motivators are loss of face and shame [20, 33, 44, 46]. Individuals often emphasise personal autonomy, freedom of choice and personal responsibility as values of personal independence in individualist cultures, and often show a preference for the independence of groups and self-directed behaviour, as these individuals attempt to maintain personal opinions and attitudes that are distinctive [39, 44]. In contrast, a sense of working within a group, interdependence and duty to a group are attitudes represented in a collectivist culture, as values in these societies stress that personal goals in groups are less important than maintaining the goals of the group. Therefore, individuals living in a collectivist society are interdependent with their in-group, and there is a collective responsibility for accountability and sharing responsibility [44, 46].

Real World Parallels: In Japan, managers of organisations often use participative programmes, employee suggestions and team decision-making or delegate responsibilities to team members and practice team working as a business strategy. Therefore, Japanese managers tend to adopt restrictive methods by expecting employees to obey and honour all management decisions, but also adopt relaxed methods by looking for consensus when issues arise, even minor issues, and ask for suggestions and ideas from employees [36]. Japanese organisations often introduce activities, such as team names, team banners, team dormitories and collective meals, to enhance productivity, as these types of activities help to integrate workers within their team and encourage effective teams. This contrasts with patterns of group working in Western countries, such as the USA, the UK, Sweden, Canada and Australia, where work teams are often self-managing, semi-autonomous or autonomous, so that team working operates as a form of self-management, and is widely applied in these countries [36]. According to Hofstede [20], there is a perception that in the USA and the UK, higher quality decisions are made by individuals, when compared to decisions made by groups.

The Sub-Strategies: This strategy contributes independence goal strategy and interdependence goal strategy.

- ***The Independence Goal Strategy:*** This strategy aims to promote self-goal, self-interest, personal responsibility and a sense of independence in cooperation. ***Target audience:*** Individuals in individualist cultures.
- ***The Interdependence Goal Strategy:*** This strategy aims to promote group-goal, group-interest, collective responsibility and a sense of interdependence in cooperation. ***Target audience:*** Individuals in collectivist cultures.

6 IdeasRoom: An Adaptive Teamwork System

Ideas can be generated when students are involved in brainstorming groups, so that the Internet tool called IdeasRoom is adopted in this study within the format of a forum for discussions, and is described as an experimental tool to promote this learning styles electronically. This teamwork brainstorming tool has the following components:

- Leader boards,
- Themes for interfaces,
- Blue, bronze, silver and gold colours to represent levels of membership
- Lists of ideas,
- Ideas to be added, and
- Sub-ideas to be added.

However, this tool also enables the use of versions that can be designed differently, and the COL version was designed to meet the preferences of collectivists, and the IND version was designed to meet the preferences of individualists. The next section provides more details and explanations, and discusses how R.I.N.G. strategies or group-based technology design strategies that are relevant in terms of cultural backgrounds inform both of these versions.

6.1 IND Interface

The RING sub-strategies of competition, individual identity, equity and independent goals are adopted in this version. Personal welcome messages, individuals' points are displayed, membership levels are highlighted, pictures and names of users are shown and themes represent these members, which are intended to enhance perceptions of uniqueness, independence and self views that are independent for the individual identity sub-strategy. Self achievement recognition and comparisons based on peer-to-peer perceptions involve points for completing activities defined as personal rewards, and levels of participation compared with other group members from personal feedback shown by gold, silver, bronze and blue colours that represent levels of membership for virtual personal achievement represented in two forms. Rewards for users are determined by participation in terms of quantity and quality with points that are awarded, and participation of users is represented by personal themes and personal membership levels, so that a member's theme is personalised by self-earned points, and shows that the equity norm has two forms. Finally, changing independent and personal goals are reflected by leader board changes and personal theme changes, and levels of personal membership are related to changing levels of participation of users that defines the independent goals sub-strategy.

6.2 COL Interface

The strategies of harmony, group identity, equality and interdependent goals form the collectivist culture R.I.N.G. sub-strategies for the COL interface. The group has a welcome message to promote the identity of the group, total points are shown for individual members and each group, membership levels for groups are shown, pictures and names of groups are shown, and group themes collect information from the group, so that belonging together, fitting in and views that are interdependent promote the group identity sub-strategy. Perceptions of belonging and interdependence group themes are related to different colours, such as gold, silver, bronze and blue as strategies for motivation. When groups compete, first ranking could be achieved simultaneously by all groups involved, and between-group competition is represented on the leader board, and in-group cooperation encourages the harmony sub-strategy [8]. To enable group comparisons, feedback about participation levels is shown when group membership levels move from one level to a different level that are represented by different colours of gold, silver, bronze and blue. Group members are awarded collective points for collective participation, so that feedback on group participation is shown by group themes and group membership levels, so the equality norm has two forms, as group reward points are awarded based on the quantity and quality of all members, which defines collective participation. Collective goals are achieved based on group positions on the leader board, and group themes and group membership levels are changed when group participation is increased by the interdependence goal sub-strategy

7 Evaluation

A factorial design experiment was conducted in a computer lab to evaluate the effectiveness of culturally adapted approaches and the design proposed in this research. In previous studies of human computer interactions, field scientist researchers and psychologist researchers often adopt factorial design in their methodologies, as these lower the likelihood of confounding variables and errors in experiments, and this indicates if variables are associated [25]. Researchers often apply factorial design when a variable that is dependent and single is studied to gain better understanding if this is affected by other independent variables. Therefore, investigations have 4 conditions when experiments have a 2×2 design, so that when testing how many conditions exist, this is associated with how many factors exist. Therefore, factorial design experiment was adopted for the evaluation stage of this study due to its suitability to analyse learners' preferences for design, learners' usability perceptions in terms of the collectivist design version or the individualist design version, and how respondents with collectivist cultural types and individualist cultural types interacted with the system. To encourage students to participate in this study, the researcher explained that each participant would receive a £10 Amazon voucher for participation. In total, 52 students agreed to participate in the study.

7.1 Hypotheses

Two hypotheses are formulated in this evaluation as follows:

Hypothesis 1: Personalised teamwork system based on user culture background (individualism - collectivism) yields significantly higher levels of perceived usability than a non-personalised system.

Hypothesis 2: One particular type of teamwork system design (IND version or COL version) is significantly preferred by students with a particular culture cognitive style (individualist or collectivist).

7.2 Measures

The Scenario Questionnaire of Cultural Orientations developed by Chirkov et al. [9] is used in this study to identify users' cultural cognitive style, which validates the findings of this current research, as this questionnaire is based on previous empirical and theoretical research studies and adopts parameters for the questionnaire that are not selected arbitrarily, and offers significant advantages for this study. Kitayama [24] argues that bias should be reduced in research that has cross-cultural associations, as the scenario format is identified, and is a valid approach to reduce or remove potential bias. The domain for this questionnaire is specifically set within an academic institution, where assessment procedures need to recognise the context of cultural backgrounds for students, and avoids the adoption of a questionnaire with a general domain. In addition, more precise predictions can be made of social life and behaviours of individuals in academic institutions when the boundaries of individuals are set specifically, so that domain specificity is another advantage. This questionnaire attempts to accurately describe situations with 4 options and 12 scenarios, and collectivism and individualism as distinct cultural backgrounds that are represented by two options. A Likert scale provides measurement from 1 or strongly disagree to 5 or strongly agree to highlight agreement levels, and teamwork learning activities enable universities to adapt and modify each scenario according to its specific context.

Brooke [6] developed the system usability scale (SUS) questionnaire that offers 5 Likert scale responses from strongly agree to strongly disagree for 10 questions, which is adopted in this current study to measure perceived levels of usability, and Tullis and Stetson [47] explain that this system usability test is used widely, is reliable and is quick to complete for business organisations and educational institutions.

The preference of design is measured by a questionnaire developed for this purpose. The questionnaire aimed to collect data about users' preferences for the design, and specifically which version of the IdeasRoom System is preferred, and the overall design of the system. The questionnaire includes 8 questions and the main question intended to answer hypothesis 2 asks users which interface they preferred more in brainstorming task 1 or brainstorming task 2 and why.

7.3 Procedure

Students who agreed to participate were asked to provide basic information to identify them for this study, such as student name, student ID and email address. Participants were informed that this information would be kept for the duration of the study and then would be destroyed or replaced with a coded system. The researcher would maintain a link that identifies students to the coded information, but this link would be kept secure and available only to the researcher. The researcher commenced the study process by thanking the respondents for their participation in this research study, and then explained the purposes and aims of the study. Participants were asked to complete a psychometric test (Scenario Questionnaire of Cultural Orientations) to identify the users' cultural cognitive styles. The researcher classified users into a particular culture cognitive style cluster (individualists or collectivists) using the cluster algorithm as described in a previous study [37].

Participants' registration with IdeasRoom system is completed by the researcher before the sessions. Five brainstorming sessions were conducted and each session involved 12 or 16 participants for up to two hours. Participants were asked to interact with the IdeasRoom system to perform brainstorming task 1 for two topics using a given username and password. The system divided participants into groups of four, and all four were asked to work together during the system as one group. Each session involved half the participants interacting with a mismatched condition and the other half interacted with a matched condition. Mismatch condition refers to users that interacted with a non-personalised interface version; for example, individualist users interacted with the COL version and collectivist users interacted with the IND version. Match condition refers to users that interacted with a personalised interface version; for example, individualist users interacted with the IND version and collectivist users interacted with the COL version.

Participants' allocation into groups was random and with consideration of the balance between the number of individualist and collectivist users in each group. After completing brainstorming task 1, each participant was given 10 min to complete an online survey, which included usability scale questions (SUS).

After the usability scale was completed that involved all participants with both versions of the IdeasRoom system (IND version and COL version), participants were asked to perform brainstorming task 2 for new two topics. In brainstorming task 2, the user condition was changed, so that those who had experienced a mismatched condition in brainstorming task 1 were then exposed to a matched condition, and those who had experienced a matched condition in brainstorming task 1 were then exposed to a mismatched condition. Brainstorming task 2 was adopted to highlight users' preferences for a specific version, as well as to give them exposure to the other version they had previously experienced. After completing brainstorming task 2, each participant was given 10 min to complete an online survey, which included preference of the design questions.

7.4 Results

The experiment was conducted with 52 participants. The participants were postgraduate students in a computer science department. In terms of cultural background types, 25 participants were classified as individualist users and 27 participants were classified as collectivist users. During task 1 brainstorming, 25 participants interacted with the IND version, 12 were individualist users (matched) and 13 were collectivist users (mismatched). Also, 27 participants interacted with the COL version, and 13 were individualist users (mismatched) and 14 were collectivist users (matched) shown in the table below. In total, 26 participants interacted with the matched version and 26 participants interacted with the mismatched version (Table 1).

Table 1. Users allocation in brainstorming Task 1.

User type/Version	IND version	COL version
Individualist users	12 (matched)	13 (mismatched)
Collectivist users	13 (mismatched)	14 (matched)

Usability

The perception of usability for IdeasRoom system was examined. The perception of usability for the IND version (Mean = 73.20, SD = 6.02) and the COL version (Mean = 73.15, SD = 7.06). A t-test was conducted for independent samples to define the differences of mean on users' perceptions of usability after interacting with the IND and the COL versions IdeasRoom system. The results show that there is no significant difference for perceived usability between the IND and COL versions. This means both versions are similar and in general, the scores for perceived usability for both versions are reasonable, because the mean is more than 70 [3], which suggests that participants found both versions easy to use and indicates overall satisfaction.

Hypothesis 1 relates to level of perceived usability between personalised and non-personalised approaches and this is examined by comparing matched and mismatched

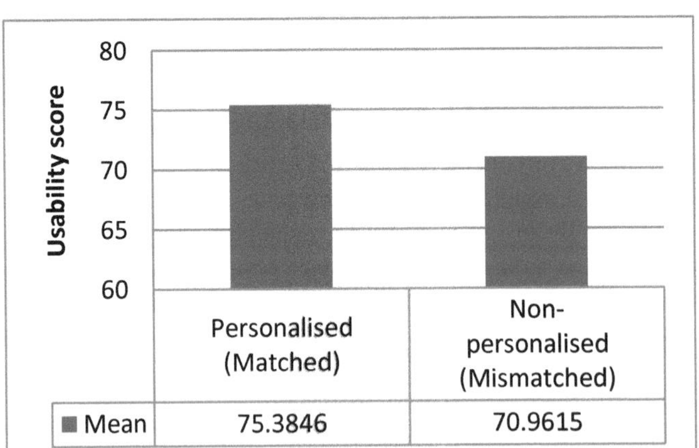

Fig. 1. Means of usability for matched and mismatched conditions.

conditions. Learning is improved when systems are perceived to be clearly usable, so that learners are motivated, engaged and satisfied with their interactions [2, 49]. To examine Hypothesis 1, a t-test was conducted for independent samples to define the differences of mean on users' perceptions of usability after interacting with the matched and mismatched versions of the teamwork system. The analysis showed that interactions with the personalised teamwork system approach were more efficient (M = 75.3846, SD = 6.73396) than the non-personalised teamwork system approach (M = 70.9615, SD = 5.57122). The Levene's test of homogeneity of variance (P = .931) showed equality of variances. There was a statistical significance of these results (MD = 4.42308, t(50) = 2.581, P = .013). The means of average perception scores for each condition is shown in the figure below (Fig. 1).

A two-way ANOVA was performed to investigate the main effects of interaction between types of users (individualists and collectivist) and the IdeasRoom versions (IND and COL) on users' perceptions of usability. The analysis showed that there was a significant interaction effect between user type (individualist vs. collectivist) and the IdeasRoom version (IND version vs. COL version) on users' perceptions of usability (F(1, 48) = 6.742, P = .012).

The figure shown below (Fig. 2) represents a pairwise comparison between user types (individualist and collectivist) and system versions (IND and COL). The results show that individualist participants perceived usability better with the IND version (personalised condition) with a mean of 76.46 scores in comparison with collectivist participants having a mean of 70.19 scores. Likewise, collectivist users perceived usability better with the COL version (personalised condition) with a mean of 74.46 scores in comparison with individualist having a mean of 71.73 scores. Therefore, when compared with the scores for the non-personalised system of teamwork, there is perceived usability at a higher level for usage of the personalised system of teamwork, which recognises cultural backgrounds of users defined as individualists or collectivists, and confirms this hypothesis.

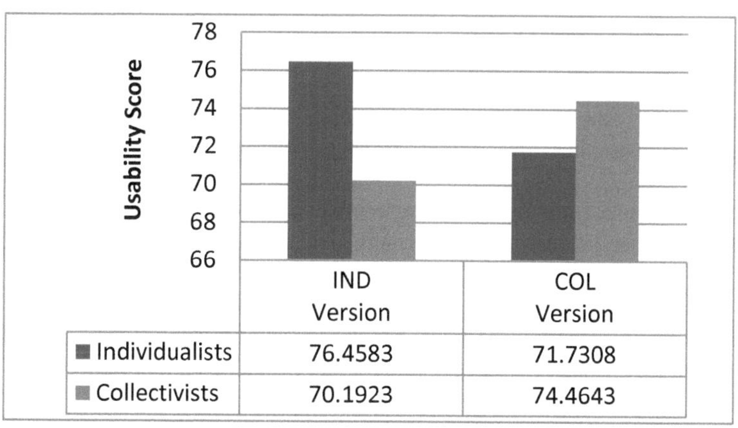

Fig. 2. Means of usability per culture type group and system version.

Design Preference

In order to examine Hypothesis 2, a chi-square test was carried out. The Independent Variable (IV) was assumed to be the user's preference selected and the Dependent Variable (DV) was the user's culture type. Since the DV was measured on a Likert-based scale of frequency, an ordinal scale (ranking the preference), and non-parametric test were chosen. The results show that there is a statistically significant difference in the frequency of preference between individualist and collectivist users ($\chi(1) = 22.194$, $p = 0.000$).

The figure shown below (Fig. 3) represents a bar chart of the medians of the two versions of the system preference frequency (IND version vs. COL version) between the two types of users (individualist users and collectivist users). This indicates that 80% of individualist participants preferred the IND version (personalised condition) compared to 20% of individualist participants who preferred the COL version (non-personalised condition). Likewise, around 85% of collectivist participants preferred the COL version (personalised condition) compared to 15% of collectivist participants who preferred the IND version (non-personalised condition).

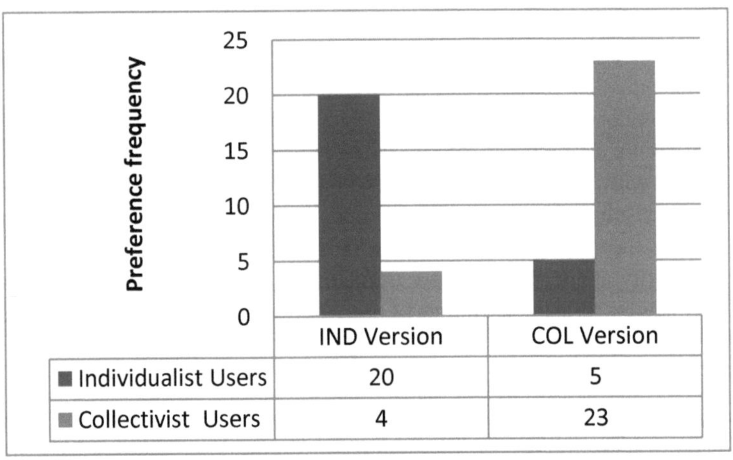

Fig. 3. Preference frequency of the two versions of the system (IND version and COL version) between two user types (individualist users and collectivist users).

Only 10% of the participants in this experiment provide qualitative data about reasons for preferring a specific version of the design. The qualitative data shows that individualist participants express some reasons for preferring the IND version, such as individually rewarding and personal achievements, while collectivist participants prefer the COL version for various reasons, such as group competition and sense of interdependency. Hypothesis 2 is also confirmed, and it can be concluded that participants' preferences for experiencing a system is matched to their cultural inclinations.

8 Conclusion

The design and evaluation of cultural adaptive eLearning system based upon individual differences in cultural cognitive backgrounds (individualism and collectivism) was summarised in this paper. This paper introduces cultural adaptive system called IdeasRoom. The IdeasRoom system has adaptations to its interface to include two different versions of design: individualist version (IND) and collectivist version (COL). The design of both versions was informed by R.I.N.G. design strategies which identified from the cross-cultural psychology literature relating to the bipolar dimension of individualism–collectivism, and through insights from interviews designed to explore cultural factors within academic teamwork in our previous studies [38].

This research study has investigated how students' cultural backgrounds, such as those identified as collectivists and those identified as individualists, have different perceptions and behaviours in teamwork learning activities in educational institutions, and that these individual differences need to be addressed when designing online learning activities that are adaptive and personalised. This study also explains that cultural adaptions can be implemented when adopting the IdeasRoom system for students' teamwork activities, as the design for this study included a COL version for collectivist users and an IND version for individualist users. The system proposed by this study presents an initial evaluation of the findings of the 52 participants who were postgraduate students to compare perceived usability of the non-personalised version and the personalised version. The findings of this study are significant, as perceived usability was higher when users experienced a learning system that had a better match to their cultural backgrounds. Therefore, this study argues that students could participate more and learn more if their learning interactions match their cultural backgrounds better, which could also motivate them better, engage them better and satisfy them better.

This investigation was based on a short-term study with a relatively small number of participants. A long-term evaluation with more participants is desirable in future research studies into this subject, which could investigate the effectiveness of the adaptive design based on cultural diversity with various aspects of teamwork activities, such as students' perceptions of free-riding behaviour and perceptions of fairness. Also, a qualitative evaluation could be conducted to evaluate the R.I.N.G. design strategies, and how participants respond to IdeasRoom features that represent the R.I.N.G. design strategies.

References

1. Alshammari, M., Anane, R., Hendley, R.J.: Adaptivity in E-learning systems. In: Proceedings - 2014 8th International Conference on Complex, Intelligent and Software Intensive Systems, CISIS 2014, pp. 79–86 (2014)
2. Ardito, C., et al.: An approach to usability evaluation of e-learning applications. Univ. Access Inf. Soc. **4**(3), 270–283 (2006)
3. Bangor, A., Kortum, P.T., Miller, J.T.: An empirical evaluation of the system usability scale. Int. J. Hum.-Comput. Interact. **24**, 574–594 (2008)

4. Bishop, J.W., Chen, X., Scott, K.D.: What drives Chinese toward teamwork? A study of US-invested companies in China (1999)
5. Boticario, J., Santos, O., Van Rosmalen, P.: Issues in developing standard-based adaptive learning management systems (2005)
6. Brooke, J.: SUS - a quick and dirty usability scale. In: Usability Evaluation in Industry, vol. 189(194), pp. 4–7 (1996)
7. Brusilovsky, P.: Adaptive hypermedia for education and training. In: Durlach, P.J., Lesgold, A.M. (eds.) Adaptive Technologies for Training and Education, p. 46. Cambridge University Press, New York (2012)
8. Cárdenas, J.C., Mantilla, C.: Between-group competition, intra-group cooperation and relative performance. Front. Behav. Neurosci. **9** (2015)
9. Chirkov, V.I., Lynch, M., Niwa, S.: Application of the scenario questionnaire of horizontal and vertical individualism and collectivism to the assessment of cultural distance and cultural fit. Int. J. Intercult. Relat. **29**(4), 469–490 (2005)
10. Cox, T.H., Lobel, S.A., McLeod, P.L.: Effects of ethnic group cultural differences on cooperative and competitive behavior on a group task. Acad. Manag. J. **34**(4), 827–847 (1991)
11. Drury, H., Kay, J., Losberg, W.: Student satisfaction with groupwork in undergraduate computer science: do things get better? In: Proceedings of the Fifth Australasian Conference on Computing Education, vol. 20, pp. 77–85. Australian Computer Society, Inc. (2003)
12. Erez, M., Earley, P.C.: Culture, self-identity, and work (1993)
13. Essalmi, F., et al.: Generalized metrics for the analysis of E-learning personalization strategies. Comput. Hum. Behav. **48**, 310–322 (2015)
14. Fadil, P.A., Williamson, S., Knudstrup, M.: A theoretical perspective of the cultural influences of individualism/collectivism, group membership, and performance variation on allocation behaviors of supervisors. Compet. Rev. Int. Bus. J. **19**(2), 134–150 (2009)
15. Galanes, G.J., Adams, K.H., Brilhart, J.K.: Effective Group Discussion: Theory and Practice. McGraw-Hill Humanities Social, New York (2003)
16. Gelfand, M.J., Erez, M., Aycan, Z.: Cross-cultural organizational behavior. Annu. Rev. Psychol. **58**, 479–514 (2007)
17. Gibbs, G.: The assessment of group work: lessons from the literature. Assessment Standards Knowledge exchange (2009)
18. Hauger, D., Köck, M.: State of the art of adaptivity in e-learning platforms. In: LWA, pp. 355–360 (2007)
19. Hofstede, G., Hofstede, G.J., Minkov, M.: Cultures and Organizations, Software of the mind. Intercultural Cooperation and Its Importance for survival (2010)
20. Hofstede, G.H.: Culture's Consequences: Comparing Values, Behaviors, Institutions and Organizations Across Nations. Sage, Thousand Oaks (2001)
21. Hofstede, G.H.: Cultures and Organizations, Software of the Mind: Intercultural Cooperation and its Importance for Survival (1996)
22. Khaled, R.: Culturally-relevant persuasive technology. Pt Design, p. 256 (2008)
23. Kim, K.-S., Moore, J.L.: Web-based learning: factors affecting students' satisfaction and learning experience. First Monday **10**(11), 115–131 (2005)
24. Kitayama, S.: Culture and basic psychological processes–toward a system view of culture: comment on Oyserman et al. (2002). Psychol. Bull. **128**(1), 89–96 (2002)
25. Lazar, J., Feng, J.H.J., Hochheiser, H.: Research Methods in Human-Computer Interaction. Wiley, New York (2010)
26. Leibbrandt, A., Gneezy, U., List, J.A.: Rise and fall of competitiveness in individualistic and collectivistic societies. In: Proceedings of the National Academy of Sciences of the United States of America, vol. 110(23), pp. 9305–9308 (2013)

27. Mann, L., Radford, M., Kanagawa, C.: Cross-cultural differences in children's use of decision rules: a comparison between Japan and Australia. J. Pers. Soc. Psychol. **49**(6), 1557–1564 (1985)
28. Markus, H.R., Kitayama, S.: Culture and the self: implications for cognition, emotion, and motivation. Psychol. Rev. **98**(2), 224–253 (1991)
29. McSweeney, B.: Hofstede's model of national cultural differences and their consequences: a triumph of faith - a failure of analysis. Hum. Relat. **55**(1), 89–118 (2002)
30. Merkin, R., Ramadan, R.: Facework in Syria and the United States: a cross-cultural comparison. Int. J. Intercult. Relat. **34**(6), 661–669 (2010)
31. Myers, S.A., et al.: Taking a trait approach to understanding college students' perceptions of group work. Coll. Stud. J. **43**(3), 822 (2009)
32. Park, O., Lee, J.: Adaptive instructional systems. In: Handbook of Research for Educational Communications and Technology, (1911), pp. 651–684 (2003)
33. Plueddemann, J.E.: Leading Across Cultures: Effective Ministry and Mission in the Global Church. InterVarsity Press, Downers Grove (2012)
34. Powell, A., Piccoli, G., Ives, B.: Virtual teams: a review of current literature and directions for future research. ACM SIGMIS Database **35**(1), 6–36 (2004)
35. Reinecke, K.: Culturally adaptive user interfaces (2010)
36. Sagie, A., Aycan, Z.: A cross-cultural analysis of participative decision-making in organizations. Hum. Relat. **56**(4), 453–473 (2003)
37. Shishah, W.: Culturally personalised approach in the teamwork design system. IJCIT Int. J. Comput. Inf. Technol. (IJCIT) **5**(4), 383–388 (2016)
38. Shishah, W., FitzGerald, E.: Incorporating cultural factors into the design of technology to support teamwork in higher education. In: CSEDU 2016, Rome, Italy (2016)
39. Shulruf, B., Hattie, J., Dixon, R.: Development of a new measurement tool for individualism and collectivism. J. Psychoeduc. Assess. **25**(4), 385–401 (2007)
40. Smith, C., Bath, D.: The role of the learning community in the development of discipline knowledge and generic graduate outcomes. High. Educ. **51**(2), 259–286 (2006)
41. Smith, G.G., et al.: Overcoming student resistance to group work: online versus face-to-face. Internet High. Educ. **14**(2), 121–128 (2011)
42. Stewart, C.: A cultural education model: design and implementation of adaptive multimedia interfaces in eLearning (2012)
43. Tielman, K., et al.: Collaborative learning in multicultural classrooms: a case study of Dutch senior secondary vocational education. J. Vocat. Educ. Train. **64**(1), 103–118 (2012)
44. Triandis, H.C.: Culture and Social Behavior. Mcgraw-Hill Book Company, New York (1994)
45. Triandis, H.C.: Individualism & Collectivism. Westview Press, Boulder (1995)
46. Triandis, H.C.: Individualism-collectivism and personality. J. Pers. **69**(6), 907–924 (2001)
47. Tullis, T.S., Stetson, J.N.: A comparison of questionnaires for assessing website usability ABSTRACT: introduction. In: Usability Professional Association Conference, pp. 1–12 (2004)
48. Tutty, J.I., Klein, J.D.: Computer-mediated instruction: a comparison of online and face-to-face collaboration. Educ. Tech. Res. Dev. **56**(2), 101–124 (2008)
49. Zaharias, P., Poylymenakou, A.: Developing a usability evaluation method for e-learning applications: beyond functional usability. Int. J. Hum. Comput. Interact. **25**(1), 75–98 (2009)

Research on Potential Features to Enhance On-line Course Materials for Student Revision

Petch Sajjacholapunt[2](✉) and Mike Joy[1]

[1] Department of Computer Science, University of Warwick, Coventry CV4 7AL, UK
m.s.joy@warwick.ac.uk

[2] Faculty of Information and Communication Technology, Mahidol University, Bangkok, Thailand
petch.saj@mahiodl.ac.th
http://www.dcs.warwick.ac.uk
https://www.ict.mahidol.ac.th/

Abstract. Providing online course materials on the course website has become standard practice in most institutions. These materials are intended to support students' study after class and especially revision before an examination. Most students download and print out these online materials uploaded by teacher, which reduces the advantages of being online. Besides which, students sometimes suffer from the stress of revising a large amount of material. Maximising the potential of these online materials as an alternative method of revision is a challenge in the area of technology enhanced learning. To address this issue and overcome the challenge, we have developed the self-revision electronic course materials framework (SRECMATs) that features direct access to specific materials through keyword browsing and keyword searching, allowing users to gain a quick overview of extracted keywords along with easy access to related materials. This feature restructures the uploaded materials and delivers intelligent online materials for students. The first prototype was developed and launched for a Design of Information Structures module in the Department of Computer Science at the University of Warwick. This paper evaluates the proposed framework in order to assess student satisfaction, understand students' perceptions of using the system prototype, and understand whether or not the developed features are appropriate for practical use.

Keywords: Online materials management · Online materials design · Course management system · Student revision

1 Introduction

Revision is one of important learning processes in a university where students study again the work that they have done, in order to prepare for an exam [15]. At this stage, it has become standard in all universities to provide online course

G. Costagliola et al. (Eds.): CSEDU 2016, CCIS 739, pp. 118–138, 2017.
DOI: 10.1007/978-3-319-63184-4_7

materials for students. One of the main purposes of providing these materials on a course website is to allow students access at any time and place for their revision. Our earlier survey results [4] suggest that students sometimes suffer from a large amount of learning materials to review in a short period of time as well as poor learning resources uploaded by teachers. Moreover, Nicol [6] found that many students cannot develop effective searches for online library resources and require support from library professionals. These issues indicate that the current online materials can be a cause of inefficient revision, which creates greater cognitive load for students as well as being time-consuming. Forsyth [7] argues that many institutions have not considered their presentation of online materials carefully due to a lack of institutional commitment to effective online delivery. In addition, designing an intelligent system to deliver online course materials requires not only knowledge about the content of materials but also programming and design skills. Fortunately, content management systems (CMS) exist which are tools that allow teachers to manage content on the website and upload materials without any programming knowledge. At present, almost every university has started to embed this system on the university website to provide simplicity and flexibility for teachers who lack website development skills. The current CMS platforms, however, only support teachers to create and upload online materials, which do not benefit students much.

We therefore endeavoured to support students by maximising the potential of online learning materials while still considering how to reduce teachers' workloads when developing and designing the system. The current study has not, however, revealed an effective way of designing appropriate features to deliver course materials for students' revision. This has left us a number of challenges to investigate potential features of online tools that students need for exploring online materials during the revision period. In order to identify these potential features, we designed a software framework called "SRECMATs". It was designed based on our literature review and results from a previous survey [4]. The basic concept of the software framework is to integrate all learning materials and provide a simple navigation system as an alternative revision method for students. Students are given the opportunity to browse, search, and navigate across integrated online learning materials in one place and in a much richer way. We also aimed to validate the proposed framework by developing and launching a system prototype in a first-year undergraduate course. The background study describing the design of the SRECMATs framework is provided in the next section followed by discussion of components of the SRECMATs framework, an evaluation of the framework, and a conclusion.

2 Background Study

To deliver appropriate online course materials that can support students during their revision, we need to understand other issues which relate to students' revision. In this section, we present a background study of related works which have influenced the design of a software framework through three research questions.

Firstly, how do students normally use online materials for revision? Secondly, what are the issues affecting current traditional course websites? Finally, how can cognitive theory support students' revision?

2.1 How Do Students Normally Use Online Materials for Revision?

In formal education, many studies have focused heavily on teaching and learning approaches such as lecture-based learning, discovery learning, hands-on learning, seminars and debates. However, only a few of them have considered how students learn during revision periods. Woloshyn [3] states that revision is a process that depends on what students have done previously. Many universities suggest best practice as regards to revision on their course website obtained from discussions with students who come for consultation. Results from analysing the UK university course websites [17–22] reveal that the common approaches for revision are:

- to make notes only on important points;
- to take time to memorise materials;
- to practise with past exam papers.

Although many universities provide general guidelines for students to perform effective revision, there are only a few pieces of research which have studied the behaviour of students during their revision. This could imply that research in this area is not yet mature. Entwistle [1] has studied the revision process and revision strategies and has captured the pattern of student revision by conducting interviews with 13 students and collecting written responses from 11 students. His results show that students perform the following tasks during revision:

- learning from original notes;
- memorising parts of the notes;
- copying notes to maintain concentration;
- summarising and condensing notes.

Later Entwistle [2] followed his previous study [1] by conducting interviews with the 28 students. The results from this second study suggested two other processes before revision: commenting on the understanding they achieved, and reviewing notes. The results of these two experiments correspond with a majority of university guidelines which suggest students engage in reflective thinking about their previous knowledge, organising notes, reviewing lecture notes, summarising and producing new notes, then memorising them. Sajjacholapunt and Joy [4] further explored a common pattern of students in using learning materials during revision periods through a questionnaire survey to extend the earlier study by Entwistle [2]. The results were used to design a conceptual framework to describe revision as shown in Fig. 1. The framework suggests that students typically start their revision with lecture slides to gain an overview, then move to past exam papers for practice or further reading of their lecture notes to gain

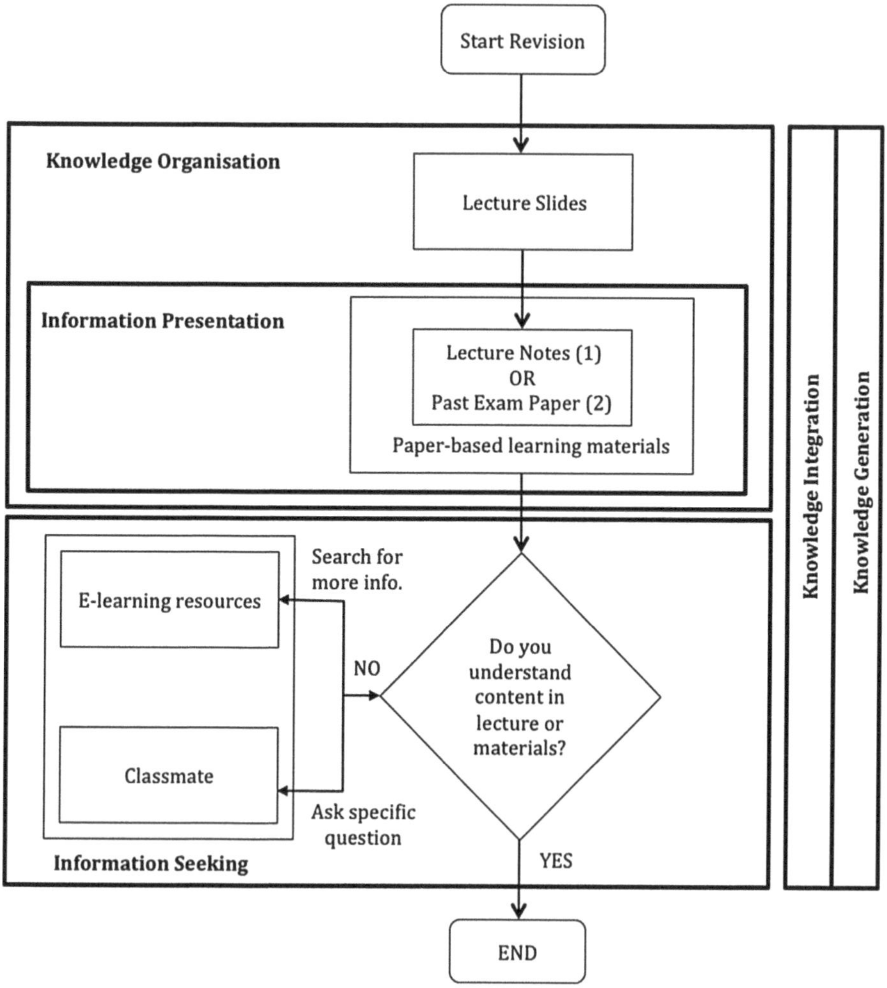

Fig. 1. Framework for a common process of using e-learning resources for revision [4].

more detailed information. If they do not understand the materials, they would search for more information online or ask their classmates. The research also revealed a potential issue for improved online course materials to address, which is that the majority of students are worried about the large quantity of learning materials to be revised. Students also mentioned that they need a tool that allows them to easily organise and navigate through the course materials. These results motivated us to devote further study about how to design an appropriate tool to support students.

2.2 What Are the Issues of Current Traditional Course Websites?

Due to the advancement of technology, most universities have provided online course websites for students. The major reasons are to provide learning materials to enable students to collaborate, and to facilitate communication with teachers. At present, a content management system (CMS) is used as a tool to support university staff, especially academics, in order to build and manage their course websites through Graphic User Interfaces (GUI). Teachers can therefore focus on content and information while remaining ignorant of programming or web design. However, the current CMSs only provide basic features such as content management, online discussion boards, and grade reports. In the case of learning materials, current CMS tools only allow teachers to upload information on the course websites. Although students can access materials at any time from anywhere, it is still not always convenient to perform revision online. Most students still print online materials and review them on paper. Thus the challenge is to improve online materials by enhancing course website features to better support students' online revision activity.

2.3 How Can Cognitive Load Theory Support Students' Revision?

Cognitive theory is an important theory related to the learning process including revision. It is about how students perceive, think, learn, understand, and know something [8]. These learning activities are relevant to the amount of information being used in the working memory which is known as cognitive load [14]. De Jong [12] states that the working memory can be overwhelmed if learning activities need too much capacity. The cognitive load, however, can have both positive and negative effects on learning. It can be classified into three types [12] that are: *intrinsic* cognitive load – refers to a difficulty and complexity of the learning material itself which is hard to change, such as content of the learning materials, *extraneous* cognitive load – refers to an unnecessary workload for learning such as searching of relevant information from learning materials contained in many different pages, and *germane* cognitive load – refers to a process or workload that benefits learning, such as the process of organising learning materials before revision. Since the intrinsic cognitive load is immutable, this project focuses only on reducing the extraneous cognitive load of students using online materials and leaving the germane cognitive load for students. In order to reduce extraneous cognitive load, different types of cognitive tools have been studied. Orey [9] classified cognitive tools aiming at supporting cognitive load from students into four categories: knowledge organisation, information presentation, information seeking, and knowledge integration. The definitions of each category are listed below.

- **Knowledge Organisation:** supporting a student in simply organising information they have, in order to understand a conceptual relationship between these pieces of information. An example of these kinds of tool is mind-mapping.

- **Information Presentation:** supporting a student to represent and view data from different aspects. These types of tools are visualisation tools such as the Google chart application.
- **Information Seeking:** supporting a student to search for specific information. This type of tool consists of recommendation systems or search engines.
- **Knowledge Integration:** supporting a student to collect and connect new knowledge to existing ones. This type of tool includes referencing tools.

These types of cognitive tools have been considered for use as a guideline to identify potential issues to improve the revision process in our previous work [5]. Our previous research also found that students have more issues regarding the readability and navigability of online materials which increase their cognitive load. Since most university course websites only consider uploading static materials to students, we thus endeavour to reduce their cognitive load by enabling better navigation features to support their revision. This would aim at reducing their cognitive load and leaving them to concentrate more on other learning skills. The next section will discuss the proposed functionality through the SRECMATs framework.

3 SRECMATs Framework

SRECMATs is a framework for a web-based tool that automatically restructures online course materials which are uploaded by the teacher by integrating and linking all materials based on keywords. The SRECMATs framework is composed of front-end services and back-end services as illustrated in Fig. 2. Details of each are discussed below.

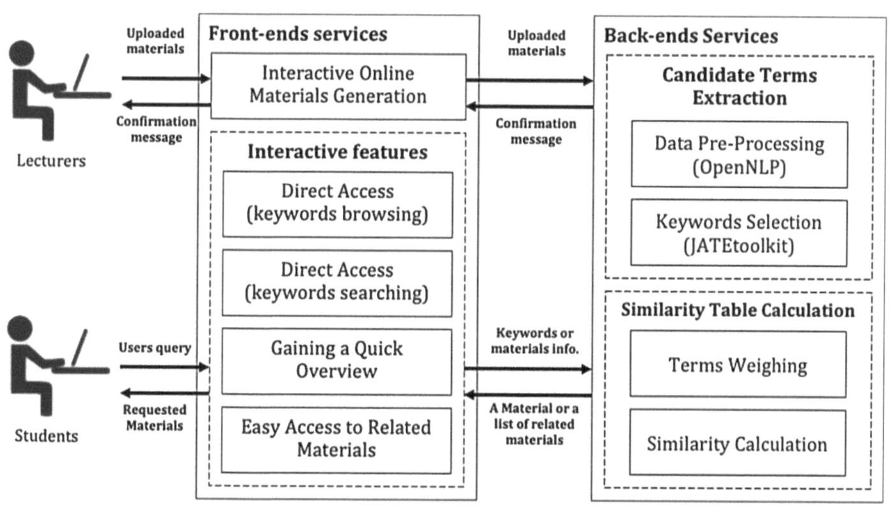

Fig. 2. The software framework for designing interactive self-revision course materials (SRECMATs).

3.1 Front-End Services

The front-end services contain components pertaining to the functionality of the system. The components of the front-end services can be divided into two types based on the user that are features for teachers and for students. For teachers, SRECMATs only provides basic components similar to CMS features which teachers can fill online with the course information and upload online materials as normal without worrying about coding. The system will automatically process these materials and publish them to students.

For students, SRECMATs provide four main features to support students' revision on the course website: direct access by using keyword browsing; direct access by using keyword searching; gaining a quick overview using keywords; easy access to the related materials. These features are mainly designed to support information seeking and information presentation tasks. Details of each feature are discussed in the following subsections.

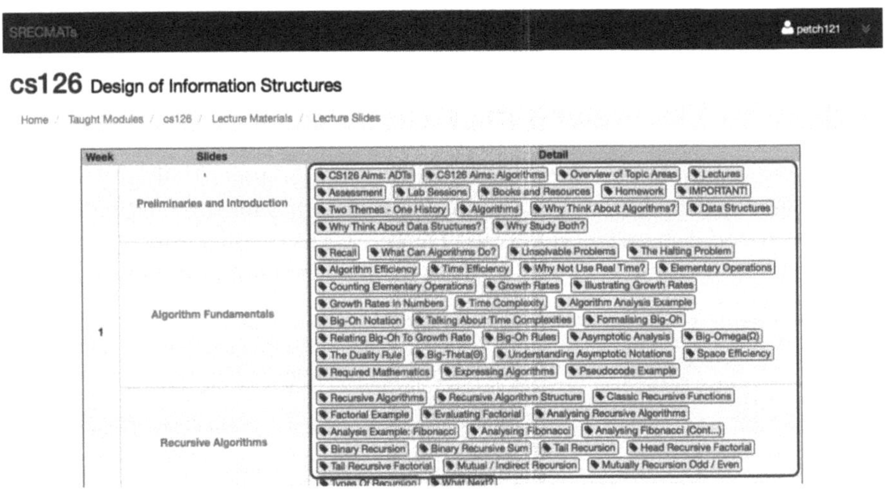

Fig. 3. Direct access by using keyword browsing.

Direct Access is a feature that allows students to have quick access to a particular page of a set of learning materials. This feature is introduced to reduce the cognitive load of the information-seeking process when students want to read about particular topics. SRECMATs provides two kinds of direct access features: keyword browsing and keyword searching. Keyword browsing is a tool that shows important keywords contained in learning materials (e.g., topic, technical terms) for students to easily find and directly navigate to a particular page as presented in Fig. 3. Keyword searching is different from keyword browsing by allowing students to type in a set of keywords (similar to Google search) into a search bar for accessing particular learning materials that correspond to keywords as presented in Fig. 4.

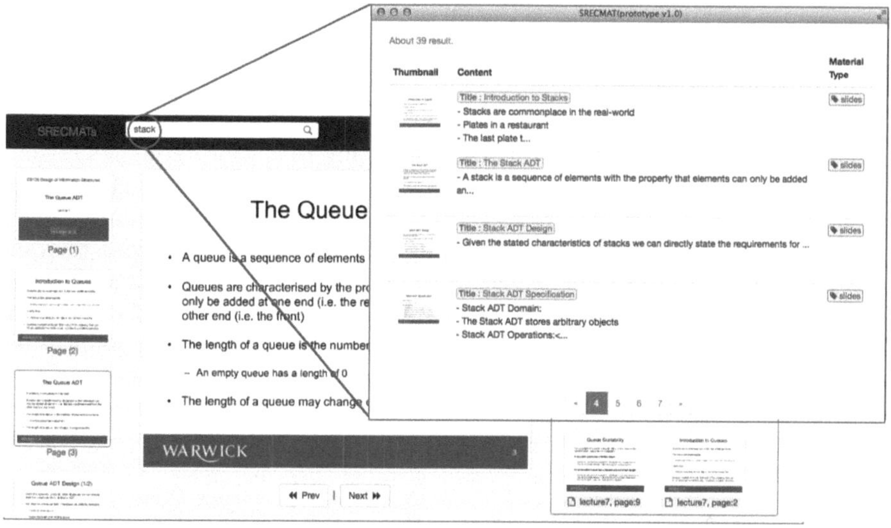

Fig. 4. Direct access by using keyword searching.

Gaining a Quick Overview is a feature that allows students to quickly get a rough idea of what a document is about. This feature is mainly introduced to reduce the cognitive load of information presentation by providing a set of keywords that are relevant to the documents as shown in Fig. 5. SRECMATs

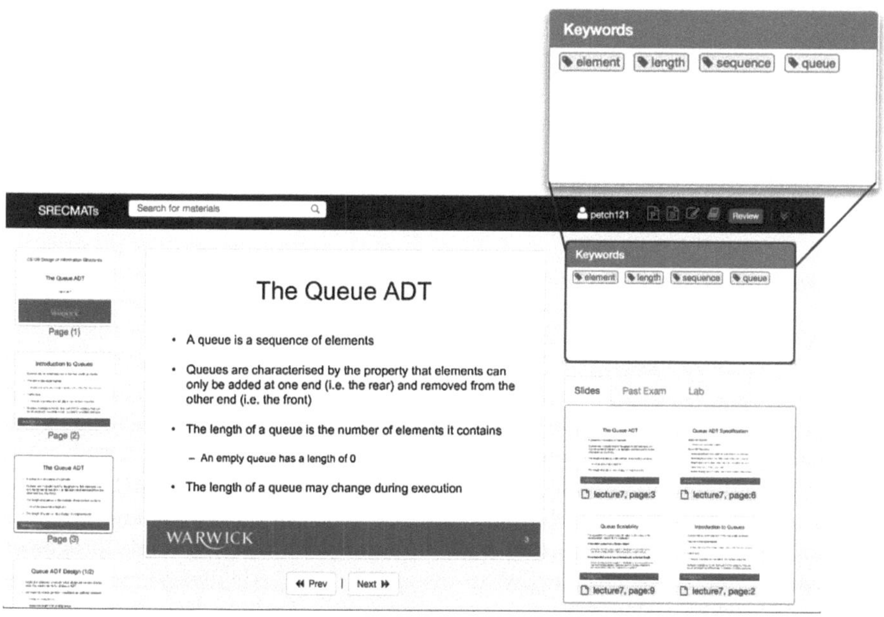

Fig. 5. Quick overview through a set of keywords.

automatically extracts a list of keywords from a document ranked based on frequency. This feature also facilitates scanning and skimming, which are important for speed-reading [10].

Easy Access to Related Materials is a feature that allows students to simply switch and quickly navigate through different kinds of materials through the navigation bar on the top-right corner as shown in Fig. 6. SRECMATs also provides a recommendation feature, which allows students to revise relevant materials quickly to gain more insight information or to practice more on a particular topic. The recommendation feature is implemented based on Natural Language Processing techniques. As with direct access features, these features aim to support students' in seeking information.

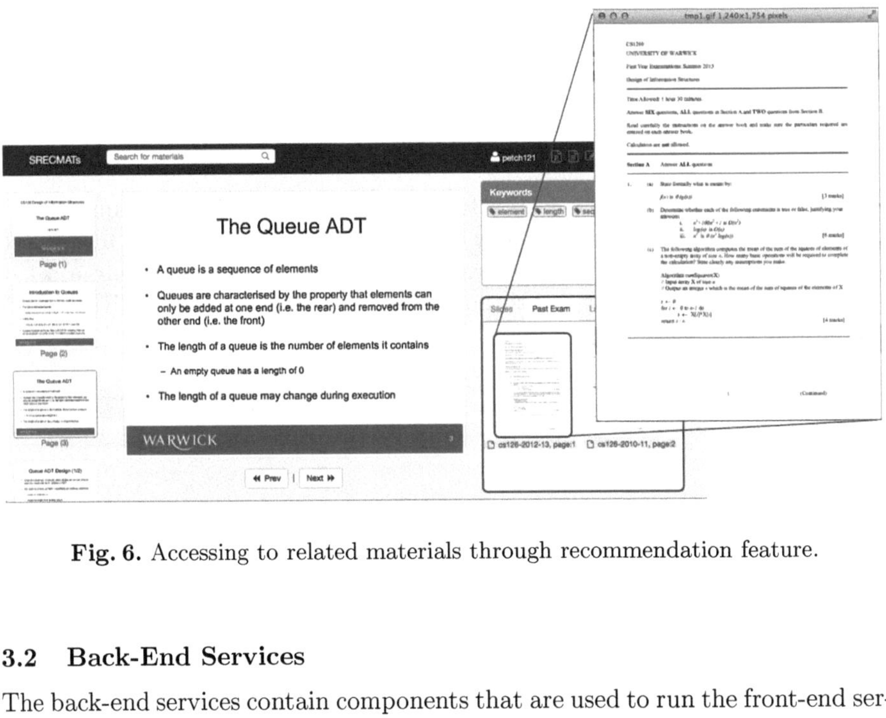

Fig. 6. Accessing to related materials through recommendation feature.

3.2 Back-End Services

The back-end services contain components that are used to run the front-end services. The HTML language, CSS bootstrap framework, and pdfViewer libraries are used to construct the front-end user interface. Direct access by keyword searching is handled by a relational database. Other features (direct access by keyword browsing, gaining a quick overview, and easy access to related materials) are constructed and processed by Natural Language Processing (NLP) tools [11]. The reason for using NLP techniques is because the majority of materials provided on the course website are in PDF format which can be simply processed as plaintext. The NLP techniques are used for automatically extracting technical terms and for calculating similarity between materials. The summaries of techniques that have been used in SRECMATs [5] are discussed below.

Table 1. Common pre-processing tasks [5].

Converted document to plain text
Sentence segmentation
Tokenisation
Part-of-speech tagging
Stemming and lemmatisation
Stop-words filtering

Candidate Term Extraction is a process for extracting candidate technical terms and topic sentences from online materials. Results of this process are: used in three purposed features that are keyword browsing where key sentences of each lecture slide and each past exam paper are extracted and used for browsing; gaining quick overview where candidate terms are used for scanning and skimming of information; and accessing related materials where candidate terms are used for calculating similarity among documents in the corpus. The candidate term extraction process is composed of two sub-processes: data pre-processing and keyword selection.

- **Data Pre-processing:** This stage prepares all materials to meet the requirements of the system. Details of the methods used in this research are presented in Table 1. Our framework focuses on processing actual learning materials (e.g., PDF format) that are commonly provided by the university, and are difficult to reuse. Therefore, we firstly convert these PDF learning materials to plain text by using iText[1], a Free Java-PDF library. We next use the open-source JATEtoolkit[2] to process documents based on NLP methods that are: sentence segmentation – breaking sentences of a paragraph in a document; tokenisation – breaking up sentences into units (words or phrase) for processing in term extraction methods; part-of-speech tagging – assigning a part-of-speech to tokenised words such as noun, verb, adjective; stemming and lemmatisation – normalising words (to a normal form); and stop-words filtering – eliminating non-relevant candidate terms based on a list of pre-defined words.
- **Keyword Selection:** After data pre-processing, we have a set of candidate terms which will be filtered to use in the system depending on requirements of the front-ended features. For *direct access*, the selected terms for lecture slides are all the topic sentences in each slide, whilst the selected terms for past exam papers are all candidate terms appeared in the index at the back of the textbook. For *gaining quick overview*, we just use all terms appearing in the index at the back of the textbook. For *accessing related materials*, we use candidate terms after pre-processing for calculating similarity.

[1] http://itextpdf.com.
[2] https://code.google.com/p/jatetoolkit/.

Similarity Table Calculation. For easy access to the materials features, especially the material recommendation one, calculating the degree of similarity between online materials is another challenge. Having obtained a set of keywords in each item, we next have to use these terms as a key feature to identify the degree of similarity between online learning materials. When students focus on a learning material, other related materials ranked by similarity score are provided for them. The degree of similarity between two learning materials, $Sim(A, B)$, is calculated through a cosine similarity formula as follows:

$$\begin{aligned} Sim(A, B) &= \frac{\vec{A} \cdot \vec{B}}{|\vec{A}||\vec{B}|} \\ &= \frac{\sum_{i=1}^{n} w_{A(i)} \times w_{B(i)}}{\sqrt{\sum_{i=1}^{n} w_{A(i)}^2} \times \sqrt{\sum_{i=1}^{n} w_{B(i)}^2}}, \end{aligned} \tag{1}$$

where $w_{U(i)}$ denotes a weight of term i in learning materials U and $\vec{U}$ is a weight of term vector $(w_{U(1)}, w_{U(2)}, ..., w_{U(n)})$.

The weight of each term in learning materials is defined based on a term weighting scheme which refers to a score of how important each term is in a document. In this first prototype, only a classical term weighting TF-IDF is considered to be used as a weight of term $w_{U(i)}$. This is to validate whether or not the classical term weighting provided sufficient accuracy results for the recommendation system. Details of the term weighting techniques that we used are summarised as follows.

- **Term Frequency** (TF) is a measure of the frequency of a candidate term that appears in the target document. For the candidate term i in learning material U, the normalised term frequency $TF(i, U)$ was derived from a fraction of the raw frequency, $freq(i, U)$, and the maximum of raw frequency of term l, which was computed over all terms in the learning material U as $\max_l freq(l, A)$ [13].

$$TF(i, U) = \frac{freq(i, U)}{\max_l freq(l, U)}. \tag{2}$$

- **Inverse Document Frequency** (IDF) is a measure of the importance of the term provided, in terms of whether the term is common (and appears in most documents), or is rare (and appears only in a few documents) as proposed by [13]. Let N be the total number of learning materials and n_i be the number of learning materials that a candidate term i appears. The inverse document frequency of term i, $IDF(i)$ is computed by [13]:

$$IDF(i) = \log \frac{N}{n_i}. \tag{3}$$

The weight of term i in learning material U is thus the product of (2) and (3).

$$w_{U(i)} = \mathit{TF\text{-}IDF}(i, U) = \mathit{TF}(i, U) \times \mathit{IDF}(i). \quad (4)$$

4 SRECMATs Evaluation

To evaluate the SRECMATs framework, we designed and launched a system prototype in 2015 with the first year undergraduate course 'Design of Information Structures' delivered by the Department of Computer Science at the University of Warwick. The system was introduced to students a month before their final examination as an alternative to existing course materials for revision but not as a replacement for the traditional course website. This study finished one day after the examination. During the use of the tool students were still able to use the traditional course website as usual. Moreover, students retained the right to decide whether to use it or not without any effects on their results. The aim of this evaluation is to understand general perceptions as well as their satisfaction pertaining to the use of the SRECMATs framework. In addition, we evaluated the usability of four main features or components provided in the SRECMATs, asking whether they are useful and beneficial to students.

4.1 Methodology

To evaluate how appropriate the provided features were in term of usefulness and benefit for students' revision, results from a usability evaluation seemed insufficient on their own. In this study we therefore decided to evaluate the SRECMATs framework based on three aspects, in order to ensure reliability and confirm the findings and results that are listed below.

- **Students Behaviour:** to obtain Students' Behaviour, the students' use of the log file was observed and analysed. SRECMATs recorded students' activities during their use of the system such as login information, navigated links, and accessed objects. We analysed this information and discovered patterns of using SRECMATs, such as how often students used the system, and how they actually accessed online materials.
- **General Perceptions:** to obtain general perceptions about the usefulness of SRECMATs, feedback regarding how satisfied students were with SRECMATs was collected by using a star rating method. After they had used SRECMATs a few times, the system automatically redirected them to a feedback survey page. The system also asked students to provide comments and suggestions to identify their perceptions of using this tool.
- **Usability Evaluation:** to evaluate usability of the system, students' feedback pertaining to a usability of the system were collected by using a questionnaire survey method. The questionnaire was designed based on a standard 5Es usability scheme to measure how easy to learn, effective, efficient, error tolerant, and engaging the system was.

4.2 Result and Discussion

Results are discussed in three sections based on the evaluation methods that are student behaviour, general perceptions, and a usability evaluation. Details of each set of results are discussed below.

Student Behaviour. In this study, we intend to observe three major activities of students using the SRECMATs system: the number of students using a tool; the time that students spent using the system; the pattern of students' navigation. The results of these observations are discussed below.

Number of Students using Tools: can indicate how interested they are in the system as well as being used as evidence to ensure that there was a sufficient number of students willing to use the SRECMATs tool for evaluating the usability. Inadequate use of tools results in difficulty claiming the benefits of tool use. There were 132 students registered on the course, and having introduced the system, 73 students registered to use the system, which is 53% of the population. However, the actual number of students using the system was 63, which is 47% of the population. Figure 7 presents a line chart showing the number of students who accessed the traditional course website (dotted line) compared with the SRECMATs system (solid line).

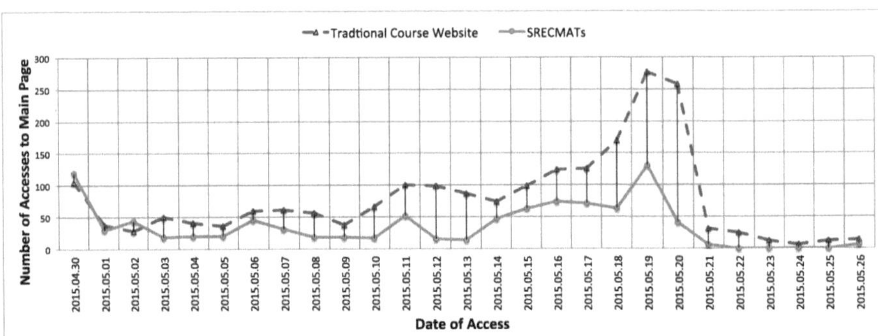

Fig. 7. Number of accessing traditional course website (red) and SRECMATs system (blue). (Color figure online)

The trend of student access to both websites is similar in that the number of accesses increased steadily from the start until it reached a peak one day before the examination. This suggests that the majority of students were likely to review material just a few days prior to the examination and only a few of them accessed online materials much earlier. In addition, the number of students who used and accessed the SRECMATs system indicates that some of them were genuinely interested in the system and were willing to use it continuously during their revision. This led us to perform a usability evaluation of the system.

Time That Students Spent: can indicate how interested students are in the system as well as their engagement behaviour. We recorded time that students spent on it between login and logout as shown in Fig. 8. We classified length of time into three groups: 0–10 mins, 11–60 mins, and more than 60 mins. The majority of students spent only 10–30 mins on the system. This may imply that students use SRECMATs for a short time as a reference tool just to recall their knowledge.

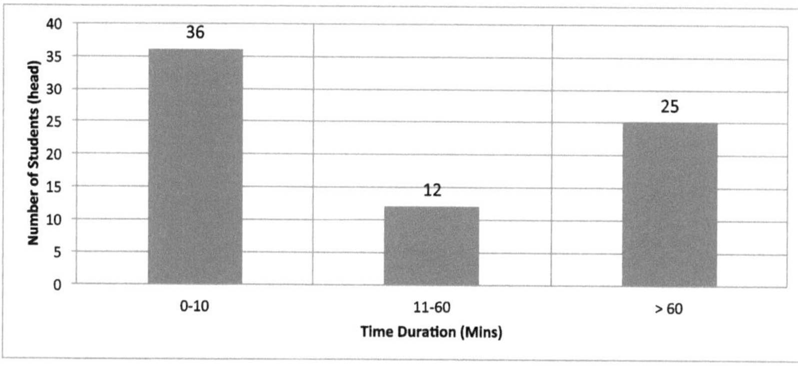

Fig. 8. Time duration students spent on the SRECMATs system.

Pattern of Students Navigation: is about what kind of materials they visited the most as well as in what order. The SRECMATs log file also records type of materials that students navigated to. The timestamps were recorded showing how they visited and left the material. From these data, we analysed and classified patterns of students' use of learning materials into four main types as shown in Table 2. These types of revision strategy are used in Fig. 9 and illustrate the numbers of students using different patterns on SRECMATs.

Considering results in Fig. 9 by ignoring Type IV, where students do not intend to use the system, it can be seen that most students used SRECMATs as a tool for referencing (Type II) by reviewing past exams and lecture slides for a short period of time. The most common navigation patterns that students do on SRECMATs are Type II and Type III where they start their revision with a past exam paper before navigating to the lecture slides. This result contradicts the previous survey in [4] where students tended to start their revision with lecture slides before past exam papers. However, this may result from students starting their revision on printed lecture slides before practising on the past exam paper materials.

Moreover, we also recorded how often students use our features to understand their preference by counting the number accessing per click. The results are presented in Fig. 10. The results, however, do not consider the quick overview feature through keywords because it does not have a physical action by students

Table 2. Description of each type of revision strategy presented in Fig. 9.

Type I:	(1) Start revision on (all) lecture slides (2) Go through past exam papers (3) Go back to specific lecture slides
Type II:	(1) Start with past exam papers (2) Go to related specific lecture slides (Quick look for reference)
Type III:	(1) Start with past exam papers (2) Go to a set of related lecture slides (Spend time reading)
Type IV:	(1) Students who do not intend to use the system but only login and navigate through few functions which do not show any revision patterns

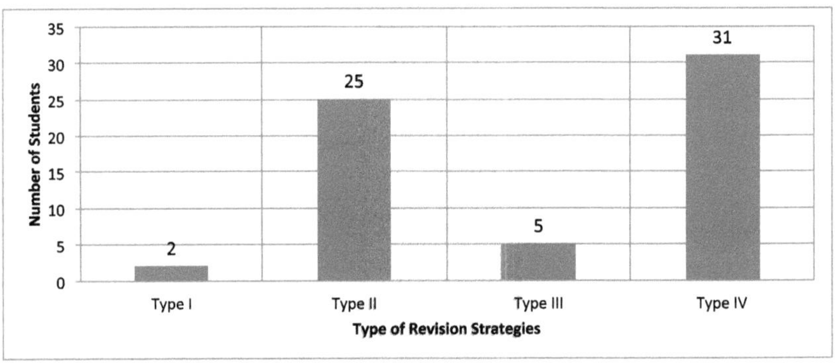

Fig. 9. Number of students performing revision strategies on the SRECMATs system.

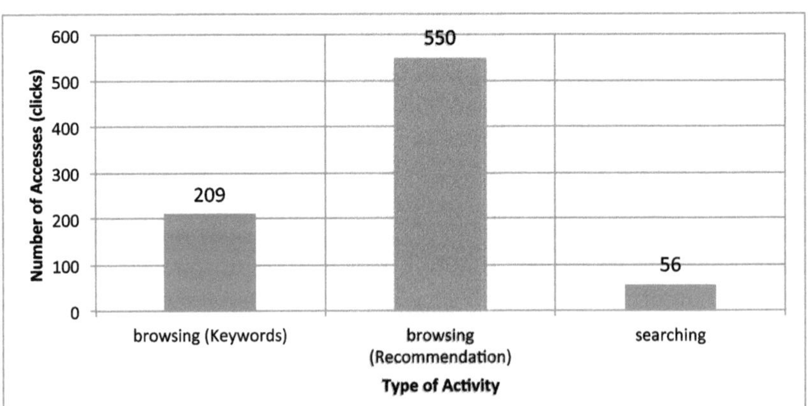

Fig. 10. Number of uses of navigation functions in the SRECMATs system.

which we can capture. It is clear that most of students access the related material feature (browsing recommendation), with 550 clicks, than the other two features (direct access through searching and browsing). This high number using the feature could be regarded two ways: either that students may literally prefer to use these features or, alternatively, that these features may provide inaccurate results and students thus need to use it many times to find what they are looking for. Therefore, we later performed usability evaluations on these features.

General Perceptions. We measured general perceptions by asking students to rate and comment on our system. The five star rating method was used where 1 star means a user is very dissatisfied and 5 stars means they are extremely satisfied with the system. Table 3 presents the rating scores from 30 students who rated the system. The other 43 students did not respond to the rating exercise.

Results from Table 3 show that a majority of students (mode) who rated the system, gave the SRECMATs system 4 stars which means that most of them were satisfied with the system. 6 students gave the system the full score of 5 stars which indicated that the system was extremely useful for them. However, there was another group of 6 students who responded with 3 stars, indicating that they felt neutral about the system. The average rating score (mean) computed from data presented in Table 3 is 4. The average score of 4 also indicates that students are likely to felt satisfied with the tool.

Table 3. Average rating of the SRECMATs system.

Rating Score	Number of students
not response	43
★	0
★★	0
★★★	6
★★★★	18
★★★★★	6

After giving a star rating, six students were willing to contribute their opinion. The comments of each student are presented below.

> **Student 1:** "It's nice that all the resources are gathered in one place, but this thing is a bit broken. When I'm looking at past papers or lecture slides, and I try to go into past exam papers or slides using the blue buttons on the top right, it never works on the first try. When it works after a couple of clicks, it goes to the right page but shows my name wrongly, and then again for some reason I have to try a couple of times before I get to the lecture/past paper I need."

Student 2: "A quick and easy way to look for the information you want in the lecture slides and the exam papers."
Student 3: "A search bar."
Student 4: "Useful for CS126, would be more interested if there were other options available too (CS136, CS137, CS140, etc.). A great idea!"
Student 5: "It's helpful to have everything in one place."
Student 6: "Clean design but the fact that the 'back' button (specifically in the Chrome browser) does not have any use may confuse people due to the fact that it's conventional that if you want to go back to the previous page, you want to use the back button. Otherwise, it's a good app!"

Apart from Student 3, the other 5 students seem to have had a good experience with the SRECMATs system. However, the comments from Student 1 and Student 6 indicated bugs found in the system. This is an issue of usability, which we will discuss more in the next section.

Usability Evaluation. After students finished the examination, they were asked to complete a questionnaire survey constituting a usability evaluation of four frontend services discussed in Sect. 3.1. The questionnaire was designed based on the "Five Es" usability scheme [16], which is composed of the following.

- **Easy to Learn:** a component to measure on how easy to use the features are.
- **Effective:** a component to measure how effective the features are in terms of completeness and accuracy.
- **Efficient:** a component to measure how efficient the features are in terms of reducing time spent on the task.

Table 4. Usability survey based on five Es scheme.

Five E's	Question?	Browsing	Searching	Recommending	Keywords Tagging
Easy to Learn	I can start using this function without any tutorial.	4.42	4.42	4	4.14
Effective	This function allows me to navigate through e-materials easily and precisely.	3.85	3.71	3.14	3.57
Efficient	This function reduces time I spend on browsing e-materials.	3.57	3.85	3.28	3.28
Error Tolerant	I found that this function disturbs my ability to navigate through e-materials	1.85	1.71	2.14	2
Engaging	I prefer to have this function on the course website.	4	4	3.28	3.28

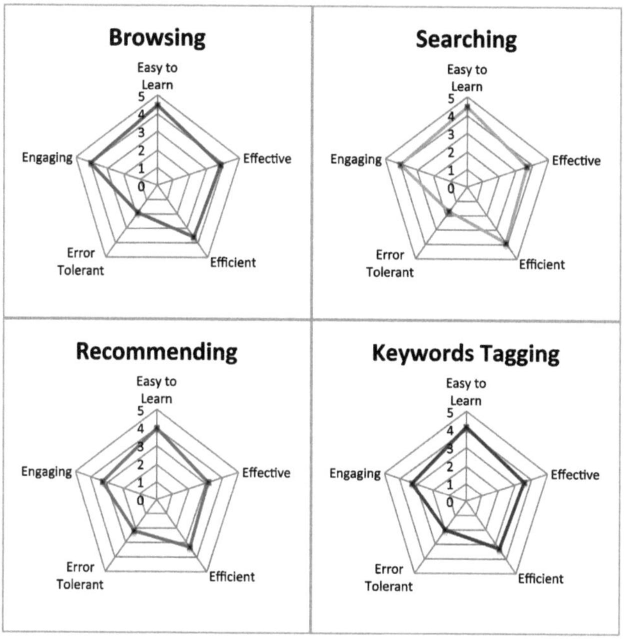

Fig. 11. Five Es evaluation scheme to evaluate usability.

- **Error Tolerance:** a component to measure how well error tolerance of the features deals with bugs or errors.
- **Engaging:** a component to measure how much a student likes engaging with these features.

Likert scales from 1–5 were used for measuring levels of the Five Es in each question (1 totally disagree, 5 totally agree). The results in Table 4 illustrate the average scores of 5Es usability evaluation of the four features provided in SRECMATs. Data from Table 4 are also converted into a radar chart as presented in Fig. 11, which allows us to simply see the strengths and weaknesses of each feature.

Easy to Learn: the average scores of how easy to learn are higher than 4.0 for all features, and especially for browsing and searching features, which suggests that all these features are easy to use without extra tutorial support being required.

Effective: the average effective scores for browsing, searching, and keyword tagging are all above 3.5 which suggests that students are satisfied with the accuracy and completeness of these features. However, the effective score of the recommending system is 3.14, which is the lowest score, and suggests a need for improvement in the accuracy of this feature.

Efficient: the trend of the average efficiency score is similar to the effective score where browsing, searching, and keyword tagging are more efficient than the recommending system. This suggests that the recommending system still lacks the capability to reduce students' time spent on navigation through related materials.

Error Tolerance: this score measures how well the features prevent errors in students' navigation. By errors we mean that the features can lead a student to a undesired direction or actual unexpected error, which can disturb navigation ability of students. The result showed that all features have average error tolerance scores below 2.5, which indicate that most students were not disturbed by errors in navigation through these features.

Engaging: the average engagement score of 4.0 (Agree) for keyword browsing and searching shows that students are willing to use these features and prefer to have them on the course website. In addition, the keyword tagging and recommending systems have engagement scores of 3.28 which are a little above the boundary, implying that these features still need to improve in many ways to attract students.

5 Conclusion

This paper presents the SRECMATs software framework as shown in Fig. 1 for utilisation and delivery of online course materials. While teachers upload materials as normal using content management systems, SRECMATs would automatically create indexes, links, and navigation paths between materials. We aim to reduce the cognitive load of students by supporting a low level of cognitive skills. Students can then focus more on the content of revision. To ensure that the SRECMATs framework has the potential to be applied in practice, we performed three studies of students' behaviour, general perceptions, and a usability evaluation.

Results of the student behaviour study show that a significant number of students registered to use the SRECMATs system. The log file activity also illustrates that they used it continuously during their revision. In addition, there was a group of students who spent more than an hour revising online. These results suggest that students were satisfied with the tool. The log file also reveals students' patterns in using learning resources, where a majority of them used SRECMATs as a reference tool to review their knowledge by starting their revision with past exam papers then going on to lecture slides but only spending a few minutes on each of the materials. Very few of them closely read all the materials page by page.

The results relating to general perceptions confirms that students are satisfied with the system from average score of star rating of 4.0. We also received positive comments from five students (out of six). However, two students mentioned issues regarding bugs and errors found on the system which need to be addressed.

The usability evaluation at the end showed that all the features are easy to learn without any extra tutorials. It also suggested that most students prefer to have direct access by using keyword browsing and keyword searching features on the course website. However, the 5Es score of easy access to related materials and gaining quick overview features are just above the borderline 3.0 score (except the error tolerance). This indicates that these features still require improvement particularly in term of effectiveness as regard to accuracy of results. Finally, positive results in regard to students' behaviour and their general perception are in conformity with results from a usability evaluation where SRECMATs framework was evaluated as useful for some groups of students and thus having potential for practical evaluation.

Although the aim of this research was achieved, there were some unavoidable limitations. The major limitation is, because of the time limit, the system evaluation was conducted only on one class of students. Moreover, results from the general perception and usability evaluations form a self-report study which may contain several potential sources of bias, such as selective memory and telescoping. Therefore, to confirm and generalise the survey results for a larger group, more experiments should be conducted.

References

1. Entwistle, N.J., Entwistle, A.: Contrasting forms of understanding for degree examinations: the student experience and its implications. High. Educ. **22**(3), 205–227 (1991)
2. Entwistle, N., Entwistle, D.: Preparing for examinations: the interplay of memorising and understanding, and the development of knowledge objects. High. Educ. Res. Dev. **22**(1), 19–41 (2003)
3. Woloshyn, V.E., Pressley, M., Schneider, W.: Elaborative-interrogation and prior-knowledge effects on learning of facts. J. Educ. Psychol. **84**(1), 115 (1992)
4. Sajjacholapunt, P., Joy, M.S.: Exploring patterns of using learning resources as a guideline to improve self-revision, pp. 5263–5271 (2014)
5. Sajjacholapunt, P., Joy, M.: Analysing features of lecture slides and past exam paper materials towards automatic associating E-materials for self-revision. In: Proceedings of 7th International Conference on Computer Supported Education (CSEDU 2015), Scitepress (2015)
6. Nicol, D., Littlejohn, A., Grierson, H.: The importance of structuring information and resources within shared workspaces during collaborative design learning. Open Learn. J. Open Distance e-Learn. **20**(1), 30–49 (2005)
7. Forsyth, I.: Teaching and Learning Materials and the Internet. Routledge, London (2014)
8. Cohen, L., Manion, L., Morrison, K., Wyse, D.: A Guide to Teaching Practice. Routledge, London (2010)
9. Orey, M.: Emerging Perspectives on Learning, Teaching and Technology. CreateSpace, North Charleston (2010)
10. Carr, N.: Author Nicholas Carr: The Web Shatters Focus, Rewires Brains, vol. 24. Wired magazine, San Francisco (2010)
11. Ricardo, B.Y., Berthier, R.N.: Modern Information Retrieval: The Concepts and Technology Behind Search, vol. 84, 2nd edn. Addision Wesley, New York (2011)

12. De Jong, T.: Cognitive load theory, educational research, and instructional design: some food for thought. Instr. Sci. **38**(2), 105–134 (2010)
13. Salton, G., Buckley, C.: Term-weighting approaches in automatic text retrieval. Inf. Process. Manage. **24**(5), 513–523 (1988)
14. Sweller, J.: Cognitive load during problem solving: effects on learning. Cogn. Sci. **12**(2), 257–285 (1988)
15. Mclntosh, C. (ed.): Cambridge Advanced Learner's Dictionary, 4th edn. Ernst Klett/Sprachen, Stuttgart (2013)
16. Quesenbery, W.: What does usability mean: looking beyond ease of use. Ann. Conf. Soc. Tech. Commun. **48**, 432–436 (2001)
17. Faculty of Humanities Study Skills, University of Manchester. Revision Strategies. http://www.humanities.manchester.ac.uk/studyskills/assessmentevaluation/assessment/revisionstrategies.html.
18. Student Learning Development, University of Leicester. Revision and exam skills. http://www2.le.ac.uk/offices/ld/resources/study/revision-exam
19. University of Oxford. Revision and examinations. https://www.ox.ac.uk/students/academic/guidance/skills/revision?wssl=1
20. University of Southampton. Exam and revision techniques. http://www.southampton.ac.uk/uni-life/choose-southampton/undergraduate/exams-revision.page
21. The University Study Advisers, University of Reading. Planning your revision. www.reading.ac.uk/internal/studyadvice/StudyResources/Exams/sta-planningrevision.aspx
22. Student Support, University of Bath. Exams and revision. http://www.bath.ac.uk/students/support/academic/exams/

Web-Based Frameworks for CLIL in Primary School: Design, Implementation, Pilot Experimentation and Results

Luca A. Ludovico[1(✉)] and Claudia Zambelli[2]

[1] Laboratorio di Informatica Musicale, Dipartimento di Informatica, Università degli Studi di Milano, Via Comelico, 39, 20135 Milano, Italy
luca.ludovico@unimi.it
[2] Università degli Studi di Milano-Bicocca, Piazza dell'Ateneo Nuovo, 1, 20126 Milano, Italy

Abstract. Content and Language Integrated Learning (CLIL) is an immersive pedagogical approach where the learners' foreign language represents the medium of classroom instruction. In this paper we will discuss its applicability to primary school, addressing children aged between 6 and 7. Such an approach, relatively novel due to the young age of students, requires ad hoc pedagogical methods, learning resources and multimedia interactive interfaces in order to foster bilingualism and – potentially – even multilingualism. This work will cover all the aspects involved, starting from an overview of the state of the art, defining the research questions, describing the design and implementation of suitable Web solutions, showing a pilot experimentation, and finally discussing the obtained results.

1 Introduction

An emerging trend in pedagogy is to propose rich educational environments based on integrated approaches, including traditional lessons, manipulative tasks, multimedia, out-of-school activities, and so on. The goal is to enhance that educational cross-component able to influence key aspects of children's growth such as expressiveness, autonomy and sociality, in accordance with the fundamental concepts of *pedagogical activism* [1].

In this sense, technology can profitably support pedagogy. Ad-hoc methodologies, techniques and devices can be designed to make children learn how to interact, listen, watch, discriminate, transpose concepts, and develop their cognitive and social skills in meaningful learning contexts. Curricular contents and multimedia can be coupled to create multi-layer learning environments aiming at the integration of skills and abilities. As stated in [2], multimedia should not be seen as a mere collection of sound, images, video and animations; rather, it is a vital, dynamic field offering new challenges, interesting problems, exciting results, and imaginative applications. The educational impact of multimedia – already addressed by a huge number of theoretical analyses, scientific works and projects – requires an explicit design effort geared to kids [3].

G. Costagliola et al. (Eds.): CSEDU 2016, CCIS 739, pp. 139–158, 2017.
DOI: 10.1007/978-3-319-63184-4_8

Integration among heterogeneous skills is also the basis of *Content and Language Integrated Learning* (CLIL), a methodology adopted in teaching situations where a foreign language is used as a medium for teaching non-language content [4]. CLIL encourages a cross fusion of didactic subjects – currently considered as a relevant educational trend [5] – by approaching content through the target language. In this sense, CLIL acts as a bridge able to connect multiple learning aspects into a coherent whole where interdisciplinary elements prevail [6].

The goal of this work is to discuss a novel approach to CLIL which takes into account and joins commonly-accepted pedagogical theories, current trends in education, multimedia, computing devices, and information systems, in order to make CLIL profitably applicable to primary school students.[1]

2 A Short Overview of CLIL

The label "CLIL" stands for classrooms where a foreign language is used as a medium of instruction in content subjects [8]. This initiative was launched in 1994 in conjunction with the European Commission, since multilingualism was – and it is still – considered at the heart of European identity, and languages are seen as a fundamental cultural aspect of European citizenship [9]. The idea was originated by a discussion among experts, above all in Finland and the Netherlands, on how to bring the language-learning excellence typical of a restricted number of institutes into mainstream government-funded schools and colleges.

CLIL aims to develop both *lower* and *higher order thinking skills* in children, according to Bloom's taxonomy of cognitive objectives [10]. CLIL strategies are mainly focused on the latter abilities – namely those skills involving analysis, evaluation and synthesis, i.e. creation of new knowledge – even if higher order thinking skills are dependent on an earlier acquisition of lower ones. Consequently, such a methodological approach is more cognitively engaging for both students and teachers. On one side, this aspect may increase the demands and difficulty of CLIL, but on the other side it leads to a higher engagement and motivation too [11].

Another point to underline is the difference between *Basic Interpersonal Communicative Skills* (BICS) and *Cognitive Academic Language Proficiency* (CALP). BICS refers to conversational fluency in a language, whereas CALP refers to student's ability to understand and express, in both oral and written modes, concepts and ideas that are relevant to success in school [12]. In CLIL, teachers have to address CALP rather than BICS, whereas students have to know both content-specific vocabulary for the topic they are learning (e.g., technical terms), and a suitable language to carry out activities during the lesson (e.g., sentence starters).

One of the key aspects in CLIL is the identification of the *input* [13]. A foreign language should provide learners with a substantial amount of comprehensible input. From this point of view, content is conveyed by the teacher as a way of

[1] This paper in an extension of a work presented at the CSEDU 2016 conference. For further details, please refer to [7].

facilitating understanding, and the input is represented by the language to which learners are exposed [14].[2]

All constructivist comprehension theories underline the importance of the input in the construction process. However, the input as such is not important for successful processing, rather for the significance it has for the learner. Cognitive psychologists argue that comprehenders can only process input successfully if they can relate it to what is already part of their own body of knowledge. Social constructivists carry their argument even further: in their opinion, only input in which comprehenders can get engaged – or involved in – can be processed and will finally lead to a construction which they can make use of [15]. These considerations are behind the design of the Web frameworks described below.

In order to provide an effective input, educators need to know what CLIL exactly is, mastering both the methodology and a specific language for contents. Consequently, ad-hoc professional training is required for teachers. Among a number of initiatives, it is worth citing *CLIL4U*[3] and the *British Council's CLIL project*.[4]

3 State of the Art

Two key aspects of this proposal are: i) CLIL in primary school education, and ii) the use of multimedia technology as a means to convey content in a foreign language.

In most educational systems which encourage an early study of a foreign language, curricular approaches are rather similar, usually consisting of general lessons that include foreign culture, art and craft activities. A great importance is given to the development of phonemic awareness and vocabulary, and these goals are traditionally achieved through reading and writing assignments.

In the educational systems open to CLIL experimentation, this methodology is usually applied to secondary (see e.g. [16–18]) or tertiary education (see e.g. [19–21]).

Conversely, the application of CLIL to very young students attending primary school is a quite novel idea. In this sense, it is worth citing a pilot project in Spanish curricular infant education described in [22]. An interesting study about CLIL across multiple educational stages, ranging from primary to tertiary level, is provided in [23]. Another relevant initiative aiming to examine the effects of foreign language exposure vs. specific language exposure was carried out in an institute offering preschool, primary and secondary schooling [24].

Some researches go even further, exploring the methodologies and tools to teach a foreign language to preschool children. For example, [25] addresses

[2] In the following, we will extend the concept of input to other aspects of our proposal, such as multimedia and digital skills.

[3] http://languages.dk/clil4u/index.html.

[4] http://www.britishcouncil.org/europe/our-work-in-europe/content-and-language-integrated-learning-clil.

preschool teachers and administrators, suggesting how to develop effective programs to create the linguistic background for early second-language exposure. Learning in an early stage of life is facilitated, so the acquisition of a foreign language can be easily integrated into the exploration of basic curricular topics such as numbers, colors, animals, etc. [26]. It is also possible to use unconventional teaching strategies such as nursery rhymes [27].

Didactic experiences expressively designed for children attending the first years of primary school can encompass engaging classroom tasks, motivating games and other activities aiming to improve their listening and speaking skills. The development of reading and writing abilities will occur later, but it will be possible to encourage such skills through a suitable evolution of the CLIL environment, thus creating a continuous educational path. In all the mentioned activities, CLIL is considered effective not only to teach curricular contents together with a foreign language, but also to foster cognitive development, communication abilities and cultural awareness, as stated in [28, 29].

4 Research Questions

This work raises research problems that are rooted into different fields, in particular pedagogy, multimedia and information technology. Consequently, the research questions we want to answer are complex, heterogeneous and transdisciplinary.

We do not aim to prove the pros neither discuss the cons presented by CLIL; in this sense, the state of the art reported in Sect. 3 should provide some interesting food for thought. Rather, our proposal makes an assumption: the possibility to effectively employ CLIL in primary school education, as demonstrated by some pilot studies cited above. Starting from this ground truth, our research moves along 3 dimensions: (i) the educational dimension, (ii) the technological dimension, and (iii) the teaching environment setting.

As it regards the educational dimension, [Q1] *how can we rethink traditional teaching tools in order to encourage CLIL-based learning?* [Q2] *Can multimedia and transmediality be integrated in order to enhance the CLIL experience?*

Concerning technological aspects, [Q3] *to what extent can the use of technological devices encourage the adoption of CLIL in primary school?* And [Q4] *how does a combined use of CLIL and multimedia technologies improve students' skills in the administered school subjects, foreign language, and digital competences?* Please note that [Q4] actually refers to this dimension as far as the focus is on technology; but if the aim is to "demix" the integration of school subjects, foreign language and multimedia technologies in order to test the acquisition of skills in each single area, this research question will better fit the educational dimension.

Moreover, we want to discover if the current proposal could/should affect the teaching environment, including the way lessons are organized and conducted, and the relationship between school and the outer world. For instance, [Q5] *what is the impact of the proposed CLIL enhancement on teaching activities?* In other words, are teachers ready and trained to accept this innovation? Are classroom settings fit for this goal, and – if not – can they be easily rearranged? Is the available equipment fit for our goals? Besides, we want to test if the integrated vision typical of CLIL can help bridge different learning environments: [Q6] *may this proposal encourage the integration of classroom lessons and out-of-school activities?*

Finally, more general research questions may arise. For example, [Q7] *to what extent can a playful environment foster creativity, collaboration and the aptitude to a learn-it-yourself approach?* [Q8] *Can we generalize the proposed strategies in order to address students of other years?*

In the following we will try to answer all these questions in order to validate our proposal, from both a theoretical and an experimental point of view. In particular, Sect. 6 will present the results of a pilot study conducted in an Italian primary school.

In general terms, there are two types of data that can shape research questions: quantitative and qualitative data. While the former type of data focuses on the numerical measurement and analysis between variables, the latter examines the social processes that give rise to the relationships, interactions, and constraints of the inquiry. In this work, quantitative data will be retrieved from both measurable aspects of classroom situations and the analysis of assessment tests administered to young students after CLIL lessons, whereas qualitative data will be mainly inferred from an interview to the teacher who adopted the proposed methodology during the pilot study.

5 A Web-Based CLIL Environment

As stated in [30], CLIL exists in different guises on a continuum where content-based education is at the softer end, and bilingual education is at the harder one. As a consequence, we can recognize *Hard (Strong) CLIL*, where teaching and learning are primarily content-driven, and *Soft (Weak) CLIL*, which is mainly language-driven. The version of CLIL we are going to adopt stands in the middle, consequently it is sometimes called *Mid (Comfortable) CLIL*: learning occurs as a combination of both language and content, and its aims can be considered dual-focused. Mid-CLIL requirements imply a mixed use of graphical and audio-visual elements (i.e. multimedia in its multiple forms), necessarily predominant due to the young age of students. A key role is played by audio, that mainly allows listening activities in the native as well in the foreign language. Moreover, audio can be used to introduce additional sounds that can reinforce learning, as in the examples below.

Computer-based solutions and technological devices can respond to the mentioned needs, since they provide those audio-visual aids required to involve young learners and to overcome the typical problems caused by an unknown language in young students. In addition to traditional tools already in use at schools (blackboards, textbooks, etc.), technological equipment such as computers and interactive boards can foster the acquisition of linguistic competence in an entertaining and motivating way.

Narrowing the field to the Web, the new possibilities offered by HTML5 – and specifically by its built-in support of audio and video – allow the creation of playful environments oriented to CLIL in primary school. JavaScript, another W3C-compliant standard, can add the interactivity required to enrich the interface from both a graphical and a functional point of view.

A Web application, compared to "traditional" software, presents a number of advantages, such as: multi-platform portability, compatibility with a wide range of devices,[5] out-of-school availability, and so on. Besides, the adoption of purely client-side technologies potentially allows teachers to distribute materials through physical media (CD-ROMs, USB pens, etc.), and users to work off-line, namely with no network connection.

In order to test the efficacy of our approach, we have designed, implemented and tested a basic Web environment dealing with typical primary-school subjects, like farm animals and musical instruments. The idea was to equip teachers with a flexible tool, easily adaptable to students' age, skill levels and didactic goals. A single class is composed by many children, each one presenting a different way to learn. In accordance with the theory of multiple intelligences [31], we aimed to provide multiple inputs, multiple interaction modes and multiple ways to employ the same Web environment, so that the resulting learning experience can be really "student-tailored".

Consequently, we embedded *different kinds of content* into each *learning resource*: multiple graphical representations, pronunciation of terms in the native and foreign language(s),[6] other contextualized audio content (animal sounds, music excerpts, etc.) and a text transcription of foreign words.

The resulting interface, shown in Fig. 1, lets teachers choose among scenarios that present a gradually increasing number of learning resources as well as a gradually increasing graphical complexity. At the moment of writing, two sample lessons – dealing with farm animals and musical instruments respectively – are available at http://clil.lim.di.unimi.it.

6 Pilot Experimentation

An early experimentation of the framework described in Sect. 5 took place at the *Istituto comprensivo Mahatma Gandhi* located in Trezzano Rosa, Italy. Two first-year classes of the primary school, made of 13 (Class A) and 15 (Class B) students, were involved in the experimentation.

Two CLIL sessions were organized during the hours of Music and Sciences, dealing with musical instruments and farm animals respectively. Lessons were administered to students approximatively of the same age, between 6 and 7. For practical and organizational reasons – the pilot study was conducted at the end

[5] A W3C-compliant application can be virtually run on desktop computers, tablets, interactive whiteboards, smartphones, and – in general – any network-connected device equipped with an HTML5 browser.

[6] Please note that a strict interpretation of CLIL would forbid the use of students' mother tongue during lessons.

of the school year – Class A participated in both sessions, whereas Class B was administered only the lesson about farm animals.

CLIL sessions were coordinated by a non-linguistic subjects' teacher, having expertise on the topics to treat, a basic ability to speak a foreign language, and knowledge about students' vocabulary.

Each CLIL session consisted of two parts: *acquisition* and *assessment*. During the former phase, taking approximatively 40 min, students were free to independently explore the Web interface, working alone or in small groups, possibly under the supervision of the teacher. By using the term *acquisition*, we want to stress that students are not only *learning* lexicon and notions on school subjects, but they are developing a number of higher-order skills, as detailed below. After the first phase, described in Sect. 6.1, students were required to undergo an anonymous assessment test that lasted about 40 min. The goals were manifold: the teacher had to check the actual learning of school subjects and foreign lexicon; the CLIL expert had to test the achievement of high order thinking skills and the development of further abilities (e.g., digital competences, scaffolding, peer collaboration, etc.); and the authors of the research wanted a measurable feedback about the effectiveness of their methodology. The results of the assessment phase have been reported in Sect. 6.2.

Fig. 1. A web framework for CLIL written in HTML5 and JavaScript.

6.1 The Acquisition Phase

The first phase was conducted by following a strict interpretation of CLIL: the teacher spoke exclusively the foreign language – in this case English – adopting necessarily a simplified lexicon and grammar. Since children could remain surprised or even confused because of the foreign language, the educator characterized the context by placing an English pennant on the teaching desk.

Due to the constraints imposed by classroom equipment, the teacher decided to concentrate the activity of each class on a single device. When in front of the computer, students had to work alone or in small groups, exploring different scenarios and finding their own way to learn (see Fig. 2). This strategy was adopted since one of the current trends of pedagogy is to turn students into the protagonists of their educational process within a self-regulated learning approach [32]. In the meanwhile, idle children were invited by the supervising teacher to observe the interface and to participate by repeating the words chosen by their classmates. The teacher acted as a *coach* by coordinating students activities, providing inputs and encouraging cooperation.

While students were engaged with learning and the teacher was supervising them, an expert with a pedagogical background conducted the observation phase. As a first result, this lesson model proved to be effective in encouraging interaction among classmates, thus reaching the goals of peer seeking, peer reviewing and cooperative learning. Due to the limited linguistic knowledge of young students, interaction necessarily occurred in their native language. Figure 3 shows a moment of dialog among classmates. Simultaneously, another type of relationship emerged in the class: the presence of the teacher was not seen by students as a constraint but rather as a guide, in the context of a supervised didactic activity.

Besides, the observation revealed some unforeseen ways to use the interface, originally designed for personal fruition in a self-regulated context. This experience showed a number of collaborative applications: for example, the possibility to launch a game where a child choose an animal sound, and classmates have to say the corresponding foreign word. This kind of activities created an atmosphere of playful involvement, motivation, and peer-to-peer incitement.

One aspect that could negatively affect the experiment was the need to provide young students with technology skills, for instance to explain in a foreign language how to navigate the Web interface. However, being *digital natives*, students showed a good mastery of technological tools, and the interfaced proved to be intuitive enough.

6.2 The Assessment Phase

In order to verify the effectiveness of our proposal, at the end of the CLIL-based acquisition phase we planned to administer a test in a paper-delivered format to children. The test was anonymous, in order to reduce stress conditions and let the learning outcomes emerge.

Fig. 2. Students exploring different scenarios.

Fig. 3. Cooperation and dialog among students in front of the interface.

The skills to investigate were primarily related to listening comprehension, since reading and writing abilities should be developed later. Consequently the document contained a very limited amount of text, it required no written answer, and contents were mainly graphical. However, pictures were significantly different from the representations shown to students in learning scenarios. In fact, the goal of the CLIL experience was not to teach the relationship occurring between a given graphical representation and its phonetic counterpart, but rather the one occurring between a concept – which can be graphically represented in different forms – and the corresponding foreign word.

The assessment was conceived to check the acquisition of different skills and test multiple intelligences. It consisted of three sections – *Listen & Choose*, *Listen & Color*, and *Listen & Draw* respectively – and the task to carry out in each section was orally explained by the teacher in simple words.

During the *Listen & Choose* assignment, the teacher indicated a given subject (i.e. an animal or a musical instrument) to be recognized among three alternatives. An example of sentence was: "Number 1: choose the pig". Students had to go to subsection 1, select one of the pictures – in this case the choice was among a bear, a pig and an elephant – and mark the right answer. This activity included a total of four multiple-choice questions. As shown in Fig. 4, answers could contain also animals not present in the scenarios, and – in any case – the graphical representation of the known animals was different from the ones previously presented to children. In this way, we tested not only the acquisition of specific lexicon, but also the development of understanding and abstracting abilities.

Concerning students' performances, children demonstrated a very good level of listening comprehension and lexicon acquisition. As it regards the recognition of animals, in Class A the wrong answers were 3 out of 52, with an error rate less than 6%, and in Class B they were 6 out of 60, with an error rate of 10%. The recognition of musical instruments was proposed only to Class A; this task was carried out with only 1 error, which means an error rate of 2% approximatively.

Fig. 4. An excerpt from the *Listen & Choose* assignment.

During the *Listen & Color* assignment, the teacher indicated through a simplified language which subject (i.e. which animal or musical instrument) had to be colored with a specific crayon. An example of sentence was: "Take your blue pencil and color the rooster". Figure 5 shows the coloring page for the test on farm animals. The associations were: blue rooster, green cow, yellow pig, brown horse, white goat, and red sheep for animals; orange violin, pink trombone, black flute, blue xylophone, green oboe, and yellow double bass for musical instruments.

One of the potential problems with this task was the discrepancy between the color a subject usually presents in the real world and the one requested by the teacher. Another obstacle was the need to recall prior knowledge, such as the name of colors in English. Reasoning skills were also stimulated by the request to use the color white, which did not correspond to any crayon. These aspects were intentionally introduced in order to foster students' higher-order thinking skills and cross-subject integration.

Fig. 5. The picture to fill during the *Listen & Color* assignment.

Students' performances on animals were impressive: both in Class A and B the assignment was completed without any error. The case of musical instruments was more difficult, nevertheless the error rate remained below 8% (6 errors out of 78 responses).

Finally, during the *Listen & Draw* assignment, the teacher suggested which subjects (i.e. which animals or musical instruments) had to be drawn on paper. An example of sentence was: "Number 1: draw a dog". Please note that the sentence challenged students not only through the use of a contextual lexicon in a foreign language, that is a basic requirement of CLIL, but also through the prior knowledge of numbers and the need for a personal reworking of graphic content, thus bridging different school subjects and competences. The sequence of animals was: 1. dog, 2. pig, 3. sheep, 4. rooster, and 5. horse; the sequence of musical instruments was: 1. piano, 2. trumpet, 3. guitar, 4. flute, and 5. drum.

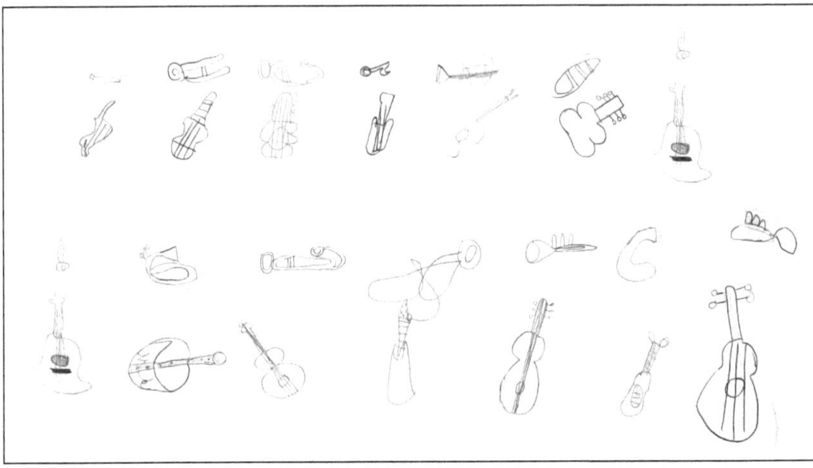

Fig. 6. The pictures of guitars and trumpets produced during the *Listen & Draw* assignment. Below the final picture, it is often visible an earlier draft.

All students from Class A and Class B completed the task. The outcomes of this section, partially shown in Fig. 6, were interesting from different perspectives: they pointed out not only which words were harder to understand, but also which subjects were more difficult to represent. Needless to say, these results cannot be evaluated ignoring the prior domain knowledge (e.g., the availability of a given musical instrument at home), the drawing skills and the level of creativity of each student.

In order to improve listening comprehension, during the assessment phase some reinforcement techniques were adopted by the teacher. First, the instructions to follow – provided using a simplified language – were uttered clearly and repeated several times. Besides, when previous knowledge had to be recalled, the teacher employed additional tools: for example, the number of the current exercise was pronounced and simultaneously written on the blackboard. Finally, ad-hoc body language and explanatory gestures proved to be particularly effective, for instance to mimic the movements of instrument players.

6.3 Interview with the Teacher

The interview with the teacher who conducted the classroom experimentation allowed us to catch those qualitative aspects of student-teacher interaction which could not have been inferred from the test.

In addition to confirming a number of issues that had emerged from the observation, such as the good level of involvement and interaction, she reported some sentences uttered by students that unveiled interesting aspects.

First, in reference to the use of the Web platform, a girl asked in Italian: «Teacher, can I do it at home, too?», thus revealing the will to spontaneously bridge school education and home activities.

Another interesting aspect noticed by the teacher during her coaching activity is a mixed use of the native and foreign language in children's interactions. For example, she heard the sentence: «Guarda, ecco il *dog*!», a mixed-language expression which can be translated as: «Look, here is the dog!».

One last point that is worth remarking is the aptitude shown by some students to anglicize unknown terms by an autonomous mental process of rule inference. For example, the Italian word "nero" – corresponding to the English word "black", unknown to students – was transformed into "ner", thus creating the same relationship that exists between "violino" and "violin". Despite this naive approach generally produces incorrect results, this case demonstrates CLIL's potential to stimulate higher order thinking skills.

7 Towards a Multi-layer Pedagogical Approach

With respect to the approach described in Sect. 5, a more advanced goal is to realize a multi-layer pedagogical environment based on the role of multimedia not only as a privileged means to convey content, but also as a way to create a complex network of correlated and synchronized information. Foreign language, multimedia and technologies are the entities to be integrated in order to foster a stratification of skills, in accordance with the theory of "four Cs" [33]: Communication (i.e. improving overall target language competence), Content (i.e. learning the knowledge and skills of the subject), Culture (i.e. building inter-cultural knowledge and understanding), and Cognition (i.e. developing thinking skills).

We can define this new proposal as "multi-layered" because it embraces different media types and media instances – each one with its own features, granularity and level of abstraction – and keeps them together in an interconnected information network. This approach was already present in the Web environment described in Sect. 5, but we would like to extend it by establishing a dense network of interconnections among the various facets of learning resources, including synchronization among timed materials.

A multi-layer structuring of information can be conferred to a Web environment through a suitable representation format. To this end, we are exploring the possibilities offered by IEEE 1599, an international standard promulgated by the Institute of Electrical and Electronics Engineers (IEEE). Originally conceived for music information, IEEE 1599 adopts XML (eXtensible Markup Language) in order to describe a music piece in all its aspects, ranging from notation to audio, aiming to potentially provide the most comprehensive description [34].

The design of a CLIL framework based on IEEE 1599 calls for a paradigm shift, but such a framework supports important improvements with respect to the proposal in Sect. 5, such as the possibility to include multiple timed contents and to experience them in a synchronized environment. While the previous interface required specific user actions to trigger events, now it is possible to use a tale, a rhyme or a song to drive their occurrences. Besides, thanks to the characteristics of IEEE 1599 originally designed for music, the user is allowed to switch current materials in real time: graphic backgrounds can be changed to increase or decrease the difficulty level without pausing the narration, the sequence of events can be altered by choosing a different kind of timed content, multiple audio tracks can be employed to illustrate different pronunciations, the language itself can be switched in the context of a multilingual lesson, etc.

An IEEE 1599 example of CLIL lessons has been uploaded to the "Music Box" section of the *EMIPIU* framework,[7] a repository of music pieces encoded in IEEE 1599 format. The comparison between a standard music case and CLIL learning material is illustrated in Fig. 7.

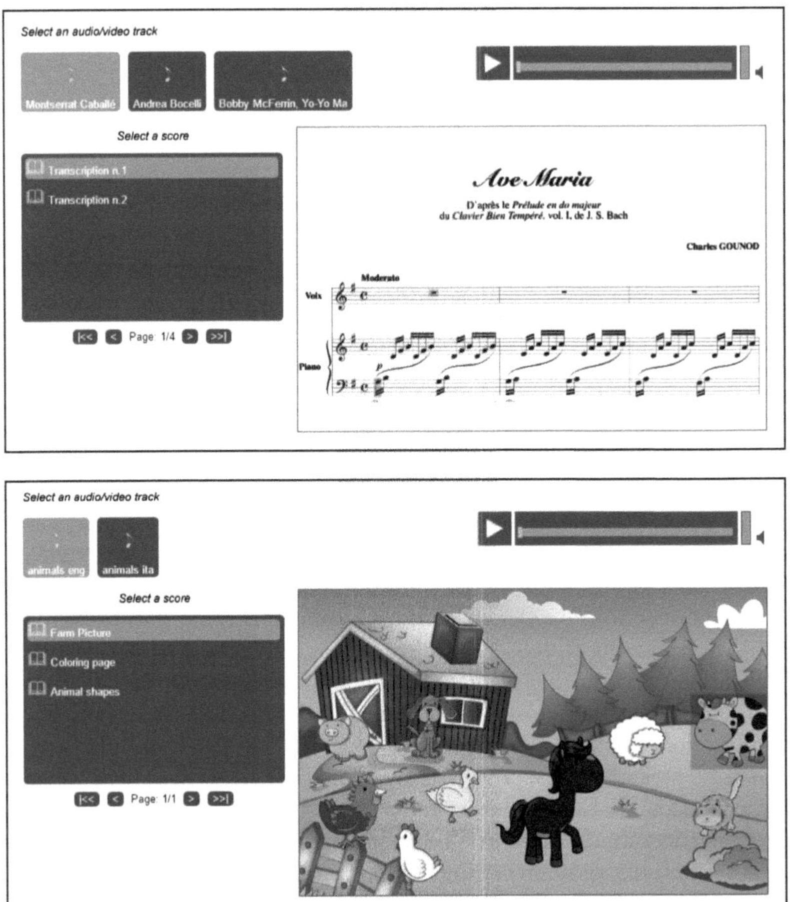

Fig. 7. A Web interface for advanced music fruition and its CLIL reinterpretation.

[7] http://emipiu.di.unimi.it.

Another field to explore is the integrated use of CLIL and music, which could be easily implemented in IEEE 1599 without any paradigm shift. Pedagogical research states that songs and rhymes can be used to teach new words, increase vocabulary, introduce a specific lexicon, and improve pronunciation [35]. Moreover, songs are memorable for a long time: a recent study confirmed the long-held belief that singing in a foreign tongue can facilitate language learning [36]. Music quite naturally provides opportunities to practice patterns, math concepts, and symbolic thinking skills, all in the context of a joyful noise, which makes it attractive and engaging even for very young children. There are multiple and heterogeneous ways to participate in music activities, and such experiences can be easily adapted for a range of developmental levels and skills depending on the learner's age [37].

Recalling the concept of *input* introduced in Sect. 2, music-based lessons offer three distinct sources of language input [38]:

1. the language used to manage classroom activities and to set up music experiences;
2. the process itself that leads to a performance;
3. the actual words and phonological features of songs, rhymes, musical stories, etc. (performed by the audience or already available as media content).

Some pilot studies about the integration of music in CLIL experiences have been already published – see e.g. [39] – but mainly as an alternative to traditional music lessons and addressing secondary-school students. As it regards future work, one of our research goals will be to transform CLIL into CLMIL – a new acronym standing for content, language and music integrated learning – and to test the efficacy of this approach in primary school.

8 Answers to Research Questions

The results achieved through a careful design, a suitable implementation and the experimentation of the aforementioned prototypes let us answer the research questions listed in Sect. 4.

[Q1] *How can we rethink traditional teaching tools in order to encourage CLIL-based learning?*
[A1] We designed and implemented two Web frameworks suitable for use by primary-school children both in classroom and out of school, in a supervised as well as in a self-regulated context. These tools are not intended to completely replace traditional teaching methodologies, but to improve their efficacy thanks to computer technologies, multimedia and interactivity.

[Q2] *Can multimedia and transmediality be integrated in order to enhance the CLIL experience?*
[A2] CLIL-based strategies encourage the use of additional content and reinforcement elements coming from different fields. Also in a traditional setting, the teacher is suggested to go beyond a standard lesson administrated in a

foreign language. Consequently, we integrated digital pictures and sounds in a framework that could recall real-life scenes, like a window open on a courtyard full of animals or a theater box in front of the orchestra. A number of scenarios have been provided, in order to challenge self-regulated children without causing frustration if the scenario was too demanding. As a result, the level of interactivity and engagement was undoubtedly higher with respect to a standard CLIL lesson.

[Q3] *To what extent can the use of technological devices encourage the adoption of CLIL in primary school?*
[A3] Thanks to their young age, digital natives showed great familiarity with technology. During the experimentation, there was no need to explain how to use Web interfaces, since children were perfectly able to navigate them and enjoy learning resources. Far from representing a limit or a constraint, the use of technological devices emphasized the playful aspects of CLIL learning.

[Q4] *How does a combined use of CLIL and multimedia technologies improve students' skills in the administered school subjects, foreign language, and digital competences?*
[A4] The encouraging outcomes of tests demonstrated the acquisition of the school subject under discussion as well as the related foreign lexicon. In other words, the basic goals of any CLIL experience were completely achieved. Moreover, computer-based activities improved the familiarity of students with technological tools, and less-skilled children were helped and encouraged by their classmates in the context of a joyful peer-to-peer cooperation.

[Q5] *What is the impact of the proposed CLIL enhancement on teaching activities? Are teachers ready and trained to accept this innovation? Are classroom settings fit for this goal, and – if not – can they be easily rearranged? Is the available equipment fit for our goals?*
[A5] Thanks to the specific training and open-mindedness of the teaching staff in the school where the experimentation was conducted, the experience was really positive. Nevertheless, answering these questions in general terms is hard: CLIL requires domain knowledge and specific training for educators, and learning resources should be the result of a collaborative work involving domain experts, linguistic subjects' teachers, pedagogues and computer developers. These aspects may clearly have an impact on the ordinary activities of a school and require the integration of missing competences or – at least – cooperation with other institutions. It is worth recalling that the pilot study described above was made possible by the agreement among a primary school, a university department of education and a computer science department. As it regards classroom equipment, the described Web frameworks are not too demanding: they require a personal computer, possibly attached to a video projector or an interactive board, and – despite the use of Web technologies – no network connection.

[Q6] *May this proposal encourage the integration of classroom lessons and out-of-school activities?*

[A6] This question can be answered from two perspectives. Concerning a teacher-driven pedagogical design that fosters cross-subject learning and encourages continuity with external activities (e.g., school trips, visits to museums, exhibitions, etc.), our approach can be easily extended by integrating the proposed interfaces with additional multimedia content, links, and suggestions for manipulative activities. A close collaboration among education experts and developers can help generate strongly-related learning resources both in the real world and in the digital domain. In a nutshell, this is what happened for the preparation of the assessment test. From the point of view of students, who in this context are considered as the protagonists of their own learning process, the described experience stimulated interest towards curricular and related non-curricular activities also outside the school environment.

[Q7] *To what extent can a playful environment foster creativity, collaboration and the aptitude to a learn-it-yourself approach?*
[A7] The pilot experimentation revealed that young students – supervised by a coaching teacher but free to express themselves in the context of self-regulated learning – showed great interest in the proposed educational activities, thanks to the multimedia and interactivity features offered by the framework. They demonstrated a natural aptitude towards collaboration, including group activities, peer-to-peer review of user actions, and encouragement. When working with classmates, children could experience the so-called *cooperative learning*. New theories of social constructivism and constructivism network argue that knowledge is acquired in a context, and – in this sense – cooperative learning encourages the development of communication skills and positive interdependence [40]. In particular, audience support was a key aspect of social interactions: "idle" children played indeed an important role in sustaining interest and passion during lessons. Support from the audience further convinced current users that what they were doing was interesting, and they somehow felt proud of themselves since they were the center of attention. Finally, as it regards creativity, students were stimulated in different ways, ranging from the availability of a number of scenarios to explore during the acquisition phase – each one presenting its own graphical aspect and a specific difficulty level – to the tasks assigned during the assessment phase. Self-regulation, cross-subject integration and out-of-school activities are issues where creativity can emerge.

[Q8] *Can we generalize the proposed strategies in order to address students of other years?*
[A8] The main obstacle we faced from a pedagogical point of view was to let very young students approach a CLIL lesson, namely a learning session completely administered in a foreign language. Since CLIL is studied and usually applied to higher school levels, extending our approach to older students has no contraindications, but rather opens up new possibilities. Examples are the integration of text contents and the consequent study of phoneme-grapheme mapping, the gradual introduction of an increasingly complex grammar and lexicon, the possibility to address multilingualism, and a better integration with other curricular subjects.

9 Conclusion

In this work we described an educational proposal for primary school based on the integration of three domains: computer technologies, multimedia, and foreign language. Since our approach makes them tightly interconnected each other, it can be difficult to establish the exact role played by each aspect: any of them could be seen as the *input*, the *means* or the *educational goal* of the initiative. This is perfectly consistent with the declared aims of CLIL methodologies, where the focus is on integration. The development of Web interfaces based on CLIL pedagogical indications proved to be an accessible, highly-customizable, open and free approach to apply CLIL strategies to primary school education.

Acknowledgements. The authors wish to acknowledge the staff of the *Istituto comprensivo Mahatma Gandhi*, Trezzano Rosa, Italy. Special thanks to the school director, Gabriella Sesana, who approved and encouraged our pilot study. This project has been partially funded by the Università degli Studi di Milano.

References

1. Dewey, J.: Art as experience. Penguin (2005)
2. Gonzalez, R., Cranitch, G., Jo, J.: Academic directions of multimedia education. Commun. ACM **43**, 89–95 (2000)
3. Druin, A., Solomon, C.: Designing Multimedia Environments for Children: Computers, Creativity, and Kids. ERIC (1996)
4. Mehisto, P., Marsh, D., Frigols, M.J.: Uncovering CLIL. Macmillan Publishers Limited, Hong Kong (2008)
5. Coyle, D., Hood, P., Marsh, D.: Content and language integrated learning. Ernst Klett Sprachen (2010)
6. Agolli, R.: A penetrating content and language integrated learning (CLIL) praxis in Italian mainstream education: Stemming novelties and visions. Res. Papers Lang. Teach. Learn. **4**, 138 (2013)
7. Ludovico, L.A., Zambelli, C.: Towards a music-based framework for content and language integrated learning in preschool. In: Proceedings of the 8th International Conference on Computer Supported Education (CSEDU 2016). SciTePress, Portugal, pp. 75–84 (2016)
8. Dalton-Puffer, C.: Discourse in Content and Language Integrated Learning (CLIL) Classrooms, vol. 20. John Benjamins Publishing, Amsterdam (2007)
9. Directorate-General for Education and Culture: Content and Language Integrated Learning (CLIL) at School in Europe. Eurydice, European Commission (2006)
10. Bloom, B.S.: Taxonomy of educational objectives. David McKay, New York 356, 1998–1999 (1956)
11. Pinner, R.: Authenticity of purpose: CLIL as a way to bring meaning and motivation into EFL contexts. Asian EFL J. **15**, 137–158 (2013)
12. Cummins, J.: BICS and CALP: empirical and theoretical status of the distinction. In: Hornberger, N.H. (ed.) Encyclopedia of Language and Education, pp. 487–499. Springer, New York (2008)
13. Krashen, S.D.: The Input Hypothesis: Issues and Implications. Addison-Wesley Longman Ltd., Boston (1985)

14. Costa, F., Coleman, J.: Integrating content and language in higher education in Italy. Ongoing research. Int. CLIL Res. J. **2010**, 19–29 (2010)
15. Wolff, D.: Integrating language and content in the language classroom: are transfer of knowledge and of language ensured? ASp la revue du GERAS **41–42**, 35–46 (2003)
16. Llinares, A., Whittaker, R.: Linguistic analysis of secondary school students' oral and written production in CLIL contexts: studying social science in english. Current Research on CLIL (2006). 28
17. Whittaker, R., Llinares, A., McCabe, A.: Written discourse development in CLIL at secondary school. Lang. Teach. Res. **15**, 343–362 (2011)
18. Costa, F., Coleman, J.A.: A survey of English-medium instruction in Italian higher education. Int. J. Bilingual Educ. Bilingualism **16**, 3–19 (2013)
19. Dafouz, E., Núñez, B., Sancho, C., Foran, D.: Integrating clil at the tertiary level: teachers reactions. Diverse Contexts-converging goals. CLIL in Europe. Frankfurt: Peter Lang, pp. 91–101 (2007)
20. Aguilar, M., Rodríguez, R.: Lecturer and student perceptions on clil at a spanish university. Int. J. Bilingual Educ. Bilingualism **15**, 183–197 (2012)
21. Strotmann, B., Bamond, V., Lopez-Lago, J.M., Bailen, M., Bonilla, S., Montesinos, F.: Improving bilingual higher education: training university professors in content and language integrated learning. Higher Learn. Res. Commun. **4**, 91–97 (2014)
22. Esteban, S.G.: Soft CLIL in infant education bilingual contexts in Spain. Int. J. Langu. Appl. Linguist. **1**, 30–36 (2015)
23. Dafouz, E.: CLIL across educational levels: experiences from primary, secondary and tertiary contexts. Richmond Publ. (2009)
24. Saladrigues, G., Llanes, À.: Examining the impact of amount of exposure on l2 development with CLIL and non-CLIL teenage students. Sintagma: revista de lingüística **26**, 133–147 (2014)
25. Tabors, P.O.: One child, two languages: A guide for preschool educators of children learning English as a second language. ERIC (1997)
26. Fernández López, P.: The use of audiovisual stories in the preschool CLIL environment. Master's thesis, Facultad de Formación del Profesorado y Educación, Universidad de Oviedo (2014)
27. Haces Tamés, B.: Nursery rhymes for content and language integrated learning in preschool education. Master's thesis, Facultad de Formación del Profesorado y Educación, Universidad de Oviedo (2015)
28. Sakurai, S.: Bilingual education in primary school: aspects of immersion, CLIL, and bilingual modules. Lang. Educ. **29**, 83–85 (2015)
29. Sokół, M.: Helping preschool and primary school children to develop phonemic awareness and bilingual literacy skills in the light of SLA theories. Master's thesis, Institute of Iberian and Ibero-American Studies and College of English Language Teacher Education, Warsaw University (2015)
30. Glušac, T.: CLIL and one-to-one classes. Content and Language Integrated Learning (CLIL) in Teaching English to Young Learners 63 (2012)
31. Gardner, H.: Frames of Mind: the Theory of Multiple Intelligences. Basic books (2011)
32. Zimmerman, B.J.: Investigating self-regulation and motivation: Historical background, methodological developments, and future prospects. Am. Educ. Res. J. **45**, 166–183 (2008)
33. Coyle, D.: Relevance of CLIL to the European Commission's language learning objectives. 2002). CLIL/EMILE the European Dimension. Finland: UniCOM (2002)

34. Baggi, D.L., Haus, G.M.: Music Navigation with Symbols and Layers: Toward Content Browsing with IEEE 1599 XML Encoding. Wiley, Hoboken (2013)
35. Atta-Alla, M.N.: Developing adult english language learners' vocabulary skills through children's rhymes and songs. English Lang. Teach. **5**, 79 (2012)
36. Ludke, K.M., Ferreira, F., Overy, K.: Singing can facilitate foreign language learning. Mem. Cogn. **42**, 41–52 (2014)
37. Parlakian, R., Lerner, C.: Beyond Twinkle, Twinkle: using music with infants and toddlers. YC Young Child. **65**, 14–19 (2010)
38. Willis, J., Paterson, A.: English through music: effective CLIL lessons for young learners (2008)
39. Kuncířová, J., Vojtková, N.: CLIL in music for secondary schools. Master's thesis, Department of English Language and Literature, Faculty of Education, Masaryk University (2013)
40. Coonan, C.M.: Insider views of the CLIL class through teacher self-observation-introspection. Int. J. Bilingual Educ. Bilingualism **10**, 625–646 (2007)

Minimizing Computing Costs of Policy Trees in a POMDP-based Intelligent Tutoring System

Fangju Wang(✉)

School of Computer Science, University of Guelph, Guelph, ON, Canada
fjwang@uoguelph.ca

Abstract. Uncertainties exist in intelligent tutoring. The partially observable Markov decision process (POMDP) model may provide useful tools for handling uncertainties. The model may enable an intelligent tutoring system (ITS) to choose optimal actions when uncertainties occur. A major difficulty in applying the POMDP model to intelligent tutoring is its computational complexity. Typically, when a technique of policy trees is used, in making a decision the number of policy trees to evaluate is exponential, and the cost of evaluating a tree is also exponential. To overcome the difficulty, we develop a new technique of policy trees, based on the features of tutoring processes. The technique can minimize the number of policy trees to evaluate in making a decision, and minimize the costs of evaluating individual trees.

Keywords: Intelligent tutoring system · Partially observable markov decision process · Policy tree · Computing cost

1 Introduction

An intelligent tutoring system (ITS) performs one-to-one, interactive teaching. It has the abilities of knowledge tracing and adaptive instruction. During a tutoring process, an ITS traces and stores the student's knowledge states, and chooses optimal tutoring actions accordingly. In recent years, ITSs have been developed as teaching aids in many fields including mathematics [1,19], physics [15], chemistry [11], computer programming [1], medical science [19], military training [7], and web-based adult education [5,10]. Students can use ITSs for learning concepts [8,12], or problem-solving skills [14], or both [19].

Information about student knowledge states plays an important role in adaptive tutoring. Unfortunately, in a practical tutoring process, student states may be uncertain to the teacher. Quite often, the teacher does not know exactly what the student's states are, and what the most beneficial tutoring actions should be [19]. For building an adaptive tutoring system, the partially observable Markov decision process (POMDP) model may provide useful tools to deal with uncertainties. It enables a system to take optimal actions even when information of states is uncertain and/or incomplete.

In a POMDP, finding the optimal solutions (or actions) is the task of *POMDP solving*. A practical technique for POMDP solving is to use *policy trees*. In a

G. Costagliola et al. (Eds.): CSEDU 2016, CCIS 739, pp. 159–178, 2017.
DOI: 10.1007/978-3-319-63184-4_9

policy tree, nodes are actions and edges are observations by the agent. The children of a node (action) are possible actions in the next step depending on what the agent observes. The technique involves evaluating alternative trees, choosing the optimal one, and taking its action(s). The technique of policy trees is still very expensive, although it is better than many others. In making a decision, the number of trees to evaluate is typically exponential [3]. The cost for evaluating a tree is exponential as well [12]. The computational complexity discourages application of a policy tree technique to practical tutoring processes.

To overcome the difficulty of computational complexity, we develop a novel technique of policy trees, aiming at minimizing the number of trees to evaluate in making a decision, and the costs for evaluating individual trees. This technique is based on the information of pedagogical orders of the contents in the instructional subject. In this paper, we first provide the background knowledge of a POMDP necessary to understand our technique, review the related work of using the POMDP model for building ITSs, with emphasis on POMDP solving, then we present our technique of policy trees, and finally we discuss some experimental results.

2 Partially Observable Markov Decision Process

2.1 POMDP and Belief Calculation

The major components of a POMDP are S, A, T, ρ, O, and Z, where S is a set of states, A is a set of actions, T is a set of state transition probabilities, ρ is a reward function, O is a set of observations, and Z is set of observation probabilities. At a point of time, the decision agent is in state $s \in S$, it takes action $a \in A$, then enters state $s' \in S$, observes $o \in O$, and receives award $r = \rho(s, a, s')$. The probability of transition from s to s' after a is $P(s'|s, a) \in T$. The probability of observing o in s' after a is $P(o|a, s') \in Z$.

A POMDP is an extension of a Markov decision process (MDP), for modeling a decision process in which states are not completely observable. In a POMDP, the agent infers state information from its actions and observations, and makes decisions based on the inferred information. O and Z are the extended components for dealing with uncertainties in observing states.

A POMDP has another new component: *belief* for representing the inferred information about states. In some literature, it is called *belief state*. A belief is defined as probability distributions over states

$$b = [b(s_1), b(s_2), ..., b(s_Q)] \tag{1}$$

where $s_i \in S$ $(1 \leq i \leq Q)$ is the ith state in S, Q is the number of states in S, $b(s_i)$ is the probability that the agent is in s_i, and $\sum_{i=1}^{Q} b(s_i) = 1$. During the decision process, the agent cannot directly observe the state at every time step, the information available is the beliefs.

The agent uses *policy* π to choose an action based on its belief:

$$a = \pi(b) \tag{2}$$

where b is the belief. When π is optimal, it returns the optimal action for b.

After the agent takes action a and enters s', it has a new belief b'. The new belief is a function of b, a, o, and s'. Since a belief is a vector (see Eq. (1)), the agent updates its belief by calculating the individual elements. The following is the formula for calculating element $b'(s')$ in b':

$$b'(s') = \sum_{s \in S} b(s)P(s'|s,a)P(o|a,s')/P(o|a) \tag{3}$$

where $P(o|a)$ is the total probability for the agent to observe o after taking a. It is calculated as

$$P(o|a) = \sum_{s \in S} b(s) \sum_{s' \in S} P(s'|s,a)P(o|a,s'). \tag{4}$$

$P(o|a)$ is used in Eq. (3) as a normalization factor so that the elements in b' sum to one.

2.2 Technique of Policy Trees

In a POMDP, finding the optimal policy is called *solving the POMDP*. For most applications, solving a POMDP is intractable [2,9]. A practical approach for POMDP-solving is using *policy trees*. Figure 1 illustrates a policy tree, in which $a_r \in A$ is the root action, o_1, o_2, ..., o_K are all the possible observations, and a is an action in A.

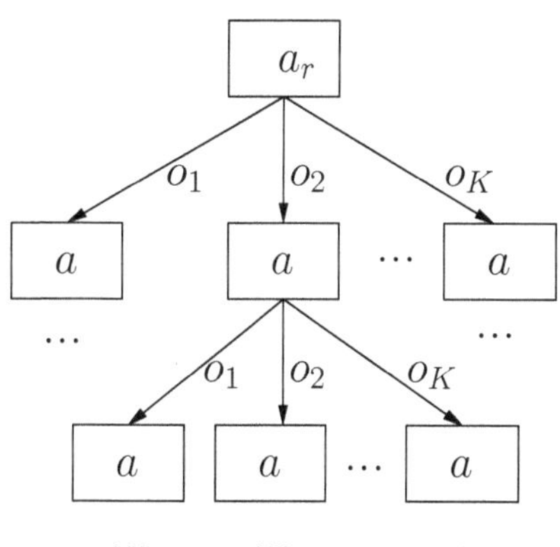

Fig. 1. A policy tree.

In a policy tree, edges are labelled with observations, and nodes are labelled with actions. At an internal node, for each observation in O, there is an edge to a node at a lower level. A node at the lower level is labelled with an action in A. Based on a policy tree, the root determines the first action to take (the root action). Assume that the observation is o after action a. The next action to take is the one connected to a by the edge labelled with o. A path in a policy tree is a sequence of "action, observation, action, observation, ..., action".

In a finite horizon POMDP of length H, a policy can be a tree of height H. The number of nodes in a policy tree of height H is

$$\sum_{t=0}^{H-1} |O|^t = \frac{|O|^H - 1}{|O| - 1} \tag{5}$$

where $|O|$ is the size of O. At each node, the number of possible actions is $|A|$. Therefore, the total number of all possible H-horizon policy trees is

$$|A|^{\frac{|O|^H - 1}{|O|-1}}. \tag{6}$$

2.3 Making Decisions with Policy Trees

In an approach of policy trees, each tree is associated with a value function, which returns the long term rewards by taking the tree. Making a decision is to find the policy tree that has the highest value, that is, the *optimal* tree. Let τ be a policy tree and s be a state. The value function of s given τ is

$$V^\tau(s) = \mathcal{R}(s, a) + \gamma \sum_{s' \in S} P(s'|s, a) \sum_{o \in O} P(o|a, s') V^{\tau(o)}(s') \tag{7}$$

where a is the root action of τ, γ is a discounting factor, o is the observation after the agent takes a, $\tau(o)$ is the subtree in τ which is connected to the node of a by the edge of o, and $\mathcal{R}(s, a)$ is the expected immediate reward after a is taken in s, calculated as

$$\mathcal{R}(s, a) = \sum_{s' \in S} P(s'|s, a) \mathcal{R}(s, a, s') \tag{8}$$

where $\mathcal{R}(s, a, s')$ is the expected immediate reward after the agent takes a in s and enters s'. The second term on the right hand side of Eq. (7) is the discounted expected value of future states.

From Eqs. (1) and (7), we have the value function of τ at b:

$$V^\tau(b) = \sum_{s \in S} b(s) V^\tau(s). \tag{9}$$

When the value functions are optimal, we have $\pi(b)$ returning the optimal policy tree $\hat{\tau}$ at b:

$$\pi(b) = \hat{\tau} = \arg\max_{\tau \in \mathcal{T}} V^\tau(b), \tag{10}$$

where $\mathcal{T}$ is the set of policy trees to evaluate in making the decision.

From Eqs. (7) and (10), we can see that making a decision requires evaluating all the policy trees in $\mathcal{T}$. As discussed, $|\mathcal{T}|$ is exponential in $|O|$, and the number of nodes in a tree is exponential in the tree height (see Eqs. (5) and (6)). In evaluating a tree, the total cost is proportional to the number of nodes. The intractability has been an obstacle to applying the policy tree approach to practical problems.

3 Related Work

The work of applying the POMDP model to computer supported education started in as early as 1990s [4]. In the early years' work, POMDPs were used to model internal mental states of individuals, and to find the best ways to teach concepts. Typically, the states of a student had a boolean attribute for each of the concepts, the actions available to the teacher were various types of teaching techniques, and the observations were the results of tests given periodically. The goal could be to teach as many of the concepts in a finite amount of time, or to minimize the time required to learn all the concepts.

The recent work related with applying POMDPs to intelligent tutoring included [6,7,12,13,17,18]. The work was commonly characterized by using POMDPs to optimize and customize teaching, but varied in the definitions of states, actions, and observations, and in the strategies of POMDP-solving. In the following, we review some representative work in more details, with emphasis on POMDP-solving.

In the work reported in [12], the researchers created a system for teaching concepts. They developed a technique of faster teaching by POMDP planning. The technique was for computing approximate POMDP policies, which selected actions to minimize the expected time for the learner to understand concepts. The researchers framed the problem of optimally selecting teaching actions by using a decision-theoretic approach, and formulated teaching as a POMDP planning problem. In the POMDP, states represented the learners' knowledge, transitions modeled how teaching actions stochastically changed the learners' knowledge, and observations indicated the probability that a learner would give a particular response to a tutorial action. Three learner models were considered in defining the state space: memoryless model, discrete model with memory, and continuous model.

For solving the POMDP, the researchers developed an online method of forward trees, which were variations of policy trees. A forward tree was constructed by interleaving branching on actions and observations. For the current belief, a forward tree was constructed to estimate the value of each pedagogical action, and the best action was chosen. The learner's response, plus the action chosen, was used to update the belief. And then a new forward search tree was constructed for selecting a new action for the updated belief. The cost of searching the full tree is exponential in the task horizon, and requires an $O(|S|^2)$ operations at each node. To reduce the number of nodes to search through, the researchers restricted the tree by sampling only a few actions. Additionally, they limited the horizon to control the depth of the tree.

The work described in [7] was aimed at making POMDP solvers feasible for real-world problems. The researchers created a data structure to describe the current mental status of a particular student. The status was made up of knowledge states and cognitive states. The knowledge states were defined in terms of gaps, which were misconceptions regarding the concepts in the instructional domain. Observations were indicators that particular gaps were present or absent. The intelligent tutor took actions to discover and remove all gaps.

The cognitive states tracked boredom, confusion, frustration, etc. The intelligent tutor accounted for a learner's cognitive state so as to remove gaps more effectively.

To facilitate POMDP solving, the researchers developed two scalable representations of POMDP states and observations: state queue and observation chain. They introduced parameter d_{jk} for describing the difficulty of tutoring concept j before concept k. By reordering the gaps to minimize the values in d, a strict total ordering over the knowledge states, or priority, could be created. A state queue only maintained a belief about the presence or absence of one gap, the one with the highest priority. The state queues allowed a POMDP to temporarily ignore less-relevant states. The state space in a POMDP using a state queue was linear, not exponential.

The existing techniques for improving POMDP solving have made good progress towards building practical POMDP based ITSs. However they had limitations. For example, as the authors of [12] concluded, computational challenges still existed in their technique of forward trees, despite sampling only a fraction of possible actions and using very short horizons. Also, how to sample the possible actions and how to shorten the horizon could be challenging problems. As the authors of [7] indicated, the methods of state queue and observation chain might cause information loss, which might in turn degrade system performance in choosing optimal actions.

4 An Intelligent Tutoring System on POMDP

4.1 An Overview

We have developed an experimental system as a test bed for our techniques, including the technique of policy trees. The system is for teaching concepts. Working with different data sets, it teaches different subjects. The ITS tutors a student at a time, in a turn-by-turn interactive way. In a tutoring process, the student asks questions about concepts, and the system chooses optimal tutoring actions based on its information about the student's knowledge states. Figure 2 illustrates some example questions and answers when the system teaches basic knowledge of software.

In a subject of science or mathematics, many concepts have prerequisites. To understand a concept well, a student must first study all its prerequisites. When the student asks about a concept, the system should determine whether it needs to teach a prerequisite for the student to make up some required knowledge, and, if so, which to teach. At a tutoring step, the *optimal* action is to teach the concept that the student requires to make up, and that the student can understand without making up any other concepts. In Fig. 2, `m3` is an optimal action.

4.2 Casting the ITS Structure onto a POMDP

The major components of the ITS include a *domain model*, a *student model*, and a *tutoring model*. The domain model contains the domain knowledge to teach.

```
t1 m1: What would you like to learn?
t2 h1: What is a database?
t3 m2: To understand "database", you may need to learn "file" first.
     May I teach "file"?
t4 h2: Yes, please.
t5 m3: A file is a set of data on some durable storage.
t6 h3: OK.
t7 m4: You may also need to know "query language".
     May I teach "query language"?
h8 h4: Yes.
t9 m5: A query language is a high-level language for querying.
t10 h5: But what is a high-level language?
t11 m6: A high-level language is a programming language independent
     of any particular type of computer, and is closer to human
     languages than assembly languages.
     May I return to "database"?
t12 h6: Yes.
t13 m7: A database is a collection of interrelated files manipulated
     by application programs written in a query language.
t14 h7: I see.
t15 m8: Other questions?
t16 h8: Yes. What is a data warehouse?
...
```

Fig. 2. System and student actions in tutoring. `m` - machine (system), `h` - human (student).

The student model represents the student's current states. The tutoring agent updates the student model while the tutoring progresses. The tutoring model contains the tutoring strategies.

We cast the student model onto the POMDP states, and represent the tutoring model as the POMDP policy. Currently, the student model contains information about knowledge states only. At any point in a tutoring process, the agent is in a POMDP state, which represents the student's current knowledge state. Since the state is not directly observable, the agent infers the information from its immediate action and observation, and represents the information as the current belief. Based on the belief, the agent uses the policy to choose the optimal action to teach the student. In the following subsections, we discuss the definitions of states, actions, and observations in the POMDP.

4.3 Defining States

We define the states in terms of the concepts in the instructional subject. In software basics, the concepts are *data*, *program*, *algorithm*, and many others. We use a boolean variable to represent each concept. This is a commonly used method for defining states [4]. In our scheme, variable $\mathcal{C}_i$ represents concept C_i. $\mathcal{C}_i$ may take two values $\surd C_i$ and $\neg C_i$. $\surd C_i$ indicates that the student understands concept C_i, while $\neg C_i$ indicates that the student does not.

A conjunctive formula of such values may represent information about a student knowledge state. For example, $(\surd C_1 \wedge \surd C_2 \wedge \neg C_3)$ represents that the student understands C_1 and C_2, but not C_3. When there are N concepts in a subject, we can use formulas of N variables to represent student knowledge states regarding the subject. For simplicity, we omit the $\wedge$ operator, and thus have formulas of the form:

$$(\mathcal{C}_1\mathcal{C}_2\mathcal{C}_3...\mathcal{C}_N) \tag{11}$$

where $\mathcal{C}_i$ may take $\surd C_i$ or $\neg C_i$ $(1 \leq i \leq N)$. We call a formula of (11) a *state formula*. It is a representation of which concepts the student understands and which concepts the students does not.

In the POMDP, each state in S is associated with a state formula. When the agent is in a state, from the formula of the state, it has the information of the student's current knowledge state. If the agent chooses tutoring actions according to the student's mastery of the concepts, the states have the Markov property. Making a decision depends only upon the current state, not on other states or the sequence of actions and observations that preceded it.

4.4 Actions and Observations

In a tutoring process, asking and answering questions are the primary actions of the student and system. Other actions are those for greeting, confirmation, acceptance, etc.

In an ITS for teaching concepts, student actions are mainly asking questions about concepts. Asking "what is a query language?" is such an action. We assume that a student action concerns only one concept. In this paper, we denote a student action of asking about concept C by $(?C)$, and use (Θ) to denote an *acceptance* action, like "I see", "Yes", "please continue", or "I am done", which indicates that the student is satisfied with a system answer.

The system actions are mainly answering questions about concepts, like "A query language is a high-level language for querying". We use $(!C)$ to denote a system action of teaching C, and use (Φ) to denote a system action that does not teach a concept, for example a greeting.

In building the ITS, we cast system actions and student actions onto POMDP actions and observations respectively. A tutoring process can thus be an interleaved sequence of actions and observations. A system action may change the student's knowledge state, that is, causes a state transition. The student action (question) in the new state is seen by the agent as an observation, which may provide information about the new state. The agent can infer information of the new state from its previous belief, its immediate action, and the student's new question.

5 An Overview of the New Technique

As discussed before, in a finite horizon POMDP of length H, the number of nodes in a policy tree is typically exponential in H, and the number of policy trees is also exponential. The goal of our research is to minimize the number of trees to evaluate when the agent makes a decision, and minimize the costs for evaluating individual trees. Our technique is based on the information of prerequisite relationships in the instructional subject.

In most science or mathematics subjects, there are pedagogical orders for teaching/learning contents. The relationships of content prerequisites are pedagogical orders. Formally, if to well understand concept C_j, a student must first understand concept C_i, we call C_i a *prerequisite* of C_j. For example, in software basics, *instruction* is a prerequisite of *machine language*, and in calculus, *function* is a prerequisite of *derivative*. A concept may have zero, one or more prerequisites, and a concept may be a prerequisite of zero, one or more other concepts. In this paper, when C_i is a prerequisite of C_j, we call C_j a *successor* of C_i.

In our research, we examined real tutoring processes between human students and teachers, in the subjects of high school pre-calculus mathematics and university computer literacy. We observed that the concepts asked by a student in successive questions usually had prerequisite/successor relationships with each other. Quite often, right after asking about a concept, a student might ask about a prerequisite of the concept. This happened when the teacher's answer made the student to realize that he/she needed to make up some knowledge. We also observed, a teacher often voluntarily taught a prerequisite that he/she considered necessary for the student to make up. Sometimes, we noticed after a teacher's answer about a concept, a student might ask about a successor of the concept originally asked. This usually happened when the student had been satisfied with the answer and wanted to learn more.

In short, in a "window" in the tutoring process, the student might just ask about a subset of related concepts, and in answering the questions the teacher might just need to teach concepts in the same subset. Recall we cast system and student actions onto POMDP actions and observations, and build policy trees out of the actions and observations, each of which concerns a concept. Our investigation suggested that we could develop a technique to reduce computing costs for making decisions, by grouping concepts, and building policy trees within concept groups.

In our technique, we partition the solution space based on concept grouping. When a tutoring session starts, the agent goes to the related subspace, and works there until the session terminates. We define a *tutoring session* as a sequence of interleaved student and system actions, which starts with a student action asking about a concept, ends with a student question accepting the system's answer, and may have in-between student/system actions concerning prerequisites of the concept asked in the first question. In Fig. 2, the sequence of questions and answers between `h1` and `h7` is a tutoring session, and `h8` starts a new session. If, before a session terminates, the student asks a question concerning a concept that has no prerequisite relationships with the concepts in the current session, the agent considers that a new session starts.

In the following, we present our technique of policy trees, which partitions the solution space into subspaces. First, we discuss concept grouping, on which the technique is based.

6 Grouping the Concepts

We group concepts in the instructional subject according to prerequisite relationships between the concepts. In a grouping result, each concept and all of its prerequisites are in the same group, or in a very small number of groups.

In the first step of grouping, we represent prerequisite relationships in a *directed acyclic graph* (*DAG*) and perform *topological sorting* on the DAG. Figure 3 illustrates a DAG representing the direct prerequisite relationships between a subset of the concepts in software basics. When a concept is included in the description of another, we consider it a direct prerequisite of the latter. The DAG was automatically generated by a procedure that can identify direct prerequisites for each concept in the concept descriptions. This set of concepts and their descriptions (or explanations) are in the appendix. (Note that the descriptions may not be complete and accurate. They are used in examples for discussing our technique only.)

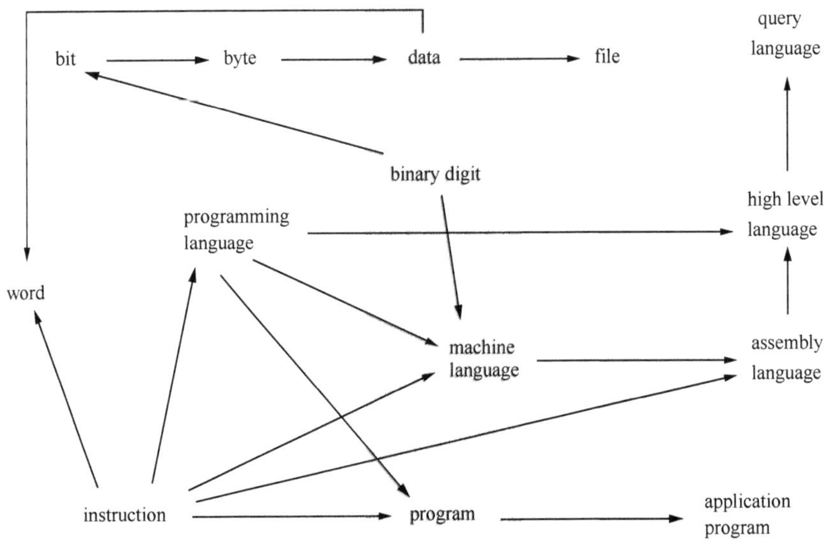

Fig. 3. The DAG representing direct prerequisite relationships in a subset of the concepts in software basics.

A result of topological sorting is an ordered sequence of the concepts in the DAG, in which the prerequisites of a concept are all on the left hand side of it. The following is a sorting result from the DAG in Fig. 3: (0) *binary digit*, (1) *instruction*, (2) *bit*, (3) *programming language*, (4) *byte*, (5) *machine language*, (6) *program*, (7) *application program*, (8) *assembly language*, (9) *data*, (10) *word*, (11) *file*, (12) *high level language*, (13) *query language*. The numbers in the parentheses are indices of the concepts in the sorted sequence. They will be used as indices in matrices as well.

In the second step, we create two matrices. The first one is the *adjacency matrix* of the DAG, denoted by M, in which $M_{ij} = 1$ if the ith concept is a direct prerequisite of the jth concept. The second matrix is M', in which $M'_{ij} = 1$ if the ith concept is a direct or indirect prerequisite of the jth concept. M' is calculated by applying a transitivity rule to M. In the matrices, the concepts are indexed according to the topological sorting result. Figure 4 illustrates matrices M and M' for the DAG in Fig. 3. Both M and M' are important information sources for constructing policy trees.

In the third step, we group concepts. Based on the grouping, we partition the state space into subspaces, which the partitioning of solution space is consistent with. In M', if the 1 s in a column are a subset of the 1 s in another column, the former is called a *contained* column. We eliminate the contained columns because the prerequisite relationships in the columns are contained in other columns. The matrix resulted from eliminating contained columns is M''. The left matrix in Fig. 5 is the M'' out of the M' in Fig. 4, with the eliminated columns replaced with "–"s.

Then, we merge the remaining columns in M'' into concept groups. The merging method is: If no less than a given percentage of the 1 s in column i

0	0	1	0	0	1	0	0	0	0	0	0	0	0
0	0	0	1	0	1	1	0	1	0	1	0	0	0
0	0	0	0	1	0	0	0	0	0	0	0	0	0
0	0	0	0	0	1	1	0	0	0	0	0	1	0
0	0	0	0	0	0	0	0	0	1	0	0	0	0
0	0	0	0	0	0	0	0	1	0	0	0	0	0
0	0	0	0	0	0	0	1	0	0	0	0	0	0
0	0	0	0	0	0	0	0	0	0	0	0	0	0
0	0	0	0	0	0	0	0	0	0	0	0	1	0
0	0	0	0	0	0	0	0	0	0	1	1	0	0
0	0	0	0	0	0	0	0	0	0	0	0	0	0
0	0	0	0	0	0	0	0	0	0	0	0	0	0
0	0	0	0	0	0	0	0	0	0	0	0	0	1
0	0	0	0	0	0	0	0	0	0	0	0	0	0

1	0	1	0	1	1	0	0	1	1	1	1	1	1
0	1	0	1	0	1	1	1	1	0	1	0	1	1
0	0	1	0	1	0	0	0	0	1	1	1	0	0
0	0	0	1	0	1	1	1	1	0	0	0	1	1
0	0	0	0	1	0	0	0	0	1	1	1	0	0
0	0	0	0	0	1	0	0	1	0	0	0	1	1
0	0	0	0	0	0	1	1	0	0	0	0	0	0
0	0	0	0	0	0	0	1	0	0	0	0	0	0
0	0	0	0	0	0	0	0	1	0	0	0	1	1
0	0	0	0	0	0	0	0	0	1	1	1	0	0
0	0	0	0	0	0	0	0	0	0	1	0	0	0
0	0	0	0	0	0	0	0	0	0	0	1	0	0
0	0	0	0	0	0	0	0	0	0	0	0	1	1
0	0	0	0	0	0	0	0	0	0	0	0	0	1

Fig. 4. Left: the adjacency matrix M of the DAG in Fig. 3; Right: the matrix M' including all direct and indirect prerequisites.

-	-	-	-	-	-	-	0	-	-	1	1	-	1
-	-	-	-	-	-	-	1	-	-	1	0	-	1
-	-	-	-	-	-	-	0	-	-	1	1	-	0
-	-	-	-	-	-	-	1	-	-	0	0	-	1
-	-	-	-	-	-	-	0	-	-	1	1	-	0
-	-	-	-	-	-	-	0	-	-	0	0	-	1
-	-	-	-	-	-	-	1	-	-	0	0	-	0
-	-	-	-	-	-	-	1	-	-	0	0	-	0
-	-	-	-	-	-	-	0	-	-	0	0	-	1
-	-	-	-	-	-	-	0	-	-	1	1	-	0
-	-	-	-	-	-	-	0	-	-	1	0	-	0
-	-	-	-	-	-	-	0	-	-	0	1	-	0
-	-	-	-	-	-	-	0	-	-	0	0	-	1
-	-	-	-	-	-	-	0	-	-	0	0	-	1

-	-	-	-	-	-	-	-	-	-	-	1	-	1
-	-	-	-	-	-	-	-	-	-	-	1	-	1
-	-	-	-	-	-	-	-	-	-	-	1	-	0
-	-	-	-	-	-	-	-	-	-	-	0	-	1
-	-	-	-	-	-	-	-	-	-	-	1	-	0
-	-	-	-	-	-	-	-	-	-	-	0	-	1
-	-	-	-	-	-	-	-	-	-	-	0	-	1
-	-	-	-	-	-	-	-	-	-	-	0	-	1
-	-	-	-	-	-	-	-	-	-	-	0	-	1
-	-	-	-	-	-	-	-	-	-	-	1	-	0
-	-	-	-	-	-	-	-	-	-	-	1	-	0
-	-	-	-	-	-	-	-	-	-	-	1	-	0
-	-	-	-	-	-	-	-	-	-	-	0	-	1
-	-	-	-	-	-	-	-	-	-	-	0	-	1

Fig. 5. Left: M'' in which the contained columns have been eliminated; Right: The result of merging columns.

match the 1 s in column j, merge column i into column j. The matrix on the right hand side in Fig. 5 shows the result of merging the columns in M''. The two columns represent two concept groups, with a 1 being a concept. We can see in the grouping result, each concept and its direct and indirect prerequisites are in the same group. As another method for reducing computing costs, we partition the POMDP state space into subspaces [16]. The method is based on concept grouping. We present the whole process of concept grouping here to show that the partitioning of solution space is on the same basis as the partitioning of state space, although the final result of concept grouping is not directly used in policy tree construction.

7 The New Technique of Policy Trees

7.1 Policy Trees and Tree Sets

In a previous section, we defined a *tutoring session*, which starts with a student question about a concept, possibly followed by questions and answers concerning prerequisites of the concept. Based on the definition, we categorize questions into *original questions* and *current questions*. An original question is the one that starts a tutoring session, and a current question is the one that the agent answers in the current step. In the tutoring session in Fig. 2, "What is a database?" is the original question, and "what is a high-level question?" is the current question at `t10`.

The concept in the original question is the one that the student originally wants to learn. The student asks a current question usually for understanding the original question. Sometimes, a current question is made by the agent when it realizes that the student needs to make up some knowledge. At the beginning of a session, the original question is also the current question.

In our discussion, we denote the original and current questions by $(?C^o)$ and $(?C^c)$ respectively, and assume $C^c \in (\wp_{C^o} \cup \{C^o\})$, where $\wp_{C^o}$ is the set of all the direct and indirect prerequisites of C^o.

For every possible pair of $(?C^o)$ and $(?C^c)$, we construct a set of policy trees. We denote the set by $\mathcal{T}_{C^c}^{C^o}$. *When the original question is* $(?C^o)$ *and current question is* $(?C^c)$, *to answer* $(?C^c)$ *the agent evaluates all, and only, the policy trees in* $\mathcal{T}_{C^c}^{C^o}$, *selects the optimal tree, and takes the root action of it.* The agent evaluates a policy tree to estimate the expected return that results from taking the root action in the current step. (See Eqs. (7), (8) and (9).)

In the set $\mathcal{T}_{C^c}^{C^o}$, there is one or more policy trees for each $C \in (\wp_{C^c} \cup \{C^c\})$. In a policy tree for C in $\mathcal{T}_{C^c}^{C^o}$, the root action is $(!C)$, and every leaf is an action for terminating the tutoring session. The terminating action is connected by an edge of (Θ) to an action of $(!C^o)$. The connected $(!C^o)$ and (Θ) represent that the student accepts the answer to the original question, and thus the tutoring session could be terminated. Figure 6 illustrates a policy tree for PL, when the original and current questions are (?ML) and (?PL) respectively, where ML stands for *machine language* and PL for *programming language*. In this tree, a thick horizontal line denotes a terminating action.

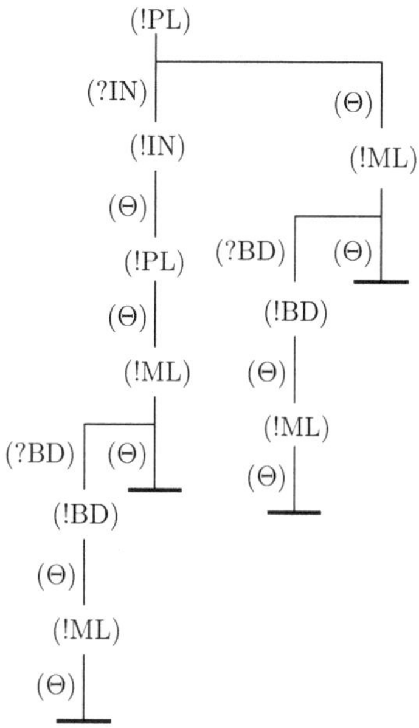

Fig. 6. A policy tree for PL when the original question is (?ML). (ML – machine language, PL – programming language, BD – binary digit, and IN – instruction.)

In a policy tree, every path from the root to a leaf is a process of tutoring. It starts with the agent's answer to the current question, and ends with the student's acceptance of the answer to the original question. A policy tree includes all such paths.

7.2 Atomic Trees

We construct a policy tree by integrating *atomic trees*. In this subsection, we discuss how to create atomic trees, and in the next subsection, how to integrate atomic trees into policy trees. In constructing a policy tree, we take into consideration the predictable student actions and the corresponding system actions in a tutoring session. As stated, we observed that student questions in a tutoring session concern concepts having prerequisite/successor relationships. Thus in a tutoring session, we can predict possible student questions.

For each concept in the instructional subject, we create an atomic tree. In the atomic tree of concept C, the root is action $(!C)$ for teaching C, and there is one or more edges for connecting the root to its children. The edges are labelled with the predictable student actions after the agent takes the root action. After $(!C)$, the predictable student actions include an *acceptance* action, and questions about the prerequisites of C. We thus label the edges with the predictable student actions (treated as observations).

Assume C has J direct and indirect prerequisites, and L direct successors ($J \geq 0, L \geq 0$, J and L are not equal to 0 at the same time). In the atomic tree of C, the root has $J+1$ edges connecting it to as many as $J+1$ children. The last edge is labelled with (Θ). When $L > 0$, the edge connects the root to a subtree in which the root action teaches one of the direct *successors* of C. When $L = 0$, the (Θ) edge connects the root to an action for terminating the tutoring session. When $J > 0$, the first J edges are for connecting the root to subtrees in which the root actions teach the J prerequisites respectively. The ith edge is labelled with $(?C_i)$, where C_i is the ith prerequisite of C $(1 \leq i \leq J)$. The edge is for connecting to a subtree, in which the root is $(!C_i)$, When $J = 0$, the atomic tree has only one edge labelled with (Θ). When creating atomic trees, we use matrix M' to find direct and indirect prerequisites for each concept, and use M to find direct successors. The matrices are calculated when we group the concepts.

Figure 7 illustrates the atomic trees of ML (machine language, top), PL (programming language, bottom left), BD (binary digit, bottom middle), and IN (instruction, bottom right), based on the DAG in Fig. 3. In an atomic tree, a triangle labelled with a concept name is a *dummy subtree*, and "Suc" stands for a successor. A dummy subtree labelled with C is not a part of the atomic tree but will be substituted with the atomic tree of C or with a system action for terminating the session, when the atomic tree is integrated into a policy tree. The substitution will be discussed later.

The semantics of the atomic tree of C is: After the agent teaches C, if the student asks a question about C_i, which is a prerequisite of C, the agent teaches C_i $(1 \leq i \leq J)$, but if the student accepts $(!C)$, the agent teaches a successor of C, or terminates the session (if C does not have a successor).

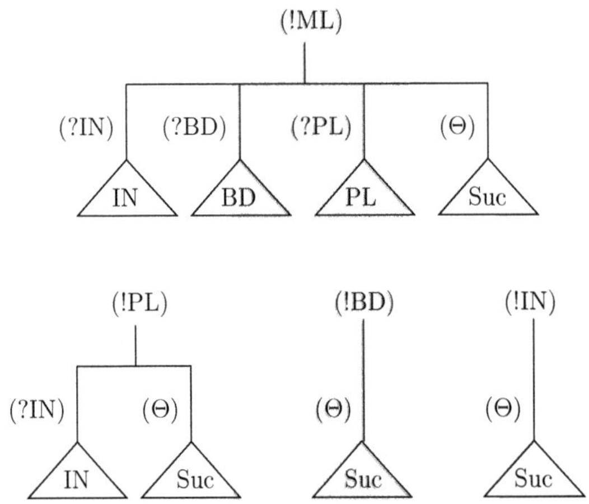

Fig. 7. Atomic trees of ML, PL, BD, and IN.

7.3 Policy Tree Construction

Now we informally discuss the algorithm for constructing a policy tree. We still denote the original and current questions by $(?C^o)$ and $(?C^c)$ respectively. We assume C^c is in $(\wp_{C^o} \cup \{C^o\})$, otherwise, we consider $(?C^c)$ starts a new tutoring session. For each pair of $(?C^o)$ and $(?C^c)$, we create policy tree set $\mathcal{T}_{C^c}^{C^o}$. For example, for the original and current question pair (?ML) and (?PL), we create tree set $\mathcal{T}_{\text{PL}}^{\text{ML}}$. When the original question is (?ML), to choose the optimal action to answer (?PL), the agent evaluates all, and only the trees in $\mathcal{T}_{\text{PL}}^{\text{ML}}$.

When we create $\mathcal{T}_{C^c}^{C^o}$, for each $C \in (\wp_{C^c} \cup \{C^c\})$, we construct one or more policy trees. We construct a policy tree for C in $\mathcal{T}_{C^c}^{C^o}$ by expanding the atomic tree of C: Substituting the dummy subtrees with atomic trees, then expanding the atomic trees, and so on, until all the leaf nodes become terminating actions. Let C have L' direct successors in $(\wp_{C^o} \cup \{C^o\})$. (To find the direct successors for C, we use the adjacency matrix M.) When $L' = 0$ or $L' = 1$, we start with one tree, in which the dummy subtree labelled with *Suc* is substituted with the terminating action ($L' = 0$), or the atomic tree of the only direct successor ($L' = 1$). When $L' > 1$, we start with L' trees, in each of which the dummy subtree labelled with *Suc* is substituted with the atomic tree of *one* of the direct successors in $(\wp_{C^o} \cup \{C^o\})$. In all the cases, a dummy subtree for a prerequisite in $(\wp_{C^c} \cup \{C^c\})$ is substituted with the atomic tree of the prerequisite.

For example, in expanding the atomic tree of PL with ML being the C^o, we substitute the dummy subtree of IN with the atomic tree of IN, and substitute the dummy subtree of *Suc* with the atomic tree of ML, which is the only direct successor of PL in $(\wp_{\text{ML}} \cup \{\text{ML}\})$. Then we expand the atomic trees of IN and ML, and so on.

When expanding an atomic tree, we may need to go up to a successor, then the successor's successor, ... In our technique, we stop at C^o. That is, we do not go up to the successor of C^o. Continue the above example of expanding the atomic of PL. When we expanding the atomic tree of ML, we do not go up to a successor of ML because ML is the C^o.

In expanding an atomic tree, we have two rules for adding a terminating action and for eliminating an edge:

- If the root of the atomic tree is $(!C^o)$, i.e. to answer the original question, substitute the dummy subtree connected by the edge of (Θ) with a terminating action.
- If the question associated with an edge has been answered in the path from the root of the policy tree, eliminate the edge without substituting the dummy subtree it connects to.

The question $(?C)$ associated with an edge has been answered, if in the path from the root to the edge, there is a node of $(!C)$ or $(!C')$ immediately followed by an edge of (Θ), where C' is a direct or indirect successor of C.

As another example of policy tree constructed by using the above procedure, Fig. 8 illustrates the policy tree for ML when the original question is (?ML), which is in $\mathcal{T}_{\text{ML}}^{\text{ML}}$.

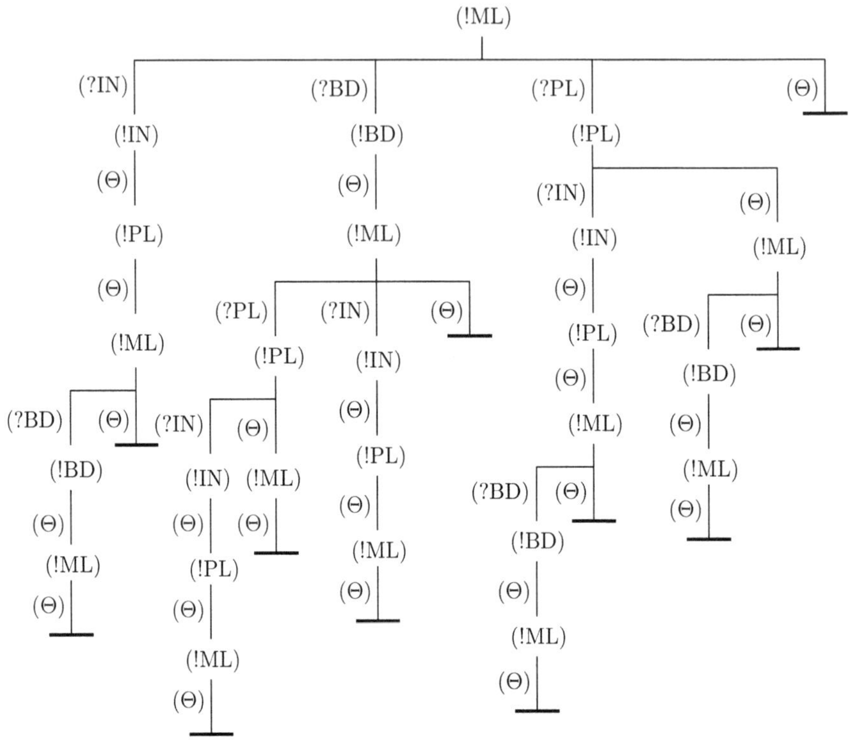

Fig. 8. A policy tree for ML when the original question is (?ML).

7.4 Choosing an Optimal Action with the Trees

All the sets of policy trees are pre-constructed and stored in a tree database. When the agent needs the optimal action to answer a question, it retrieves the database, gets the tree set for the original and current questions, and evaluate the trees in the set to find the optimal. In general, when the original question is $(?C^o)$ and the agent needs to answer the current question $(?C^c)$, it evaluates all the policy trees in $\mathcal{T}_{C^c}^{C^o}$ based on its current belief, and finds the tree that has the highest value (optimal tree). When choosing the optimal policy tree by using Eq. (10), we substitute $\mathcal{T}$ with $\mathcal{T}_{C^c}^{C^o}$.

A policy tree is not a tutoring plan that the agent will follow in the future. It is the strategy for the current step. After choosing the optimal tree, the agent takes the root action. Then it has a new current question, or terminates the session, depending on the student action (observation):

- If the student action is $(?C)$, the agent considers $(?C)$ as the new current question;
- If the student action is (Θ), and the (Θ) connects to $(!C)$ in the tree, the agent considers $(?C)$ as the new current question;

– If the student action is (Θ), and the (Θ) edge connects to a terminating action in the tree, the agent terminates the tutoring session.

To answer the new current question which is determined by using the above rules, the agent chooses an action in the same way, i.e. by evaluating a set of policy trees, and so on. Continue the example in which (?ML) and (?PL) are the original and current questions. If the policy tree in Fig. 6 is the optimal, the agent takes its root action (!PL). After (!PL), if the student action is (Θ), the agent follows the edge of (Θ) in the tree, and has (!ML) as the new current question. It evaluates the trees in $\mathcal{T}_{\text{ML}}^{\text{ML}}$, and continues until it takes a terminating action. If after (!PL) the student action is (?IN), the agent considers (?IN) as the new current question. It evaluates the trees in $\mathcal{T}_{\text{IN}}^{\text{ML}}$, and continues until it takes a terminating action.

8 Experiments and Analysis

We conducted the experiments by using the experimental ITS described before, which teaches concepts in software basics. Currently, keyboard and screen are used for system input and output. It interactively teaches a student at a time, answering the student's questions about the concepts. When the student asks a question about a concept that has prerequisites, the system chooses an optimal strategy to teach. A POMDP is the engine to make decisions based on information (belief) about the student's current knowledge states.

We use "rejection rate" to evaluate how the students satisfy the system's answers. After the system teaches a concept, if the student asks a question about a prerequisite of the concept, or says something like "I already know this concept", we consider that the student rejects the system action, and thus the action is not optimal. For a student, the rejection rate is defined as the ratio of the number of system actions rejected by the student to the total number of system actions for teaching him/her.

Encouraging results have been achieved. Compared with directly teaching the concept asked by the student, or randomly choosing a prerequisite to start with, the teaching based on students' knowledge states has achieved better result. The rejection rates have dropped significantly. We do not discuss the performance in adaptive teaching here, for this paper mainly addresses the problem of solution space.

The data set used to generate the following results includes about 90 concepts in software basics. The concepts have zero to five direct prerequisites. Based on the prerequisite/successor relationships, we partition the state space into six sub-spaces [16]. Also based on the prerequisite/successor relationships, the policy tree construction algorithm created six groups of tree sets. Table 1 lists the numbers of concepts, numbers of tree sets, numbers of policy trees, and maximum tree heights in the sub-spaces. The construction of policy trees does not rely on the result of state space partitioning. Since both space partitioning and tree construction are based on concept prerequisite/successor relationships,

Table 1. Numbers of concepts, tree sets, trees, and tree heights in sub-spaces.

Sub-space	# of concepts	# of tree sets	# of trees	Max height
1	21	231	1,771	30
2	23	276	2,300	18
3	20	210	1,540	26
4	27	378	3,654	35
5	25	325	2,925	32
6	26	378	3,744	37

the concepts in a policy tree are in the same subspace. Thus we consider that the solution space is split into the same number of subspaces.

In the experiments, the average number of policy trees (τs) in a tree set ($\mathcal{T}$) is less than ten. The average height of the policy trees is less than 20. The maximum number of edges at a node is the number of concepts in a subspace plus one (the acceptance action). The actual numbers of edges at nodes are much smaller than the numbers of concepts in subspaces. Many edges have been eliminated in policy tree construction (as described in the subsection of tree construction). In a decision step, the number of policy trees to evaluate, the heights of the trees, and the numbers of edges at nodes depend on the concept in the current question. For a concept near the lower end (having less prerequisites) the three numbers are small. For a concept near the higher end (having more prerequisites) the three numbers are big. For the higher end concepts, there is room for further improvement. We include this in our future work.

When making a decision, the agent evaluates a small number of trees. The average is less than 10 in the experiments. This does not create major efficiency problems for a modern computer. When the experimental ITS runs on a desktop computer with an Intel Core i5 3.2 GHz 64 bit processor and 16GB RAM, the response time for answering a question is less than 300 milliseconds. This includes the time for calculating a new belief, choosing a policy tree, and accessing the database of domain model. For a tutoring system, such response time could be considered acceptable.

9 Conclusion

Our policy tree technique can minimize the number of policy trees to evaluate in choosing an action. When looking for a strategy to answer a question, the agent needs to evaluate a set of pre-constructed policy trees, determined by the original and current questions. The set includes only the policy trees for the concepts in the current question and some of its prerequisites and successors. They are the concepts that the student may want to learn after asking the original question. The set does not include the policy trees that are unrelated to the tutoring session. In addition, since the policy trees to be evaluated include related concepts only, and unnecessary edges are pruned when the trees are constructed, the costs for evaluating individual trees can be minimized. The results in our initial experiments have showed that the technique is effective in addressing the problem of exponential solution space.

The technique is based on the nature of education processes, and thus especially suitable for building systems for education. The technique can be applied to any tutoring tasks in which the subjects have pedagogical orders in the contents.

Acknowledgements.. This research is supported by the Natural Sciences and Engineering Research Council of Canada (NSERC).

Appendix I: Sample Concepts and Descriptions

- A **binary digit** is 0 or 1.
- A **bit** is the smallest unit of information on a computer. It can hold one of the two values of binary digits.
- A **byte** consists of eight consecutive bits.
- **Data** represents information, stored on a computer as sequences of bytes.
- A **word** is a fixed-sized piece of data handled as a unit by the instruction set or the hardware of the processor.
- A **file** is a collection of data. It has a name.
- An **instruction** is a coded command to the computer to perform a specified function.
- A **programming language** is an artificial language designed to communicate instructions to a computer.
- A **machine language** is a programming language, in which each instruction is represented as binary digits.
- An **assembly language** has the same structure and set of instructions as a machine language, with the instructions represented by names.
- A **high-level language** is a programming language independent of any particular type of computer, and is closer to human languages than assembly languages.
- A **query language** is a high-level language for querying.
- A **program** is a sequence of instructions written in a programming language, for performing a specified task with a computer.
- An **application program** is a program developed for performing a specific task directly for the user.

References

1. Anderson, J.R., Corbett, A.T., Koedinger, K.R., Peeelletier, R.: Cognitive tutors: lessons learned. J. Learn. Sci. **4**(2), 167–207 (1995)
2. Braziunas, D.: POMDP solution methods: a survey. Technical report, Department of Computer Science, University of Toronto (2003)

3. Carlin, A., Zilberstein, S.: Observation compression in DEC-POMDP policy trees. In: Proceedings of the 7th International Joint Conference on Autonomous Agents and Multi-agent Systems, pp. 31–45(2008)
4. Cassandra, A. A survey of POMDP applications. In: Working Notes of AAAI 1998 Fall Symposium on Planning with Partially Observable Markov Decision Process, pp. 17–24(1998)
5. Cheung, B., Hui, L., Zhang, J., Yiu, S.M.: SmartTutor: an intelligent tutoring system in web-based adult education. J. Syst. Softw. **68**, 11–25 (2003). Elsevier
6. Chinaei, H.R., Chaib-draa, B., Lamontagne, L.: Learning observation models for dialogue POMDPs. In: Kosseim, L., Inkpen, D. (eds.) AI 2012. LNCS, vol. 7310, pp. 280–286. Springer, Heidelberg (2012). doi:10.1007/978-3-642-30353-1_24
7. Folsom-Kovarik, J.T., Sukthankar, G., Schatz, S.: Tractable POMDP representations for intelligent tutoring systems. ACM Trans. Intell. Syst. Technol. (TIST) - Special Section on Agent Communication, Trust in Multiagent Systems, Intelligent Tutoring and Coaching Systems Archive **4**(2), 29 (2013)
8. Jeremic, Z., Jovanovic, J., Gasevic, D.: Evaluating an intelligent tutoring systemfor design patterns: the DEPTHS experience. Educ. Technol. Soc. **12**(2), 111–130 (2009)
9. Littman, M.L.: A tutorial on partially observable Markov decision processes. J. Math. Psychol. **53**, 119–125 (2009)
10. McLaren, B.M., DeLeeuw, K.E., Mayer, R.E.: Polite web-based intelligent tutors: can they improve learning in classrooms? Comput. Educ. **56**(3), 574–584 (2011)
11. McLaren, B.M., van Gog, T., Ganoe, C., Karabinos, M., Yaron, D.: The efficiency of worked examples compared to erroneous examples, tutored problem solving, and problem solving in classroom experiments. Comput. Hum. Behav. **55**, 87–99 (2016)
12. Rafferty, A.N., Brunskill, E., Griffiths, T.L., Shafto, P.: Faster teaching by POMDP planning. In: Biswas, G., Bull, S., Kay, J., Mitrovic, A. (eds.) AIED 2011. LNCS (LNAI), vol. 6738, pp. 280–287. Springer, Heidelberg (2011). doi:10.1007/978-3-642-21869-9_37
13. Theocharous, G., Beckwith, R., Butko, N., Philipose, M.: Tractable POMDP planning algorithms for optimal teaching in SPAIS. In: IJCAI PAIR Workshop (2009)
14. VanLehn, K.: Intelligent turoring systems for continuous, embedded assessment. In: Dwyer, C. (ed.) The Future of Assessment: Shaping Teaching and Learning, pp. 113–138. Erlbaum, Mahwah (2008)
15. VanLehn, K., van de Sande, B., Shelby, R., Gershman, S.: The Andes physics tutoring system: an experiment in Freedom. In: Nkambou, R., Bourdeau, J., Mizoguchi, R. (eds.) Advances in Intelligent Tutoring Systems. SCI, vol. 308, pp. 421–443. Springer, Heidelberg (2010). doi:10.1007/978-3-642-14363-2_21
16. Wang, F.: Handling exponential state space in a POMDP-based intelligent tutoring system. In: Proceedings of 6th International Conference on E-Service and Knowledge Management (IIAI ESKM 2015), pp. 67–72 (2015)
17. Williams, J.D., Poupart, P., Young, S.: Factored partially observable Markov decision processes for dialogue management. In: Proceedings of Knowledge and Reasoning in Practical Dialogue Systems (2005)
18. Williams, J.D., Young, S.: Partially observable Markov decision processes for spoken dialog systems. Comput. Speech Lang. **21**, 393–422 (2007). Elsevier
19. Woolf, B.P.: Building Intelligent Interactive Tutors. Morgan Kaufmann Publishers, Burlington (2009)

Can Digital Games Help Seniors Improve Their Quality of Life?

Louise Sauvé[1(✉)], Lise Renaud[2], David Kaufman[3], and Emmanuel Duplàa[4]

[1] Département Éducation, Télé-Université/SAVIE, Québec, Canada
louisesauve25@gmail.com
[2] Faculté de Communication, UQAM, Montréal, Canada
renaud.lise@uqam.ca
[3] Faculty of Education, Simon Fraser University, Burnaby, Canada
dkaufman@sfu.ca
[4] Faculty of Education, University of Ottawa, Ottawa, Canada
eduplaa@uottawa.ca

Abstract. This developmental research study aimed to design, implement and evaluate an online educational game to improve the quality of life for seniors aged 55 years and older. The game Live Well, Live Healthy! (cvje2.savie.ca) is a Bingo game in which the learning content in the study is integrated into the mechanism of the game. A "pre-test/post-test" single group methodology measured the impact of the game on three dimensions of quality of life: psychological, physical, and social. A total of 56 seniors played for a week in multiplayer mode involving real-time interaction with at least two other participants. The results indicated that the educational game improved the seniors' perception of a majority of the variables concerning the three dimensions: physical (fatigue, sleep, eating habits); social well-being (building ties, social connectedness, friendships) and psychological well-being (depression, difficulty doing activities, mood and feeling of being loved). Some variables (sadness, isolation, proximity to family and physical habits) generated a weak perception of positive benefits for these seniors.

Keywords: Online games · Seniors · Benefits · Quality of life

1 Introduction

1.1 Background

The aging population represents a serious challenge for healthcare systems and social insurance in the 21st century. Aging seniors are facing the decline of their physical and cognitive abilities, loss of long-term companions and social support, changes in their familial or professional environment, changing lifestyles, and the increased likelihood of developing chronic and disabling diseases. But what are we doing to improve the quality of life for seniors? Can online educational games help them age better?

G. Costagliola et al. (Eds.): CSEDU 2016, CCIS 739, pp. 179–192, 2017.
DOI: 10.1007/978-3-319-63184-4_10

1.2 Purpose of the Study

Our study aims to measure the benefits of an online educational game designed for seniors concerning their quality of life.

1.3 Research Questions

The study investigated the following research questions:

- What is the impact of the educational game on the perception of the seniors' physical condition?
- What is the impact of the educational game on the perception of the seniors' psychological state?
- What is the impact of the educational game on the perception of the seniors' social environment?

2 Literature Review

An investigation by CEFRIO in Quebec indicated that over a third of seniors aged 55 and over use the Internet to play digital games either alone or in groups [1]. Given this interest, we wondered whether the use of online educational games could be beneficial for improving seniors' quality of life.

Quality of life is a global concept describing the daily life of people, taking into account their emotional and social functions as well as purely physical conditions. Even though there does not seem to be a consensus on its definition [2], the most widely used definition comes from the World Health Organization [3], which defines Quality of Life as "…individuals' perception of their position in life in the context of the culture and the value systems in which they live and in relation to their goals, expectations, standards and concerns. It is a broad ranging concept affected in a complex way by the person's physical health, psychological state, level of independence, social relationships, personal beliefs and their relationship to salient features of their environment."(p. 1).

This concept takes into account four dimensions: physical (autonomy and physical abilities), psychological (isolation, depression, emotion), relational (family, social, professional), and symptomatic (impact of a disease and its treatment). Surveys [4, 5] have revealed that a majority of seniors consider psychological well-being, involvement in social activities, and physical health as conditions for successfully aging. Finally, Turcotte and Schellenberg [6, p. 51] observe that "active participation in society can also be compromised if a person has difficulty hearing, seeing, walking, climbing stairs, bending, learning or doing similar activities. All these difficulties, if cumulative, can greatly impair the quality of life of a person of any age."

Digital games are becoming increasingly popular with seniors [7, 8]. According to the World Health Organization [9], digital games can influence both seniors' health, viewed through a broad, biopsychosocial perspective, and their ability to perform activities in their current environment.

What does the literature say concerning the impact of digital games as it pertains to the physical, psychological and social aspects of seniors' quality of life? Some studies on the impacts of digital games on an active lifestyle (i.e., the ability to maintain physical and functional independence) have shown beneficial effects on the quality of life of seniors [10–12]. Other research has examined the contribution of games using the Nintendo Wii game console to seniors' performance of physical and functional tasks, with mixed results: some studies [13–15, 31] concluded that improvements were apparent; however, others [16, 17] found no improvements.

Social interaction and social support are frequently identified as key aspects of seniors' quality of life [18–21]. Seniors are already active users of interactive technologies, and they are able to use digital games and to easily learn to do so [22]. Studies are showing increasingly that digital games are a means of social interaction that may improve the quality of life of seniors [1, 23–30]. Whitcomb [32] found that games develop social relationships and a sense of well-being among seniors while providing an enjoyable way to spend time. Astell [33] suggested that digital games and interactive technologies (Skype, Facebook, etc.) offer social connections, especially for elderly people suffering from dementia.

Regarding physiological aspects, Allaire et al. [34] found a significant difference between gaming (moderate and occasional) and non-gaming seniors, concerning socio-affective dimensions such as mood and depression. In addition, Wollersheim et al. [35] reported that digital games break down isolation as well as decrease feelings of loneliness.

Despite these findings, few studies have addressed the psychological aspects of quality of life.

It is difficult to draw conclusions from current empirical studies because there is little overlap in these studies. This is due to several factors:

- the variation in participants' demographic data; for example, the number (1–1000 respondents), age (45 to 87), educational level (secondary to university);
- the ratio of men to women (more women than men participate in most studies);
- the diversity of research methodologies;
- the use of various measuring instruments (few studies use the same instruments);
- the choice of digital games, which are not always developed for seniors.

What happens if we experiment on an educational game with learning content dealing with nutrition and prevention, in addition to the three quality of life dimensions: physical (physical activity benefits in the development of autonomy and physical abilities), psychological (actions to take to reduce anxiety, depression, emotions) and relational (the contribution of the social environment - family, social, professional - for the well-being of seniors)? Can such a game change the perceptions of seniors towards the benefits that educational games can bring by educating them about the actions they can take to improve their quality of life?

3 Game Description

The game used in this experiment is based on the game Bingo, which was the game most frequently mentioned as played by participants in a recent survey of 932 Canadian seniors [36]. Figure 1 shows the Live Well, Live Healthy! game interface, which is divided into three parts: (a) the Bingo card, rules and tutorial; (b) information on the game's progress: the type of game, randomly drawn ball, and the Bingo button for ending the game; and (c) information related to the players' actions: players' names and scores, as well as the microphone and chat control buttons.

Fig. 1. Live well, live healthy!

The Live Well, Live Healthy! game was developed using a generic shell for educational games (http://cvje2concepteur.savie.ca). The game's educational objectives are the following: to increase knowledge about nutrition and physical activities, to decrease risk situations (or to improve prevention situations) and to identify the importance of social interactions with friends and family members.

The game offers a mechanism to display a question every time the number of a randomly drawn ball is on one or more of the players' cards. If the player answers the question correctly, a token appears in the box and the player earns points (20 points for an easy question, 30 points for an average question and 50 points for a difficult question). If the player does not answer the question correctly, the token will not appear in the box and the player loses half the points allocated to the question. The 92 questions included in the game are distributed as follows: physical state (31 questions about nutrition, 24 about physical activities), psychological aspect (18 questions) and the social environment (19 questions).

The Live Well, Live Healthy! game provides feedback to support the learning of its preset content. Immediate feedback, related to each learning task, allows players to identify successful activities and those they have failed.

The game incorporates mechanisms (Fig. 2) that: (1) highlight the results of each learning activity (success or failure) through visual or audible feedback (A) such as a smiling face or a sad one and positive or negative tone (i.e a signal that indicates whether the action in the game has been made correctly or not by the player) and (2) the correct and incorrect answers through textual (B),visual or audible (C) feedback on the content of the learning activity or provide additional information to sustain interest in the case of positive responses; and (3) allow players to see what they have learned by providing an overview of the results of the game's learning activities, together with teaching materials to review subject matter that has not been learned.

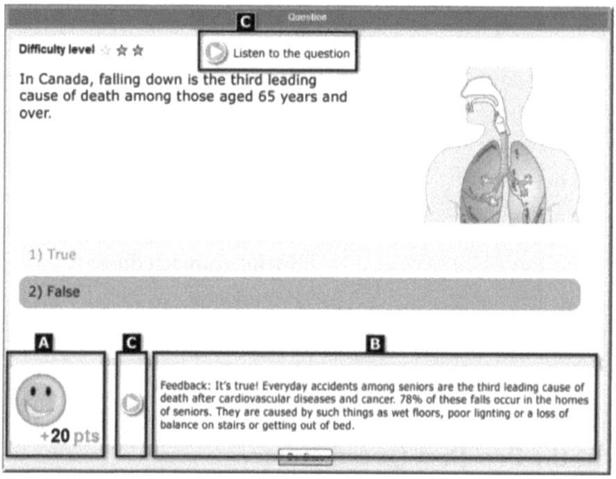

Fig. 2. Question card.

For more details about this digital game and a good preview, see [37]. This game (http://cvje2.savie.ca) promotes active living and healthy eating habits among seniors while giving them opportunities to interact with others as it illustrates these themes with good quality images and animations.

4 Methodology

Opting for a single group pre- and post-test protocol, our study measured the physical, psychological and social dimensions of quality of life. Remembering that quality of life is a subjective concept and the apprehension of the construct itself is complex, the definition of quality of life adopted in the study specified the items that the study retained to measure the impact of the game.

Likert scales were used to obtain the construct of quality of life (Table 1). To facilitate data collection, we opted for a self-administered questionnaire, making it preferable to limit the number of questions and minimize the time needed to fill out the questionnaire.

Table 1. Quality of life dimensions.

Quality of life dimensions	Items measured
Physical state	Sleep
	Tiredness
	Eating habits
	Physical activity habits
Psychological aspect	Depression
	Isolation
	Feeling loved
	Mood
	Sadness
	Ease in doing activities
Social environment	Strengthening ties
	Social connectedness
	Friendship
	Interactions with family
	Interactions with friends

4.1 Handing Out the Pre/ Post Questionnaires

A 15-item questionnaire was used for data collection. The questions were formed as a Likert scale with five levels (5 = strongly agree, 4 = agree, 3 = neutral, 2 = disagree and 1 = strongly disagree). The questions were designed to determine the perceptions of the participants towards the benefits of playing online concerning physical, social and psychological well-being. The reliability of the instrument was determined using the Cronbach's alpha index of internal consistency ($\alpha = 0.87$). Its validity was established by calculating the Pearson correlation coefficient between items belonging to the same dimension. The four items in the "Physical state" dimension showed significant correlations among themselves, as did the five items comprising the "Social environment" dimension. Significant correlations between the six items belonging to the "Psychological aspect" dimension amounted to 66%.

The pretest was completed prior to the seniors' participation in the Live Well, Live Healthy! game. Seniors were invited to play at least four games over a period of one month. Following their participation, they then completed the post-test.

4.2 Sample

It is very difficult to find objective definitions of the terms "senior" or "elderly". "The new definitions proposed by experts are not yet getting consensual approval" [6, p.8]. For our study, we selected two sample criteria: a minimum age of 55 and that of being retired.

Turcotte and Schellenberg [6] identified two types of seniors: those who are currently 65, the threshold that delineates the elderly according to Statistics Canada, and those who are considered the next generation of seniors, adults aged between 55 and 64.

Beaudoin et al. [1] also chose the age of 55 and over to designate seniors. Given this trend, we chose to form two age groups: 55 to 64 and 64 years and older.

On the retirement aspect, Turcotte and Schellenberg [6] found that people aged 56 and over who are retired have more time to devote to their home computer. In a recent study in Australia by Brand et al. [38], nearly one player in five was likely to be aged 51 and over. They found that the reasons and motivations why players choose to play vary by age group, suggesting that stages of life play an important role in the act of playing games. Following these authors' suggestions, we focused on retired people, who were more available and interested in participating in the experiment.

Recruiting our sample of seniors aged 55 and over was carried out through elderly associations and retirement homes. The experiments were done on site during social activities organized by the associations or in the residences' living room. Computer equipment was made available to the participants. The project was approved by the ethics committee at each of the authors' universities. All participants signed a consent form and were able at any time to interrupt their participation without any prejudice. A list of available human resources in their region was provided to them if needed.

4.3 Analysis

The analysis comprised the calculation of frequencies and percentages for each question. The Fisher's exact test was used to determine the significance of the differences between the responses of the pretest and post-test. Since the variables were not normally distributed, the use of parametric tests such as the paired samples t-test was discarded.

5 Results

Of the 67 participants of the study, 56 (83%) completed the pre- and post-test questionnaires in their entirety, providing all the required information. Table 2 shows the analysis of the 56 respondents.

Table 2. Sample characteristics (sex, age group and level of online gaming skills (n = 56)*.

Age group	Level of online gaming skills	Men	Women	TOTAL
55–64	Beginner	4	10	14
	Intermediary	2	4	6
	Subtotal	*6*	*14*	*20*
65 and over	Beginner	8	18	26
	Intermediary	1	9	10
	Subtotal	*9*	*27*	*36*
TOTAL		15	41	56

The sample included 41 women and 15 men. 20 participants (36%) are aged 64 or under and 36 subjects (64%) are 65 or older. 40 players have stated they are "beginners" in relation to their level of online gaming skills, while 16 participants were considered "intermediate" (Initially we presented three skill levels. Two respondents were "experts." Given the low numbers, we decided to integrate them with the intermediate players). Note that the initial trial period was one month and that seniors were invited to play at least one game per week for a minimum of four games with two other participants. However, the technological constraints of the locations for the experiment (little or no computer equipment or connectivity) reduced the experimental period to one week. All seniors played at least one game, 79% of them played two games and 21% of seniors played four games.

In the following subsections we present the perceptions of participants (n = 56) regarding the effects of playing online on their quality of life. These effects are grouped according to the previously described dimensions: physical state, psychological aspects and social environment. Table 3 shows the results related to these three dimensions.

Table 3. Results in connection with the three dimensions regarding quality of life (n = 56).

Item	Mean		
Physical state	Pre	Post	*p*
Fatigue	2.95	3.57	0.069
Sleep	3.44	3.80	0.031
Eating Habits	4.05	4.20	0.083
Physical Activity Habits	2.18	2.53	0.462
Social Environment			
Strengthening Ties	2.90	3.79	0.001
Social Connectedness	3.32	3.44	0.056
Friendship	3.03	3.79	0.003
Interactions with family	3.72	3.95	0.621
Interactions with Friends	3.69	4.13	0.064
Psychological Aspects			
Depression	3.76	4.21	0.022
Ease of Doing Activities	3.55	4.00	0.156
Mood	3.84	4.33	0.011
Isolation	3.79	4.15	0.158
Sadness	3.86	4.23	0.167
Feeling Loved	4.24	4.37	0.016

5.1 Perceptions About the Effects of Playing Online on Psychological Well-Being

Regarding the effects of the game on the players' physical state, the results show an increase in the means of the four items on this dimension, resulting in an improvement in participants' perceptions towards physical well-being.

Fatigue. The average of the pre-test (2.95) showed a more neutral perception of the effects that playing online has on fatigue while the post-test average increased by 0.62 to place it in the favourable range (strongly agree or agree). The percentage of participants who thought that playing online does not tire them after a few hours of playing went from 43% in the pretest to 63% in the post-test. These differences are significant (Fisher's exact test, $p = 0.069$).

Sleep. The general assessment of the impact of online games on sleep also improved. Generally, participants believe that online play does not affect their sleep. Although the pretest average (3.44) showed an already favourable position on this, it strengthened and increased by 0.36 in the post-test. This difference is significant (Fisher's exact test, p = 0.031).

Eating Habits. Both before and after playing online, the widespread opinion was that this activity does not encourage participants to skip meals. This perception was strengthened in participants (average rose from 4.05 to 4.20). The proportion of participants who were of the opinion that online gaming had no effect on feeding habits has gone from 84% in the pretest to 93% in the post-test. These differences are significant (Fisher's exact test, p = 0.083).

Physical Activity Habits. The perception of a positive effect from the game on physical activity was rather low. Before playing, only 12% of participants were of the opinion that online gaming encourages them to be more active. Although this proportion increased to 27% in the post-test, the average remains in the negative range (2.18 in the pre-test and 2.53 in the post-test). The result of Fisher's exact test shows that these differences are not significant (p = 0.462).

5.2 Perceptions About the Effects of Playing Online on Social Well-Being

In regard to the effects of gaming on the social environment of the participants, the responses show an improvement in perception in this regard. Indeed, there was an increase in the averages of the five items included in this dimension.

Strengthening Ties. With 36% in the pre-test to 75% in the post-test, the rate of participants who agreed with the idea that the game allows them to strengthen their ties increased significantly (p = 0.001). The average had an increase of 0.89. In other words, the perception of the game as a means of strengthening social ties has changed favourably.

Perception of Social Connectedness. Online gaming promotes a social connectedness with others. The pretest average (3.32) and post-test (3.44) support this assertion. The proportion of participants in agreement was 52% before playing and 66% thereafter. These differences are significant (Fisher's exact test, p = 0.056).

Friendship. In connection with the two preceding items, the rate of participants who were of the opinion that online play allows them to have friends has increased significantly (from 40% in the pretest to 73% in the post-test). The average increased by 0.76 and answers converged more around the average. These differences are significant (Fisher's exact test, p = 0.003).

Interactions with Family. The perception towards interactions with family remains in the positive range. The average pretest was 3.72 and had an increase of 0.23. However, the Fisher exact test does not conclude that these differences are significant (p = 0.621). If NSP is considered (42 in the pretest and 29 in the post-test), the significance improves, but remains slightly nonsignificant (p = 0.139 > 0.100).

Interactions with Friends. In the same vein, the results suggest that there has been a consolidation of the perception of interactions with friends. In the pretest, 74% of participants found this perception favourable. The percentage increased to 88% in the post-test. These differences are significant (Fisher's exact test, p = 0.064).

5.3 Perceptions About the Effects of Playing Online on Psychological Well-Being

Regarding the effects of the game on psychological well-being, although three of the six items that make up this dimension do not show significant differences, we see significant increases in the averages.

Depression. According to participants' responses before they used the game, 74% of participants indicated they did not feel depressed in the current week. In contrast, 17% said they felt depressed. These proportions changed significantly after using the game. The percentage of participants who expressed not being depressed increased to 88% while only one participant responded unfavourably. These differences are significant (Fisher's exact test, $p = 0.022$).

Ease of Doing Activities. The day after the experiment, participants did not think that their daily activities required an effort, and this was found both in the pre-test (average of 3.55) and in the post-test (4.00). Although there was an increase of 0.45 in the average, the Fisher exact test does not confirm significant differences ($p = 0.15683$). Yet it should be noted that the NSP increased from 7 in the pretest to 15 in the post-test, which had an impact on the significance of the differences (If NSP is included, the Fisher exact test $p = 0.069$ is less than 0.100, then the differences may be considered significant).

Mood. The responses suggest that the game had a positive effect on the moods of participants. The rate of participants who expressed feeling in a good mood had a significant increase (0.012). It rose from 77% to 88%. These differences are significant (Fisher's exact test, $p = 0.012$).

Isolation. The percentage of participants who indicated they do not feel alone rose from 74% in the pretest to 90% in the post-test. In the same vein, the average was 3.79 and increased to 4.15. Nevertheless, these differences cannot be considered significant ($p = 0.158 > 0.100$).

Sadness. Similar to the previous item, the percentage of participants who said they did not feel sadness has gone from 81% in the pretest to 88% in the post-test. Similarly, the average was 3.86 and went up to 4.23 for an increase 0.37. However, the Fisher exact test showed no significant difference ($p = 0.167$.).

Feeling Loved. Participants in the study felt loved. The answers show that this perception was positive both before and after the use of the game. This is confirmed by the averages of the pretest (4.24) and the post-test (4.37) and by the participant's rate of agreement (95% in the pretest and 90% in the post-test). These differences are significant (Fisher's exact test, $p = 0.016$).

6 Discussion

We recall that the content of the Live Well, Live Healthy! game addresses three dimensions of the quality of life (physical state, psychological aspect, and social environment) in the form of closed questions.

Overall, the results showed significant differences in a majority of the variables that were analyzed. Playing the Live Well, Live Healthy! game online resulted in the participants' improved perception of their quality of life along these dimensions. Our hypothesis that digital games improve seniors' quality of life was therefore confirmed regarding its physical, social and psychological aspects. Digital game development aimed at seniors is promising. However, certain items seem questionable. What about the non-significant variables?

Our respondents reported that the playing online gave them no incentive to be more active. It is true that most online games, whether for individual or group play, are not combined with physical devices such as Nintendo Wii and Microsoft Kinect Xbox 360 which, according to Daniel [17] and Singh et al. [15], promote improvement in physical conditioning. Game interactions in Live Well, Live Healthy! are done using a touch-screen or mouse. The game content covers how to adopt good physical habits. It seems that this way of educating seniors, that is, by offering models of good physical habits without putting them into action from within the game, maintains their perceptions that online games do not encourage them to be more active.

As for their psychological state, playing online for a limited period does not seem to change the perception of seniors who feel isolated and sad. It is interesting to note that participants who reported feeling in a better mood after playing an educational game, which Rosenberg et al. [39] linked to enjoyment in playing the game, should have normally felt less sad as well, but this was not the case. We would hypothesize that the source of their sadness is more due to their social isolation caused by lack of contact with friends and/or family [35] and that their gameplay did not change this situation during the period of our intervention.

Despite the interaction of respondents with others who were not family members during the game, it seems that those who had this perception before the game did not change it as a result of their participation in the Live Well, Live Healthy! game. These results lead us to question the time allowed to seniors for playing. Given technological constraints (participants had little or no computer equipment nor sufficient connectivity at their disposal, particularly in their seniors residences), we limited the playing time to one week in order to move the equipment to the different locations. This may explain the results that were obtained. Most studies done with seniors that have obtained positive results on the cognitive, social, psychological or physical level [40] experimented on the games for a period of at least three weeks. Only the study done by Seçer and Satyen [41] obtained no significant difference when they experimented on their game over a period of two to three weeks.

In terms of the social environment, playing online maintained their perception towards the proximity of family but nothing more. However, during the testing of the game, few seniors played with their families; they mostly experimented with friends and people around them at the residence. Can the context of the experiment explain the participants' unchanging perception of this aspect? This is a question for further research.

7 Conclusions

The results of our study indicate that educational games among seniors can lead to an improved perception of their quality of life that encompasses the following aspects: physical state (fatigue, sleep, eating habits); social well-being (strengthening ties, social connectedness, friendship and interaction with friends) and psychological well-being (depression, ease of doing activities, mood and feeling loved). As for sadness, isolation, interactions with family and physical habits, the perception of a positive effect remains weak among seniors.

While showing very positive results regarding the three dimensions of the study, several limitations have nuanced our findings: the small number of respondents (n = 56), the experimental time (one week), the limited number of games in which respondents participated (between one and four games). Similarly, the use of a board game designed with learning objectives and offered online limits the generalizability of our results for the same type of games.

Further studies should be made to overcome these limitations and consider the impact of online educational games on seniors.

Acknowledgements. We would like to thank the research assistants involved with this study: Samuel Venière for recruitment and data collection in the field, Aurélie Faticati for the literature review and Gustavo Adolfo Angulo Mendoza for the statistical analysis of the data of the study.

We also thank the Social Sciences and Humanities Research Council of Canada (SSHRC) and the AGE-WELL NCE Inc., a member of Canada's Networks of Centres of Excellence program, for their financial support of this research.

References

1. Beaudoin, J., Kooli, N., Thomas, F., Arlabosse, B., Couture, A., Danjou, R.: Génération @: Portrait de l'utilisation d'internet et de l'ordinateur par les aînés internautes du Québec: CEFRIO, Québec (2011). http://www.cefrio.qc.ca/media/uploader/Rapport_generationa_internautes_qc.pdf
2. Kuyken, W.: WHOQOL group: the world health organization quality of life assessment (WHOQOL): Position paper from the world health organization. Soc. Sci. Med. **41**(10), 1403–1409 (1995)
3. WHOQOL Group: Study protocol for the World Health Organization project to develop a quality of life assessment instrument (WHOQOL). Qual Life Res 2(2), pp. 153–159 (1993) doi:10.1007/BF00435734
4. Bowling, A., Dieppe, P.: What is successful ageing and who should define it? BMJ **331**, 1548–1551 (2005). doi:10.1136/bmj.331.7531.1548
5. Chen, S.C., Huang, Y.G.L., Chiang, I.T.: Using somatosensory video games to promote quality of life for the elderly with disabilities. In: Proceedings, the IEEE 4th International Conference on Digital Game and Intelligent Toy Enhanced Learning (Digitel), pp. 258–262. IEEE, Takamatsu (2012)
6. Turcotte, M., Schellenberg, G.: Un portrait des aînés au Canada [A portrait of seniors in Canada] Statistiques Canada, Ottawa (2006)
7. Diaz-Orueta, U., Facal, D., Nap, H., Ranga, M.-M.: What is the key for older people to show interest in playing digital learning games? Initial qualitative findings from the LEAGE project on a multicultural European sample. Games Health J. **1**(2), 115–123 (2012). doi:10.1089/g4h.2011.0024
8. Nacke, L.E., Nacke, A., Lindley, C.A.: Brain training for silver gamers: Effects of age and game form on effectiveness, efficiency, self-assessment and gameplay experience. Cyberpsychol. Behav. **12**(5), 493–499 (2009). doi:10.1089/cpb.2009.0013
9. World Health Organization: International classification of functioning, disability and health (ICF). World Health Organization, Geneva (2001). http://www.who.int/classifications/icf/en/

10. Figueira, H., Figueira, J., Mello, D., Dantas, E.: Quality of life throughout aging. Acta Medica Lituanica **15**, 169–172 (2008)
11. Freitas, C.M., Santiago, M.S., Viana, A.T., Leão, A.C., Freyre, C.: Motivational aspects that influence the elderly to enroll on and continue participating in physical exercise programs. Revista Brasileira de Cine-antropometria Desempenho Humano 9(1), 92–100 (2007) https://periodicos.ufsc.br/index.php/rbcdh/article/view/4037
12. Pernambuco, C.S., Rodrigues, B.M., Bezerra, J.C.P., Carrielo, A., de Oliveira Fernandes, A.D., de Souza Vale, R.G., Dantas, E.H.M.: Quality of life, elderly and physical activity. Health **4**(2), 88–93 (2012). doi:10.4236/health.2012.42014
13. Jorgensen, M.G., Laessoe, U., Hendriksen, C., Nielson, O.B.F., Aagaard, P.: Efficacy of Nintendo Wii training on mechanical leg muscle function and postural balance in community-dwelling older adults: A randomized controlled trial. J. Gerontol. A Biol. Sci. Med. Sci. **68**(7), 845–852 (2013). doi:10.1093/gerona/gls222
14. Maillot, P., Perrot, A., Hartley, A.: Effects of interactive physical-activity video-game training on physical and cognitive function in older adults. Psychol. Aging **27**(3), 589–600 (2012). doi:10.1037/a0026268
15. Singh, D.K.A., Rajaratnam, B.S., Palaniswamy, V., Raman, V.P., Bong, P.S., Pearson, H.: Effects of balance-focused interactive games compared to therapeutic balance classes for older women. Climacteric **16**(1), 141–146 (2013). doi:10.3109/13697137.2012.664832
16. Bieryla, K.A., Dold, N.M.: Feasibility of Wii Fit training to improve clinical measures of balance in older adults. Clin. Interv. Aging **8**, 775–781 (2013). doi:10.2147/CIA.S46164
17. Daniel, K.: Wii-hab for pre-frail older adults. Rehabil. Nurs. **37**(4), 195–201 (2012). doi:10.1002/rnj.25
18. Adams, K.B., Liebrandt, S., Moon, H.: A critical review of the literature on social and leisure activity and well-being in later life. Ageing Soc. **31**(4), 683–712 (2011). doi:10.1017/S0144686X10001091
19. Heylin, L.: The older, the lonelier? Risk factors for social loneliness in old age. Ageing Soc. **30**(7), 1177–1196 (2010). doi:10.1017/S0144686X10000292
20. Reichstadt, J., Sengupta, G., Depp, C., Palinkas, L.A., Jeste, D.V.: Older adults' perspectives on successful aging: Qualitative interviews. Am. J. Geriatr. Psychiatry **18**(7), 567–575 (2010)
21. Theurer, K., Wister, A.: Altruistic behaviour and social capital as predictors of well-being among older Canadians. Ageing Soc. **30**(1), 157–181 (2010). doi:10.1017/S0144686X09008848
22. Pew Internet and American Life Project: Demographics of Internet users. Pew Research Center, Washington, DC (2011). http://pewinternet.org/Static-Pages/Trend-Data/Whos-Online.aspx
23. De Schutter, R., Abeele V.V.: Designing meaningful within the psycho-social context of older adults. In: Abeele, V.V., Zaman, B., Obrist, M., IJsselsteijn, W. (eds.) Proceedings of the 3rd International Conference on Fun and Games, Fun and Games 2010, pp. 84–93. ACM, New York (2010)
24. De Schutter, B.: Never too old to play: The appeal of digital games to an older audience. Games Cult. **6**(2), 155–170 (2011). doi:10.1177/1555412010364978
25. Ijsselsteijn, W., Nap, H.H., Kort, Y., Poels, K.: Digital game design for elderly users. In: Kapralos, B., Katchabaw, M., Rajnovich J. (eds.) Proceedings of the 2007 Conference on Future Play, pp. 17–22. ACM, New York (2007)
26. Khoo, E., Cheok, A.: Age invaders: Intergenerational mixed reality family game. IJVR 5(2), 45–50 (2006). http://mixedrealitylab.org/projects/all-projects/age-invaders/
27. Khoo, E.T., Merritt, T., Cheok, A.D.: Designing physical and social intergenerational family entertainment. Interact. Comput. **21**(1–2), 76–87 (2009). doi:10.1016/j.intcom.2008.10.009

28. Mahmud, A.A., Mubin, O., Shahid, S., Martens, J.-B.: Designing and evaluating the tabletop game experience for senior citizens. In: Proceedings of the 5th Nordic Conference on Human-Computer Interaction Building Bridges - NordiCHI 2008, pp. 403–406. ACM Press, New York (2008)
29. Stebbins, R.: Serious Leisure: A Perspective for Our Time. Transaction Publishers, New Brunswick (2007)
30. Stowe, J.D., Cooney, T.M.: Examining rowe and kahn's concept of successful aging: Importance of taking a life course perspective. Gerontologist **55**(1), 43–50 (2015). doi: 10.1093/geront/gnu055
31. Theng, Y.-L., Chua, P.H., Pham, T.P.: Wii as entertainment and socialisation aids for mental and social health of the elderly. In: Extended Abstracts on Human Factors in Computing Systems CHIEA 2012, pp. 691–702 (2012). doi:10.1145/2212776.2212840
32. Whitcomb, G.R.: Computer games for the elderly. In: Rosenberg, R.S. (ed.) Proceedings of the Conference on Computers and the Quality of Life, CQL 1990, pp. 112–115. ACM, New York (1990). doi:10.1145/97344.97401
33. Astell, A.J.: Technology and fun for a happy old age. In: Sixsmith, A., Gutman, G. (eds.) Technologies for Active Aging, pp. 169–187. Springer, New York (2013)
34. Allaire, J.C., McLaughlin, A.C., Trujillo, A., Whitlock, L.A., Laporte, L., Gandy, M.: Successful aging through digital games: Socioemotional differences between older adult gamers and non-gamers. Comput. Human Behav. **29**(4), 1302–1306 (2013). doi:10.1016/j.chb.2013.01.014
35. Wollersheim, D., Merkes, M., Shields, N., Liamputtong, P., Wallis, L., Reynolds, F., Koh, L.: Physical and psychosocial effects of Wii video game use among older women. IJETS **8**(2), 85–98 (2010)
36. Kaufman, D., Sauvé, L., Renaud, L., Duplàa, E.: Enquête auprès des aînés canadiens sur les bénéfiques que les jeux numériques ou non leur apportent [Survey of Canadian seniors to determine the benefits derived from digital games]. Research report. TÉLUQ, UQAM, Simon Fraser University, University of Ottawa, Québec (2014)
37. Sauvé, L., Renaud, L., Kaufman, D., Duplàa, E.: Validation of the educational game for seniors: "Live Well, Live Healthy!". Procedia Soc. Behav. Sci. 176, 674–682 (2015). Elsevier Ltd., Chicago (2015). doi:10.1016/j.sbspro.2015.01.526
38. Brand, J.E., Lorentz, P., Mathew, T.: Digital Australia 2014. Interactive Games and Entertainment Association and Bond University, Eveleigh, Australia (2014). http://www.igea.net/2013/10/digital-australia-2014/
39. Rosenberg, D., Depp, C.A., Vahia, I.V., Reichstadt, J., Palmer, B.W., Kerr, J., Norman, G., Jeste, D.V.: Exergames for subsyndromal depression in older adults: A pilot study of a novel intervention. Am. J. Geriatr. Psychiatry **18**(3), 221–226 (2010)
40. Sauvé, L., Renaud, L., Venière, S., Mendozo, G.A.: Rapport d'expérimentation du jeu Vivons bien, vivons sainement! [Experimentation report on the game Live Well, Live Healthy]: Télé-université and UQAM, Québec (2015)
41. Seçer, I., Satyen, L.: Video game training and reaction time skills among older adults. Act. Adapt. Aging **38**(3), 220–236 (2014). doi:10.1080/01924788.2014.935908

Skramble: An Embeddable Python Programming Environment for Use in Learning Systems

Henry Miskin(✉) and Anandha Gopalan

Department of Computing, Imperial College London,
180 Queens Gate, London SW7 2RH, UK
hpm14@ic.ac.uk, a.gopalan@imperial.ac.uk

Abstract. Computing has recently been introduced as a core subject in British schools, meaning that children need to learn computer programming. Teachers have to be prepared to deliver the new curriculum and children need the correct environment and support to succeed. This paper discusses TuringLab, a challenge-based learning system for the Python programming language and proposes Skramble, an embeddable Python programming environment for use within existing learning systems. TuringLab has been used to teach children how to programme at a number of volunteer-led coding clubs. Children engaged well with the system, and the volunteers, who acted as teachers in these sessions, found it an extremely valuable educational tool. Skramble is an open source environment and is designed to abstract functionality such as code execution, error handling, syntax analysis, code testing, output capture and package management: allowing this feature-rich environment to be easily integrated into existing learning systems.

Keywords: Computer programming · Information technology · Open source · Online learning · Python programming

1 Introduction

Technology is transforming the world in which we live and children of the future need to be provided with the knowledge and skills to keep up with this change. The ability to understand the underlying functionality of technology has become a required skill of the modern world [1]. This growing importance of computing knowledge is reflected in the British Curriculum, as computing has recently been introduced as a core subject in both primary and secondary education [2]. Children from the age of 5 need to learn to programme [3] and beyond the age of 11, children are required to learn a syntax-based programming language [4].

Teachers have to deliver the new computing curriculum, which is a daunting prospect as many teachers do not have a formal background in computer science. Students must be taught both the fundamentals of computer science and computer programming: the practical element of computing [5]. A recent study found that although teachers are very enthused by the new curriculum, many do not feel confident in teaching it [6].

G. Costagliola et al. (Eds.): CSEDU 2016, CCIS 739, pp. 193–213, 2017.
DOI: 10.1007/978-3-319-63184-4_11

To support teachers in delivering the new computing curriculum, there are a number of resources available for teaching the fundamental concepts of computing [7]. In addition the Computing at School (CAS) group provides support for the delivery of computer science content in the classroom through a community of educators who share resources and best practices [8].

Many websites are available to help children learn to programme; they are well-developed, interactive and initially engaging. The tutorials provided on such sites incrementally build skills to develop programming concepts [9]. Fully online courses have been found to achieve positive results [10], however they are limited in how effectively they maintain the engagement of children, as is shown by high attrition rates [11].

Current systems seldom offer collaboration or interaction, with the result that each child operates as a discrete unit. Furthermore, their highly structured tutorials provide very little ability for teachers to influence the content which the children consume. As a result, current tools are not always applicable to a classroom environment and cannot be used for bespoke or cross-curricular projects.

Although the current offerings for learning to programme do not always fit into the classroom, many teachers are making use of Virtual Learning Environments (VLEs) to assist teaching and curriculum delivery [12]. These tools allow teachers to manage a virtual classroom, provide many collaborative features and have been well received by students, teachers and parents. External tools which provide assessment or rich media can be incorporated through the Learning Tool Interoperability (LTI) standard [13].

The learning environment provided by existing VLEs give classrooms the intersection between the interactivity of online courses and the adaptability and engagement of physical teaching. VLEs already reduce the work required for teachers to set and assess work, which makes them an attractive proposition for teachers. However, they currently do not provide the tools necessary to help teachers in delivering the practical elements of the new computing curriculum (teaching programming) while maintaining teacher involvement and control. There is a need for a programming environment that could be integrated into existing learning systems and could be used alongside ordinary teaching.

This paper outlines TuringLab, a system for learning Python programming and proposes Skramble, an adaptable and embeddable Python programming environment. TuringLab was used at a number of volunteer-led programming sessions, children not only returned week on week to the session, but they also continued to use the system outside of structured sessions. Iterative feedback from the children testing and using this software has enabled the current version to be fine-tuned to the needs of real classroom situations. Where the limitations of TuringLab lie in its inability to integrate with existing learning systems, Skramble provides an advanced programming environment which can be integrated with existing systems. Skramble abstracts complex functionality such as syntax analysis, code execution, error handling, and output capture for any host system to easily make use of.

2 Background

The merits of Skramble are dependent on how well it can integrate with current learning systems and teaching practices. To devise an adaptive programming environment which has the features to create an educational learning environment, a number of learning theories from existing literature are discussed first (Sect. 2.1) after which existing systems which are used to teach children to programme are reviewed (Sect. 2.2).

2.1 Existing Literature

The Skramble editor is a tool designed for use when teaching computing to students. Literature on learning theory and learning to programme was reviewed to consider how children could learn computing most effectively using Skramble. In this section, existing literature relevant to Skramble is discussed.

Learning Theory. The three most common learning theories (behaviourism, cognitivism and constructivism) can be used as a basis for understanding the practices that are applicable to e-learning. The implications of these theories on e-learning is reported from a number of sources in [14]. The findings from each of the common learning theories is presented throughout this section.

From a behaviourist approach the material to be learnt needs to be carefully broken down. Additionally, learners need to be told the outcomes of learning and assessed to check that they have met their required outcomes [15].

Formative assessment which is outlined in [16], as a means of tailoring learning activities based on the completion of previous outcomes of learning, allows learning to be tailored to students based on their individual progress and difficulties. Strategies to facilitate assessment for learning are outlined in [17–19] and include providing explicit learning objectives to pupils, making use of peer assessment and providing immediate feedback to pupils.

The cognitive school of learning suggests that learning material should be received in the form of sensations before perception and processing. The location and display of information is key to the learning outcomes while the difficulty of the material should match the cognitive ability of the learner [20].

Maintaining the difficulty of the material at the correct cognitive level for a learner is referred to as the zone of proximal development, where children are identified as needing the correct scaffolding through challenge completion [21,22]. This is further developed in [23,24] where the two zones of proximal development are outlined: the cognitive and motivation zones, which suggests the need for children's motivation to be maintained. A student's motivation is broken down into attention, relevance, confidence and satisfaction [25].

Constructivists see learners as active agents in the discovery of knowledge where learners should be in control of their learning. Instructors have to provide good interactive instructions and learning needs to be meaningful and illustrative for the learners [14].

Active learning is identified in [26] as a type of learning where the student is the agent of discovery which corresponds closely to the constructivist school of learning. Strategies and environments which most befit active learning are outlined in [27,28]; all advocate authentic, meaningful, collaborative and achievable tasks which call upon higher order cognition, cross-curricular knowledge and a focus on the task at hand as opposed to assessment.

The role of technology in learning is discussed in [29–31], where the authors describe how technology has immense capacity to create quality learners who are well placed to solve real-world problems and in doing so develop deeper knowledge. This is achieved through the interactive and resourceful use of technology and by seeking out knowledge relating to the problem at hand. The flexibility of remote learning in higher education was found to benefit students as it created a better learning philosophy [32–34].

Learning to Programme. Learning to programme is a complicated task which requires the learner to configure a programming environment, comprehend the syntax and additionally consider how to approach the problem at hand.

Learning to programme can be made more accessible through the use of a visual programming language. Scratch is a popular block-based programming environment [35]. Students using Scratch have showed sustained engagement with programming and independently discovered programming concepts [36,37].

The successes of the Scratch system could be due to motivation, simplification and support, which are identified in [38] as key to making programming more accessible. These findings relate closely to the cognitive school of learning where students are identified as needing to remain within the zone of proximal development.

Learning to programme is considered from different psychological perspectives in [39,40] who concur that successful learning is the result of feedback from practicing in an environment which assists in the identification and recovery from errors.

From a behaviourist approach, programming can also be simplified by tutorial-style interactions that allow students to learn to programme syntax languages. This can help students who are not familiar with the syntax of a language, however it can be found to provide too much assistance to students completing problems [41].

Learning to programme is considered from a constructivist approach in [42] where constructive and collaborative learning were seen to increase attainment. The findings in [43] support this and outline a number of practical approaches to achieving constructivist learning. A guide in [44] outlines advice for programming in schools and suggests that much learning of programming happens through guided exploration.

Summary. The existing literature on learning theory and learning to programme provide many requirements for the ideal learning system when learning to programme, many of these requirements were integrated within

TuringLab. Skramble however needs to provide the optimal programming environment within any learning system, in this section the features which Skramble must expose to a host learning system are discussed.

The behaviourist school of learning defines that the hosting system needs to clearly define learning outcomes and assess their completion of these learning outcomes. This means that Skramble must allow test cases to be defined by the hosting system so that the correctness of the task can be easily verified to affirm that students have completed their learning outcomes.

To correspond with recommendations from the cognitivist perspectives, the hosting system needs to again display learning outcomes but additionally suggest challenge difficulty. To enable the challenge difficulty to be inferred over time Skramble needs to provide feedback to the hosting system as to how challenging users found the task at hand. Having clearly defined difficulty allows students to select challenges of appropriate difficulty and for which they have already been introduced to the concepts.

A key requirement identified both from cognitive learning theory and pragmatic experience of learning to programme is the need to make programming accessible. With reference to syntax programming, this outlines the need to assist students in recovering from errors. Additionally, this indicates that challenges need to create meaningful outputs. Therefore Skramble needs to provide error support and graphical output.

From the perspective of the constructivist theory of learning the requirement to create an active learning environment is presented. This means that Skramble should be able to provide reference materials which are relevant to the task at hand, to allow this the hosting system must be able to define which technologies or external packages are needed to solve the problem so that Skramble can provide the relevant documentation.

The requirements identified from the existing literature define some of the overall specifications of Skramble. These requirements along with the aim of Skramble to be integrated into an existing learning system and used alongside ordinary teaching provide the basis for reviewing and understand existing systems.

2.2 Existing Systems

In this section, existing systems are critically assessed to determine how best to achieve the requirements identified for Skramble in Sect. 2.1. The systems considered generally provide online environments where users can write and run code within their browser, however they are often stand-alone environments which do not interface with existing learning systems.

Figure 1 shows a broad overview of the existing systems. The dashed circles depict the four major functionalities identified in the existing systems. These systems are arranged in a Venn diagram to display each system's relation to a functionality. The labels applied to the functionalities are explained below.

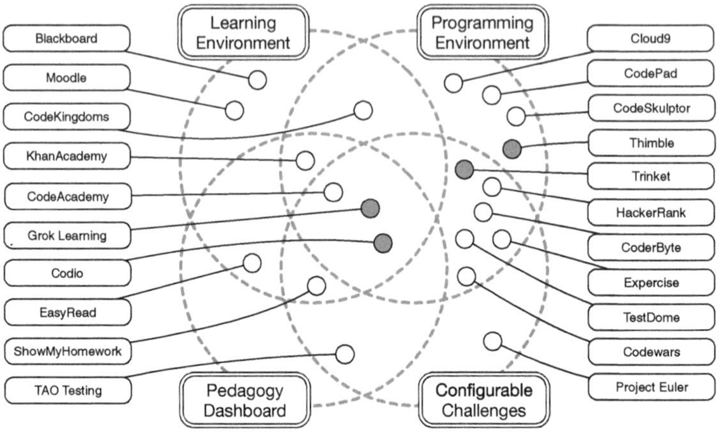

Fig. 1. Venn diagram showing related existing systems.

Learning environment relates to any system which includes teaching material, be that predefined or teacher-created. These systems in general have a large amount of content and are intended for learners to remain within the infrastructure for learning, exercises and testing. Given the aim of Skramble to integrate with existing learning systems it is essential to review them.

Programming environment encompasses systems which have the facility to write and run code. Most systems with this feature also have the ability to test code against predefined or user-specified test cases. Systems with advanced programming environments are important to review in order to consider how to create meaningful and complex challenges while still supporting the students.

Pedagogy dashboard defines any system which has a dashboard through which teachers can view metrics on their pupils. These metrics relate to how a user is interacting with programming tasks and what learning progressions are being made through these interactions. To allow teachers to formatively assess their students, a feature-rich pedagogy dashboard is important. Allowing teachers to differentiate students means they can be kept at the correct cognitive level.

Configurable challenges specifies systems which give users the ability to add customised problem definitions. Problem definitions contain a rich text description of the problem and, more often than not, testing criteria to define when a problem is complete. Reviewing approaches to defining and assessing challenges means that Skramble can make use of elegant challenge specifications which are not too time-consuming for teachers to create.

The aim of Skramble is to create a programming environment which can be used with existing learning systems. The interface through which Skramble is integrated in existing learning systems will have to allow teachers to configure programming tasks or challenges and make it possible for the programming environment to provide feedback on how well the given programming task has been completed. The shaded circles indicate systems which are of interest to the development of Skramble. These systems include Trinket, Thimble, Grok Learning and Codio. A brief analysis of the beneficial features of each of these systems is outlined below.

Trinket[1] is an embeddable code editor and programming environment which allows students to programme using either Python or web technologies. Trinket can be integrated with any website through an iframe, making it incredibly versatile, however it does not provide any feedback on a student's completion of a given task. Trinket executes all code on the browser, making it responsive and able to provide graphical output from executing code.

Thimble[2] is an open source platform for students to create and share projects using web technologies. Thimble uses the Bramble[3] editor which provides a very advanced editing environment for website creation. Thimble is a self-standing website and is designed as a playground with no specific tasks, which makes it very similar to the Scratch system.

Grok Learning[4] is a stand-alone web-based learning platform for Python programming. It includes courses and assignments with assessed programming tasks and a dashboard is available for teachers to monitor student progress. The code is executed on a server using websockets, therefore there is no graphical output, however the full Python programming language can be used.

Codio[5] is a web-based integrated development environment for students to learn and practice programming. Students can enroll in courses tailored to teach different programming languages. Teachers can create custom programming environments and challenges. Student progress and engagement can be analysed through a teacher dashboard. Codio has limited ability to be embedded in existing learning systems, however the adaptability of the programming environment and inclusion of a teacher dashboard make this a very versatile stand-alone system.

Summary. Existing systems were reviewed to understand how other systems have implemented requirements for a programming environment. In general the existing systems provide advanced programming environments which are engaging for children to use, however they either provide their own learning system complete with feedback on student progress or the feedback (if at all) they provide is not appropriate. Skramble must provide an equally advanced programming environment which allows students to discover computing concepts through challenge and exploration. However, Skramble must also allow integration with existing learning systems, thus making it easy for teachers to adopt it in their current classroom practices.

[1] https://trinket.io/.
[2] https://thimble.mozilla.org/.
[3] http://blog.humphd.org/thimble-and-bramble/.
[4] https://groklearning.com.
[5] https://codio.com/.

3 Design

This section details the design process which TuringLab, the case study system went through to fulfil requirements and features identified in Sect. 2. A participatory design process was used during development.

The design process began with requirement gathering from children at volunteer-run programming clubs before development was commenced and this feedback continued throughout the software development life-cycle.

The current design of the TuringLab system is the result of a number of iterations using the lessons from previous stages of the design process to improve the system and features. Feedback collected from children during the design process was in the form of open ended questions to achieve the greatest insight into how children used the software.

1. **Functional Mockup**
   A functional mockup was created as early as possible. This allowed children to access a number of programming challenges and view the solutions. This functionality was provided on a single page, with the specification of the challenge included in the comments section of the code. Children got confused by the cluttered interface and did not naturally read the comments contained within the code to understand what was required in the challenge.
2. **Alpha Design**
   The alpha design split the selection of challenges and completion of challenges onto separate pages and displayed the challenge specification separately to the code. This version allowed children to write code on their browser and run or test the code on the server. The system was not suitably responsive for children who often ran the challenges many times during completion; both the lack of graphical output and inclusion of code testing made the children lose engagement very quickly. The benefits of testing from an educator's perspective did not outweigh the lack of engagement from children.
3. **Beta Design**
   The beta design moved code execution from the server to the client. This meant the system was far more responsive for the users and outputs to running code could be displayed graphically. In previous trials only a selection of children used the system and they quickly lost engagement. In this version all the children learning Python used the system and maintained engagement and enjoyed the outputs they produced. The graphical outputs seemed to assist children in gaining familiarity with the concepts of iteration and selection. Running code on the client meant challenges were of reduced complexity and were not tested; however, this was worthwhile to maintain child engagement.
4. **Current Design**
   The current design takes much the same form as the beta design; however, provides an interface for teachers to overview the progress which children were making when completing challenges. This means that teachers can see errors and solutions in real time. The volunteers assisting with the coding sessions found these features very beneficial in order to provide the proper scaffolding;

however, the greatest benefit was to encourage discussion following a session. Children were asked to run their favorite solutions and then took it in turns to explain how they had achieved the output which was displayed on the large screen.

Every stage of the design process which the TuringLab system went through informed the implementation of the features within the system. Many proposed features for Skramble were added as a result of feedback from students using the TuringLab system. By approaching the design of Skramble from the point of view of its application and benefit to a learning system, has helped formalise feature requirements by what is needed from the perspective of an end user.

Figure 2 shows the current student interface looks in the TuringLab system and how the different screens are linked to one another. This interface is comprised of three main screens: selecting a group, selecting a challenge within a group and completing a challenge. When completing a challenge, children are able to access a help page, run the challenge code and access different versions of the code. Important features to note for Skramble is the ability to access help relating to the challenge at hand.

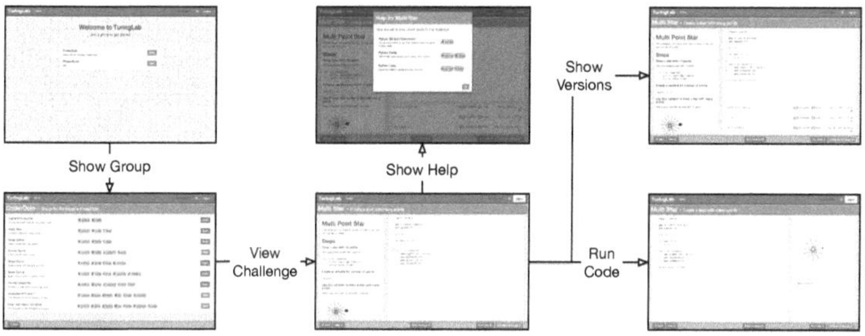

Fig. 2. Student interface user interaction flow.

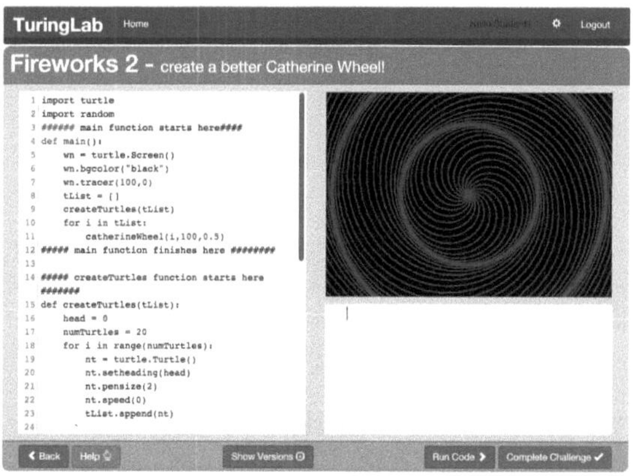

Fig. 3. Student running code screen.

Figure 3 shows the screen when a child has run a challenge. The interface contained within the central section of the screen (including the code editor, graphical output and terminal) shown is similar to what will be provided by Skramble. The code editor is to the left and provides full syntax highlighting. The output of the code is on the right and provides a graphical output in the form of the Python Turtle[6] graphics and a terminal output which displays print messages and allows children to provide standard input.

4 Implementation

This section outlines the proposed implementation of Skramble. The requirements for Skramble were heavily informed from the implementation of the TuringLab system which was completed incrementally alongside the design process. This allowed the TuringLab system to transform quickly based on the requirements identified at different stages of the design process without having to modify the interface through which the programming environment is integrated within the system. The design process from Sect. 3 serves as further requirements gathering and design specification for Skramble.

Skramble is heavily based on Bramble[7], an editor adapted by Mozilla from Brackets[8], an open source editor created by Adobe. To allow Python code to be executed, Scramble makes use of the Skulpt[9] library which is a JavaScript library used to compile Python code to JavaScipt; thus allowing Python code to be executed on the client side.

The overall architecture of Skramble can be seen in Fig. 4. This diagram shows the central core of Skramble and the different interfaces which are available to a learning system when interacting with Skramble. As with the Bramble

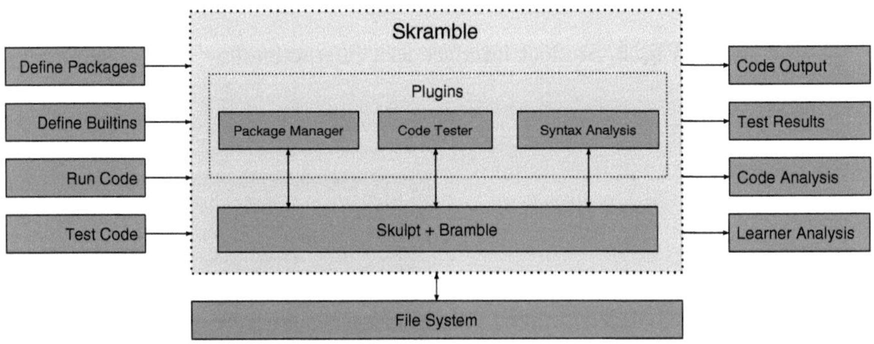

Fig. 4. System architecture.

[6] https://docs.python.org/3.4/library/turtle.html.
[7] https://github.com/mozilla/brackets.
[8] https://github.com/adobe/brackets.
[9] http://www.skulpt.org/.

editor, Skramble is designed to be hosted within an environment through use of an iframe. To allow communication between the host environment and the editor, post messages are used to communicate with the iframe.

The Bramble editor is integrated with a host environment in a very similar way, however, Skramble adds further functionality to that interface making it suitable for both running and testing Python code. Additionally the interface through which plugins are integrated with Bramble provide the perfect ability to create isolated additions to the code editor which can perform advanced functionality or analysis of the code.

Any learning system which hosts Skramble is provided with full control of the file system. This means that Skramble does not store any data on users or programming tasks, therefore, there is no requirement for a separate database or storage system. Though this leaves complexity to the learning system it ensures a very clean interface with the code editor.

The learning system which hosts Skramble is able to configure which package dependencies are required or define Python built-in functions using either Python or JavaScript. The built-in functions provided to Skramble are available globally when executing the Python code and these could overwrite existing Python functionality or provide an interface to external APIs.

There are a number of interfaces through which Skramble can be requested to perform an action. Code can be run using Skramble and when the code has finished executing both the graphical output and terminal output are returned to the learning system. Code can be tested using Skramble based on test cases defined in the file system when tests are completed test results are returned to the learning system, as appropriate.

Through use of a syntax analysis plugin Skramble can provide static code analysis on the code base contained within the editor. This static analysis is used internally within Skramble to advise the user when there is an error with their code. Additionally, the results of this analysis are sent to the learning system which hosts Skramble through emitting an event. The Bramble editor provides an event emitter interface which informs the hosting environment when code has been changed or ran. Skramble provides the same events alongside additional events for when code has finished running, errors have occurred or code analysis has been completed.

Whenever the host system modifies packages or built-in functions using the Skramble interfaces the file system is updated to reflect these changes. As a result the programming environment is persisted entirely through the file system. This is a very important system design decision as it allows the code in any Skramble editor to be shared with any system using the Skramble editor. Therefore teachers using different learning systems to deliver content are easily able to share resources with other teachers.

Potential mechanisms to integrate the Skramble editor with learning systems are shown in Fig. 5. Skramble can be directly embedded within a host learning system, embedded using the LTI 2.0 standard using a wrapper or embedded using an iframe wrapper.

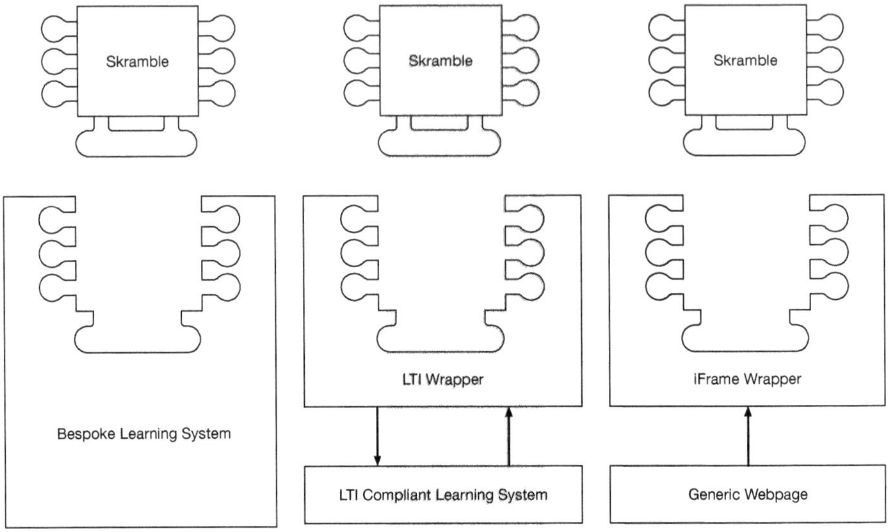

Fig. 5. System integration.

In the first example, the Skramble environment is being used in a bespoke learning system where the host manages the data which Skramble uses. The host learning system can interact with any of the interfaces provided by Skramble giving precise control of the embedded editor.

In the second example the Skramble environment is being integrated through the LTI 2.0 standard. Here the LTI wrapper system otherwise known as the tool provider manages the Skramble editor data, interacts with the Skramble interfaces and also provides authorisation. When the tool is launched by the LTI compliant learning system it provides user details so as the tool provider can expose the correct editor environment.

The final example is in many ways similar to the LTI integration, the wrapper system manages interaction with Skramble and provide user authorisation. In this example however the learning system or generic website cannot provide details of the student using the system therefore a user would have to login to the wrapper system to access, edit and run their stored code.

5 Evaluation

TuringLab was used to assess the required features and potential integration for Skramble. This approach was taken to ensure that development of Skramble is effective and to the most part the features are known a priori. In this section, TuringLab is evaluated to reflect on the beneficial pedagogical features of the Python programming environment. This analysis is discussed in relation to the future development of Skramble.

TuringLab was designed from a user centered approach; children attended volunteer-led programming clubs and made use of the system to learn Python. At a number of the programing clubs, children also learnt Scratch[10]. When learning Scratch, an interface was provided to give the children well-scaffolded projects to work on, which recorded their progress in a similar way to the TuringLab system.

From discussions with children during the process of developing TuringLab, it was clear that having a graphical output for their programmes in the form of Python Turtle graphics was very important. This meant children could easily detect errors in their solution through visual comparison and the output to their code was something that they could be proud of. Furthermore, the visual output allowed non technical volunteers to both reason about issues in a child's code and see merit in complex creations. This observation supports the requirement identified in Sect. 2 to have meaningful output from code execution.

Feedback on the TuringLab system was collected over the course of 8 programming clubs. These programming clubs were funded by the Department of Computing at Imperial College London and therefore were free to attend and did not require attendees to bring any computer equipment. The first 3 sessions were Python only mixed sessions which had a largely male demographic, the following 5 sessions allowed children to select between Scratch and Python programming but was for girls only.

Over the 5 sessions a total of 122 responses were collected from attendees. Given that a number of individuals were repeat attendees this equated to 70 unique respondents completing feedback on the programming clubs; 21 of these unique respondents reviewed the Scratch system and 49 reviewed the Python system.

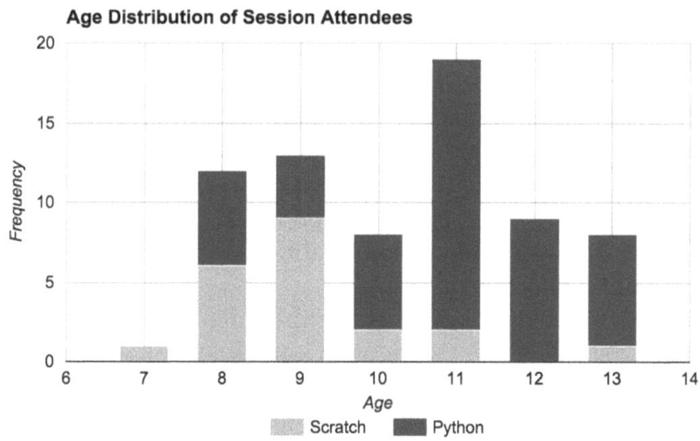

Fig. 6. Comparison of programming language choice for attendees of different ages.

[10] https://scratch.mit.edu/.

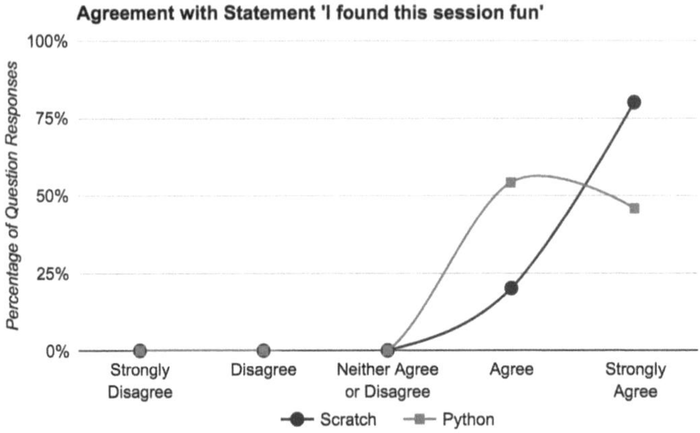

Fig. 7. Comparison of agreement with statement ‘I found this session fun’.

Figure 6 shows the number of children learning Python using TuringLab and the number of children learning Scratch. It can be seen that generally older children chose to learn Python whereas younger children favoured Scratch. However, children of all ages learnt both Python and Scratch suggesting both languages are appealing to children between the ages of 7 to 13.

Throughout the project a focus of the system has been to create an environment which children enjoy using and which maintains their engagement. To find out the level of enjoyment and therefore potential long term engagement, children were questioned on how enjoyable the session was. Figure 7 shows that children found the session slightly more enjoyable when using Scratch than Python but overall enjoyed learning both.

In Fig. 7, it can be seen that the programing clubs facilitate a high level of engagement from children; however, as the children were not found to enjoy using the Python system as much as the Scratch system it shows that there are potential areas of improvement. The issues with TuringLab may be due to not having the correct amount of scaffolding to support children through the challenges or that younger children find syntax programming more challenging than block programming. This presents a potential plugin for Skramble, which could be realised through a block-based editor for the Python Turtle library, similar to the Trinket block code editor[11].

Figure 8 shows the extent to which children agree that the error messages were easy to understand. From this figure it can be seen that there are a number of respondents that did not find the error messages easy to understand. This presents the need for Skramble to provide more readable error messages. This improvement would not necessarily reduce the error rate but it would allow children to recover from errors more easily through having the correct scaffolding available. Reducing the need to seek help from a teacher is vital to encourage

[11] https://trinket.io/blocks.

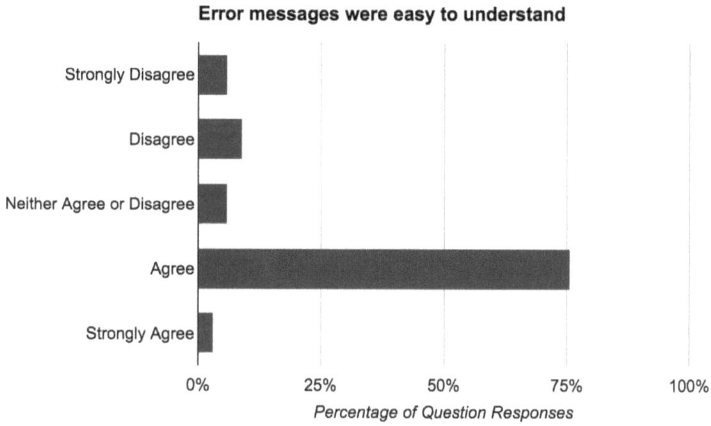

Fig. 8. Children agreement with statement 'Error messages were easy to understand'.

an active learning environment, where children can work at their own pace on challenges of their choice.

Figure 9 shows the number of children using the system who clicked on an error message for more information. Clicking on the error message provides further syntax analysis of the error message, while currently syntax analysis only checks correct parenthesis matching. The large number of children that clicked on error messages shows the importance of providing further assistance to the children to recover from errors within Skramble. Furthermore, this shows the importance of allowing plugins to be added to the Skramble editor, which can easily provide further functionality, be that created by senior teachers, academics or other children.

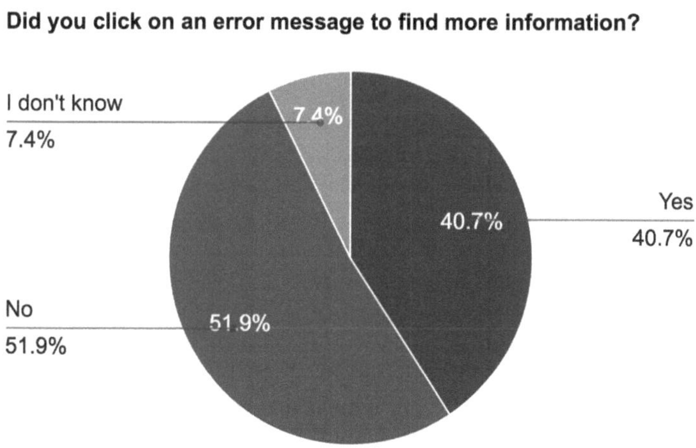

Fig. 9. Pie chart showing the proportion of children who clicked on error messages.

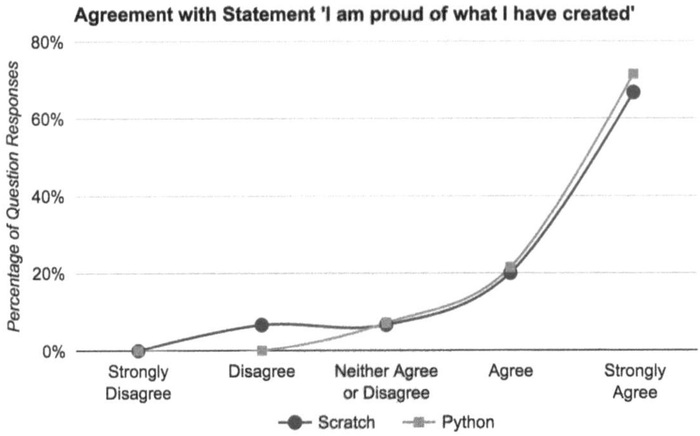

Fig. 10. Comparison of agreement with statement 'I am proud of what I have created'.

It can be seen in Fig. 10 that in general children are equally proud of what they have created in both Scratch and Python. This result is surprising, since children are able to create games and animation using Scratch whereas with Python they create far less appealing projects (in the time available during the programming clubs), but which are also more challenging. This result suggests that children are proud of completing challenging projects which feel more difficult or meaningful.

Figure 11 depicts the proportion of respondents who made use of the help button within the TuringLab system. The help button brings up resources related to the current challenge. Given that a third of children used the help button it suggests that the system nurtures an active learning environment for some of the children. This feedback does not, however suggest if the help resources were useful in resolving the issues faced. Given the number of children using the help feature and the desired adaptability of the Skramble editor, this affirms the need to have reference material available from within the programming environment which does not need to be added by the teacher.

Figure 12 shows a spiral created by a child during one of the sessions. The child was very proud of the work completed which could be seen from the passion with which they explained the spiral at the end of the class. The teacher display mode facilitates children discussing their favorite creations during the session. This requirement for teachers and children to be able to showcase work is a feature that needs to be present in Skramble.

Figure 13 shows the open ended responses when children who programmed using Python were are asked 'What do you like best about coding?'. There are a number of statements related to the end product, including one response which states 'YOU CAN DO ANYTHING'. This is a key point about providing a child friendly Python programing environment, in that children are supported but not limited in what they can create. This also shows the need to allow external built-in functionality to be defined, which will mean that there truly is no limit to the possible output from the children.

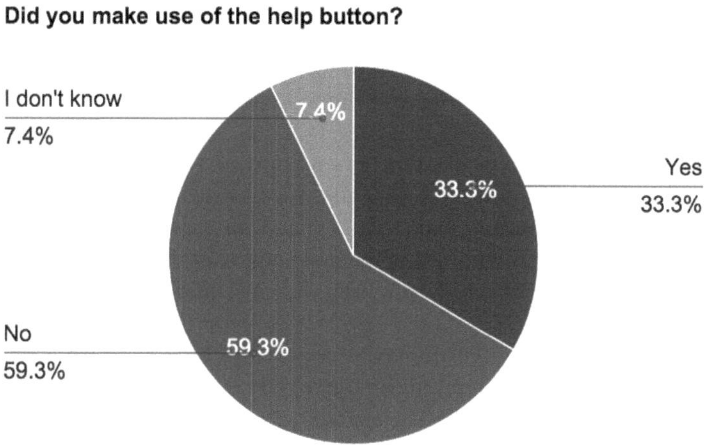

Fig. 11. Pie chart showing the proportion of children who made use of the help interface.

Fig. 12. Example of children work created on TuringLab.

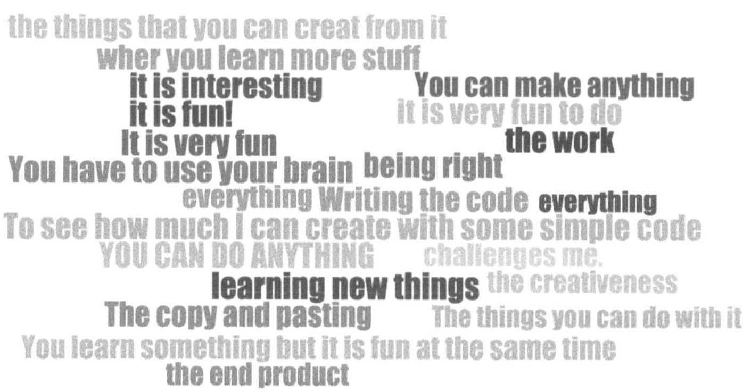

Fig. 13. Word cloud of student responses to question 'What do you like best about coding?'.

6 Conclusions

This paper outlined TuringLab, a system for learning Python programming and proposed Skramble, an adaptable and embeddable Python programming environment.

TuringLab was used to assist teachers as part of their standard teaching in delivering the practical elements of the computing curriculum through the setting and assessing of programming exercises. TuringLab was designed as a pedagogical system for children to complete programming exercises in a challenge-based programming environment which provides support and assistance during their completion of challenges.

Overall the feedback for TuringLab was positive. It is clear from the sessions (and the ensuing feedback) that children enjoyed using TuringLab and a number of children have returned both to TuringLab outside of the programming sessions and to the sessions the following weeks. Given that the children are proud of their final results it is clear that the system is providing children with interesting and hard challenges. This is likely to have been afforded by the ability of TuringLab to display a graphical output from the code execution.

TuringLab showcases the need for a Python programming environment which can be used in learning systems. TuringLab is a system which children have engaged with and enjoyed using over the course of a number of programming clubs. There are however, a number of enhancements to the Python programming environment which will be provided by Skramble and these advancements are detailed in Sect. 7. These extensions will allow TuringLab to provide greater assistance to children when they are seen to struggle and hence facilitate more complex challenges.

Skramble is based on existing open source projects and provides a feature-rich programming environment that abstracts functionality such as syntax analysis, code execution, error handling, and output capture. The features identified for inclusion within the Skramble programming environment are those which have been seen to provide the greatest educational benefit to users of the TuringLab system. The system architectural decisions made in the conceptualisation of Skramble were made with a mind for usability, adaptability and expansivity.

The Skramble editor can be used and integrated into many learning environments (through the use of the Learning Tool Interoperability standard or through the use of an iframe wrapper), while allowing for resources to be shared across these environments. This gives great power to educators by allowing them to not only create resources but also to share them. By building upon an open source editor which has a standardised interface for plugins, we open up the potential for Skramble to be extended by allowing for the addition of many beneficial packages, as necessary.

7 Future Work

In this Section the road-map for improving Python code execution using Skulpt and the development of Skramble is discussed. Having completed and evaluated

TuringLab, there are a number of improvements to be made particularly in how the Skulpt library is used to execute Python code and these improvements will be integrated during the development of Skramble.

First and foremost, Skramble must develop on the Bramble editor to include the ability to execute Python code. This fundamental requirement means that the Skulpt library is integrated into Bramble to give both terminal interaction and show graphical output from executing code. Following this, external interfaces will be added to Skramble to allow its basic integration with a learning system. This will bring Skramble to the level that the TuringLab Python programming environment currently resides.

Following basic integration with a learning system the Skulpt library will be modified to allow more than a single source file to be included in the project. This functionality is built into the Bramble editor, however this will need to be integrated with the Skulpt library. Allowing multiple files will mean the programming environment can provide advanced helper functions without confusing or distracting children.

Having extended Skramble to allow for more than a single source file, the next step is to extend it further in order for it to provide more advanced error messages than those shown from the Skulpt library. These improvements will mainly be to reduce the occurrence of 'Bad Input' as an error message as this is not understandable (or useful) to novice programmers. Once the error messages have been improved, a basic plugin will be created to provide the syntax analysis which is found in TuringLab. The purpose of this plugin is to give the foundations to more advanced syntax analysis plugins without the need to modify the entire Skramble source code.

The next stage of the Skramble development timeline is to allow Skulpt to import external libraries for use by children, but these have to be individually configured for use with Skulpt. This is the approach taken by the Trinket[12] team to allow components of numpy[13] and matplotlib[14] to be accessible through Skulpt. This is the approach that will be taken to allow external packages using Skramble.

Finally, when Skramble provides the proposed Python programming environment, its features will need to be tested and iterated upon. To give students the ability to use and interact with Skramble, the open source project Thimble (See footnote 2) will be modified to use Skramble as opposed to Bramble. This provides a quick approach to creating a system which children can interact with.

References

1. Stergioulas, L.K., Drenoyianni, H.: Pursuing Digital Literacy in Compulsory Education. New Literacies and Digital Epistemologies, vol. 43. Peter Lang Publishing Inc., New York (2011)

[12] https://trinket.io/python.
[13] http://www.numpy.org/.
[14] http://matplotlib.org/.

2. Gove, M.: Michael Gove speaks about computing and education technology (2014). https://www.gov.uk/government/speeches/michael-gove-speaks-about-computing-and-education-technology. Accessed 27 Aug 2015
3. Cellan-Jones, R.: A computing revolution in schools, September 2014. http://www.bbc.co.uk/news/technology-29010511. Accessed 4 Jun 2015
4. Department for Education. National curriculum in England: computing programmes of study, September 2013. https://www.gov.uk/government/publications/national-curriculum-in-england-computing-programmes-of-study. Accessed 4 Jun 2015
5. Jones, S.P.: Code to joy. Times Educ. Suppl. (2015)
6. Computing at School. Computing Teachers Call For More Training Amidst Concerns Pupils Know More Than Them, January 2015. http://www.computingatschool.org.uk/index.php?id=current-news&post=quickstart-launch-2. Accessed 4 Jun 2015
7. OurICT. Ten Resources for Teaching Computer Science (2015). http://www.ourict.co.uk/teaching-computer-science/. Accessed 22 Aug 2015
8. Brown, N.C.C., Kölling, M., Crick, T., Jones, S.P., Humphreys, S., Sentance, S.: Bringing computer science back into schools: lessons from the UK. Special Interest Group on Computer Science Education (2013)
9. EdSurge. Teaching Kids to Code (2015). https://www.edsurge.com/research/guides/teaching-kids-to-code. Accessed 14 Oct 2015
10. Flanagan, J.: 10 places in Britain where you can learn how to write computer code (2013). http://www.theguardian.com/technology/2013/oct/14/learn-how-to-code. Accessed 27 Aug 2015
11. Zheng, S., Rosson, M.B., Shih, P.C., Carroll, J.M.: Understanding student motivation, behaviors and perceptions in MOOCs. In: ACM Conference on Computer Supported Cooperative Work & Social Computing, March 2015
12. Ofsted. Virtual learning environments: an evaluation of their development in a sample of educational settings (2009)
13. EDUCAUSE. 7 things you should know about learning tools interoperability. Technical report, EDUCAUSE (2013)
14. Alzaghoul, A.F.: The implication of the learning theories on implementing e-learning courses. Res. Bull. Jordan ACM **11**(11), 27–30 (2012)
15. Mödritscher, F.: e-Learning theories in practice: a comparison of three. Sci. Technol., 3–18 (2006)
16. Black, P., Wiliam, D.: Inside the Black Box: Raising Standards Through Classroom Assessment. Granada Learning, London (1998)
17. Black, P., Harrison, C., Lee, C., Marshall, B., Wiliam, D.: Assessment For Learning: Putting it into Practice. McGraw-Hill Education, London (2003)
18. Cooper, D., Adams, K.: Talk about Assessment: Strategies and Tools to Improve Learning. Thomson/Nelson, Toronto (2007)
19. Knight, J.: The assessment for learning strategy. Technical report, Department for children, schools and families (2008)
20. Anderson, T.: The Theory and Practice of Online Learning. Athabasca University Press, Athabasca (2008)
21. Vygotsky, L.: Mind in Society: The Development of Higher Psychological Processes. Harvard University Press, Cambridge (1978)
22. Wood, D.: How Children Think and Learn: The Social Context of Cognitive Development. Blackwell, Oxford (1998)

23. Brophy, J.: Toward a model of the value aspects of motivation in education: developing appreciation for particular learning domains and activities. Educ. Psychol. **34**(2), 75–85 (1999)
24. Juriševič, M.: Creativity in the zone of proximal motivational development. In: Facilitating Effective Student Learning Through Teacher Research and Innovation, pp. 415–429 (2010)
25. Keller, J.M., Suzuki, K.: Use of the ARCS Motivation Model in courseware design (1988)
26. Adler, M.J.: The Paideia Proposal: An Education Manifesto. Macmillan, New York (1982)
27. Brophy, J.E.: Synthesis of research on strategies for motivating students to learn. Educ. Leadersh. **5**(2), 40–48 (1987)
28. Scott Grabinger, R., Dunlap, J.C.: Rich environments for active learning: a definition. Res. Learn. Technol. **3**(2), 5–34 (1995)
29. Huffaker, D.A., Calvert, S.L.: The new science of learning: active learning, metacognition, and transfer of knowledge in e-learning applications. J. Educ. Comput. Res. **29**(3), 325–334 (2003)
30. Pearlman, B.: Making 21st century schools creating learner-centered schoolplaces/workplaces for a new culture of students at work. Educ. Technol. **49**(5), 14–19 (2009)
31. Walser, N.: Spotlight on Technology in Education. Harvard Education Letter Spotlight, vol. 7. Harvard Educational Publishing Group, Cambridge (2011)
32. Twigg, C.A.: Quality, Cost and Access: The Case for Redesign. Prentice-Hall, New Jersey (2002)
33. Gordon, N.: Flexible pedagogies: technology-enhanced learning (2014)
34. Arkorful, V., Abaidoo, N.: The role of e-learning, advantages and disadvantages of its adoption in higher education. Int. J. Instr. Technol. Distance Learn., 29 (2015)
35. Maloney, J., Burd, L., Kafai, Y.: Scratch: a sneak preview. In: Creating, Connecting and Collaborating Through Computing (2004)
36. Maloney, J.H., Peppler, K., Kafai, Y.: Programming by choice: urban youth learning programming with scratch. In: ACM SIGCSE Technical Symposium on Computer Science Education (2008)
37. Franklin, D., Conrad, P., Boe, B., Nilsen, K.: Assessment of computer science learning in a scratch-based outreach program. In: Proceeding of the 44th ACM Technical Symposium on Computer Science Education (2013)
38. Kelleher, C., Pausch, R.: Lowering the barriers to programming: a taxonomy of programming environments and languages for novice programmers. ACM Comput. Surv. (CSUR) **37**, 83–137 (2005)
39. Hoc, J.-M., Nguyen-Xuan, A.: Language semantics, mental models and analogy. Psychol. Program. **10**, 139–156 (1990)
40. Gomes, A., Mendes, A.J.N.: Learning to program-difficulties and solutions. In: International Conference on Engineering Education, pp. 1–5 (2007)
41. Deek, F.P., McHugh, J.A.: A survey and critical analysis of tools for learning programming. Comput. Sci. Educ. **8**(2), 130–178 (1998)
42. Van Gorp, M.J., Grissom, S.: An empirical evaluation of using constructive classroom activities to teach introductory programming. Comput. Sci. Educ. **11**(3), 247–260 (2001)
43. Sentance, S., Csizmadia, A.: Computing in the curriculum: challenges and strategies from a teacher's perspective. Educ. Inf. Technol. **22**, 469–495 (2016)
44. Kemp, P., Dorling, M., Humphreys, S., Hunt, S., Jackson, C.: Computing in the national curriculum: a guide for secondary teachers (2014)

Hybrid Ranking Method for E-Learning Platform Selection: A Flexible Approach

Soraya Chachoua(✉) and Nouredine Tamani(✉)

L3i Laboratory, University of La Rochelle, La Rochelle, France
{soraya.chachoua,nouredine.tamani}@univ-lr.fr, ntamani@gmail.com

Abstract. E-Learning platforms comparison helps users select the most suitable platform according to their individual pedagogical needs and objectives. However, from decision support perspective, selecting the optimal platform in terms of tools and services that meet user's requirements still remain difficult to achieve. Thus, we investigate in this paper an e-Learning evaluation method based on a symbolic approach using preference operators and Qualitative Weight and Sum method (QWS) [1] providing a total order among the considered e-Learning systems. However, even the totality ensured by the preference operators we developed, they are still not sufficient from decision making perspective, since they can return a ranking in which several alternatives are all equally and indistinguishably (un)satisfactory. Therefore, we combine our symbolic approach with a flexible ranking method based on linguistic quantifiers and fuzzy quantified propositions along with two new parameters for quality assessment refinement, called *least satisfactory proportion* and *greatest satisfactory proportion*, denoted by *lsp* and *gsp* respectively, to be able to discriminate among alternatives evaluated as equal. The hybrid method obtained can significantly refine the ranking providing users with valuable information to help them make decisions.

1 Introduction and Motivation

The past decade has seen many changes in educational and industrial training methods along with the increasing of the number of users having diverse needs and objectives, and the large adoption of communication and information technologies. Thus, a large number of free and commercial e-Learning systems have been developed in different areas such as education [2], language learning [3], business training [4,5], medicine [6,7] and public administrations [8], etc. which provide on/off-line and remote training making user training more flexible and easier. The multitude of e-learning platforms developed for a single domain (such as in language learning, for instance, we can distinguish tens of e-Learning applications and on-line platforms like *babel*, *busuu*, *duolingo*, *ef*, *tell me more*, *Pimsleur*, etc.) makes it difficult to objectively select the more suitable one according to one's pedagogical needs and objectives.

The choice of a suitable system based on criteria describing the considered e-Learning platforms is of great help for users. Standards and norms such as

G. Costagliola et al. (Eds.): CSEDU 2016, CCIS 739, pp. 214–236, 2017.
DOI: 10.1007/978-3-319-63184-4_12

SCORM[1], QTI[2], IMS[3], etc. define e-Learning quality properties, such as adaptability, sustainability, interoperability and reusability. We refer the reader to [9] for an e-Learning platform evaluation based on the SCORM specification. In addition, many other evaluation approaches have been proposed such as [10], in which the framework considers two models: one addresses the different ways to produce learning processes in an e-Learning system, which has been reused in [11], and the other characterizes the different evaluation criteria of learning models as introduced in [12].

Qualitative methods have also been considered for e-Learning systems evaluation. The most commonly used approach is Qualitative Weight and Sum, denoted by QWS [1]. It relies on a list of weighted criteria [13,14] for the evaluation of e-Learning systems. In practice, it is based on qualitative weight symbols expressing six levels of importance, namely: E for *essential*, $*$ for *extremely valuable*, # for *very valuable*, + for *valuable*, | for *marginally valuable*, and 0 for *not valuable*. Hence, e-Learning system performance is measured by symbolic weights attached to some criteria [13], such that low-weighted criteria cannot overpower high-weighted ones. For instance, if a criterion weighted #, the platform can only be judged # or lesser (+, | or 0) but not $*$ or higher. To obtain a global evaluation for a platform, QWS approach aggregates the symbols attached to criteria through a simple counting, which is finally used to rank the considered e-Learning systems. Because of the naive aggregation function used by the approach, the result may be counterintuitive and not clear to explain and justify. For example, let us suppose three e-Learning systems, denoted by e_1, e_2, e_3 respectively, for which the aggregation function delivers the results as summarized in Table 1. It is easy to conclude that e_1 is better than e_2, since e_1 is better than e_2 on symbol $*$ and both tied the score for the other symbols. But, it is not that easy to say whether e_1 is better than e_3 or not, because even though e_1 performs well on symbol $*$, e_3 is much more better than $e1$ on symbols # and +. Therefore, further analysis has to be conducted to conclude. As some e-Learning systems are not comparable, then the approach delivers a pre-order over the evaluated platforms.

Table 1. Example of e-Learning system aggregation results.

	E	$*$	#	+	|	0
e_1	-	3	4	-	2	-
e_2	-	2	4	-	2	-
e_3	-	2	8	1	2	-

To deal with this issue, one can consider the Analytic Hierarchy Process (AHP) method [14]. AHP is used to deal with complex decision-making

[1] SCORM: Sharable Content Object Reference Model, http://scorm.com.
[2] QTI: Question and Test Interoperability, http://www.imsglobal.org.
[3] IMS: Instructional Management Systems, http://www.imsglobal.org.

processes. It translates the symbols defined in QWS into values as detailed in Table 2, borrowed from [1]. Thus, AHP captures both subjective and objective values, checks their consistency and reduces bias decision making in evaluating e-Learning systems [15]. The criteria are gathered up by category and subcategory. Results of feature category or subcategory evaluation computed by the weighted calculation functions are percentages of the form of a real number as described in [14]. For example, let us say that the percentage returned for the feature *Chat* is 14%; then, according to Table 2, the judgment of this result is between "marginally valuable" and "valuable", but which the user should consider. The percentages returned can be difficult to interpret for the comparison of e-Learning platforms when several attributes have to be dealt with.

Table 2. QWS symbols translated into AHP weights.

	QWS	Weight in AHP
Essential	*E*	5
Extremely valuable	*	4
Very valuable	#	3
Valuable	+	2
Marginally valuable	|	1
Not valuable	0	0

These above methods return results which can be less expressive and non-intuitive enough from a user standpoint for system quality assessment and ranking. Therefore, we investigate in this paper methods for e-Learning systems assessment and ranking combining QWS values, symbolic preference relations and comparison operators, which have been proved to be total orders allowing to rank a set of e-Learning platforms from the most to the least optimal, helping the end user to make a decision. Notwithstanding, the practical application of approach we proposed revealed a limitation from decision making standpoint, in the sense that a large set of alternatives can be evaluated as equally (un)satisfactory owing to its purely qualitative nature. A need for an hybrid approach mixing both qualitative and quantitative behaviors is then underlined and a flexible solution is also developed based on fuzzy set theory [16] as a first attempt to provide a possible feasible solution.

Indeed, fuzzy sets approach is considered here as a formal theoretical basis since fuzzy sets are simultaneously quantitative and qualitative, and provide a general model for user preference expression and interpretation based on fuzzy predicates such as *high*, *expensive*, *young*, etc. Particular kind of fuzzy conditions, called quantified propositions, involving linguistic quantifiers have also been defined. A quantified proposition is based on a linguistic quantifier, which expresses a compromise between the universal quantifier ($\forall$) and the existential quantifier ($\exists$). A linguistic quantifier refers to expressions such as *most*, *almost all*, *around 4*, etc. For instance, the sentence *"find colleges that have most of their alumni are professionally successful"* involves a quantified proposition defined by the linguistic quantifier *most of*, and expresses both quantity and quality in terms of what extent the expression is evaluated as true. The closer to 1 the evaluation is, the better. We consider the criteria describing e-Learning platforms as a fuzzy set of important criteria (from the user perspective) then we compute for each platform the truth value of the following fuzzy quantified proposition: *"almost_all the criteria are important"*. This truth value expresses a quantitative evaluation of the alternatives in the sense that it corresponds to the extend platform's criteria are evaluated as important by the user. After that, we define two new parameters to assess the quality of the subsets of criteria satisfying the truth value of the quantified proposition. They are denoted lsp and gsp and stand for *the least satisfactory proportion* and *the greatest satisfactory proportion* respectively. These parameters are used to break ties among equally evaluated alternatives (based on the truth value of the considered fuzzy quantified proposition) from qualitative point of view. The hybrid approach obtained shows a significant refinement of the final ranking which can greatly help users make decision for e-Learning platform selection.

It is note worthy that this paper is an extended version of our previous research paper [17].

The remainder of the paper is structured as follows. Section 2 details our symbolic-based approach for e-Learning systems evaluation. Section 3 presents an illustrative example of our approach to evaluate and to rank a set of open-source e-Learning systems. In Sect. 4, a reminder of linguistic quantifiers and the interpretation of fuzzy quantified propositions for preference expression and modeling are introduced. Section 5 details the application of the fuzzy quantification based approach to our application context (ranking e-Learning platforms), while introducing the new parameters for ranking refinement. Finally, Sect. 6 concludes the paper and introduces some future work.

2 Hybrid E-Learning System Evaluation Approach

In this section, we detail our approach for e-Learning platform evaluation and ranking relying on symbols borrowed from QWS method and qualitative preference relation and comparison operators. In Subsect. 2.1, we introduce our evaluation approach and in Subsect. 2.2, we show the use of our approach for e-learning platform ranking.

2.1 Symbolic Approach for E-Learning Platforms Evaluation

We define the evaluation symbols as follows.

Definition 1 (Evaluation Symbols). *The evaluation symbols as defined in QWS approach are: E = essential, * = extremely valuable, # = very valuable, + = valuable, | = marginally valuable and 0 = not valuable. We denote by* $\mathcal{S} = \{E, *, \#, +, |, 0\}$ *an ordered set of evaluation symbols.*

We define a preference relations *more preferred than or equal to*, denoted by $\succeq$, and *less preferred than or equal to*, denoted by $\preceq$, over the evaluation symbol set $\mathcal{S}$ as follows.

Definition 2 (Preference Relations $\succeq$ and $\preceq$). *Let $\mathcal{S} = \{E, *, \#, +, |, 0\}$ be an ordered set of evaluation symbols such that: $pos_{\mathcal{S}}(E) = 1$, $pos_{\mathcal{S}}(*) = 2$, $pos_{\mathcal{S}}(\#) = 3$, $pos_{\mathcal{S}}(+) = 4$, $pos_{\mathcal{S}}(|) = 5$, $pos_{\mathcal{S}}(0) = 6$, where $pos_{\mathcal{S}}(\centerdot)$ stands for the position of symbol $\centerdot$ in set $\mathcal{S}$.*
We define the preference relation more preferred than or equal to, *denoted by $\succeq$, over $\mathcal{S}$ as:*

$$\forall (a, b) \in \mathcal{S}^2 : a \succeq b \text{ iff } pos_{\mathcal{S}}(a) \leq pos_{\mathcal{S}}(b) \tag{1}$$

The preference relation less preferred than or equal to, *denoted $\preceq$, is defined as:*

$$\forall (a, b) \in \mathcal{S}^2 : a \preceq b \text{ iff } pos_{\mathcal{S}}(a) \geq pos_{\mathcal{S}}(b) \tag{2}$$

We can easily prove both preference relations $\succeq$ and $\preceq$ are total orders.

Property 1 (Total Order Properties). The preference relations $\succeq$ and $\preceq$ are total orders.

Proof. The proof of property 1 is detailed in Appendix A.

Based on the above defined preference relations, we define two comparison operators named $prefMin$ and $prefMax$, so that it will be possible to compare systems on each criterion describing them. These operators will serve as means to aggregate the evaluations obtained for system criteria.

Definition 3 *($prefMax$ and $prefMin$ Comparison Operators). $prefMax$ and $prefMin$ operators are defined by formulas* (3) *and* (4) *respectively.*
The function $prefMax$ is defined by the following formula (3).

$$\begin{aligned} &\mathcal{S} \times \mathcal{S} \rightarrow \mathcal{S} \\ &(a, b) \mapsto max(a, b) = \begin{cases} a & if\ (a \succeq b) \\ b & otherwise. \end{cases} \end{aligned} \tag{3}$$

The function $prefMin$ is defined by the following formula (4).

$$\begin{aligned} &\mathcal{S} \times \mathcal{S} \rightarrow \mathcal{S} \\ &(a, b) \mapsto min(a, b) = \begin{cases} a & if\ (a \preceq b) \\ b & otherwise. \end{cases} \end{aligned} \tag{4}$$

When we apply the comparison operators $prefMax$ and $prefMin$ over our symbolic set $\mathcal{S}$, we obtain Table 3.

Property 2 ($prefMax$ properties). $prefMax$ is associative, commutative, idempotent, it has E as absorbent element and 0 as neutral element.

Proof. Proofs of $prefMax$ properties are detailed in Appendix A.

Property 3 ($prefMin$ properties). $prefMin$ is associative, commutative, idempotent, it has 0 as absorbent element and E as neutral element.

Proof. Proofs of $prefMin$ properties are detailed in Appendix A.

Table 3. The operators $prefMax$ and $prefMin$ table.

$prefMax$	E	*	#	+	|	0
E	E	E	E	E	E	E
*	E	*	*	*	*	*
#	E	*	#	#	#	#
+	E	*	#	+	+	+
|	E	*	#	+	|	|
0	E	*	#	+	|	0

$prefMin$	E	*	#	+	|	0
E	E	*	#	+	|	0
*	*	*	#	+	|	0
#	#	#	#	+	|	0
+	+	+	+	+	|	0
|	|	|	|	|	|	0
0	0	0	0	0	0	0

2.2 Using Our Comparison Operators to Rank E-Learning Systems

The evaluation of e-Learning platforms is based on categories, each of which defines some criteria as defined in [18], for example the category *Communication tools*, and their criterion such as *Chat*. Categories and their criteria are summarized in Table 4. The five categories considered in platform evaluation are:

- Communication tools
- Software and installation
- Administrative tools and security
- Hardware presentation tools
- Management features

To evaluate each category, we use the comparison operators $prefMax$ and $prefMin$. But to evaluate a considered e-Learning system, we need the evaluation of the five categories. For that purpose, we define two aggregation operators, called $prefMinMax$ and $prefMaxMin$, which are based on our comparison operators.

Definition 4 *($prefMinMax$). Let $\mathcal{A}$ be a matrix of n lines and m columns of evaluation symbols of $\mathcal{S}$. We define the minimum guaranteed satisfaction value as follows.*

We denote a matrix from $\mathcal{A}$ as:

$$A = (a_{ij})_{\substack{1 \leq i \leq m \\ 1 \leq j \leq n}} \text{ and } a_{ij} \in \mathcal{S}$$

We define $prefMinMax$ of A as:

$$\begin{aligned} \mathcal{S}^{m \times n} &\to \mathcal{S} \\ A &\mapsto prefMinMax(A) = \\ &\quad prefMin_{1 \leq i \leq m}(prefMax_{1 \leq j \leq n}(a_{ij})) \end{aligned} \tag{5}$$

Definition 5 *($prefMaxMin$). We define the maximum possible satisfaction value of $\mathcal{S}^{m\times n}$ as $prefMaxMin$:*

$$\mathcal{S}^{m\times n} \to \mathcal{S}$$
$$A \mapsto prefMaxMin(A) = prefMax_{1\leq i\leq m}(prefMin_{1\leq j\leq n}(a_{ij})) \quad (6)$$

The $prefMinMax$ operator computes the least optimistic value amongst the criteria, whereas $prefMaxMin$ operator computes the greatest pessimistic value amongst the criteria.

3 Illustrative Example

We apply our e-Learning systems evaluation approach to a set of nine open-source e-Learning platforms below, and which have been tested and compared [19–22].

1. Claroline: version 1.9.2, http://www.claroline.net
2. Dokeos: version 2.1.1, http://www.dokeos.com/fr
3. eFront: version 3.6.11, http://www.efrontlearning.net
4. ILIAS: version 4.1.3, http://www.ilias.de
5. Open ELMS: version 7, http://www.openelms.org
6. Ganesha: version 4.5, http://www.ganesha.fr
7. Olat: version 7.2.1, http://www.olat.org
8. AnaXagora: version 3.5, http://www.anaxagora.tudor.lu
9. Sakai: version 10.4, https://sakaiproject.org

Each criterion takes a symbolic value from the set $\mathcal{S}$ based on users opinions community. To obtain the evaluation of each criterion, we have carried out surveys in our university involving under-graduated students (small group of 10 students), who have tested each e-learning platform during a training session (2 h).

Table 4. Overview of the hierarchy categories and their criteria.

Category	Communication tools					Software & Installation				Administrative tools and Security								Hardware Presentation tools				Management features			
Criterion	Chat	Forum	Mail	Video conference	Calendar	Downloading	Installation	Assistance	Documentation	Courses administration	Tracking progress	Online registration	Learning path creation	Report	Learning path organisation	Test evaluation	Security	Announcements	Learning Objects	Exercices	Content import	Multi course management	Multi user management	Evaluation management	User Group

We are aware that the process is subjective and a different panel of students or users can express different opinions about the e-Learning platforms. We recall that this data collection aims at illustrating the use of our approach. The values obtained for each criterion in its category are summarized in Table 7. The application of our approach on the set of considered systems is performed as follows.

Table 5. *prefMin* and *prefMax* results for Communication Tools category.

	Communication tools						
	chat	**Forum**	**Mail**	**Conference Video**	**Calendar**	*prefMin*	*prefMax*
Claroline	#	#	+	#	+	+	#
Dokeos	*	+	+	*	*	+	*
eFront	|	#	#	+	+	|	#
ILIAS	#	+	+	0	+	0	#
Open ELMS	0	0	*	0	0	0	*
Ganesha	#	#	+	0	0	0	#
Olat	*	*	*	0	*	0	*
AnaXagora	#	#	#	0	+	0	#
Sakai	*	#	*	*	#	#	*

1. for each category in Table 4 we compute values of *prefMin* and *prefMax* for all functionalities based on Definition 3. In Table 5, we display the results obtained by applying our approach on the category "Communication Tools" for our considered set of e-learning platforms.
2. for each category in Table 7 we compute values of *prefMaxMin* and *prefMinMax*. Results of both operators are displayed in Table 6.

According to Table 6,

- we obtain the following ranking if we consider *prefMaxMin* operator:
  (Claroline $\simeq$ Dokeos $\simeq$ eFront $\simeq$ Ganesha $\simeq$ Sakai) $\succ$
  (Ilias $\simeq$ Open ELMS $\simeq$ Olat $\simeq$ AnaXagora)
  such that Claroline, Dokeos, eFront, Ganesha, Sakai equally ranked at the top and outperform Ilias, Open ELMS, Olat, AnaXagora systems, which are ranked at the second position.
- we obtain the following ranking if we consider *prefMinMax* operator:
  Sakai $\succ$ (Claroline $\simeq$ Dokeos $\simeq$ Olat) $\succ$ (eFront $\simeq$ ILIAS $\simeq$ Open ELMS $\simeq$ Ganesha $\simeq$ AnaXagora)
  such that Sakai is the best e-learning system and ranked at the top; then Claroline, Dokeos and Olat are equally ranked at the second position, and also better ranked that eFront, ILIAS, Open ELMS, Ganesha and AnaXagora systems, ranked at the third position.

Table 6. Results of *prefMaxMin* and *prefMinMax* computation over the considered set of e-Learning platforms.

	Communication tools	Software & Installation	Administrative tools and Security	Hardware presentation tools	Management features	*prefMaxMin*	*prefMinMax*
	prefMin	*prefMin*	*prefMin*	*prefMin*	*prefMin*		
Claroline	+	+	+	#	+	#	#
Dokeos	+	|	|	#	+	#	#
eFront	|	#	|	|	|	#	+
ILIAS	0	|	|	0	|	|	+
Open ELMS	0	|	|	0	0	|	+
Ganesha	0	|	+	0	#	#	+
Olat	0	|	|	0	|	|	#
AnaXagora	0	|	|	0	|	|	+
Sakai	#	|	|	0	|	#	*

Furthermore, users can make a choice based on either *prefMaxMin* or *prefMinMax* operators or can combine the results returned by both operators. For instance, in our illustrative example, Claroline, Dokeos, eFront, Ganesha and Sakai are equally optimal platforms according to *prefMaxMin* operator, whereas Sakai is the optimal one according to *prefMinMax* operator. If we consider both operators, we notice that Sakai performs better since it is ranked at the top according to both operators.

For decision making support point a view, it would be interesting to have the possibility to distinguish between the similar or equally ranked options (e-learning systems in our case). The symbolic preference relations used in our case divide a set of items into classes of equivalent items (having the same ranking position). But, what if we combine to the approach a flexible quantitative dimension which refines the ranking in each class of equivalence and permits distinguishing among systems belonging to the same class.

We explore in what follows the opportunity to make use of a fuzzy approach for e-Learning platform ranking. Fuzzy sets theory and fuzzy logics have been widely proved to be powerful theoretical basis to model flexibility and to compute user preferences [23].

Table 7. E-Learning platform's features symbolic evaluation.

	Communication tools					Software & Installation				Administrative tools and Security								Hardware presentation tools				Management features			
	chat	**Forum**	**Mail**	**Video conference**	**Calendar**	**Downloading**	**Installation**	**Assistance**	**Documentation**	**Courses administration**	**Tracking progress**	**Online registration**	**Learning path creation**	**Report**	**Learning path organisation**	**Test evaluation**	**Security**	**Announcements**	**Learning Objects**	**Exercises**	**Content import**	**Multi course management**	**Multi user management**	**Evaluation management**	**User group**
Claroline	#	#	+	#	+	*	+	#	*	#	#	+	+	*	+	#	#	*	*	#	*	+	+	+	#
Dokeos	*	+	+	*	*	#	|	+	+	+	E	+	|	E	|	#	#	*	*	#	*	+	+	E	+
eFront	|	#	#	+	+	*	#	#	#	|	*	+	#	*	#	#	#	|	+	+	+	+	|	+	|
ILIAS	#	+	+	0	+	+	|	|	|	|	+	#	|	|	|	|	#	0	#	+	0	+	|	+	|
Open ELMS	0	0	*	0	0	+	|	+	+	|	#	+	+	#	|	*	|	0	*	0	#	0	0	#	#
Ganesha	#	#	+	0	0	+	|	+	+	#	E	|	+	E	#	#	+	0	#	0	#	#	#	#	#
Olat	*	*	*	0	*	+	|	|	#	#	*	|	+	#	|	#	#	0	*	*	*	|	+	*	*
AnaXagora	#	#	#	0	+	+	|	+	|	#	*	|	*	+	#	#	+	0	+	#	|	|	#	#	*
Sakai	*	#	*	*	#	*	|	*	|	E	*	|	E	*	*	*	|	*	#	0	#	|	#	E	*

4 Fuzzy Quantifier Based Ranking Method

In this section we briefly recall the basis concepts upon which our approach is built. Subsection 4.1 reminds the main definitions related to fuzzy sets. Subsection 4.2 recalls the definitions of linguistic quantifiers. Subsection 4.3 summarizes concepts about fuzzy quantified propositions. Finally, Subsect. 4.4 details the decomposition-based approach as our main tool for the evaluation of fuzzy quantified propositions of the form "Q X are A".

4.1 Fuzzy Set Theory

Fuzzy set theory introduced by Zadeh [16] to express the gradual membership of an element to a set.

Formally, a fuzzy set F is defined on a referential U by a membership function $\mu_F : U \mapsto [0,1]$ such that $\mu_F(x)$ denotes the membership grade of x in F. In particular, $\mu_F(x) = 1$ denotes the full membership of x in F, $\mu_F(x) = 0$ expresses the absolute non-membership and when $0 < \mu_F(x) < 1$, it reflects a partial membership (the closer to 1 $\mu_F(x)$, the more x belongs to F).

The core of F is $Core(F) = \{x \in F : \mu_F(x) = 1\}$ and its support is $Support(F) = \{x \in F : \mu_F(x) > 0\}$. If a fuzzy set is a discrete set then it is denoted $F = \{(x_1, \mu_F(x_1)), ..., (x_n, \mu_F(x_n))\}$, otherwise, it is characterized by its membership function, in practice often a trapezoidal function.

The union $\cup$ and the intersection $\cap$ operators are defined by a couple of a t-norm and a t-conorm, such as (min, max). Let F, G be two fuzzy sets, $\mu_{F \cup G}(x) = max(\mu_F(x), \mu_G(x))$, $\mu_{F \cap G}(x) = min(\mu_F(x), \mu_G(x))$, and the complement of F, denoted F^c, is $\mu_{F^c}(x) = 1 - \mu_F(x)$.

The logical counterparts of $\cap$, $\cup$ and the complement are respectively $\wedge, \vee$ and $\neg$. Other operators have also been defined such as fuzzy implications [24].

4.2 Fuzzy Linguistic Quantifiers

Linguistic quantifiers express fuzzy quantities such as most, almost all, around 4, several, much, not many, few, etc. They express a flexible quantification between the existential quantifier ($\exists$) and the universal quantifier ($\forall$). A linguistic quantifier Q can be absolute or relative:

- Absolute quantifiers such as "at least 3", "at most 5" and "around 4" express a number and their interpretation do not depend on the cardinality of the set X. Such quantifiers are defined as follows:

$$\mu_Q : \mathbb{R}|\mathbb{N} \rightarrow [0,1]$$
$$x \mapsto \mu_Q(x)$$

- Relative quantifiers such as "few", "almost all" and "around half" express a proportion and their interpretation depend on the cardinality of the set X. Their generic definition is as follows:

$$\mu_Q : [0,1] \rightarrow [0,1]$$
$$x \mapsto \mu_Q(x)$$

where μ_Q is the truth-value of the quantifier Q applied on x elements; x can refer to either a quantity or a proportion.

A linguistic quantifier can also be increasing or decreasing. Q is an increasing quantifier if the truth-value of the quantified proposition in which it is involved does not decrease if the satisfaction to fuzzy predicate A by elements of X increases. "at least 3", "almost all" and "most of" are examples of increasing quantifiers. A quantifier Q is a decreasing quantifier if the truth-value of the quantified proposition in which it is involved does not increase if the satisfaction to fuzzy predicate A by elements of X increases. "at most 3", "few" and "at most half" are examples of decreasing quantifiers. A quantifier is monotonic if it is either increasing or decreasing. Non-monotonic or unimodal quantifiers could also be pointed out. They refer to quantities such as "around 5", "around a quarter", etc.

The evaluation of a quantified statement amounts to determine its gradual truth-value (in the unit interval $[0,1]$). Propositions of the form "Q B X are A" raise an interpretation issue when the fuzzy set B tends to the empty set. Therefore, we only detail hereinafter the evaluation of quantified propositions of the form "Q X are A".

4.3 Fuzzy Quantified Propositions

Linguistic quantifiers allow the definition of fuzzy quantified propositions by combining fuzzy predicates and quantifications. Let Q, X, A and B be respectively a linguistic quantifier, a set of elements and two fuzzy predicates. A fuzzy quantified proposition can have one of following forms "Q X are A" or "Q B X are A". The former means that among elements of X, there are Q elements that satisfy the fuzzy predicate A, as in the proposition "most of e-learning platforms are well-designed", and the latter means that among elements of X that satisfying B, there are Q elements that satisfy A, as in the proposition "at least 5 of big e-learning platforms are expensive".

Many approaches have been proposed to evaluate statements of type "Q X are A", but any evaluation of fuzzy quantified propositions should verify some properties to express user preferences. The following four properties are the most important ones to be satisfied by any interpretation and evaluation approach (see [25] for more details about properties).

Property 4 (Existential Quantifier Definition). The interpretation of fuzzy quantified propositions should be able to derive the interpretation of the existential quantifier-based proposition: "$\exists X$ are A", such that "$\exists$" is an absolute quantifier that is defined as follows:

$$\mu_{\exists}(x) = \begin{cases} 0 & if\, x = 0 \\ 1 & otherwise \end{cases} \tag{7}$$

The evaluation of a proposition of the form "$\exists X$ are A" is $sup_{x \in X} \mu_A(x)$.

Property 5 (Universal Quantifier Definition). The interpretation of fuzzy quantified propositions should be able to derive the interpretation of the universal quantifier-based proposition: "$\forall X$ are A". "$\forall$" is a relative quantifier that is defined as follows:

$$\mu_{\forall}(x) = \begin{cases} 1 & if\, x = 1 \\ 0 & otherwise \end{cases} \tag{8}$$

The evaluation of a proposition of the form "$\forall X$ are A" is $inf_{x \in X} \mu_A(x)$.

The other properties are related to monotony. A quantified proposition evaluation should be monotone along with both linguistic quantifiers and fuzzy predicates involved.

The following interpretations of fuzzy quantified propositions are suitable for user preference expression and evaluation, since they verify the regular properties introduced in [25]:

- the decomposition based approach [26],
- OWA-based approach [27],
- fuzzy integral (Choquet/Sugeno) based approach [25]. It has been shown in [25] that the Choquet (resp. Sugeno) fuzzy integral-based approach is equivalent to the decomposition-based approach (resp. OWA-based approach).

In the following subsection, we introduce the decomposition-based approach because it is the basis of our flexible ranking methods. The interpretation based on OWA approach is left for future works.

4.4 The Decomposition-Based Approach

The decomposition-based approach has been proposed by Yager in [26] for the evaluation of fuzzy quantified propositions of the forms "Q X are A", in which Q is an increasing quantifier. Let "$P : Q$ X are A" be a fuzzy quantified proposition such that Q is an increasing linguistic quantifier. The decomposition-based approach computes its truth-value, denoted by θ_P, based on the best regular (crisp) subset $E \subseteq X$ which contains Q elements that satisfy the condition A.

Therefore, we obtain the following formula (1) if Q is an absolute quantifier and formula (2) if Q is a relative one:

$$\theta_P = max_{i\in\{1,...,n\}} min(\mu_A(x_i), \mu_Q(i)) \tag{9}$$

$$\theta_P = max_{i\in\{1,...,n\}} min(\mu_A(x_i), \mu_Q(\frac{i}{n})) \tag{10}$$

where $\mu_A(x_1) \geq \mu_A(x_2) \geq ... \geq \mu_A(x_n)$.

Remark 1. The decomposition-based approach considers only increasing quantifiers. When Q is decreasing, the evaluation of a proposition of the form "Q X are A" could be deduced from the evaluation of the derived proposition "Q' X are not A", where Q' is the antonym of Q; such as the proposition "At most 3 platforms are expensive", which could be evaluated using the equivalent proposition "At least 4 platforms are not expensive".

5 Application to e-Learning System Ranking

We apply our linguistic quantifier based ranking method to our context of e-learning platforms ranking.

Let us model an e-Learning platform p_j as a set of couples of (*criterion*, *value*) as follows $p_j = \{(c_{j1}, v_{j1}), (c_{j2}, v_{j2}), ..., (c_{jn}, v_{jn})\}$ where c_{ji} with $i \in \{1, ..., n\}$ is a criterion and v_{ij} its value given by a user to express the importance of platform functionalities. Therefore, we define a platform satisfaction degree, denoted by $\theta(p_j)$ as the truth value of the following fuzzy quantified proposition:

"*Almost all criteria are important*"

Its evaluation is given by using the decomposition-based approach through the formula (11) as follows:

$$\theta(p_j) = max_{i=1,...,n}(min(\mu_{imp}(c'_{ij}), \mu_{allmost\_all}(\frac{i}{n}))) \tag{11}$$

$\mu_{imp}(c_{ij})$ is the degree of importance of criterion i of platform j, and $\mu_{imp}(c'_{i1}) \geq \mu_{imp}(c'_{i2}) \geq ... \geq \mu_p(c'_{in})$ are the ascending raking of the criteria according to their evaluation $\mu_{imp}(c_{ij})$.

The ranking rule is as *"the closer to* 1 θ *is the top ranked the platform will be"*. The underlying preference relation is defined as follows:

Definition 6 (Preference Relation $\tilde{\succeq}$). *Let p_i and p_j are two e-learning platforms. Then, $p_i \tilde{\succeq} p_j$ if and only if $\theta(p_i) \geq \theta(p_j)$.*

Remark 2. It is easy to prove that the preference relation $\tilde{\succeq}$ is a total order.

To apply our fuzzy quantifier based ranking method on the set of considered platforms, we need to map the evaluation symbols of Table 7 to the unit interval $[0, 1]$; for instance, we can consider the following mapping: $(E, 1), (*, 0.8), (\#, 0.6), (+, 0.4), (|, 0.2), (0, 0)$. The second requirement is to define the linguistic quantifier "almost_all" by its membership function. For instance, Fig. 1 illustrates an example of membership function of the considered quantifier. It represents the following function defined on $[0, 1]$:

$$\mu_{almost\_all}(x) = \begin{cases} 0 & if\, x \in [0, 0.5] \\ \frac{5}{2}(x - \frac{1}{2}) & if\, x \in [0.5, 0.9] \\ 1 & if\, x \in [0.9, 1] \end{cases}$$

Example 1. We evaluate the considered criterion for the platform "Sakai" according to its symbolic evaluation of Table 7 based on the linguistic quantifier *almost_all* of Fig. 1. Let F be a fuzzy set of "Sakai" criteria such that:

$$S = \{(c_1, 0.8), (c_2, 0.6), 0.8/C_3, 0.8/C_4, 0.6/C_5, 0.8/C_6, 0.2/C_7, 0.8/C_8, 0.2/C_9, 1/C_{10}, 0.8/C_{11}, 0.2/C_{12}, 1/C_{13}, 0.8/C_{14}, 0.8/C_{15}, 0.8/C_{16}, 0.2/C_{17}, 0.8/C_{18}, 0.6/C_{19}, 0/C_{20}, 0.6/C_{21}, 0.2/C_{22}, 0.6/C_{23}, 1/C_{24}, 0.8/C_{25}\}$$

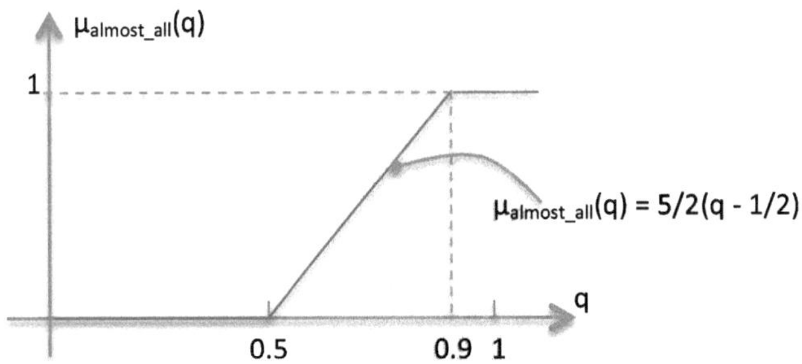

Fig. 1. Example of definition of the quantifier *almost_all.*

The ascendant ranking of important criteria is:
$C_{10} \geq C_{13} \geq C_{24} \geq C_1 \geq C_3 \geq C_4 \geq C_6 \geq C_8 \geq C_{11} \geq C_{14} \geq C_{15} \geq C_{16} \geq C_{18} \geq C_{25} \geq C_2 \geq C_5 \geq C_{19} \geq C_{21} \geq C_{23} \geq C_7 \geq C_9 \geq C_{12} \geq C_{17} \geq C_{22} \geq C_{20}$

Formula (11) is then applied as follows:

$$
\begin{aligned}
\theta(Sakai) = max(&\\
&min(\mu_{Imp}(c_{10}), \mu_{almost\_all}(0.04)), min(\mu_{Imp}(c_{13}), \mu_{almost\_all}(0.08)),\\
&min(\mu_{Imp}(c_{24}), \mu_{almost\_all}(0.12)), min(\mu_{Imp}(c_{1}), \mu_{almost\_all}(0.16)),\\
&min(\mu_{Imp}(c_{3}), \mu_{almost\_all}(0.2)), min(\mu_{Imp}(c_{4}), \mu_{almost\_all}(0.24)),\\
&min(\mu_{Imp}(c_{6}), \mu_{almost\_all}(0.28)), min(\mu_{Imp}(c_{8}), \mu_{almost\_all}(0.32)),\\
&min(\mu_{Imp}(c_{11}), \mu_{almost\_all}(0.36)), min(\mu_{Imp}(c_{14}), \mu_{almost\_all}(0.4)),\\
&min(\mu_{Imp}(c_{15}), \mu_{almost\_all}(0.44)), min(\mu_{Imp}(c_{16}), \mu_{almost\_all}(0.48)),\\
&min(\mu_{Imp}(c_{18}), \mu_{almost\_all}(0.52)), min(\mu_{Imp}(c_{25}), \mu_{almost\_all}(0.56)),\\
&min(\mu_{Imp}(c_{2}), \mu_{almost\_all}(0.6)), min(\mu_{Imp}(c_{5}), \mu_{almost\_all}(0.64)),\\
&min(\mu_{Imp}(c_{19}), \mu_{almost\_all}(0.68)), (\mu_{Imp}(c_{21}), \mu_{almost\_all}(0.72)),\\
&min(\mu_{Imp}(c_{23}), \mu_{almost\_all}(0.76)), min(\mu_{Imp}(c_{7}), \mu_{almost\_all}(0.8)),\\
&min(\mu_{Imp}(c_{9}), \mu_{almost\_all}(0.84)), min(\mu_{Imp}(c_{12}), \mu_{almost\_all}(0.88)),\\
&min(\mu_{Imp}(c_{17}), \mu_{almost\_all}(0.92)), min(\mu_{Imp}(c_{22}), \mu_{almost\_all}(0.96)),\\
&min(\mu_{Imp}(c_{20}), \mu_{almost\_all}(1)))\\
&= max(\\
&min(1,0), min(1,0), min(1,0), min(0.8,0), min(0.8,0), min(0.8,0),\\
&min(0.8,0), min(0.8,0), min(0.8,0), min(0.8,0), min(0.8,0),\\
&min(0.8,0), min(0.8,0.05), min(0.8,0.15), min(0.6,0.25),\\
&min(0.6,0.35), min(0.6,0.45), min(0.6,0.55), min(0.6,0.65),\\
&min(0.2,0.75), min(0.2,0.85), min(0.2,1), min(0.2,1), min(0.2,1),\\
&min(0,1) = max(0,0,0,0,0,0,0,0,0,0,0,0,0.05,0.15,0.25,0.35,\\
&0.45,0.55,0.6,0.2,0.2,0.2,0.2,0.2,0) = 0.6
\end{aligned}
$$

By using the same membership function as in Example 1, we compute truth-value ($\theta(P)$) for each considered platform of our set of e-Learning systems. Results are displayed in Table 8.

According to these results, we obtain the following ranking for:
Sakai $\tilde{\succ}$ (Claroline $\tilde{\simeq}$ Dokeos $\tilde{\simeq}$ eFront $\tilde{\simeq}$ Olat $\tilde{\simeq}$ Ganesha $\tilde{\simeq}$ AnaXagora) $\tilde{\succ}$ (ILIAS $\tilde{\simeq}$ Open ELMS).

We notice that according to the quantification, we also obtain none distinguishable platforms (Claroline $\tilde{\simeq}$ Dokeos $\tilde{\simeq}$ eFront $\tilde{\simeq}$ Olat $\tilde{\simeq}$ Ganesha $\tilde{\simeq}$ AnaXagora) and (ILIAS $\tilde{\simeq}$ Open ELMS). But, in this case, we can make use of additional information to refine our ranking. Indeed, the result returned by the decomposition based approach can be interpreted also as the supremum satisfaction degree we can obtain for an element x (a platform in our example), along with the minimum subset of criteria which satisfy the fuzzy condition considered in the quantified proposition and its corresponding proportion to the entire set of criteria.

Table 8. E-Learning platform's features fuzzy evaluation.

	Communication tools					Software & Installation				Administrative tools and Security								Hardware presentation tools				Management features				$\theta(P)$
	chat	Forum	Mail	Video conference	Calendar	Downloading	Installation	Assistance	Documentation	Courses administration	Tracking progress	Online registration	Learning path creation	Report	Learning path organization	Test evaluation	Security	Announcements	Learning Objects	Exercises	Content import	Multi course management	Multi user management	Evaluation management	User group	
Claroline	0.6	0.6	0.4	0.6	0.4	0.8	0.4	0.6	0.8	0.6	0.6	0.4	0.4	0.8	0.4	0.6	0.6	0.8	0.8	0.6	0.8	0.4	0.4	0.4	0.6	0.4
Dokeos	0.8	0.4	0.4	0.8	0.8	0.6	0.2	0.4	0.4	0.4	1	0.4	0.2	1	0.2	0.6	0.6	0.8	0.8	0.6	0.8	0.4	0.4	1	0.4	0.4
eFront	0.2	0.6	0.6	0.4	0.4	0.8	0.6	0.6	0.6	0.2	0.8	0.4	0.6	0.8	0.6	0.6	0.6	0.2	0.4	0.4	0.4	0.4	0.2	0.4	0.2	0.4
ILIAS	0.6	0.4	0.4	0	0.4	0.4	0.2	0.2	0.2	0.2	0.4	0.6	0.2	0.2	0.2	0.2	0.6	0	0.6	0.4	0	0.4	0.2	0.4	0.2	0.2
Open ELMS	0	0	0.8	0	0	0.4	0.2	0.4	0.4	0.2	0.6	0.4	0.4	0.6	0.2	0.8	0.2	0	0.8	0	0.6	0	0	0.6	0.6	0.2
Ganesha	0.6	0.6	0.4	0	0	0.4	0.2	0.4	0.4	0.6	1	0.2	0.4	1	0.6	0.6	0.4	0	0.6	0	0.6	0.6	0.6	0.6	0.6	0.4
Olat	0.8	0.8	0.8	0	0.8	0.4	0.2	0.2	0.6	0.6	0.8	0.2	0.4	0.6	0.2	0.6	0.6	0	0.8	0.8	0.8	0.2	0.4	0.8	0.8	0.4
AnaXagora	0.6	0.6	0.6	0	0.4	0.4	0.2	0.4	0.2	0.6	0.8	0.2	0.8	0.4	0.6	0.6	0.4	0	0.4	0.6	0.2	0.2	0.6	0.6	0.8	0.4
Sakai	0.8	0.6	0.8	0.8	0.6	0.8	0.2	0.8	0.2	1	0.8	0.2	1	0.8	0.8	0.8	0.2	0.8	0.6	0	0.6	0.2	0.6	1	0.8	0.6

For instance, in Example 1, the degree returned is 0.6 from the 19th greatest criteria, and the minimum set of criteria satisfying the quantified proposition is: $C' = \{C_{10}, C_{13}, C_{24}, C_1, C_3, C_4, C_6, C_8, C_{11}, C_{14}, C_{15}, C_{16}, C_{18}, C_{25}, C_2, C_5, C_{19}, C_{21}, C_{23}\}$, which corresponds to 76% of the criteria. We also notice that it is the maximum set of criteria which maximises the satisfaction degree. That means that the addition of any other criterion does not improve the satisfaction degree at all. Then, we define the least satisfaction proportion and greatest satisfaction proportion parameters (denoted by lsp and gsp respectively). Let us first define the following concepts:

- "$P : Q\ C$ is A" is a fuzzy quantified proposition with Q is a linguistic quantifier, C is a crisp set of m elements, and A a fuzzy predicate,
- $C^{\geq} = [C_1, ..., C_m]$ such that $\mu_A(C_1) \geq \mu_A(C_2) \geq ... \geq \mu_A(C_m)$ is ascendantly ordered vector of elements of C regarding the fuzzy predicate A,

Definition 7 (Least Satisfaction Proportion lsp). *The least satisfaction proportion is* $lsp = \frac{J}{m}$, *where* $J = min\{k : k = 1, ..., m \wedge \theta_P = min(\mu_A(C^{\geq}_k), Q(\frac{k}{m}))\}$.

Definition 8 (Greatest Satisfaction Proportion gsp). *The greatest satisfaction proportion is* $gsp = \frac{\mathcal{J}}{m}$, *where* $\mathcal{J} = max\{k : k = 1, ..., m \wedge \theta_P = min(\mu_A(C^{\geq}_k), Q(\frac{k}{m}))\}$.

Once these parameters are defined, we can make use of them for element ranking as stated by the following proposition.

Proposition 1. *Let c_i and c_k two elements of C of fuzzy quantified proposition of the form "$P : Q\ C$ is A".*

(a) If $lsp(c_i) < lsp(c_k)$ then $c_k \succ c_i$
(b) If $lsp(c_i) = lsp(c_k) \wedge gsp(c_i) > gsp(c_k)$ than $c_i \succ c_k$
(c) If $lsp(c_i) = lsp(c_k) \wedge gsp(c_i) = gsp(c_k)$ than $c_i \simeq c_k$

Proof. The proof of Proposition 1 can be easily obtained based on the monotony (increasing) property of the quantifier Q.

Example 2. We apply Proposition 1 on the set of similar platforms of Table 8 obtained in the previous example. The results are displayed in Table 9.

The sub-ranking is then: Claroline $\tilde{\succ}$ Dokeos $\tilde{\succ}$ eFront $\tilde{\succ}$ Ganesha $\tilde{\succ}$ (Olat $\tilde{\simeq}$ AnaXagora) $\tilde{\succ}$ ILIAS $\tilde{\succ}$ Open ELMS.

The obtained ranking is more refined and allow selecting top k e-learning platforms by combining both qualitative and quantitative measures.

Table 9. *lsp* and *gsp* for similar platforms.

Platform	*lsp*	*gsp*
Claroline	0.68	1
Dokeos	0.68	0.88
eFront	0.68	0.80
Ganesha	0.68	0.76
Olat	0.68	0.72
AnaXagora	0.68	0.72
ILIAS	0.60	0.88
Open ELMS	0.60	0.68

6 Conclusion and Future Work

In this paper, we have investigated two approaches for alternative ranking applied on e-Learning platform selection: a preference relation-based approach and flexible approach based on fuzzy quantification. We have illustrated the idea of their combination for ranking refinement which significantly help users make decision according to their needs and objectives. Practically, we have considered categories to describe each e-Learning system; each of which defines some criteria over well-known properties of these systems. We applied our approach on a set of open source e-Learning systems for which we have gathered through short surveys their evaluation on the considered criteria. The first approach assesses the quality of an e-Learning system by considering its maximum possible satisfaction and/or its minimum guaranteed satisfaction. These values are finally used to rank the alternatives from the most to the least satisfactory, and to deliver to the user one or several optimal systems. In the case of several alternatives are delivered as equally satisfactory, we consider the second approach, more flexible from computation point of view, to refine the ranking. The approach makes use of linguistic quantifiers and fuzzy quantified propositions to compute for each alternative an aggregated value corresponding to what extend its criteria are evaluated as important by the user. In addition, we defined two new parameters for ranking refinement called *least satisfactory proportion* and *greatest satisfactory proportion*, denoted by *lsp* and *gsp* respectively, to assess the quality of the subset of criteria evaluated as important by the user for each alternative.

For future directions, it is still to undertake a larger survey to evaluate the platforms as accurate as possible. It is also worthy to consider user profiles when performing surveys in such a way that we obtain different values for different profiles. A profile can be defined over a population of users based on their interests and training objectives. From theoretical point of the view, the study of the properties of *lsp* and *gsp* such as monotony and their relationship with the definition of the linguistic quantifier involved in the fuzzy quantified proposition can reveal the potential of these parameters for proportion quality evaluation in fuzzy quantified propositions.

A Appendix

Proof of Property 1 Total Order

We only prove hereinafter the property for the preference relation $\succeq$. The proof of the property for the preference relation $\preceq$ is similar to the one of $\succeq$.

Proof 1 ($\succeq$ is Total Order). The preference relation $\succeq$ is a total order iff:

1. $\succeq$ is reflexive
2. $\succeq$ is antisymmetric
3. $\succeq$ is transitive

1. Relation $\succeq$ is reflexive iff $\forall a \in \mathcal{S} : a \succeq a$. Therefore, a $\succeq$ a iff $pos_{\mathcal{S}}(a) \leq pos_{\mathcal{S}}(a)$ which is verified for the comparison operator $\leq$ since $\leq$ is reflexive. Then $\succeq$ is reflexive.
2. Relation $\succeq$ is antisymmetric iff $\forall a, b \in \mathcal{S} : a = b$. Then:
   a $\succeq$ b $\wedge$ b $\succeq$ a iff $pos_{\mathcal{S}}(a) \leq pos_{\mathcal{S}}(b) \wedge pos_{\mathcal{S}}(b) \leq pos_{\mathcal{S}}(a)$ which is verified for $\leq$ since $\leq$ is antisymmetric.
   Then $\succeq$ is antisymmetric.
3. $\succeq$ is transitive iff $\forall a, b, c \in \mathcal{S} : a \succeq b \wedge b \succeq c \Rightarrow a \succeq c$. As a $\succeq$ b $\wedge$ b $\succeq$ c then $pos_{\mathcal{S}}(a) \leq pos_{\mathcal{S}}(b) \wedge pos_{\mathcal{S}}(b) \leq pos_{\mathcal{S}}(c)$. Therefore, $pos_{\mathcal{S}}(a) \leq pos_{\mathcal{S}}(c)$ since $\leq$ is transitive. That means that $a \succeq c$ and $\succeq$ is transitive.

Proof of $prefMax$ Properties

Proof 2 ($prefMax$ Properties)

1. $prefMax$ is associative on $\mathcal{S}$:
   $\forall a, b, c \in \mathcal{S}$, then: $prefMax(prefMax(a, b), c) = prefMax(a, prefMax(b, c))$. We denote by I the left term $PrefMax(PrefMax(a, b), c)$ and by II the right term $PrefMax(a, PrefMax(b, c))$.
   Table 10 shows results of evaluation of the left and the right terms, which are identical. Therefore $prefMax$ is associative.
2. $prefMax$ is commutative iff $\forall a, b \in \mathcal{S} : prefMax(a, b) = prefMax(b, a)$.
   From Table 3, the $prefMax$ matrix is symmetric so $prefMax$ is commutative.
3. $prefMax$ is idempotent iff $\forall a \in \mathcal{S}$:
   $prefMax(a, a) = a$.
   From the main diagonal of Table 3, we conclude that $prefMax$ is idempotent.
4. $prefMax$ has 0 as neutral element iff $\forall a \in \mathcal{S}$:
   $prefMax(a, 0) = a$.
   Table 3 shows that $prefMax$ has 0 as neutral element.
5. $prefMax$ has E as absorbent element iff $\forall a \in \mathcal{S} : prefMax(a, E) = E$.
   Table 3 also shows that $prefMax$ has E as absorbent element.

Table 10. Formula results for the property of associativity of prefMax operator.

	I	II
$a \succeq b \wedge a \succeq c$	a	$\Rightarrow a \succeq prefMax(b, c) \Rightarrow II = a$
$a \succeq b \wedge c \succeq a$	c	$\Rightarrow c \succeq b$ (transivity) $prefMax(b, c) = c \Rightarrow II = c$ since $c \succeq a$
$b \succeq a \wedge b \succeq c$	b	$prefMax(b, c) = b \Rightarrow II = b$ since $b \succeq a$
$b \succeq a \wedge c \succeq b$	c	$prefMax(b, c) = c \wedge c \succeq a$ (transitivity) $\Rightarrow II = c$

Proof of $prefMin$ Properties

Proof 3 ($prefMin$ Properties)

1. $prefMin$ is associative on $\mathcal{S}$:
   $\forall a, b, c \in \mathcal{S}$: $prefMin(prefMin(a, b), c) = prefMin(a, prefMin(b, c))$. We denote by I the left term $PrefMin(PrefMin(a, b), c)$ and by II the right term $PrefMin(a, PrefMin(b, c))$.
   Table 11 shows results of evaluation of the left and the right terms, which are identical. Therefore $prefMin$ is associative.
2. $prefMin$ is commutative iff $\forall a, b \in \mathcal{S} : prefMin(a, b) = prefMin(b, a)$.
   From Table 3, the $prefMax$ matrix is symmetric so $prefMin$ is commutative.
3. $prefMin$ is idempotent iff $\forall a \in \mathcal{S} : prefMin(a, a) = a$.
   From the main diagonal of Table 3, we conclude that $prefMin$ is idempotent.
4. $prefMin$ has E as neutral element iff $\forall a \in \mathcal{S}$:
   $prefMin(a, 0) = a$.
   Table 3 shows that $prefMin$ has E as neutral element.
5. $prefMin$ has 0 as absorbent element iff $\forall a \in \mathcal{S}$:
   $prefMin(a, E) = E$.
   Table 3 also shows that $prefMin$ has 0 as absorbent element.

Table 11. Formula results for the property of associativity of prefMin operator.

	I	II
$a \succeq b \wedge b \succeq c$	c	$\Rightarrow a \succeq prefMin(b, c) \Rightarrow II = c$ since $a \succeq c$
$a \succeq b \wedge c \succeq b$	b	$\Rightarrow a \succeq prefMin(b, c) \Rightarrow II = b$ since $a \succeq b$
$b \succeq a \wedge a \succeq c$	c	$\Rightarrow b \succeq c$ (transivity) $prefMin(b, c) = c \Rightarrow II = c$ since $a \succeq c$
$b \succeq a \wedge c \succeq a$	a	a is the smallest symbol between a, b and c, so $II = a$

References

1. Stufflebeam, D.L.: Empowerment evaluation, objectivist evaluation, and evaluation standards: where the future of evaluation should not go and where it needs to go. Eval. Pract. **15**, 321–338 (1994)
2. Venkataraman, S., Sivakumar, S.: Engaging students in group based learning through e-learning techniques in higher education system. Int. J. Emerg. Trends Sci. Technol. **2**, 1741–1746 (2015)
3. Bañados, E.: A blended-learning pedagogical model for teaching and learning efl successfully through an online interactive multimedia environment. Calico J. **23**, 533–550 (2013)
4. Colace, F., Santo, M.D., Pietrosanto, A.: Evaluation models for e-learning platform: an ahp approach (2006)
5. Ubell, R.: Engineers turn to E-Learning. IEEE Spectr. **37**, 59–61 (2000)
6. Schneider, A., Albers, P., Mattheis, V.M.: E-Learning en urologie: Mise en oeuvre de l'apprentissage et l'enseignement Platform CASUS - Avez patients virtuels conduire a une amélioration des résultats d'apprentissage d'une étude randomisée chez les étudiants, vol. 94. Karger AG, Basel (2015)
7. Hannan, T.M.: Politique-en-pratique pour la polyarthrite rhumatoide: étude randomisée d'essai et la cohorte controlée de e-learning visant une meilleure gestion de la physiothérapie (2013)
8. Stoffregena, J., Pawlowski, J.M., Pirkkalainen, H.: A barrier framework for open e-learning in public administrations (2015)
9. García, F.B., Jorge, A.H.: Evaluating e-learning platforms through scorm specifications. In: IADIS Virtual Multi Conference on Computer Science and Information Systems (MCCSIS 2006), IADIS (2006)
10. Britain, S., Liber, O.: A framework for pedagogical evaluation of virtual learning environments (2004)
11. Laurillard, D.: Rethinking University Teaching: A Conversational Framework for the Effective Use of Learning Technologies. Routledge, London (2013)
12. Liber, O., Olivier, B., Britain, S.: The toomol project: supporting a personalised and conversational approach to learning. Comput. Educ. **34**, 327–333 (2000)
13. Graf, S., List, B.: An evaluation of open source e-learning platforms stressing adaptation issues. In: Proceedings of the 5th IEEE International Conference on Advanced Learning Technologies, ICALT 2005, pp. 163–165, IEEE Computer Press (2005)
14. Hamtini, T.M., Fakhouri, H.N.: Evaluation of open-source e-learning platforms based on the qualitative weight and sum approach and analytic hierarchy process. Technical report (2012). http://www.iiis.org/CDs2012/CD2012SCI/IMSCI_2012/PapersPdf/EA418WG.pdf. Accessed 21 May 2013
15. Maruthur, N.M., Joy, S.M., Dolan, J.G., Shihab, H.M., Singh, S.: Use of the analytic hierarchy process for medication decision-making in type 2 diabetes. PloS One **10**, e0126625 (2015)
16. Zadeh, L.: Fuzzy sets. Inf. Control **8**, 338–353 (1965)
17. Chachoua, S., Tamani, N., Malki, J., Estraillier, P.: e-learning platform ranking method using a symbolic approach based on preference relations. In: Proceedings of the 8th International Conference on Computer Supported Education, pp. 114–122 (2016)

18. Atthirawong, W., MacCarthy, B.: An application of the analytical hierarchy process to international location decision-making. In: Gregory, M. (ed.) Proceedings of The 7th Annual Cambridge International Manufacturing Symposium: Restructuring Global Manufacturing, pp. 1–18. University of Cambridge, Cambridge (2002)
19. Lebrun, M., Docq, F., Smidts, D., et al.: Claroline, une plate-forme d'enseignement et d'apprentissage pour stimuler le développement pédagogique des enseignants et la qualité des enseignements: premières approches. In: Colloque de l'AIPU, Montpellier (2008)
20. Reiter, S., Kohlbecker, J., Watrinet, M.L.: Anaxagora: a step forward in e-learning. In: ECEL2006-5th European Conference on elearning: ECEL2006, p. 291. Academic Conferences Limited (2006)
21. Dogbe Semanou, D.A.K., Durand, A., Leproust, M., Vanderstichel, H.: Etude comparative de plates-formes de formation à distance. le cadre du Projet@ 2L Octobre (2007)
22. Laforcade, C.P., Oubahssi, L.: Étude comparative de plates-formes de formation à distance (2014)
23. Greco, S., Pereira, R.A.M., Squillante, M., Yager, R.R.: Preferences and Decisions: Models and Application, vol. 257. Springer, Heidelberg (2010)
24. Bouchon-Meunier, B., Dubois, D., Godo, L., Prade, H.: Fuzzy set and possibility theory in approximate and plausible reasoning. In: Bezdek, J.C., Dubois, D., Prade, H. (eds.) Fuzzy Sets in Approximate Reasoning and Information Systems. The Handbook of Fuzzy Sets, pp. 27–31. Kluwer Academic Publishers, Dordrecht (1999)
25. Liétard, L.: Contribution à l'interrogation flexible de bases de données: Etude des propositions quantifiées floues. Ph.D. thesis (1995)
26. Yager, R.R.: General multiple-objective decision functions and linguistically quantified statements. Int. J. Man Mach. Stud. **21**, 389–400 (1984)
27. Yager, R.R.: Fuzzy quotient operators for fuzzy relational data bases. Fuzzy Engineering toward Human Friendly Systems **1**, 13–15 (1991)

Interactive and Narrative Data Visualisation for Presentation-Based Knowledge Transfer

Reinout Roels(✉), Yves Baeten, and Beat Signer

Web and Information Systems Engineering Lab, Vrije Universiteit Brussel,
Pleinlaan 2, 1050 Brussels, Belgium
{rroels,bsigner}@vub.ac.be

Abstract. In recent years, presentation tools such as Apple's Keynote or Microsoft PowerPoint play an important role in knowledge transfer. Despite the fact that over the last decade we have witnessed various technological advances and new media types, existing presentation tools still mainly support the presenter-driven delivery of static content. On the other hand, research in information visualisation illustrates that interactive data exploration and storytelling can significantly improve the extraction and transfer of knowledge from raw data sets. Our goal is to improve data-driven knowledge transfer in presentation tools by applying existing information visualisation concepts. Therefore, we derived a set of general requirements for interactive information visualisation in presentation tools. A prototype of a presentation tool which addresses these requirements has been developed based on the MindXpres presentation platform. Ultimately, the presented requirements might serve third-party slideware vendors as input for improving support for data-driven knowledge transfer in existing presentation tools.

Keywords: Presentations · Slideware · Narrative visualisation · Interactive visualisation · Data exploration

1 Introduction

The field of information visualisation investigates graphical data representations that reinforce human cognition and help us in detecting causal relationships between data. Recent technological advances led to more dynamic and interactive information visualisations. Current development therefore emphasises on providing users more control over the visualisation process in order to enable the interactive exploration and discovery of meaningful relations between data points.

Storytelling has shown to be an effective approach for sharing insights gained by studying specific data sets [1]. Facts that have been tied together as part of a story are easier to present as well as more memorable by the audience. Therefore, we have seen the rise of so-called narrative visualisations or visualisations that help us to tell stories with data [2]. For example, educational textbooks often contain various charts and diagrams in order to support the message that

G. Costagliola et al. (Eds.): CSEDU 2016, CCIS 739, pp. 237–258, 2017.
DOI: 10.1007/978-3-319-63184-4_13

the text is trying to convey. These narrative visualisations have been adapted for recent media and are becoming more dynamic. For instance, news on the television might use animated graphs to show changes in oil prices or election results whereas online news articles might be complemented by user-controllable interactive visualisations.

A common medium used for narrative visualisations are the slide decks created with presentation tools such as PowerPoint. With more than 30 million PowerPoint presentations produced every day [3], we cannot deny the role that presentation tools play in knowledge transfer. These tools allow us to display content such as text, images or charts. Nevertheless, unlike other digital media, presentation tools do not exploit recent techniques for interactive information visualisation to their full potential. We have seen little evolution in the core ideologies of presentation tools which were originally designed for the production of physical photographic slides. For example, most slide decks are still linear sequences of spatially restricted slides with static content. However, from a technological point of view, there is no reason why some of these limitations should still apply. Visualisation techniques such as zoomable user interfaces allow us to get rid of spatial boundaries. Furthermore, hardware such as tablets, smartphones or digital pens support the non-linear presentation of content and enable various forms of real-time interactions with a presentation's content. Nevertheless, existing workarounds for implementing this functionality either require too much time and effort or force the presenter to use some third-party tools during presentation time which interrupts the flow of the narrative.

We address some of the discussed shortcomings of current presentation tools and introduce an interactive data visualisation solution for the MindXpres presentation tool. By applying well-established concepts from information visualisation and visual storytelling, we aim to provide more effective narrative visualisations in presentations. Our interactive data visualisation solution for MindXpres supports the predefinition of a series of views for a given data set as well as transitions between these views in order to support the narrative. In contrast to existing presentation tools, the visualised data and visualisation parameters can be changed between each step of the narrative. For instance, the chart type (e.g. bar chart or pie chart) can be changed, filters can be applied on the data or the focus might be adjusted. Furthermore, the same functionality remains available at presentation time, allowing the presenter to break free from any predefined visualisation series in order to explore and discuss the data without restrictions. By applying established information visualisation guidelines and techniques, the resulting presentation helps the audience to strengthen their mental model and enhances the effectiveness of knowledge transfer. In addition, our proposed approach does not only reduce the time needed to create compelling narratives based on a raw data set, but also results in a shift towards audience-driven narratives.

In Sect. 2 we discuss information visualisation and narrative visualisation concepts in more detail, relate them to existing presentation tools and discuss shortcomings of existing presentation tools. We then propose enhancements for some of these shortcomings in Sect. 3 and derive a number of general requirements for interactive narrative information visualisation in presentation tools. Section 4 provides some details about our prototype implementation for the MindXpres presentation tool, which is followed by a use case in Sect. 5 in order to illustrate some of our prototype's functionality. We conclude with a discussion and outline of future work.

2 Background

The advent of modern media such as television and computers have enabled more dynamic and interactive visualisations. Similar to these visualisations we see on television also major newspapers have adopted the concept of graphical storytelling and sometimes allow users to interact with the visualisation. For instance, the BBC[1], The Telegraph[2] and The New York Times[3] accompany some of their articles with interactive visualisations. An article in The Economist calls it "*melding the skills of computer science, statistics, artistic design and storytelling*" [4]. In this section we take a look at existing information visualisation and narrative visualisation concepts and explain why they work well. After presenting some related tools, we outline their limitations in the context of presentation-based knowledge transfer.

2.1 Interactive Visualisation

An important goal of information visualisation is to strengthen a viewer's understanding of the underlying data, which might be hard to interpret in its raw form. Abstract data representations can offer a high-level overview and help us to reinforce our mental model [5]. Such graphical representations make use of our highly developed ability to process the continuous stream of information-rich signals captured by our eyes [6]. Concepts such as shape, colour, size or distance are intuitive to us and the interpretation of some of these concepts comes naturally. Research in this domain led to Gestalt psychology, a research field that identified a series of laws helping us to understand these natural interpretations [7]. For instance, when comparing objects in a visualisation, it is clear that a larger object represents a larger quantity or something of higher importance. Similarly, objects that are spatially close to each other are likely to be more related than objects with a larger distance in between them. The field of information visualisation tries to exploit these findings in order to facilitate knowledge transfer. Few [8] proposed a classification of eight messages that one might want to show using quantitative data, together with the type of visualisation that is suitable for each message. The messages include time series, rankings, part-to-whole, deviation, distribution, correlation, geospatial messages and nominal comparison.

1 http://www.bbc.com/news/11628973.
2 http://www.telegraph.co.uk/news/interactive-graphics/.
3 http://www.nytimes.com/interactive/2015/us/year-in-interactive-storytelling.html.

The formation of a mental model can further be augmented by allowing the user to interact with the data [6]. The significance of interaction while processing information was illustrated in Gibson's cookie cutter experiment [9] and is often used as a classic example to prove the relevance of interaction in information visualisation. Gibson concluded that our brain performs better as active explorer, even if the act of exploring requires additional coordination and processing. Interaction techniques in information visualisation can be seen as the features that provide users with the ability to directly or indirectly manipulate and interpret representations. Note that this also includes menu interfaces that allow users to manipulate the representation and, for instance, switch to another chart type or sort a bar chart in descending order [10]. Furthermore, Dix and Ellis [11] emphasise two important principles in interacting with visualisations. The first principle "*same representation, changing parameters*" states that users should be able to interactively change parameters of the presentation. The second principle "*same data, changing representation*" implies that a user should be able to switch between conceptually different data visualisations. Various representations can be appropriate for different types of data and each representation needs to be tuned for its purpose.

There are various academic studies about different interaction techniques such as zooming or filtering which resulted in the categorisation of frequently used techniques in information visualisation. One of the widely accepted classifications was independently proposed by both Siirtola [12] and Yi [10]. Even though the authors did not collaborate, the proposed interaction categories are very similar:

- *Select*: mark something as interesting
- *Explore*: show something else
- *Reconfigure*: show a different arrangement
- *Encode*: show a different representation
- *Abstract/Elaborate*: show more or less details
- *Filter*: show something conditionally
- *Connect*: show related items

2.2 Narrative Visualisation

Interactive visualisation techniques cover the exploration and analysis of data but there is also a need for presenting and communicating data effectively. As stated by Kosara, "*tying facts together into a story is one of the most effective ways of presenting them and making a point*" [1]. The main reason for using stories is the fact that they are known to be a popular way of conserving information and passing it on. Not only do narratives preserve and advertise information, they also act as an adhesive between facts to make them memorable [13]. Segel and Heer [2] further provide a classification of the different approaches and design techniques used in news media to visually tell stories.

In the context of presentations, narrative visualisations are mainly author driven. The scenes and scenarios are linear and predefined by the presenter, messages and conclusions are explicitly mentioned and the audience has little to no influence on the story. This contrasts with reader-driven narratives found in other contexts where there is no prescribed ordering, the free interaction and exploration is central and possible interpretations are left to the reader. Segel and Heer state that ideally, visual narrative genres must balance a narrative—intended by the author—with story discovery by the reader [2]. Kosara confirms that this also holds true for collaborative settings where stories can not only be used to support discussion and decision making, but also during the analysis process. Hence, stories can serve as a source for drawing conclusions, similar to the narrated history of an event [1].

Note that narrative visualisations can be manipulated to emphasise specific messages during free exploration. For instance, Hullman and Diakopoulos [14] identified a number of approaches and design techniques for prioritising particular interpretations in visualisations. These findings imply that narrative visualisations can be designed to deliver a predefined message without explicitly giving the message away.

2.3 Existing Visualisation Tools

Even though the visualisation of information in graphs is an important feature of current presentation tools, existing presentation solutions clearly lack the interactive or narrative aspects discussed earlier in this section. PowerPoint makes it easy to visualise numbers stored in a spreadsheet and provides a lot of freedom in terms of chart types and styling options. Nevertheless, the final result of this process is always a static graph. Of course, as with any content in PowerPoint, it is possible to apply transitions (e.g. fade in or slide out) and motion path animation effects. These effects can either be applied to the complete chart or, depending on the type of chart, to smaller parts within the chart. By using these transitions and motion path animations as a workaround, authors can compose basic narratives by, for example, making parts of a pie chart appear one by one. However, this approach has several shortcomings. First of all, it requires a major authoring effort since animations have to be manually applied to the different parts in order to achieve the desired effect. Furthermore, things might get even more complicated when changes have to be made at a later stage. In order to switch to another chart type, it might further be necessary to define multiple versions of the graph with the corresponding transitions between them. Second, if we depend on these transition effects, the result consists of a predefined sequence of states and there is no way to deviate from this fixed path. While it can be desirable to predefine a path through the data, it might also be beneficiary to have the flexibility to show alternative unprepared variations when answering unexpected questions. Last but not least, it is important to note that a chart is rendered only when the underlying data or configuration is changed at authoring time, but from then on the chart has to be considered a collection of static images. This implies that any effects only operate on the graphical level but cannot do anything that would require the components of the chart to adapt between steps. We can make the bars of a bar chart appear one by one but it is impossible to apply modifiers to the information or configuration that defines the graph. For example, we cannot just switch to another chart type, change the scale of a graph or filter out specific values as a step in the animation. There are third-party plug-ins such as oomfo[4] or think-cell[5] which add even more options for creating charts, but one has to be aware that these third-party plug-ins typically only add additional authoring and styling features for designing what will ultimately result in a static chart with the same limitations. So far we have only discussed charts in PowerPoint but we came to similar conclusions for alternative presentation tools such as Apple's Keynote[6] or Prezi[7].

In terms of academic work, there are a number of tools based on the interactive visualisation principles discussed earlier. Notable examples are VICKI [15], Spotfire [16] and GGobi [17]. While these are promising tools founded on the principles of proven concepts, they also show a number of shortcomings which make them less suited for use in presentations. First of all, these solutions were built as standalone applications and their interfaces are not optimised for use during a presentation. The presenter has to leave the presentation and switch to another application which interrupts the flow. These tools also consist of multiple windows and have complex menus that do not translate well to the limited resolution offered by most projectors. In addition, significant interaction is needed to operate the tools, requiring the presenter to focus on the software and use the keyboard or mouse to go through a series of actions to switch between desired visualisations. It is evident that these solutions focus on the interactive exploration part, but the ability to use them as narrative visualisation tools is rather limited. Commercial solutions with similar restrictions include IBM's Many Eyes [18] and Tableau[8]. Note that the previously mentioned GGobi also provides an Application Programming Interface (API) that allows programmers to embed and pragmatically interact with visualisations. There are other development frameworks such as UC Berkeley's prefuse visualization toolkit[9] for the Java programming language or the popular D3[10] JavaScript library. While these frameworks offer a broad range of features for modern data visualisation, they are usually used for building standalone applications. More importantly, they require the programming of the desired visualisation which is not suitable for the majority of presenters.

Hans Rosling's 2006 TED talk entitled 'The Best Stats You've Ever Seen' [19] is an excellent example of the fact that it is possible to build a presentation around dynamic and interactive data visualisation. During his talk, Rosling made the point that there is so much data related to human development trends but it is difficult to educate people and transfer knowledge about current issues

[4] http://oomfo.com.
[5] http://www.think-cell.com/en/products/.
[6] http://www.apple.com/mac/keynote/.
[7] https://prezi.com.
[8] http://www.tableau.com.
[9] https://github.com/prefuse/Prefuse.
[10] http://d3js.org.

if we cannot present these statistics in an accessible way. For his presentation, he used a proprietary tool (now forming part of the Gapminder[11] suite) that allowed him to animate and visualise data over time, switch between chart types or highlight areas of interest and annotate them. The success of the talk can partly be attributed to Rosling's energetic personality and compelling arguments, but also his novel approach to presenting data gained a lot of attention [1] and has been explored in great detail. Robertson later showed that animated transitions can have a negative effect on a viewer's ability to follow trends [20], but because these animated transitions are entertaining and capture the attention, they work well in front of a live audience. While Rosling's 2006 TED talk was definitely a major step in the right direction, the Gapminder series of tools also has some shortcomings. First of all, once more they are standalone applications and require a presenter to switch between presentation and tool. More importantly, these tools were specifically built for educating people about certain topics related to human development. This implies that the data sets are fixed and the functionality and visualisations are tweaked for drawing conclusions from geographic and demographic data over time. Other tools have been built for specific use cases, including the MediaViz [21] platform for visualising data relevant to online media studies. Similarly, ArtVis [22] is a tool for exploring European art over time on a map-based visualisation. GeoTime [23] represents another geography-based visualisation tool focussing on creating a visual story out of geo-temporal events. While GeoTime is one of the few tools where the creation of a narrative out of a raw data set lies in its core, its use is limited due to the focus on geo-temporal data only.

The discussed related work highlights the added value of interactive and narrative visualisations even if we have to conclude that existing presentation tools do not offer the necessary support for applying such narrative visualisations in practice. There are some workarounds such as creating multiple static charts with manually-defined transitions between them, but often presenters are not willing to make this effort and rather opt for a less dynamic narrative. Alternatively, it is possible to use stand-alone tools which were not designed to be used in the context of live presentations and can therefore not easily be applied as tools for narrative visualisations.

3 Requirements

Research in the field of information visualisation and narrative visualisation shows that the use of specific visualisation techniques can lead to improved knowledge transfer. However, as discussed earlier we see that existing presentation tools do not exploit these visualisation techniques to their full potential. Our goal is to close this gap and to apply lessons learned from interactive information visualisation as well as narrative visualisation in order to improve presentation-based knowledge transfer. Based on the presented related work and the shortcomings of existing

[11] http://www.gapminder.org/downloads/.

presentation solutions discussed in Sect. 2, we derived a set of requirements for interactive information visualisation in presentation tools:

R1: Integration in Presentation Tools. As slide decks are one of the most frequently used media for transferring knowledge in education and business settings, it is preferable to directly integrate interactive visualisations into a presentation rather than relying on third-party applications. If an interactive visualisation is not integrated into the presentation tool, the presenter is forced to switch between applications which takes time and interrupts the presentation flow.

R2: Focus on Proven Techniques and Guidelines. Popular presentation tools put their main focus on aesthetics and looks but the offered features are not always beneficial in terms of knowledge transfer. For instance, the ability to show three-dimensional bar charts or pie charts has been proven to cause longer interpretation times and may even be interpreted incorrectly [24,25]. Similarly, Tufte [26] argues that most graphical bells and whistles (what he calls "chartjunk") increase the signal-to-noise ratio and dilute the message one wants to deliver. Presentation tools should not only create visually appealing visualisations but also support the presenter in creating visualisations that focus on strengthening the viewer's mental modal and transferring knowledge more efficiently. Therefore, a presentation tool should offer features based on the message that the presenter is trying to pass on, for instance based on Few's classifications introduced earlier [8]. Note that this is not only relevant for static visualisations but should also apply to the currently non-existent interactive features by, for example, basing ourselves on Siirtola's classification of relevant tasks for data exploration [12].

R3: Interactive Visualisations as Support for Oral Narratives. When using interactive and dynamic visualisations as support for an oral narrative, it is desirable to be able to predefine a sequence of views for a given data set and to step through these views during the presentation. In addition to simple enter and exit animations offered by existing tools, it is important to be able to apply the two interaction principles by Dix and Ellis [11] introduced earlier. This implies that it should be possible to modify parameters in between the steps of a presentation (e.g. change the scale or apply a filter on the data) and to change the data representation (e.g. by switching to another chart type). By allowing the presenter to define such a sequence of states, they can synchronise the visualisation state with the oral narrative at preparation time and ensure that limited interaction with the computer is needed during the presentation.

R4: Unscripted Data Exploration. In addition to stepping through the predefined states of a visualisation, the presenter should also be able to change the representation or parameters at any time during a presentation. Segel and Heer [2] pointed out the importance of balancing the narrative intended by the author with story discovery by the reader. This also applies to certain presentation styles where questions or discussions with the audience can drive the presentation. Therefore, a presentation tool should also allow the presenter to interact with the visualisation during the presentation with the same set of interactions offered at authoring time. Since the resolution (screen real estate) and interaction is limited during a presentation, special care needs to be taken to offer the available interactions in a way that does not clutter the visualisation and can be controlled without intensive user input.

R5: Interactivity after the Presentation. As mentioned earlier, readers or audience members should not be excluded from the interaction. This does not only apply during a presentation but should be valid for a slide deck's entire lifetime. For example, in higher education slide decks are often offered as part of the study material. A student reviewing the slides at home should at least be able to play back the visualisation as it was defined by the presenter. Ideally, students should also have the option to freely navigate the data in order to clarify any doubts they may have and to strengthen their mental model by exploring the data set. Another use case is the inverted or flipped classroom setting where activities that are typically considered homework become central during class and the teacher merely guides the completion of these activities [27]. By offering students the interactive slide decks that were used in the pre-recorded lectures, they are not only able to replicate situations from the videos, but they also have a tool for further data exploration in order to come to their own conclusions.

4 Implementation

In this section we discuss the technical details of the interactive and narrative visualisation extension for the MindXpres presentation tool by revisiting the requirements presented in Sect. 3 and showing how our prototype addresses these requirements.

Requirement R1 states that the visualisation should be integrated in the presentation tool in order that the presenter does not have to switch between external third-party applications. Our interactive data visualisation prototype has been implemented as a plug-in for the MindXpres presentation tool [28,29]. MindXpres was developed to overcome the limited extensibility of well-known slideware tools such as PowerPoint or Keynote and to offer a rapid prototyping platform for novel presentation ideas. While PowerPoint offers an Application Programming Interface (API), it enforces the usage of a linear sequence of slides with relatively static content which makes it difficult to experiment with radically new ideas for next generation presentation tools. In contrast, the highly modular MindXpres architecture allows any component to be replaced and new components and functionality can easily be added. For instance, users may choose to use a plug-in that visualises content using a zoomable user interface (ZUI) or they can use a plug-in that visualises the same content in a classic linear fashion as in existing slideware.

As shown in Fig. 1, the core MindXpres engine provides various abstractions that allow plug-in creators to focus on their ideas instead of having to reimplement the basic functionality. The graphics engine, for example, provides functionality related to the visualisation of content which drive features such as the ZUI and

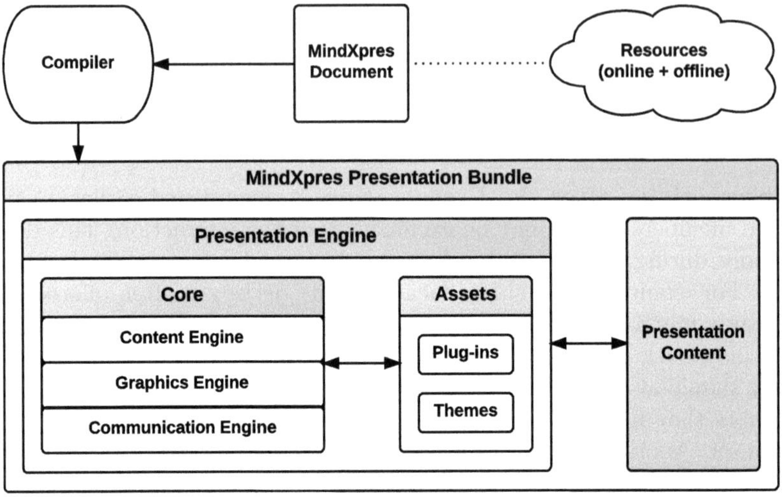

Fig. 1. MindXpres architecture.

interactive rich media visualisation plug-ins. The communication engine allows instances of a MindXpres presentation to form networks which enables plug-ins to communicate across devices and supports audience-driven functionality such as polls, quizzes or screen mirroring [30]. MindXpres uses HTML5 and related technologies for enhanced portability and plug-ins are written entirely in JavaScript. Although a graphical editor is under development, MindXpres presentations are currently defined in an XML-based declarative language similar to the LaTeX language that is used for the authoring of text documents. Listing 1.1 shows an example of a presentation in the XML authoring language. The goal is that a user can focus on the authoring of the content whereas the presentation tool deals with the layout and styling. While MindXpres comes with a default set of plug-ins for basic components such as images, bullet lists, videos or slides, it is easy to add plug-ins for new content types. Note that these plug-ins also extend the vocabulary used in the MindXpres document format. More specifically, a plug-in can add new XML tags to be used in the document format and the plug-in then takes responsibility for visualising content placed within these tags.

```
<presentation>
  <slide title="Vannevar Bush">
    <bulletlist>
      <item>March 1890 - June 1974</item>
      <item>Founder of Raytheon</item>
    </bulletlist>
    <image file="bush.jpg"/>
    <quote source="As We May Think (1945)">
      A record, if it is to be useful to science, must be continuously
      extended, it must be stored, and above all it must be consulted.
    </quote>
  </slide>
</presentation>
```

Listing 1.1. MindXpres presentation in XML.

In the past, MindXpres has been used for implementing new presentation components such as for the interactive visualisation of source code [31]. For the presented interactive data visualisation, we have taken a similar approach by implementing a data visualisation plug-in for MindXpres. Since MindXpres is based on client-side web technology, we did not have to start from scratch but could make use of existing visualisation libraries. As a starting point, we used Bostock's Data-Driven Documents (D3) JavaScript library [32] which supports complex data-driven visualisations through code. The library uses the widely supported SVG, HTML and CSS standards to generate the desired visualisation. D3 is a powerful solution offering control over every possible aspect, but it is also quite complex to use since even a simple static bar chart requires tens, if not hundreds of lines of code [33]. For this reason, we also use the C3.js JavaScript library[12], a D3-based reusable chart library that provides abstractions for most of the common chart types out of the box. Based on C3's API, one can control the state of a chart such as focusing on a data series, selecting data points, showing or hiding the data series or updating the data. With these features it is possible to change the chart in response to events such as user input or temporal triggers. Since MindXpres makes it possible to create highly dynamic and interactive plug-ins to integrate content directly in the slides (or other containers), *Requirement R1* is easily met.

Requirement R2 is the driving force behind the set of features and functionality that is offered to end users. We have already described how techniques and guidelines that contribute to the transfer of knowledge should be prioritised and this is reflected in what a user can do and sees as an end result. First of all, the default representations of the various charts and graphs are styled according to existing guidelines such as those by Tufte [26]. These guidelines include, for instance, the use of plain backgrounds or colour schemes that are composed of contrasting colours. We further made sure that enough graph and chart types are supported in order to represent all types of data characteristics a presenter might want to show to their audience. Therefore, we based ourselves on Few's classification [8] which defines the following ways for showing specific data characteristics:

- *Nominal Comparison*: compare categorised data in no particular order
- *Time Series*: visualise series of data over time
- *Ranking*: compare categorised data ordered by size
- *Part-to-Whole*: display categorised data as a ratio of the total
- *Deviation*: compare categorised data to a specific reference measure
- *Frequency Distribution*: show the count of occurrence in specific ranges
- *Correlation*: show statistical relationship between pairs of variables

Bar charts enable nominal comparisons, rankings, frequency distributions (histograms) and deviation (since bars can also go below the horizontal axis). Line charts further allow us to visualise time series, and the area under each line can optionally be filled with a colour. As an addition to bar charts, box

[12] http://c3js.org.

plots can also be used for showing deviation. Pie charts, regular bar charts and stacked bar charts allow the user to visualise how categories relate to the total amount of data. Finally, scatter plots are provided for showing correlation. Related work such as zGapMinder, ArtVis [22], GeoTime [23] and MediaViz [21] further highlights that geographical data should not be ignored. Our visualisation plug-in therefore supports different map-based visualisations such as bubble maps, choropleth maps as well as maps with pie chart overlays.

Requirement R3 demands that the visualisation and parameters should be changeable so that different views of the same data can be presented efficiently. The data to be used in a visualisation can be specified in two ways. It can either be directly defined in the MindXpres XML language or an external file can be provided. By default, D3 supports the loading of data in plain text, JSON, XML, HTML, CSV and TSV format. We have extended this list of formats with support for Excel spreadsheets by implementing a compile-time trigger in the MindXpres plug-in. The compiler converts any referenced spreadsheet data to JSON and bundles it with the presentation, which makes it easier for the JavaScript plug-in to process the data at runtime.

After providing a data set, the author can define the visualisation's starting state. This includes the setting a chart type, specifying the parts of the data to be shown initially as well as configuring specific chart components such as the zoom level, axes or legends. Subsequently, the author can define additional visualisation states to match their narrative. During the presentation, the presenter will be able to step through these states and the plug-in automatically applies the settings specified for each state. Note that any part of the configuration can

Table 1. Implemented abstractions for manipulating a visualisation.

Parameters	Description and abstractions
Highlighting	Highlighting and fading out specific elements[focus, defocus]
Visibility	Showing and hiding specific elements [show, hide]
Data sources	Load and unload data sets [load, unload, unload_all]
Data display	Data or group display settings [show, hide, set_name, set_colour]
Axis settings	Assign data group and display settings to axes [group, label, min, max, range]
Filtering	Apply or remove filter to data [apply_filter, remove_filter]
Selecting	Selecting or unselecting data [select, unselect]
Representation	Transform visualisation to a specified chart or map type [set_chart_type]
Grouping	Combine columns or groups into a new group [make_group]
Sorting	Sort data based on specified group [sort]
Gridlines	Settings for horizontal or vertical grid lines [set_spacing, enable, disable]
Regions	Select intervals on an axis for side by side display [add, remove]
Legend	Legend visibility and groups to be included [show, hide, set_groups]
Tooltip	Turn tooltip on or off [show, hide]
View area	View manipulation (zooming or panning) [set_zoom, set_x, set_y]
Chart size	Resize the chart to a given height and width [resize]
Chart rendering	Request a refresh or clear everything [redraw, clear]

change between states. This includes the data set, chart type as well as other parameters that cannot be changed in conventional presentation tools. In order to hide the complexity of the used D3 and C3 libraries, we provide abstractions for useful configuration changes in accordance to the interaction techniques provided by Yi et al. [10]. Table 1 highlights a list of abstractions implemented by our prototype, which make it easier for a presenter to define the transformations needed to bring the visualisation to the next desired state. Further, Listing 1.3, which is discussed in more detail later, shows an example of how a visualisation and its states are defined in the XML language. In this example the data is retrieved from an external file but the visualisation states are defined in the XML language. Note that the data could also be defined in the XML document itself and on the other hand the configuration could be defined in an external file.

While quantitative data can all be treated in the same way for operations such as averaging, grouping, filtering and visualising, additional work was required to support data representing geographical locations. When an abstraction related to geographical data is invoked, the relevant subset of data is automatically examined. If the data is numerical and within a certain range, it is assumed that the data represents coordinates and nothing further needs to be done. In the case that the data is in textual form, reverse geocoding is applied. This implies that the text is converted into coordinates in order that strings that represent a location (e.g. "*Belgium*" or "*Fifth Avenue New York*") can be used in the visualisation. In the current implementation the reverse geocoding is performed via the Google Maps Geocoding API[13] which requires a connection to the Internet. However, in future implementations we could also provide a local database for offline lookups. The result of the reverse geocoding process is a set of coordinates that can be used in the visualisation. The map-based visualisations are also based on D3.js. Our plug-in includes a file that contains the topological data needed for visualising countries and continents. These boundaries can also be used by the plug-in to classify coordinates by region. An extension called D3 Geo Projection[14] allows us to easily map geographic coordinates to pixel coordinates in the map viewport while taking the map's current projection method, scale and rotation into account. It was further necessary to define some operations specifically for coordinates, such as operations for calculating the distance between coordinates or finding the centre of a list of coordinates (the centroid).

In order to fulfil *Requirement R4*, the presenter is free to apply unscheduled abstractions at any time during a presentation. Some of the abstractions are triggered via the mouse. For example, by hovering over an element, the element is highlighted and the corresponding tooltip is shown. Similarly, data groups can be hidden or shown by clicking on the relevant group in the legend. However, note that not all interactions can be offered via non-intrusive mouse actions. For this reason we have integrated an interaction menu that allows the presenter to

[13] https://developers.google.com/maps/documentation/geocoding/start.
[14] https://github.com/d3/d3-3.x-api-reference/blob/master/Geo-Projections.md.

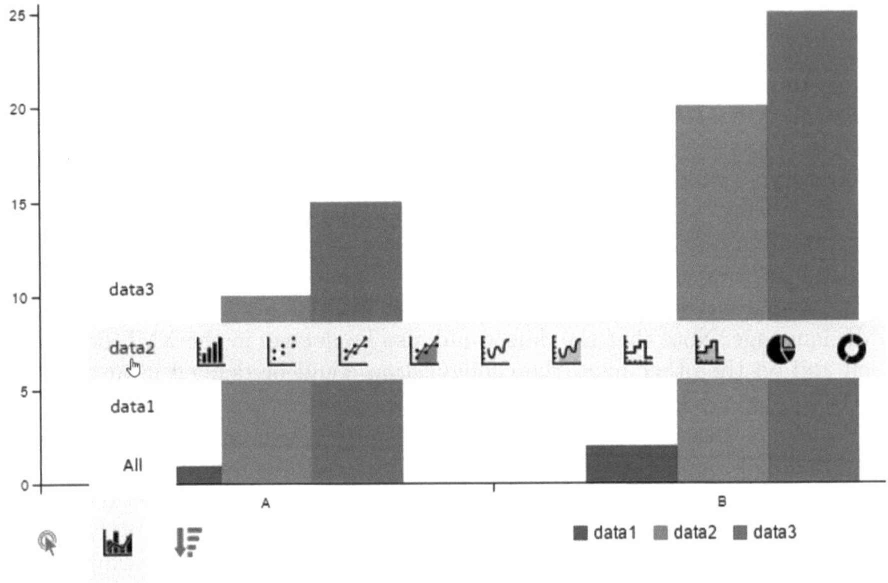

Fig. 2. Interaction menu at presentation time.

perform any of the offered interaction abstractions during the presentation as illustrated in Fig. 2.

Last but not least, *Requirement R5* has been addressed by allowing the audience to play back the visualisation at home and freely explore it. Since MindXpres is based on web technologies, a MindXpres presentation bundle can easily be made accessible online and accessed by any device running a web browser. A viewers can iterate through the predefined states as set up by the presenter, but they also have access to the menu for manually applying any of the provided abstractions. This helps a viewer to strengthen their mental model as they are free to examine the data from different angles in case something is not clear.

5 Use Case

In order to demonstrate the benefits of our interactive data visualisation plug-in, we present a short scenario that demonstrates how one can use the plug-in to create a narrative visualisation. In contrast to existing presentation tools, a presenter only needs to create one visualisation with one data set for which they define a sequence of views that support their oral narrative. This not only requires much less time and effort than existing workarounds, but it also makes it easier to apply changes at a later point in time. In the presented scenario, the goal is to compare the tax and social burdens of salaried employees in the 27 member states of the European Union. As a starting point, a JSON file that contains the relevant data for the year 2014 is used [34]. A small snippet of the

JSON content is shown in Listing 1.2. A dynamic and interactive visualisation is then used to illustrate the extra money an employer has to pay in order that an employee will receive exactly one euro after taxes. Since the presentation is going to be delivered to a Belgian audience, the presenter starts with an explanation of the tax situation in Belgium. At first, a simple chart is shown in Fig. 3(a) with a blue bar representing the one euro the employee receives.

```
[
  ["Austria",1,0.5,0.32,0.29],
  ["Belgium",1,0.62,0.5,0.22],
  ["Bulgaria",1,0.22,0.11,0.16],
  ...
  ["Spain",1,0.39,0.21,0.08],
  ["Sweden",1,0.42,0.33,0],
  ["United Kingdom",1,0.14,0.2,0.12]
]
```

Listing 1.2. A snippet of the JSON data used in the scenario.

In a next step, the presenter introduces the concept of employer social security and adds it to the chart in the form of the orange extension to the original blue bar in Fig. 3(b), in order to provide an idea of the proportions. Note that the scale of the horizontal axis automatically adjusts and now shows a linear scale from 0 to the total costs of 1.6 euro so far. The same procedure is repeated for the income tax (green) and the employee social security (red), introducing one item at a time in order to keep the audience focussed on the explanations (Fig. 3(c)). The exact values of the different parts that make up the bar are shown in a small table when the mouse cursor is hovered over the bar. In a next step, the presenter transforms the visualisation into a pie chart which shows the ratio of each part as a percentage, revealing that an employee only receives 42.7% of what the employer pays as shown in Fig. 3(d).

In order to get a better understanding of what these values mean, the presenter switches back to a bar chart and compares the Belgian with the average EU employer costs as illustrated in Fig. 3(e). In order to show the variation in employer costs across Europe, the presenter can zoom out and show all the countries in the data set side by side as highlighted in Fig. 3(f). By default the countries are ordered alphabetically and if the list is too long to fit on the screen, the presenter can drag up and down to scroll in the list. Note that at any point the presenter can zoom back to a single country, for instance Cyprus, in order to explain why it is the country with the lowest employer costs as shown in Fig. 3(g). Finally, the presenter decides to show the full list again, but this time sorted by total employer costs in order to point out the cheapest and most expensive countries from the perspective of an employer as highlighted in Fig. 3(h).

So far the presenter has only used graphs to explore the data and spatial properties have not been taken into account. For instance, it might be interesting to see whether the location plays a role and if countries that are close to Belgium have similar high taxes. Figure 4 shows an alternative map-based visualisation with Belgium and its neighbouring countries. For each country the centroid is calculated and a pie chart containing the different tax ratios is shown in the centre of the country's boundaries. Note that the presenter never had to deal

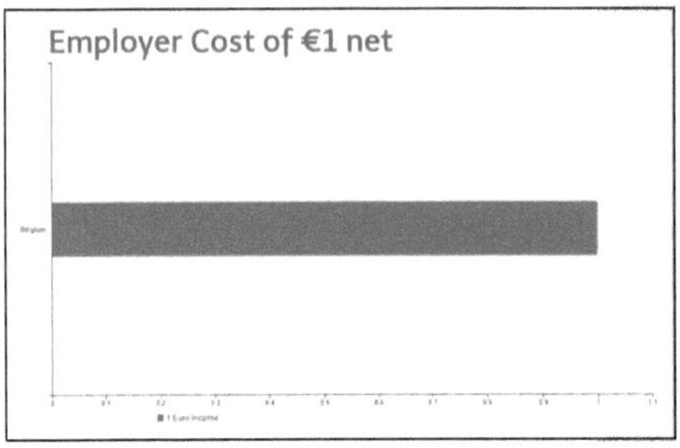

(a) One Euro received by employee

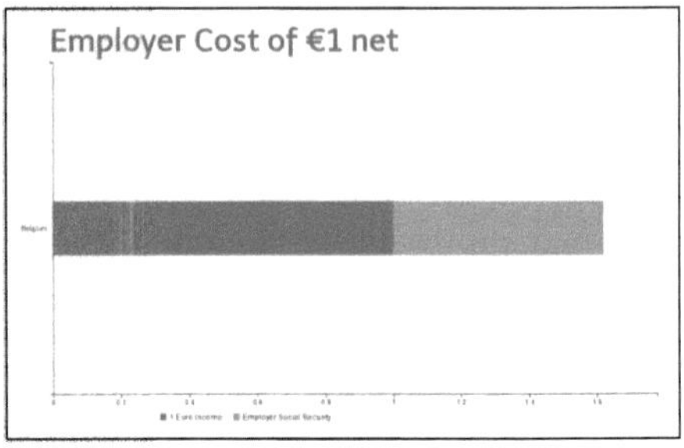

(b) Add employer social security

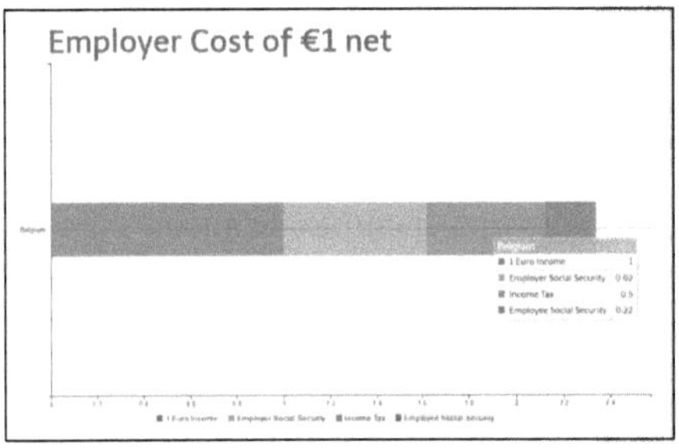

(c) Add income tax and employee social security

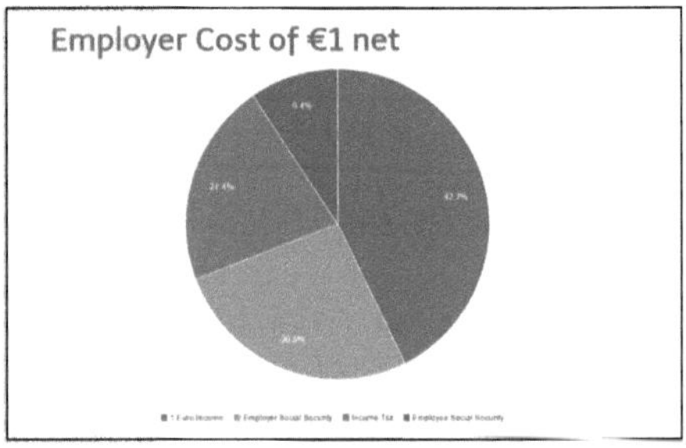

(d) Switch to pie chart

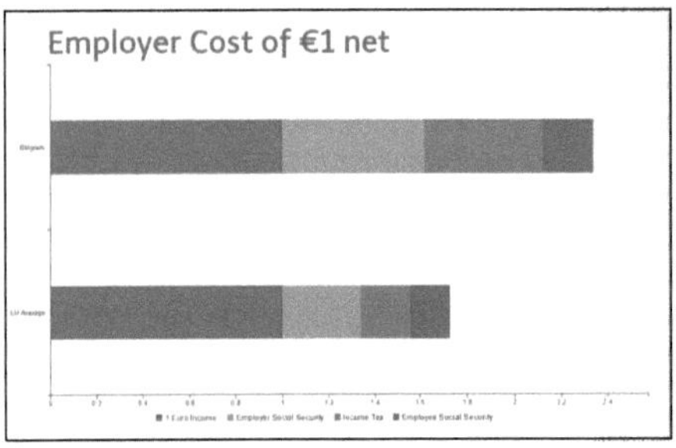

(e) Compare with EU average

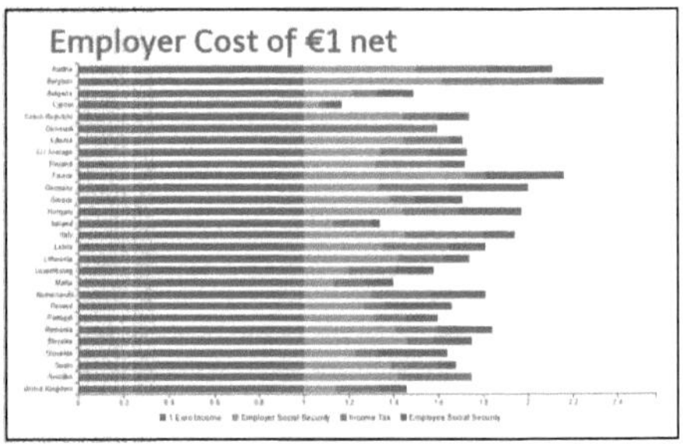

(f) All countries (alphabetically)

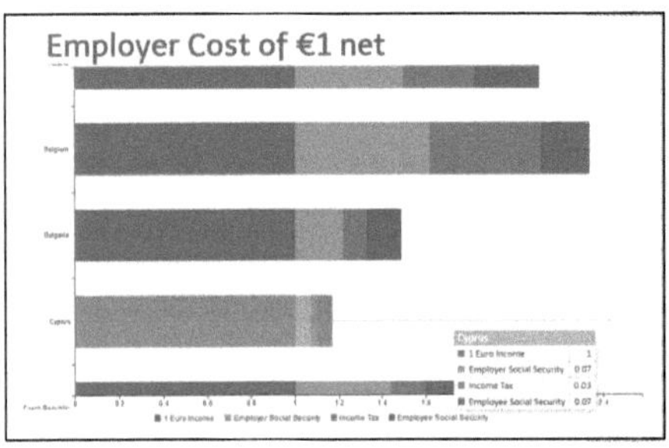

(g) Zoom in

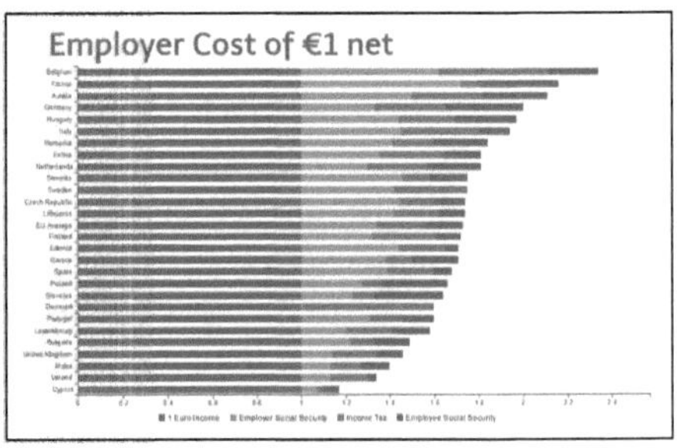

(h) All countries (sorted by value)

Fig. 3. Various graph-based phases of a visualisation for EU employer costs. (Color figure online)

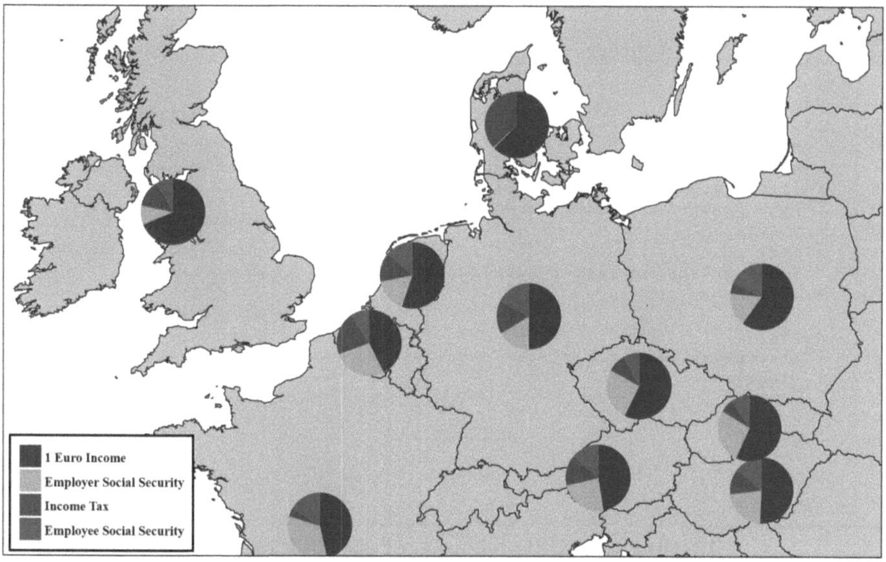

Fig. 4. A map-based visualisation of the EU employer costs.

with any coordinates as the tool automatically applied reverse geocoding based on the country names contained in the country column of the data set and deduced that the granularity of the categorisation was at the level of countries.

Note that even without the narrative, a viewer might still derive the implicit messages that the presenter would normally present orally (e.g. "*Belgium employees receive less than half of what the employer pays*", or "*employer costs in Belgium are very high compared to the rest of Europe*"). This is in line with the findings of Hullman and Diakopoulos who state that narrative visualisations can be designed to deliver predefined implicit messages [14]. It further demonstrates the potential value of our interactive data visualisation plug-in for audience members who review the slides after the delivery of a presentation (e.g. students using the slides as study material) as they can play back the sequence and come to the intended conclusions without the oral narrative.

Listing 1.3 shows how the discussed scenario has been defined in the XML-based MindXpres authoring language. The illustrated XML snippet forms part of a larger XML document defining the entire presentation. The `infovis` tag on the first line tells the MindXpres compiler and runtime engine that our information visualisation plug-in has to be invoked in order to process the child tags and render the relevant content. The `data` tag then specifies the data file to be used by the plug-in. Finally, a list of visualisation states or views are provided.

```
<infovis>
 <data file="tax_eu.csv"></data>
 <config>
  <view>
   <chart type="bar"variant="stacked"/>
   <axis dim="x"group="socialtax"/>
   <axis dim="y"group="countries"/>
   <filter group="countries"value="Belgium"/>
   <show group="socialtax"sub="income"/>
  </view>
  <view>
    <show group="socialtax"sub="security1"/>
  </view>
  ...
  <view>
   <show group="socialtax"sub="security2"/>
  </view>
  <view>
   <chart type="pie" />
  </view>
  ...
 </config>
</infovis>
```

Listing 1.3. XML definition of visualisation states.

By default the first view in the list will be used as an initial state, resulting in the chart shown in Fig. 3(a). The succeeding views contain instructions on how to adapt the visualisation for subsequent visualisation states. In this case, subgroups of data are made visible and since the chart type is a stacked bar chart, they will be added to the relevant bars. When the author wants to switch to a pie chart, the `chart` tag is used to set a new chart type. Note that any settings from previous views, such as the filter put in place to select only data from Belgium, are still valid. In this case, axis settings are also kept but are ignored as they are not relevant for a pie chart. Nevertheless, when we switch back to a bar chart in a later view, the earlier axis settings still apply. The rest of the states shown in the scenario are achieved in a similar manner and are mainly the result of applying filter and sorting instructions.

6 Discussion and Conclusion

Information visualisation has become more dynamic and interactive by adapting to recent media for content delivery. We started by discussing the benefits of dynamic and interactive visualisations and have presented the relevant concepts that contribute to their success. In particular we have shown how narratives can be used to make data more memorable and how a viewer's mental model can be strengthened by allowing them to interact with the data. However, we identified that the benefits of such interactive visualisations are currently not applied to their full potential in the context of presentation tools. This can partially be attributed to a lack of technical support. For instance, in a popular presentation tool such as PowerPoint there are many different chart types, but the result is always a static view which is unsuitable for data exploration or narrative visualisation. There are a number of workarounds including the use of basic enter and exit animations but unfortunately one cannot make changes to the underlying data or visualisation parameters during these animations.

Related work shows many interesting tools for the exploration of data but hardly any of them have been adapted for usage in a presentation. In particular, these tools are often specialised stand-alone applications with a complex user interface and have little to no support for creating visualisations that support a narrative. Based on the investigated related work and established interactive and narrative visualisation techniques, we derived a set of five requirements for interactive data visualisation in the context of presentations. We have further presented the implementation of an interactive and narrative visualisation prototype that meets these requirements and has been realised as a generic data visualisation plug-in for the MindXpres presentation tool. The discussed plug-in allows presenters to directly embed interactive and narrative visualisations into their presentation. In order to support a variety of different data sets and visualisation styles, we have defined a number of generic abstractions for changing specific aspects of a visualisation. The presenter can use these abstractions to predefine a series of visualisation states supporting their story but they can also be applied freely during the delivery of a presentation. Note that the provided abstractions are not restricted to the data representation (e.g. chart type or zoom level) but also allow the underlying data to be manipulated. For instance, data can be filtered, sorted or added in order to better fit the message the presenter is trying to deliver. Thereby, interactive visualisations as support for an oral narrative can be created with minimal effort, in contrast to existing slideware such as PowerPoint where a new graph would have to be created for each state. Our approach also shows benefits when changes have to be made to the narrative and when the visualisations need to be adapted. Since nowadays slide decks form an important part of the reference material that is provided to students, the plug-in not only allows them to play back the visualisation at home but further enables them to freely explore the data in order to clarify any questions they might have and to strengthen their mental model.

The features that our solution offers to end users are based on well-established techniques and guidelines for information visualisation. For example, we ensured to provide support for all the message types that can be visualised using quantitative data, as defined by Few [8]. This has been achieved by supporting a wide range of common chart types (and their variations) such as line, bar or pie charts as well as scatter plots. Furthermore, we support map-based visualisations such as bubble charts and choropleth maps to illustrate spatial date relations. Our current solutions also supports all the interaction techniques defined by Yi [10] except for techniques related to the *connect* principle, which would allow viewers to show items which are related to a selected one. The support of this principle has proven to be non-trivial as there is no similarity metrics that works for all data and contexts. Further investigation is needed to see how we might abstract this particular interaction technique in the future.

In correspondence with the declarative content authoring approach of the MindXpres presentation platform, the presented plug-in extends the XML-based MindXpres authoring language in order to define interactive and narrative visualisations based on raw data sets. However, in the near future we foresee a graphical authoring component. The interaction menu for real-time modifications shown earlier in Fig. 2 has potential for being used at authoring time. A visualisation sequence could, for instance, be defined as a sequence of snapshots created by using the menu to specify the desired visualisation states.

In conclusion, the presented MindXpres extension represents a major step towards applying the benefits of interactive data exploration and storytelling to the domain of presentation tools. The benefits of applying interactive and narrative visualisations in presentations has been illustrated in a use case where we also highlighted the flexibility of our approach. Even if our current prototype has been developed as a plug-in for the MindXpres presentation platform, we are convinced that our findings and proposed abstractions for data exploration are general enough and can also be applied to other presentation tools. Furthermore, the requirements that we have defined for interactive information visualisation in presentation tools might serve third-party slideware vendors as input for improving their existing products in order to improve the oral knowledge transfer when presenting specific data sets.

References

1. Kosara, R., Mackinlay, J.: Storytelling: the next step for visualization. Computer **46**, 44–50 (2013)
2. Segel, E., Heer, J.: Narrative visualization: telling stories with data. IEEE Trans. Visual Comput. Graphics **16**, 1139–1148 (2010)
3. Parker, I.: Absolute powerpoint: can a software package edit our thoughts. The New Yorker **28**, 76–87 (2001)
4. Show Me - New Ways of Visualising Data. The Economist (2010). http://www.economist.com/node/15557455. Accessed 29 Jun 2016
5. Zhicheng, L., Stasko, J.T.: Mental models, visual reasoning and interaction in information visualization: a top-down perspective. IEEE Trans. Visual Comput. Graphics **16**, 999–1008 (2010)
6. Ware, C.: Information Visualization: Perception for Design, 3rd edn. Elsevier, Amsterdam (2012)
7. Ellis, W.D.: A Source Book of Gestalt Psychology. Psychology Press, New York (1999)
8. Few, S.: Show Me the Numbers: Designing Tables and Graphs to Enlighten, 2nd edn. Analytics Press, Burlingame (2004)
9. Gibson, J.J.: Observations on active touch. Psychol. Rev. **69**, 477 (1962)
10. Yi, J.S., Kang, Y.A., Stasko, J., Jacko, J.: Toward a deeper understanding of the role of interaction in information visualization. IEEE Trans. Visual Comput. Graphics **13**, 1224–1231 (2007)
11. Dix, A., Ellis, G.: Starting simple: adding value to static visualisation through simple interaction (1998)
12. Siirtola, H.: Interactive visualization of multidimensional data. Ph.D. thesis, University of Tampere (2007)

13. Austin, M.: Useful Fictions: Evolution, Anxiety, and the Origins of Literature. University of Nebraska Press, Lincoln (2011)
14. Hullman, J., Diakopoulos, N.: Visualization rhetoric: framing effects in narrative visualization. IEEE Trans. Visual Comput. Graphics **17**, 2231–2240 (2011)
15. Dawkes, H., Tweedie, L.A., Spence, B.: VICKI: The VIsualisation Construction KIt. In: AVI 1996, Workshop on Advanced Visual Interfaces. ACM (1996)
16. Ahlberg, C.: Spotfire: an information exploration environment. ACM SIGMOD Rec. **25**, 25–29 (1996)
17. Swayne, D.F., Lang, D.T., Buja, A., Cook, D.: GGobi: evolving from XGobi into an extensible framework for interactive data visualization. Comput. Stat. Data Anal. **43**, 423–444 (2003)
18. Viegas, F.B., Wattenberg, M., van Ham, F., Kriss, J., McKeon, M.: ManyEyes: a site for visualization at internet scale. IEEE Trans. Visual Comput. Graphics **13**, 1121–1128 (2007)
19. Rosling, H.: TED Talk: Hans Rosling Shows The Best Stats You've Ever Seen (2006). www.ted.com
20. Robertson, G., Fernandez, R., Fisher, D., Lee, B., Stasko, J.: Effectiveness of animation in trend visualization. IEEE Trans. Visual Comput. Graphics **14**, 1325–1332 (2008)
21. Devezas, T., Nunes, S., Rodríguez, M.T.: MediaViz: an interactive visualization platform for online media studies. In: HIC 2015, International Workshop on Human-Centric Independent Computing. ACM (2015)
22. Dumas, B., Moerman, B., Trullemans, S., Signer, B.: ArtVis: combining advanced visualisation and tangible interaction for the exploration, analysis and browsing of digital artwork collections. In: AVI 2014, 12th International Working Conference on Advanced Visual Interfaces. ACM (2014)
23. Eccles, R., Kapler, T., Harper, R., Wright, W.: Stories in GeoTime. In: VAST 2007, IEEE Symposium on Visual Analytics Science and Technology. IEEE (2007)
24. Siegrist, M.: The use or misuse of three-dimensional graphs to represent lower-dimensional data. Behav. Inf. Technol. **15**, 96–100 (1996)
25. Fischer, M.H.: Do irrelevant depth cues affect the comprehension of bar graphs? Appl. Cogn. Psychol. **14**, 151–162 (2000)
26. Tufte, E.R., Graves-Morris, P.: The Visual Display of Quantitative Information, 2nd edn. Graphics Press, Cheshire (1983)
27. Bishop, J.L., Verleger, M.A.: The flipped classroom: a survey of the research. In: ASEE 2013, 120th American Society for Engineering Education Conference (2013)
28. Roels, R., Signer, B.: MindXpres: an extensible content-driven cross-media presentation platform. In: Benatallah, B., Bestavros, A., Manolopoulos, Y., Vakali, A., Zhang, Y. (eds.) WISE 2014. LNCS, vol. 8787, pp. 215–230. Springer, Cham (2014). doi:10.1007/978-3-319-11746-1_16
29. Roels, R., Baeten, Y., Signer, B.: An interactive data visualisation approach for next generation presentation tools: towards rich presentation-based data exploration and storytelling. In: CSEDU 2016, 8th International Conference on Computer Supported Education. SCITEPRESS (2016)
30. Roels, R., Signer, B.: A unified communication platform for enriching and enhancing presentations with active learning components. In: ICALT 2014, 14th IEEE International Conference on Advanced Learning Technologies. IEEE (2014)
31. Roels, R., Mestereaga, P., Signer, B.: Towards enhanced presentation-based teaching of programming - an interactive source code visualisation approach. In: CSEDU 2015, 7th International Conference on Computer Supported Education. SCITEPRESS (2015)

32. Bostock, M., Ogievetsky, V., Heer, J.: D3 data-driven documents. IEEE Trans. Visual Comput. Graphics **17**, 2301–2309 (2011)
33. Bostock, M.: Let's Make a Bar Chart (2013). http://bost.ocks.org/mike/bar/. Accessed 29 Jun 2016
34. Rogers, J., Philippe, C.: The Tax Burden of Typical Workers in the EU 28, vol. 17. New Direction, Brussels (2014)

Feedback Authoring for Exploratory Activities: The Case of a Logo-Based 3D Microworld

Sokratis Karkalas[1](✉), Manolis Mavrikis[1], Marios Xenos[2], and Chronis Kynigos[2]

[1] UCL Knowledge Lab, UCL Institute of Education, London WC1N 3QS, UK
{s.karkalas,m.mavrikis}@ucl.ac.uk

[2] Educational Technology Lab, National Kapodistrian University of Athens, Athens, Greece
{mariosxenos,kynigos}@ppp.uoa.gr

Abstract. This paper presents AuthELO an authoring environment that can be used for the configuration of logging and authoring of automated feedback for exploratory learning objects (ELOs). ELOs are web components (widgets) that can be integrated with learning platforms to synthesise highly interactive learning environments. AuthELO has been developed in the context of the MCSquared project that is developing a platform for authoring interactive educational e-books. This platform comprises an extendable set of diverse widgets that can be used to generate instances of exploratory activities that can be employed in various learning scenarios. AuthELO was designed and developed to provide a simple, common and efficient authoring interface that can normalise the diversity of these widgets and give the ability to non-experts to easily develop or customise the feedback that is provided to students using a data-driven approach. In this paper we describe the architecture and design characteristics of AuthELO and a small-scale evaluation with activities in a logo-based 3D microworld called Malt+. We reflect on both the challenges of the authoring process and the pedagogical potential of the feedback when these activities are used by students.

Keywords: Feedback authoring · Exploratory learning environments

1 Introduction

Authoring educational interactive tasks is a challenging and time consuming endeavour particularly if they include some form of adaptive or intelligent support to the learner. While there is an abundance of tools that allow non-expert developers, such as educational designers or teachers, to author their preferred activities, these are limited to static content or to pre-defined question-answer activities. As we review in Sect. 2, researchers in the field of Intelligent Tutoring Systems are looking into the development of tools that ease the authoring process for ITS but have largely remained in the realm of structured interaction.

G. Costagliola et al. (Eds.): CSEDU 2016, CCIS 739, pp. 259–278, 2017.
DOI: 10.1007/978-3-319-63184-4_14

We are interested in highly interactive, exploratory activities that take place within open learning environments including microworlds [1,2]. Although such environments can be effective in supporting learners' development of conceptual knowledge, they require significant amount of human or computer support [3]. Despite the fact that research in the area has demonstrated that it is possible to delegate part of this support to intelligent components (e.g. [4,5]), there have been little attempts to reduce the entry threshold for both programmers and end-users [6].

This paper presents AuthELO, a tool for authoring exploratory learning objects (ELOs), configuring the logging and programming the automated feedback they provide. This tool has been developed in the context of the Mathematical Creativity Squared (MCSquared) EU-funded project (http://mc2-project.eu/) that is developing a platform for authoring interactive educational e-books. This platform comprises an extendable set of diverse widgets that can be used to generate instances of exploratory learning activities that can be employed in various learning scenarios. In this project we designed and developed a tool that is able to provide a simple, common and efficient authoring interface that can normalise the heterogeneity of these widgets and reduces the time it takes and the skills required to program the feedback that can be provided to students based on their interaction.

Section 3 presents the development methodology that underpins the design of AuthELO. Sections 4 and 5 present the architecture and the tool in detail. Section 6 presents an evaluation of the current prototype with a logo-based microworld (Malt+) and Sect. 7 concludes the paper and briefly discusses our next steps.

2 Related Work

The development of learning material that is interactive and provides automated intelligent feedback to the students falls naturally into the category of ITS authoring systems. There have been many such systems developed in the past. Database-related tutors like SQL-Tutor, EER-Tutor and Normit [7] are cases that follow the constraint-based modelling approach. To author web- and constraint-based tutors [8] developed ASPIRE. The use of simulation-based authoring is presented in [9]. An approach that is used for the development of adaptive hypermedia is presented in [10]. An attempt to lower significantly the skill threshold required is the model-tracing approach [6]. Most of these approaches, although different, they converge in that they all presuppose the use of low level technical expertise for the authoring. Systems that require no programming include the ASSISTment Builder [11] and Redeem[12]. The latter is an approach that combines existing material with teaching expertise to develop simple intelligent ITSs. A mixed system that supports the development of two types of ITSs is CTAT [13,14]. It supports the development of cognitive tutors and example-tracing tutors. The latter case requires no programming at all.

All of these systems are typically domain-specific solutions that may require low level technical expertise and usually offer fairly limited and not easily generalisable output. That seriously limits the applicability of these tools to a wider range of learning scenarios. One of the most recent developments in the field is the Generalized Intelligent Framework for Tutoring (GIFT) [15] that provides tools to support various elements of the authoring process. Although GIFT targets domain experts with little or no knowledge of computer programming or instructional design, at the moment it mostly enables rapid development of expert models and other domain knowledge. This results in a fully-fledged ITS that depends on the services provided by GIFT. That may limit the re-usability of the authoring tool with other learning platforms or may be beyond what is needed or what is possible with limited resources (e.g. of a teacher wanting to adapt a simple activity). At a conceptual and architectural level our system resembles SEPIA [16]. SEPIA is designed so that automated support can be added in the form of an epiphytic application that is external to the learning environment. Integration does not require changes in the target environment and interoperation is not based on domain specific models and tools.

From an end-user pespective, the most relevant solution to our approach, and the one that seems to require the least amount of cognitive load for the author, is the example-tracing approach [13]. The author develops feedback by executing the activity like a student. This provides the author with a tree-like view that is representative of the current state of the student. The author can then annotate the diagram and determine the behaviour of the tutor. The disadvantage of this approach is that it is domain-specific and not generalisable beyond structured tasks that have a relatively limited range of possible alternative paths. In an exploratory learning environment these paths are potentially infinite.

In our system we follow the example-tracing approach but we are not using the visualisation part simply because it is impossible to represent visually all the possible states in such diverse domains and open environments. Our tool must be generic enough so that it can be used with exploratory learning environments. Support is expected to be task-dependent but tasks may not be structured. Authoring must be based on data that becomes available as the student interacts with the environment. The author generates data and utilises this information in order to form sensible rules for the generation of feedback. These rules are currently expressed through programming but our intention is to provide a service that can be accessible through different levels of specificity. That will make the system usable by authors with different levels of expertise without compromising the ability to intervene at the lowest level if necessary. A high level language that is specialised in feedback authoring and a visual programming shell will be the high level constructs that will make it easily accessible to non-technical users.

3 Methodology

In this project the main objective is to design and develop an authoring tool for the engineering of automated (intelligent) support for online learning activities.

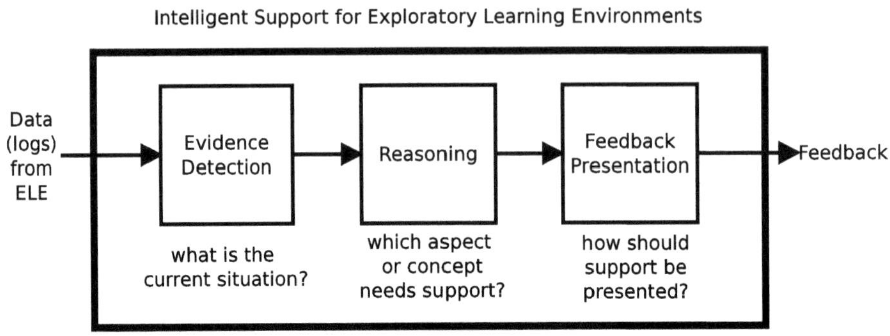

Fig. 1. Conceptual data flow of support for exploratory learning. From [5].

As mentioned, we are interested in highly interactive 'widgets' that can either be standalone activities or live in the context of an e-book. Such widgets offer learning opportunities through exploration and discovery of knowledge in an unstructured manner (Fig. 1).

The methodology we have followed for the design and development of Auth-ELO is based on previous work presented in [5]. This approach is based on the premise that the complexity of the task can be reduced and made manageable through the compartmentalisation of different concerns regarding the different aspects of the problem. In practice this can be done by focusing on the three most important questions related to support:

- What is the situation now? (evidence)
- Which aspect needs support? (reasoning)
- How should the support be presented for maximum efficacy? (presentation)

Each one of these questions corresponds to different aspects of the problem and thus may require different approaches and expertise. Considering these aspects separately reduces the skill threshold required to deal with the problem in its entirety. Typically, in this scheme, the development of support moves towards the opposite direction of the data flow. Designers would start from the presentation and the process would gradually move towards the development of components that produce evidence. In this project the presentation is designed based on the assumption that an exploratory learning system should not intervene in the process in an intrusive manner [3]. Support should not be provided in order to manipulate the students and control their behaviour. The system should be discreet and inform the users for potential issues but not interrupt the learning process. On the other hand support should always be available on demand. Students may not be able to exploit the full potential of such learning environments if there is not enough support available to direct them [17,18]. In this tool support is provided after the student initiates the process. We also provide the learning platform the ability to use the same functionality in order to display informative messages to the users regarding the current state of the activity.

The focus of this work is on reasoning and the acquisition of evidence that can support it. For the former we collected a number of use cases of specific learning activities developed in GeoGebra[1], Malt+[2] and FractionsLab[3]. Expert designers and educators provided us with complete usage scenarios for each activity that include potential student misconceptions, landmarks that can indicate important states of the constructions and the respective feedback that the system is expected to provide to students. This information helped us form the initial requirements for the reasoning part and they have also been transformed into batteries of tests for the technical evaluation of the software.

The data acquisition part comes after because it depends on the reasoning part. Having all the information about the needs of the reasoning part enables us to identify the requirements for the evidence part. The challenges we identified for that part follow:

- need for methods to make the widgets generate the required data
- need for methods to transfer this data between tiers
- need for methods to efficiently store that data in the tool and make it processable so that it can be used for answering queries to the reasoning part

4 Architecture

The tool is a native HTML5 application with no external dependencies and is physically decoupled from learning platforms. It does not implement any platform-specific or proprietary functionality and therefore its service is not limited to an existing platform. It has been designed in a way so that its functionality can be provided in a service oriented approach using standardised communication protocols and data formats. After the tool is virtually integrated with a learning platform from the users' perspective the whole system looks unified and homogeneous. Integration is seamless and requires nothing more that setting up a url along with the parameters that provide information on how to instantiate the learning object to be configured and where to store the configuration data. This information is stored in the learning platform and is used whenever an author wants to configure logging and automated feedback for a learning object.

The author initiates this process in the learning platform and implicitly gets redirected to AuthELO. From that point on the tool takes over. It creates an instance of the widget that lives in its own private and secure space (sandbox). The two software components operate as independent applications in parallel (asynchronously) within the same browser instance. The glue between them is another component that is called Web Integration & Interoperability Layer (WIIL). WIIL as the name suggests, is a web component that can be used to integrate other web components with a platform. It can also provide a simple yet efficient communication mechanism so that the integrated components can

[1] https://www.geogebra.org/.
[2] http://etl.ppp.uoa.gr/malt2/.
[3] http://fractionslab.lkl.ac.uk/.

be interoperable. This is described in [19]. An earlier version of the WIIL and its potential usage was presented in [20].

Upon instantiation, the widget sends to AuthELO its widget-specific metadata. That is information about the types of elements that can exist in the widget environment and the types of events that these elements can generate. This data is maintained in local in-memory databases[4] at the AuthELO side of the browser. AuthELO uses this information to construct dynamically a graphical user interface for the configuration of logging. Something that needs to be noted here is the dynamic nature of this process. There are no presumptions about the information that is received from the widgets. Different widgets may provide different metadata and that, in turn, may result in the formation of different interfaces.

This GUI is immediately usable by the author. The author can set up data logging rules that have immediate effect on how the instance behaves. The rules are stored in local databases in AuthELO and they are also sent to the widget so that the respective event handlers can be registered. After registration, the widget is able to generate data according to what the author prescribed in the configuration interface. This data becomes directly available to the author for inspection through the WIIL (see activity log in Fig. 2). The author uses this information to make decisions about what feedback needs to be provided to the students (Fig. 8). This part of the configuration is also stored in local databases.

The logging and feedback configuration is then passed by the tool to the learning platform, so that these settings can become available to the actual widget instances that are going to be used by students. The learning platform

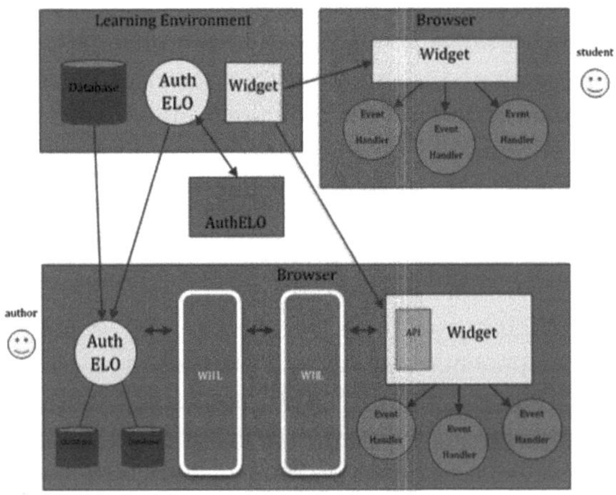

Fig. 2. AuthELO's architecture.

[4] We used TaffyDB (http://www.taffydb.com/) — an open source, lightweight and efficient NoSQL database.

sends these settings as part of the initialisation parameters during the widget launch process.

5 The AuthELO Tool

AuthELO is designed to provide a generic interface between web-based learning objects, learning platforms and authors that want to synthesise exploratory learning activities with them. The design is based on the following five main requirements:

- Authors must be able to dynamically configure what data will be logged by a learning object during a session with a user. This can be data generated from interactions between the user and the widget and derivative data that gets generated by the widget itself as a result of some event.
- Authors must be able to specify rules about real-time feedback that should be provided to the students. These rules should be based on log data that is dynamically generated as the student engages with the activity.
- It should be possible for authors to configure all the available widgets through a common interface. This interface should be able to hide the diversity of potentially heterogeneous learning components that might be offered in the system.
- The tool must not impose barriers in terms of skills and technological expertise. Teachers with a certain degree of IT literacy should be able to use it for authoring of interactive learning material.

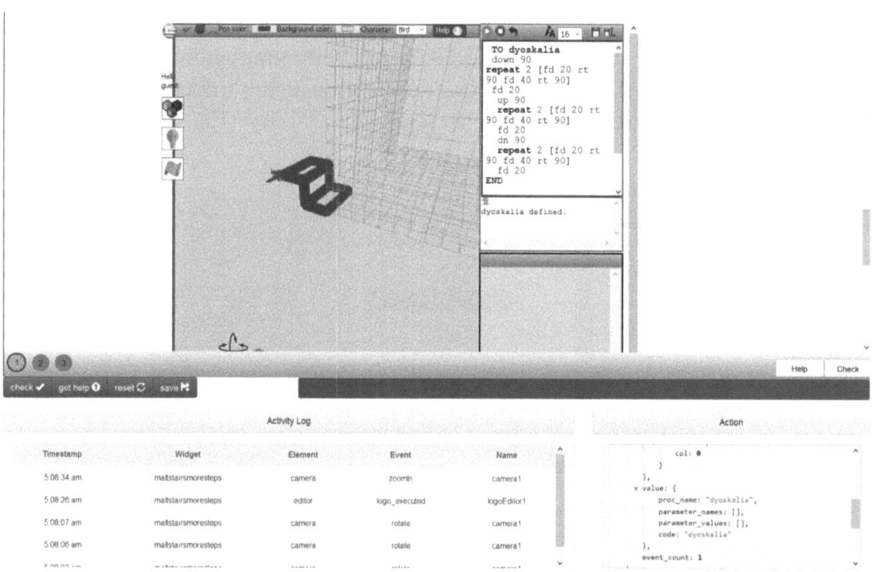

Fig. 3. The authoring interface provides a live instance of the activity along with a toolset for testing and debugging.

- The tool must be able to offer opportunities for exploratory authoring of feedback reducing the cognitive load that is expected for non-structured tasks of exploratory activities.

The general aim of this project is to provide a tool that offers the following:

- It is simple to use
- It can be used with diverse learning components
- It can be used effectively to configure feedback for non-structured tasks in exploratory learning environments

5.1 The Authoring Interface

When the tool gets instantiated it looks like Fig. 3. The authoring interface is provided as a triplet of tabs named ‘widget’, ‘logging’ and ‘feedback’. The first page (widget) provides a visual of the activity along with a basic toolset that can be used for testing and debugging. In the middle of the page there is a live instance of the widget that represents the activity that is going to be presented to the student through the learning platform. The author can interact with it in the same way that a student would and experiment with different configurations until the result satisfies the learning objectives that have been set. During this interaction the author can see what data gets generated and display messages useful for debugging.

5.2 Authoring Logging

Configuration options for logging are given in the homonymous tab-page. This page is dynamically constructed by the application using information retrieved from the live widget instance that represents the activity (Fig. 4).

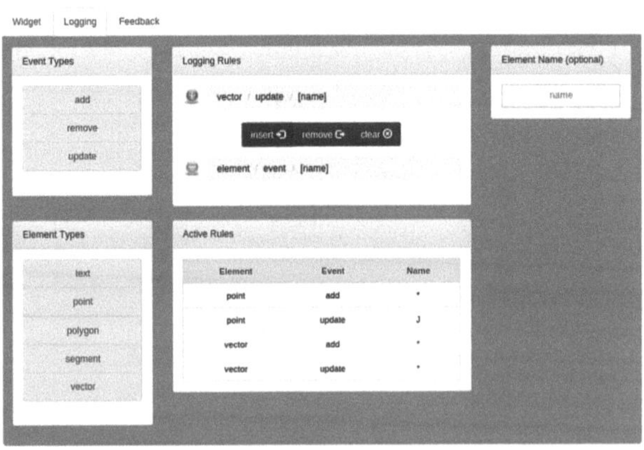

Fig. 4. Logging Configuration.

That means that this part of the tool dynamically changes for different widgets or widgets that contain different constructions. The aim is to for the tool to work with different widget 'instances' i.e. different configurations of the same widget but for different activities. The challenge is that these instances contain different types of elements able to generate different types of events. The tool is able to dynamically query the instance and obtain all the information that is necessary to reconstruct itself and adapt to the individual characteristics and needs of the activity. But how can that be possible? Widgets may be third party components that do not provide standard communication interfaces and data formats. So how do we deal with diversity? There is no magic behind this wonderful feature. Communication and interoperability between the tool and widget instances go through WIIL [19]. In that layer we can reshape APIs and semantically enhance the metadata that is received from instances whenever that is deemed necessary. That takes care of diversity but what happens if the initial construction that is given for the activity does not contain all the necessary elements and events? The assumption is that the tool queries the live instance and retrieves information about what is currently present in the construction. For that part there is no easy answer. You either get the widget implementers to expose a method that provides information about all the possible elements and events for that particular widget or you get the activity author to create extra elements that may need to be recorded in the log files and hide them from the user. In this particular implementation we followed the second approach simply because it would be impossible to force widget vendors to change their implementations and it would be impractical to visualise endless lists of element and event types that would not be used in the activity. Cluttering the authoring interface with unnecessary information would compromise the usability of the tool.

In this page the author can see a list of the element types that are supported by the widget along with the types of events that these elements can generate. These lists are presented as sequences of buttons. The author can press a button and select an element or an event type. When that happens the name of the selected entity appears in the 'logging rules' section next to the plus sign.

The rules have immediate effect on how the instance behaves. They are stored in local databases in AuthELO and they are also sent to the widget so that the respective event handlers can be registered. WIIL takes care of the underlying operations for that. After registration, the widget is able to generate data according to what the author prescribed. In Fig. 5 we can see where new rules are formed. A combination of an element type with an event type gives us a valid rule. The author can optionally provide a name for a specific element if needed. If the rule is ready, it can be inserted by pressing the button 'insert'. The rule in Fig. 5 instructs the system to generate events when the value of the point element 'A' changes.

If we want to generate update events for any element of a point type then we can omit the name. If we attempt to insert a more generic rule than one that

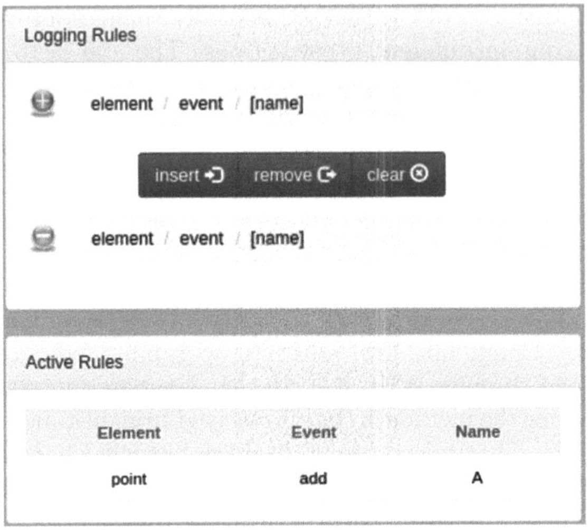

Fig. 5. Rule insertion.

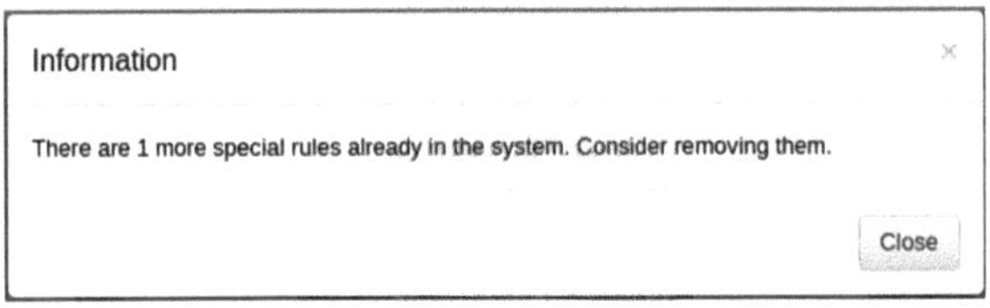

Fig. 6. More general rule.

already exists then the system will give us a warning message but it will allow the operation (Fig. 6).

The opposite is not true. If we attempt to insert a more specific rule than one that already exists then the system will not perform the operation because it will not have any effect at all (Fig. 7).

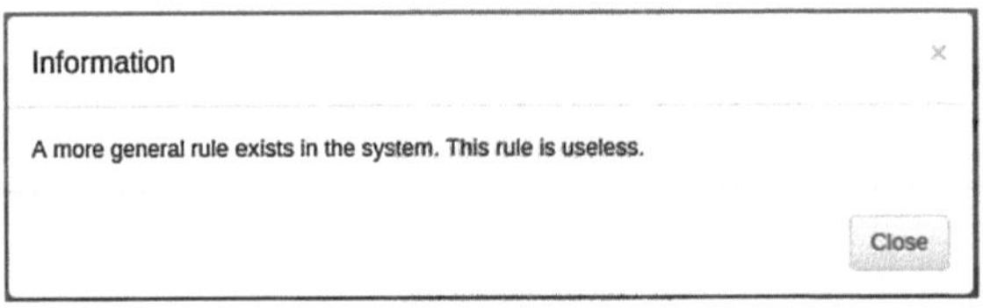

Fig. 7. More special rule.

If the rule is exactly the same as an already existing one the system will reject it. If a rule needs to be removed then the author can select it by clicking on the list

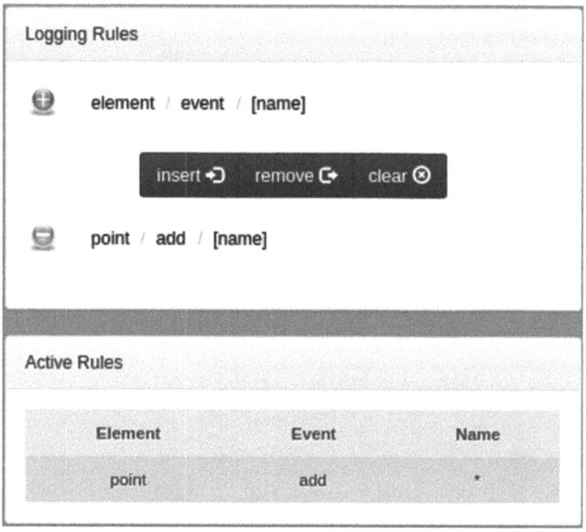

Fig. 8. Rule removal.

in the 'Active Rules' section. The selected rule will then appear in the 'Logging Rules' section next to the minus sign. The rule can be deleted by pressing the 'remove' button.

When a rule is inserted it gets immediately activated. That means that the author can go back to the 'Widget' tab and start generating data by interacting with the widget. The data appears at the bottom of the page.

5.3 Authoring Feedback

The configuration or authoring of feedback can be done through the editor that is provided in the 'Feedback' tab-page (see Fig. 9). In this part the author can utilise the data generated and displayed in the 'Widget' tab-page and specify rules that state what needs to be done if certain conditions are satisfied. In this version of the tool these rules must be expressed in JavaScript. This is done through a specialised editor that provides support to the author and basic error checking[5]. This way the author can dynamically inject new functionality into the system.

Feedback is presented either through an area under the widget instance or through an intelligent assistant that looks like an owl and displays the message in a bubble (see Fig. 10). Authors simply have to change a parameter when they call the function to display the message in order to select one or the other.

After the implementation of feedback rules, the author can go back to the 'Widget' tab and test the feedback. If the author makes a mistake the system

[5] We incorporated the ace editor (http://ace.c9.io) which is a high performance web-based JavaScript tool. The tool is parameterized to process JavaScript code and display it accordingly. It is equipped with syntax highlighters, automatic code indentation, and code quality control and syntax checking that is based on the well-known tool JSHint (http://jshint.com/).

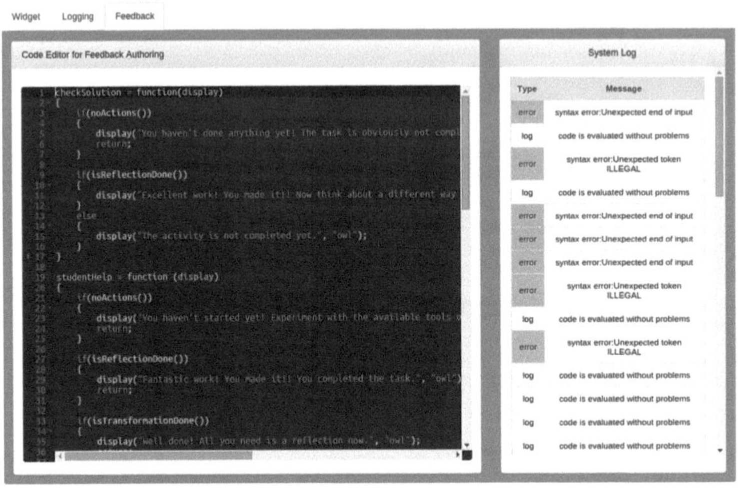

Fig. 9. Feedback authoring through a specialised editor and system log.

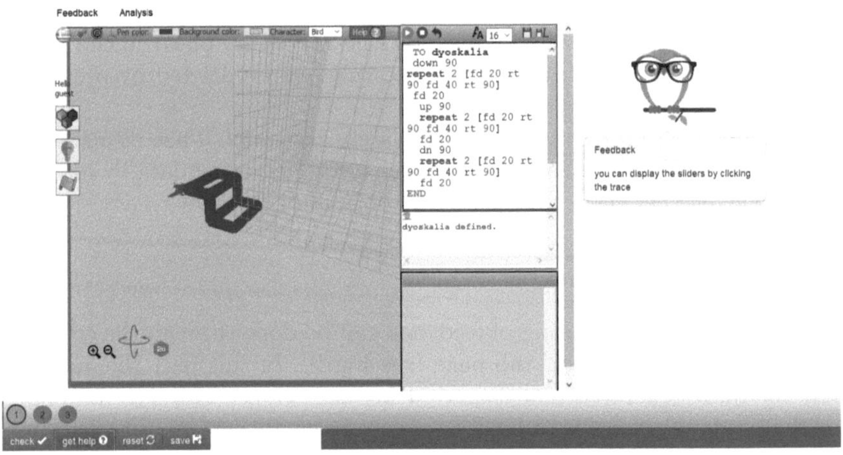

Fig. 10. Help messages.

displays an error notification under the column named 'System Log' indicating the problem. In this case the changes are not saved and the new functionality is not applied.

Something that needs to be noted here is that this part of the tool is work in progress. We are working towards an intuitive and simple user interface that would not require high-level of programming expertise from an author (particularly a teacher). In the meantime, both in order to test the system but also to ensure that it can be immediately used in the context of the project, we exposed a part of the actual JavaScript code that is used to provide the feedback. This does not affect the usability of the system at this stage, only requires a level of expertise from the author that should be able to at least understand JavaScript syntax.

6 Prototype Evaluation

AuthELO is currently being used as the standard tool in the MCSquared platform for the development of automated feedback. MCSquared is an active project and that means that AuthELO is continuously being used and evaluated in practice by a large community of learning designers. The people involved in this process form Communities of Interest (CoIs) and continuously utilise the MCSquared platform to produce new learning material and evaluate it in the classroom. Different CoIs may have a different orientation, specialise in a certain domain and utilise a certain set of ELOs for their productions. In this paper we present the work that has been done by the Greek COI that specialises in constructionist activities with narrative and utilises the ELO Malt+ for the development of learning materials.

6.1 Malt+

Malt+ is an exploratory learning environment that utilises programming to design 3D dynamic graphic models. It consists of a programming editor, a 3D scene and a dynamic variation tool. Learning designers can build domain specific Malt+ widgets (e.g. in mathematics, informatics etc.) that offer students opportunities to explore, redesign and test their own assumptions in order to approach a solution. An avatar on the 3D scene moves and draws shapes and models based on programming code that is executed in the editor. The variation tool can dynamically change the resulting model by changing the programming parameters providing a way to explore modifications in a continual and direct way. As there is a camera available that can change the perspective, activities may exploit the 3D space from the beginning or may start in 2D space and switch to 3D space dynamically. Depending on the activity goals, the presented problem may have more than one solution, it may be solved with multiple alternative programming strategies and as a consequence of those multiple different learning paths may be followed.

A large number of Malt+ widgets have already been produced and studies have examined the functionalities and prospects this environment provides. In [21], the study identifies the role of logo programming in meaning generation in mathematical thinking and points out how reconstruction of a program and its 3D result could affect generalization. Another study [22] has evidenced that the ability to explore and symbolically represent movements and shapes with Logo, engage students in notions of the conceptual field of curvature in space. The role of dynamic manipulation of a 3D shape the environment offers, has also been studied when students exploring the dynamic aspects of an angle [23].

6.2 The Activities

A typical scenario with Malt+ is to present a 'half-baked' microworld to the students and ask them to amend and/or augment it in order to derive a complete construction or fix problems with the existing one. A 'half-baked' microworld [24] is incomplete by design, provoking students to build a new artifact that has more meaning for them. Through this process the students engage with the material, the concepts and the techniques involved in an experiential way and discover knowledge themselves. For this evaluation the Greek CoI developed two such activity scenarios named `Staircases` and `Chand Baori`.

Staircases. The e-book `Staircases` puts the student in the position of an architect who designs different types of staircases. This activity is offered in an e-book that provides a series of activities starting from indentifying the characteristics of a stairs and ending with building complex stair types.

This activity comprises two tasks that are interrelated. The beginning of the second part presupposes the completion of the first part. Both tasks have been implemented in the same Malt+ instance. The first part presents a semi-defined (broken) staircase and asks students to explore the staircase parameters, indentify their role in the shape and amend them to build a well-defined staircase. The second part asks the students to find a way to generalise the previous solution so that it can be used for the construction of well-defined staircase with any number of steps. Students use a predefined program to do their experimentations and modify it to provide a solution (Fig. 11).

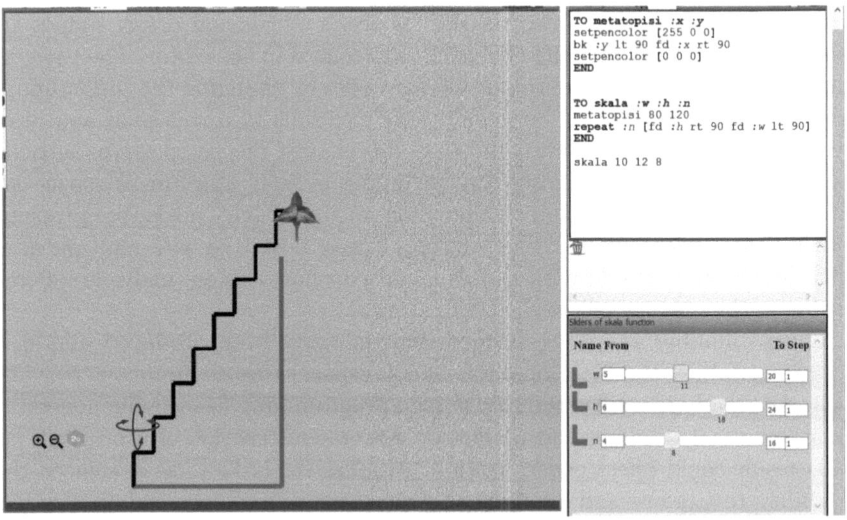

Fig. 11. The staircases activity in Malt+.

Chand Baori. The activity `Chand Baori` asks students to build a 7-step double staircase as Chand Baori stairs looks like. The activity starts with a small program that draws 2 steps on the 3D space. Students have to indentify the programming code that draws each step, replicate it to draw more steps and find a solution to change direction and move down after the top of the stairs. In this activity depending on the students programming skills or the target group, totally different strategies can be followed. Thus, a solution may contain only simple repeated commands or loop structures or subroutines or combination of them (Fig. 12).

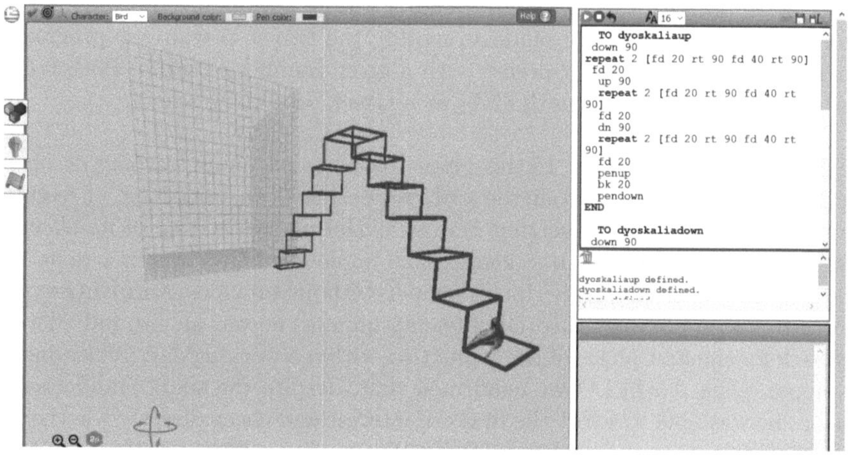

Fig. 12. The chand baori activity in Malt+.

6.3 Challenges

The challenges we were faced with during this process were multifaceted. A technical challenge was to inform AuthELO about the particular set of element types and their respective event types that may be found in a Malt+ environment. Despite the fact that Malt+ is a very sophisticated ELO it does not natively support an API through which this information can be acquired. The solution was to semantically enhance it in AuthELO through WIIL [19]. For this, a formal description of nine element and four event types was formulated after using Malt+ in various scenarios without any logging rules applied.

Another challenge was to address the requirement of providing feedback for two distinct and interrelated subtasks implemented in the same Malt+ instance. The Staircases activity poses such a requirement. The learner is presented with two questions that have to be followed in succession. The automated feedback component must be able to distinguish between the two and suppress feedback if the first part is not complete. In this case it is expected to direct the learner to finish the first subtask.

6.4 The Evaluation Study

Methodology and Material. In order to design the essential guidelines and find any possible weak points of the feedback system, we conducted two studies in real world conditions: A pilot study and an evaluation study. In both studies we exploited four activities that were designed as exploratory activities with Malt+ widgets. The theme of those activities was 3D staircase design using logo programming code. In the first activity students have to identify the correlation between the different geometrical characteristics of a staircase and modify the logo code to build a generic staircase program. In the second activity they have to modify a logo program to extend a two-step stair to a seven-step staircase. In the third activity the goal is to design a seven-step double staircase (Chand Baori). In the final activity students modify the two-step staircase program in order to draw any double staircase with a given number of stairs. Both studies took place in after school math clubs at a Greek secondary school.

Design and Pilot Phase. In this phase, based on the main learning designer's experience and feedback from the CoI, we designed an initial set of feedback messages with the goal of getting first an initial understanding of its effectiveness from a pilot study with students. The implementation was first done by a relatively experienced JavaScript developer without previous AuthELO experience. After a preparatory tutorial of twenty minutes he was able to fully develop feedback for the first phase of the evaluation within a working day. Observing the developer using AuthELO we confirmed that, despite the short familiarisation session, he was able to select the items of interest and check directly whether the widget generates the data required. Reflecting on the usage he mostly commented on the ease of authoring thanks to fact that data gets displayed dynamically as he interacted with the widget. As there was no need to consult the widget documentation for anything or to switch context and query the back-end database he confirmed our design rationale that this reduces the overall time, particularly because otherwise one needs to spend a significant amount of time going through the events that generate data — especially in the context of exploratory learning objects. This is not something we can expect the average teacher to have the training or time to do hence the involvement of a developer at this initial phase.

Having designed the feedback, eight students participated in a pilot study, allocated in 4 groups. From this experiment we collected 547 indicators. All students had previous experience with Malt+ environments but they were presented these particular activities for the first time. The main goals of the pilot study was to:

- identify possible problematic or difficult situations that the intelligent support system should recognise during the activity
- identify sample solution paths the students follow in order to acquire evidence and generalise the designed feedback
- study the students' reactions and the level of acceptance of such a system

After the first iteration, the data collected was analysed along with the tutors' observations and a revision of the feedback was introduced by both the teacher and the original designer. This time it took them approximately two hours to amend the initial design and align it with the new requirements. The effort in this phase focused on providing simple, generic but relevant and helpful feedback. The main advantage of AuthELO as suggested by the teacher taking part in the study was the transparency introduced by being able to see the various feedback rules and feedback messages and discuss them with the original developer. This made him confident that in subsequent iterations he would be able to make modifications through the MCSquared platform himself.

Feedback is always available but it provided on demand. That means that students initiate the process when they feel they need assistance. Due to space limitations we are not describing all the details of the feedback defined but we quote three indicative feedback design decisions for the 'baori' activity:

1. If the time elapsed since the student began interacting with the microworld is less than 30% of the estimated completion time for the activity and the camera has not been used yet the system prompts the student to use it before any other help is given. If the camera has already been used more than 20 times and the sliders are not used then the system prompts the user to try the sliders.
2. If the number of loops identified in the function is more than two then the system gives a hint about possible unecessary code repetition and suggests the user to think about reusability of code.
3. If a function is properly defined but is not called repetitively the system suggests the user to rethink about the reasoning behind the design of the function and how it is supposed to be utilised by the rest of the program. This is obviously related to the previous suggestion (reusability of code).

Testing the Redesign. During the second phase we examined the automated feedback generated both from a technical and from an educational point of view. We also tried to identify the cause of possible failures to provide the required level of help.

From a technical point of view there were no problems experienced during the process. AuthELO was able to express all the different types of feedback required regardless of complexity and the activity player was able to generate the correct feedback at all times.

From an educational point of view the preliminary analysis shows the following:

- Students tend to avoid getting help even if they are encouraged to do so. It is very important therefore to carefully introduce any feedback affordances to students and to discuss with them their purpose.
- Due to the exploratory nature of the activities, students may miss opportunities, get lost and ultimately abandon the activities. Designers, therefore, may need to consider when to design feedback that intervenes in appropriate times as suggested in [3].
- A feedback message that does not meet the 'expectations' of the students could act as an inhibitor of asking further help from the system. It is important, therefore, to design feedback messages carefully and to allow designers and teachers to modify them easily and frequently based on their expertise.

A possible interpretation of the above follows:

- Computer users and especially students are not familiar with the process of asking the system for help. In fact, there is an almost common belief that the system can provide only general help and users have to read a lot of help text to find a useful hint. In our study another factor that may affect the student behavior is that the study sample was part of a special student club where members 'play' with technologies and mathematics and therefore they prefer to explore and try rather than ask the system for ready-made help.
- Students seem to get disappointed very quickly from a given help message that does not seem to be helpful enough. They get a negative 'sense of help' and avoid asking for more.
- It is very hard for the author to identify all possible situations in an exploratory environment so in some cases the feedback may have general guidelines and not specific hints at least initially. Feedback authoring in this case should always be an iterative process that stops when the level of support in relation to the level of expected support is deemed adequate.
- There are cases, especially during the beginning of the activity, where the author might deliberately not provide very 'targeted' help. Students in this case may perceive this behaviour as a weakness of the system and loose their confidence in it. A possible consequence of that might be that the students ignore further help messages provided by the system because they see it as unworthy of their attention.

We can see how designing automated feedback for an ELO is a difficult and time-consuming process with potentially uncertain results and how an tool like AuthELO facilitates not only the authoring process but also the possibility of easily modifying feedback design and investigating its efficacy.

7 Conclusions

In this paper we presented a tool that can be used to author automated feedback on ELOs. The tool provides a very simple yet effective interface through which learning designers can configure data logging and authoring rules for feedback. The system is developed as a web-based stand-alone application that is available as a service and can be integrated seamlessly with any learning platform with minimal development or administrative overhead. AuthELO has been thoroughly tested for usability and robustness and its final version is being used as the standard feedback authoring tool for key web-based interactive widgets of the MCSquared project. In this paper we presented an evaluation study that was performed on an e-book that combines multiple instances of the 3D Logo microworld MALT+. The findings of this study suggest that AuthELO satisfies its original design goals as it enables easy development of feedback for complex exploratory learning activities whereas at the same time it is expressive enough to formulate rules for any type of feedback required. According to the study participants, it significantly reduces the cognitive load for both developers and teachers and therefore it seems to lower the entry threshold for potential interested designers who want to create or modify feedback on exploratory activities. The tool can also be used by low skilled teachers with limited or no programming expertise to configure or tweak pre-defined feedback. The findings also suggest that the tool has the potential to enhance author performance and productivity.

In the next version we envisage to provide the same service through a more sophisticated environment that will be a combination of visual programming and a high level language especially designed for expressing feedback. We expect these changes to lower the entry threshold for potential users even further.

Acknowledgements. The research leading to these results has received funding from the European Union Seventh Framework Programme (FP7/2007-2013) under grant agreement N°610467 - project 'M C Squared'. This publication reflects only the authors' views and the European Union is not liable for any use that may be made of the information contained therein

References

1. Healy, L., Kynigos, C.: Charting the microworld territory over time: design and construction in mathematics education. ZDM **42**, 63–76 (2010)
2. Mavrikis, M., Noss, R., Hoyles, C., Geraniou, E.: Sowing the seeds of algebraic generalization: designing epistemic affordances for an intelligent microworld. J. Comput. Assist. Learn. **29**, 68–84 (2013)
3. Mavrikis, M., Gutierrez-Santos, S., Geraniou, E., Noss, R.: Design requirements, student perception indicators and validation metrics for intelligent exploratory learning environments. Pers. Ubiquit. Comput. **17**, 1605–1620 (2013)
4. Bunt, A., Conati, C., Huggett, M., Muldner, K.: On improving the effectiveness of open learning environments through tailored support for exploration. In: 10th World Conference of Artificial Intelligence and Education, AIED 2001 (2001)
5. Gutierrez-Santos, S., Mavrikis, M., Magoulas, G.D., et al.: A separation of concerns for engineering intelligent support for exploratory learning environments. J. Res. Pract. Inf. Technol. **44**, 347 (2012)
6. Blessing, S., Gilbert, S., Ourada, S., Ritter, S.: Lowering the bar for creating model-tracing intelligent tutoring systems. Front. Artif. Intell. Appl. **158**, 443 (2007)
7. Mitrovic, A.: Fifteen years of constraint-based tutors: what we have achieved and where we are going. User Model. User-Adap. Inter. **22**, 39–72 (2012)
8. Mitrovic, A., Martin, B., Suraweera, P., Zakharov, K., Milik, N., Holland, J., McGuigan, N.: Aspire: an authoring system and deployment environment for constraint-based tutors (2009)
9. Munro, A.: Authoring simulation-centered learning environments with rides and vivids. In: Murray, T., Blessing, S.B., Ainsworth, S. (eds.) Authoring Tools for Advanced Technology Learning Environments, pp. 61–91. Springer, Dordrecht (2003)
10. Brusilovsky, P.: Developing adaptive educational hypermedia systems: from design models to authoring tools. In: Murray, T., Blessing, S.B., Ainsworth, S. (eds.) Authoring tools for advanced technology Learning Environments, pp. 377–409. Springer, Dordrecht (2003)

11. Razzaq, L., Patvarczki, J., Almeida, S.F., Vartak, M., Feng, M., Heffernan, N.T., Koedinger, K.R.: The assistment builder: supporting the life cycle of tutoring system content creation. IEEE Trans. Learn. Technol. **2**, 157–166 (2009)
12. Ainsworth, S., Major, N., Grimshaw, S., Hayes, M., Underwood, J., Williams, B., Wood, D.: Redeem: simple intelligent tutoring systems from usable tools. In: Murray, T., Blessing, S.B., Ainsworth, S. (eds.) Authoring Tools for Advanced Technology Learning Environments, pp. 205–232. Springer, Dordrecht (2003)
13. Aleven, V., Mclaren, B.M., Sewall, J., Koedinger, K.R.: A new paradigm for intelligent tutoring systems: example-tracing tutors. Int. J. Artif. Intell. Educ. **19**, 105–154 (2009)
14. Koedinger, K.R., Aleven, V., Heffernan, N., McLaren, B., Hockenberry, M.: Opening the door to non-programmers: authoring intelligent tutor behavior by demonstration. In: Lester, J.C., Vicari, R.M., Paraguaçu, F. (eds.) ITS 2004. LNCS, vol. 3220, pp. 162–174. Springer, Heidelberg (2004). doi:10.1007/978-3-540-30139-4_16
15. Sottilare, R.A., Goldberg, B.S., Brawner, K.W., Holden, H.K.: A modular framework to support the authoring and assessment of adaptive computer-based tutoring systems (cbts). In: Proceedings of the Interservice/Industry Training, Simulation, and Education Conference (2012)
16. Ginon, B., Thai, L.V., Jean-Daubias, S., Lefevre, M., Champin, P.-A.: Adding epiphytic assistance systems in learning applications using the SEPIA system. In: Rensing, C., Freitas, S., Ley, T., Muñoz-Merino, P.J. (eds.) EC-TEL 2014. LNCS, vol. 8719, pp. 138–151. Springer, Cham (2014). doi:10.1007/978-3-319-11200-8_11
17. Mayer, R.E.: Should there be a three-strikes rule against pure discovery learning? Am. Psychol. **59**, 14 (2004)
18. Klahr, D., Nigam, M.: The equivalence of learning paths in early science instruction effects of direct instruction and discovery learning. Psychol. Sci. **15**, 661–667 (2004)
19. Karkalas, S., Mavrikis, M., Charlton, P.: The web integration & interoperability layer (wiil). turning web content into learning content using a lightweight integration and interoperability technique. In: 7th International Conference on Knowledge Engineering and Ontology Development (KEOD) (2015)
20. Karkalas, S., Bokhove, C., Charlton, P., Mavrikis, M.: Towards configurable learning analytics for constructionist mathematical e-books. In: Intelligent Support in Exploratory and Open-ended Learning Environments Learning Analytics for Project Based and Experiential Learning Scenarios, p. 17(2015)
21. Diamantidis, D., Economakou, K., Kaitsoti, A., Kynigos, C., Moustaki, F.: Social creativity and meaning generation in a constructionist environment. In: CERME 9-Ninth Congress of the European Society for Research in Mathematics Education, pp. 2340–2346 (2015)
22. Zantzos, I., Kynigos, C.: Differential approximation of a cylindrical helix by secondary school students. In: Proceedings of the Constructionism 2012 Conference - Theory, Practice and Impact. National and Kapodistrian University of Athens, Athens (2012)
23. Latsi, M., Kynigos, C.: Meanings about dynamic aspects of angle while changing perspectives in a simulated 3d space. In: Proceedings of the 35th Conference of the International Group for the Psychology of Mathematics Education, Ankara, Turkey (2011)
24. Kynigos, C., et al.: Half-baked logo microworlds as boundary objects in integrated design. Inf. Educ. Int. J. **6**, 335–359 (2007)

The Side Effect of Learning Analytics: An Empirical Study on e-Learning Technologies and User Privacy

Madeth May[1(✉)], Sébastien Iksal[1], and Claus A. Usener[2]

[1] UBL University of Maine – EA4023, Avenue Olivier Messiaen, LIUM Research Laboratory, 72085 Le Mans, France
{madeth.may,sebastien.iksal}@univ-lemans.fr
[2] University of Münster, Leonardo-Campus 3, 48149 Münster, Germany
usener@ercis.de

Abstract. Student monitoring, the most common practice in Learning Analytics (LA), has become easier and more efficient thanks to the use of tracking approach that consists of collecting data of users and of their interactions throughout learning platforms. While LA gives considerable assistance to the tutors in the tasks of monitoring online learning, it also creates major drawbacks for the learners. For instance, tracking approach in LA raises many privacy questions. As for the learners, knowing that their personal data are being used, even for educational purposes, they could radically change their perception on e-learning technologies. Not to mention that these concerns would have a strong impact, sometimes very negatively, on not only their behaviors but also their learning outcomes. To better understand the side effect of LA, more particularly the privacy issues in e-learning, the research effort presented in this paper covers two main aspects. First, it outlines various tracking approaches in e-learning. Second, it analyzes how the learners perceive the use of their personal data and the related privacy issues. To do so, an experiment has been carried out with the participation of students from three different universities in France and one university in Germany. The major contribution of this paper is the awareness-raising of privacy concerns in exploiting tracking data in e-learning, which are often overlooked by researchers and learning content providers.

Keywords: Data analysis · Data indicator · Ethics in e-learning · Learning analytics · Privacy issues in e-learning · Tracking data

1 Introduction

In 2011, when we first presented a study on security and privacy issues in e-learning [1], we pointed out the lack of data protection measures from the learning content providers. We also discussed how users relied on trust when accessing to their online learning platforms, and how technical solutions still had their limitation in terms of privacy protection. Since then, we continue to expand our research scope by focusing more on users and their perception on the use of their personal data in various educational settings. More precisely, our research team studies how privacy concerns would affect user behavior during the learning process. The study presented in this paper combines

G. Costagliola et al. (Eds.): CSEDU 2016, CCIS 739, pp. 279–295, 2017.
DOI: 10.1007/978-3-319-63184-4_15

existing research findings with the empirical data acquired throughout an experiment that we have conducted with the participation of students from three universities in France and one university in Germany.

Our research approach is to take a closer look at Learning Analytics and the technologies that support it. More precisely, the user-tracking technologies that provide great assistance in terms of student monitoring while creating at the same time negative impact on the learning experiences. By focusing on the learners' perception of tracking technologies used in the majority of e-learning platforms, the study presented in the paper is the first attempt to understand what cause privacy concerns and how learners perceive them.

It is worth mentioning that the purpose of this paper is to share scientific findings based on field studies and empirical data. Our research team has no intention to make any claim regarding how to definitely solve privacy matters that one might encounter accordingly to a variety of factors, including institution's regulations, learning contexts and cultural points of view. This paper is not meant to address new research challenges either, but to assist the participants in the learning process, including researchers and learning content providers in acquiring a better understanding of privacy matters when it comes to making use of tracking data in e-learning. Our goal is to raise awareness of the issues in question, which are often neglected in the research efforts that involve user tracking and personal data analysis.

This paper is structured as follows. The second section provides an overview of our research work that emphasizes on user-tracking approach and data visualization. An example of using tracking data from a previous study is presented in the same section. A general discussion on user tracking approach is made in the third section. It is based on a number of related works, which help us gain a broader perspective on what causes privacy concerns. The fourth section is dedicated to our experiment. Data analysis and commenting on results are made in the same section. In the last section, we draw a conclusion and highlight future work.

2 Research Context

2.1 User Tracking Approach in Learning Analytics

E-learning has been evolving rapidly, from purely Web-based to mobile and ubiquitous learning experiences, thus providing even more personalized solutions that better suit each individual need. For that reason, institutions, teachers and learners seemingly embrace e-learning [2] and consider it among the most innovative learning mediums [3]. In fact, within the past ten years, we witness a strong ongoing growth of research interests in e-learning [4, 5] and the emergence of technologies that better support user interactivity [6] and content sharing [7].

In order to make e-learning more practical and more efficient in terms of student monitoring, other research efforts like [8, 9] focus more on user tracking approach that consists of collecting data of users and of their activities within learning platforms. As discussed in our previous work [10], using a tracking mechanism to observe the learning process has been proven to be a reliable support to both instructors and learners, particularly in e-learning contexts [11]. To state an example, by monitoring an e-learning session, the instructors are able to follow the activities being undertaken by the learners and to observe their behaviors on learning resource consumption [12]. As for the students, having records of their own activities allows them to keep track of their individual progress, their interactions among other students as well as their achievements throughout the learning session [13].

Acknowledging the contributing factor of "user tracking approach" to high quality teaching and learning guidance in e-learning as pointed out by [14], researchers and learning content providers choose to integrate systematically a tracking system in their educational settings. To back up this claim, the most recent studies of [15, 16] review a variety of learning platforms that make use of students' tracking data for different purposes, among which are student assessment and evaluation. Further evidence on how user tracking approach is broadly used to help enhance e-learning can be found in the research works of [17–21].

Implementing user tracking systems in e-learning has been done in numerous ways as identified by [9, 22–24]. With the progress being made in regard to the tracking mechanism, the technique of collecting data has become more sophisticated and powerful while being effortless to be deployed in an existing e-learning environment. In the meantime, such progress has increased privacy questions, which lead to a situation where security and privacy protection are becoming crucial for the users. Hence, it is relevant to our research interests to determine users' concerns and to investigate their needs in terms of privacy provision.

2.2 Previous Works

Our research team works on learning environments and studies numerous research questions related to "Modeling the Observation of Usage Tracks and their Analysis". Our goal is to better observe and analyze users' activities by exploiting the user declaration model and user-tracking data [11, 25].

A part of our research work involves user tracking on e-learning platforms where Computer Mediated-Communication tools (i.e., forums, chat, newsgroups, wiki, etc.) are widely used to foster learning activities and to compensate the lack of face-to-face interactions among the participants [26]. We proposed an explicit tracking approach to assist the conceptual design and implementation of a tracking system for a variety of Web-based communication tools [27]. The proposed approach was built upon a tracking mechanism that simultaneously collects fine-grained data from both client and server sides. On top of that, the tracking process can be made on different levels of Human-Computer Interactions, which allows us to characterize the nature of the acquired data (i.e., user's action, user-machine interaction or system event) and to conduct the analysis accordingly. The technical aspects of the tracking approach in question can be found in [28].

Tracking data analysis is very often associated to data-mining, but one of our proposals is also to consider the analysis as a prescriptive approach [29]. We proposed a formal description of data indicators and more generally observational data according to the description of observational needs given by the participants in the learning process.

This kind of tracking data analysis focused on the following questions: (i) what is interesting to observe, (ii) why it is important, what is the observational goal (assessment, regulation, adaptation, re-engineering, reflexivity), and (iii) what is the most efficient way of data presentation for improving the comprehension of indicators? The Usage Tracking Language (UTL) [11] aims to be neutral regarding learning technologies in order to describe the analysis process and the corresponding data. It is based on generic models and a processor to corporate tracking data and compute indicators.

For the sake of comprehension, "data indicator" refers to a piece of information, extracted from a set of tracking data. Generally computed in graphical representations, a data indicator features the process of the considered "cognitive system" learning activity, the characteristics or the quality of the interaction being performed on a learning environment [30]. Data indicators provide means of abstracting and visualizing the information that they feature. Obtaining data indicators is a complex process. It involves many phases, among which the transformation of data indicators in graphical representations.

2.3 Data Indicators in Learning Analytics

Another part of our research effort focuses on tracking data exploitation where research challenges were studied in [10]. Our goal is to make use of the collected tracking data in order to help the participants explore their past and ongoing activities on a learning platform. With the technical support in terms of data analysis and visualization, the participants could not only examine their activities, but also make an assessment of their effectiveness, achievements, etc. We identified 4 observation goals for our tracking tools: reengineering, adaptation, assessment and reflexivity. All participants in the learning process can classify their observational needs at least in one of these goals.

The need of data analysis and visualization tools can be briefly explained as follows. With the current support of e-learning that prioritizes content sharing and user communication [6, 7], the participants are compelled to neglect some fundamental facets of online learning, such as self-monitoring and self-evaluation. Additionally, despite the learning possibilities provided by an e-learning platform, the participants are unable to fully control their activities in the way they used to do in a traditional classroom. Not to mention the fully online interaction between the participants that makes the supervision tasks very laborious for the instructors. Last but not least, while the learners usually encounter difficulties in getting feedbacks on their own activities, the instructors, on the other hand, are often constrained by the lack of technical assistance to conduct a proper analysis on the learners' tracking data.

Having studied these issues, we addressed the importance of technical supports in tracking data analysis and visualization in order to enhance e-learning experiences for both the instructors and the learners. Therefore, we have designed and developed TrAVis (Tracking Data Analysis and Visualization tools) for the instructors who are in need of supervising learners' activities [25], and also for the learners who seek to self-monitor during their learning sessions [31]. We have also designed and implemented UTL to support tracking data analysis. For instance, UTL enables the tutors to specify their observational needs in a learning session and to compute data indicators used to better monitor and evaluate the latter.

To illustrate how tracking data analysis could contribute to e-learning enhancement in terms of student monitoring, we give below an example of a "data indicator" representing a group activities on a learning platform supported by Moodle. The following data indicators are modeled and computed by UTL. They illustrate activities of 2 groups of students while navigating lecture modules according to a given learning scenario. If taken a closer look, such data indicators allow a comparison of different aspects of group activities. For instance, we can easily point out that in group A, the students had enough time to use all modules. On the other hand, the group B had more difficulties to navigate between modules. While there might not be enough information to make further conclusion, it is still very useful for the teacher to have data indicators that help them to better analyze and understand the activities of each group of students.

Another example of data indicators is shown in Fig. 2. Generated by TrAVis, the data indicators provide a visualization of two groups of students on three forums that have the same structure, dedicated to group collaboration. Each radar graph, filled in with a distinct color, provides a quick perception of the forum and its access frequency, number of active participants, threads, messages, and files, etc. Hence, the teacher can

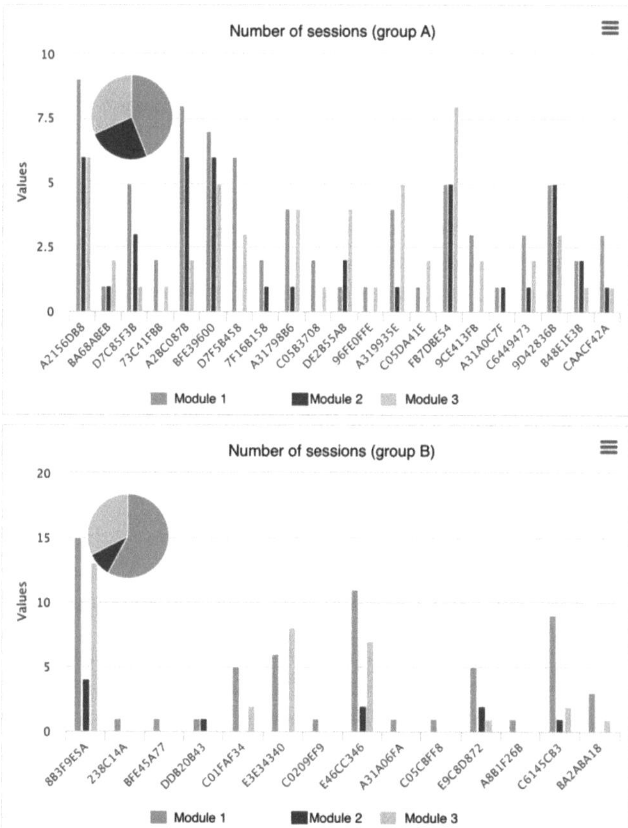

Fig. 1. Example of data indicator with UTL.

make use of these indicators to analyze the interactions among the students. On top of that, the given quantitative information allows the teachers to evaluate the collaboration level of each group. For instance, Fig. 2 shows that group A has more intense interactions than group B in almost the three forums. Such indications can be used to (i) compare the participation rates of both groups during the collaborative task or (ii) to evaluate the productivity rates of one group in relation to another, according to the number of created threads and shared files. More data indicators and their analysis can be found in [10].

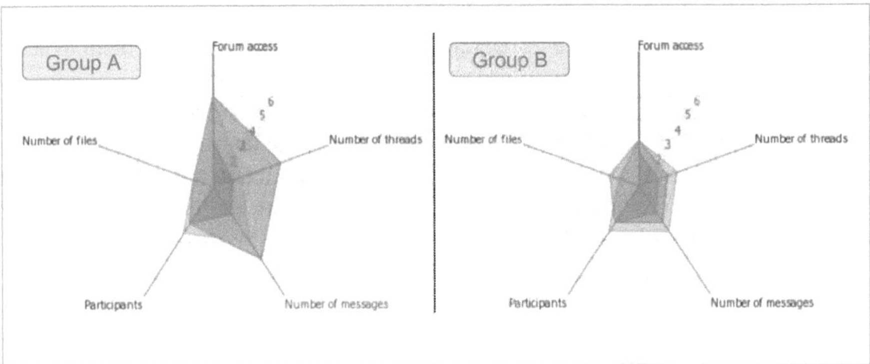

Fig. 2. An example of data indicators that analyze the participation level of two groups of students.

To sum up, data indicators computed from e-learning tracking data provide means of awareness, assessment and evaluation of a learning situation. However, obtaining data indicators involves a complex procedure that starts with a tracking technique. Indeed, the latter is crucial to the whole data gathering process and always has an impact on the production of quality and substantial data indicators. Consequently, most tracking techniques that are robust and efficient in collecting users' data are at the same time very intrusive [9, 23]. To gain a broader perspective on how tracking approaches could cause privacy issues, the study we present in the following section covers a number of research works with examples of how tracking data are used.

3 Related Works

3.1 The Correlation Between Learning Analytics and Privacy Concerns

Using data indicator in the analysis process enables one to synthesize, infer and interpret the information that it features. In e-learning, while it gives considerable assistance to the tutors in the tasks of monitoring online learning, it also creates major drawbacks for the learners. For an example, some learners who are cautious about privacy matters would become apprehensive of being traced and of having no control over how their personal data are being exploited. Yet, they have to accept the undesirable inconveniences of having their data scrutinized so that they could receive in return the assistance when needed. To better understand this phenomenon, a literature study has been conducted on a number of research works where data indicators computed from e-learning tracking data are being exploited by the tutors to gain awareness, to make an assessment and to evaluate learners' activities.

Starting with Argunaut [32], which is an awareness tool, built to keep track of online interaction. It provides data indicators of collaborative learning activities, thus allowing the instructors to examine the behavioral aspects of each individual student during a collaborative task. It should be noted that the awareness indicators of users' collaboration were first found in the research effort of [33], which demonstrate how data indicators on the interaction links could give awareness of the discussion depth and of the student's learning attitude. Later, we have studied iHelp [34], another awareness tool that shares the same characteristics of Argunaut. iHelp assists the instructor in supervising the communication process among the learners.

Besides gaining awareness, making an assessment of learners' activities is also compulsory. For that matter, [35, 36] suggested an analysis of various aspects of an individual or a group activities. For example, the instructor can make an appreciation of the participation level of an individual or a group of learners based on the number of messages exchanged among the group. On the other hand, [37] proposes a platform that offers means to analyze the temporal and spatial dimensions of learners' interactions on a communication tool. As for the data indicators, they are computed in a form of activity map, enabling the instructor to observe and assess communication characteristics such as the degree of participation of a learner, compared to the whole group.

Regarding the evaluation tools that provide data indicators on students' activities and their outcomes, CourseVis [38] provides the instructor with means of evaluating the social aspect of each student in a learning session. Not too far from CourseVis in terms of data analysis and visualization, DIAS (Discussion Interaction Analysis System) of [39] is another evaluation system that helps the instructors investigate learners' interactions on a communication tool. Data indicators computed by DIAS mainly serve for the evaluation of the social dimension of each learner. In the same context, GISMO, a Graphical Interactive Student Monitoring tool, developed by [8], proposed another way to visualize behavioral and social data of learners' activities. Its objective is to help instructors evaluate the involvement of the learners during the course activities on a learning platform (e.g. Moodle). For a more complex learning environment like MOOC, Coffrin et al., [40] made use of data indicators to classify student types and to analyze students' engagement and performance throughout their learning process. Last but not least, Glass (Gradient's Learning Analytics System), a Web-based visualization platform [41] that offers the possibilities to keep track of students' activities on different tools used in a learning setting. Data indicators provided by Glass are meant to assist the instructors in evaluating the students on how active they are and how they perform in a given learning context.

Thus far, our primary observation regarding the existing tools is that most of them aim to better support the instructors in exploiting learners' tracking data. To do so, they explore every possible piece of information related to the learner's activity in order to accordingly generate significant data indicators on the latter. The intrusive characteristics of each tool allow, on the one hand, a pertinent analysis on learners' activities, but causes major privacy concerns on the other hand [42]. While some recent research efforts like [43, 44] took into account the need of users in controlling how their personal data are being used, only a few are accessible by the learners. This is due to their restricted user rights from a technical standpoint, as well as their roles in the learning process. As a result, the learners always comply with the regulations of the e-learning platform and put their trust on the latter [45]. Consequently, the privacy concerns remain to be addressed as the learners are not always in the position to determine what data to share and whom to share with. This is not to mention that in some circumstances, the learners were not informed of the use of their tracking data either for instructional or research purposes.

Another observation is relevant to the strong focus of the previous works, placed on the efficiency of the tracking approach and the data indicators. The privacy concerns seem to be overlooked. Nonetheless, these concerns have a direct impact on the learner behavior as studied by [46]. Sharing the same concerns as [47], our research team has been studying the learner's perception on privacy issues, which usually cause some changes to the behavioral aspects of each individual activity in e-learning. For instance, the confidentiality and anonymity play an important role in learner engagement and performance as an individual or a group. Without necessary protection measures, learners are becoming too afraid to be exposed to what meant to help them learn in the first place as found in the studies of [42, 43].

3.2 Identifying the Privacy Concerns

According to [48], privacy concerns are mainly caused by the use of technologies. As a matter of fact, with the growth of new platforms, new learning opportunities can be created along with new problems. The participants usually require technical knowledge of how technologies work in order to understand the privacy levels and threats. Nevertheless, the lack of information and technical supports in that matter causes the most privacy concerns.

Learning service and content providers also bear the responsibility of intensifying the privacy issues. The participants frequently ask the question how their personal data are stored and protected by the learning content providers. As found in the study of [49], the participants are primarily concerned with trust assessment of learning environments they are using, and with the protection of their sensitive data.

The study of [47] pointed out that privacy issues are also related to the participant consent, data ownership, confidentiality and anonymity. The participants expressed their concerns regarding how information collected throughout the learning process would be kept secure and private. The confidentiality is part of the privacy protection that refers to participants' right to control the access of their tracking data as well as other information about them. Regarding the anonymity, most participants are unaware of their right to request the removal of any characteristics (i.e., name, address, affiliated institutions, geographical areas, etc.) that would allow them to be identified.

Our findings reveal that most participants regret not being part of the decision-making on what information to be collected, what to be used, and for what purpose. Despite the compromise they have to make when consuming resources on an e-learning platform, the participants expect to have choices to accept to be traced, to deny the use of their data or to limit access to some users.

Privacy issues also concern the security threats of technologies we are using. Indeed, the participants are exposed to a risk of data and identity theft. Such issues make participants doubt the confidentiality and data protection measures proposed by their affiliated institutions or learning content providers. Research evidence can be found in the study of [50].

Our study also took an interest in mobile e-learning where security and privacy threats remain challenging despite technological progress made on ubiquitous learning. This is due to the fact that granting access to mobile devices on learning contents opens doors to security threats that have not been taken into account by the learning service providers. The diversity of mobile devices and their security protection measures are varied in accordance with the operating system, the application used and user own measures to protect their privacy. Research data from the study of Young [51] cover the privacy preservation for mobile e-learning. Yong pointed out the security threats regarding ubiquitous learning and the privacy preservation techniques for the learners.

To summarize, security and privacy levels differ in various learning environments and depend on types of learning activities being conducted by the participants. For instance, a collaborative learning situation where interactions between participants are inevitable and their exchanges of both personal and collaborative data are intense, a strong protection of participants' privacy could only be done on a particular environment that is specifically built for such situation as found in [52] on establishing a privacy-aware collaborative learning environment.

In practice, it is not always straightforward or simple to promise absolute privacy, confidentiality and anonymity when using open e-learning environment. However, identifying the privacy levels clearly and their relative protection measures allow us to set rules and policies in terms of user tracking.

4 Case Study

4.1 Setup and Participants

On top of the study we made on existing research works, we have conducted a semi-controlled experiment where TrAVis was used to analyze and visualize tracking data collected on a Moodle learning platform. Our main goal is to acquire an overview of student perception on privacy issues when their personal data are being used in an authentic learning situation. Our clear intention is to consult the students who are naturally concerned about their data in an actual practice setting instead of interviewing some random students. As a matter of fact, every student who participates in our experiment uses online learning platform on a regular basis. A total of 178 students from three universities in France and one university in Germany participated in our study.

Most participants have sufficient knowledge in Computer Sciences and e-learning technologies. Each one of them is clearly explained the purpose of the study and how their tracking data are being treated. Having acknowledged the necessity of protecting the participants' personal data, we choose to discuss in this paper the findings from a general perspective. Experimental data will be presented without distinguishing the groups of participants, their respective university, and academic background. Furthermore, any sensitive information susceptible to identify the participants or the level of their implication in the study will be intentionally left out.

4.2 Procedure

The participants were assigned the task of using Moodle to organize their group activities. They were also encouraged to use a discussion forum, already integrated into Moodle, to perform their communication activities. Depend on their affiliated university, the participants had between one and two weeks to complete the assigned task. They were then asked to use TrAVis to analyze their personal data gathered during the period of the experiment. We also provided to the participants technical assistance in choosing tracking data to analyze and in visualizing data indicators on their past activities.

At the end of the experiment session, the participants were solicited to answer a questionnaire with over twenty questions, which emphasizes on three main aspects: (i) their perception of privacy issues in e-learning, (ii) their general knowledge on tracking approaches and tracking data analysis, and (iii) their request for privacy protection measures.

4.3 Experimental Data

The most significant data from the questionnaire that reflect how students perceive the privacy and security issues in e-learning are illustrated in Fig. 3. What gets our attention the most is the belief of the participants that an anti-virus or an anti-spyware would help them overcome the privacy issues in e-learning. Indeed, 34% of the participants claimed to have a good protection system that prevents their personal data from being collected. Such misunderstanding is a big part due to the lack of technical knowledge on how a

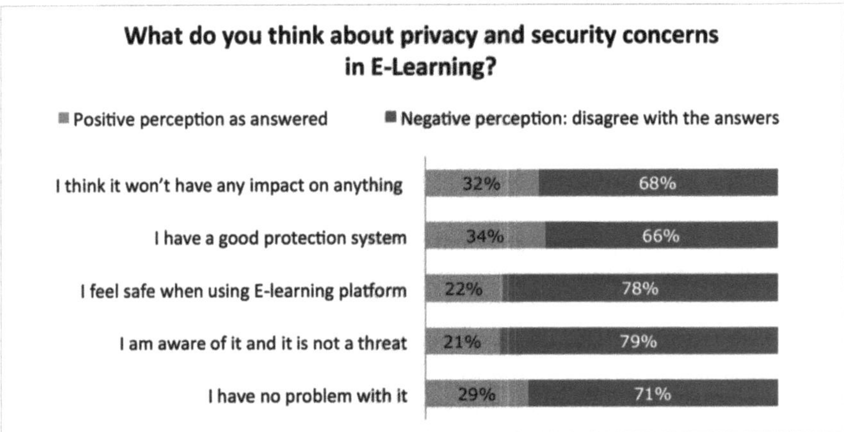

Fig. 3. Student perception on privacy and security concerns in e-learning.

tracking mechanism works. It is also because the privacy issues are very confusing for the participants. For instance, the most frequently asked question during our experiment was whether or not they were tracked when using a browser in incognito or private mode to access their online learning environment. In fact, most participants do not have a clear perception on the tracking process and its correlation to the privacy concerns.

Although the majority of the participants seem to figure out the most common security aspects in e-learning technologies, they still have difficulty identifying the related threats. As confirmed the data from the fourth and fifth rows in Fig. 3, only 21% claimed to have knowledge of the tracking process and considered it without harm to their private data. Respectively, 29% admitted that they have neither privacy nor security preoccupation in e-learning. On the contrary, over 78% disagreed with the previous claims and felt unsafe when using e-learning regardless the tracking process being deployed or not.

Figure 3 also reveals interesting data that support our hypothesis regarding the impact of user-tracking approach on user behavior in e-learning. 68% of the participants expressed their fears towards a learning environment with an integrated tracking system. The participants recognized that the latter had sometimes affected how they perform certain types of activities. For example, they suggest limiting private activity or reducing public intervention like on a discussion forum, so that they would leave the least of their traces possible on an open e-learning environment.

The second analysis we made on the data from the questionnaire focuses on the participants' general knowledge on tracking approach and tracking data analysis. As illustrated in Fig. 4, we find the most familiar tracking approaches used on Web-based learning environments. With the exception of the browsing history, which 69% of the participants are aware of, the rest of the tracking approaches are either new or unclear to the participants. 18 to 44% declared that they have only heard of the tracking system,

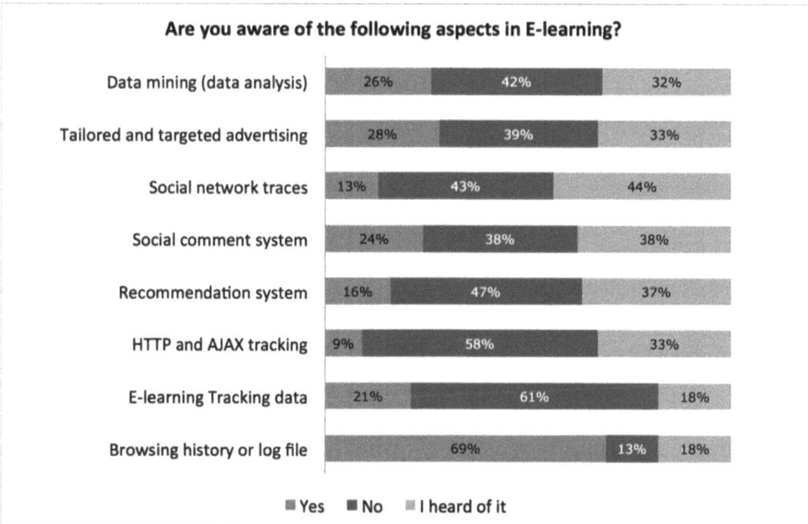

Fig. 4. Student awareness of user-tracking approach and tracking data analysis in e-learning.

but they had no idea of what it is and how it works. What is more intriguing is that 61% of the participants are not common to a tracking system in e-learning and are unaware of its existence.

Judging from the experiences of the participants in online learning and social environments, we expected to witness a higher positive response rate to the questions on tailored advertising, social network traces and social comment system (cf. row 2, 3 and 4 in Fig. 4). Nonetheless, only 13% understand what social traces are and 28% are aware of the targeted advertisements. The social comment system is sometimes used in an online learning environment (e.g., blog, wiki), only 24% realized that their personal information from their social network account (e.g., Facebook, Google +) are being used in their e-learning environment. While 30% are familiar with such tracking possibility, another 30% have no clue of it.

If we take a closer look at some more complex notions like HTTP and AJAX tracking, only 9% of the participants acknowledged its usage on a large scale in Web-based e-learning platforms. In the meantime, over 58% ignored that their activities could be monitored on both client and server sides thanks to HTTP and AJAX tracking system. As for the data analysis, the participants seem to be more familiar with data mining as confirmed 26% of them while another 32% mentioned that they only have heard of it. Still, 42% did not have knowledge of various analyses being made on their tracking data by the researchers, the instructors or the learning content providers.

The third objective of our experiment is to explore different privacy protection measures as seen by the participants, to help them get beyond privacy concerns. Table 1 shows the most demanding features regarding personal data protection, consent agreement, anonymous use of learning services, ethics legislation and awareness raising. On a scale of 0 to 5, the participants expressed the least and the most important privacy protection measures.

Table 1. Most requested features in terms of privacy and personal data protection.

Importance level	0	1	2	3	4	5
Awareness raising	0%	2%	15%	15%	33%	35%
Avoidance of personal data	2%	5%	10%	16%	18%	49%
Data protection	6%	11%	15%	22%	18%	28%
Anonymous access	10%	7%	18%	13%	33%	19%
Data access management	2%	12%	5%	33%	30%	18%
Right to be forgotten	9%	9%	11%	23%	27%	21%
Guarantees from content provider	0%	6%	33%	29%	18%	14%
Consent agreement	0%	3%	12%	33%	14%	38%
Ethics legislation	19%	29%	14%	13%	13%	12%

Interesting information can be retrieved from Table 1. Examples include "avoidance of personal data" and "consent agreement", which are both strongly relevant to privacy concerns in e-learning. In fact, consent is one of the keystones of privacy research practices in e-learning. Somehow, we were surprised to learn that most of the participants had never been reached out by anyone to sign a consent form. Yet, they have been regularly using Moodle, and their tracking data have been exploited in both educational and research settings.

The data from Table 1 also show that the participants consider "user data protection" and "anonymity" among the most important privacy provisions. As for "personal data protection", the participants requested to be informed of the tracking process. According to the participants, being aware of the latter is the key to reducing privacy concerns.

If take a closer look at how the participants perceive tracking approach in e-learning, while 49% of them claim that user tracking as a big threat, only 12% believe that ethics legislation could help them control the visibility and the use of their sensitive data. Interestingly, we have found similar results in our previous study [1] that user tracking is not welcome even when users receive personalized content and assistance in return.

To wrap up, this study enables us to gain a broader perspective of the most crucial aspects regarding privacy concerns in e-learning. While we still need to conduct more analysis on the experimental data we have acquired, the early findings point to the most critical measures to undertake to keep users informed of the privacy issues and to help them avoid confronting one. The study we made thus far also inspires us to explore a proper solution for our research work, which implicates user tracking and data analysis.

5 Conclusion

The research effort we presented in this paper analyzes existing findings and experimental data obtained from a case study on privacy issues in e-learning. While attempting to demonstrate, with research evidence, the benefits of a user tracking approach to e-learning enhancements, we also point out the necessity of gaining an insight on the privacy concerns that most participants encounter in their daily learning activities.

We also address the lack of guidance for the participants to acquire a better understanding on privacy levels and threats. Data from our study reveal that the participants have a very negative perception on e-learning technologies when it comes to privacy and data protection. We recognize that avoidance of personal data is the most requested privacy provision, enabling students to anonymously access to e-learning platforms. However, we should also point out that a learning application aims at assisting students and so they cannot act in full anonymity. For that reason, participants in our study were always informed of the tracking process and given the right to control access to their data. On top of that, we always have a clear policy regarding the use of student tracking data in research and instructional purposes. For instance, the consent agreement is compulsory for the students and only authorized and anonymous data are used in our publications. We have no intention to make any claims regarding how to definitely solve privacy issues that one might encounter. Nonetheless, we hope to raise awareness of researchers, pedagogical teams and other e-learning practitioners in terms of user tracking and data analysis.

What we have also learned from the current study is that the research trends in Learning Analytics tend to focus more on technologies. To us, it is worth questioning our research strategy that places technologies ahead of the users, their actual needs and their concerns with privacy. LA has been indeed positively welcomed by the e-learning community and practitioners, but has also been indirectly forcing users to constantly readjust themselves to newly created environments and technologies. Are we actually adapting to technologies? If so, why is it not the other way around?

Privacy concerns remain one of the main research challenges in LA. Therefore, our future work will focus on a more in-depth analysis of the current experimental data to explore other aspects like ethics in e-learning. We are also attempting to quantify and qualify the impact of the privacy issues on the behavioral, social and cognitive aspects of online learning. To do so, research colleagues from France, Germany and Greece are collaborating on an experiment to study the evolvement of privacy questions and their associated threats by taking into account both ethical and cultural points of view.

References

1. May, M., George, S.: Privacy concerns in e-learning: is using tracking system a threat? Int. J. Inf. Educ. Technol. **1**, 1–8 (2011)
2. Popovici, A., Mironov, C.: Students' perception on using eLearning technologies. Procedia – Soc. Behav. Sci. **180**, 1514–1519 (2015)
3. Gaur, S., Chaudhary, A., Mittal, M.: A comparative study of e-learning technique with traditional teaching techniques. Int. J. Innovative Res. Electr. Electron. Instrum. Control Eng. **3**, 23–25 (2015)
4. Scott, P., Vanoirbeek, C.: Technology-Enhanced Learning (2007)
5. Manson, P.: Technology-Enhanced Learning: Supporting Learning in the 21st Century (2007)
6. Gamage, D., Fernando, S., Perera, I.: Factors affecting to effective eLearning: learners perspective. Sci. Res. J. (SCIRJ) **2**, 42–48 (2014)
7. Lau, R.W.H., Yen, N.Y., Li, F., Wah, B.: Recent development in multimedia e-learning technologies. World Wide Web **17**, 189–198 (2013)
8. Mazza, R., Botturi, L.: Monitoring an online course with the GISMO tool: a case study. Int. J. Interact. Learn. Res. **18**, 251–265 (2007)
9. Corbi, A.: Review of current student-monitoring techniques used in eLearning-focused recommender systems and learning analytics. Int. J. Artif. Intell. Interact. Multimedia **2**, 44–52 (2014)
10. May, M., George, S., Prévôt, P.: TrAVis to enhance online tutoring and learning activities: real time visualization of students tracking data. Int. J. Interact. Technol. Smart Educ. **8**, 52–69 (2011)
11. Choquet, C., Iksal, S.: Modeling tracks for the model driven reengineering of a TEL system. JILR **18**, 161–184 (2007)
12. Gómez-Aguilar, D.A., Hernández-García, Á., García-Peñalvo, F.J., Therón, R.: Tap into visual analysis of customization of grouping of activities in eLearning. Comput. Hum. Behav. **47**, 60–67 (2015)
13. Qahmash, A.I.: The impact of e-learning as educational method on student's learning progress. J. Emerg. Trends Comput. Inf. Sci. **4**, 601–605 (2013)
14. Jermann, P., Soller, A., Muehlenbrock, M.: From mirroring to guiding: a review of state of the art technology for supporting collaborative learning. In: Proceedings of the First European Conference on Computer-Supported Collaborative Learning, Maastricht, The Netherlands, pp. 324–331 (2001)

15. Martinez Mones, A., Dimitriadis, Y., Morch, A., Ludvigsen, S., Herrer, A., Hoppe, U., Barros, B., Verdejo, F., Hulshof, C., Jong, T., Fessakis, G., Petrou, A., Dimitracopoulou, A., Lund, K., Baker, M., Jermann, P., Dillenbourg, P., Kollias, V., Vosniadou, S.: State of the art on interaction analysis: interaction analysis indicators. Interaction & Collaboration Analysis Supporting Teachers and Students' Self-regulation, 148 pages (2004)
16. Alowayr, A., Badii, A.: Review of monitoring tools for e-learning platforms. Int. J. Comput. Sci. Inf. Technol. **6**, 79–86 (2014)
17. Burdescu, D.D., Mihăescu, M.C.: Building intelligent e-learning systems by activity monitoring and analysis. In: Tsihrintzis, G.A., Jain, L.C. (eds.) Multimedia Services in Intelligent Environments, pp. 153–174. Springer, Heidelberg (2010)
18. Hardy, J., Antonioletti, M., Bates, S.: E-learner tracking: tools for discovering learner behavior. In: IASTED International Conference on Web-based Education, Austria, pp. 458–463 (2004)
19. Jeske, D., Backhaus, J., Stamov Roßnagel, C.: Self-regulation during e-learning: using behavioural evidence from navigation log files. J. Comput. Assist. Learn. **30**, 272–284 (2014)
20. Mehra, S.: Emerging trends in learning management systems. Int. J. Comput. Sci. Issues **12**, 79–83 (2015)
21. Softic, S., Taraghi, B., Ebner, M., Vocht, L., Mannens, E., Walle, R.: Monitoring learning activities in PLE using semantic modelling of learner behaviour. In: Holzinger, A., Ziefle, M., Hitz, M., Debevc, M. (eds.) SouthCHI 2013. LNCS, vol. 7946, pp. 74–90. Springer, Heidelberg (2013). doi:10.1007/978-3-642-39062-3_5
22. Kim, J.., Gunn, D.., Schuh, E., Phillips, B., Pagulayan, R.., Wixon, D.: Tracking real-time user experience (TRUE): a comprehensive instrumentation solution for complex systems. In: SIGCHI Conference on Human Factors in Computing Systems, Florence, Italy, pp. 443–452 (2008)
23. Popescu, E., Cioiu, D.: Instructor support for monitoring and visualizing students' activity in a social learning environment. In: 2012 IEEE 12th International Conference on Advanced Learning Technologies (ICALT), pp. 371–373 (2012)
24. Pozzi, F., Manca, S., Persico, D., Sarti, L.: A general framework for tracking and analysing learning processes in computer-supported collaborative learning environments. Innovations Educ. Teach. Int. **44**, 169–179 (2007)
25. May, M., George, S., Prévôt, P.: TrAVis to enhance online tutoring and learning activities: real time visualization of students tracking data. In: IADIS International Conference on E-learning, Freiburg, Germany, pp. 57–64 (2010)
26. Berge, Z., Collins, M.: Computer-mediated communication and the online classroom in distance learning. Compu.-Mediated Commun. Mag. **2**, 6 (1995)
27. May, M., George, S., Prévôt, P.: A closer look at tracking human & computer interactions in web-based communications. ITSE **5**, 170–188 (2008)
28. May, M., George, S., Prévôt, P.: Tracking human-computer interactions in e-learning: an application to computer mediated communications. In: IADIS International Conference on Interfaces and Human Computer Interaction, Freiburg, Germany, pp. 163–170 (2010)
29. Lekira, A., Després, C., Jacoboni, P., Choquet, C., Iksal, S.: Using indicators during synchronous tutoring of practical work. In: The 11th IEEE International Conference on Advanced Learning Technologies, pp. 568–572 (2011)
30. Dimitracopoulou, A.: Computer based interaction analysis supporting self-regulation: achievements and prospects of an emerging research direction. Technol. Inst. Cognition Learn. (TICL) **6**, 291–314 (2008)

31. May, M., George, S.: Using learning tracking data to support students' self-monitoring. In: International Conference on Computer Supported Education, Noordwijkerhout, The Netherlands, pp. 46–55 (2011)
32. de Groot, R., Drachman, R., Hever, R., Schwarz, B., Hoppe, U., Harrer, A., De Laat, M., Wegerif, R., McLaren, B., Baurens, B.: Computer supported moderation of e-discussions: the ARGUNAUT approach. In: International Conference of Computer Supported Collaborative Learning, New Jersey, USA, pp. 165–167 (2007)
33. Gerosa, M.., Pimentel, M., Fuks, H., Lucena, G.: Analyzing discourse structure to coordinate educational forums. In: The 7th International Conference on Intelligent Tutoring Systems, Maceiò, Alagoas, Brazil, pp. 262–272 (2004)
34. Brooks, C., Panesar, R., Greer, J.: Awareness and collaboration in the iHelp courses content management system. In: Nejdl, W., Tochtermann, K. (eds.) EC-TEL 2006. LNCS, vol. 4227, pp. 34–44. Springer, Heidelberg (2006). doi:10.1007/11876663_5
35. Donath, J.: A semantic approach to visualizing online conversations. Commun. ACM **45**, 45–49 (2002)
36. Shaul, M.: Assessing online discussion forum participation. Int. J. Inf. Commun. Technol. Educ. **3**, 39–46 (2007)
37. Gibbs, W., Olexa, V., Bernas, R.: A visualization tool for managing and studying online communications. Int. J. Educ. Technol. Soc. **9**, 232–243 (2006)
38. Mazza, R., Dimitrova, V.: CourseVis: externalising student information to facilitate instructors in distance learning. In: Artificial Intelligence in Education, Sydney, Australia, pp. 279–86 (2003)
39. Bratitsis, T., Dimitracopoulou, A.: Data recording and usage interaction analysis in asynchronous discussions: the D.I.A.S. system. In: Proceedings of the 12th International Conference on Artificial Intelligence in Education AIED, Workshop Usage Analysis in Learning Systems, Amsterdam, The Netherlands, 9 pages (2005)
40. Coffrin, C., Corrin, L., de Barba, P., Kennedy, G.: Visualizing patterns of student engagement and performance in MOOCs. In: Proceedings of the Fourth International Conference on Learning Analytics And Knowledge, pp. 83–92. ACM, New York (2014)
41. Leony, D., Pardo, A., de la Fuente Valentín, L., de Castro, D.S., Kloos, C.D.: GLASS: a learning analytics visualization tool. In: Proceedings of the 2Nd International Conference on Learning Analytics and Knowledge, pp. 162–163. ACM, New York (2012)
42. Bandara, I., Ioras, F., Maher, K.: Cyber security concerns in e-learning education. In: ICERI2014 Proceedings, pp. 728–734 (2014)
43. Esposito, A.: Research ethics in emerging forms of online learning: issues arising from a hypothetical study on a MOOC. Electron. J. e-Learning **10**, 315–325 (2012)
44. Ivanova, M., Grosseck, G., Holotescu, C.: Researching data privacy models in eLearning. In: 2015 International Conference on Information Technology Based Higher Education and Training (ITHET), pp. 1–6 (2015)
45. Roca, J.C., García, J.J., de la Vega, J.J., JC: The importance of perceived trust, security and privacy in online trading systems. Info. Mngmnt. Comp. Secur. **17**, 96–113 (2009)
46. Brown, T.: Ethics in eLearning. In: Workshop for Net Business Ethics, Honolulu, Hawaii, pp. 1–6 (2008)
47. Kanuka, H., Anderson, T.: Ethical issues in qualitative e-learning research. Int. J. Qual. Methods **6**, 1–14 (2007)
48. Klobucar, T., Jenabi, M., Kaibel, A., Karapidis, A.: Security and Privacy Issues in Technology Enhanced Learning. IOS Press, Amsterdam (2007)

49. Anwar, M., Greer, J.: Reputation management in privacy-enhanced e-learning. In: Proceedings of the 3rd Annual Scientific Conference of the LORNET Research Network, Montreal, Canada, 6 pages (2006)
50. Ben Arfa Rabai, L., Rjaibi, N., Ben Aissa, A.: Quantifying security threats for e-learning systems. In: 2012 International Conference on Education and e-Learning Innovations (ICEELI), pp. 1–6. IEEE (2012)
51. Yong, J.: Security and privacy preservation for mobile e-learning via digital identity attributes. J. Univ. Comput. Sci. **17**, 296–310 (2011)
52. Borcea-Pfitzmann, K., Liesebach, K., Pfitzmann, A.: Establishing a privacy-aware collaborative eLearning environment. In: Proceedings of the EADTU Annual Conference 2005: Towards Lisbon 2010: Collaboration for Innovative Content in Lifelong Open and Flexible Learning, 8 pages, Rome (2005)

Social Network Analytics in Formal and Informal Learning Environments with EduBridge Social

Luciana Oliveira[1(✉)] and Álvaro Figueira[2]

[1] CRACS / INESC TEC & CEOS.PP, Polytechnic of Porto, Rua Jaime Lopes Amorim, Porto, Portugal
lgo@eu.ipp.pt

[2] CRACS/INESC TEC, University of Porto, Porto, Portugal
arf@dcc.fc.up.pt

Abstract. The integration of social media in education has been raising new challenges for teachers, students and organizations, in both traditional and technology-mediated learnings settings. Formal higher education contexts are still mostly anchored and locked up in institutional LMS, despite the innumerous educational digressions that educators have been conducting throughout social media networks. One of the biggest challenges in contemporary educational needs consists on managing the integration, validation and reporting on educational processes, goals and student performance, when they are widely spread in several formal and informal contexts. In this chapter a system for the integration of LMS and social media is presented, as well as evidence on its practical usage. A set of social network analytics are also brought forward as features that are currently being added to the referred system.

Keywords: Social student relationship management · Educational communication · LMS · Facebook groups · Moodle · Learning analytics · Social network analysis

1 Introduction

The tendency to value and strategically frame the development of social interactions transcends the transactional and organizational needs and environment of organizations at large, and of Higher Education institutions in particular. It is a clear reflection on how communication has been evolving since the growth and intensification of the use of social media platforms, that impacts on how society at large relates to organizations and, on a micro level, on how individuals relate to each other. It reveals a strengthening of the relationships between publics and organizations and also the intensification of two-way communication streams. In fact, social media has been redefining how we relate to each other as humans and how we as humans relate to the organizations that serve us [1]. It has been imposing a two-way dialog that brings people together to discover and share information, share ideas and build communities of people that share the same interests.

The concept of Social Student Relationship Management (Social SRM) consists of a particularization of the Social CRM concept, applied to the relationship between

G. Costagliola et al. (Eds.): CSEDU 2016, CCIS 739, pp. 296–316, 2017.
DOI: 10.1007/978-3-319-63184-4_16

educational providers (such as schools, universities and training centres) and students supported by social media platforms.

Social SRM aims at amplifying the formal and informal bonds between students and schools, expanding their interactions into social conversations, and strengthening educational ties through the development of collaborative conversations that provide mutually beneficial value and that, ultimately, allows for the growth of social and educational communities. It places organizations, teachers and staff in student's digital natural environment, engaging them in personalized dialogs that reinforce students' role as empowered participatory individuals in organizational strategic development and also in the management of their learning opportunities.

The educational dimension of Social SRM comprises the set of relationship and interactions between teachers and students, in social media, in the domain of teaching-learning communication, in the classroom administration and in the students' social integration. As a subsystem of internal organizational communication it brings organizational culture into the relationship and builds upon it, since "students' experiences depend on their social class backgrounds, the responses of school staff to their behaviour within schools, and the actions of students and staff that create school cultures" [2].

We believe that the quality of the communication in a learning system significantly impacts on its efficiency and that the state-of-the-art information technologies, mainly social media, offers unlimited resources for the communication's streamlining and diversification of formal and informal learning [3].

Social media has been boosting educators to drive formal learning contexts into social networks aiming at the development of learning communities that allow for collaborative exploration and reflection of ideas, in a cooperative and supportive atmosphere [4]. Besides offering participants the potential to benefit from a ready source of peer support it also provides the necessary emotional support [5] to allow for communities' social inclusion.

In the next section of this paper we present the background of the Social SRM concept and the educational domains of its application, since our main focus resides on the communicative/dialogical nature of the interactions happening inside the learning communities.

In Sect. 3 a case study focused on the educational use of Facebook groups is presented, consolidating the main dimensions of the Social SRM concept, where the need for a management/interaction system is raised. In Sect. 4 we present the EduBridge Social system which aims to bridge educational environments with social networks. We begin by describing the system's architecture, how it integrates with Moodle and Facebook, and how authentication is managed. In Sect. 5 we detail the main aspects of the system's interface and the system's relevance/contribution in terms of potential to improve the management of the educational environment for teachers. In Sect. 6 we present set of analytics, social network analysis and visualizations which are currently be added to the system. Finally, in the last section we present our conclusions and future work.

2 Background on Social SRM

The concept of Social SRM builds upon previous research on the use of Facebook groups in education, as reported by [6]. In order to fully clarify it, it is essential to present its three main components.

2.1 Teaching-Learning Communication

In this domain communication serves as a vehicle for reaching educational goals. It encompasses formal educational communication, which is sustained by a curriculum and pedagogic model with clear indications of contents, methods, requirements and assessment, and the informal educational communication, which is not institutionalized, methodical, structured, intentional and sustained by a previous definition of pedagogic goals. Informal educational communication is more prone to social media environments, thus it's important to understand that the absence of a curriculum and pedagogic model doesn't annul its educational potential. The spontaneous, simple conversation and group discussion that characterizes informal communication may produce educational effects, when contributing to behavioural changes in individuals.

2.2 Classroom Administration

This domain is in direct dependency of the organizational administrative communication that regulates learning tasks, schedules and procedures. Social media has proven to be an excellent tool for classroom administration, in terms of processes clarification and celerity, student responsiveness and time economy. This is heavily sustained by the amount of time and attention students dedicate to social media.

2.3 Student Social Integration

This dimension is aimed at fostering the formation of the sense of belonging and ultimately the development of a learning community. It consists of the most pure form of social interaction, relying heavily on the establishment of meaningful conversations that allow for the development of social and emotional bonds. From the teachers' point of view, and as a community builder/manager, it requires an engaging, motivational, cooperative and personal/informal communication approach that is favoured in social media environments.

Educational Social SRM comprises a set of communication domains that aim to foster student integration and avoid disengagement or dropout. It contributes to setting a welcoming school climate prone to success and completion, which has been defined as "...the quality and character of school life experiences and reflects norms, goals, values interpersonal relationships, teaching, learning and leadership practices, and organizational structures" [7]. For instance, in a blended learning environment, social media provides two-way exchanges between the classroom and the virtual interaction environment in the relationship building process – both environments being interchangeably reinforced.

3 Facebook Groups in Education

In this section we present evidence on previous research [6] conducted on the use of Facebook groups, as an extension of the classroom teacher-student relationship, into a more dynamic and informal environment.

The aim of this case study was to discover, investigate and assess the three components of the educational dimension of Social SRM mentioned in the previous section. Research also allowed to obtain insights on the benefits, challenges and tech needs for a broader implementation of this methodology.

The study was carried out during two semesters, in three different subjects from the first, second and third year from two different courses. The courses were held in traditional classroom, with Moodle support. A Facebook group was created for each class and the students were invited to join. Though participation was not mandatory, all of the students having a Facebook profile joined the groups, except for 3 students who didn't own a Facebook profile and didn't wish to own one. Among the three classes there were 99 students (grouped in 52, 34 and 13 participants) and one teacher interacting in three separate Facebook groups. Facebook groups were introduced to students as a complimentary support platform in the first class of the semester and not as a replacement for the institutional LMS, as Wang proposes [8].

We must stress that the focus resided on the communicative/dialogical nature of the interactions happening inside the learning communities, mainly because there was no particular objective assigned to participants when these communities were formed. Students were invited to join a "support community" where anything could happen, in order to assure that dialogue and relationships were spontaneous and self-motivated, as already defended by some authors [9]. Students were encouraged to bring any subject they found relevant to the group.

All the groups' interactions were retrieved from Facebook, using the available API. In this process, the following fields were collected on each groups' feed: post id, post author, post message, post type and corresponding #comments and #likes. The posts were classified in 5 main subject categories, which were created to fit the natural and dynamic discussions that emerged in the groups: (1) course administration, (2) posts related to course contents/curriculum, (3) course unrelated personal interests/projects, (4) posts related to academic training and personal development and (5) social messages. Additionally, in order to better understand these results and to dig into personal perspectives, students were surveyed.

Concerning the domain of educational communication and its specificities in the social media environment, in the case study, the three Social SRM dimensions were not equitably detected: messages related to teaching-learning and course administration rounded up to 40% each and messages aimed at the student social integration rounded only up to 20%. Still, it was possible to identify several positive impacts from the implementation of the above mentioned methodology, which were consolidated with survey responses.

When asked if they would like to connect and communicate with other teachers on Facebook, 89% of the students responded affirmatively. When asked why, these mentioned mainly: the celerity in responses/clarification of doubts, the increased interaction with the teacher, the improvement of the communication with the teacher, the easiness to keep up and the increased visibility/sense of presence of course activities, discussions and administration, the enlarged team spirit and the fact that teachers post relevant content in course's scientific domain.

Students were also questioned about their perspectives on the social relationship they maintain with their teachers, in order to provide a fuller picture on the importance of the social dimension of this relationship. 94% of the students believes that a good social relationship between teacher and students is fundamental for academic success and that teachers do not invest enough on the formation of these relationships (74%). 93% of the students would like other teachers to use Facebook for educational and social purposes, increasing teacher-student interactions.

When asked about the Facebook group usefulness, effectiveness, communication and relationship potential, students reported that it contributes to a better working relationship with peers (96%), it increases the socialization potential among classmates (92%), it provides a better social and professional relationship with the teacher (96%), it increase their motivation to learn (84%) and that they feel more actively participating and engaged in course activities (90%), that their peers value their contributions in the Facebook group (89%) and that, in the Facebook group, the class works as cooperative team (91%). Engagement in Facebook has also been shown to be closely related to an increase in college students' social capital, especially for those with low self-esteem and life satisfaction [9].

On the teacher perspective, the extension of classroom communication into social media can provide real benefits, but it can also pose some challenges. Using Facebook groups to answer students' questions and doubts can be real time-effective, since clarification becomes widely available for everyone. When it comes to requiring student's attention or immediate actions, social media offers excellent celerity as students respond almost immediately. Facebook groups also allowed shy/introverted students to become more actively engaged in discussions and, though it may be possible to discuss details associated to teacher-student privacy, it can be quite useful to understand the student general state of mind, general interests and social background context, which becomes accessible.

On the other hand, the teacher may face some challenges during the extension of classroom communication into social media, such as: compromising their privacy on the network, students expecting quicker responses and student active engagement may require a lot of moderation time. In these environments it is convenient to lower the level of relationship formality, which may conflict with a very formal classroom teacher attitude and/or intrapersonal communication style.

Cultural issues must also be raised. There is a profound heritage of formality and vertical relationships in HEI's cultural environment which may pose additional challenges to the proposed methodology. In order to address these challenges further research should focus on determining how informal should teacher-student interactions be on social media, providing clear guidelines resulting from the convergence of mutual expectations.

The conducted study also revealed that, in order to efficiently manage and assess social students' relationships, teachers need suitable monitoring and analysis tools/ applications.

In our perspective, and based on students' and teachers' perceptions on the use of social networks as complimentary educational systems, the teacher is the agent facing the bigger challenges. In fact, students naturally and easily accommodate several dimensions of their lives in social networks (personal, professional, social, educational), and are very open to changes. However, on top of the previously mentioned challenges that teachers may face, there is also the need to institutionally and educationally legitimize the use of social networks, since some teachers refuse to adopt concurrent non-institutional systems, such as the school's LMS. This lays on top of deep cultural issues and on the organization's proneness to adopt/adjust to new technologies.

Given this scenery, we believe to be of the utmost importance to bridge between the well-established LMS and the also well-established social networks (ex. Facebook), taking advantage of pre-acquired habits, knowledge and sense of control, which is currently offered to teachers. We believe that providing the current LMS with insights and features that allow teachers to manage and perceive the dynamics of students' interactions on social media, to manage them and to make educational sense of them, may, in fact, facilitate and potentiate the inclusion of social networks on the best service of education.

At this stage, and in this paper, our main focus is to provide teachers with resources to validate the use of social media in their educational settings. Though research emerges at a quick pace, teachers' technology adoption pace and the process of integrating a wider variety of technologies in their pedagogical framework is considerably slower. In fact, despite the advances in research and the proven evidence of the benefits of the educational use of social media in education, it doesn't necessarily mean that there is a corresponding widespread adoption of it. Therefore, we believe that, at a first instance, it is necessary to gather teachers' consensus by fomenting a shift in practices (for instance, through teacher training) and secondly by providing a technological solution that assures the maintenance of the validity, security and institutional recognition of the required shift in pedagogical practices. Research outputs from the work of [6] were already converted into several teacher dissemination, training and demonstration initiatives, thus its outputs are being actively offered to educational professionals and actually being incorporated in their practices. In order to consolidate this process, an urgent technological development is crucial in order to facilitate the necessary shift, and this is why, for now, teachers are at the centre of our main concerns, since they are the main catalyst agents.

On the following section, we present the architecture of the EduBridge system, built to fulfill the above mentioned needs.

4 System's Architecture

Our proposed system bridges one learning management system with a social network. Our approach was to focus on the popular of these two systems. According to its popularity and maturity, we naturally picked Moodle and Facebook.

The proposed system is based on a set of Moodle blocks that share a communications engine and a database stored locally. The system's architecture is based on the model – view-control pattern, implemented through five modules. In this case, the 'view' is produced by each module. However, the 'control' is hierarchically spread through the top level-module down to the leaves modules. This organization is depicted in Fig. 1. As a top layer we have the communications module (googleoauther2) which establishes a connection between Moodle and Facebook through the Facebook's authentication mechanism, using the user's credentials. Then, the control is passed to the module fbgroups to retrieve the groups owned by the user. This module is also responsible for creating lists of users belonging to the groups and to set some counters for usage statistics. The module fbcomments retrieves all the posts and comments that were posted in timeline of the selected group. Finally, the modules fbstats and fbtotalstats present the local statistics, and global statistics, about the selected group or all the considered groups, respectively.

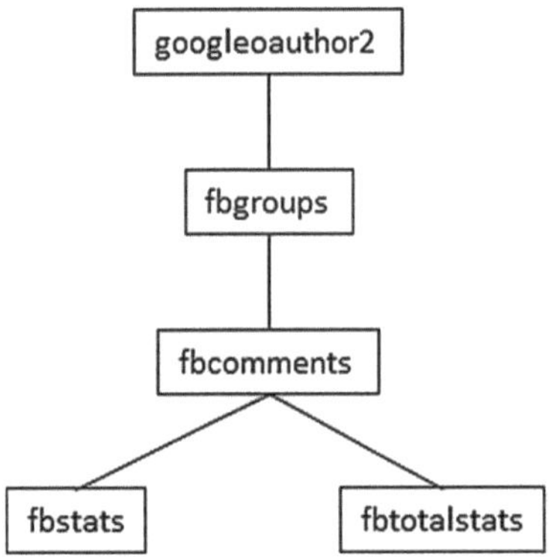

Fig. 1. The system's 5 modules.

These modules were implemented as simple Moodle blocks. The reasons for this decision mainly relied on:

- It's easier to maintain modular code;
- Moodle blocks have enough capabilities to include code which is centrally administrated, and that can share a common access to specific tables in the database;
- The blocks positioning system is quite customizable in versions after Moodle 2.8 making it simpler to be adapted to the visual organization's preferences of each user.

4.1 Integration Between Systems

Our system uses the Facebook API to access specific data using the user's credentials. In our case we need to access data related to the groups created by a specific user. Therefore, during authentication, Facebook asks for consent to use the user_managed_groups permission of the API. Once this permission is granted by the user, it is stored and is never asked again to the user.

The 5 modules are integrated into Moodle in the form of blocks. Each one has to be stored (manually) in a specific Moodle folder in the file system. However, after restart of the system, they are all detected by Moodle, and automatically integrated in registered blocks list. We believe this organization makes the code easier to maintain, and to deploy into another instance of Moodle very easily.

We must stress that the systematic (though expected) evolution of the Facebook API makes the integration with other systems dependant on which permissions are available. It is usual to have a certain permission granted for one version of the API, and in another the right to access that permission is revoked.

4.2 Authentication

Once authentication is completed in Moodle, the user needs to authenticate himself in Facebook, using the Facebook authentication mechanism.

This is a persistent mechanism as while the user is logged into Moodle, it does not need to authenticate again in Facebook. The "cookies" created by the system ensure a validation time of 30 days.

Although there is just one pair of credentials to use the API, and to communicate with Facebook, the communicating token is shared by all users of the Moodle system. However, access is only possible to the groups created by that specific user. For example, groups that weren't created, but just subscribed will not be considered by the system. Hopefully this won't prevent the further developments we intend to introduce in the system.

4.3 Using Moodle Modulesas Blocks

Moodle blocks are plugins that load in the right-hand side or left-hand side column of a Moodle site, and display information to the user in a rectangular block. Each side column can have zero, one or multiple blocks loaded. Examples of built-in Moodle blocks include: HTML content, calendars, menus, course lists, etc. A diagram illustrating the standard areas of Moodle is depicted in Fig. 2.

Blocks are programmed by extending the PHP class block_base, introducing a init() procedure, and assigning content to the block by using function get_content(). An important advantage of using blocks is that there is already support to "capabilities". Therefore, blocks may invoke the get_context_instance to understand what kind of permissions that particular user has. This allows us to use different accesses to the system (administrator, teacher, students) in very straight forward way. For example, we want to hide the system blocks for non-authorized access.

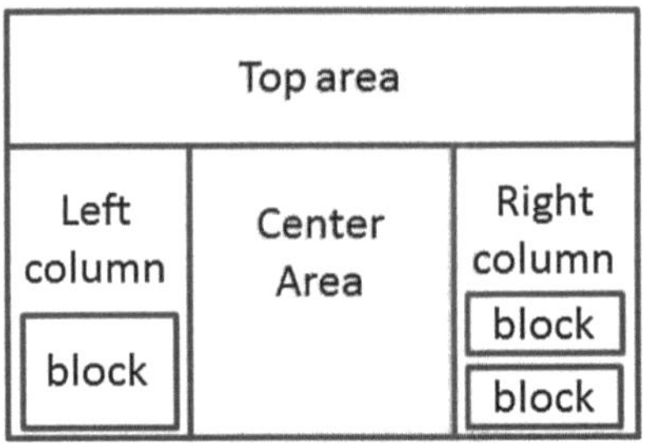

Fig. 2. The standard Moodle layout.

Finally, because blocks can be moved in the Moodle standard layout, they can be repositioned during execution time, which makes it easy to the user to choose the most comfortable way of displaying them.

4.4 Database Tables

Moodle supports a variety of SQL databases by providing an abstraction layer, based on specific code libraries, which allow the programmer to access every type allowed database in the same way.

Every data table in Moodle has one common integer element: the id. This id is unique in the whole Moodle database which means that it serves as a primary key, but also as a foreign key to any table. This situation is a core rule to Moodle database programming.

```
<?xml version="1.0" encoding="UTF-8" ?>
<XMLDB PATH="blocks/fbcomments/db" VERSION="20141207"
COMMENT="XMLDB file for Moodle blocks/fbcomments/db"
xmlns:xsi="http://www.w3.org/2001/XMLSchema-instance"
xsi:noNamespaceSchemaLoca-
tion="../../../lib/xmldb/xmldb.xsd"
>
<TABLES>
 <TABLE NAME="fb_user_ids" COMMENT="user identity pro-
viders">
  <FIELDS>
   <FIELD NAME="id" TYPE="int" LENGTH="10"
NOTNULL="true" SEQUENCE="true"/>
   <FIELD NAME="fbid" TYPE="char" LENGTH="125"
NOTNULL="true" SEQUENCE="false"/>
   <FIELD NAME="courseid" TYPE="char" LENGTH="125"
NOTNULL="true" SEQUENCE="false"/>
   <FIELD NAME="groupid" TYPE="char" LENGTH="125"
NOTNULL="true" SEQUENCE="false"/>
   <FIELD NAME="groupname" TYPE="char" LENGTH="125"
NOTNULL="true" SEQUENCE="false"/>
   </FIELDS>
   <KEYS>
    <KEY NAME="primary" TYPE="primary" FIELDS="id"/>
   </KEYS>
</TABLE>
```

Fig. 3. Part of file install.xml.

Almost all plugins have a hook to the database in the form of a subfolder named 'db' that contains files which manage data tables specific to the plugin (or block). The db folder typically contains the files install.xml, upgrade.php and access.php. The install.xml defines the tables required for the system (in Fig. 3 we present part of install.xml of block fbcomments).

The file upgrade.php contains instruction to update table elements, while file access.php defines the capabilities associated with the block.

The system runs with the support of 4 new database tables, as illustrated in Fig. 4. Tables fb_group_stats and fb_users_id are used mainly for computing statistics; fb_appinfo is used to share Facebook access among users, and; auth_googleauth2_user_idps is used for users' authentication.

	fb_group_stats
K:	group_id: VARCHAR
	user_id_mp:VARCHAR
	user_id_mc:VARCHAR
	user_id_mp_name:VARCHAR
	user_id_mc_name:VARCHAR
	c_likes:INTEGER
	p_likes:INTEGER
	n_comments:INTEGER
	n_posts:INTEGER
	last_event:VARCHAR

	fb_users_id
	fbid:VARCHAR
	courseid:VARCHAR
K:	groupid:VARCHAR
	groupname:VARCHAR

	fb_appinfo
K:	id:INTEGER
	num:INTEGER
	appid:VARCHAR
	appsecret:VARCHAR

	auth_googleauth2_user_idps
K:	userid:INTEGER
	provideruserid:VARCHAR
	provider:VARCHAR
	accesstoken:VARCHAR

Fig. 4. EduBridge Social database tables.

Note that although figures, videos and audio do appear in the Moodle block, they are not stored locally. Instead, all these "heavy" media elements are loaded on demand.

5 Interface

The system's interface is composed of a four-set Moodle blocks which users, particularly teachers, can display and manage in their Moodle Dashboard (known as "My home" up to Moodle's 2.8 version). This aims at framing the system in the most recent Moodle's philosophy for managing the teacher's educational workspace.

The four blocks are designated as: "Facebook Groups", "Facebook Posts & Comments", "Facebooks Statistics" and "Total Statistics".

The block's behaviour is interdependent, thought the information displayed on all four blocks is adjusted to users' interaction with the block "Facebook Groups".

The "Facebook Groups" block (Fig. 5) retrieves the list of groups that the authenticated user manages on Facebook. This means that all educational and personal groups are displayed and accessible through Moodle's interface. This is also the main block among the four-set, since it allows teachers to arrange the information and views to be generated.

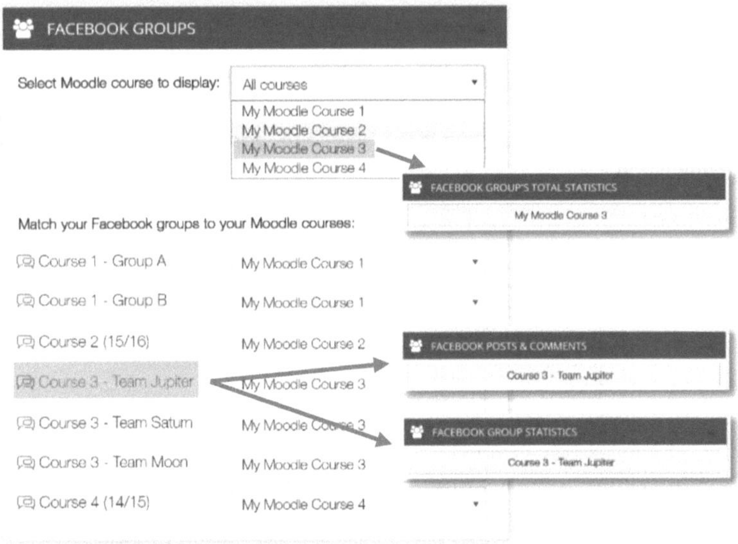

Fig. 5. "Facebook Groups" block.

In order to provide teachers with tools to (1) separate personal from educational groups and (2) arrange and match the groups to their courses on Moodle a set of drop-down matching boxes were incorporated.

The ability to match Facebook Groups to Moodle courses is also aimed at providing teachers with greater flexibility to accommodate the need for diversity of educational scenarios, concerning the arrangement of students in wider or narrower social learning networks. Assigned to the same Moodle course it is possible to have one or more Facebook groups, whether the teacher intends to arrange the class into separate visible or non-visible teams. This is also aimed at providing teachers with the same Moodle course participants' management features, concerning the creation of course level groups.

As illustrated on Fig. 6, a dropdown box presents teachers the full list of his/her own Moodle courses, which can be assigned to each Facebook's group. Having students arranged into separate Facebook groups will allow teachers to monitor each group's performance individually and to assess each group's participant commitment and contributions to the assigned projects/activities, which is displayed on the "Facebook Statistics" and "Total Statistics" block. Figure 4 presents a real case scenario in which the teacher only uses one Facebook group per Moodle course. However, it is possible to have other grouping configurations, such as the need to create several Facebook groups belonging to the same Moodle course, thus this feature was added the "Facebook

Groups" module. This allows the analysis of interactions developed in separate groups that belong to the same class/course, particularly in courses in which students are assigned concurrent and separate projects development and in individual/group assessment is needed.

Fig. 6. "Facebook Posts and Comments" block.

The system also provides teacher with the ability to access all the group's posts and interactions on Moodle's Dashboard, through the block "Facebook Posts and Comments" (Fig. 6). This block's main purpose is to increase the level of integration between the two platforms, since it eliminates the need to access a second environment (Facebook) in order to check updates and new user's interactions, which may or may not require action.

It is recommended that this block is displayed on the Dashboard's central area, as illustrated in Fig. 2, given the amount and of information it provides, which includes every posts' text and other visual static or dynamic multimedia content.

For each post it is possible to access the post author, post date, time and post comments. For the sake of economy of page height, comments are collapsed by default, and can be further expanded by the user, as illustrated in Fig. 6.

For each comment, the block displays the comment author, date, time, likes, comment's likes and replies.

The "Group Statistics" block offers teachers statistical data concerning the group's total number of posts, total number of posts, median of comments per post, retrieves the group's most recent post and comment and also the most popular post, which is the post with more likes, as illustrated in Fig. 7. This block also displays user interaction statistics, providing relevant information for student's performance assessment.

Fig. 7. "Group Statistics" block (a).

Statistical information about student's performance is organized in two sections (Fig. 8): "Users who posted" new messages in the group and the corresponding amount of likes and "Users who commented", that is, the users who interacted with the messages posted on the same group, by posting replies of liking comments.

Users (teacher and students) are ranked by the amount of interaction they generate in the group. Rankings of users' statistical data are particularly useful during the teaching-leaning process and specifically relevant for student continuous or final assessment.

For instance, a user may post a lot of messages in the group, but may not receive feedback at all (that is, the content may not be relevant for that community) and/or may not interact at all with other users' messages (that is, he/she may not find other user's content relevant and/or this may be an indicator of lack of interest, inexistence of group sense of belonging, etc.).

Fig. 8. "Group Statistics" user's interactions section (b).

On the other hand, a user may not introduce any content at all in the group, but he/she may be an active and valuable member to the community, either by commenting, replying to comments (i.e., fostering discussion) or liking his/her colleagues' messages.

It is up to the teacher to consider the weight of these parameters in assessing individual or group performance (if assessment is applicable).

The fourth block, "Facebook Total Statistics" (Fig. 9), displays the global statistics for the Moodle course selected on the "Facebook Groups" block. In case two or more Facebook groups are assigned to the same Moodle course, this block will provide the teacher the aggregated statistics for that set of groups. This feature is particularly relevant

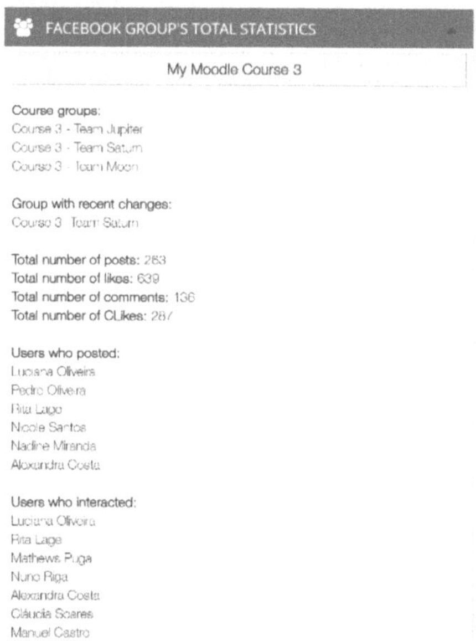

Fig. 9. "Facebook Total Statistics" block.

when the teacher intends to have the class divided into groups and uses several Facebook groups to guide and support each group separately.

This block is also useful for teacher needing aggregated statistics for all his/her Facebook groups or for personalized sets of groups, which are matched in the "Facebook Groups" block.

6 Social Network Analytics and Visualization

6.1 Types of Interactions

We recall that we retrieved the posts for the first semester of 2013, which comprehend posts/comments between September 2013 and January 2014. The results are presented in Table 1.

Table 1. Analytics of the retrieved posts.

	Posts	Comments	Likes
Number of	162	772	727
Post type:			
Link	30	80	113
Photo	35	263	205
Status	90	413	372
Video	7	16	37

These results forecast on the type of content which is more prone to generate higher participation and engagement for that community in particular and which are the most common types of interactions. If we look at the results independently of the effort, we come to the conclusion that status updates and photos lead to more interactions. However, if we consider these results proportionally to the effort in posting, then post type "photo" is the most prone to generate higher levels of interaction: whereas "status" messages generate an average of 4 "comments" and "likes", "photo" type posts are able to collect, in average, 8 "comments" and 6 "likes".

This analysis can be done on-the-fly while using the system, and can provide teachers with relevant information regarding the type of post they should choose when looking to increase their interaction with other group members. The analysis is also relevant for teachers looking to develop comparisons among several groups he/she manages, to outline a specific group profile and to transfer knowledge, as group manager, from one group into another.

6.2 Frequency of Interactions

Analysing the posting frequency/intensity in the course of the semester allows us to identify peaks of intensity of communication/interaction occurring in the group. From the graph shown on Fig. 10, we can see that this number varies between 1 and 7.

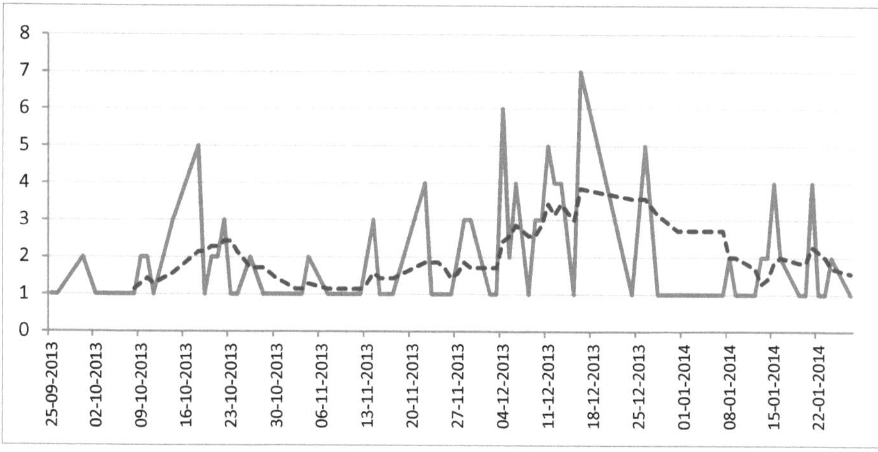

Fig. 10. Facebook group posting frequency. (Color figure online)

Particularly in the case study presented, by analysing the solid blue line, it is possible to identify 4 distinct moments: one in early October, one in late November, one in December and one in mid, late January. The dotted red line depicts a moving average of the interactions in periods of 7 days. This line indicates a global interaction per week leading us to conclude basically the same but with slower variations and less peaks showing clearly the most intensive interactions periods of the year. These lines provide teachers with the detection of the most intense working periods along the semester. It also reveals how students organize class projects and which could be the most productive periods. In this case, students were assigned a four-month collaborative project and an individual project. On early October, higher interactions are related to deciding the themes and teams for the collaborative project. Peaks on late November and throughout December are related to intra and inter team discussions and teacher solicitations for the development of the projects. The peaks detected on the first and third week of December indicate the higher stages of project development closer to its due date.

Depending on the results obtained in formal assessment and the quality of these peaks of interactions, teachers might feel necessary to make adjustments to course schedules and to try to anticipate or delay certain peaks aiming at improve the overall performance of students and of the learning process.

This combination of results from both environments is of the highest importance for the assessment of the overall conduction of a course, particularly for the teacher. It also allows the teacher to evaluate the potential offered by each of the environments and to better plan for future integrations. When using several educational environments teachers should be aware of the added value these bring into the educational context and should also be able to report on and to account for it.

6.3 Daily Interactions' Periods

One of the main advantages of Social Media Networks, particularly Facebook, is its ability and easiness to fit into student's daily digital environment. Educators' ability to take advantage of this scenario may return higher student involvement in the learning process and higher proximity between the academic and personal life for students, allowing for bigger interchanges. Social media is also a privileged environment for news/content sharing. Whether it consists on specialized/technical or generic content, real-life events, case studies or curiosities, its incorporation in educational groups is a one or two clicks process. Therefore, educational groups on Social Media benefit from the speed and diversity of content permanently emerging on the network.

As reported by other studies [10], best times to post on Facebook are early in the morning, between work and dinner hours and between dinner and bedtime. Data from our case study (as illustrated in Fig. 11) consolidates these indicators, reinforcing the period between around 4 p.m. as the most active in group interactions. As mentioned above, this educational context is benefiting from Social Media constant usage habits. However, the regression line shows that in a year period students tend to interact earlier. Comparing the initial date with the final one, the average interactions occur about an hour earlier in the day.

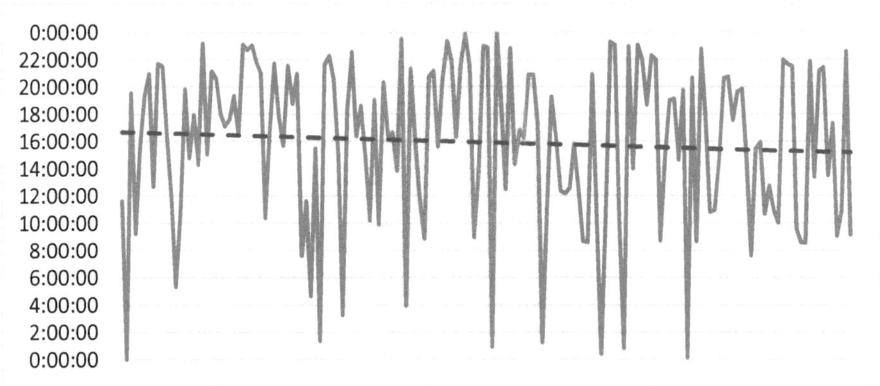

Fig. 11. Interactions per hour of the day.

Analysing the most active and fruitful time slots when looking to foster interactions is a valuable insight for teachers, whether it is knowledge acquired from previous group analysis or is related the group under analysis. Though every group may tend to develop a very intrinsic interaction profile, which may be more or less permeable to internal or external factors, the collection of insights and knowledge gathered by the teacher are of high instrumental value for the development of learning communities' management skills.

6.4 Visualising Interactions

Traces of activity left by social media users can facilitate perceptions on individual behaviour, social relationships, and community efficiency [11]. Tools and processes to analyse social traces are essential for enabling educators to study and nurture meaningful and sustainable social interactions occurring in learning communities.

In the case study under analysis we have a Facebook group with 42 participants, which correspond to the 42 nodes of the social graph represented in Fig. 12. There are 556 established connections (in the form of a 'comment-to' or 'reply-to') between group members, but only 51 are unique. This is why some connections are thicker than others, to depict a repeated connection. There are 150 self-loops, which mean that some group participants do comment, or reply, to their own posts, or comments.

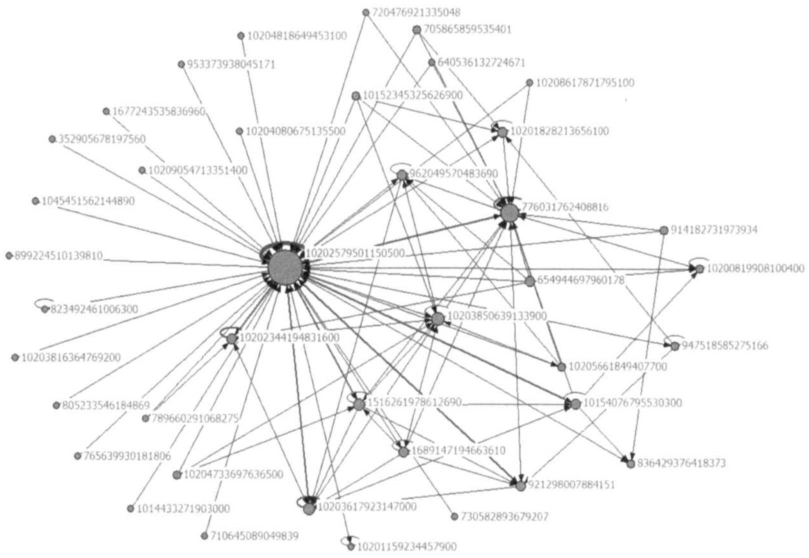

Fig. 12. The social graph.

Identities on the social graph have been anonymised, and converted to masked Facebook profile IDs, in order to assure confidentiality. In our representation of the network we adhere to the format proposed in [12]. As it can be seen in Fig. 12, some nodes are bigger than others. This happens because we set the size of each node to be proportional to its out-degree (note that the graph is directed). Therefore, the biggest the node size, the largest is its out-degree. This metric is a simple way to find out the most participative people in the group. We can also easily find which node ("102…50500" – the teacher) bridges all the others, although node "776…08816" (student) is also important in the network. Another conclusion that we can deduct from the graphic is that only a minority of nodes (apart from the teacher) are connected to other nodes. I.e., students do not frequently engage in each other conversations or are not very solicited. However, there are about 15 exceptions (15 nodes) to this rule.

The previous analysis also leads us to identify a graph density of about 6%. This value levels to a poorly connected network, which is a characteristic of Ego-Networks or of high-centralized networks. On the other hand, the maximum geodesic distance is 3, while the average geodesic distance reduces to 1.9, which means that we can, on average, reach any other node in less than two hops. Therefore, despite not being a dense network, it is well connected (because of the high centralization index).

Clearly, there are nodes with more connections and connected with denser parts of the network. Those nodes (students) allow the information to propagate fast, and make the network more responsive to posts. Mapping this situation to the academic world and students, this means that these students are indispensable to have success in communicating to the whole class. As a side note, it is curious to note that all these subgraphs include self-loops, which means that these students are willing to create answers in their own posts or comments, fostering discussion around topics that they brought to the group. Clearly, this group and its interactions are very teacher centric. There are a few students generating interactions among peers but the bridge element is the teacher.

7 Discussion

Educational insights on graph interaction analysis provide teachers with knowledge on which type of community has developed or is being developed. Many considerations could be built on this topic: weather the interactions should be teacher or student centred, which are not our main purpose. We can however stress that knowledge on this aspect is both relevant for teachers and for students, namely: to identify the type of community, its main intervenient, the origin of interactions and how oneself relates to the others in that group.

The proposed methodology, previous research outputs and presented system allowed for the development and implementation of "How to use Facebook groups in education" workshops. The workshops were conducted by the researchers and were aimed at the pedagogical and technological development of teachers. A lack of pedagogical validity was detected during this dissemination phase, which lead us to the need of incorporating new features in the already established LMS (Moodle). A very relevant detail, which is not frequently mentioned in literature, and is of the utmost importance to this scenario, is the discrepancy between the pace of research and its concrete/tangible corresponding transfer into the educational context. In some organizational cultures, the proneness to adopt or adapt to new pedagogical methodologies/technologies is very slow. This was recognized by researchers during the initial stages of introduction of institutional LMS in education [13], when teachers' proneness to adopt technology mediated education was a hot topic. This means that, despite the advances in research, priorities should also rely on the academic and day-to-day practices, thus it is not our intent to contribute to the persistent gap between researchers and practitioners. Our main goal, is to capacitate and actually facilitate the adjustment of teachers to new tendencies. In our perspective, this can only be accomplished by capacitating the well-known environments with new features, reducing the notion of risk that teachers often associate to pedagogical innovation.

8 Conclusions and Future Work

In this chapter the concept of Social Student Relationship Management was presented as the ground foundation for the development of social and learning interactions on learning communities. Research conducted on the teacher/student and student/student interactions on Facebook groups has revealed a high potential for the development of several types of learning communities: teacher centered; mostly instrumental and aimed at administrating the traditional and virtual classroom; and, or essentially, focused on social informal interactions that reveal high potential for personal integration and knowledge exchange. In this chapter, we have presented one case study where it is possible to detect a unique balance of interactions inside a community.

These results and the needs assessment, that was performed during early dissemination of the methodology, led us to create a system that bridges Moodle with Facebook groups. The proposed architecture is based on the model-view-controller which can be applied to most social networks with minimal effort. The system's user interface was also described with several examples taken from its real usage.

The tangible output of this research consists of an asset to capacitate Moodle, extend its features and foster its interoperability with emerging technologies, thus research main focus relies on the development and monitoring of learning communities in social media networks.

Current technical development of the system includes both the optimization of the Moodle blocks presented in this paper and the addition of features presented in section six, namely the vizualization of the types of interactions occurring on the network. We believe that vizualization of the construction, structure, dimension and evolution of the network is of high relevance for teachers and for students. Time span visualization as well as network current status may allow teachers to identify risks and opportunities in community development, such as marginalized or low performance students, but also high performing students requiring additional challenging tasks, both aimed at preventing frustration and/or dropout. For students, the vizualization of their position in the network, as well as rankings-based analytics could serve self-assessment and performance benchmarking tools. The effects of such tools on motivation to learn and improve student performance or to foster dropout are, however, not clear at the moment and lack extensive research, which we believe will be possible to conduct in a near future.

Social network analytics is, in fact, a current hot topic which we aim to address on the teacher and student perspective, aiming at providing a validated tool for formal and informal learning management and assessment.

Acknowledgements. This work is supported by the ERDF – European Regional Development Fund through the COMPETE Programme (operational programme for competitiveness) and by National Funds through the FCT (Portuguese Foundation for Science and Technology) within project "Reminds/UTAP-ICDT/EEI-CTP/0022/2014".

References

1. Reuben, R.: The use of social media in higher education for marketing and communications: a guide for professionals in higher education. EduGuru (2008)
2. Parsons, T.: The school class as a social system. In: Ballantine, J., Spade, J. (eds.) Schools and Society: A Sociological Approach to Education, pp. 35–40. SAGE Publications, Thousand Oaks (2014)
3. Dorin, B., Razvan, B., Bogdan, P.: The role of the web technologies in connection to the communication's streamlining and diversification between the actors of a learning system. In: Monica, P., Bogdan, P. (eds.) Social Media in Higher Education: Teaching in Web 20, pp. 216–236. IGI Global, Hershey (2013)
4. Palloff, R.M., Pratt, K.: Online learning communities in perspective. In: Luppicini, R. (ed.) Online Learning Communities, pp. 3–15. Information Age Publishing, Charlotte (2007)
5. Sawyer, R.K.: The Cambridge Handbook of the Learning Sciences. Cambridge University Press, Cambridge (2005)
6. Oliveira, L.: Social student relationship management in higher education: extending educational and organisational communication into social Media. In: 9th Annual International Technology, Education and Development Conference. IATED, Madrid (2015)
7. Bryant, V.C., et al.: School as haven: transforming school environments into welcoming learning communities. Child Youth Serv. Rev. **35**(5), 848–855 (2013)
8. Wang, Q., et al.: Using the Facebook group as a learning management system: An exploratory study. Br. J. Edu. Technol. **43**(3), 428–438 (2012)
9. Deng, L., Tavares, N.J.: From Moodle to Facebook: exploring students' motivation and experiences in online communities. Comput. Educ. **68**, 167–176 (2013)
10. Cormier, D.: When Is the Best Time to Post on Facebook? (2013). http://www.socialmediatoday.com/content/when-best-time-post-facebook
11. Hansen, D.L., et al.: Do you know the way to SNA? A process model for analyzing and visualizing social media network data. In: 2012 International Conference on Social Informatics (Social Informatics). IEEE (2012)
12. Silva, A., Figueira, Á.: Depicting online interactions in learning communities. In: 2012 IEEE Global Engineering Education Conference (EDUCON). IEEE (2012)
13. Rogers, E.M.: Diffusion of Innovations. Simon and Schuster, New York (2010)

A Model Driven Approach to Business Process-Based Learning

Venkatapathy Subramanian[1,2](✉) and Antonia Bertolino[2]

[1] GSSI, L'aquila, Italy
venkatapathy.s@gssi.infn.it
[2] CNR-ISTI, Pisa, Italy
antonia.bertolino@isti.cnr.it

Abstract. In modern information society, workers need to continuously update and improve their knowledge and competences, and new means for supporting effective learning in the workplace are sought. In this work, we describe a process-based approach to e-learning centered around the well-established Business Process Management discipline. In short, we propose that business process models are used to represent the organizational knowledge and the learning contents. We adapt such models to specific learning needs, by augmenting the business process with a learning path specification that outlines learners objectives, activities and expected outcomes. The key idea then is that a learning session corresponds to simulation and monitoring of a route on a defined learning path. To develop such a process-based e-learning platform we leverage Model Driven Engineering technology allowing for efficient model transformation and platform development. We illustrate the approach on a realistic case study.

Keywords: Business Process Management · Learning path · Workflow learning · Workplace learning · Model-Driven Engineering · Model transformation

1 Introduction

In the modern knowledge society, advanced education plays a key role. At all ages and in varying contexts we are called to master and process a great amount of information and capacities, some very specialized, which are continuously communicated thanks to pervasive Information and Communication Technologies (ICT). As a matter of fact, learning is no longer confined to formal courses in school or University, but happens more and more as a continuous and lifelong process.

Indeed, advanced countries see investing in people education and qualification as a necessary condition to overcome the economic crisis and support innovation and future recovery. One significant part of adult education needs to take place at work, where people must continuously develop new skills and competences to overcome evolution of processes and technology. A culture of collaborative

G. Costagliola et al. (Eds.): CSEDU 2016, CCIS 739, pp. 317–335, 2017.
DOI: 10.1007/978-3-319-63184-4_17

workplace learning must be shared between employers and workers from different offices and organizations under a win-win strategy.

Hence, the need arises for putting in place means to support workplace learning, while successful individual learning becomes an important parameter for the successful functioning of an organization. In recent years, many training and e-learning methods and frameworks are developed to help the employees of an organization to learn about the business activities they are involved in. However the training and e-learning sessions may be not as successful as aimed because:

- often the training session is out of working time, implying that workers need to devote extra-work time that is demanding and exhausting
- the learning curve for the training session itself is steep and apart from their business activities and hence workers are hesitant to take up the task
- setting up a learning environment similar to the working environment is very difficult for the company and usually costly and so workplace training becomes difficult for the company to setup

Organizations look for alternative approaches to train the employees that can address the above issues. The solution should be workflow learning in which employees can take lessons while they are at work. Cross, characterised workflow learning as learning that *"employs smart" software to guide, inform, and assist workers to do their jobs better.* [10] Workplaces are now considered as learning environments that focus on the *"interaction between the affordances and constraints of the social setting, on the one hand, and the agency and biography of the individual participant, on the other"*. [5] In that case, workflow learning can be used as workplace learning as its main goal is to optimize the business process.

However, to develop e-learning systems based on workflow learning, we need to look beyond current e-learning practices that focus only on content creation, towards those that focus on the business process or the workflow. Conventional e-learning systems mainly focus on content-based pedagogy and only provide ways for knowledge transfer. They do not put emphasis on the process of learning, whereas, workflow learning is strongly related to the business process of the organization.

The discipline of Business Process Management can provide missing links to design such process-based learning systems [10]. Business Process Management (BPM) is a management science that helps in improving corporate performance by managing and optimizing a company's business process. [27] Main activities of BPM include: process modeling, implementation, execution and analysis. One important feature of BPM is its process-oriented model-driven approach to design and implement the business processes.

We propose BPM as a means to develop workplace learning and training within an organization. BPM has matured for the last couple of decades and has penetrated many large scale organizations in their design of business process as well as the related software applications needed to execute the processes. Thus many facilities needed for using a BPMS to design a learning systems are already in place such as collaborative execution between different users, web-service integration, and similar. However BPM is not originally conceived for learning. In this work, we focus on extending BPM so that it can be used for workplace learning. In particular, we introduce a learning path specification that can be embedded into a BPM systems. We call it as Business Process Management-based Learning System (BPMLS).

A preliminary version of this work appeared as [23], in which we first introduced a specification of learning path over the standard BPMN specification. Here we provide an extended description of our research goals and results, and in particular we use a model-driven approach [4] to design the learning path specification and to extend BPMS for the design of the learning system. BPM also employs Model-Driven Engineering principles and so it is easier to use them for BPMLS too. We use Eclipse Modeling Framework (EMF) for building modeling tools for learning path specification and transform them into business process models so that BPMS can be extended for execution of process models with learning parameters. After some background notions in Sect. 2, in Sect. 3 we introduce our learning path mapped on BPM models and describe the BPMLS framework that can be used for declaring and assessing learning activities of workplace learners. In Sect. 4 we explain the transformation technique used within our framework. In Sect. 5 we evaluate the prototype of our framework on a realistic example. Related work and Conclusions sections complete the paper.

2 Background

This section provides an overview of background concepts and technologies that are at basis of our work. In particular, our approach uses and combines concepts and definitions related to:

- Business Process Management discipline;
- Business Activity Monitoring system;
- Model-driven Engineering approach;
- Workplace Learning approach;
- Learning Path specification.

In [1], van der Aalst and coauthors define **Business Process Management** (BPM) as a discipline *supporting business processes using methods, techniques, and software to design, enact, control, and analyze operational processes involving humans, organizations, applications, documents and other sources of information.*

BPM spans over a complex life-cycle including stages of design, configuration, enactment, and diagnosis [1]. A **Business Process Management System** (BPMS) is a suite of software tools that leverage BPM concepts and support the BPM life-cycle.

BPMS frameworks provide tools for: *i.* Process modeling, *ii.* Process Execution, and *iii.* Business Activity Monitoring [1], among others. Using a BPMS, process models are automated as workflow models that can be executed by a process engine [25], where a workflow may contain a sequence of business activities, the work of a person, group, or any business applications.

In particular, **Business Process Management Notation** 2.0 [6] (in the following referred to simply as BPMN) is a widely used standardized graphical notation for modeling executable business processes in a workflow.

Business Activity Monitoring (BAM) software can provide real-time access to critical business performance indicators for business activities executed by BPMS. BAM collects data of interest during the run-time business process execution. By using Complex Event Processing (CEP) techniques [7] BAM can later derive higher level business events from the composition of observed simple events. The collected data can be correlated to Key Performance Indicators (KPIs) and Goals defined for the process models [8,17].

Due to the complexity involved in building software systems, there is a paradigm shift in software development methodologies used to develop such systems. One such methodology that focuses on using of models to develop software is Model-Driven Engineering (MDE). A model is an abstract representation of essential functionality that needs to be implemented. The core of MDE is use of models as primary artifacts in software development, and use of (automated) model transformation techniques to transform one model to another [4]. Models can be helpful for a developer because they allow them to abstract away from a specific development technology in early stages. Later, the models can be transformed to a specific execution language by applying model-to-code transformation. This transformation is done using metamodels that are defined as models of models [20]. Transformation from model-to-code will be done using tools, which will generate code from the design models that the developer use to refine further.

MDE will be the core software-development principle of this work. We will use a customized modeling language called learning path specification to design and implement process-centric e-learning platform using BPMS. Eclipse Modeling Framework (EMF) is the modeling framework that will be used for MDA-based design along with its e-core model for model specification. For model transformation between learning and business process model, we will use ATLAS Transformation Language. See more details in Sect. 4.

Within the learning context, a **learning path** is a sequence of activities and learning objectives customized to the needs and competencies of a learner [14]. It can be described as the route, chosen by a learner through a range of learning activities, which allows them to build knowledge progressively [9]. It should contain a *learnflow*, which gives orchestration details for learning activities, roles and other learning resources [19], as well as learning objectives or outcomes.

Many platform-independent Educational Modeling Languages have been proposed to describe a learning path. IMS Global Consortium released the IMS-Learning Design (LD) specification that allows for defining the learning path as a Unit of Learning (UOL) [13]. In [14], Janssen and coauthors introduce a generic learning path model that is mapped to IMS-LD.

The aim of this paper is to introduce a model-driven approach to workplace learning that integrates the learning path specification into BPMS. Our framework draws together the key concepts and definitions from BPM discipline, MDE technology as well as workplace Learning approaches explained above.

3 Framework and Architecture

BPM provides a process-centric approach to the development of software framework for business. Although in principle the standard BPMN notation could be used to design the business processes a user wants to learn, it cannot directly be used for designing suitable learning models.

Jassen and coauthors [14] list the general requirements of a learning path specification. It must:

1. enable the description of actions that lead to certain learning outcomes
2. describe these actions based on the competency of the learner
3. facilitate identification of different learning paths leading to the learning outcomes

The above requirements are not addressed expressly in BPMN since it was originally conceived for different purposes. When it comes to defining learning path for business process models, specification of learnflow and learning objectives differ due to the following reasons:

- Learning flow for workplace learning should align to the business activities of an organization. What an employee learns should conform to the business process sequence rules established by the organization.
- Learning objectives of workplace learning should be correlated to Key Performance Indicators (KPIs) of business activities that are executed during the learning process.
- Learning path should be able to capture different business scenarios of the same business process. An employee's business activity may change based on the inputs he receives during the business process execution

We developed a learning path specification extending BPMN [23] which can be used to design learning objects on top of business process models. Our learning path specification acts as a scaffolding knowledge framework on top business process models for defining learning goals and requirements. The key aspects and requirements mentioned previously are also captured in our learning path specification. Our specification maps KPIs of business processes to objectives of the learning path. We extended the BPMN metamodel with the introduction of classes and attributes related to a learning path. Figure 1 represents the meta-model of our learning path specification. In the figure, classes with gray background are related to the BPMN model. Classes with the yellow background (those that we introduce) are related to the learning path specification. Since we extended the BPMN model, our learning path specification can be integrated to

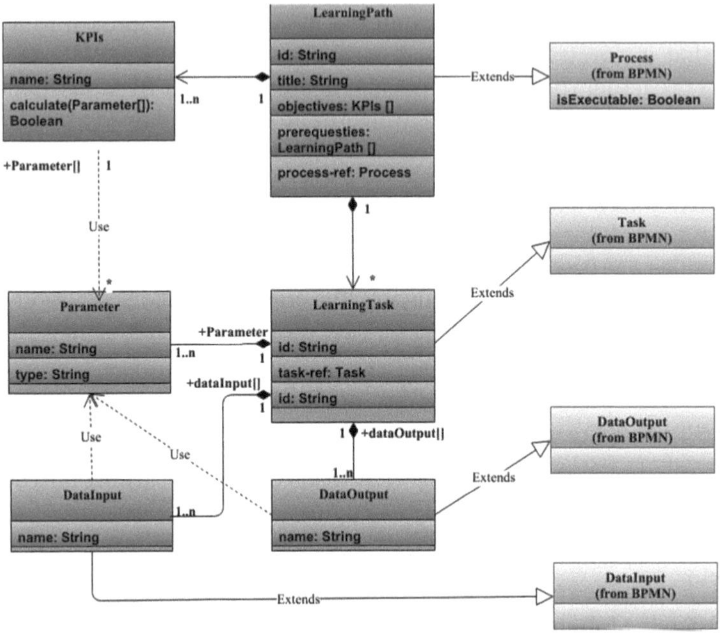

Fig. 1. Learning Path Specification for Business Process Model.

BPMS for workplace learning. More details of our specification can be found in our previous work [23].

We also proposed an architectural framework called Business Process Management Learning System (BPMLS) that uses our learning models for modeling and execution. The framework is conceived such that an employee who needs to learn about a business process can log into the system and will find an environment mimicking the real business process for learning purposes. It will also help developers to build process-based models with learning goals and requirements for individual learners, based on the requirement of the employees. They can design learning models using our proposed learning path specification. The framework will provide methods to define learning path as well as to execute and monitor the learning progress during a learning session.

The overall framework of our BPMLS is given in Fig. 3. The architecture covers three phases of a BPM life-cycle, namely Modeling, Execution and Monitoring. During the modeling phase, learning paths are defined for a given process model based on our specification. Every learning object will contain the learning path model as well as its corresponding business process model. Learning models created can be executed in Process execution engine of BPMLS. Process execution consists of a learning path initiator to choose the best path for a user based on his competencies and requirements, and process execution engine. During the process execution, the actual business scenarios are mimicked through simulated business services component. Monitoring phase involves keeping track of the various learning activities happening within BPMLS, and providing feedback and learning suggestions to the user. Monitoring uses BAM techniques to monitor the learning path execution and provides real-time results of the learning progress.

3.1 Prototype

We developed a prototype based on our proposed BPMLS architecture [23,24]. The prototype included a custom learning path model based on our specification, Apache Activiti as process execution engine [22] and Drools Fusion based CEP engine for monitoring [11]. A overview of the relation between objects of different components such as learning path model, BPMN model, events and Drools Fusion CEP rules is provided in Fig. 2. A Business Process Model defined using BPMN.2.0 specification can have one or more Learning Paths. Each instance of Learning Path model represents one learning session, and executes a process instance in BPMLS, with KPIs and monitoring parameters defined by the Learning Path model. Learning Paths fulfill learning objectives which are represented as KPIs. KPIs are used to evaluate key business metrics that are crucial during the execution of the process instance. Mapping KPIs to Learning objectives ensures that learning sessions caters to the business goals of the organization. KPIs are callable functions, which are included in CEP rules for monitoring purposes. Events, used in CEP rules, are created for all the learning process and tasks, and are used to track learning progress.

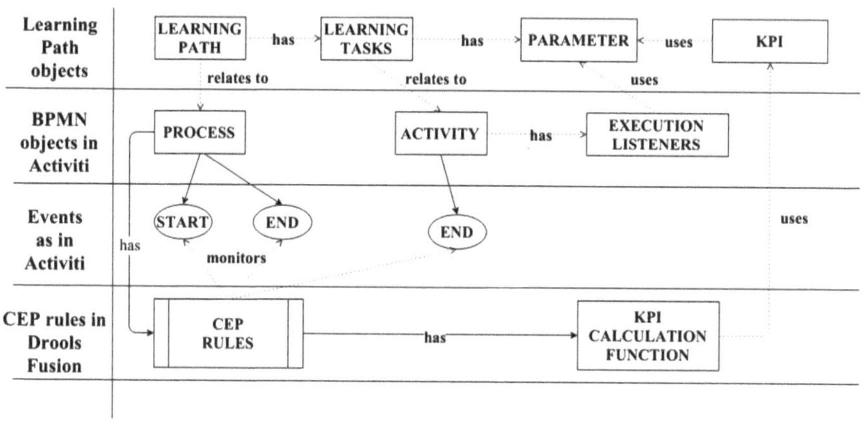

Fig. 2. Overview of relation between objects of different components.

3.2 Model Transformation

The proposed specification is an extension of BPMS with learning specifications. Since several BPMS platform already exist, we decided to reuse an existing BPMN execution platforms to design BPMLS. We followed a MDE approach for developing our BPMLS.

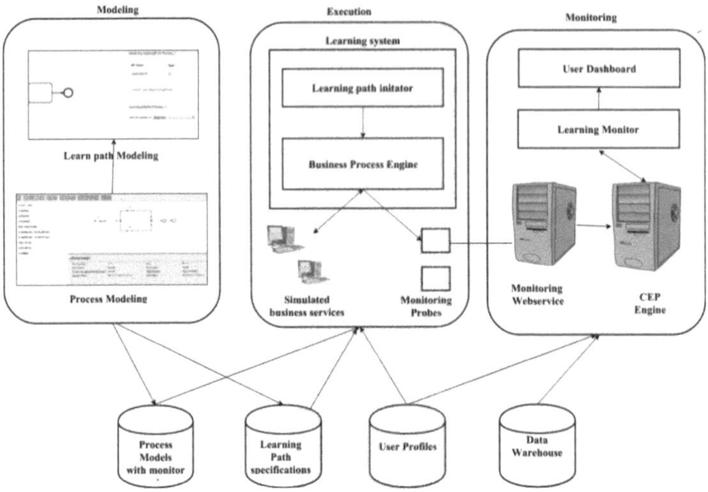

Fig. 3. Framework of BPMS based learning and monitoring system.

One of the main tasks within the development of BPMLS using MDA is model transformation. Within our context, model transformation is used to derive BPMN models with appropriate learning parameters based on the learning path provided for the same. The goal of our model transformation technique is to accept both the learning path model as well as its referenced business process model and provide outputs that can be executed within BPMS compliant process engine. The output will be again a business process model (model-to-model transformation) that is customized for a given learning objective.

An overview of the model transformation is represented in Fig. 4. In the next section we describe in detail the ATL Model Transformation technique and the algorithm used within BPMLS.

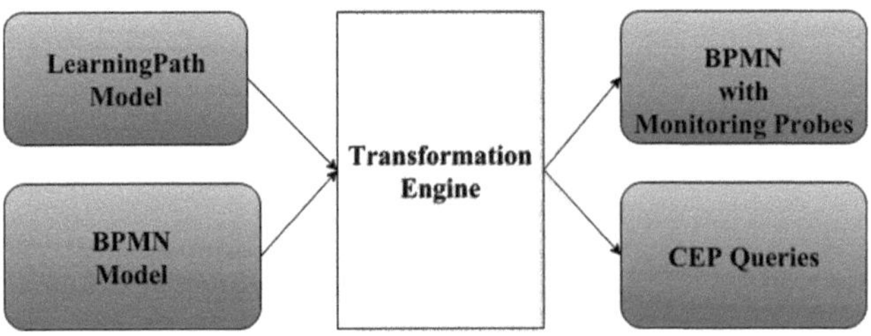

Fig. 4. Overview of model transformation.

4 ATL Transformation

We provide here technical details about the model transformation. Readers that are not interested to technology behind the framework can skip this section.

(ATLAS Transformation Language) is a transformation language developed as a part of the AMMA (ATLAS Model Management Architecture) platform [3]. It is build on top of Eclipse Modeling Framework (EMF), which is a modeling framework based on structure data. ATL is a hybrid transformation language that contains a mixture of declarative and imperative constructs. Model transformation in MDE conforms to a model transformation pattern, represented in Fig. 5 [3].

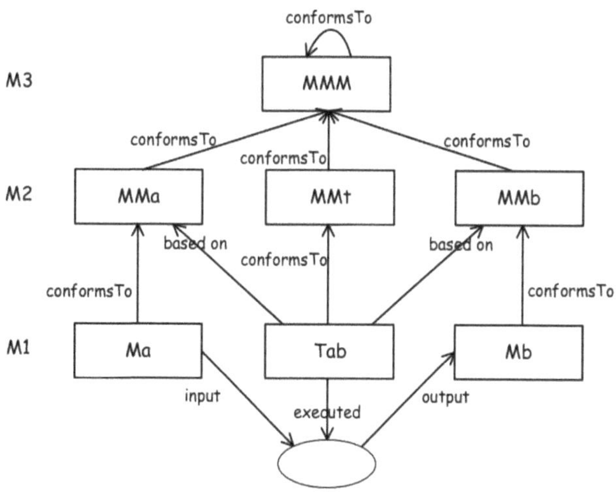

Fig. 5. Overview of model transformation.

The transformation happens during the execution of the TAB program. With reference to Fig. 5, the output is Mb from Ma. All three models Tab, Ma, Mb conform to their respective metamodels- MMt, MMa, MMb. And all metamodels conform to MMM, the metametamodel. ATL in the context of the above transformation patten is shown in Fig. 6. It is same as the given transformation pattern, with the relations program mma2mmb.atl to Tab, ATL to MMt and MMM to MOF.

Bezivin et al. provide seven classifications of transformation and the proposed transformation is a hybrid mixture Level 2 and Level 6. The general representation of the transformation is given as,

Mb2MbT: Ma,Mb -> Mc; MMa = MMc; MM where,

Ma is BPMN metamodel, *Mb* is the proposed learning path specification and *Mc* is the target BPMN model. The metamodels *MMc* and *MMa* are strictly

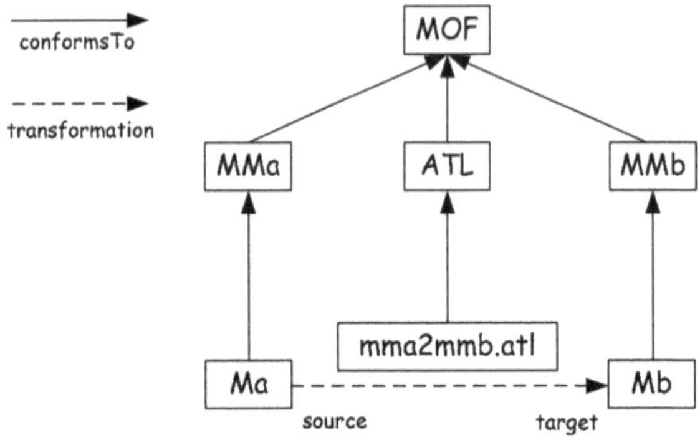

Fig. 6. Overview of model transformation.

identical and hence the transformation relationship between *Ma* and *Mc* is endogenous. In case of model *MMc* and *MMb* it can be considered as unconstrained exogenous transformation.

The algorithm for learning path to business process model is given in Listing below.

Algorithm 1. Learning path model to Business process Model transformation

---

```
Data: In1:Instance of Learning Path; In2: Business Process Model.
Result: OT1
initialization:
Copy In2 -> Ot1;
forall the LearningTask in IN1 do
    if In1.LearningTask.hasDataInput then
        Create OT1.UserTask.DataInput;
        Copy IN1.LearningTask.DataInput -> OT1.UserTask.DataInput;
    end
    if In1.LearningTask.hasDataOnput then
        Create OT1.UserTask.DataOutput;
        Create IN1.LearningTask.DataOutput -> OT1.UserTask.DataOutput;
    end
    if IN1.LearningTask.hasParameters() then
        Create OT1.UserTask.extensibleElement;
        forall the IN1.Parameters do
            Create OT1.Parameter;
            Copy IN1.Parameters -> OT1.Parameter;
        end
    end
end
```

During the initialization of the algorithm, an exact copy of the input BPMN model IN2, is created as the output. Then algorithm copies the learning tasks and its corresponding learning parameters of the input IN1 into the BPMN model ON1. The result is a business model customized with learning parameters that can be used for executing and monitoring.

In the standard BPMN.2.0, only generic classes of monitoring parameters have been defined and it is up to BPMS adopters to provide concrete implementation of a working monitoring framework. Also, the specification introduces an extensibility mechanism that allows extending standard BPMN elements with additional attributes. [6] This is to allow the modeling tools specify non-standard elements to satisfy a specific need. This is important for us because, the above algorithm is based on the extensible attributes provided in Apache Activiti. The learning path specification has provision to provide specific input and expected output to a learning task, and it requires the extensible attributes adopted by implementers of BPMN model such as Apache Activiti.

The transformation can be separated in two parts: one is transformation from learning path model to business process model. This is done using the algorithm provided in Listing 1. The transformation is simple and can be described as in the following pseudo-code:

LearningTask -> UserTask
Parameter -> Activiti:FormProperty
DataInput -> DataInputAssociation
DataOutput -> DataOutputAssociation

The second part of the transformation involves definition of JavaObjects required in Activiti mapping to the attributes above. Apache Activiti is written Java and might require Java classes depending on the requirement. For example, to pass the parameters value to CEP engine during execution, Apache Activiti provides with mechanism to execute external Java Code, called execution listeners. The following table lists the Java classes required for each of the parameter above and their relation to BPMN specification.

Learning path	BPMN	Java code
LearningTask	UserTask extensionElements	none
Parameter	Activiti:FormProperty activiti:executionListener	Class extending EventListener
KPI	Activiti:executionListener	Class extending EventListener and CEP Queries
DataInput Dataoutput	dataInputAssociation dataOutputAssociation	Java Variable or Complex Java Object

5 Evaluation

In this section we will see a motivational example, to understand the learning path specification that was defined earlier. We also evaluate the transformation algorithm defined earlier as well as our BPMLS framework.

The seventh European Union Framework Program (FP7) provided funding opportunities for many organizations within Europe to support Research and Development. Organizations working within FP7 programs should understand the complexity involved during the successful execution of their projects. Understanding the different processes involved is crucial for the success of the project. For example, participants in an EU financed project are obliged to report periodic budgeting activities for the tasks performed within the project. This process is quite complex but yet extremely important for the employees of the organization to understand. Workplace learning for such scenarios is the need of the hour for such organizations. We will consider below a motivational example that will highlight the usefulness of our learning path specification workplace learning for the above scenario. Figure 7 represents a simplified BPMN model for the periodic budgeting report of an organization that is involved in the FP7 project.

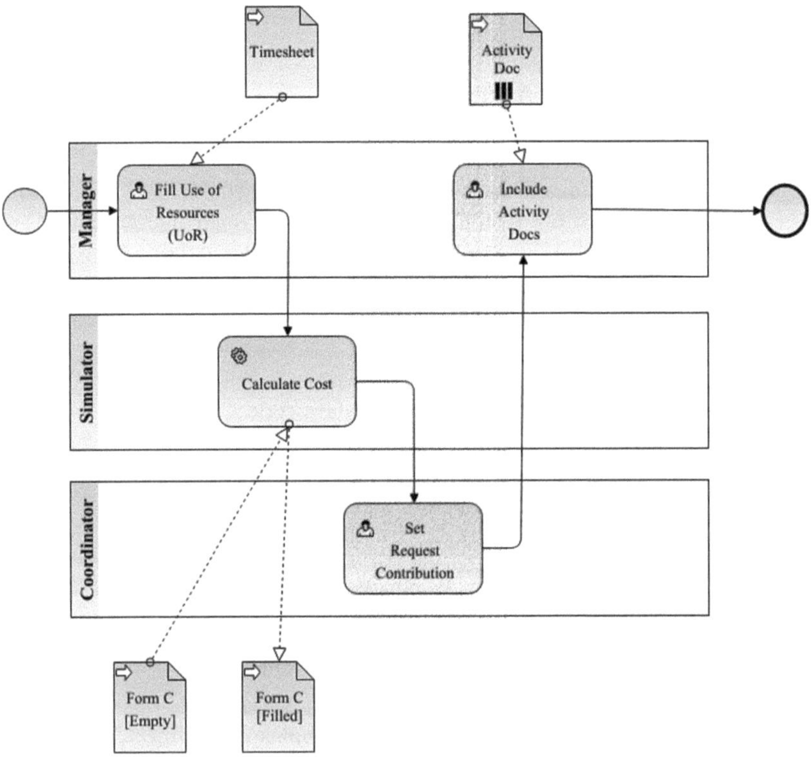

Fig. 7. Example process-periodic budgeting report.

It is a collaborative process between a project manager and a project coordinator. In the first task 'Fill Use of Resources (UoR)', the project manager has to fill a predefined timesheet form to reflect the different resources used for the project during a particular period. Next task is an automated service task (typically a web-service call), that mimic the process to calculate project costs based on the timesheet filled earlier. At the end of the 'Calculate Cost' task, a filled 'Form C' document will be provided to Project Coordinator. The coordinator will set a contribution in the next task called 'Set Request Contribution' based on the details available in Form C. In the final step, the manager has to attach a list project activity documents relevant to the project. The task is called 'Include Activity Docs' in the business process model. With the submission, the process will be completed.

Though it is a simplified version of EU budget reporting, the above example is still complex enough to be reproduced in a standard Learning Management System (LMS). We will see how our BPMLS framework makes it easier for creating a learning environment for such scenarios.

5.1 Learning Path for Periodic Budget Reporting

Our first goal is to provide a learning path specification for the above example. Figure 9 provides the instance model of the Learning Path specification. The instance captures one learning scenario for the example. The learning path is created for the budgeting scenario of 'Project X'. The details of the sample project scenario is provided as **DataInput** to the learning task 'Fill Use of Resource'. Note that in the representational figure just the name of the project is provided. However additional details can be provided as an array of **DataInput** object (not provided in the figure for the sake of brevity). The learning task also contains a **Parameter** object called 'Total Time' that will be used within **KPI**. 'Set Request Contribution' is another learning task of the learning path specification. It also contains

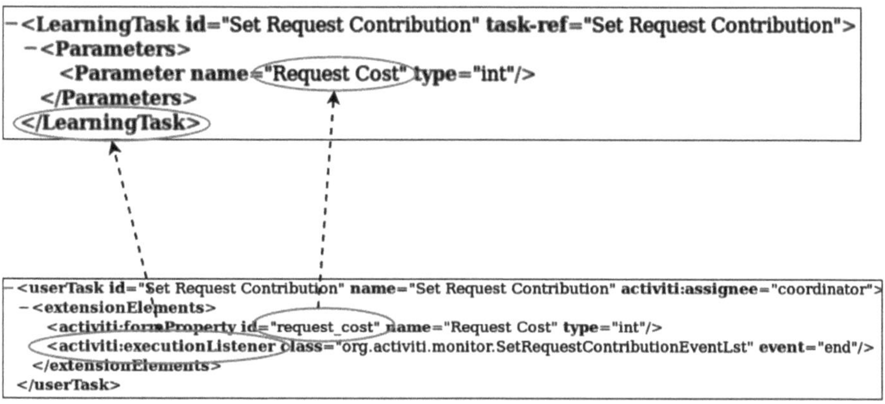

Fig. 8. Transformation for a learning task.

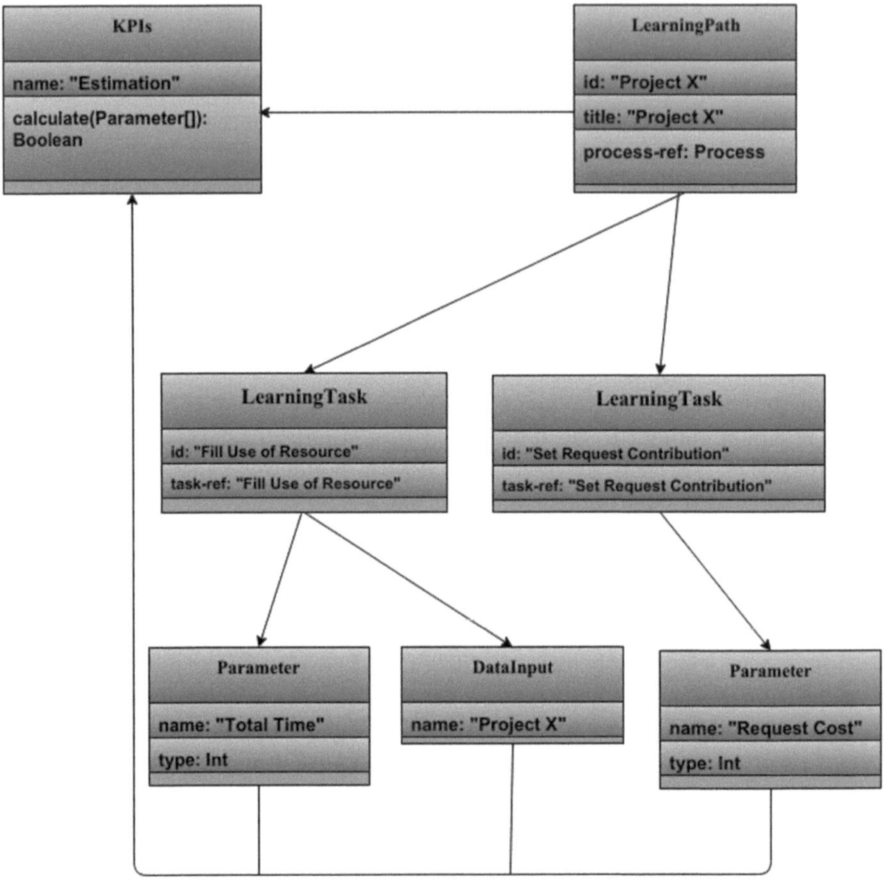

Fig. 9. Learning path specification-periodic budgeting report.

a **Parameter** object called 'Request Cost' to capture the cost set by the project coordinator.

Both the **Parameter** objects are used within the calculate function of **KPI** class which is defined as: $TotalTime < 100\ \ \&\&\ RequestCost < 10000$.

The KPI function verifies if the collaborators of the ' Project X' is able to fill the forms accurately. In our specification, KPIs are used to monitor if the 'Total Time' entered by the project manager is less than 100 (hours) and the 'Request Cost' entered by the project cost is less than 10000 (Euros). And this KPI is set as learning objective of our learning path specification. This way our learning path specification can ensure that the learning scenario caters to the business goals of the organization.

5.2 Designing the Learning Path and Its Transformation to BPMN Model

The learning path specification defined earlier is designed using the EMF to get the learning path instance in ecore model. This provided to the ATL transformation algorithm defined in Sect. 4. The output is an BPMN model with customized parameters for learning purpose. An example instance of transformation is given in Fig. 8. Notice that the *Parameter* of the *Learning-Task* is converted into *extensionElement* of the BPMN model. Event Listeners are created for the learning task in the figure. This is to monitor when the user finishes the execution of a learning task or a given learning path.

Challenges in Transformation. The transformation described here is a unidirectional transformation to transform a learning model into a business process model. We are currently not focusing on bidirectional transformation which will be completed in the future work. However this unidirectional transformation is not without challenges. One major challenge during the transformation is creation of Activiti listeners for each of the User task involved in learning, and creating the skeleton in the process execution archive. The creation of Java classes is done manually for now, and need to be automated for an effective transformation technique.

5.3 Prototype Evaluation

A prototype was developed to evaluate the learning path model transformation and assessment techniques. Learning path specification are created as mentioned above. Model transformation is performed in a semi-automated way, where the BPMN models are generated automatically and later manually updated with the additional learning tasks parameters. We already have developed a semi-automated model transformation technique in our work, and currently we are in the process of automating the transformation technique.

For the Process Execution Engine, as mentioned we used Apache Activiti, an open-source Java-Based BPM Platform [22]. For learning path monitoring we used Drools Fusion [11] based CEP engine. Apache Activiti Explorer was used to design, and execute the process models. Learning path model and its corresponding business process models, CEP rules were created separately. The explorer interface was modified to detect and display the learning progress to the users. Figure 10 provides a screenshot in which the 'Fill Use of Resources' task is executed. Figure 11 provides a screenshot of a simplified web page where the progress of the learner is registered.

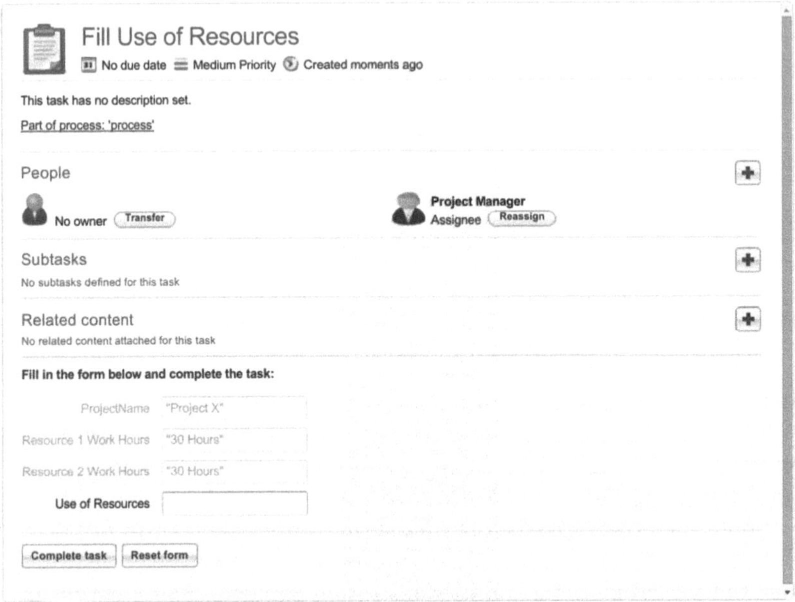

Fig. 10. Learning path specification-periodic budgeting report.

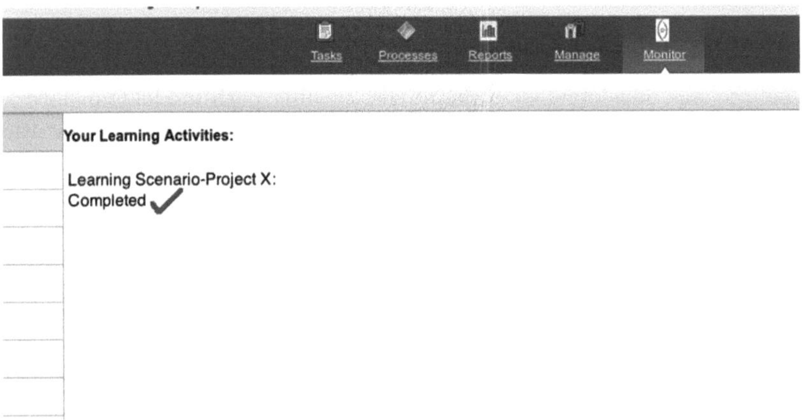

Fig. 11. Monitoring-periodic budgeting report.

6 Related Work

Using BPM concepts for the management of collaborative learning processes have long been considered by the research community. Marino and coauthors [19] proposed a method to transform learning design models defined using the IMS-LD specification to business process execution model called XML Process Definition Language. The goal was to use IMS-LD for defining a learning design and use business process engine as a delivery platform for the learning designs. In [16], Karampiperis and coauthors examine using of BPMN as a common representation notation for learning flows modeled using Business Process Execution Language (BPEL) and present an algorithm for transforming BPEL Workflows to IMS-LD learning flows.

Vantroys and Peter [26] presented Cooperative Open Workflow (COW), a flexible workflow engine that can be used to transform IMS-LD into XPDL designs to enact the learning models in the platform. Another e-learning platform called Flex-el [18], is also been built on top of workflow technology. It provides a unique environment for teachers to design and develop process-centric courses and to monitor student progress. Project TRAILER, BPMN is used as a model to define a methodology and developing tools to learning as well as the management of competences and skills acquired through informal learning experiences, both from the perspective of the user and the institution or company [12,21].

Above discussed methodologies and platforms focus on using BPM techniques and technologies for designing learning specifications for academic scenarios and do not focus on workplace learning.

Regarding learning path specification, Janssen and coauthors proposed learning path information model that can represent a formal learning path model. [15] However, the specification is generic and does not address the requirements of workplace learning based on BPM. We already raised the issues in Sect. 6.

As far as we know none of the existing work focus on using BAM for workplace learning monitoring. In their work, Adesina et al. focus on visually tracking the learning progresses of a cohort of students in a Virtual Learning Process Environment (VLPE) based on the Business Process Management (BPM) conceptual framework. [2] Their work focus on learning specifications for academic scenarios and do not focus on workplace learning. Tracking the learning progress also do not leverage upon BAM systems.

Our work defines a precise specification that can be used for defining learning path for business process models, as well as transformation techniques for using standard business activity monitoring techniques to monitor learning progress of an employee.

7 Conclusions

Workplace learning is an actual need for employees who are required to constantly improve their knowledge on the business process they are involved in. Workflow learning can help in building intelligent software to guide, inform, and assist workers to do their jobs better. Workflow learning is indeed the perfect fit for the employees as it is done during the work and the goal of it is to improve the business process. The discipline of Business Process Management can help in designing process-based learning systems for workplace learning. Our work aims at exploiting this potential of BPM to support effective and realistic workplace learning activities. This work details and extends our previous work [23], that introduced a specification of learning path extending the standard BPMN specification. In this extended work along with the Learning Path specification and BPMLS, we also focus on a model-driven approach to the development of the proposed framework. The model-driven approach focuses on defining a transformation relationship between the learning path specification and its corresponding business process models. This gives us the advantage of building learning system that are compliant to the existing model-driven BPMS systems.

To the best of our knowledge there is no existing proposal for adapting BPMS to learning needs. Our work stays within the context of the European Learn PAd project, that aims at exploiting enriched BPMN models for deriving both recommender systems and simulation sessions used expressly for learning the modeled sequence of tasks. We are currently refining platform implementation, and testing it on several scenarios defined within the Learn PAd project.

Acknowledgements. This research has been partially supported from the European Union's Seventh Framework Programme [FP7/2007–2013] under Grant Agreement N. 619583 (Project Learn PAd - Model Based Social Learning for Public Administrations).

References

1. Aalst, W.M.P., Hofstede, A.H.M., Weske, M.: Business process management: a survey. In: Aalst, W.M.P., Weske, M. (eds.) BPM 2003. LNCS, vol. 2678, pp. 1–12. Springer, Heidelberg (2003). doi:10.1007/3-540-44895-0_1
2. Adesina, A., Molloy, D.: Virtual learning process environment: cohort analytics for learning and learning processes. In: World Academy of Science, Engineering and Technology 65 (2012)
3. Allilaire, F., Bézivin, J., Jouault, F., Kurtev, I.: Atl-eclipse support for model transformation. In: Proceedings of the Eclipse Technology eXchange workshop (eTX) at the ECOOP 2006 Conference, Nantes, France. vol. 66. Citeseer (2006)
4. Beydeda, S., Book, M., Gruhn, V., et al.: Model-Driven Software Development, vol. 15. Springer, Heidelberg (2005)
5. Billett, S.: Workplace participatory practices: conceptualising workplaces as learning environments. J. Workplace Learn. **16**(6), 312–324 (2004)
6. bpmn.org: Business process modeling notations (2011). http://www.omg.org/spec/BPMN/2.0/. Accessed 7 Nov 2015
7. Buchmann, A., Koldehofe, B.: Complex event processing. it-Information Technology Methoden und innovative Anwendungen der Informatik und Informationstechnik **51**(5), 241–242 (2009)
8. Calabro, A., Lonetti, F., Marchetti, E.: Monitoring of business process execution based on performance indicators. In: 2015 41st Euromicro Conference on Software Engineering and Advanced Applications (SEAA), pp. 255–258. IEEE (2015)
9. Clement, J.: Model based learning as a key research area for science education. Int. J. Sci. Educ. **22**(9), 1041–1053 (2000)
10. Cross, J.: Workflow learning. http://elearnmag.acm.org/featured.cfm?aid=1013188. Accessed 26 July 2016
11. Drools Fusion 6.0.3: Drools Fusion: Complex Event Processor (2015). http://www.jboss.org/drools/drools-fusion.html Accessed 27 Nov 2015

12. García-Peñalvo, F.J., González, M.Á.C., Zangrando, V., Holgado, A.G., Seoane, A.M., Forment, M.A., Galanis, N., Brouns, F., Vogten, H., Griffiths, D., et al.: Trailer project (tagging, recognition, acknowledgment of informal learning experiences) a methodology to make learners' informal learning activities visible to the institutions. J. UCS **19**(11), 1661–1683 (2013)
13. IMS-Global: Ims- learnind design (2003). http://www.imsglobal.org/learningdesign/index.html. Accessed 7 Nov 2015
14. Janssen, J., Berlanga, A., Vogten, H., Koper, R.: Towards a learning path specification. Int. J. Continuing Eng. Educ. Life Long Learn. **18**(1), 77–97 (2008)
15. Janssen, J., Hermans, H., Berlanga, A.J., Koper, R.: Learning path information model (2008). Accessed 9 Nov 2008
16. Karampiperis, P., Sampson, D.: Towards a common graphical language for learning flows: transforming BPEL to IMS learning design level a representations. In: Seventh IEEE International Conference on Advanced Learning Technologies, ICALT 2007, pp. 798–800. IEEE (2007)
17. Koetter, F., Kochanowski, M.: Goal-oriented model-driven business process monitoring using ProGoalML. In: Abramowicz, W., Kriksciuniene, D., Sakalauskas, V. (eds.) BIS 2012. LNBIP, vol. 117, pp. 72–83. Springer, Heidelberg (2012). doi:10.1007/978-3-642-30359-3_7
18. Lin, J., Ho, C., Sadiq, W., Orlowska, M.E.: Using workflow technology to manage flexible e-learning services. J. Educ. Technol. Soc. **5**(4), 116–123 (2002)
19. Mariño, O., Casallas, R., Villalobos, J., Correal, D., Contamines, J.: Bridging the gap between e-learning modeling and delivery through the transformation of learnflows into workflows. In: Pierre, S. (eds.) E-Learning Networked Environments and Architectures, pp. 27–59. Springer, New York (2007)
20. Mellor, S.J., Clark, T., Futagami, T.: Model-driven development: guest editors' introduction. IEEE Softw. **20**(5), 14–18 (2003)
21. Penalvo, F.J.G., Zangrando, V., Holgado, A.G., Gonzalez, M.A.C., Pardo, A.S., Griffiths, D., Forment, M.A., Mykowska, A., Janssen, J., Alves, G.R., et al.: Trailer project overview: tagging, recognition and acknowledgment of informal learning experiences. In: 2012 International Symposium on Computers in Education (SIIE), pp. 1–6. IEEE (2012)
22. Rademakers, T.: Activiti in Action: Executable business processes in BPMN 2.0. Manning Publications Co. (2012)
23. Subramanian, V., Bertolino, A.: Learning path specification forworkplace learning based on business process management. In: Proceedings of the 8th International Conference on Computer Supported Education, pp. 172–180 (2016)
24. Subramanian, V., Bertolino, A.: Monitoring of learning path for business process models. In: Proceedings of the International Workshop on domAin specific Model-based AppRoaches to vErificaTion and validaTiOn, pp. 62–72 (2016)
25. Van Der Aalst, W., Van Hee, K.M.: Workflow Management: Models, Methods, and Systems. MIT press, Cambridge (2004)
26. Vantroys, T., Peter, Y.: COW, a flexible platform for the enactment of learning scenarios. In: Favela, J., Decouchant, D. (eds.) CRIWG 2003. LNCS, vol. 2806, pp. 168–182. Springer, Heidelberg (2003). doi:10.1007/978-3-540-39850-9_15
27. Wikipedia: Business process management – wikipedia, the free encyclopedia (2016). https://en.wikipedia.org/w/index.php?title=Business_process_management&oldid=726367379. Accessed 26 July 2016

Approaches to Detecting and Utilizing Play and Learning Styles in Adaptive Educational Games

Renny S.N. Lindberg[1] and Teemu H. Laine[2](✉)

[1] Department of Computer Science, Vrije Universiteit Brussel, Brussels, Belgium
renny.lindberg@gmail.com

[2] Department of Computer Science, Electrical and Space Engineering, Luleå University of Technology, Skellefteå, Sweden
teemu@ubilife.net

Abstract. Games have emerged as promising tools to make learning more fun. Pedagogical effectiveness of an educational game can increase if its behavior changes according to learners' play and learning styles. Several models for categorizing learning and play styles exist, but not many studies simultaneously detect and utilize both style groups. To alleviate this, as the first contribution, we analyzed and compared existing learning and play style models, and chose the most suitable one from each group. Personality style models were also discussed. We then created a questionnaire based on Honey and Mumford's Learning Style Questionnaire and Bartle's Player Types, and collected data from 127 South Korean elementary school children. The results indicated that specific play styles were clearly more dominant (Killer 18%, Achiever 24%, Explorer 32%, Socializer 41%), whereas dominant learning styles were distributed more evenly (Activist 33%, Reflector 37%, Theorist 20% and Pragmatist 25%). As the second contribution, we presented the foundations of a generic adaptation model for utilizing learning and play styles for designing adaptive educational games.

Keywords: Learning styles · Play styles · Personality types · Educational games · Adaptation · Questionnaire

1 Introduction

Digital games have risen to new heights as general entertainment and have also expanded beyond the field of leisure to more serious venues. For example, games have been utilized as educational tools [10,41,44] and as catalysts for people to do physical exercise [31,36]. Games that have other purpose than pure entertainment are generally referred to as serious games. Within the umbrella term of serious games, game-based learning, in particular, is a heavily trodden research field. There exists significant evidence that utilizing games in education can have positive effects on learning and motivation [3,10,12,20,23,41,44].

G. Costagliola et al. (Eds.): CSEDU 2016, CCIS 739, pp. 336–358, 2017.
DOI: 10.1007/978-3-319-63184-4_18

While researching education technologies and pedagogy in general, it is not uncommon to come across different learning style models and discussions for and against them. Researchers have proposed several models [11] for mapping out various learning styles. Learning style models can be used to understand the differences among heterogeneous learners and thereby optimize a learning environment for each learning style.

There are several game genres – ranging from first-person shooters (FPS) to large-scale country-governing simulations, and from role-playing games (RPG) to sport games – that cater to vastly different play styles. For example, a majority of FPS games expect a combination of aggressiveness and cunning, whereas a typical RPG expects the player to have a strategic mindset. Several models have been proposed to categorize players according to what style of gameplay they prefer [4–6, 29, 40]. Perhaps due to the novelty of gaming research field, there are not many validated play style models that tackle the heterogeneity among players.

Several studies have been conducted that focus on either play styles [33, 43] or learning styles [7, 27]. However, we were unable to find studies that consider both styles for making educational games adaptive. There are three reasons for adapting educational games based on the learner's play and learning styles. Firstly, adaptive educational games could offer learning materials in a way that the learner would be more attuned to receiving and processing. Secondly, offering a suitable play style for the learner would make the game mechanics easier to understand, thus reducing the learning curve. Thirdly, well-aligned play and learning styles, through which learning materials and gameplay are provided, could increase the learner's motivation to continue playing the game and thereby increase the possibility for them to enter the flow state [35].

While we focus on merging play and learning styles, we also discuss some personality style models, as they occasionally appear in gaming and education studies [11, 26].

This work is part of a three-year (2015–2018) research project, which aims at developing a learner-aware adaptation framework for game-based programming education. We have previously published a version of this paper at the CSEDU 2016 conference [30]. In this updated version, we first present an extended review of models for learning and play styles. As a new contribution, personality style models are also discussed. Secondly, based on the review, we select one learning style model and one play style model for developing a questionnaire that detects children's play and learning styles. Thirdly, we present an analysis of data that were collected from 127 South Korean elementary school students using the questionnaire. Fourthly, as a new contribution, we proposed a generic approach for adapting gameplay and learning content in educational games based on the learner's learning and play styles. These results can be of interest to educational game developers, educators and game researchers.

2 Learning Style Models

Learning styles have been researched by scholars for decades during which dozens of models have been proposed [11]. In the following, we present three popular learning style models – where popularity was deemed based on their citation counts – that were considered in this study.

2.1 Kolb's Learning Style Inventory

One of the most widely known learning style models was created by Kolb, who published his Learning Style Inventory (LSI) in 1984 [25]. The model was made for general use and aimed at individuals to identify the way they learn [24]. The LSI model defines four distinct learning styles as follows:

- Accommodator (CE/AE): Prefers practical, hands-on approach to problems.
- Converger (AC/AE): Prefers hands-on approach to applying theories.
- Diverger (CE/RO): Prefers discussing and thinking the problem through.
- Assimilator (AC/RO): Prefers reasoning and theoretical approach.

Kolb's learning styles are based on a four-stage learning cycle consisting of: Concrete Experience (CE), Reflective Observation (RO), Abstract Conceptualization (AC) and Active Experimentation (AE). Essentially, the four learning styles are combinations of these four stages. For instance, Accommodator is a combination of Concrete Experience and Active Experimentation [25]. Since its emergence, LSI has been developed further; its latest specifications were published in 2005 [24].

2.2 Honey and Mumford Learning Style Questionnaire

Honey and Mumford [18] built their Learning Style Questionnaire (LSQ) on top of Kolb's LSI. Their purpose was to use the model in the context of management of work spaces. Honey and Mumford redefined LSI's four learning styles as:

- Activist: Learns by doing; prefers a practical approach.
- Theorist: Learns by an analytical approach; needs to understand the theory first.
- Pragmatist: Needs to see a connection between the theory and the task at hand; prefers to apply theory in real life.
- Reflector: An observer who does not directly interact, but rather collects data from multiple sources.

Honey and Mumford's model has a four-stage cyclical form with the following stages: (i) Having an experience, (ii) Reviewing the experience, (iii) Concluding from the experience, and (iv) Planning the next steps. Their model suggests that different people are more attuned to different stages, thus individual learning processes should be adapted accordingly.

2.3 Felder-Silverman Learning Styles Model

Originally aimed specifically at engineering students, Felder-Silverman Learning Styles Model was created by Felder and Silverman [14] and later improved upon by Felder and Soloman, who used the model to derive a questionnaire instrument named as Index of Learning Styles (ILS) [15]. The model maps learners into four dimensions: (i) Active and Reflective, (ii) Sensing and Intuitive, (iii) Visual and Verbal, and (iv) Sequential and Global. The extremes of these dimensions are defined as:

- Active learner: Hands-on approach, discussing about the project; likes group work.
- Reflective learner: Thinks about the problem quietly at first; prefers working alone.
- Sensory learner: Likes to learn facts; enjoys solving problems with well-established methods.
- Intuitive learner: Enjoys discovering the connections between problems; good with abstraction.
- Visual learner: Remembers best anything that they have seen, such as images, flow charts and diagrams.
- Verbal learner: Gets more out of words, both written and spoken.
- Sequential learner: Approaches a problem in a stepwise manner, solving one sub-problem at a time.
- Global learner: Move forward in large jumps, absorbing materials in a seemingly random manner.

It is worth noting that "Verbal" was "Auditory" in the original model; the term "Verbal" was proposed by Felder and Solomon in ILS [15]. Furthermore, within one dimension, such as Active-Reflective, a person may converge towards one of the extremes or diverge away from both extremes.

2.4 Comparison of Learning Style Models

Table 1 shows how the aforementioned learning style models compare to each other. Because Honey and Mumford's model was built on top of Kolb's model, they are strongly similar. Felder and Silverman's model describes its styles in a slightly different manner. Their model assumes that learners draw tendencies from four dimensions. Essentially, the first two dimensions have similarities with Kolb's as well as Honey and Mumford's styles. In Active-Reflective dimension, the connections are obvious, and despite using different names, Intuitive maps quite comfortably with Assimilating and Theorist, and Sensing connects to Converging and Pragmatist.

3 Play Style Models

Compared to learning styles, play styles have not received that much attention from researchers. In the following section, we describe four play style models, which have been proposed and used in game studies.

3.1 Bartle Player Types

Perhaps the best known play style model was described by Bartle in his paper "Hearts, Clubs, Diamonds, Spades: Players who suit MUDs" [4]. Bartle created his model by analyzing players in Multi-User Dungeon (MUD) games. Since its emergence, the model has been often cited in game-related studies across game genres. The Bartle Player Types (BPT) model defines four play styles: Killer, Achiever, Explorer and Socializer. These four styles are distributed in corners of a two-dimensional space where the X-axis represents Player – World and the Y-axis denotes Acting – Interacting. The characteristics of the four styles are:

- Killer: Aggressive predators who enjoy harassing other players. To some extent they socialize with other Killers, explore the game and gather resources, but these are only means to an end. Being in control and dominating the game are also appealing to Killers.
- Achiever: Solely focused on beating the game as perfectly as possible. In a multiplayer game this typically means gathering resources and level-ups, whereas in a single player game the focus would be to clear every achievement and the game perfectly.
- Explorer: Interested in mapping the game mechanics inside and outside. Inside means discovering every corner of the game, and outside refers to utilizing bugs that might give benefits to the player.
- Socializer: Are into the game nearly solely to use it as a communication forum to connect and talk with other players. Other game mechanics represent merely a backdrop to achieve this goal.

Despite originally being intended to be a model for mapping sociocentric behavior of players in multiplayer games, BPT can also be used to discover the

Table 1. Comparison of learning style models.

Kolb	Honey & Mumford	Felder & Silverman
Accommodating	***Activist***	***Active***
Practical, social	Practical, social	Practical, social
Diverging	***Reflector***	***Reflective***
Observation, social	Observation, prefers pairs	Observation, prefers working alone
Assimilating	***Theorist***	***Intuitive***
Theoretical, analytical, not very social	Theoretical, analytical, facts	Innovative, abstract learning, theoretical
Converging	***Pragmatist***	***Sensing***
Apply theory to practical solutions	Apply theory to practical solutions	Facts, theoretical
n/a	n/a	***Sequential – Global***
n/a	n/a	***Visual – Verbal***

dominant play style of an individual playing single player game. This view is supported by the emergence of newer models that are bear similarities to BPT, such as DGD1 and Four Keys, which are described in the following sections.

While Bartle did not create a questionnaire for his model, the Bartle Test questionnaire was proposed by Andreasen and Downey [2]. Bartle Test is based on binary choice questions following the style "I would rather do this or that", and it has gained significant popularity as a play style mapping tool within gaming communities.

3.2 Demographic Game Design Model (DGD1 and DGD2)

The first Demographic Game Design Model (DGD1) was revealed in book "21st-Century Game Design" by Bateman and Boon [5]. It was intended for identifying player preferences that could help development of games that cater to different demographic groups [39]. DGD1 comprises four play styles:

- Wanderer: Associated with experience and identity. They enjoy new experiences and discovering the game area or story elements rather than challenging gameplay, which they tolerate in order to advance in the game.
- Conqueror: Aim to defeat the games they play. They enjoy challenges introduced by the game and the pay off when overcoming those challenges.
- Manager: Aim to master the game and understand its gameplay mechanics. They do not care much about winning the game, but rather to reach a point where there is nothing new to learn.
- Participant: Associated with immersing themselves into a game world through social interaction with other players or with non-player characters. Any game that gives emotional feedback (good or bad) appeals to this play style.

The DGD1 model is dependent on the Myers-Briggs Type Indicator that describes 16 different personality types (see Sect. 4.1) [38]. The DGD1 model was developed further into DGD2, which aimed at improving upon DGD1. This upgrade mainly affected how the survey was built and how resulting data was analyzied, thus no changes to the original play styles were made [6].

3.3 BrainHex

BrainHex is based on the foundations of DGD1 and DGD2 [40] and it distinguishes seven play styles: Seeker, Mastermind, Socializer, Daredevil, Survivor, Achiever and Conqueror. Only one play style, Conqueror, was kept from the older DGD1 and DGD2 models; however, Nacke et al. [39] suggested that Manager, Wanderer and Participant styles in DGD1/DGD2 correspond to Mastermind, Seeker and Socializer of BrainHex, respectively. Hence, the three new play styles introduced in BrainHex are:

- Survivor: Enjoy the thrill of horror games and other games that exert feelings of terror during gameplay.

- Daredevil: Enjoy fast-paced thrill-seeking games in which the levels' terrain and design can be abstract and the player has to rush forward and react to the game area. In some ways this is similar to Survivor with the difference that enjoyment is drawn from positive experiences rather than negative.
- Achiever: Achiever is equivalent to Bartle's original depiction of the namesake style and as much is stated by the researchers themselves [40]. Achievers enjoy finishing the game and they are not above endless'grinding' to clear the game perfectly.

3.4 Four Fun Keys

Lazzaro published her Four Fun Keys (4FK) model in a conference paper "Why We Play Games: Four Keys to More Emotion without Story" [29] in which she discussed the emotions created by gameplay. The 4FK model's approach to categorizing players is based on different emotions that games may evoke in them. Lazzaro's four styles are:

- Hard Fun: Players of this style relish challenges and beating games by using their wits. It is important to note that a challenging game with lots of luck-based components would not appeal to this play style.
- Easy Fun: These players enjoy exploration and figuring out the game. Games that open gradually by making the player explore are especially appealing to this play style. They are interested in the game's story and generally get attached to their game character.
- Altered States/Serious Fun: The game is a tool to pass time, to clear thoughts, or to change one's mental state. Games that can be played without much effort are appealing to this play style.
- People Factor/People Fun: Play games to socialize and spend time with friends. The game itself is not important. Players of this style also encompass people who do not enjoy playing games alone, but who enjoy gathering together with friends to play games.

3.5 Comparison of Play Styles

As Table 2 shows, certain similarities can be drawn between BPT and other play style models. The authors of BrainHex also admit some of these similarities [40] and explain how much their model is related to BPT. It must be noted that while Table 2 reveals connections among play styles, it does not indicate strengths of those connections. We placed DGD2's Manager between BPT's Achiever and Explorer based on its definition. In BrainHex, Manager was discarded alongside with Wanderer, and five new styles were added in their place. BrainHex's Achiever is essentially the same than its namesake in BPT. Manager and Seeker both connect to BPT's Explorer; Manager shares Explorer's general curiosity to see how things work, and Seeker is curious about the game world. Additionally, BrainHex's two new play styles– Daredevil and Survivor – loosely relate to BPT's Explorer; players of one of these niche styles are seeking a specific emotion: horror or thrill.

Table 2. Comparison of play styles.

Bartle player types	DGD1 & DGD2	BrainHex	Four fun keys
Killer	***Conqueror***	***Conqueror***	***Serious Fun***
Aggressive, unsocial, control	Competitive, perfectionist, strategy-oriented	Challenge-seeking, aggressive	Stimulation, excitement, avoiding boredom
Achiever	***Manager***	***Achiever***	***Hard Fun***
Competitive, perfectionist, social, hard-working	Control, understanding of game mechanics	Goal-oriented, long-term achievements, "ticking boxes", ultimate completion	Competitive, perfectionist, strategy-oriented
Explorer		***Mastermind***	***Easy Fun***
Exploration in game, understanding of game mechanics, unaggressive		Strategic, problem solving, understanding of mechanics	Exploration in the game, social, enjoys puzzles, excitement and adventure, wanting to figure it out
	Wanderer	***Seeker***	
	Experience-seeking, impulsive, exploring	Curious, exploration in game	
		Daredevil	
		Thrill-seeking	
		Survivor	
		Terror-seeking	
Socializer	***Participant***	***Socializer***	***People Fun***
Very social, cooperative, unaggressive, trusting, communication, game not important	Very social, immersion-seeking, cooperative	People-seeking, communication, trusting	Very social, communication, game not important

Connections can also be drawn between 4FK and BPT, but not so directly as with the previously mentioned DGD1, DGD2 and BrainHex. Three 4FK styles have similarities with BPT styles as follows: People Fun is close to BPT's Socializer; Hard Fun shares some similarities with BPT's Achiever in terms of the player wanting to beat the game; Easy Fun's focus on exploration and curiosity draws parallels to BPT's Explorer. Serious Fun does not tie to any specific BPT style. Essentially, any type of game that allows the player to attain a sense of joy and to avoid boredom is Serious Fun.

4 Personality Style Models

While the above models describe different styles for learning and playing, there also exist personality style models that attempt to categorize individuals into predefined personality groups. Learning and play styles often have connections to personality styles, hence we introduce three of them in this section.

4.1 Myers-Briggs Type Indicator

Myers-Briggs Type Indicator is based on Jung's psychological type theory [19], which specifies six types divided into three groups: Introversion – Extraversion, Sensing – Intuition, and Thinking – Feeling. According to Jung, one of the two in each group is a dominant type. Myers-Briggs proposed a fourth group to complement Jung's theory: Judging – Perceiving. The four groups are as follows:

Extraversion – Introversion: defines the person's focus. An introvert is interested in their internal world, reflecting on it. Introverts are generally thoughtful persons and can lack the interest of joining others' activities. Extravert is the opposite whose focus is mainly on the external world and its stimuli.

Sensing – Intuition: In this context, sensing is something that the person can see or physically feel through stimuli, whereas intuition is more of an undisclosed feeling, or a hunch.

Thinking – Feeling: This is the preference of how the person makes behavioral judgments either by using logic or emotions as the decisive factor.

Judging – Perceiving: This defines how the obtained information is processed. Judging people have strict guidelines that they follow, whereas Perceiving people are more likely to improvise and can easily veer off from their current path, if the situation calls for it.

Myers-Briggs defines 16 personality types that are combinations of the aforementioned four groups. These personality types are named by combining the first letters of dominant types. For instance, the Introversion-Sensing-Feeling-Judging personality is referred to as ISFJ. As a widely used model, Myers-Briggs Type Indicator shares conceptual similarities with some learning style models and play style models [8,37].

4.2 Big 5

The core concept of the Big 5 model is that human personality traits can be narrowed down to five broad dimensions, as follows:

Openness to Experience: How curious, creative and complex the person is, or whether the person is conventional, down-to-earth with narrow interests [42].

Conscientiousness: How well-organized, disciplined and careful the person is.

Extraversion: This is similar to Jung's description of Extraversion and Introversion, with an added notion of social aspects of these personality types. Extraverts are seeking people out and being talkative, whereas Introverts are likely doing the opposite.

Agreeableness: This covers social aspects of the individual on scales of outgoing vs. detached. Furthermore, it defines how trusting and compassionate the person is towards others, or alternatively, how argumentative and challenging they are.

Neuroticism: How emotionally volatile the person is, and whether emotions have control over their decisions and actions.

Furnham's comparative study [16] found similarities between Big 5 and Myers-Briggs Type Indicator as follows: Agreeableness is similar to Thinking-Feeling, Conscientiousness to Judging-Perceiving, Extraversion to Extraversion-Introversion, and Openness to Sensing-Intuitive. To the best of our knowledge, the Big 5 model does not directly relate to any specific learning or play style model. However, it has close resemblance to Myers-Briggs Type Indicator, and research exists on establishing connections between Big 5, BPT, and Kolb's learning styles [26].

4.3 Keirsey Temperament Sorter

In their book "Please understand me" [21], Keirsey and Bates proposed the Keirsey Temperament Sorter (KTS), a personality questionnaire for identifying temperaments. KTS has similarities to Myers-Briggs Type Indicator [38], and it defines four temperaments as:

- Artisan: Partical persons who like working with their hands. They are adventurous in the nature and always looking for new challenges.
- Guardian: Social persons who are serious about their duties and responsibilities. They believe in following the rules and cooperating with others.
- Rational: Persons who tend to be pragmatic and focus on problem solving. They also have insatiable hunger for accomplishing their goals and work tirelessly on ongoing projects.
- Idealist: They believe that friendly cooperation is the best way to achieve one's goals. They shy away from conflicts as these upset them.

"Please Understand Me II" [22] placed these temperaments into a two-dimensional space akin to BPT. The X-axis represents Internals versus Externals and the Y-Axis comprises Change versus Structure.

5 An Instrument for Detecting Learning and Play Styles

In order to build an instrument for detecting learning and play styles, we first selected representative learning and play style models based on their respective comparisons. For detecting learning styles, we chose Honey and Mumford's LSQ because it is well established and validated. The comparison conducted by Coffield et al. [11] indicated that LSQ and Kolb's model stand on an equal footing. However, we chose the former because it has simpler terms describing the four styles.

The BPT model was chosen mainly due to the lack of validated competing models and also to avoid unnecessary complexity that would ensue from using models that define play styles overly detailed, such as the BrainHex model [40]. Despite having originally been intended as a tool for analyzing sociocentric interaction among people within multiplayer games, BPT can be used to define play styles in single player games, as was shown in Sect. 3.1.

After choosing the models, we created a questionnaire in English and later translated it to Korean. A Korean elementary school teacher helped in validating the questionnaire in two ways. First, she confirmed the clarity of the statements in English. Second, after translation of the questionnaire to Korean, she validated the statements to ensure that the language used was appropriate to the target students' comprehension ability.

After a demographics section, the questionnaire is divided into three parts. The first part measures gaming habits of the respondents, including how much they play games, their preferred game genres, and their favorite game titles. The purpose of this part is to get an overview of the landscape of digital gaming among elementary school students in the target context.

The second part focuses on identifying play styles. It is based on the aforementioned Bartle Test. We transformed the Bartle Test's binary choice statements into four-point Likert scale ("Strongly Agree", "Somewhat Agree", "Somewhat Disagree", "Strongly Disagree") to allow greater flexibility and depth for answering and data analysis. Furthermore, as respondents of elementary school students, we simplified the statements in order to decrease the chances of misunderstanding. Another reason why rewording the statements was necessary was due to the Bartle Test's original purpose of being used for multiplayer gamers; our questionnaire does not make any assumptions of the types of games the respondents like to play.

Table 3. Examples of questionnaire statements.

Play style	Question
Killer	"I enjoy games where I can make and destroy what I want (For example: Minecraft)"
Achiever	"I enjoy collecting items/money in the game"
Explorer	"I enjoy exploring the whole game area"
Socializer	"Playing together with a friend is more important than the game itself"
Learning style	
Activist	"I enjoy new challenges"
Reflector	"In group assignments I rather listen to others' opinions first before giving my own"
Theorist	"I need to confirm things myself that people tell me as facts"
Pragmatist	"If I can't use an idea in the real world, I find it boring"

The third part of the questionnaire focuses on mapping learning styles. It is a shorter version of Honey and Mumford's LSQ with simplified language. We applied Likert scale statements instead of yes/no statements, which were originally used to determine a dominant learning style. Rewording the statements, which were originally aimed at adults, was necessary so as to make them easier for children to understand. This rewording was done carefully in order to retain original meanings of the statements used by Honey and Mumford.

Our questionnaire contains four statements for each style, thus there are 16 statements per model. The original Bartle's Test has 41 statements, and the number of statements in LSQ is either 40 or 80, depending on the version. Both original questionnaires were deemed to be too long because children are known to have short attention spans [1]. Table 3 show example questions from each style section of our questionnaire.

6 Evaluation

As we have shown above, there are several learning and play style models which could be used for making educational games more adaptive. In this section, we present an evaluation of play and learning styles among South Korean elementary school students using the aforementioned instrument.

6.1 Research Design

Participants. The test group consisted of 127 South Korean elementary school students of whom 33 were from 3rd grade (10 years old) and the remaining 94 were from 5th grade (12 years old). The ages follow the Korean age reckoning system where a person is one year old at the time of birth. The test group had a nearly equal gender distribution with one undisclosed, 61 females and 65 males.

Data Collection and Pre-processing. After receiving appropriate permissions to conduct an experiment at a South Korean public elementary school, questionnaire papers were distributed to students in four classes by teachers who briefly explained the purpose of the questionnaire to their students. The students were encouraged to ask questions should they find any question difficult to understand. The teachers remained in the classrooms for the duration data collection in order to answer any questions raised by the students.

The questionnaire data consisted of 127 responses, which were pruned down to 100 (46 Females, 53 Males, 1 undisclosed) for play style and learn style analyses. Pruning was done by disregarding questionnaires that were not properly filled, that is, multiple blank answers or "Strongly Disagree" or "Strongly Agree" in all statements. For play time analysis, we were able to use the entire data set.

6.2 Results

The following sections present the results of our questionnaire data analysis. After describing the results of play time analysis, we show how play and learning styles manifested themselves among the respondents.

Play Time. In the gaming habits part of the questionnaire, we investigated how much the respondents spend time playing video games. Figure 1 illustrates the respondents' estimations of their video game playing time on a scale of 1–6 where 1 depicts daily playing and 6 indicates never playing. Mean (μ) and standard deviation (σ) values are also reported. Answers within the range of 1 to 3 can be considered regular to semi-regular playing and 4–6 from irregular to rarely or never. There were clearly more males who played games regularly (52/65 answered between 1–3), whereas among females the distribution was nearly equal (30/61 answered between 1–3).

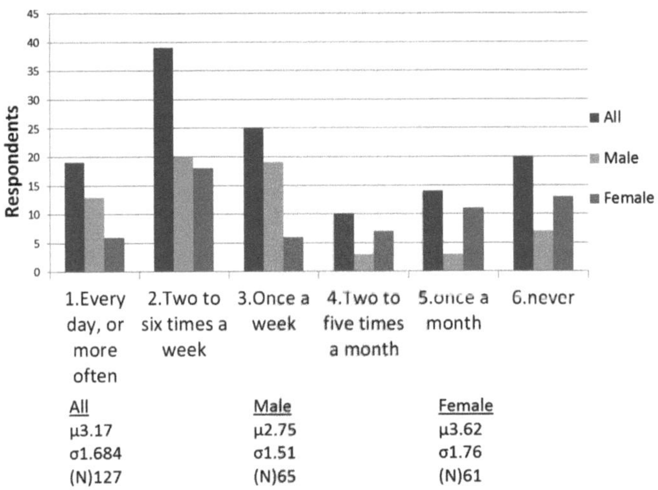

Fig. 1. How regularly do respondents play video games.

Play Styles. The play style part of the questionnaire was divided into four sections based on BPT: Killer, Achiever, Explorer and Socializer. There was no option given to skip any of the statements separately, but if the respondent stated that they do not play games at all, they could jump directly to the learning style part.

In order to identify a dominant play style, we used a point system in which we assigned 1, 0.5, −0.5 and −1 points for Strongly Agree, Somewhat Agree, Somewhat Disagree and Strongly Disagree, respectively. The points in each style category were then added up, and the style with the highest points was designated as the respondent's dominant play style. This was done so as to see which style would be the strongest style for each respondent. If there were two or more equally strong styles, all of them were included in the counts of dominant styles. Secondary styles can also be identified through the point system, but they are not reported here. Figure 2 shows a histogram of dominant play styles among the respondents. Socializer was clearly the most common play style, followed by Explorer. Interestingly, only five Killers were identified among females, whereas the number of Killers was more than twice of that among males. Nevertheless,

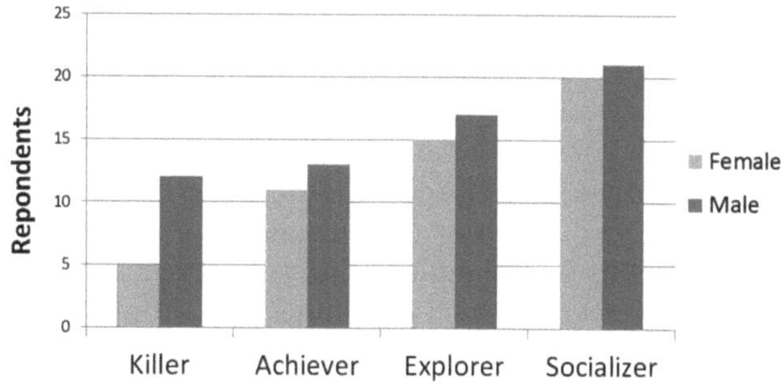

Fig. 2. Distribution of dominant play styles.

Killer was the least common style. This result is exemplified by the Killer statement "I enjoy teasing other players in a multiplayer game", which was rejected by 72% and 89% of males and females, respectively.

Learning Styles. Similarly to the play style part of the questionnaire, the learning style part consisted of 16 statements, four for each learning style: Activist, Reflector, Theorist and Pragmatist. We identified the dominant learning styles using the same point system than with the play styles above. Figure 3 illustrates the distribution of dominant learning styles. Activist and Reflector styles are clearly more common compared to Pragmatist and the least popular Theorist. Moreover, the results indicate that males are more practical and active than females, whereas females tend to prefer theories and contemplation than compared to males.

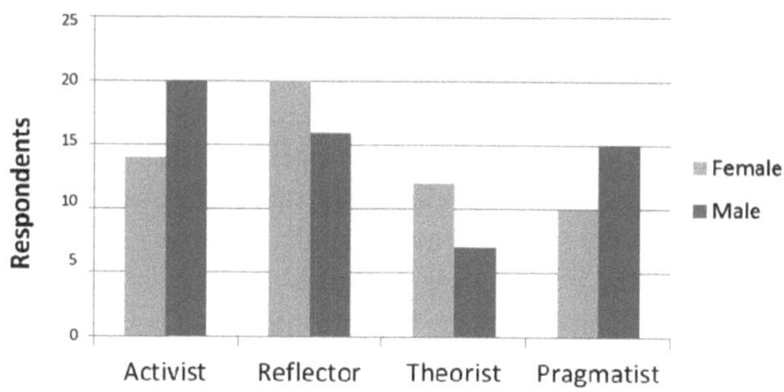

Fig. 3. Distribution of dominant learning styles.

7 Towards an Adaptation Model for Educational Games

Making an adaptive game is a demanding process in which game designers are normally faced by two options, or a partial embrace of both. The first option is that the adaption is built into each part of the game by hand, which means that multiple versions of the same game scenario (e.g., level, mission, quest, or task) are created to offer a higher degree of personalized gameplay and learning content. One example of this are RPGs that try to adapt their world to mirror the good, the evil or the neutral actions of the player. Though some RPGs do also use automation in their design, such as generating dungeons, they typically rely heavily on pre-designed scenarios. For instance, the dialogue offered by non-player characters (NPC) is something that has to be predefined beforehand and NPC behavior must be coded for each encounter. The script of a dialogue-heavy RPG named *Planescape: Torment* reportedly contained 800 000 words [17]. As another example, the player of *Dragon Age: Origins* must choose which race they belong to, and depending on the selection a ready-made tutorial for that specific race is shown.

The second option for making a game adaptive is that the game scenarios and content are generated automatically by a game engine based on predetermined adaptation rules. Roguelike games, such as *Nethack* or *Darkest Dungeons*, are good examples of this. In these games the player must survive through dungeons that are procedurally generated and might follow specific rules about when and where valuable items are likely appear and how tough and numerous enemy monsters are. This degree of automation, as we call it, shows that both of the aforementioned approaches have their benefits and drawbacks. The first approach can offer the most personalized experience from start to finish, both in form of actual game content and educational topics, but it takes a significant time and resources to make and would be hard to adjust to new content or game topics later on. The second approach of automatically generated content, on one hand, solves this issue, since one needs only to define a topic, source materials, and some rules on how to generate adapted content for the game. On the other hand, it tends to suffer from the opposite, as the game itself tends to be more generic and the specifying rules can be a complex endeavor.

As an answer to these issues, we propose an adaptation approach that is somewhat safer for dynamic content that is likely to change in the future, as is the case with many educational materials. Conceptually, our approach is located in between the two aforementioned adaptation options. It provides the same game scenario structure for each player, while performing adaptation of gameplay and learning content within the scenario at runtime. Below we explain the details of our adaptation approach, which aims to adapt an educational game based on the player's learning style and play style. Our approach is intended to be generic enough to be usable for creating different types of educational games. It forms the foundations of an adaptation model for educational games, which we are currently working on.

In our adaptation approach, play style affects how gameplay is presented to the player. By offering the same game scenarios to all play style classes and only affecting what will be in those scenarios, such as types and numbers of enemies, NPCs and obstacles, we can adapt gameplay to two out of four play style classes: Killers and Achievers. Additionally, Explorer and Socializer styles are supported by adjusting the game's user interface with what is generally known as'fog-of-war' in video games (i.e. hiding objects that are beyond the player's line of sight), and by offering options for socializing with NPCs or other players, respectively. Table 4 illustrates the general idea of how play style adaptation can be done with our approach. Essentially, to cover all four play styles, we suggest to manipulate both the user interface and the game world.

Table 4. Adaptation to play styles.

Play style	User interface	Game world
Killer	Stronger audiovisual destruction effects	High number of enemies and destructible obstacles
Achiever	Tracking of high score and collectibles	Moderate number of enemies and high number of destructible obstacles; collectible items and achievements
Explorer	Fog-of-War	Low number of enemies and obstacles; hidden paths and assets
Socializer	Chat/dialogue	Low number enemies and low number of obstacles; non-player characters (NPCs) and additional in-game dialogue

A more challenging part of adaption is how to handle learning styles because there is no consensus on the most effective way of presenting educational content in games. The concepts of gamification and edutainment typically involve a singular approach of delivering learning materials in a preordained format that does not change much as the game progresses. Furthermore, the usage of learning styles is often discussed in form of applying them to traditional classroom environments. There are, however, several adaptive tutoring systems that are based on Honey and Mumford's model or other learning style models [9,13,28].

Our adaptation to learning styles is based on Magoulas et al.'s [32] work on INSPIRE, an adaptive educational hypermedia system [28]. INSPIRE utilizes the Component Display Theory [34], which proposes three levels of learner performance based on how advanced the learner is in learning a given concept: (i) *Remember* or memorize a new concept, (ii) *Use* or apply previously memorized concepts to solve a problem, and (iii) *Find* or create new concepts. INSPIRE divides learning materials into three presentation groups within the *Remember* level: (i) Question, (ii) Example, (iii) Theory. The *Use* level has four presentation groups for learning content: (i) Activity, (ii) Example,(iii) Theory (iv) Exercise. Magoulas et al. also proposed learning activities for the *Find* level (e.g., simulations, exploration and case studies) but they did not explicitly specify presentation groups for it [32]. The order in which learning contents are presented is determined based on the learner's learning style.

When devising our adaptation approach, some changes to the INSPIRE's adaptation model were necessary due to rather stark differences between educational games and e-learning systems. We combined the *Remember* and *Use* levels

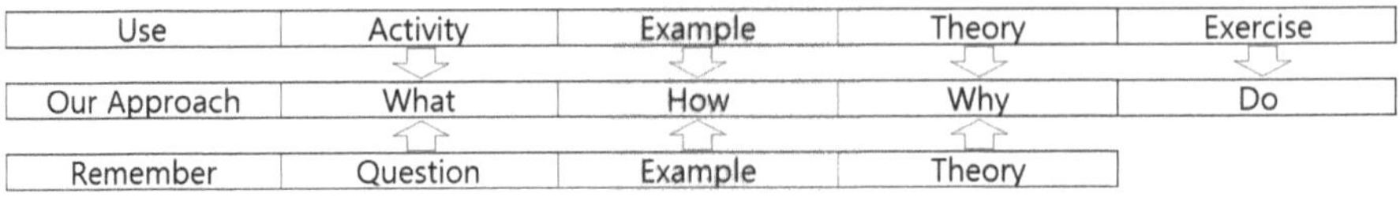

Fig. 4. Presentation groups in the proposed adaptation approach.

Table 5. Example of learning style adaptation in a Super Mario game.

Learning style	Step 1	Step 2	Step 3	Step 4
Activist	Objective is explained: solve adding fractions (WHAT)	Game starts (DO)	Short explanation of how an adding fractions problem can be solved is hidden behind a hint button. (HOW)	Short explanation of adding fractions and its uses in other contexts (WHY)
Reflector	Short explanation of adding fractions and its uses in other contexts (WHY)	Short explanation of how an adding fractions problem can be solved (HOW)	Objective is explained: solve adding fractions (WHAT)	Game starts (DO)
Theorist	Objective is explained: solve adding fractions (WHAT)	Short explanation of adding fractions and its uses in other contexts (WHY)	Short explanation of how an adding fractions problem can be solved (HOW)	Game starts (DO)
Pragmatist	Short explanation of how an adding fractions problem can be solved (HOW)	Short explanation of adding fractions and its uses in other contexts (WHY)	Objective is explained: solve adding fractions (WHAT)	Game starts (DO)

because educational gameplay often requires novice learners to memorize new concepts in order to apply them to problem solving. Moreover, these levels share similar presentation groups. We left out the *Find* level because the purpose of the proposed adaptation approach is to use it for elementary school programming education games that focus on teaching basic programming concepts. The original presentation groups were also modified as shown in Fig. 4. We combined the Question group from *Remember* and the Activity group from *Use* into a new group called *What*, as in "What do I need to do?" We kept the Example and Theory groups from *Remember* and *Use*, and named them *How*, as in "How can I do it?", and *Why*, as in "Why did I do that?", respectively. Lastly, the Exercise group from *Use* was named *Do*, as in "Doing it". The following list describes these groups with example contents.

Table 6. Example of play style adaptation in a Super Mario game.

Play style	User interface	Game world
Unadapted	Unadapted	3x Enemies 5x Destructible obstacles
Killer	Nothing asides controllers; special effects on destroyed obstacles and enemies	8 x Enemies 10 x Destructible obstacles
Achiever	Show accumulated points and collected items	5 x Enemies 8 x Destructible obstacles Achievements given for destroying all obstacles in level and for collecting items around the level
Explorer	Game map showing only visited places, hiding the rest	3 x Enemies 5 x Destructible Obstacles Each level has one secret room and Easter eggs (hidden features)
Socializer	Chat with other players, or show feed from online community	2 x Enemies 0 x Destructible obstacles NPCs with dialogues

- Text and Image (or other media) representing WHAT the player is supposed to do, essentially the learning challenge.
- A short video tutorial (or other media) showing HOW the player may approach the challenge. It may show how a similar, possibly simpler, problem is solved. In a game, this also teaches the player about game mechanics.
- Answering WHY the player did what they did by presenting them a short explanation of the learned concept and its uses in other contexts.
- DO play the game and solve the learning challenge. Gameplay can be considered to be a hands-on part of the learning process.

The presentation groups will be activated in an order that is appropriate to the player's learning style. To determine a suitable order for each style, we followed the *Use* level's original ordering [32]. Tables 5 and 6 exemplify how an imaginary version of Super Mario game for learning adding fractions could be adapted using our adaptation approach.

8 Discussion

The evaluation presented above sheds some light on the play and learning styles among South Korean elementary school students. The results were as we expected in the sense that there were no single dominant learning and play styles that would significantly shadow the other styles. Instead, most respondents had several fairly strong styles. A consequence of this is that an adaptive educational game does not necessarily have to strictly follow one learning/play style combination throughout the game, but it could also alternate between multiple styles that are identified to be strong in the player. This allows the creation of versatile adaptive games that could change even between repeated game sessions.

Finding the underlying reasons for negative answers to the Killer statement "I enjoy teasing other players in a multiplayer game" requires further research, but we have initial ideas to guide future research. On one hand, it is reasonable to assume that some students might have felt the need to mask their negative behavior. On the other hand, a third grade teacher commented that her students are particularly eager to help each other, thus indicating altruistic mindsets, which is clearly against what the Killer style represents. It would be interesting to conduct a future study to see whether the results would be similar with older students who are likely to consume more "killer" games, such as first-person shooters. Similarly, it would be meaningful to investigate whether differences exists among cultural groups.

The popularity of Socializer can be partially explained by the collective Korean culture and the general tendency of children to prefer playing games together. The popularity of Explorer may have been influenced by the natural curiosity of children. To draw any relevant conclusions on what caused these two styles to be the most common dominant styles would requires additional research within the same age group and among older learners.

Currently, the questionnaire is aimed at elementary school children, which is why we limited the number of questions to four per learning/play style. Using a low number of questions bears some disadvantages, such as suboptimal accuracy and lack internal consistency validation. However, the time taken for filling in a concise questionnaire is less likely to exceed the children's attention span. If the questionnaire would be aimed at teenagers or adults, it would be reasonable to include more questions to increase accuracy and enable internal consistency validation. But if the questionnaire is to be used within a game, then a lengthy questionnaire might severely damage gameplay experience.

The lack of validation for reliability and internal consistency should be considered in the future versions of the questionnaire. Reliability metrics, such as Cronbach Alpha, can only be performed on data set having statements that measure the same property. In its current form, our questionnaire is minimized so that the statements for any given style are measuring different properties related to that style. However, since we based our questionnaire on previously tested models, it is reasonable to assume that the chosen questions, albeit simplified for the use of children, have a sufficient degree of reliability.

In Evaluation, we mapped the respondents within learning and play style models. This mapping indicates what kind of stimuli might enhance the respondents' immersion and increase learning efficiency. In the next step of this research project, we aim to use these results for making an adaptive educational game prototype and evaluate it with elementary school children. Essentially, for such an adaptive game to use learning and play style models in an effective way, the game should present a questionnaire at the beginning, make calculations to deduce learning and play styles, and utilize the identified styles to adapt gameplay and game content. The questionnaire could be disguised in form of a character building dialogue in order to connect it closely to the game world. It would be even better if the game could automatically learn about play and learning styles of the player during gameplay, and consequently generate the game world and educational content. Doing so would allow the removal of the questionnaire, thus making the game engaging from the start.

The proposed adaptation approach can simplify design processes of adaptive educational games by providing basic methods for adapting game mechanics and provisioning learning content according to play and learning styles. Although our approach can be useful in many educational game projects, there may be cases that require a tailored adaptation. Furthermore, our adaptation approach may not be optimal for some game genres because they support poorly specific play styles. For example, it would feel artificial to force a casual game, such as Candy Crush Saga, to support Socializers. Essentially, if a game is to support all styles, it must be designed as such from the beginning. A game that only supports some specific styles may in some ways be more efficient as it allows a more in-depth approach to these styles. This, however, bears a risk of the game to be efficient only with players who are aligned with the styles used.

At the moment of writing this paper, we are working on an adaptive game prototype for programming education based on the proposed adaptation approach. In the game, the same scenario will be offered to players having different play and learning styles, but the manners in which game scenario and learning contents are presented and interacted with differ among the styles.

9 Conclusions

In this study we crafted a questionnaire to detect elementary school students' play and learning styles in order to create adaptive educational games. After performing an analysis and comparison of popular learning and play style models, including also personality style models, we crafted a questionnaire based on the Bartle Test questionnaire and the Honey and Mumford's Learning Style Questionnaire. The questions were simplified and modified to use Likert scale statements. The data collected with the questionnaire revealed the distribution of dominant learning and play styles among South Korean elementary school students.

Our questionnaire is significant because until now most of previous learning style and play style mapping instruments were created for older respondents and the two style groups were rarely combined. While the questionnaire yielded results that are useful for understanding the types of learners and players in South Korea, we intend to perform further studies in other countries so as to compare the results between cultures. Moreover, in order to understand the interplay among learning styles and play styles, a study on intra-model and inter-model relationships is needed.

Based on Bartle's play styles and Honey and Mumford's learning styles, we proposed an adaptation approach for educational games that could be applied to different topics and game genres. We have begun developing a prototype game for programming education that utilizes the proposed questionnaire and adaptation approach. The game consists of a main game and educational puzzles that teach different programming concepts, such as variables, loops and if-else conditionals. The puzzles will be adapted based on detected learning style, and play style adaptation is applied to the main game. The efficiency and effectiveness of the proposed adaptation approach will be evaluated in the future once the prototype game is finished.

References

1. Abadzi, H.: Efficient learning for the poor: new insights into literacy acquisition for children. Int. Rev. Educ. **54**, 581–604 (2008). Washington, DC: The World Bank, Washington D.C
2. Andersen, E., Downey, B.: The MUD personality test. MUD Companion **1**, 33–35 (2001)
3. Arnab, S., Brown, K., Clarke, S., Dunwell, I., Lim, T., Suttie, N., Louchart, S., Hendrix, M., De Freitas, S.: The development approach of a pedagogically-driven serious game to support Relationship and Sex Education (RSE) within a classroom setting. Comput. Educ. **69**, 15–30 (2013)
4. Bartle, R.: Hearts, clubs, diamonds, and spades: players who suit MUDs. J. MUD Res. **1**(1), 19 (1996)
5. Bateman, C., Boon, R.: 21st Century Game Design, 1st edn. Charles River Media, Hingham (2005)
6. Bateman, C., Lowenhaupt, R., Nacke, L.E.: Player typology in theory and practice. In: Proceedings of DiGRA 2011 Conference: Think Design Play, pp. 1–24 (2011)
7. Bontchev, B., Vassileva, D.: Learning objects types dependability on styles of learning. In: Proceedings of 8th WSEAS International Conference, pp. 227–234 (2011)
8. Briggs, K.C.: Myers-Briggs Type Indicator. Consulting Psychologist Press, Inc., Palo Alto (1977)
9. Canavan, J.: Personalised E-Learning through learning style aware adaptive systems. Thesis, p. 0 (2005)
10. Coenen, T., Mostmans, L., Naessens, K.: MuseUs: case study of a pervasive cultural heritage serious game. J. Comput. Cult. Herit. **6**(2), 1–19 (2013)
11. Coffield, F., Moseley, D., Hall, E., Ecclestone, K.: Should we be using learning styles? What research has to say to practice. Technical report, Learning and Skills Research Centre, London (2004). www.LSRC.ac.uk
12. Connolly, T.M., Boyle, E.A., Macarthur, E., Hainey, T., Boyle, J.M.: A systematic literature review of empirical evidence on computer games and serious games. Comput. Educ. **59**(2), 661–686 (2012)
13. Del Corso, D., Ovcin, E., Morrone, G., Gianesini, D., Salojarvi, S., Kvist, T.: 3DE: an environment for the development of learner-centered custom educational packages. In: Proceedings - Frontiers in Education Conference, vol. 2, pp. F2C/21–F2C/26 (2001)
14. Felder, R.M.: Learning and teaching styles in engineering education. Eng. Educ. **78**(7), 674–681 (1988)
15. Felder, R.M., Spurlin, J.: Applications, reliability and validity of the index of learning styles. Int. J. Eng. Educ. **21**(1), 103–112 (2005)

16. Furnham, A.: The big five versus the big four: the relationship between the Myers-Briggs Type Indicator (MBTI) and NEO-PI five factor model of personality. Pers. Individ. Differ. **21**(2), 303–307 (1996)
17. Gillen, K.: Retrospective: Planescape Torment (2010). https://www.rockpapershotgun.com/2010/09/28/re-retrospective-planescape-torment/
18. Honey, P., Mumford, A.: The Manual of Learning Styles, 3rd edn. Peter Honey Publications, Maidenhead (1982)
19. Jung, C.G.: Psychological Types: The Collected Works, vol. 6. Routledge and Kegan Paul, London (1971)
20. Ke, F., Grabowski, B.: Gameplaying for maths learning: cooperative or not? Brit. J. Educ. Technol. **38**(2), 249–259 (2007)
21. Keirsey, D., Bates, M.: Please Understand Me: Character and Temperament Types, 5th edn. Prometheus Nemesis Book Company, Del Mar (1984)
22. Keirsey, D., Bates, M.: Please Understand Me: Temperament, Character, Intelligence. Prometheus Nemesis Book Company, Del Mar (1998)
23. Kim, B., Park, H., Baek, Y.: Not just fun, but serious strategies: using meta-cognitive strategies in game-based learning. Comput. Educ. **52**(4), 800–810 (2009)
24. Kolb, A.Y., Kolb, D.A.: The Kolb Learning Style Inventory - Version 3.1 2005 Technical Specifications, vol. 200. Hay Resource Direct, Boston (2005)
25. Kolb, D.A.: Experential Learning: Experience as the Source of Learning and Development. Prentice Hall, Englewood Cliffs (1984)
26. Konert, J., Göbel, S., Steinmetz, R.: Modeling the player, learner and personality: independency of the models of Bartle, Kolb and NEO-FFI (Big5) and the implications for game based learning. In: Proceedings of the 7th European Conference on Games Based Learning, pp. 329–335 (2013)
27. Koops, M., Hoevenaar, M.: Conceptual change during a serious game: using a lemniscate model to compare strategies in a physics game. Simul. Gaming **44**(4), 544–561 (2012)
28. Papanikolaou, K.A., Grigoriadou, M., Kornilakis, H., Magoulas, G.D.: INSPIRE: an INtelligent system for personalized instruction in a remote environment. In: Reich, S., Tzagarakis, M.M., Bra, P.M.E. (eds.) AH 2001. LNCS, vol. 2266, pp. 215–225. Springer, Heidelberg (2002). doi:10.1007/3-540-45844-1_21
29. Lazzaro, N.: Why we play games: four keys to more emotion without story. In: Game Developers Conference, July 2004
30. Lindberg, R.S.N., Laine, T.H.: Detecting play and learning styles for adaptive educational games. In: 8th International Conference on Computer Supported Education, vol. 1, pp. 181–189. SCITEPRESS Science and Technology Publications (2016)
31. Macvean, A., Robertson, J.: iFitQuest: a school based study of a mobile location-aware exergame for adolescents. In: Proceedings of the 14th International Conference on Human-Computer Interaction with Mobile Devices and Services - Mobile-HCI 2012, p. 359 (2012)
32. Magoulas, G., Papanikolaou, K., Grigoriadou, M.: Adaptive web-based learning: accommodating individual differences through system's adaptation. Brit. J. Educ. Technol. **34**(4), 511–527 (2003)
33. McMahon, N., Wyeth, P., Johnson, D.: Personality and player types in fallout new vegas. In: Proceedings of the 4th International Conference on Fun and Games - FnG 2012, pp. 113–116 (2012)
34. Merrill, M.D.: "Component Display Theory". Instructional-Design Theories and Models: An Overview of Their Current Status, 1st edn. Lawrence Erlbaum Associates, London (1983)

35. Mirvis, P.H.: Flow: The Psychology of Optimal Experience, vol. 16, 1st edn. Harper & Row, New York (1991)
36. Morelli, T., Foley, J., Lieberman, L.: Pet-N-Punch: upper body tactile/audio exergame to engage children with visual impairments into physical activity. Proc. Graph. Interface **2011**, 223–230 (2011)
37. Myers, I., Myers, P.: Gifts Differing: Understanding Personality Type. Nicholas Brealey Publishing, London (2010)
38. Myers, I.B.: The Myers-Briggs Type Indicator: Manual (1962). Consulting Psychologists Press, Palo Alto (1962)
39. Nacke, L.E., Bateman, C., Mandryk, R.L.: BrainHex: preliminary results from a neurobiological gamer typology survey. In: Anacleto, J.C., Fels, S., Graham, N., Kapralos, B., Saif El-Nasr, M., Stanley, K. (eds.) ICEC 2011. LNCS, vol. 6972, pp. 288–293. Springer, Heidelberg (2011). doi:10.1007/978-3-642-24500-8_31
40. Nacke, L.E., Bateman, C., Mandryk, R.L.: BrainHex: a neurobiological gamer typology survey. Entertain. Comput. **5**(1), 55–62 (2014)
41. Nygren, E., Sutinen, E., Blignaut, A.S., Laine, T.H., Els, C.J.: Motivations for play in the UFractions mobile game in three countries. Int. J. Mob. Blended Learn. **4**(2), 30–48 (2012)
42. Oliver, J., Sanjay, S.: The big five trait taxonomy: history, measurement, and theoretical perspectives. Handb. Pers. Theor. Res. **2**, 102–138 (1999)
43. Orji, R., Vassileva, J., Mandryk, R.L.: Modeling the efficacy of persuasive strategies for different gamer types in serious games for health. User Model. User Adap. Interact. **24**(5), 453–498 (2014)
44. Popescu, M.M., Romero, M., Usart, M., National, C.I.: Using serious games in adult education serious business for serious people-the metavals game case study. Learning **2**(1), 68–72 (2011)

Towards Efficient Teacher Assisted Assignment Marking Using Ranking Metrics

Nils Ulltveit-Moe[1(✉)], Terje Gjøsæter[2(✉)], Sigurd Assev[1(✉)], and Halvard Øysæd[1(✉)]

[1] Department of Information and Communication Technology, University of Agder, Jon Lilletuns vei 9, 4879 Grimstad, Norway
{nils.ulltveit-moe,sigurd.m.assev,halvard.oysad}@uia.no
[2] NC-Spectrum, Kviteseidgata 18, 3850 Kviteseid, Norway
terje.gjosater@nc-spectrum.no

Abstract. This paper describes a tool with supporting methodology for efficient teacher assisted marking of open assignments based on student answer ranking metrics. It includes a methodology for how to design tasks for markability. This improves marking efficienty and reduces cognitive strain for the teacher during marking, and also allows for easily giving feedback to students on common pitfalls and misconceptions to improve both the learning outcome for the students as well as the teacher's productivity by reducing the time needed for marking open assignments. An advantage with the method is that it is language agnostic as well as generally being agnostic to the discipline of the course being assessed. The ranking metrics also provide implicit plagiarism detection.

Keywords: Entropy · Cross assignment marking · Learning Management Systems · Efficient teaching methods

1 Introduction

This paper presents a method for teacher assisted marking of answers to open text-based questions based on ranking metrics. It furthermore describes how the opportunistic web-scraper based assessment method FrontScraper described in [17], can be evolved into a robust cross-platform assessment plugin module for existing Learning Management Systems (LMS). This will be done as part of an upcoming research project NOVMARK - Novel Methods and Metrics for Assisted Marking of Student Work.

The assessment improvement process supported by the LMS plugin is described in Fig. 1. The objective of the project is designing an innovative tool and methodology for teacher assisted grading of open-ended tasks. This includes the following steps in a continuous improvement cycle to improve both teacher

G. Costagliola et al. (Eds.): CSEDU 2016, CCIS 739, pp. 359–379, 2017.
DOI: 10.1007/978-3-319-63184-4_19

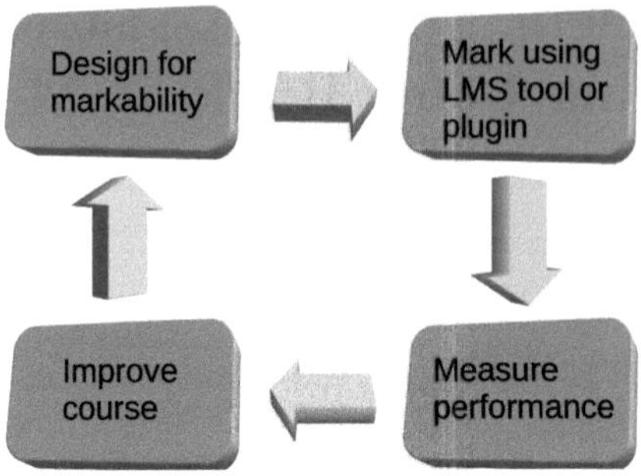

Fig. 1. Assessment improvement process.

efficiency during marking as well as the course itself based on knowledge on how well students have learnt different learning outcomes. This includes:

- Design of student tasks for markability, so that these tasks more easily can be marked using the LMS tool or plugin FrontScraper and also so that the teacher most efficiently can mark the given tasks whilst giving the students an opportunity to demonstrate knowledge at different levels.
- Use the tool for teacher-assisted marking of student tasks, to speed up the assessment process by sorting the assignments roughly according to expected student knowledge, and also increase consistency by considering data from past student evaluations.
- Use data from the tool to measure student performance for getting feedback on how well students have understood various learning objectives in the course. Measured performance also includes timing data from the assessment process itself.
- Improve the course based on data from the assessment database of the tool. Identification of common fault modes for students can be used to improve the teaching to reduce the risks that the students fall into these pitfalls or learn misconceptions. The students can also be made aware of these common misconceptions during the course. Timing data from the tool can furthermore be used to identify bottlenecks during assessment in order to improve the assessment process itself.

This allows both the marking and course to undergo a continuous improvement process in a similar way as the well-known Plan Do Study Act (PDSA) method of improvement [12], where the teacher both learns how to improve the course content as well as how to improve own efficiency when teaching as well as when marking.

The method and tool does not aim at performing automatic grading. However, it still allows for faster marking of open-ended tasks with more consistent outcome and less cognitive load for the teacher during marking. An objective should be that the teacher only marks the differences between similar answers or answer archetypes instead of having to use energy on analysing the same answer several times at different times during marking. The approach allows for managing feedback to students to improve the learning outcome over time.

1.1 Motivation

Teachers and professors use a significant amount of their work time on marking assignments, as the following order estimate (or Fermi estimate) indicates. The biggest potential for the assessment method is in secondary and tertiary education, since these use open-ended questions to a greater degree than primary education. According to Eurostat there were 40 million students and 3.2 million teachers in primary and secondary education in 2013 [8]. Assuming that each student on average hands in approximately 60 exercises per year (four exercises and exam for six subjects per year), and that the teacher uses on average 15 min to mark each open-ended assignment, then in total 600 million work hours will be used on marking each year, corresponding to 347000 teacher positions.

If 20% of the exercises work for the method, and the saving time is 30% (4.5 min), then effort corresponding to 36 million hours or 20900 full teacher positions can be saved per year. This is a significant effort that can be used for better purposes, for example to improve the teaching, if the proposed method is deployed on a large scale.

We asked researchers on the social media ResearchGate what they meant was the most efficient method of designing and marking student assignments[1]. There was in general no consensus between teachers on this, however the researchers and professors had several good suggestions. Some claimed that multiple choice and short answer questions were the way to go, however others meant that multiple choice has limited use, since it only can be used to assess superficial knowledge. Others suggested that problem solving and case studies are the best ways for final student examinations, where you have a project as part of the evaluation. In general several good practices was suggested, such as assessing the student while learning (formative assessment) as well as when the student has learnt (summative assessment), as well as techniques for keeping focus whilst marking such as lock the door, unplug the phone and do not worry about decimals. Some also suggested planning with student peer review, following guidelines on what the students should focus at. This is obviously one way to reduce the teacher load, since the problem of marking the assignments then partially can be outsourced to the students.

Which assessment method you choose will however have a significant impact on the teacher - multiple choice questions are extremely teacher efficient, since they can be marked automatically. More open-ended questions in general takes longer time to mark, and are harder to mark efficiently. There have been some attempts on automatically marking open-ended essays, for example [9,13,20]. However the general consensus so far is that such methods are not sufficiently reliable to be used in practice. Our approach is aiming for a more modest goal - improve the efficiency of tool assisted marking.

Two important good practices that were suggested in the answers were to mark subassignments instead of each answer as well as sorting the papers according to marks for each section. This avoids that the teacher has to jump between

[1] https://www.researchgate.net/post/What_is_the_most_efficient_way_of_designing_and_marking_student_assignments.

good and poor students all the time and it reduces the cognitive load for the teacher by having to focus at one subtask at the time. The FrontScraper tool automates this good practice to improve marking speed and precision.

1.2 Problem Description

One of the more laborious tasks for a teacher is to mark and grade assignments and exams. We view this as a task that fundamentally does not scale, and with large courses with hundreds of students a simple exercise report can produce thousands of pages that have to be read and evaluated. Often the reading of hundreds of similar, but not equal answers can feel quite frustrating, and this can furthermore lead to impaired judgement. We, and many with us, have experienced this, however there does not appear to be any readily available solutions for mitigating this problem. There has been extensive research into how the evaluation process can be used to benefit the students, as well as some early research on automated grading, however there is less research on how to do the marking process more efficiently.

Most teachers or professors would probably agree that their evaluation of student assignments is not perfect. Teachers are only humans, and can have good days and bad days. The marking precision and performance can change accordingly. Several different biases can therefore occur when marking many assignments, for example:

- The teacher acquires new insight in the topic during the marking.
- Marking slips, or is skewed over time;
- The teacher loses attention while assessing the assignments;
- The teacher mixes in own knowledge when interpreting vague or overly brief answers;

All these factors may lead to this undesired result: The teacher fails to give a correct assessment of the answer, and thus may give it an incorrect grade.

Our vision is to simplify the marking process by providing the teacher with a technique and methodology for marking assignments more efficiently. The method provides a tentative ranking of student answers to sub-assignments based on their amount and diversity of information amongst others using an information-theoretic metric based on Shannon entropy.

2 Methodology and Tools for Improved Marking Efficiency

A methodology and supporting tool (FrontScraper) is used to support teacher assisted evaluation of open tasks. This includes designing tasks for markability, which means that assignments are designed and planned in a way that facilitates an efficient and precise marking process, as well as tool support for reducing the cognitive load and number of mental context switches that the teacher needs to do whilst marking.

In the future the methodology and tools should be more closely integrated as an LMS plugin to support multiple types of assignments, for example textual answers, multiple choice answers which can be marked automatically, software programming exercises and mathematical assignments. The method also provides more consistent feedback and grade to students with essentially the same type of answer and the same misconceptions.

2.1 Planning and Designing Assignments

When planning and designing assignments, the teacher should aim at testing for knowledge at different levels in Bloom's taxonomy of knowledge [2]. Testing for learnt facts is at the lower end of Bloom's taxonomy and can be done using simpler means such as multiple choice questions. Testing for understanding can however be done in a better and more reliable way using more open ended questions. This also avoids certain pitfalls with multiple choice based questions. It has for example been claimed that certain students with dyslexia may be disadvantaged, since they do not perceive the finer points of the questions and therefore more easily selects the wrong answer[2]. However later research claims that properly designed multiple choice questions, designed with accessibility in mind, does not give significantly different results from more open ended questions [14]. It is therefore important to plan and design the assignment both with accessibility and markability in mind. One advantage with more open ended questions is that it is easier to understand the student's fault mode or misconceptions with such questions. The teacher can then give the student more credit if they for example have given a good reasoning, but has missed or misunderstood some parts of the question.

Planning the assignments well includes letting the students know what you expect from them, so that the learning objectives and assessment criteria are consistent. Pretesting the assignments on a colleague is a good method for testing how well an assignment works.

We think it is important to develop the assignments so that they are not too open-ended or complex, since this can make the marking unnecessarily complex, and it can also make it difficult to compare the performance of the students. If a sub-assignment appears to be too complex, then it should be split it into smaller, more manageable sub-assignments. This also reduces the number of combinations of fault modes that you need to give feedback about, which facilitates a more targeted student feedback.

2.2 Clear Acceptance Criteria

To make the job as a teacher more efficient, we postulate a need to set some clear acceptance criteria on what an acceptable answer consists of. Without these criteria, one could end up with answers that are more difficult and labour intensive to mark than strictly necessary. A necessary criterion for tool-supported

[2] http://news.bbc.co.uk/2/hi/uk_news/magazine/7531132.stm.

marking methods, is that the answer follows a clearly defined format that can be parsed by the teaching support tools. This means that the following mandatory acceptance criteria must be followed:

- The student is clearly identified on the assignment.
- Verification that the answer follows the required report template.

A standardised exercise template is therefore a necessary requirement for more efficient assignment marking. The teacher could add other optional acceptance criteria as well, for example:

- Proper citations are being used, and quoted references are reasonable. A plagiarism checking tool (e.g. Sherlock or Ephorus) can be used to detect suspicious cases. Serious plagiarism instances can then be investigated and rejected from the marking.
- Set a maximum page or word limit for the answer, so that the student risks that the answer is not being marked beyond the maximum page limit. Such a maximum page limit is common both in research when writing scientific papers or project applications, as well as when writing articles for newspapers. Many universities have such limits as well. A page limit forces the students to think and prioritise the most important information. This also means that the students cannot easily choose an easy way out like cooking existing web resources, such as Wikipedia.

Those who write too voluminously will then need to learn to condense the answer, something that should increase the learning outcome. It would also prepare the student for the exam, when strict time limits can make voluminous writing a bad strategy. Such criteria may increase the quality of the answers, and at the same time make the job of evaluating them less arduous. The LMS needs an automatic test module to verify these constraints before accepting a student submission. In our case, such a test module could for example be implemented using the T-Flip assessment method which originally was intended used for testing software assignments [1].

2.3 Marking Principles

In principle, the teacher should only need to mark the same answer once. Similar answers should ideally be compared, and only significant differences should be checked, instead of the teacher having to mark hundreds of minor variants over the same theme. The assignment marking strategy should be able to identify the correct knowledge level of the students, to avoid too loose or strict judgement. The marking strategy should also be able to separate out the areas teachers think are easy doing first - marking the clear answers (very good or very bad). This means that the more fuzzy category or categories in the middle more easily may be done once the experience from the good and bad answers have been acquired.

A good strategy for the teacher or assessor is to mark one part assignment/sub-assignment at a time, to avoid mental context switch between different assignments. This ensures that the teacher more easily can keep different answer alternatives in mind and avoid having to write down and search for suitable comment alternatives to the answers. This makes it easier to remember the different types of answers to the sub-assignment on different levels.

2.4 Use of Our FrontScraper Tool

Figure 2 shows the FrontScraper tool in use. The FrontScraper console, which is used to manage the marking process, is shown in the upper right part of the picture. The console shows the list of comments that have been given to previous students for the given assignment. Console commands can be used to navigate to the next student, previous student, a given student etc. The learning management system (LMS) ClassFronter is shown to the left of the picture. It shows the feedback comments, evaluation and grade of the student being marked. The student answer being marked (anonymised) is shown in the lower right part of the picture. FrontScraper supports displaying the answer as text, as a least common denominator between different document formats, as well as displaying the original student answer.

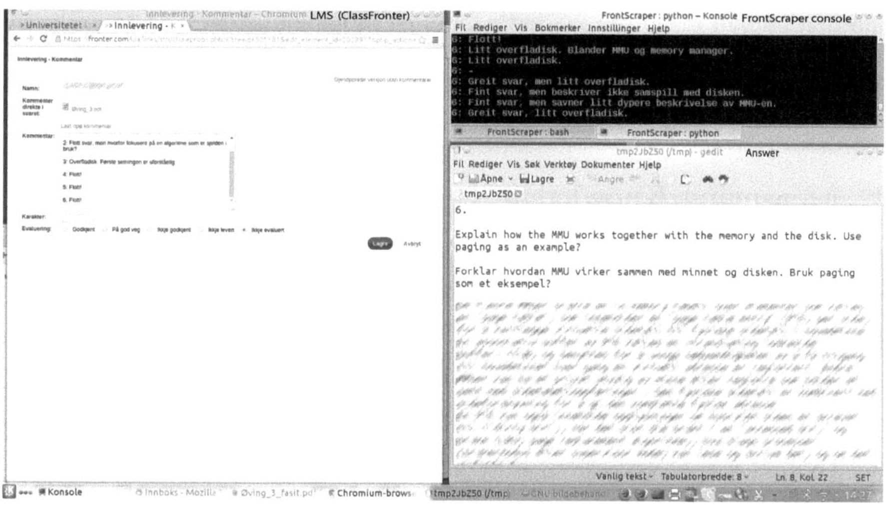

Fig. 2. FrontScraper tool (web scraper mode) used to mark student assignment.

The tool supports the marking process by downloading, parsing and splitting the student assignments into sub-assignments. It furthermore sorts the students according to an information entropy based "knowledge" metric, which ensures that the most comprehensive, and usually the best solutions, will be marked first. These are usually more motivating to mark for the teacher since it is rewarding to see how much the students have learnt, and the teacher might learn something from good answers as well. In addition, the marking speed typically increases as less and less comprehensive answers are marked, as illustrated in Fig. 13. The tool furthermore maintains a list of comment alternatives to different answers, sorted by usage frequency, which allows reusing earlier comments to give more consistent feedback to the students. Avoiding having to type in the same comment several times increases productivity.

Another advantage is that similar answers tend to be grouped together, which increases the efficiency even further, since the same comment then in many cases can be used for consecutive answers. The reason for this is that the entropy metric has the desirable property that a small document change will result in a small change in entropy [15]. This allows similar answers to be marked together, which improves the marking speed.

Other advantages with this approach, is that it allows the teacher to get through one or more sub-assignments in one day, which reduces the risk of judgements sliding over time. The tool maintains a list of distinct answers per assignment, which makes it easy to copy and paste previous answers where this is applicable.

The teacher can keep a note of different comments covering common failure modes for the students, and share these with the students. This allows the students to learn about common pitfalls based on past experience. Storing this information will make the teacher's marking more consistent over time. In the future it would even be an advantage to share information about common student failure modes, and how to avoid these between teachers to perform more efficient and focused teaching.

3 Measuring Knowledge

This section describes how knowledge can be measured. It gives an introduction to the information-theoretic model of knowledge as motivation for the entropy-based knowledge metric. This is then used as a measure of the amount of information in student answers.

What is knowledge? According to Dretske's information theoretic epistemology, mental facts can be defined as follows [5,7]:

(1) All mental facts are representational facts, and
(2) All representational facts are facts about *informational functions*.

With this definition of information in hand, Dretske gives the following definition of knowledge:

K knows that s is F = K's belief that s is F is caused (or causally sustained) by the information that s is F.

During an exam, assignment or test, a student reproduces her knowledge, which essentially means writing down information stating his or her belief of the causal relationships of gained information during the course. When the teacher has marked the assignment and the student reads the results, then her beliefs become knowledge.

Thus, according to Dretske, exams or assignments consist of information. By using information metrics, in this case information entropy, we get a measurable function representing a student's knowledge. Note that the teacher still is needed as an evaluator, since an information metric is not able to express whether the student's beliefs are *relevant or correct*, and only *relevant alternatives* should be considered according to Dretske [6].

It can furthermore be observed that these informational functions exist as representational facts. These representational facts are manifested by sentences of words in the student's answer. We do not aim at measuring the exact meaning of the students answer, but a good approximation of the complexity of the answer is word entropy, considering only the words that contribute to the factual information. The words that do not contribute significantly to factual information for a language L are called stop-words, denoted by S_L. There are standardised stop-word lists for different languages, for example the words "a, about, above, after,..." in English[3].

The representational facts, here denoted by X, can then be expressed more formally as the relative complement (or set difference) $W \backslash S_L$ between all words W in the answer A, $W \subset A$, and the set of stop-words S_L that are assumed to not contribute to the representational facts for the domain knowledge in a given natural language L. As long as the stop-words do not overlap significantly within the given factual knowledge domain, then the stop-words can be merged for a set of natural languages $\{L1, L2, ..., LN\}$, so that $X = A \backslash (S_{L1} \cup S_{L2} ... \cup S_{LN})$. Norway needs to consider the stop-words of three languages: $S_{Bokmål}$, $S_{Nynorsk}$ and $S_{English}$. The proposed information metric for measuring student answer knowledge can therefore be expressed as the word (or concept) Shannon entropy $H(X)$ for a set of words (or concepts) χ:

$$H(X) = \sum_{x \in \mathcal{X}} P[X = x] log \frac{1}{P[X = x]} \tag{1}$$

An advantage with an information theoretic metric for coarse-sifting through answers, is that it is largely agnostic to the underlying written language. For Norwegian universities this is important, since answers can be in either of the two Norwegian languages (Bokmål or Nynorsk) or English. In Northern Norway, Sami may additionally be used.

4 System Architecture

The original system architecture of FrontScraper is shown in Fig. 3. FrontScraper is implemented in Python and uses the Selenium WebDriver[4] as a web-scraper for interfacing towards the web interface of the Learning Management System (LMS) ClassFronter [17]. This allows for tight integration with the LMS, and at the same time allows FrontScraper to manage the marking and navigation

[3] Stop-word lists: https://code.google.com/archive/p/stop-words/.

[4] Selenium WebDriver: http://seleniumhq.org.

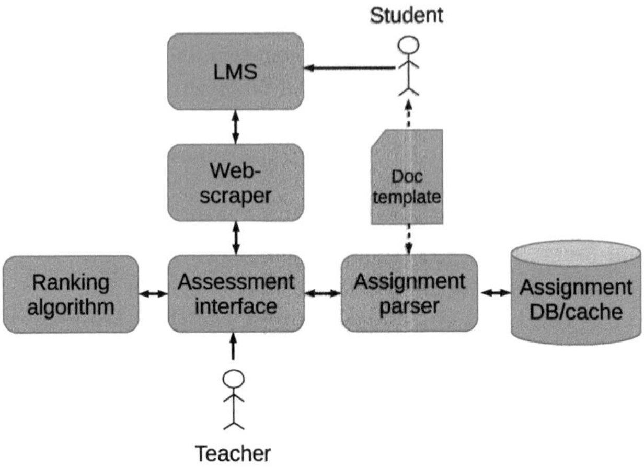

Fig. 3. Web scraper system architecture (original FrontScraper).

between students using the assessment interface. A disadvantage with the original solution, is that the web scraper is quite fragile, and easily breaks if the LMS web pages change. In order to mitigate this, an off-line mode was added to FrontScraper as shown in Fig. 4. This allows the tool to be used on assignments exported from the LMS in .zip format. An assessment database (PostgreSQL database) was added for offline mode to store grades and comments to the individual sub-assignments during marking. The assessment database has also been integrated with the web scraper module to store the data history when the tool operates in web scraper mode. The assessment database stores historic data for subsequent data analysis, for example to correlate assessment metrics with grade to identify the best metric or to analyse the marking performance or grade distribution of different courses or over different years. The offline mode has the advantage that the tool can be used by personnel who have not got access to the LMS, such as external examiners, and it reduces the strain on the LMS without loss of assessment functionality. In the future, we plan to add support for a standardised interface towards the LMS, such as LTI to allow the assessment tool to be used as an integrated plugin to the LMS.

The assessment interface is used for identifying and downloading the student assignment, as well as navigating between student answers. The current set of sub-assignments being marked are ranked according to the Shannon entropy based ranking algorithm. The ranking algorithm disregards stop-words in the languages being considered (Norwegian, Nynorsk and English) and creates a unique index per word. The algorithm then calculates the entropy of the word index and ranks the assignments from high to low entropy, so that the teacher starts with marking the typically most comprehensive answers first. Caching of student assignments is supported in the assignment database/cache to reduce the LMS load when performing marking across sub-assignments. The assignment parser is used to parse the student assignment according to a supported document template used for student assignments. It is mandatory for the students

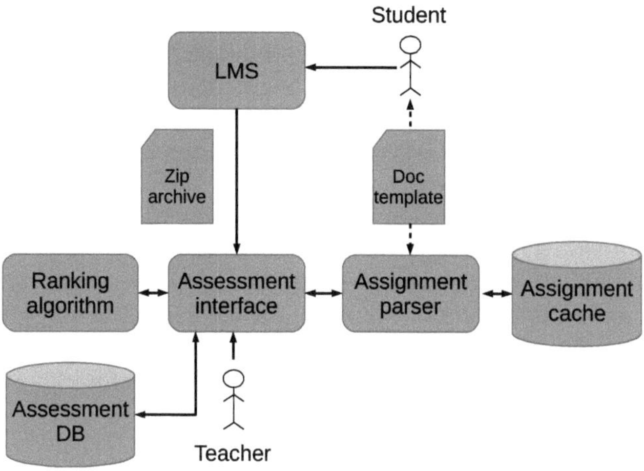

Fig. 4. Off-line system architecture.

to use a supported document template so that FrontScraper is able to reliably detect the sub-assignments of the student answers when marking. FrontScraper supports a sanity check (checkAssignments.py) which can be used to verify that the student answers are being split into the expected number of sub-assignments.

4.1 Marking Algorithm

The marking algorithm works from a high-level perspective as follows: First, the web-scraper is initialised, which starts up the browser connected to the LMS. The teacher can then log in to the LMS and go to the hand-in folder to be marked in a new browser tab. FrontScraper then reads information about all M students $\{s_1, s_2, \ldots, s_M\}$ in the hand-in folder, and then reads the submitted answers $A = \{a_1, a_2, ..., a_M\}$ from the students. The tool initially tries to read the cached answer in the assignment database/cache, and if the document is not cached, then it is read directly from the LMS. This reduces the load of running FrontScraper on the LMS. The tool then splits each the assignment into N sub-assignments $\{a_{1,1}, a_{1,2}, ..., a_{M,N}\}$ and caches the results in the assignment database/cache.

Then each word of the current sub-answer $a_{i,j}$ is converted into a unique integer word code $w_{i,j} = wordCode(a_{i,j})$ for each word in the answer that is not in the set of stop-words, which are ignored. The first word is assigned word code 1, the second distinct word code 2, and so on... For example, the text "A computer file system stores information in a computer." has the non-stop words "computer file system stores information computer". The word code for this text string would be $w_{i,j} = \{1, 2, 3, 4, 5, 1\}$. This is implemented using a dictionary which stores the next word code for any words not in the dictionary. This means that each word code representing a word essentially is one symbol in the entropy calculations. After that the ranking algorithm is then calculated on the list of word codes representing the current sub-assignment $a_{i,j}$ being marked, i.e. $r_{i,j} = rank(w_{i,j})$. For Shannon entropy, the ranking function would for example be $r_{i,j} = H(w_{i,j})$. The list of assignments being marked is then sorted according to the rank r_i of the given sub-assignment i algorithm being marked, so that the teacher starts with marking the typically most comprehensive answers and ends with the typically least comprehensive answers of the sub-assignment.

The tool then iterates through the sorted assignments and lets the teacher mark the candidate. The teacher can choose from the palette of previous answers for the given sub-assignment to speed up the feedback to the students. The algorithm in addition supports commands for navigating to the *previous, next, first* and *last* candidate as well as *candidate i*. Finally, when all sub-assignments have been marked, then the teacher can set the final grade for each student based on the comments and results for all sub-assignments.

5 Experiments

The experiments in this paper is based on the DAT103 Operating System course at our University in spring 2016. The experiments differ from the experiments in [17] by investigating whether there is a correlation between the entropy metrics per subanswer whereas the original paper investigated correlation per answer for a whole assignment. One can expect different results as well as more noise by focusing on more fine-grained information. In addition, the paper aims at performing a preliminary investigation on which entropy metric that is best at estimating student answer quality by performing an ordinal logistic regression analysis of how well the metrics fit the data. The experiments include the results from marking two assignments: assignment 2 and 3, which was marked by different teachers. Assignment 2 was marked without the FrontScraper tool and assignment 3 with it. The data set contains the results from 1471 marked subanswer (675 by teacher 1 and 796 by teacher 2). There were 76 students participating in exercise 2 and 72 students in exercise 3. Figures 5 and 6 show

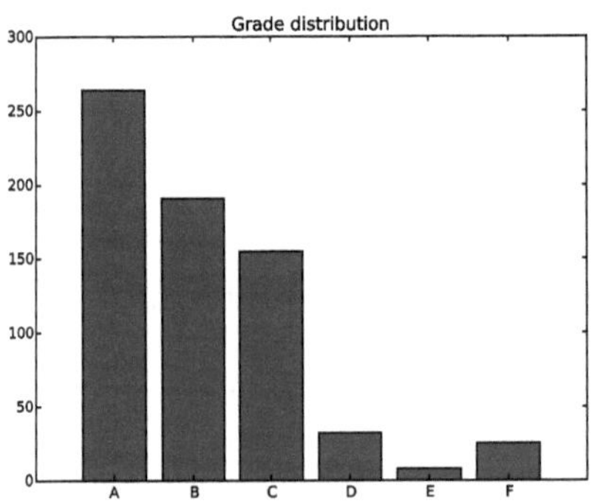

Fig. 5. Assignment 2 grade distribution per subassignment.

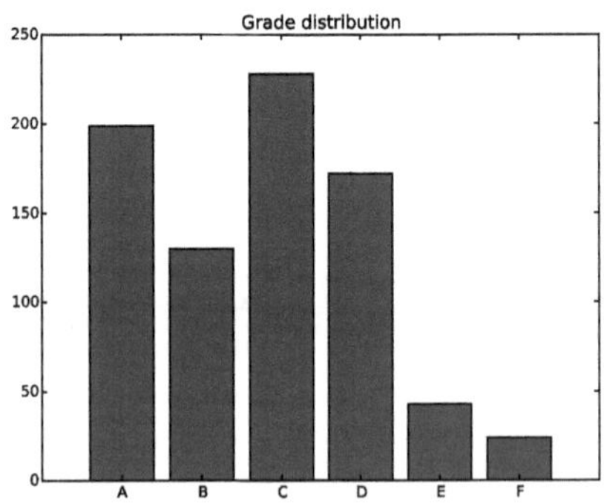

Fig. 6. Assignment 3 grade distribution per subassignment

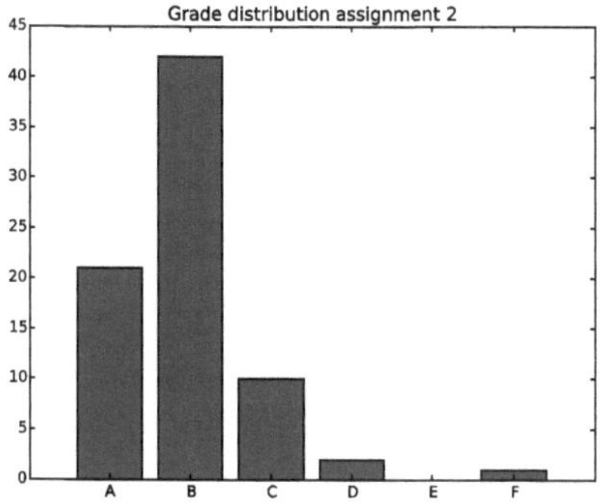

Fig. 7. Grade distribution for entire assignment 2.

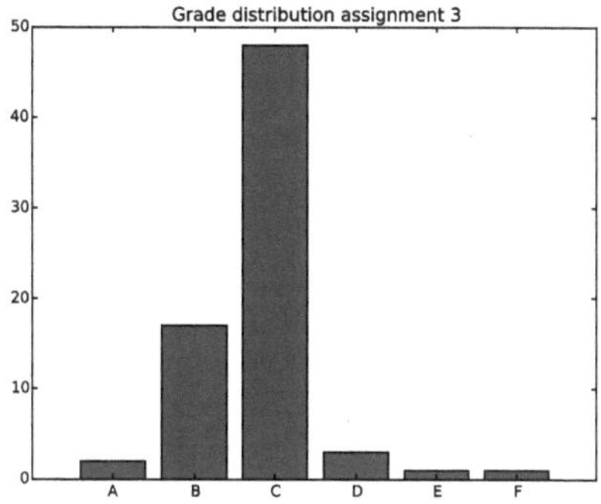

Fig. 8. Grade distribution for entire assignment 3.

the grade distribution for assignment 2 and 3 respectively. Both distributions are biased towards better grades, however these results are per sub-answer for a hand-in exercise. The overall grade for all students is less skewed as shown in Figs. 7 and 8, since a typical student will have a mix of different grades for the subanswer of an assignment.

Figures 9 and 10 show how the Shannon entropy $H(X)$ correlates with grade. The first figure shows the results of assignment 2 marked by teacher 1 without FrontScraper and the second figure shows the results of assignment 3 marked by teacher 2 using FrontScraper. Both figures show that the entropy increases with increasing grade from grade E to A for both assignments, corresponding to increasing information in the answer. The results for grade F is however different. F shows both high entropy and large variation. The reason for this is probably that there are many ways to fail. Some students have very good answers, but they were plagiarised. Other students failed because of empty answers. There were also students that misunderstood the question or guessed the answer in this category. This is a new finding compared to the original paper, which focused on the entropy of the entire assignment. This effect becomes more apparent when focusing on whether individual subassignments fail.

A limitation with entropy as a measure of information content, is that the entropy only depends on word frequencies. It is therefore possible to have a very brief answer with high entropy. The extreme example is an answer with a distinct set of unique words (e.g. "I do not know the answer"), which would have a word entropy of 1. One way to mitigate this problem, is to also consider the length of the student answer in words $|X|$ as part of the heuristic on how comprehensive the student answer is. It is however recommendable to penalize overly long answers. One way to do this, is to multiply the entropy with the square root of the word length, so that the indicator considers a combination of information diversity and content length, however penalizing the benefit of overly long answers. This also avoids the risk that some comprehensive answers that use a relatively simple language get a too poor ranking, for example if the student uses longer descriptions with fewer words in the explanation. The advantage with this metric is that it allows for coarse-sifting student answers from poor, via medium to good answers.

Figures 11 and 12 show boxplots with the correlation between grade and the square root of word length $\sqrt{|X|}$ for assignment 2 and 3 respectively. The trend is the same as for plain entropy, indicating that many students lose out due to writing too brief answers rather than writing good answers. This is however an assignment that is an open book exam - the candidates have all information available. It is therefore perhaps not the best test of their own acquired knowledge, since they could pick existing good answers as long as they referenced them properly. Entropy might have more of an effect in a closed exam, where the students own knowledge is tested to a greater degree, and not their ability to put together existing information. Investigating this is however left as future work.

Ordinal logistic regression is a statistical method that can be used to identify which of the metrics that fit the marked grade best. An advantage with this method is that it assumes that the grade scale is an ordinal scale, but it does not make any assumptions about the distance between the grades apart from the order. Based on the preanalysis where it was identified that grade F does not fit the model, then we aim at performing the regression analysis for the remaining grades E, C, D, B, A. The practical meaning of this is that the proposed metrics will be poorer at predicting F grades (failures), which will occur randomly among the students. The exception is the special case of empty answers which fits the model.

Table 1. Ordinal logistic regression analysis of grade described by metric candidates.

Model	Std. error	Wald Z	LRχ^2	$Pr(>\chi^2)$
Assignment 2				
$Grade \sim H(X)$	0.09	7.8	57	<0.0001
$Grade \sim \sqrt{\lvert X\rvert}$	0.31	9.2	99	<0.0001
$Grade \sim \sqrt{\lvert X\rvert} \cdot H(X)$	0.03	8.6	85	<0.0001
Assignment 3				
$Grade \sim H(X)$	0.10	8.7	79	<0.0001
$Grade \sim \sqrt{\lvert X\rvert}$	0.37	10.3	119	<0.0001
$Grade \sim \sqrt{\lvert X\rvert} \cdot H(X)$	0.04	9.8	104	<0.0001

The ordinal logistic regression model (lrm) in R is then used to estimate the parameters of the model using the maximum likelihood approach. This paper does not repeat the underlying well-known theory [19]. We tested different models using ordinal logistic regression, as shown in Table 1. Models with two degrees of freedom ($Grade \sim \sqrt{|X|} + H(X)$) was rejected, since the entropy factor then was not statistically significant ($P = 0.08$). However both entropy $H(X)$, square

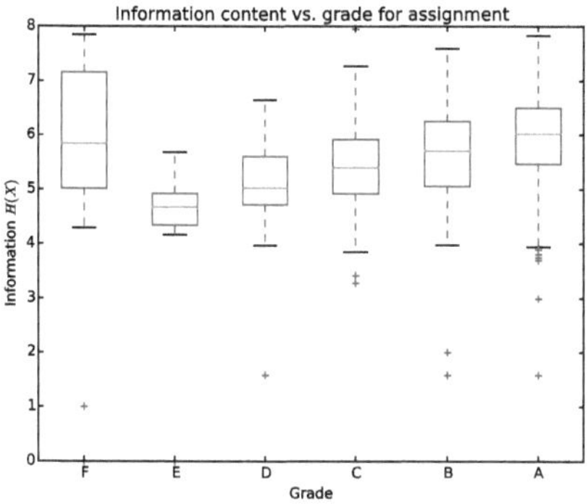

Fig. 9. $H(X)$ for assignment 2 as a function of grade marked without FrontScraper.

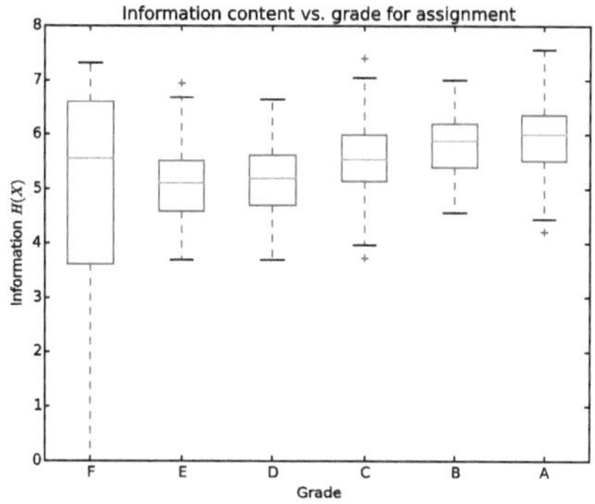

Fig. 10. $H(X)$ for assignment 3 as a function of grade marked with FrontScraper.

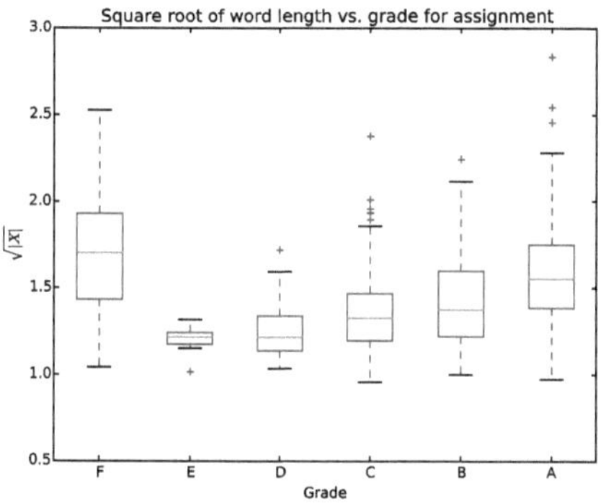

Fig. 11. Square root of word length $\sqrt{|X|}$ for assignment 2 as a function of grade marked without FrontScraper.

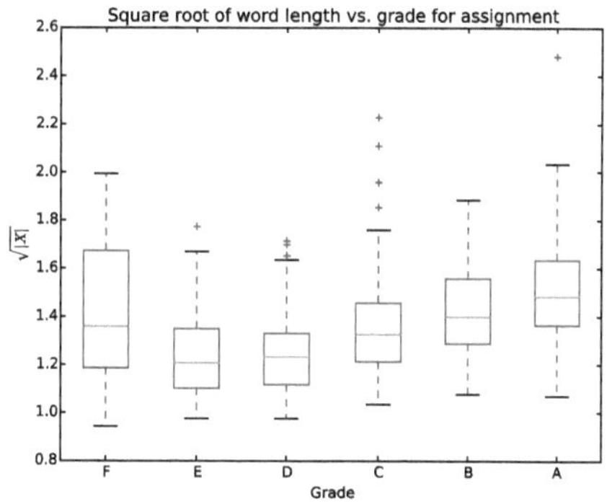

Fig. 12. Square root of word length $\sqrt{|X|}$ for assignment 3 as a function of grade marked with FrontScraper.

root of word length $\sqrt{|X|}$ as well as the length corrected entropy $\sqrt{|X|} \cdot H(X)$ are all statistically significant. The overall best metric according to the regression analysis is the square root of word length. Future research involve investigating whether entropy term weighting based on past assessments as well as reinforced learning can be used to improve the ranking function.

It may be possible to do even better using knowledge-based marking strategies, such as Latent Semantic Analysis (LSA) which also considers semantic clues from the words in the text [9,10,13,20], however this is at the expense of having to build up a suitable set of good model answers. An advantage with our simple metric, is that it works without a database of model answers. Our method can in the future be extended with more advanced ranking algorithms such as LSA by building on the database of already marked answers.

Figure 13 shows the time used per subassignment during the marking of assignment 3. Only one teacher marked this subassignment using the

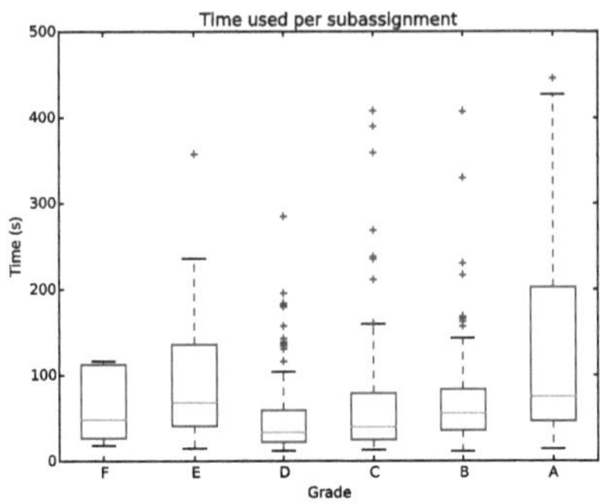

Fig. 13. Time used for marking subassignments as a function of grade.

FrontScraper tool in offline mode. 72 students were marked, and there were 9 subassignments in it, in total 648 answers were marked, excluding a multiple choice assignment that can be marked automatically. In general, it does not make sense to use this approach for marking multiple-choice questions, since the entropy of the answer cannot be used to distinguish between the candidates (there were only two boxes ticked in the answer - the entropy metric does not care where these are ticked.) The boxplot shows the median, upper and lower quartile and min/max values as well as outliers marked with crosses. The figure only shows marking time up to 500 s to avoid outliers such as when the teacher takes a break or the freetime between working days. The median marking time per task is 48 s, meaning that the 648 subassignment should be possible to mark in approximately 7.6 effective hours if the examiner can focus 100% on the job. The marking of this assignment required more time than this in practice (4.4 days), since the off-line version of FrontScraper was developed and debugged in parallel with the marking.

A-candidates required the most effort to mark (median grade 74 s). These candidates typically wrote very good answers, but also usually more complex and longer answers than other students. The distribution for A candidates is heavily skewed towards longer marking times, since these candidates may come with new information that must be checked for relevance by the teacher before a grade can be set. B, C and D candidates take successively shorter time to mark (median B = 55 s, C = 37 s and D = 31 s), typically because of less reading time due to shorter answers that lacked some of the information in better answers. This quantifies the effect the examiner has experienced, that the marking speed generally increases as the poorer and shorter answers are being marked. E and F candidates took longer to assess (median E = 65 s, F = 46 s) since these answers were vague and mostly nonrelevant, making them harder to assess for the examiner. There are however relatively few such answers (22 F's and 39 E's), so these do not impact the overall marking time so much. The bulk of the candidates have a subanswer grade in the range B, C and D, which are relatively fast to mark.

6 Discussion

The main innovations in the assessment method and tools is allowing for marking of subassignments sorted according to information content. This minimises mental context switching and fatigue for the teacher, and gives more consistent grading. The tool supports navigating between answers and also supports giving students feedback and information about performance and common fault modes whilst marking as shown in Table 2. The table shows that the most commonly occurring problem is that students have misconceptions about the topic being taught, followed by the student mixing knowledge meaning that a concept has not been properly learnt, and third incomplete answer to the assignment. The teacher can then work on mitigating these and other identified problems during the subsequent course, allowing for feedback to improve the course in subsequent years.

Table 2. Top ten fault modes identified during marking of Assignment 3.

#	Fault mode
26	Misconceptions
19	Mixes knowledge
18	Did not answer part of the assignment
11	Candidate guesses answer
11	Plagiarism
11	Uncertain/poor explanation
8	Language translation problem
3	Candidate did not answer the question
3	Excessively long answer

The entropy metrics ensure that similar answers typically are grouped together and also has the nice property that the metric correlates roughly with grade. An advantage is that the solution is language independent, since this is one of the main obstacles for including such metrics by most LMS vendors.

Marking assignments "across" sub-assignments has the advantage that the teacher tends to use the grade scale more consistently, since the teacher compares each sub-assignment with others on a fair ground, instead of being biased by previous answers by the student. This avoids the risk that the teacher becomes overcautious if a student has a bad start on the assignment. Furthermore, if the teacher has a poor day, then this affects all students more equally by marking across sub-assignment answers, than if marking of entire assignments is being used. It must furthermore be emphasised that the ranking method requires manual quality assurance by the teacher. It is not suitable for automatic grading since it would be possible for the student to manipulate the ranking by writing varying, but not necessarily relevant text.

An additional benefit by using this approach, is that sub-assignments that are equal or very similar typically will be marked next to each other, which makes it easy to detect plagiarism in the form of copying of answers between students.

7 Related Works

Our approach uses a methodology for improved planning, definition and grading of assignments and exams that uses an entropy-based metric for ranking assignments, together with a supporting tool for marking across sub-assignments.

Another popular approach for performing automatic grading of essays and similar answer texts is using Latent Semantic Analysis (LSA) [9,13,20]. This method aims at performing automatic grading of the content by comparing the answers to select learning material and human-graded essays. Our approach does not aim at performing automatic grading, but rather being a system for improved content organisation and support for teacher based grading. Our approach is simple compared to LSA, however it also has the advantage of being general, language independent and not requiring the pre-training to learn the concepts required for automatic grading as LSA does. A limitation with our solution is, however that it uses a simple heuristic measure of answer complexity based on information diversity and length, and does not attempt to understand the text semantics.

An ontology-based hierarchical knowledge metric for student learning assessment was proposed by [3]. This metric operates with four different knowledge levels and defines a knowledge metric loosely based on Shannon entropy. It furthermore uses a semantic measure of similarity based on [11]. The metric is relatively complex, and not easy to calculate automatically. The paper only presents results from a case study. Our solution is simpler, based on pure Shannon word entropy and easy to automate. Our experiments show that the metric is useful for improving the speed of teacher-supported assessment.

Probabilistic Latent Semantic Analysis (PLSA) is a statistical technique for the analysis of co-occurrence of words. The parameters of PLSA are learnt using Expectation Maximisation based unsupervised clustering. This method has been implemented in the automatic essay grading system AEA [10]. Both LSA and PLSA can use entropy-based term weighting in order to give higher values to words that are more important [10].

There are several code quality assessment systems that are useful for automatic feedback to student's submitted code for programming exercises. They are however usually restricted to evaluating code in one specific programming language. These tools may be based on error checking, code metrics, machine learning, or a combination of these [1].

Other methods that have been suggested are amongst others k-nearest neighbour, Naïve Bayes, artificial neural networks and decision tree for classifying programming exercises as either well written or poorly written [1,18].

A different, but somewhat related area of research, is the quantitative analysis of different grading policies in education [16]. This research suggests that the entropy of a grading scheme measures the amount of information carried by a student's grade and therefore a grading scheme should be chosen which maximises the entropy of the student grades, whilst also having high consistency in the grading over time. This research uses entropy for a different purpose than our paper, since it is used for theoretical analysis of the performance of different grading schemes.

Moodle supports Turnitin's GradeMark, which can be integrated with a plagiarism checking tool and allows the instructors to grade and mark up papers using a set of standard and custom comments [4]. Our approach is different by providing a work-flow that marks across sub-answers using an information metric that allows for coarse sorting the assignments into the comprehensive and the superficial ones, which aids in determining the correct overall level of the group. It inherently has the desirable property of clustering answers that are very similar, which increases the marking speed, since similar answers can get similar comments.

8 Conclusions

This paper introduces a method and tool for marking open text-based questions based on answer ranking metrics. The tool FrontScraper is originally based on a web scraper which interacts with ClassFronter. It supports navigating between answers and keeps a list of unique answers given to students. It also caches results locally to reduce the load on the LMS.

An offline mode was added to create a more robust solution that is independent of LMS implementation and to allow external examiners to assess the student tasks without requiring a user on the LMS. This also avoids the strain on the LMS when using the system and it allows for a solution that is independent of LMS.

FrontScraper increases the marking speed and precision significantly by supporting marking sub-assignments instead of whole assignments. This also reduces the risk of grade slipping, and it ensures that a bad day for the teacher affects students more fairly. The knowledge metric sorts answers roughly from good to poor grade and allows for implicit plagiarism detection since equal answers come side-by-side and similar answers typically are close to each other. The method is relatively simple but robust, since it does not rely on reinforced learning, which would require an existing database of answers.

9 Future Work

Future work includes a larger evaluation of FrontScraper using more comprehensive experiments. This also includes testing and adapting the tool to different subjects and disciplines. We furthermore envisage that by storing information about grade and common fault modes, then the assessment database being built up using this tool can be used to support a transition towards machine supported grading based on for example LSA in the future. This also includes combining the solution with other pedagogical methods, such as peer-to-peer evaluation and formative assessment to inspire high-quality student answers.

Future work also involves improving the tool, user interface and LMS integration, supporting user-centered design to remove bottlenecks whilst marking as well as supporting standardised LMS interfaces such as LTI or xAPI. The project also aims at highlighting the difference between student answers in the future, to make it easier to achieve the objective of marking only the differences in text between answers.

A follow-up project aims at disseminating the solution world-wide based on an open source reference implementation and collaboration with a commercial LMS vendor.

References

1. Barstad, V., Goodwin, M., Gjøsæter, T.: Predicting source code quality with static analysis and machine learning. In: Proceedings of NIK 2014. Norsk Informatikkonferanse (2014)
2. Bloom, B.S., Others, A.: Handbook on Formative and Summative Evaluation of Student Learning. McGraw-Hill, New York (1971)
3. Braham, R.: A knowledge metric with applications to learning assessment. In: Proceedings of KEOD 2010, pp. 5–9. SciTePress - Science and Technology Publications (2010)
4. Buckley, E., Cowap, L.: An evaluation of the use of Turnitin for electronic submission and marking and as a formative feedback tool from an educator's perspective. Br. J. Educ. Tech. **44**(4), 562–570 (2013)
5. Dretske, F.: Knowledge and the Flow of Information. MIT Press, Cambridge (1981)
6. Dretske, F.: Perception, Knowledge and Belief: Selected Essays. Cambridge University Press, Cambridge (2000)
7. Dretske, F.I.: Naturalizing the Mind. MIT Press, Cambridge (1997)
8. Eurostat: Education and training in the EU - facts and figures (2013)
9. Foltz, P.W., Laham, D., Landauer, T.K., Foltz, P.W., Laham, D., Landauer, T.K.: Automated essay scoring: applications to educational technology. In: Proceedings of EdMedia 1999, vol. 1999, pp. 939–944 (1999)
10. Kakkonen, T., Myller, N., Timonen, J., Sutinen, E.: Automatic essay grading with probabilistic latent semantic analysis. In: Proceedings of the Second Workshop on Building Educational Applications Using NLP, EdAppsNLP 2005, pp. 29–36. Association for Computational Linguistics, Stroudsburg (2005)
11. Lin, D.: An information-theoretic definition of similarity. In: Proceedings of the 15th International Conference on Machine Learning, pp. 296–304. Morgan Kaufmann (1998)
12. Moen, R.D., Nolan, T.W., Provost, L.P.: Quality Improvement Through Planned Experimentation. McGraw-Hill, New York (1999)
13. Rehder, B., Schreiner, M.E., Wolfe, M.B.W., Laham, D., Landauer, T.K., Kintsch, W.: Using latent semantic analysis to assess knowledge: some technical considerations. Discourse Process. **25**(2–3), 337–354 (1998)
14. Ricketts, C., Brice, J., Coombes, L.: Are multiple choice tests fair to medical students with specific learning disabilities? Adv. Health Sci. Educ. **15**(2), 265–275 (2009)

15. Shannon, C.E.: A mathematical theory of communication. Bell Syst. Tech. J. **27**(379–423), 623–656 (1948)
16. Sikora, A.S.: Mathematical theory of student assessment through grading (2015)
17. Ulltveit-Moe, N., Assev, S., Gjøsæter, T., Øysæd, H.: Streamlining assessment using a knowledge metric. In: Proceedings of CSEDU 2016, pp. 190–197. SCITEPRESS - Science and Technology Publications (2016)
18. Valenti, S., Neri, F., Cucchiarelli, A., Valenti, S., Neri, F., Cucchiarelli, A.: An overview of current research on automated essay grading. J. Inf. Technol. Educ. Res. **2**(1), 319–330 (2003)
19. Winship, C., Mare, R.D.: Regression models with ordinal variables. Am. Sociol. Rev. **49**, 513–524 (1984)
20. Zen, K., Iskandar, D., Linang, O.: Using Latent Semantic Analysis for automated grading programming assignments. In: 2011 International Conference on Semantic Technology and Information Retrieval (STAIR), pp. 82–88 (2011)

The Problem Distiller Tool: Supporting Teachers in Uncovering Why Their Students Have Problems Understanding Threshold Concepts

Sara Cruz[1], José Alberto Lencastre[1(✉)], Clara Coutinho[1], Gill Clough[2], and Anne Adams[2]

[1] Institute of Education, University of Minho, Braga, Portugal
sara.acruz@gmail.com,
{jlencastre,ccoutinho}@ie.uminho.pt
[2] Institute of Educational Technology, Open University, Milton Keynes, UK
{gill.clough,anne.adms}@open.ac.uk

Abstract. This study explored the use of a web-based tool entitled 'Problem Distiller' designed to support teachers in uncovering why their students have problems understanding Threshold Concepts. Data collected involved interviews with two math teachers, invited to experiment the Problem Distiller tool and Think Aloud protocol. Content analysis was used to process and analyse the collected data. Findings show that teachers found it helpful when the information they entered through the Problem Distiller was fed back as they constructed an online diagnostic quiz. Focusing on the teachers' understanding of why the students have problems is an effective way of tackling the barriers posed by Threshold Concepts and can be integrated with existing strategies and teaching approaches.

Keywords: Threshold Concepts · Tricky Topics · Technology-enhanced learning · Deeper understanding

1 Introduction

Threshold Concepts are fundamental topics in education without which students cannot progress in the subject [8]. They frequently contain 'troublesome knowledge' that students struggle to understand, sometimes taking refuge in memorisation (without understanding). Threshold Concepts can be so hard to comprehend that they can create in students a state of anxiety and confusion [15], and lead them to fail or give up a subject altogether [12]. Although Threshold Concepts have been identified in different disciplines, these topics are particularly common in STEM - Science, Technology, Engineering and Mathematics-, and they are often the reason that leads the students to give up studying subjects in these areas.

How to identify a Threshold Concept and distinguish them from other learning topics has provoked debate between academics. According to Meyer and Land [14], a concept is likely to be threshold if it has one or more of the following criteria:

G. Costagliola et al. (Eds.): CSEDU 2016, CCIS 739, pp. 380–401, 2017.
DOI: 10.1007/978-3-319-63184-4_20

- **Transformative** – once understood, it *potentially* causes a significant shift in the perception of a subject (or part thereof); sometimes it may even transform one's personal identity.
- **Irreversible** – it is unlikely that a Threshold Concept is forgotten or unlearned once acquired due to transformation.
- **Integrative** – a Threshold Concept is able to expose "the previously hidden interrelatedness of something".
- **Bounded** – a Threshold Concept can have borders with other Threshold Concept which help to define disciplinary areas.
- **Troublesome** – they may be counter-intuitive (common sense understanding vs. expert understanding).

It is unclear how many of these five characteristics are required to define a concept as a Threshold Concept. Nevertheless, the authors emphasize that once understood the Threshold Concept allows the student to be able to solve problems with degree of advanced difficulty [16].

Thus, enabling the student to comprehend a Threshold Concept is a concern for any teacher. Understanding the causes of the students' difficulty helps the teacher to help them and also to adopt appropriate teaching strategies to support the student in overcoming these difficulties.

In this paper we review the JuxtaLearn Problem Distiller, a tool designed to support teachers in uncovering why their students have problems understanding Threshold Concepts. The tool displays a set of tabbed panes "prompting teachers to reflect on and select possible reasons why their students might be having a particular problem, connecting all the information entered to the appropriate tricky topic and stumbling block or blocks" ([2], p. 6). In the JuxtaLearn project 'Tricky Topic' was the name we use to refer to the Threshold Concepts identified by the teacher in their practice with students. For a deeper understanding of this approach see: "Threshold Concepts Vs. Tricky Topics" [9].

In Sect. 2, we present examples of studies with different modes for identifying Threshold Concepts. The Sect. 3, we present the Problem Distiller Tool, the JuxtaLearn approach to adapt theories of Threshold Concepts into teachers' practices. In Sect. 4, we present the methods for the data collection and analysis processes. In Sect. 5 we present our main results and reflections. We conclude in Sect. 6 with a synthesis and proposals for future work.

2 Review of Studies

Much academic effort has been devoted to theoretically understanding and identifying Threshold Concepts, but little of this has translated into their practical application in educational settings.

Loertscher, Green, Lewis, Lin and Minderhout [11] conducted a study involving 75 teachers and 50 students, where involved an iterative process intended to identify threshold concepts in biochemistry. These authors used a process to identify threshold concepts that consists of five phases: (phase 1) pilot student focus group interviews, (phase 2) interdisciplinary life sciences workshop, (phase 3) biochemistry core collaborators workshop and dissemination workshop, (phase 4) student focus group interviews and (phase 5) data analysis and determination of a working list of threshold concepts. Using this process, they were able to identify threshold concepts that are fundamental to the deeper understanding of biochemistry but are also strongly related to fundamental concepts of chemistry and biology.

Meyer, Knight, Callaghan and Baldock [16] conducted a case study which used a data triangulation approach to identify threshold concepts that students should understand before solving specific problems of a civil engineering course. For collection purposes teachers took part in dialogue on understanding and conceptual capacity enabling learning for all participants in the process. They concluded that involving the various course stakeholders in an analysis about conceptual understanding and capacity makes learning achievable to all process participants. It also provides a basis for pedagogies and evaluations to facilitate advanced results in students.

Barradell and Kennedy-Jones [6] introduced a conceptual model that integrates three components: the (i) students learning, the (ii) threshold concepts and (iii) curriculum. According to this holistic model, when students talk about the threshold concepts they encounter various ideas. When these ideas are understood as part of a whole, they provide a more systematic way of thinking about how to improve educational practice.

JuxtaLearn approach focuses on adapting theories of Threshold Concepts into teachers' practical application with Tricky Topics, so that they can be integrated with the practice-based approach of teachers.

3 The Problem Distiller Tool

Co-developed with teachers, and included in the CLIPIT - the Web Space for the JuxtaLearn project-, the Tricky Topic Tool (Fig. 1) is an "in progress" online database with a catalogue of Threshold Concepts and /or Tricky Topics shaped by teachers from their perspective and based on their practice.

After several trials done in the UK and Portugal, the CLIPIT has a database with a lot of Tricky Topics.

This list of Threshold Concepts is under construction. If a Threshold Concept does not already exist in the Tricky Topic Tool, added, for example, by another teacher, the teacher can add one that fits their students' learning problems. In order to populate the Tricky Topic Tool the teacher has to enter the name of the Tricky Topic and write a description of the student's specific problem with that topic (Fig. 1).

Once the teacher adds the Tricky Topic she/he can link it into some 'Stumbling Blocks', i.e. learning barriers he thinks that the problem can be broken down into and which are commonly found by her/his students, using another feature of the Tricky Topic Tool: The Problem Distiller (Fig. 2). It is easy for the teacher to reuse a listed concept that has already been identified and added to the Tricky Topic Tool by another teacher and to add, remove or change an already described challenges in the platform for their students.

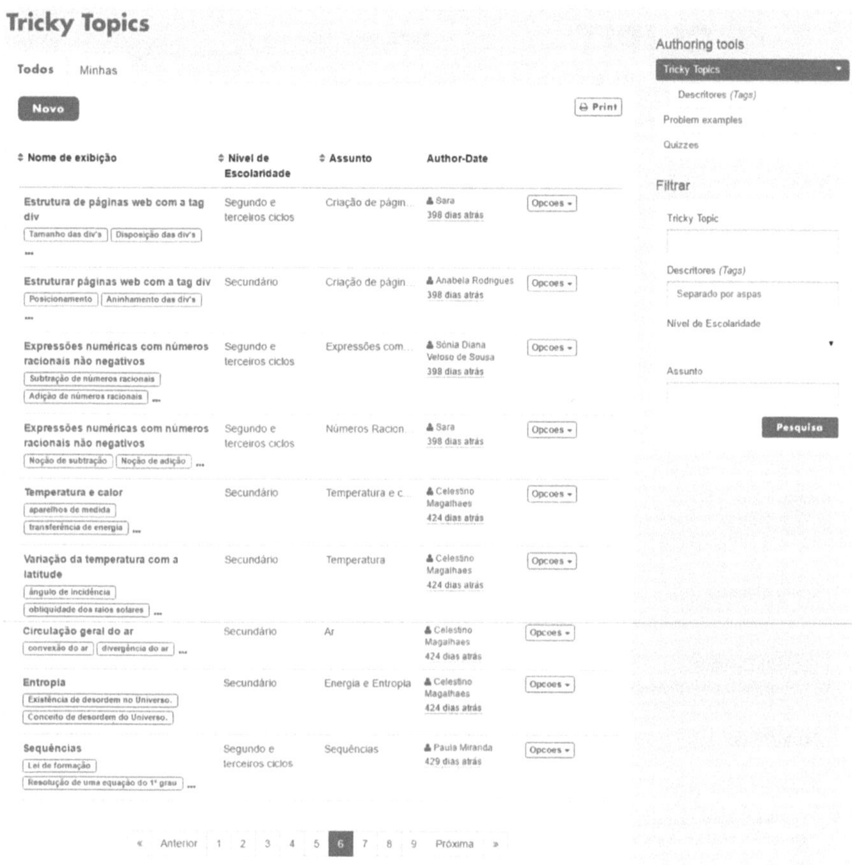

Fig. 1. Tricky topic database.

The Problem examples are classified using four categories that were obtained during the first cycle of activities – interviews, workshops - conducted with teachers in the UK. These four categories are: 'Terminology', 'Intuitive Beliefs', 'Incomplete pre-knowledge' and 'Complementary Concepts'. This information is passed through to the quiz question authoring tool, focusing the question authoring on probing the students' understanding rather than simply mapping directly onto a topic as taught in class [2].

The category 'Terminology' refers to the fact that "in all the subjects explored during the interviews and workshops, terminology was a big issue, everyday terms acquiring a different meaning when used as part of a scientific discourse, new scientific terms being introduced, one term meaning different things in different contexts, multiple scientific terms used to refer to the same thing" (JuxtaLearn Project Deliverable Report D2.1 – Taxonomy).

The category 'Intuitive Beliefs' refers to "informal, intuitive ways of thinking about the world which are strongly biased toward causal explanations. In many cases, as students advance in their understanding of science and technology subjects, they need

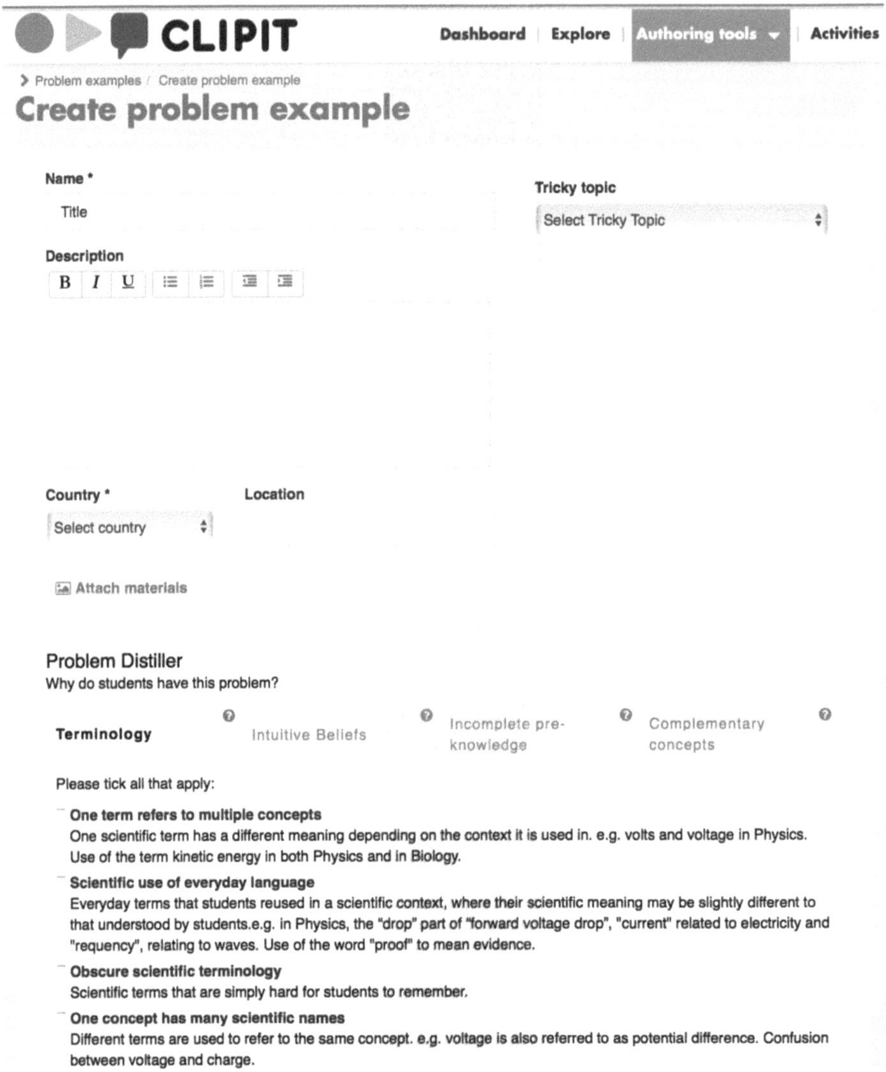

Fig. 2. Problem distiller tool.

to grasp principles which are fundamentally counter-intuitive. Such barriers can be very difficult to overcome as often the students and teachers do not realise they are there" (JuxtaLearn Project Deliverable Report D2.1 – Taxonomy).

The category 'Incomplete pre-knowledge' refers to situations "Where students either lacked an understanding of, or had an incomplete or flawed understanding of underpinning topics, or scientific method, process or discourse. For example, to understand genetic drift in biology, students need a pre-knowledge of the process of natural selection. Misunderstandings may also occur when teacher and student do not share the same scientific discourse, with students believing they have understood when, in reality, their understanding is based on a misinterpretation of what has been said" (JuxtaLearn Project Deliverable Report D2.1 – Taxonomy).

The category 'Complementary Concepts', refers to "chunks of information that students need to learn alongside the Threshold Concept. They are smaller, effectively 'sub-concepts' that a student needs to understand in order to grasp the overall Threshold Concept. For example, when learning about potential difference in physics, students also need to know about current, volts, voltage and Ohm's law. Sometimes such underpinning pre-knowledge is taught at the same time as the Threshold Concept, sometimes it is assumed that students have learned it already. When an understanding of essential concepts is missing or flawed, this can inhibit understanding of topics that rely on it" (JuxtaLearn Project Deliverable Report D2.1 – Taxonomy).

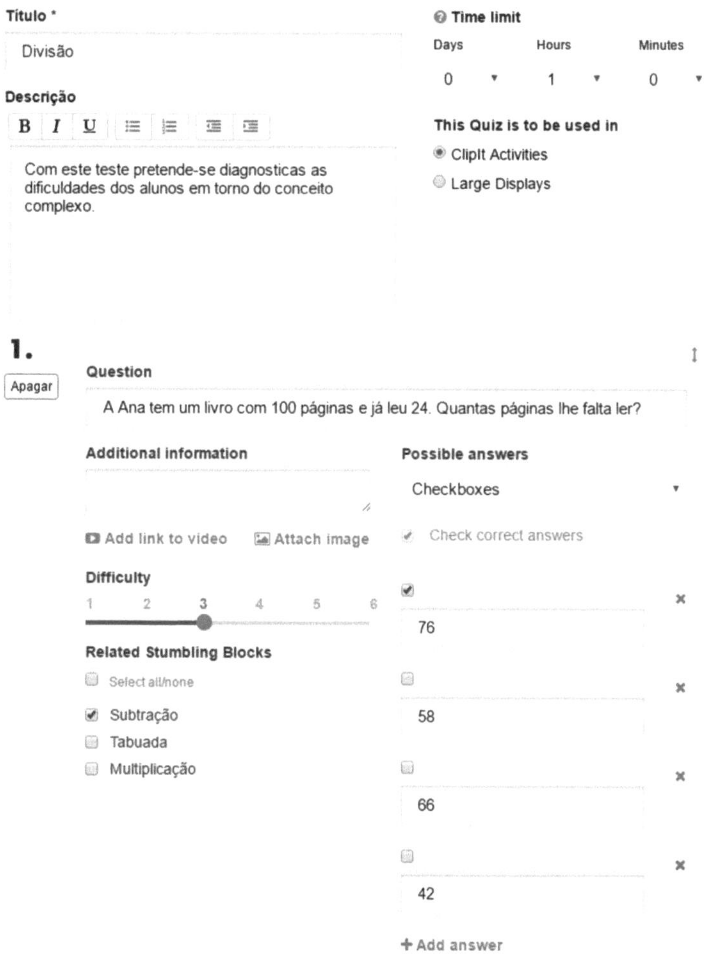

Fig. 3. Teacher's interface when designing the questions in the CLIPIT.

The Problem Distiller quiz creation stage uses the student's problems and their associated Stumbling Blocks as cues to guide the teacher in creating questions that address these specific concerns. The teacher is scaffolded to write questions that specifically target the identified stumbling blocks in order to verify if the student has the difficulties identified for the Threshold Concept. These questions form a diagnostic quiz that is effective at uncovering fundamental misconceptions (Fig. 3). The first step when creating a question for the quiz is to select the Tricky Topic and the Stumbling Blocks that the question will target. This step displays all the information related to that question: (1) stumbling blocks, (2) example of the student problems, and (3) suggested causes. For each of the Stumbling Blocks, the teacher has to create at least one question so that all the problem areas are covered. As the teacher creates the quiz, she/he links each question to one or more related Stumbling Blocks (the *why* factor), selecting the question type - multiple choices, checkboxes, true/false or numeric-, the possible options, and the correct answer. The teacher can also choose the difficulty of the test, include images and videos, and a timeout for the student to perform the quiz. The finished quiz is created and stored in CLIPIT and and made available for reuse by other teachers.

The connection between the Stumbling Blocks determines the complexity weighting of each question in the quiz and produces a radar chart visualisation for each student who has completed the quiz. This radar chart is a graphical translation of learning analytics and gives the teacher (and the student) a visual analysis of the level of the student's understanding on the Threshold Concept. In the quiz, complex questions can be connected to several Stumbling Blocks, whereas a simple question is connected to only one Stumbling Block. When the students take the diagnostic quiz, the visualised results show where the gaps in their knowledge are. The visualisation of the radar chart shows to the student his or her level of understanding of that concept in a form that is easy to understand (Fig. 4).

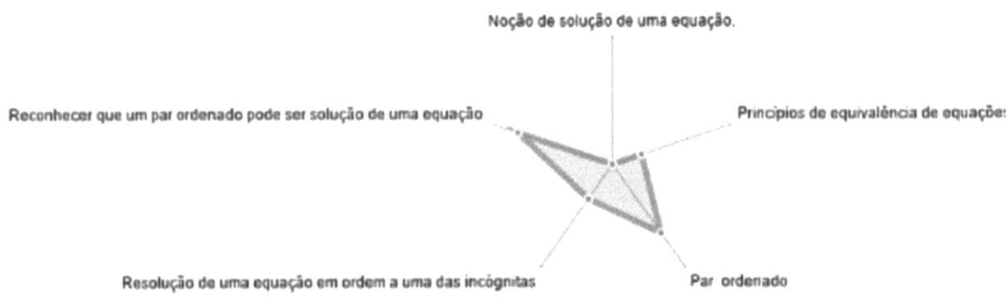

Fig. 4. Initial radar chart after performing the diagnostic quiz.

This radar chart represents the depth of the students' understanding of the 'Tricky Topic' and its connection with its various obstacles. For teachers, the radar chart flags up areas badly understood by the student, allowing them to adapt their teaching and implement intervention strategies to improve success in students learning. So, based on the diagnostic quiz information, the teacher can set up specific materials to overcome the identified difficulties, propose and differentiated tasks for knowledge consolidation, encourage the student's progress in the areas where she/he has more difficulties in order to strengthen the understanding of the 'Tricky Topics'.

At the end of the learning process the student may take another quiz on the same Tricky Topic to assess their learning progress (Fig. 5).

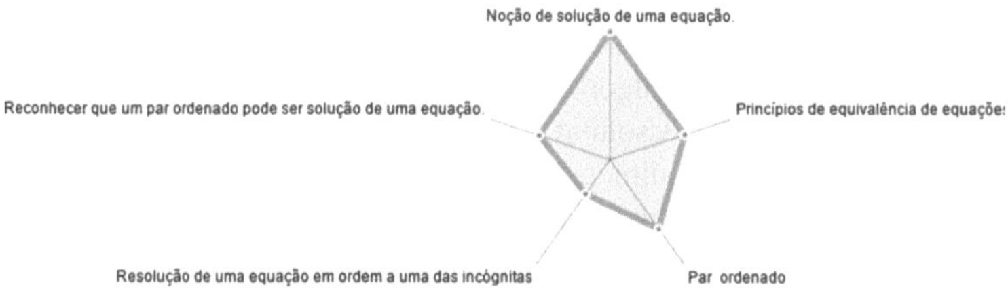

Fig. 5. Final radar chart after taking the quiz a second time.

If the students take a second diagnostic quiz, after the teacher has worked with them to overcome the weaknesses highlighted by the first diagnostic quiz, both student and teacher can easily see whether their difficulties have been overcome. We see in Fig. 5 that the student's understanding of the stumbling blocks, as illustrated by the vertices in the radar chart, has improved. Comparing the post-quiz example shown in Fig. 5 to the diagnostic quiz result shown in Fig. 4, one stumbling block has been completely overcome, reflecting the fact that that the student answered all the questions related to that problem correctly.

Comparing the diagnostic radar chart and the final radar chart, the teacher can analyse the evolution of student learning. In this case, the understanding of 'Tricky Topics' improved essentially on two of its obstacle levels, the "notion of solution of an equation" and the "principles of equation equivalence". While becoming aware of the improvement of the student, the teacher can plan teaching strategies that build deeper knowledge about the concept for the student.

4 Method

Data collection involved interviews with two math teachers from Elementary school (5th and 6th grades). The first teacher (T1) is a male, in his fifties, and teaches in a school in Marco de Canaveses, near the city of Porto in the north of Portugal. The other teacher (T2) is a female of forty-six years old, teaching in a school in the city of Braga. Both teachers have worked in teaching their entire working career.

Data was collected through structured interviews (20 min each) with the support of the Problem Distiller tool and Think Aloud protocol [21]. Based on their teaching practice they identified the math 'Tricky Topics' that were problematic for their students, and checked if the 'Tricky Topics' were already listed in the database (The Tricky Topic Tool). If not, we explained how to generate a new 'Tricky Topic'. Then, with the guidance of the Problem Distiller tool, the teachers divided each 'Tricky Topic' into stumbling blocks, and wrote a brief description of students' specific problems. The aim was to ensure that each interview presented the teachers with exactly the same questions in the same order (the JuxtaLearn taxonomy). This guarantees that answers can be reliably aggregated and that comparisons can be made with confidence between the two teachers.

For the processing and analysis of the obtained data, we performed a content analysis [5], as it allows for logical deductions based on the data obtained. The teachers' utterances were recorded and transcribed for the analysis. During the process, set of dimensions and categories emerged from data: (i) algorithm, (ii) basic operations, (iii) teaching method in the 1st level of education, (iv) reasoning and (v) use of the calculator.

It is interesting to notice that dimensions ii and iv are also reported in the literature of 'Division' [10, 17, 22]. In the dimension 'a' (algorithm), we analysed the relationship between the difficulty in the division operation and knowledge that students have of the division algorithm. In this dimension, we represent the speeches of teachers by "T1.a" or "T2.a". In dimension 'o' (operations), we analyse the relationship between the difficulty in the division operation and the students' knowledge of basic operations and we represent the speeches of teachers by "T1.o" or "T2.o". In dimension 'm' (method), we analyse the relationship between the difficulties in operating with diagnosed division in students and the teaching method in the 1st level of education. In this dimension, we represent the speeches of teachers by "T1.m" or "T2.m". In dimension 'r' (reasoning), we analyse the relationship between the difficulties in operating with the division and thinking capacity demonstrated by students. In this dimension we represent the speeches of teachers by "T1.r" or "T2.r". In dimension 'c' (calculator), we analyse the relationship between the difficulties in operating with the division and the use of calculators by students. In this dimension, we represent the utterances of teachers by "T1.c" or "T2.c". The utterances were numbered according to their occurrences in the text.

4.1 Data Collection

In this section, we describe the use of the Problem Distiller tool with two math teachers we interviewed for our study. We used the tool to help the teachers reflect on the causes of the student problems they had identified. When teachers expressed problems explaining why their students had difficulty understanding the Threshold Concept or 'Tricky Topic', they were guided by the Problem Distiller tool to identify the 'Stumbling Blocks'.

Both teachers said that the Tricky Topic 'division operation' is a Threshold Concept, at least for their students. T1 identified the following Stumbling Blocks: (1) organise calculations, (2) adding notion, (3) multiplication and (4) subtraction. After the teacher had reflected on the Threshold Concept through the mind map, he filled the CLIPIT with it. Below we present the mind map (Fig. 6) created by this teacher, and the Threshold Concept in the Tricky Topic Tool (Fig. 7).

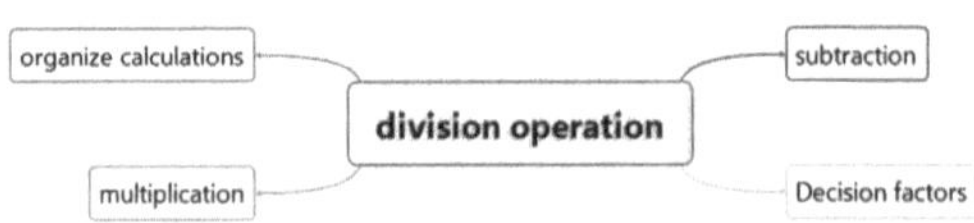

Fig. 6. Tricky topic and their stumbling blocks to T1.

Fig. 7. CLIPIT interface where the threshold concept and the 'Stumbling Blocks', and also a description of the concept.

For the Tricky Topic 'division operation', T2 identified the following Stumbling Blocks: (1) subtraction, (2) multiplication tables and (3) multiplication. Again, after the teacher had reflected on the Threshold Concept through the mind map, populated CLIPIT with it. Below we present a mind map (Fig. 8) created by this teacher, and the Threshold Concept in the Tricky Topic Tool (Fig. 9).

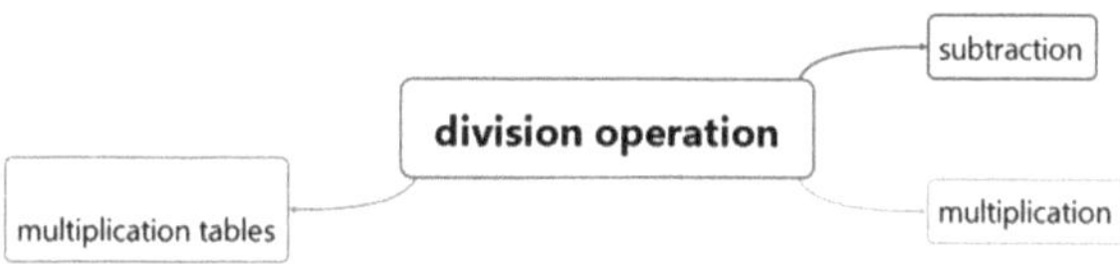

Fig. 8. Tricky topic and their stumbling blocks to T2.

Fig. 9. CLIPIT interface where the threshold concept and the 'Stumbling Blocks', and also a description of the concept.

During the interviews the Problem Distiller tool guided the teacher in identifying the causes of student's misunderstandings, adding particular examples of student's difficulties based on the teachers' experience with former students (Fig. 10).

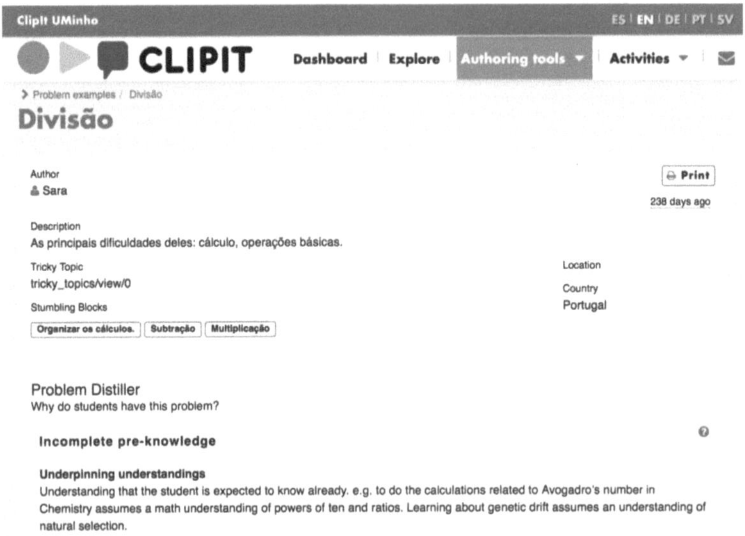

Fig. 10. CLIPIT interface: tricky topic and the 'Stumbling Blocks'.

Once identified the Threshold Concept the first reaction of both teachers (T1 and T2) when we asked them the reasons for these student's difficulties was a profound "silence". Then we showed the teachers the tabs with the following categories: Terminology, Intuitive Beliefs, Incomplete Pre-knowledge, and Complementary Concepts. Thus, we helped them to analyse each of these categories. Regarding the T1, he selected the "Incomplete pre-knowledge" and the "Underpinning understandings", corresponding to the problem "Understanding what the student is expected to know already. e.g., to do the calculations related to Avogadro's number in Chemistry assume the math understanding of powers of ten and ratios. Learning about genetic drift assumes an understanding of natural selection". Regarding T2, she selected the "Intuitive Beliefs" and the "causal flawed reasoning", corresponding to the problem "Reasoning based on the assumption of goal or purpose, e.g., birds have wings so they can fly. Genes turn off in order to enable the cell to develop properly. Inappropriate assumption of cause and effect, e.g., release an object along a curved path, and it will keep in the curve, rocks are so pointy that animals will not sit on Them and crush Them". This teacher also selected the "Incomplete pre-knowledge" and the "Underpinning understandings" with the same problem of T1.

Thus, one of the teachers (T2) identified in their students two types of problems for the same Threshold Concept, and one of these problems is the same as defined by T1. The Tricky Topic Tool and the Problem Distiller Tool allowed each teacher to see the problems identified by other teachers and thus reflect on the problems of their students compared to others.

As they made selections from the Problem Distiller Tool, teachers were identifying problems that students typically encounter in understanding the 'concept of division' and were also able to reflect on *why* these problems occur and how they can might be solved in the classroom with proper teaching and learning interventions.

Table 1. Category of analysis.

Category of analysis	N	Evidences
Algorithm	6	"Students do not know the algorithm implementation rules and do not know how to decompose a number" (T1.a1) "The Euclidean algorithm requires students to do successive divisions. The difficulties for them are huge. They can apply the algorithm realize the algorithm because it forces you to do successive divisions" (T1.a2) "In the division operation, students have many difficulties, mainly because most students cannot understand the division by two numbers" (T1.a3). "Students have difficulty in applying the divide operation algorithm and the location of elements: divider, rest, quotient and divisor" (T2.a1). "In the algorithm, students also have difficulty in organizing values in the process of division" (T2.a2). "Difficulty in organizing calculations when they are split" (T2.a3).
Basic operations	5	"Students have more difficulties in what we call the basic prerequisites, this is, the level of basic operations: addition, subtraction, multiplication and division. Of these four operations, where they appear the greatest difficulties is the division" (T1.o1) "The main difficulties of them: calculation, basic operations. We may say so, students know how to add, they know how to subtract, but in multiplication there are already great difficulties. If we are talking in the room, mainly by two numbers, mainly by two numbers I say that most students cannot do" (T1.o2) "I think mainly, the great difficulty is their basic operations, they confuse the signs of rules of multiplication or division. In mathematics master who does not add up, subtract, multiply and divide, how will dominate powers? how will dominate the other things?" (T1.o3). "Few can convert fractions to decimals, They have many difficulties" (T1.o4). "Students need to learn to add, subtract, multiply, are concepts and procedures that have many difficulties and if they have difficulties, not having the basic knowledge required, these difficulties still will aggravate" (T2.o1).

(*continued*)

Table 1. *(continued)*

Category of analysis	N	Evidences
Teaching method in the 1st level of education	1	"Students come in different primary schools accustomed to different methods, some learn through successive subtractions others by adding the reverse" (T2.m1)
Reasoning	6	"They have to use the implicit reasoning in the division operation they fail to do." (T1.r1) "The difficulties appear, for example, conversions of fractions to decimals" (T1.r2) "Mathematics is a discipline that requires training, this is, students do exercises and give up the first difficulty of the exercises. And the difficulties begin to be increasing. If the student fails to follow the matter in 5th grade, how will you get there ahead? The difficulties are increasing and not only gets what the student learns in school." (T1.r3) "Can apply to real life situations and they see that is applicable for them, and with these real-life situations carrying her later for more complicated mathematical concepts and more difficult for them to understand" (T1. r4). They cannot perceive, and the difficulty of abstraction combined with the lack of prerequisites to make the division is a problem that cannot overcome this difficulty (T2.r1). "Students have a hard mental calculation, especially in multiplication and division" (T2.r2). "I notice that students not able to find the successive divisions and do not know the multiplication table" (T2. r3).
Using Calculator	3	"The problem here is often the use of calculating machine or non-use of the adding machine (T1.c1). "If you have difficulties, with the use of the machine, these difficulties will still worsen because they do not have why not use the calculator." (T1.c2) "Then they get used to using the machine and forget what they previously learned" (T2.c1)

For a deeper analysis on the teacher's utterances (Think Aloud protocol), we prepared a content analysis. The content analysis was developed according to the phases suggested by Bardin [5]. Table 1 presents teachers' utterances according to five categories considered in the analysis.

There appear to be a greater number of evidences in the dimension "Algorithm" and "Reasoning". However, it turns out that there is only one evidence for the dimension teaching method in the 1st level of education. Teachers see the lack of knowledge in the algorithm as a deterrent for students to perform division operations. They point to students' "*difficulty in applying the divide operation algorithm and the location of elements: divider, rest, quotient and divisor*" (T2.a1), and claim that in "*the division operation students have many difficulties*" (T1.a3). In their view, students need to spend more time learning the algorithm, realizing that they "*do not know the algorithm implementation rules and do not know how to decompose a number*" (T1.a1). In a subject such as the Euclidean algorithm, taught in 5th grade, teachers recommend "*obliging students to do successive divisions*" (T1.a2), pointing out that students have great difficulties in doing this. Students also have a lot of difficulties on "*the organization of values in the process of division*" (T2.a2) and on "*organization of calculations*" (T2.a3) when they are making the division operation.

Teachers see the lack of knowledge of basic operations as an issue that prevents the students from performing division operations. Students present "*difficulties in terms of basic knowledge: addition, subtraction, multiplication and division*" (T1.o1). The development of skills in the basic operations is seen as essential if the student can work with division, because "*in mathematics, for students who do not master the add, subtract, multiply and divide, how will they master powers?, how will they overcome the other things?*" (T1.o3). Teachers said that students had difficulties to converting a minute into seconds or to convert an hour into minutes. They noticed also that if they ask students to do any form of division "*mainly by two numbers, most students cannot*" (T1.o2). Students also have many difficulties in "*converting fractions to decimals*" (T1.o4). The competence of using an algorithm is compulsory according to the Portuguese educational policies, but students are not prepared or able to learn them and so difficulties rise: "*if they [the students] have difficulties, not having the basic knowledge required, these difficulties still will aggravate*" (T2.o1).

Only in the category "t*eaching method in the 1st level of education*", one of the teachers pointed out that the learning division using didactic methods can leads to later difficulties when working with division. Also, the fact that students often come from "*different primary schools, accustomed to different methods*" (T2.m1) are also problems associated with the Tricky Topic.

Teachers understand that "*the difficulty of abstraction coupled with a lack of basic knowledge*" (T2.r1) presents a problem of understanding when students attempt to acquire new knowledge. The students "*have to use the implicit reasoning in the division operation and they fail to do so*" (T1.r1). The need for the student to remember the notion of a multiple number and know how to apply the division algorithm are factors that hinder students' ability to perform the division operation. According to the teachers, students present "*difficulty in mental calculation, especially in multiplication and division*" (T2.r2) and "*are not able to find the successive divisions*" (T2.r3). The fact that the students "*do not know the multiplication tables*" (T2.r3) is also a pointed problem for students unable to do a division. The discipline of Mathematics "*requires training, this is, students do exercises and give up the first difficulty of the exercises. And the difficulties begin to increase.. If the student cannot understand the content in 5th grade, how will they move forward? The difficulties increase and not only gets what the student learns in school.*" (T1.r3). To improve understanding and visualization, teachers call for situations where students: "*can apply maths to real life situations and develop a sound understand in context, building on this understanding to learn more complicated mathematical concepts*" (T1.r4).

Teachers see the use of calculators in 5th grade to 6th grade as an easier alternative adopted by students to perform division. They find that the "*use of calculator or non-use of the adding machine*" (T1.c1), can lead students to forget the algorithm. The students that use the calculator a lot "*forget what they previously learned about the algorithm*" (T2.c1). According to participant teachers, if students have difficulties and use the calculator, their understanding of the fundamental concepts in division will diminish and their ability to perform division without the aid of a calculator will get worse.

The teachers are faced with students who present a great diversity in terms of learning achieved, and who manifest different ways of thinking and learning. It is therefore increasingly necessary to implement differentiated phases with strategies tailored to the needs of each student. Thus, to see if the Tricky Topic stumbling blocks problems corresponded to those shown by their students, T2 selected a group of ten students (6 girls and 4 boys), from one of his classes which had the 'concept of division' as a TrickyTopic. Thus, after identifying the Stumbling Blocks associated with Tricky Topic, the professor created a diagnostic quiz and had these students take that quiz. The teacher's radar chart contains a scale, allowing a more detailed interpretation of the quiz results.

From image in Fig. 11 we can see that this student answered all subtraction questions correctly, as shown by the corresponding subtraction vertex being coincident with the apex of the triangle. However, he only answered correctly on just over half of the answers involving multiplication. This radar chart visualization suggests the student has difficulty with multiplication that may be related to his difficulty with times tables. This radar chart allows the teacher to see where the student has difficulties and adapt strategies to help him overcome the difficulties. Given that each radar chart is specific for each student, the teacher can customize teaching strategies. Another example is shown on the Fig. 12.

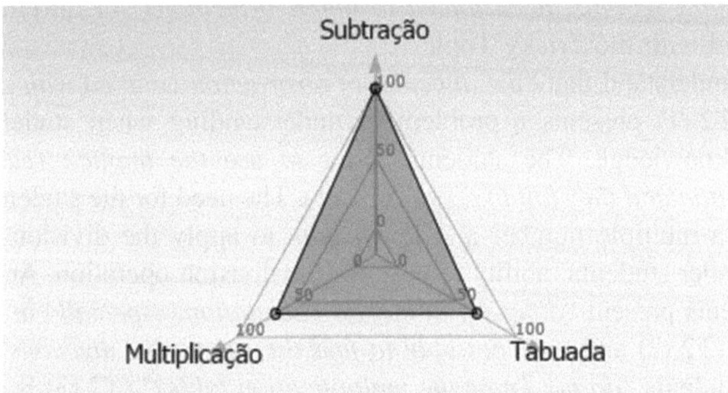

Fig. 11. Radar chartfor student 4in theteacher's interface (T2).

From the radar chart in Fig. 12, the teacher can see that the student answered correctly all questions that involved subtraction, but failed on more than half of questions that involved multiplication or knowledge of the times tables.

The same way, by analysing the graphical radar chart presented in Fig. 13, the teacher can see that the student answered correctly to the questions of quiz that involved subtraction operations, but answered correctly only half of the questions that involved multiplication operations or that involved the knowledge of times tables.

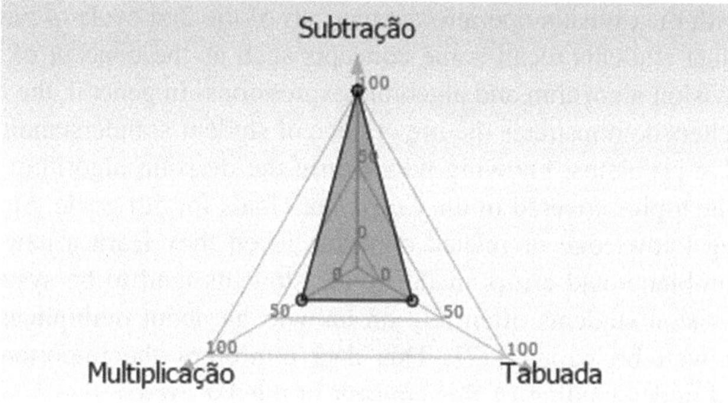

Fig. 12. Radar chart after performing the diagnostic quiz – student 1.

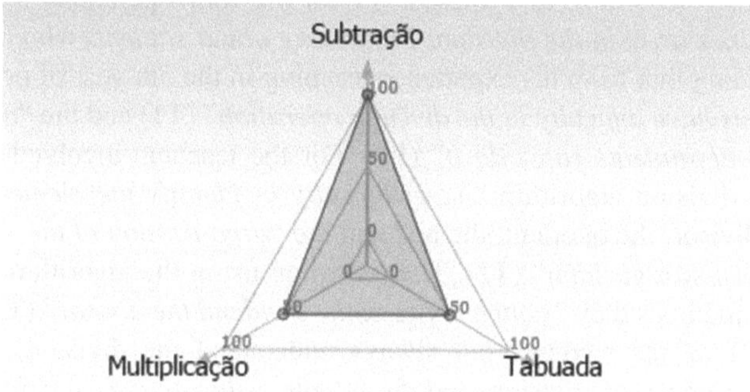

Fig. 13. Radar chart after performing the diagnostic quiz – student 2.

5 Discussion

Throughout the first years of school, students develop a sense of number, but it is only in their 3rd, 4th and 5th grade that more emphasis is given to the development of skills in multiplication and division. Many students demonstrate problems in learning the division [13]. Understanding the implicit thinking in a division operation, from a mathematical point of view, involves knowledge of other simple operations such as addition and multiplication skills. The division and multiplication operations, although simple, reveal some complexity at cognitive level when presented in problematic situations, because the values have new meanings and the figures presented are sometimes differently exploited [17]. One of the fundamental knowledge in the teaching of mathematics is the calculation of the four basic operations: addition, subtraction, multiplication and division. As the student develops the sense of number, she/he should be able to establish a rationale involving numbers [18]. By using the Tricky Topic Tool we identified together with these two teachers the concept of division as complex concept for students.

To work with the division operation at the start of the 2nd cycle of basic education, it is assumed that students recall some concepts such as the concept of multiple of a number, the division algorithm and algebraic expressions. In general, the data collected from these teachers demonstrates the importance of student's understanding of division in order to solve problems, knowing how to use the division algorithm to keep pace with some of the topics covered in the Curricular Goals for 5th grade. Students tend to use the existing knowledge or related concepts when they learn a new concept and therefore the problems and errors made by the students tend to be systematic. Thus, when doing division students often rely on knowledge about multiplication and division that may well be wrong [17]. This data reinforces the importance of giving students a solid understanding of this concept in the 1st cycle.

In Portugal, the concept of division is covered for the first time in the curricular goals in the 2nd year of primary school. The concept of division is once again addressed in the 3rd, 4th and 5th grade where other concepts will be combined relating to this operation. According to Professor T1 on the four operations addressed, "*the greatest difficulties arise in the division, I'm talking about students who are in the fifth year*" (T1). Adding that from his experience teaching in the 5th year of primary school, "*90% of students have difficulty in the division operation*" (T1) and the "*division of two numbers, 99% of students can't do it*" (P1). For the teachers involved in our study, sometimes the division algorithm "*have difficulty in identify the elements*" (T1), the dividend, the divisor, the quotient, the rest and the "*organization of the elements when making the division algorithm*" (T2). That is, when using the algorithm to work with the division, sometimes they "*switch between the dividend the divisor*" (T2). According to Professor P1 as the students not always understand the division, "*they do not recognize the process of division and forget the value that is carried*" (T2). The division algorithm, is a set of processes that follow the same order in similar situations [7] and it's not always understood by the students.

The fact that they do not know their multiplication tables and are not able to perform a multiplication limits the students' ability to work on concepts and procedures (e.g. division) that need those auxiliary calculations. The poor performance of students not only in understanding necessary strategies, but also in using them to solve a problem leads them to give up. Therefore it is essential to teach students these important processes and strategies that help them solve the problems in a more effective and efficient way [17]. Zhao et al. [22] in a study which looked at Chinese and Flemish students to know what it takes to master the four basic arithmetic operations (addition, subtraction, multiplication and division), identified that students demonstrated gaps in the four basic operations.

The division operation involves dividing a given number of equal parts. During the early years of school students learn the meaning of the division, understand the effects of dividing by integers, use and understand the notion that the division operation is the inverse operation of multiplication [18]. According to the results, the fact that students cannot resolve a task or problem involving a division appears to discourage students and prevent them from progressing. Also Montague [17] states that the division operation is a mathematical procedure with some complexity and understanding division therefore involves understanding the other mathematical operations. Many children have difficulties in using the traditional division algorithm. And when the operation is necessary in mathematical problems, many students give up. Unlike the addition operation, multiplication or subtraction, the division algorithm involves the knowledge and identification of four terms dividend, divisor, quotient and rest. These terms can also cause difficulties for the students as the teachers stated in the Tricky Topic tool when they list the understanding issues that are commonly found in students. From the point of view of these teachers "*the great difficulty of the students is the basic operation*" (T1). To develop the competence of calculation through division operation, students need to have knowledge in terms of counting and arithmetic operations such as multiplication tables. Arguments were put forward by both teachers when identifying the difficulties that students have when performing division. They mention that students sometimes fail to "*identify the elements in the division*" (P2) and on the 5th year students are expected to "*work with conversions and the Euclidean algorithm.*" (T1). According to Arends [3], an effective teacher must in addition to other duties, be able to list a set of good practice and be able to think about the process of teaching. The mathematical knowledge of the teacher is essential to teach the division operation in order to be able to identify students' difficulties and realize in which algorithm stage is this difficulty [10]. The teacher plays a fundamental role so that students can understand the mathematical meaning of the division, the procedures involved in the operation, using the correct terminology and an appropriate mathematical language. By using Tricky Topic Tool we promote thinking moments on teachers around the Tricky Topic, the ability to recall moments of work between students and difficulties in the construction of knowledge about the concept of division.

Students' problems often identified by these teachers refer to difficulties in terms of successive subtraction to solve tasks associated with the division; including "*not able to find the successive divisions*" (T2) and "*Euclidean's algorithm requires to do successive divisions.*" (T1). For Montague [17] the use of additions and successive subtraction is a strategy used by children who learn division and which is based on pre-existing knowledge about addition, subtraction and multiplication. The teachers also mentioned the fact that students are not aware to the inverse relationship between multiplication and division, can also be a problem to the understanding of division operation. They also report that students usually manifest difficulty operating between numbers written in the form of fraction, because "*do not realize the meaning of the elements in the fraction*" (T2), have difficulty to "*identify the dividend and the divisor*" (T1). To suit the results obtained by Unlu and Ertekin [20] who investigated the knowledge of a group of mathematics teachers on the division between numbers written in the form of fraction, they realized that the knowledge about the division operation with fractions does not go beyond functional knowledge. These teachers were able to apply the rules and the process inherent in the division, but were unable to explain its meaning.

Through the use of Problem Distiller tool with teachers, we realized that the understanding of essential concepts around the Tricky Topic division "*sometimes it depends on a badly learned concept*" (T2). Presuppose the use of "*already acquired knowledge of division*" (T1) as new knowledge is being developed. The lack of essential concepts, fundamental knowledge that is related to the Tricky Topic, without which the student cannot understand, was pointed out on Problem Distiller tool as one of the causes for the difficulties in the division operation. Teachers mentioned the lack of knowledge about the scientific method and the lack of support and understanding prior knowledge that the student needs to improve to understand the Tricky Topic. The lack of complementary knowledge to the division operation from the point of view of these teachers can also be a problem. They noted also that some imperfect reasoning around the division and intuitive ways of thinking about the division process can evenly become an obstacle to the understanding of division. The reflection upon the causes for the understanding of problems detected in students, allowed teachers to increase the level of awareness about the knowledge of the student.

Teaching the "division operation" not only involves knowing how to use the traditional algorithm but also understand the division operation in different situations, understand the relationship between division and multiplication and simultaneously develop a network of numerical relationships around this operation. Even the teachers who teach mathematics in the 1st and on the 2nd grades admit that the division is a difficult operation to teach to their students and their learning process is sometimes confused with the mechanization of rules associated with the algorithm instead of understanding the division operation [13]. The acquisition of mathematical knowledge allows us to develop reasoning, structure thinking and help future students to think and to decide. Understanding how students learn and how teachers teach mathematical concepts is of fundamental importance for the individual student progress and the organizations to which he belongs.

The Tricky Topic tool guided the teachers in the identification of the Threshold Concept and corresponding Stumbling Blocks. The Problem Distiller tool supports them in thinking through the students' difficulties, reflecting on possible causes for those difficulties, and on ways to overcome them. This was because the connections of each Tricky Topic in the Problem Distiller tool allowed teachers to divide the concept into smaller parts (the Stumbling Blocks), and establish a critical and reflective look at the teaching and learning of division operation based in the four areas identified as problematical for students: "Terminology", "Intuitive Beliefs", "Incomplete pre-knowledge" and "Complementary Concepts".

From our perspective, this process was essential to find ways to enable an effective and consolidated teaching about the tricky topic. The difficulties listed by the teachers match the data in the literature, particularly those obtained by Montague [17], by Zhao et al. [22] and Fernandes and Martins [10]. Also the NCTM [18] states that from the 3rd to 5th grade, students need to understand in greater depth the multiplicative nature of the number system. The results suggest that the obstacles associated with Tricky Topic identified by teachers are similar to the difficulties described in the literature about learning the division operation.

The results showed that the use of Problem Distiller prompted teachers to think outside their comfort zone. From the perception of teachers, we can say that the division operation is a Tricky Topic for the students, and the data obtained so far allow us to conclude that it is a Threshold Concept according to the criteria listed by Meyer and Land [14]. Linking the perception of teachers with the criteria listed by Meyer and Land [14] for which a concept is a threshold, we found out upon teachers' voices:

- Can be seen as **Transformative**, given that by understanding the division operation students will be able to "*use in everyday situations*" (T2) and "*to make conversions for example*" (T1);
- It is **Irreversible** once learned is difficult to be forgotten; however teachers recognise that "*the abusive use of calculator*" (T1) can lead to loss of an algorithm learned in the first cycle;
- Being the division operation a key operation to for example "*do successive divisions in Euclidean algorithm*" (T1), to respond to "*problematic situations of everyday life*" (T2), it is suggested that it is **Integrative**;
- When the division operation is used to as the basis for understanding of other mathematical concepts. The misunderstanding in division can "*compound the difficulties*" (T1), because if students "*do not have the necessary base knowledge, their difficulties in learning related concepts will increase*" (T2), suggesting that the division operation may be **Bounded**.
- Failure to understand the concept or "*confusion problems with the multiplication operation*" (T2) for example may indicate that it is a **Troublesome**, an incorrect understanding can lead to counterintuitive relations.

6 Conclusion

The JuxtaLearn project created an easy to use interactive online tool called Tricky Topic Tool to help teachers identify Threshold Concepts, and a Problem Distiller Tool to help teachers uncover the reasons why their students have problems understanding Threshold Concepts. This paper described the sessions carried out with two math teachers working with these two apps. The two tools guided the work with these teachers.

The teachers found it helpful when the information they entered through the Problem Distiller was fed back to scaffold their questions construction as they constructed an online diagnostic quiz. These prompts made it easy for them to write questions that probed to reveal whether or not their students' had a deep understanding of the Tricky Topic.

The tools are easy to use so once teachers understand the process of identifying a Tricky Topic and breaking it down into its constituent stumbling blocks, which does not happen with the methods described by other studies, such as the work of Loertscher et al. [11], based on workshops, focus groups or interviews. The Tricky Topic Tool and Problem Distiller offer a fast process which can be applied to a concrete situation: an entire class, a group of students in the class, or an individual student. This allows teachers to individualize intervention and can help differentiate pedagogical strategy.

From the students' point of view, the tool allows the student to take control and manage their learning, taking control of their personalised learning pathway. The answers to the quizzes and the results as visualised in the radar chart, allow the student to understand and reflect on the difficulties that she/he has associated to that Threshold Concept, and determine for themselves what needs to be improved.

Lastly, we would like to attest that digital technology can play a significant role in transforming teaching and learning practices for teachers and students. The JuxtaLearn project recognises that teachers are always engaged in enhancing how they teach and how their students learn. An essential part of this continuous improvement in how we enable students to learn effectively must be to embed digital technology further.

Although we are huge believers in the purposeful integration of technology in classrooms to enhance teaching and learning, we must resist the temptation to think that this is the solution to solve all learning problems. Of course, the pedagogy comes first, supported by technology initiatives with a real plan for implementation and evaluation of effectiveness. No lack of planning is likely to result and achieve productive outcomes.

Proposals for Future Work

JuxtaLearn will use the potential of 'learning analytics' to personalise the learning processes. The results of these analyses will serve several purposes, such as (1) guidance of pedagogical decisions (selection of themes and examples), (2) supervision support for teachers based on accumulated learning traces, (3) reflection support for students and teachers.

Acknowledgements. The research leading to these results has received funding from the European Community's Seventh Framework Programme under grant agreement no. 317964 JUXTALEARN. We would like to thank the interviewed teachers for their valuable collaboration.

References

1. Adams, A., Rogers, Y., Coughlan, T., Van-der-Linden, J., Clough, G., Martin, E., Collins, T.: Teenager needs in technology enhanced learning. In: Workshop on Methods of Working with Teenagers in Interaction Design, CHI 2013, Paris, France (2013)
2. Adams, A., Clough, G.: The E-assessment burger: supporting the before and after in E-assessment systems. Interact. Des. Archit.(s) J.-IxD&A **25**, 39–57 (2015)
3. Arends, R.I.: Aprender a ensinar. McGrawHill, Lisboa (2008)
4. Clough, G., Adams, A., Cruz, S., Lencastre, J.A., Coutinho, C.: I just don't understand why they don't understand: bridging the gaps in student learning. Brit. J. Educ. Technol. (2015). Submitted for evaluation
5. Bardin, L., de Conteúdo, A.: Lisboa: Edições, p. 70 (2013)
6. Barradell, S., Kennedy-Jones, M.: Threshold concepts, student learning and curriculum: making connections between theory and practice. Innov. Educ. Teach. Int. **52**, 1–10 (2013)
7. Brocardo, J., Serrazina, L.: O sentido do número no currículo de matemática. O sentido do número: Reflexões que entrecruzam teoria e prática, pp. 97–115 (2008)
8. Cousin, G.: An introduction to threshold concepts. Planet, p. 17 (2006). http://www.sddu.leeds.ac.uk/uploaded/learning-teaching-docs/teachtalk/5-12-2008/cousin_threshold_concepts.pdf
9. Cruz, S., Lencastre, J.A., Coutinho, C., Clough, G., Adams, A.: Threshold concepts vs. tricky topics - exploring the causes of student's misunderstandings with the problem distiller tool. In: Uhomoibhi, J., Costagliola, G., Zvacek, S., McLaren, B.M. (eds.) Proceedings of CSEDU 2016, 8th International Conference on Computer Supported Education, vol. 1, pp. 205–215, Rome, IT, SCITEPRESS (2016)

10. Fernandes, D.R., Martins, F.M.: Reflexão acerca do ensino do algoritmo da divisão inteira: proposta didática. Educação e Formação **9**, 174–197 (2014)
11. Loertscher, J., Green, D., Lewis, J.E., Lin, S., Minderhout, V.: Identification of threshold concepts for biochemistry. CBE-Life Sci. Educ. **13**(3), 516–528 (2014)
12. Machiocha, A.: Teaching research methods: threshold concept. In: 13th European Conference on Research Methods for Business and Management, pp. 260–265, London (2014)
13. Mendes, F.: A aprendizagem da divisão: um olhar sobre os procedimentos usados pelos alunos. Da Investigação às Práticas **3**(2), 5–30 (2013)
14. Meyer, J., Land, R.: Threshold concepts and troublesome knowledge: linkages to ways of thinking and practising within the disciplines. In: Rust, C. (ed.) Improving student Learning - Theory and Practice Ten Years on, pp. 412–424. Oxford Centre for Staff and Learning Development (OCSLD), Oxford (2003)
15. Meyer, J., Land, R.: Overcoming barriers to student understanding: threshold concepts and Troublesome Knowledge. In: Meyer, J., Land, R. (eds.) Overcoming Barriers to Student Understanding: Threshold concepts and Toublesome Knowledge, pp. 19–32. Routledge, London and New York (2006)
16. Meyer, J.H., Knight, D.B., Callaghan, D.P., Baldock, T.E.: An empirical exploration of metacognitive assessment activities in a third-year civil engineering hydraulics course. Eur. J. Eng. Educ. **40**(3), 309–327 (2015)
17. Montague, M.: Teaching division to students with learning disabilities: a constructivist approach, exceptionality: a special. Educ. J. **11**(3), 165–175 (2003)
18. National Council of Teachers of Mathematics: Princípios e Normas Para a Matemática Escolar. APM, Lisboa (2008)
19. Squire, S., Bryant, P.: The influence of sharing on children's initial concept of division. J. Exp. Child Psychol. **81**, 1–43 (2002)
20. Unlu, M., Ertekin, E.: Why do pre-service teachers pose multiplication problems instead of division problems in fractions? Procedia Soc. Behav. Sci. **46**, 490–494 (2012)
21. Van Someren, M.W., Barnard, Y., Sandberg, J.: The Think Aloud Method: A Practical Guide to Modeling Cognitive Processes. Academic Press, London (1994)
22. Zhao, N., Valcke, M., Desoete, A., Burny, E., Imbo, I.: Differences between Flemish and Chinese primary students' mastery of basic arithmetic operations. Educ. Psychol. **34**(7), 818–837 (2014)

Designing Teacher Education Programs that Produce ICT Ready Graduates

Kathy Jordan(✉) and Jennifer Elsden-Clifton

RMIT, Melbourne, Australia
kathy.jordan@rmit.edu.au

Abstract. Teacher education providers have an important role to play in preparing the next generation of teachers to be able to use ICT in their future teaching practice. Government reports and research have consistently argued that graduates are ill-prepared in their use of ICT [1]. In Australia an increasing regulatory environment means that teacher education providers need to design programs that target the attainment of specific ICT professional standards. To contribute to the discussion of ICT challenges in teacher education, this small-scale study investigated where 69 pre-service teachers acquired the ICT skills/resources commonly used in primary and secondary schools. Findings suggest that many of the generalized skills/resources were learned in their everyday life prior to undertaking their teaching program, and that they acquired a lesser number through their university coursework and/or professional experience placements. A number of implications for teacher education conclude this paper.

Keywords: ICT · Teacher education · Pre-service teacher

1 Introduction

For some time now the use of ICT in schools has been advocated, often on the grounds that such use will have a positive impact on student learning and equip them with the needed skills for a high-tech future workplace [2]. In turn, the role of initial teacher education has been to design programs to ensure that future teachers have this necessary skill set. Literature suggests that teacher education programs can provide experiences that have the potential to shape pre-service teachers' knowledge and beliefs in relation to teaching and learning with ICT, and this will ultimately impact on their future teaching practice [3–5]. As Tondeur et al. [5] argue a "crucial factor influencing new teachers' adoption of technology is the quantity and quality of pre-service technology experiences included in their teacher education programmes".

Recently in Australia, a report from the Teacher Education Ministerial Advisory Group (TEMAG); Action Now: Classroom Ready Teachers [1] was released. This was the latest in a long line of government reports and inquiries into teacher education in Australia. TEMAG, established in 2014, aimed to provide advice on the quality of teacher training in Australia and identified recommendations to better prepare teachers with the practical skills needed for the classroom.

G. Costagliola et al. (Eds.): CSEDU 2016, CCIS 739, pp. 402–419, 2017.
DOI: 10.1007/978-3-319-63184-4_21

National accreditation of teacher education in Australia is also having considerable impact on how providers design their programs [6]. Previously each state and territory had separate teacher registration boards and their focus on ICT varied considerably [7]. In 2011, the Australian Government introduced a national approach to accreditation regulated by the Australian Institute for Teaching and School Leadership (AITSL). To be nationally accredited, providers need to design their programs to meet a number of Program Standards as well as a set of national professional standards. These seven Australian Professional Standards for Graduate Teachers stipulate what teachers should know and be able to do as a graduating teacher. The Table 1 below presents the standards and descriptors relevant to ICT.

Table 1. ICT focused Australian professional standards for teachers.

Standard 2	Know the content and how to teach it	2.6 Implement teaching strategies for using ICT to expand curriculum learning opportunities for students
Standard 3	Plan for and implement effective teaching and learning	3.4 Demonstrate knowledge of a range of resources, including ICT, that engage students in their learning
Standard 4	Create and maintain supportive and safe learning environments	4.5 Demonstrate an understanding of the relevant issues and the strategies available to support the safe, responsible and ethical use of ICT in learning and teaching

With national accreditation, the provider's role is explicit: to design programs so that upon graduation pre-service teachers have met these professional standards, including ICT related standards. For example graduates need to know how to use ICT resources to engage students in their learning. Teacher education providers (through their provision of coursework and professional experience) are perceived as being responsible for developing these standards, however, what has been missing is an examination and acknowledgement of the prior knowledge and skills that pre-service teachers bring to their teacher education program. This omission is particularly pertinent when we consider that many pre-service teachers have considerable knowledge of technologies from their personal and social lives, as well as from their prior work and study. This raises a number of questions: How might pre-service teachers' prior knowledge influence program design in teacher education? What technology skills and knowledge do they bring? How do they learn ICT skills, through university coursework and professional experience - in school settings, personal life or workplace? How might teacher education use these prior skills to address the regulatory environment shaping ICT in programs?

In addressing these questions this chapter draws on literature from within teacher education and ICT. It begins by discussing the current issues facing teacher education in addressing the regulatory and industry demands of creating teachers who are proficient integrators of technology. It then discusses the common approaches used within teacher education programs to prepare ICT-ready graduates and the role and place of practical experience (practicum) in this development. The chapter then examines a survey completed by 69 pre-service teachers enrolled in primary or secondary teacher education programs at RMIT University, Victoria Australia. This survey focused on where pre-service teachers acquired the skills to use a set of ICT applications and resources (i.e. through coursework, professional experience, workplace, personal life etc.). Findings are presented and the relationship between the setting and type of resource is examined. A discussion around how pre-service teachers' prior and current ICT skills and knowledge could be considered in the design of teacher education programs concludes this chapter.

2 Technology Within Teacher Education

Historically, teacher education policy and practice seems to have been behind that of schools [8]. In 1998 the Australian Council of Deans in Education recommended that graduates should know how to use technologies [7]. At this time, state and territory education departments set guidelines for beginning teachers around personal skills and classroom strategies related to integrating ICT. This had considerable influence over the design of teacher education programs.

In 2009, the Australian Government commissioned an investigation into pre-service teacher experiences in using ICT, the barriers to its use and ways to improve teacher education programs [9]. An online survey for teacher mentors (practicing teachers who support pre-service teachers while they are on placement in schools), teacher education staff and pre-service teachers was one of the key means of data collection for the report. A number of key points were raised by the 125 respondents including concerns that most teacher education programs focused on how to use technologies rather than focusing on how to integrate them into practice; while some ICT specific courses involved staff modeling good practice, most general education courses did not; that technologies commonly used in schools were not being used in universities; difficulties in finding teacher mentors who were ICT competent; and there was a lack of assessment of pre-service teacher ICT competence. In its Executive Summary the report commented that:

> The evidence presented in this paper strongly points to fundamental systemic flaws in the pre-service teacher education system in Australia in terms of developing teacher competence in embedding ICTs in pedagogy and practice [9].

We are mindful that it can be too easy to blame teacher education providers and fail to duly recognize the complexity that is teacher education. While research clearly shows that educating the next generation of teachers is neither simple nor straightforward [4], a dominant discourse still permeates much of policy. This discourse adopts a narrow view of what teacher education providers should do, and focuses on the provision of the tools of technology and how to operate them, rather than how and why technology can be used to support learning. It also does not give due recognition to the possible obstacles that teachers face as they engage with technologies in their practice [4, 5].

Some time ago Ertmer [10], in discussing this issue, classified the numerous barriers to teacher use of ICT into two categories: extrinsic (first order) and intrinsic (second order). Within extrinsic barriers she included lack of time, lack of resources, inadequate training, and technical support; within intrinsic barriers she included beliefs and views about ICT and teaching and learning. Later, and with other researchers, she categorized enablers into two categories [11]: extrinsic enablers including access to hardware and software, as well as technical and peer support; and intrinsic enablers including personal beliefs, self-efficacy and previous experiences with ICT. Ertmer's research provides a highly influential account of the complexities that teachers face as they integrate ICT into their practice. Mirzajani et al. [12], in their review of obstacles impacting on pre-service teachers, categorized these obstacles into three types: Resource related obstacles, Institutional obstacles and Attitudinal obstacles. Resource related obstacles include lack of access to ICT hardware and software, lack of training and support to use ICT, lack of knowledge and skills, and lack of leadership. Institutional obstacles include lack of financial commitment, lack of time, and lack of incentives and commitment. Attitudinal obstacles include resistance to change, negative attitudes and self-efficacy.

It is also important to recognize that teacher education providers face a number of challenges in this area. These include lack of funding, lack of leadership and vision, the need to have staff commitment to the enterprise, the need to provide on-going professional learning, as well as the need for teaching spaces that facilitate effective practice [13]. One of the key challenges is that teacher education providers struggle to have staff with the necessary skill set to use and model best practice [14]. Many courses are taught by enthusiastic individuals rather than mainstream practitioners [14], and many classes are taught by sessional staff who may or may not have an interest or skills in using ICT effectively. Haydn [4] suggests that the competence of teacher educator staff is one of the most defining factors in whether teachers in their first year of practice use ICT or not. It has been suggested that the lack of quality teacher educators using ICT in their practice is because they are 'digital immigrants' [15]. According to the view made popular by Prensky [15] and others, the so-called 'digital immigrants', have come later to using ICT, and find using these tools foreign. This is contrasted with the 'digital natives', who have grown up with technology, and are accustomed to using technologies in their day-to-day lives. While this view has been debated and many of its claims rejected as myths [16, 17], it is still often included and quoted in the dominant discourse.

Recently, all 39 Australian universities, in what was acknowledged as a rare commitment to collaboration, worked together with other partners such as the Australian Institute for Teaching and School Leadership (AITSL), the Australian Council of Deans of Education (ACDE), the Australian Council for Computers in Education (ACCE), and Education Services Australia (ESA) to target ICT proficiency of graduate teachers across Australia. The Teaching Teachers for the Future (TTF) Project was one of four initiatives funded through the ICT Innovation Fund (ICTIF) and focused on:

> … systematic change in the ICT proficiency of graduate teachers in Australia by building the ICT capacity of teacher educators and developing resources to provide rich professional learning and digital exemplar packages [18].

The 15 month long, $8 million project, had three components: building explicit *ICTE Dimensions* to complement the Australian Professional Standards for Graduate

Teachers; developing twelve digital resource packages; and mapping current practices through the review of course documents. The number of stakeholders who committed to this project and their willingness to work together illustrates the challenge in preparing ICT-ready graduates.

Within the rhetoric about failure, challenges and obstacles, the role that pre-service teachers play in their own education and professional learning has been underplayed. Many pre-service teachers in Australia do not directly enter teacher education from school. Rather, many are older, have completed other study, have worked in other jobs, and have families. Suffice to say, this cohort already have technological knowledge and skills acquired from their prior work and study. Although many use technologies in their day-to-day lives, particularly social technologies this does not mean that they are equipped to use them in school settings [13]. As commented by Redmond, Albion and Maroulis [19]:

> … Technical skills in the use of ICTs continue to be important but, as the skill levels of students entering teacher preparation programs continue to rise, pedagogical considerations related to ICTs are increasingly viewed as more important.

A recent study by Delaney et al. [20] of 220 pre-service science teachers in their first semester of study at two Australian Universities, found that though many were familiar many types of technologies, they were not able to transfer their knowledge to the classroom setting. The challenge then for teacher education providers is how to design programs that recognize and build on the pre-service teacher's prior knowledge (gained from prior work, study and their personal lives), and transfer it to the classroom context. Also, the extent to which teacher education providers should be responsible for developing the skill-set of the next generation of educators needs to be considered, and to what extent pre-service teachers should assume some responsibility.

2.1 Approaches to Teaching ICT

In the past it was often assumed that pre-service teachers only needed to have technical-know-how to integrate ICT into their practice. Teacher education providers often met this challenge by designing skills-based courses that focused on teaching pre-service teacher how to operate and use technologies. Bakir [3] cites a survey of 1,439 United States institutions which revealed that 85% of programs offered an educational technology course that focused on basic technical skills. Skills-based courses have been criticized for their limitations in teaching pre-service teachers to apply ICT in practice [3, 21].

Mishra and Koehler [22] argue that we need to think differently about technology knowledge. Rather than narrowly defining it as the technical know-how to operate particular technology tools, these researchers argue that it also involves recognizing that technologies are not neutral and that their designs and capacities can both enable and constrain particular practice [23]. Mishra and Koehler argue that teachers need a deeper understanding of technology and a need for that knowledge to continuingly evolve and develop. They suggest that today, pre-service teachers need a complex knowledge set, one that involves the interconnection of technological, pedagogical and content knowledge, referred to as the TPACK model. As they explain:

> Understanding that introducing new educational technologies into the learning process changes more than the tools used—and that this has deep implications for the nature of content-area learning, as well as the pedagogical approaches among which teachers can select—is an important and often overlooked aspect of many technology integration approaches used to date [23].

Tondeur, et al. [5] suggest that, "Teacher education programmes have struggled with selecting and implementing the most effective strategies" to support pre-service teachers develop their ICT competence. Steketee's [21] review, while conducted some time ago, suggests that teacher education providers have used four main approaches. The first is the 'ICT skills development approach' where a specific course is used to upskill pre-service teachers to use ICT. While acknowledging that having skills is important, Steketee comments that this approach does not mean that pre-service teachers can apply these skills in practice. The second approach, the 'ICT pedagogy approach', aims to do just this; it uses a specific course to teach pre-service teachers how to incorporate ICT. While she suggests this is a strength of this approach, she identifies transference into classroom practice again as an issue. The third approach, the 'subject-specific approach', moves away from the discrete course approach and embeds ICT into specific subjects or disciplines. Steketee suggests that though this approach does enable pre-service teachers to develop practical knowledge of integrating ICT, putting this into practice during professional experience (practicum) is hindered. The fourth approach, the 'practice driven approach', is intended to address this. Commenting favorably on the authenticity of this approach, she does suggest it is weakened by the need to have a shared commitment to use ICT by university teachers, pre-service teachers, and teacher mentors in schools.

The site of professional experience/practice is also generally acknowledged as vital for the development of pre-service teachers' practical skills in teaching ICT and seen as a key learning space for teacher education, however, this is an extremely complex area which we will now examine.

2.2 Practical Experience and ICT

Teacher education providers in Australia traditionally design their programs with two components; a coursework component, typically taught on site at the university, and a practicum component whereby pre-service teachers undertake supervised professional experience in school settings [1]. This separation of theory and practice, coursework and practicum, complicates the development of pre-service teacher learning.

Practicum is an important way for pre-service teachers to develop skills in using ICT. It is through these experiences that they can build their knowledge and learn how to integrate ICT into their future practice [3]. Grove [24] comments that:

> [T]he student teaching field experience is a critical component in the preparation of student teachers as a means of establishing ICT practices they will use in future settings. The experience provides a hands-on opportunity for student teachers to put what they know into action as they transfer, apply and refine the theory they have learned into lessons for their students. It is in this critical period that they construct their understanding of teacher practice.

Yet, how the practicum should be designed and implemented, and its relationship to university coursework is heavily contested by policy makers, practicing teachers, university educators and students themselves. Zeichner [25] suggests that teacher education providers have very little involvement in the details, often seeing it as an administrative task rather than a site for learning. Furthermore, he suggests that teacher education providers have little knowledge of what happens in schools. Darling-Hammond [26] similarly suggests that:

> … [the practicum] side of teacher education has been fairly haphazard, depending on the idiosyncrasies of loosely selected placements with little guidance about what happens in them and little connection to university work.

Research also suggests that a number of factors impact on the value of the practicum in supporting pre-service teachers to gain knowledge and skills in applying ICT to their practice. According to Brown and Warschauer [27]:

> During field placements, the use of technology was considerably constrained by over-whelming demands placed on student teachers, thus perpetuating the peripheral role of technology in a teacher preparation experience.

They suggested factors such as access to technology as well as teacher mentor capacity to model successful practice, along with curriculum demands, pressure to cover content, and the need to meet standards and prepare for testing were all influential. The six pre-service teachers in their study mainly used ICT for low-end uses, such as word processing and internet searches. Martinovic and Zhang [28] in the second year of their study concluded that 61 of the 64 pre-service teachers used only one type of ICT from a selected list while on practicum. Furthermore they suggested that the lack of teacher mentors who could successfully model technology integration was one of the root causes of this singular use. As they stated:

> [W]here technology was available, its use depended solely on the classroom teachers' will and skill. Some teachers were noted to give students a web site to surf through and obtain information; some used technology only towards the end of a class as a time filler – after other materials were already covered.

3 Methodology

This chapter is essentially concerned with where pre-service teachers develop their ICT toolkit and was guided by the following research questions:

1. Where do pre-service teachers learn how to use a defined list of ICT resources? Do they learn how to use these resources in one particular setting more than others? If so, which setting was more often used? Which setting was least used?
2. Is there a relationship between the setting and type of resource?
3. As a result of these findings, what are some implications for teacher education programs?

This chapter draws on findings from a self-assessed survey completed by 69 pre-service teachers enrolled in primary or secondary teacher education programs at

RMIT University, Victoria Australia. The survey instrument was adapted from a larger instrument used by practicing teachers as a professional learning tool to benchmark their ICT confidence and skill [29]. This instrument has been used for a number of years and includes a list of ICT tools/resources that can be categorized as both General-Type resources (those that could be used in everyday lives, such as Twitter), as well as Education-Type resources (those more particular to the classroom such as interactive whiteboards). The list was reviewed by the authors and resources not considered particularly relevant to pre-service teachers were removed, resulting in 32 items being included in the adapted instrument. It should be noted, that while we considered that these resources might be relevant to pre-service teachers, we did not assume that they would know them all. The survey was administered online using Qualtrics software via a link sent by email.

The survey had a number of sections, one section asked pre-service teachers to indicate whether they knew what each of the listed ICT tools/resources was and what it did (a yes/no scale was used); another section asked them to report their level of skill in using the tools/resources (using a four-point scale: not at all/a little/some/a lot). The results of the survey have been reported elsewhere [2] but a summary is useful to this discussion. The survey data showed that pre-service teachers knew many of the General-Type resources and had quite a high level of skill in using them, including social media technologies such as networking sites, intelligent maps and digital cameras. They had a lesser knowledge and skill level in using Education-Type resources. A third section of the survey, and the focus of this chapter, asked the pre-service teachers to indicate where they had learned to use the listed ICT tools/resources. They were given five options: Coursework, Practicum, Prior Study, Prior Work, or Personal/Social Life.

4 Findings

Survey results relating to where pre-service teachers learned how to use the listed resources are presented as percentage data in Table 2 below. In the following discussion, we begin by reporting on the setting or location of their learning and then in turn report on the specific resources learned in these settings/locations. Finally, we report on the relationship between setting and type of resource (General-Type or Education-Type resource).

4.1 Site of Learning

As seen in Table 2, the pre-service teachers surveyed largely learned how to use the listed ICT resources in their Personal/Social Life. They indicated higher percentages in this setting in relation to 22 of the 32 resources, however this varied by resource.

Participants indicated higher percentages in learning to use resources during Coursework on five occasions. When it came to learning how to use resources on Practicum, participants recorded higher percentages in relation to only three resources. They did not record a higher percentage in relation to any of the resources in their Prior

Table 2. Where pre-service teachers learned to use the resource as percentages.

	Coursework %	Practicum %	Prior Study %	Prior Work %	Personal/Social Life %
Digital Learning Resources (websites, interactives, movies, images)	21	10	10	10	49
The DEECD website (Department of Education website)	77	7	2	9	5
FUSE (Department of Education repository for teachers)	25	50	13	0	13
EduSTAR (DET suite of ICT applications pre-loaded onto teacher notebooks)	29	64	0	4	4
Discussion Forums, Chat and RSS Feeds	29	0	4	8	58
Blogs	24	2	3	0	71
Wikis	57	2	4	7	30
Microblogging e.g. Twitter	39	3	0	0	58
Ning	69	6	0	6	19
Intelligent maps e.g. Google Maps	6	0	0	3	90
Online Surveys and Polls e.g. Survey Monkey	35	4	10	18	33
Social Bookmarking e.g. Delicious, Pinterest, Symbaloo	26	5	0	2	67
Social Networking Website e.g. Facebook	3	0	0	3	94
Video Sharing e.g. Teacher Tube	25	10	2	4	58
Online Conferences e.g. Blackboard Collaborate, Google Hangout	63	3	16	8	11

(*continued*)

Table 2. (*continued*)

	Coursework %	Practicum %	Prior Study %	Prior Work %	Personal/Social Life %
Video Conferencing	15	5	5	20	55
Voice Over Internet Protocol (VoIP) e.g. Skype	4	0	0	9	88
Wireless Internet Access for Learning and Teaching	15	24	7	9	45
Interactive Whiteboard (IWB)	26	47	10	12	5
Robotics Equipment e.g. Lego robotics	17	0	33	8	42
Gaming Consoles	2	0	0	4	94
Digital Cameras - still/video	2	0	2	3	93
GPS (Global Positioning Software)	2	2	0	6	90
Netbooks (mini tablets funded by the Department of Education)	6	22	2	3	67
Mobile Phones for Educational Use	28	11	2	6	53
iPod, iTouch or other MP3 players	3	3	3	3	87
Tablet e.g. iPad	8	7	2	2	82
eBook Reader e.g. Kindle	2	10	2	6	80
Learner Response Devices e.g. Quiz Dom	20	10	30	20	20
Smart Pens or Digital Pens	19	19	23	8	31
Digital Learning Portfolio	26	26	11	16	21
Voice Recognition Software	9	3	13	9	66

Work but they did indicate a higher percentage in a Prior Study setting on one occasion.

Coursework and Personal/Social Life were selected as the setting for learning for each of the listed resources. However, this was not the case with the other three settings, Practicum was not selected for seven of the listed resources, Prior Study for nine, and Prior Work for three. Thus, the order of the setting where students learned to use different ICT resources was Personal/Social Lives, then Coursework, followed by Practicum, Prior Work and then Prior Study.

4.2 ICT Resources

As stated in the previous section, a higher percentage of participants learned how to use the listed resources in their Personal/Social Lives compared to the other settings or spaces. The following section focuses on the ICT resources in relation to the setting indicated as the place of learning.

With the Personal/Social setting this ranged from 31% who learned how to use Smart Pens, to 94% who learned how to use Gaming Consoles as well as Social Networking Websites. Eighty per cent or more of the participants learned how to use nine resources in the Personal/Social Lives setting rather than other settings. These were: Gaming Consoles (94%), Social Networking Website (94%), Digital Cameras (93%), Intelligent Maps (90%), GPS (90%), VoIP (88%), iPod, iTouch or other MP3 player (87%), Tablet (82%) and eBook Reader (80%). Around 60% to 70% of participants indicated they learned how to use four main resources in the Personal/Social Lives setting. These were: Voice Recognition Software (66%), Netbooks (67%), Social Bookmarking (67%) and Blogs (71%). Around 40% to 50% reported learning eight resources: Robotics Equipment (42%), Wireless Internet Access (45%), Digital Learning Resources (49%), Mobile Phones (53%), and Video Conferencing (55%), with Video Sharing, Discussion Forums and Microblogging all recorded by some 58% of pre-service teachers.

A higher percentage of participants reported they had learned how to use six resources in the Coursework setting, rather than other settings. These were: DEECD Website (77%), NING (69%), Online Conferences (63%), Wikis (57%), and Online Surveys (35%), and Digital Learning Portfolio (26%). Participants reported higher percentage rates in learning three resources during Practicum. These were: Edustar (64%), and FUSE (50%), (both are websites designed by the government to support teachers), and Interactive Whiteboards (IWB) (47%). A higher percentage of participants reported learning how to use one resource in their Prior Study and this was in relation to Learner Response Devices (30%).

4.3 Relationship Between Location of Learning and Type of Resource

In this third section we analyze and report on the relationship between the learning setting (Coursework, Practicum, Prior Study, Prior Work, or Personal/Social Life) and the type of resource, whether General-Type resource or Education-Type resource.

Predictably, participants learned how to use General-Type resources, i.e., those that are accessible in their every-day personal/social lives, such as GPS, and Social Networking, Digital Learning Resources. They reported less learning of Education-Type resources, those more applicable to specific education settings. These were, Wireless Internet Access for Learning and Teaching, Netbooks (mini tablets funded by the Department of Education) and Mobile Phones for Educational Use.

In a Coursework setting, pre-service teachers reported learning how to use Education-Type resources such as Department of Education and Government websites and Digital Learning Portfolio. They also reported learning how to use General-Type resources including Online Conferences, Wikis and Online Surveys. In Practicum settings, participants reported learning about three Education-Type resources, Edustar, FUSE and IWBs. In the Prior Study setting they reported learning about one resource, Learner Response Devices, which falls in the General-Type resource.

As a general trend, pre-service teachers were more likely to report learning to use a resource in one of the listed settings, rather than across the five. This is shown in patterns in their rating of resources, particularly the differences between the highest rated setting and the second highest. There was a 70% difference between the highest rated resource and second highest resource in relation to nine of the resources. For example, Social Networking Website was learned by 94% of participants in their Personal/Social Life, with only 3% indicating they learned it in either Coursework or Prior Work. Gaming Consoles, was learned by 94% of participants in their Personal/Social Life and only 4% in Prior Study. A final example is iPod, iTouch or other MP3 player, where by 87% indicated they had learned in their Personal/Social Life compared to 3% who indicated they had learned how to use this resource in each of the other four settings. There were, however, some exceptions to this pattern. For example, 35% of the participants indicated they learned how to use Online Surveys in Coursework and 33% indicated they did so in Personal/Social Life. Another example is Robotics Equipment, with 42% of participants reporting they learned how to use this in their Personal/Social Life, along with 33% who reported learning in Prior Study.

There were a few occasions when the pre-service teachers did indicate that they learned how to use a resource in multiple locations. For example, Learner Response Devices was reported being learned by 20% of participants in three settings (Personal/Social Life, Coursework and Prior Work), Smart Pens was reported being learned by 31% in Personal/Social Life, 23% in Prior Study and 19% both in Coursework and Practicum. Digital Learning Portfolio was learned by 26% of participants both in Coursework and Practicum and 21% in Personal/Social Life.

This general trend of learning to use a resource in one setting (rather than multiple settings) is also shown by patterns of non-selection of a setting. This was the case in relation to 14 of the listed resources. For example, Practicum as a setting was not selected on seven occasions, e.g. Discussion Forums, Intelligent Maps, Social Networking Website, VOIP, Robotics Equipment, Gaming Consoles and Digital Cameras. Prior Work as a setting was not selected on three occasions, e.g. FUSE, Blogs, and Microblogging. Prior Study was not selected on eight occasions, e.g. Edustar, Ning, Intelligent Maps, Social Bookmarking, Social Networking Websites, VOIP, Gaming Consoles, and GPS. This pattern is also shown by very low rates of selection of a setting (2%, 3% or 4%) in relation to 22 resources.

5 Discussion

Literature to date has generally shown that teacher education providers have struggled to produce ICT competent graduates [4]. In particular, the often-used approach of a stand-alone educational technology course has been the source of contention [5, 30], so too, the skill level of teaching staff and their capacity to model practice. In Australia, teacher education providers are facing increasing pressure to achieve greater consistency across providers and to ensure effective integration of the practicum experience and the learning that takes place at the university. For some time, this pressure has also included the expectation to prepare future educators with the ICT skills and knowledge to implement this into their future classroom practice. National accreditation requirements are also having considerable impact on the design, and delivery of teacher education programs [31]. These standards, which stipulate what graduates should know and be able to do, have turned this expectation into a requirement for all providers. Yet in the past, teacher education providers have been found wanting when it comes to preparing pre-service teachers to use ICT in their teaching practice. Thus as Henderson et al. [6] suggest, providers are likely to be challenged to meet the demands of the current regulatory environment.

> Although there is no doubt that there are some individual teacher educators and exemplary institutions which would be more effective than others, it is not unreasonable to make the claim that pre-service teacher education as a whole risks failing in their mission to adequately prepare prospective teacher graduates [6].

Against this background of increasing pressure, greater accountability and criticism of past efforts, a considerable body of research has shown that achieving this ICT expectation is complex. Research has shown for example that a range of factors act as barriers or enablers [10, 11] to pre-service teacher appropriation of ICT. There is also increasing recognition in research that technical know-how, while necessary, does not accurately define the complex knowledge-set required [22] for classroom practice. Arguably then, greater recognition of this complexity could enable more complex approaches to be developed including those that enable interconnection of coursework and practicum.

This study suggests that pre-service teachers primarily learned how to use particular resources in their Personal/Social Lives rather than through their teacher education programs. For the most part these were General-Type resources learned in this setting. Pre-service teachers were also likely to learn how to use a given resource in one location, rather than across multiple locations. So, rather than learning how to use these resources being through coursework as in the past, (and as assumed in reports such as TEMAG), pre-service teachers bring considerable knowledge with them before they even start their teacher education program. As such, the results of this small-scale study could have a bearing on how teacher education programs are designed and delivered. For example, it suggests that providers could focus more on how to incorporate prior knowledge of resources to the school context, and what knowledge (pedagogy, content and technology) pre-service teachers then require.

Responsibility for developing pre-service teachers' ICT skills and knowledge, continues to rest with teacher education providers. There has been little consideration that pre-service teachers should have some accountability for their own development of ICT knowledge and skills. Also, there has been little attention given to the prior knowledge and skills they do bring with them to their teacher education program.

This study reveals a number of tensions. On the one hand teacher education providers are expected to prepare graduates who have the knowledge and skills to teach in schools, including having an ICT skill-set, and it is often assumed in research and reports that practicum provides productive learning opportunities for pre-service teachers yet, very few of the pre-service teachers in this study, reported that they learned how to use ICT resources during their placement in schools. Reports such as TEMAG [1], advise teacher education providers to make more use of school settings, in order to facilitate more practical skills but this study indicates practicum may not have provided these particular pre-service teachers with many ICT learning opportunities. There is a mismatch between the rhetoric around ICT expectations and practice.

This study highlights that pre-service teachers can learn how to use ICT resources in a range of locations, not just through a teacher education program as mandated by national accreditation requirements. This is not to suggest that having this technological knowledge is all that is required to integrate ICT into practice. Rather to the contrary, as the research by Mishra and Koehler [22] has shown, a complex set of interconnected knowledge is required involving the interplay of technology, pedagogy and content knowledge. This has implications for the design of teacher education programs.

In the past, teacher education programs often used a single-techno-centric course to teach pre-service teachers how to use ICT. These courses typically focused on how to operate various technologies, often in context-neutral ways, rather than teaching how to integrate them into specific settings. The current rate of development of new technologies continues to increase, as such, it is impossible for pre-service teachers to know and be able to use all the technologies that are on the market. Rather, as has been suggested by numerous researchers, pre-service teachers need to learn how to appropriate technologies into their practice, many of which are General-Type resources, and not those specifically designed for education contexts. Rather than pre-service teachers focusing on learning about technologies and how to use them, Mishra and Koehler [22] argue that programs need to be designed so that pre-service teachers have opportunities to engage in 'deep play' with technologies so as to be capable of seeing new uses and applications.

This study shows that General-Type resources were most known by the pre-service teachers who took part, whereas Education-Type resources were not. This raises the question of where will pre-service teachers learn how to use these Education-Type resources? The TEMAG report [1] recommends greater connections between providers and practicum sites (schools). This study indicates that the perceived benefits of learning how to integrate ICT when in a school setting may be ill conceived and not readily achievable. Indeed, it could be argued that this study challenges the implicit assumption in reports that greater connection with schools will lead to greater practice of ICT skills.

This study raises further questions about how ICT can be embedded into both components of teacher education programs; the coursework and the practicum component. Given that it is assumed that knowledge and skills are taught in both these locations, it is interesting that these settings were not utilized to any great extent as the source of pre-service teacher ICT knowledge. Teacher education providers perhaps need to move away from seeing themselves as the source of all knowledge regarding the use ICT in teaching practice, and have a greater acknowledgement that this knowledge and skill can be learned in a range of settings. We recommend further investigation into how teacher education providers can best design programs to take advantage of the multiple settings/locations in which this knowledge can be learned.

6 Limitations

It is important to note that this study has a number of limitations. First it is only a small-scale study involving a small number of pre-service teachers. A study with more participants could be of value. The selection of participants was made on a voluntary basis and only those who had undertaken at least one practicum were invited. However, secondary pre-service teachers only had a four-week practicum block and primary pre-service teachers had twice this amount, two blocks of four weeks each time. Therefore, there was a difference in the amount of practicum experience that could have influenced results. As well, the amount of time spent on Practicum was not equitable with that spent on Coursework. Furthermore, these participants were drawn from two different programs, but the data did not differentiate by program.

Another limitation in this study is the trustworthiness of self-reported data. Participants may have over-stated, or indeed under-stated, where they learned how to use the resources. There are also a number of possible limitations to the survey question which asked: 'Where I developed this skill' which could have been interpreted as referring to 'first learned' or 'most learned' which may have skewed results. In addition, as participants could only select one of the five listed locations, they could therefore not rank locations.

7 Conclusion

Teacher education providers have long been challenged to support the development of graduates to have the knowledge and skill to use ICT in their practice. While we acknowledge the challenges that providers have had in the past, and continue to face in an increasing regulatory environment, we are optimistic that more effective approaches to the design of teacher education programs will be achieved, and so too, the capacity of graduates to use ICT in their practice. This chapter contributes to the ongoing debate around how teacher education providers can educate the future educators. Having knowledge of where pre-service teachers learn how to use ICT resources, including the prior knowledge that they bring with them is an important consideration in the framing of teacher education programs.

This small-scale study found that pre-service teachers enter teacher education programs with a range of technological know-how learned from their personal and social lives. This poses a number of challenges for teacher education providers. First, providers need to recognize and utilize this prior knowledge in the design of their programs. Second, they need to do so without overly emphasizing technological knowledge in the effective use of ICT. Third, how to teach pre-service teachers how to interconnect their technological knowledge with pedagogical and content knowledge.

This study has a number of implications for teacher education providers. First, given that pre-service teachers gain considerable knowledge of General-Type resources in their Personal/Social Lives, teacher educator providers could concentrate more on embedding Education-Type resources into Coursework settings. This embedding could be across the lifespan of a program which would enable progression in learning and consistency in approach, a strategy advocated in research by Bakir [3] and Tondeur et al. [5]. Second, while research has suggested that the Practicum can be a site for learning how to use ICT resources, this study revealed limited use of this setting. As such further opportunities to explore the use of this setting could be undertaken.

This study provides evidence that pre-service teachers can learn how to use ICT resources in a range of settings/locations and that they can and do learn how to use resources prior to the commencement of their program. It suggests that considerable benefit to learning can be lost if due acknowledgement of the importance of pre-service teacher personal and social lives are not taken into consideration when planning and designing programs. While small and exploratory, this study provides some insights for future teacher education programs in Australia as understanding where pre-service teachers learn how to use ICT resources should be a consideration in program design and also beneficial in complying with national professional standards and accreditation requirements.

References

1. Australian Government Department of Education, Action now: Classroom ready teachers - Report of the Teacher Education Ministerial Advisory Group (TEMAG) (2015)
2. Jordan, K., Compton, L.: Pre-service teacher ICT skill-set: not a simple issue. In: EdMedia: World Conference on Educational Media and Technology, Kona, Hawaii, 19–22 October 2015, pp. 799–806, Waynesville, North Carolina, United States (2015)
3. Bakir, N.: An exploration of contemporary realities of technology and teacher education: Lessons learned. J. Digital Learn. Teach. Educ. **31**(3), 117–130 (2015)
4. Haydn, T.: How do you get pre-service teachers to become 'good at ICT' in their subject teaching? The views of expert practitioners. Technol. Pedagogy Educ. **23**(4), 455–469 (2014)
5. Tondeur, J., van Braak, J., Sang, G., Voogt, J., Fisser, P., Ottenbreit-Leftwich, A.: Preparing pre-service teachers to integrate technology in education: a synthesis of qualitative evidence. Comput. Educ. **59**(1), 134–144 (2012)
6. Henderson, M., Bellis, N., Cerovac, M., Lancaster, G.: Collaborative inquiry: Building pre-service teachers' capacity for ICT pedagogical integration. Aust. Educ. Comput. **27**(3), 69–75 (2013)
7. Pearson, J.: Information and communications technologies and teacher education in Australia. Technol. Pedagogy Educ. **12**(1), 39–58 (2003)
8. Downes, T., Perry, B., Sherwood, C.: IT in education and teacher education in Australia. J. Comput. Assist. Learn. **11**(1), 23–34 (1995)

9. Department of Education Employment and Workplace Relations (DEEWR): Hot topic: ICT in pre-service teacher training: strategic ICT advisory service. Education.au limited, SA (2009)
10. Ertmer, P.A.: Addressing first-and second-order barriers to change: strategies for technology integration. Educ. Tech. Res. Dev. **47**(4), 47–61 (1999)
11. Ertmer, P.A., Ottenbreit-Leftwich, A., York, C.S.: Exemplary technology-using teachers: perceptions of factors influencing success. J. Comput. Teach. Educ. **23**(2), 55–61 (2006)
12. Mirzajani, H., Mahmud, R., Ayub, A.F.M., Wong, S.L.: A review of research literature on obstacles that prevent use of ICT in pre-service teachers' educational courses. Int. J. Educ. Literacy Stud. **3**(2), 25 (2015)
13. Cheal, J., Geer, R., White, B.: The preparedness of pre-service teachers to use ICT in the classroom. In: Australian Teacher Education Association, pp. 1–8 (2012)
14. Albion, P., Redmond, P.: Teaching by example? Integrating ICT in teacher education. In: Proceedings of the 2008 Australian Computers in Education Conference, Australian Council for Computers in Education (2008)
15. Prensky, M.: Digital natives, digital immigrants part 1. Horizon **9**(5), 1–6 (2001)
16. Bennett, S., Maton, K., Kervin, L.: The 'digital natives' debate: a critical review of the evidence. Br. J. Edu. Technol. **39**(5), 775–786 (2008)
17. Selwyn, N.: The digital native-myth and reality. In: Aslib Proceedings, pp. 364–379. Emerald Group Publishing Ltd (2009)
18. Finger, G., Jamieson-Proctor, R., Cavanagh, R., Albion, P., Bond, T., Fitzgerald, R., Romeo, G., Lloyd, M.M.: Teaching teachers for the future (TTF) project TPACK survey: summary of the key findings. Aust. Educ. Comput. **27**(3), 13–25 (2012)
19. Redmond, P., Albion, P., Maroulis, J.: Intentions v reality: preservice ICT integration during professional experience. In: Society for Information Technology & Teacher Education International Conference, Phoenix, USA, 1–5 Mar 2005, pp. 1566–1571 (2005)
20. Delaney, S., Trapani, F., Chandler, P., Redman, C.: Contemporary practices of technology and its affordances: perceptions of pre-service teachers on the utilization of technology in teaching and learning practice. In EDULEARN14 Proceedings, pp. 2472–2481 (2014)
21. Steketee, C.: Integrating ICT as an integral teaching and learning tool into pre-service teacher training courses. Issues Educ. Res. **15**(1), 101–113 (2005)
22. Mishra, P., Koehler, M.: Technological pedagogical content knowledge: a framework for teacher knowledge. Teach. Coll. Rec. **108**(6), 1017–1054 (2006)
23. Harris, J., Mishra, P., Koehler, M.: Teachers' technological pedagogical content knowledge and learning activity types: curriculum-based technology integration reframed. J. Res. Technol. Educ. **41**(4), 393–416 (2009)
24. Grove, K.J.: Student teacher ICT use: field experience placements and mentor teacher influences. In: OECD ICT and Teacher Training Expert Meeting, Paris, France, October (2008)
25. Zeichner, K.: Rethinking the connections between campus courses and field experiences in college-and university-based teacher education. J. Teach. Educ. **61**(1–2), 89–99 (2010)
26. Darling-Hammond, L.: Teacher education and the American future. J. Teach. Educ. **61**(1–2), 35–47 (2010)
27. Brown, D., Warschauer, M.: From the university to the elementary classroom: students' experiences in learning to integrate technology in instruction. J. Technol. Teach. Educ. **14**(3), 599 (2006)
28. Martinovic, D., Zhang, Z.: Situating ICT in the teacher education program: Overcoming challenges, fulfilling expectations. Teach. Teach. Educ. **28**(3), 461–469 (2012)

29. Department of Education and Early Childhood Development (DEECD): The ePotential Survey Questions. http://epotential.education.vic.gov.au/webdata/ePotential%20User%20Guides%20Survey%20Questions.pdf
30. Kay, R.A.: Formative analysis of how preservice teachers learn to use technology. J. Comput. Assist. Learn. **23**(5), 366–383 (2007)
31. Australian Institute for Teaching and School Leadership (AITSL): Accreditation of initial teacher education programs in Australia: standards and procedures. Ministerial Council for Education, Early Childhood Development and Youth Affairs (MCEECDYA), Carlton South, Vic (2011)

Interval Type-2 Fuzzy Logic Systems for Evaluating Students' Academic Performance

Ibahim A. Hameed[1,2(✉)], Mohanad Elhoushy[2], and Ottar L. Osen[1]

[1] Faculty of Engineering and Natural Sciences, Department of Automation Engineering (AIR), Norwegian University of Science and Technology (NTNU), Larsgårdsvegen 2, 6009 Ålesund, Norway
ibib@ntnu.no

[2] Faculty of Electronic Engineering, Department of Industrial Electronics and Control Engineering, Menofia University, Menouf 32952, Egypt

Abstract. Assessment method sends messages to students to define and priorities what is important to learn and ultimately how they spend their time leaning it. Traditional grading methods are largely based on *human judgments*, which tend to be subjective. In addition, it is based on sharp criteria instead of fuzzy criteria and suffers from erroneous scores assigned by indifferent or inexperienced examiners, which represent a rich source of uncertainties, which might impair the credibility of the system. In an attempt to reduce uncertainties and provide more objective, reliable, and precise grading, a sophisticated assessment approach based on *type-2* fuzzy set theory is developed. In this paper, interval type-2 (IT2) fuzzy sets, which are a special case of the general T2 fuzzy sets, are used. The transparency and capabilities of type-2 fuzzy sets in handling uncertainties is expected to provide an evaluation system able to justify and raise the quality and consistency of assessment judgments. A simplified implementation of interval type-2 fuzzy system using the basic knowledge of type-1 fuzzy is presented. A comparison between the use of type-1, interval type-2 fuzzy systems and the simplified IT2 fuzzy systems in reducing uncertainties and providing more transparent and fair assessment that can reflect needs of individual students and foster development is presented.

Keywords: Interval Type-2 Fuzzy Sets (IT2FSs) · Footprint-of-Uncertainty (FOU) · Fuzzy grading system · Intelligent evaluation · Learning achievement · Transparent assessment

1 Introduction

As highlighted by Boud [2], assessment methods and requirements probably have a greater influence on how and what students learn than any other factor.

This paper is an extended and revised version of a paper presented at the 8th International Conference on Computer Supported Education (CSEDU 2016), Rome, Italy, 21–23 April 2016 [1].

G. Costagliola et al. (Eds.): CSEDU 2016, CCIS 739, pp. 420–441, 2017.
DOI: 10.1007/978-3-319-63184-4_22

This influence may become of greater importance than the impact of teaching materials itself. A high quality, reliable and transparent assessment system supports and improves student lifelong learning and ensures that all students receive fair treatment in order not to limit students' present and future opportunities. The evaluation of a students' learning achievement is done over years and provides the basis for certification of individual achievement, therefore, it should regularly reviewed and improved to ensure that the systems are educationally beneficial to all students [3,17]. Students' evaluation and scoring are largely based on human judgments, which tend to be subjective, and hence represents a rich source of uncertainties. Assessment process, as well, is suffering from uncertainty due to assigning erroneous grades and indifferent and inexperienced practices. Uncertainty is an attribute of information [5]. More often than not, the decision-relevant information is subjected to uncertainty arising from different sources. Consequently, decisions involve an undeniable amount of risk [6].

In an attempt to reduce the uncertainty in the students' assessment process, several attempts have been made in the last decade to use fuzzy set theory in educational evaluation. Biswas [7] presented two methods for students' answerscripts evaluation using fuzzy sets; a fuzzy evaluation method and a generalized fuzzy evaluation method and a matching function. Echauz and Vachtsevanos [8] proposed a fuzzy logic system for translating traditional scores into letter-grades. Law [9] built a fuzzy structure model for education grading system with its algorithm to aggregate different test scores in order to produce a single score for individual student. Wilson, Karr and Freeman [10] presented an automatic grading system based on fuzzy rules and genetic algorithms. Chen and Lee [11] presented two methods for applying fuzzy sets to overcome the problem of rewarding two different fuzzy marks the same total score that could arise from Biswas' method [7]. Ma and Zhou [12] proposed a fuzzy set approach to assess the outcomes of student-centered learning using the evaluation of their peers and lecturer.

Weon and Kim [13] presented an evaluation strategy based on fuzzy MFs. They pointed out that the system for students' achievement evaluation should consider the three important factors of the questions that the students answer: the difficulty, the importance, and the complexity. Weon and Kim used singleton functions to describe the factors of each question reflecting the effect of the three factors individually, but not collectively. Wang and Chen [14] presented a method for evaluating students' answerscripts using fuzzy numbers associated with degrees of confidence of the evaluator. Bai and Chen [15] proposed a method to automatically construct the grade MFs of fuzzy rules for evaluating student's learning achievement. Bai and Chen [16] proposed a method for applying fuzzy MFs and fuzzy rules for the same purpose. Bai and Chen [16] pointed out that the difficulty factor is a very subjective parameter and may cause an argument about fairness in evaluation. To solve the subjectivity of the difficulty factor of Weon and Kim's method [13], they obtained the difficulty as a function of accuracy of the student's answer script and time consumed to answer. However, their method still has the subjectivity problem, since the results in scores and ranks are heavily depend on the values of several weights that are determined by the subjective knowledge of domain experts.

Saleh and Kim [3] proposed three nodes fuzzy logic approach based on Mamdani's fuzzy inference engine and the center of gravity (COG) defuzzification technique as an alternative to Bai and Chen's method [16]. The transparency and objective nature of the fuzzy system makes their method easy to understand and enables teachers to explain the results of evaluation to persuade skeptic students. Hameed [17] proposed using Gaussian MFs as an alternative of the triangle MFs used in Saleh and Kim [3]. A sensitivity study showed that using Gaussian MFs with standard deviation higher than 0.4 provide more reliable and robust evaluation system which is able to provide new ranking orders without changing students' scores. Hameed [18] introduced a fuzzy system to automatically evaluate and improve fairness of multiple-choice questions (MCQs) based Exams. Hameed [19] presented a simplified implementation of interval type-2 fuzzy system and used it in evaluating student's academic achievement.

In this paper, various fuzzy logic approaches for students evaluation are proposed. Interval type-2 fuzzy logic (T2FL) system and its simplified implementation are proposed as an evaluation. The general framework of T2 fuzzy reasoning allows handling much of the uncertainty inherited in students' evaluations systems. T2FL has better capabilities in reducing the amount of uncertainty in a system due to its ability in handling linguistic uncertainties by modeling vagueness and unreliability of information [20]. In this paper, a new implementation of the three-nodes fuzzy evaluation system presented in Saleh and Kim [3] and Hameed [17] using T2FSs will be presented. A simplified implementation of IT2FSs will be presented. An example will be given to highlight the differences between traditional, T1FSs- and T2FSs-based approaches.

The paper is organized as follows: a review of existing evaluation approaches is presented in Sect. 2. The proposed interval type-2 fuzzy logic based evaluation system and its simplified implementation using the basic knowledge of T1FSs are presented in Sect. 3. In Sect. 4, results of the approaches presented in Sects. 2 and 3 applied to a real world example are presented. Comparisons between different approaches, concluding remarks and future work are presented in Sect. 5.

2 Review of Evaluation Approaches

2.1 Conventional Grading Approach

In conventional grading, only students' grades which are obtained after grading their answer sheets are used in the evaluation. Assume that there are n students to answer m questions. Accuracy rates of students' answerscripts (student's scores in each question divided by the maximum score assigned to this question) are the basis for evaluation. We get an accuracy rate matrix of dimension $m \times n$,

$$A = [a_{ij}] \tag{1}$$

where $a_{ij} \in [0, 1]$ denotes the accuracy rate of student j on question i. Time rates of students (the time used by a student to solve a question divided by the maximum time allowed to solve this question) is another basis to be considered in evaluation. We get a time rate matrix of dimension $m \times n$,

$$T = [t_{ij}] \tag{2}$$

where $t_{ij} \in [0, 1]$ denotes the time rate of student j on question i. We are also given a grade vector of the exam questions of dimension $m \times 1$,

$$G = [g_i] \tag{3}$$

where $g_i \in [0, 100]$ denotes the assigned maximum score of question i satisfying:

$$\sum_{i=1}^{m} g_i = 100$$

Based on the accuracy rate matrix A and the grade vector G, we can obtain the total score vector, S, of dimension $n \times 1$, for n students using the equation:

$$S = [s_j] = A^T G \tag{4}$$

where A^T denotes the transpose of A, $s_j \in [0, 100]$ is the total score of student j. For each individual student, s_j, can be obtained as:

$$s_j = \sum_{i=1}^{m} a_{ij} \times g_i$$

The classical rank of students is then obtained by sorting the values of S in a descending order. In this approach, the time used in solving each question is not considered.

2.2 Conventional Fuzzy Grading Approach

In fuzzy grading, other factors such as the *answer-time*, *complexity* and *importance* of the exam's questions are considered. The *answer-time*, t_{ij}, described by Eq. 2, is defined as the time used by student j for solving question i. Complexity, c_i, of a question, i, is an indication of how much deep learning and complex skills are required to solve or answer that question correctly in the permitted time. Complexity vector, C, of dimension $m \times 1$ can be represented as:

$$C = [c_i] \tag{5}$$

where $c_i \in [0, 1]$, 0 means that question i lacks complexity while 1 means that it lacks simplicity. The value of c_i for question i is assigned by domain expert (i.e., teachers or examiners) as a crisp value between 0 and 1. c_i can also be expressed as a fuzzy numbers rather than crisp numbers using k fuzzy sets. In this case, complexity matrix, C, of dimension $m \times K$ can be represented as:

$$C = [c_{ik}] \tag{6}$$

where $c_{ik} = \mu_{A_k}(x)$, $\mu_{A_k}(x)$ is a membership function for a fuzzy set A_k where each element x on the universe of discourse X is mapped into a value between 0 and 1, called the grade of membership of the element in X to the fuzzy set A_k. it is worth noting that, if the C does not provided by domain expert in the form of fuzzy numbers, a fuzzification process is required for C to be of $m \times K$ dimension.

Importance is another factor assigned by the domain expert (i.e., teachers and/or examiners) as an indication of the question's importance to the building structure of the study curriculum. Curriculum is a systematic and intended packaging of competencies that learners should acquire through learning. Curriculum contributes to the development of thinking skills and the acquisition of relevant knowledge that learners need to apply in the context of their studies, daily life and careers. Importance vector, I, of dimension $m \times 1$ can be represented as:

$$I = [i_i] \tag{7}$$

where $i_i \in [0, 1]$, 0 means less importance and 1 means more importance to the curriculum. The value of i_i assigned by the domain expert to question i could be in the form of a crisp value in the range between 0 and 1. i_i can also be expressed as a fuzzy numbers rather than crisp numbers using k fuzzy sets. In this case, the importance matrix, I, of dimension $m \times K$ can be represented as:

$$I = [i_{ik}] \tag{8}$$

where $i_{ik} = \mu_{B_k}(x)$, $\mu_{B_k}(x)$ is a membership function for a fuzzy set B_k where each element x on the universe of discourse X is mapped into a value between 0 and 1, called the grade of membership of the element in X to the fuzzy set B_k. it is worth noting that, if the I does not provided by domain expert in the form of fuzzy numbers, a fuzzifiction process is required for I to be of $m \times K$ dimension. Bai and Chen presented an approach in which adjustment vector, W, of dimension $m \times 1$ is computed in terms of the aforementioned factors and used to adjust questions' grades assigned by the domain expert [15,16].

2.3 Three-Nodes Based Fuzzy Evaluation System

The fuzzy grading approach presented in Sect. 2.2 can be implemented using three fuzzy nodes, namely, *difficulty* node, *answer-cost* node, and *adjustment* node, as it is shown Fig. 1 [3].

Inputs to the system, in its left hand side, are given either by exam results or domain expert (i.e., teachers or examiners). Each node of the system behaves like a traditional fuzzy logic controller (FLC) with two scalable inputs and one output, as it is shown in Fig. 2. It maps a two-to-one fuzzy relation by inference

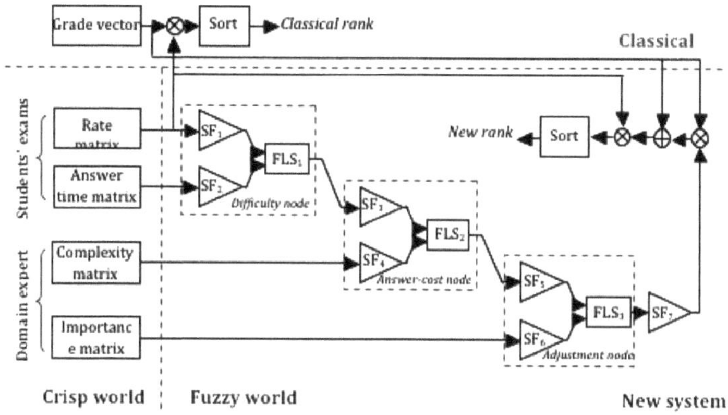

Fig. 1. Block diagram of the three nodes fuzzy evaluation system.

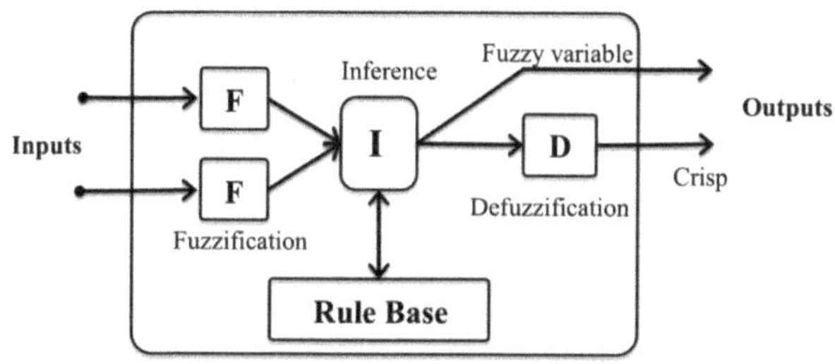

Fig. 2. Node representation as a FLC.

through a given rule bases, shown in Tables 1 and 2 where 1, 2, 3, 4 and 5 stands for the five linguistic labels or levels low, more or less low, medium, more or less high and high, respectively. The inputs are fuzzified based on the predefined defined levels (fuzzy sets) shown in Fig. 3.

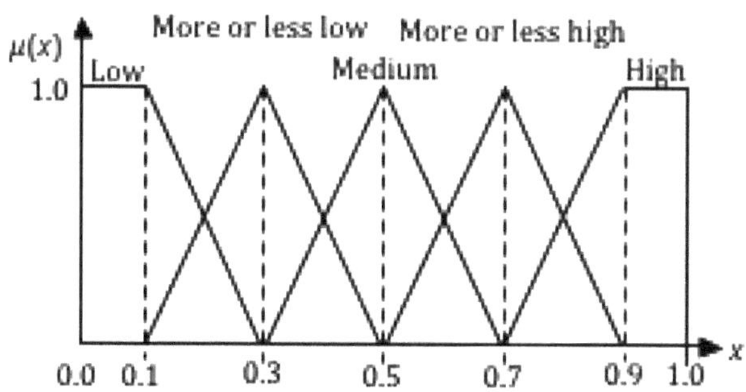

Fig. 3. Triangular membership functions of the five levels (i.e., five MFs).

In the first node, both inputs are given by students' exam result, whereas in the later nodes, one input is the output of its previous node while the other is given by a domain expert gives the other input. The output of each node can be in the form of a crisp value (defuzzified) or in the form of a fuzzy value (i.e., linguistic variables with a degree of membership). Each node has two scale factors (SFs) that can be chosen in a manner to reflect the degree of importance of each input. In this paper, SFs are chosen to be unity to reflect the equal influence of each input on the output.Fuzzy sets (FSs) are sets whose elements have degrees of membership, and were first introduced by Zadeh in 1965 as an extension of the classical notion of set [21]. The inputs are fuzzified based on the predefined defined levels (fuzzy sets) shown in Fig. 3. The fuzzy rules to infer difficulty in terms of accuracy and time rate is shown in Table 1. The fuzzy rule base to infer answer-cost in terms of difficulty and complexity and adjustment in terms of answer-cost and importance, respectively, is shown in Table 2. The surface views of the fuzzy rule bases, given in Tables 1 and 2, are shown in Figs. 4 and 5, respectively. Here, each fuzzy node proceeds in following four steps.

Table 1. Fuzzy rule base to infer difficulty.

Accuracy	Time rate				
	1	2	3	5	5
1	3	4	4	5	5
2	2	3	4	4	5
3	2	2	3	4	4
4	1	2	2	3	4
5	1	1	2	2	3

Table 2. Fuzzy rule base to infer answer-cost/adjustment.

Difficulty/Answer-cost	Complexity/Importance				
	1	2	3	4	5
1	1	1	2	2	3
2	1	2	2	3	4
3	2	2	3	4	4
4	2	3	4	4	5
5	3	4	4	5	5

Step 1. Fuzzification step in which inputs, if given in crisp values, the degree to which these inputs belong to each of the appropriate fuzzy sets is determined. Triangular MF is the commonly used due to its simplicity and easy computation. We note that the same five fuzzy sets, shown in Fig. 3, are applied to represent the accuracy, the time rate, the difficulty, the complexity, and the adjustment of questions in the fuzzy domain.

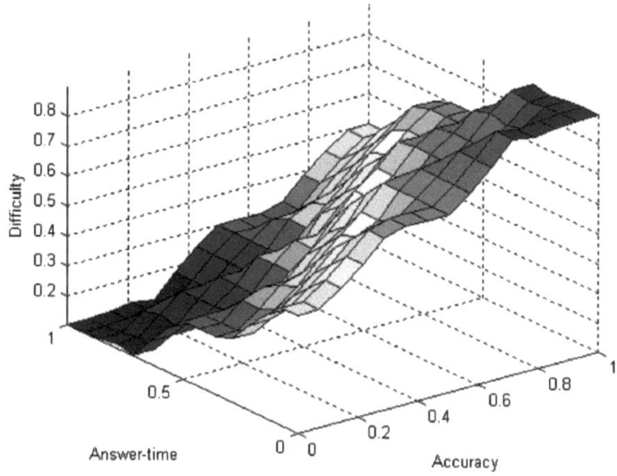

Fig. 4. Surface view of rule base of Table 1 (i.e., difficulty).

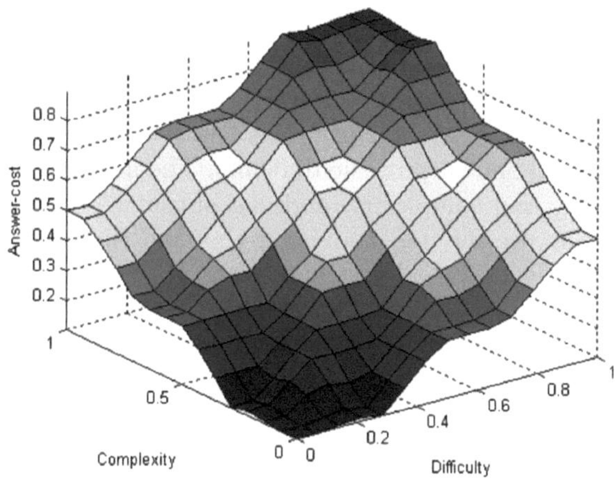

Fig. 5. Surface view of rule base of Table 2 (i.e., answer-cost and adjustment).

Step 2. Rule evaluation where the fuzzified inputs are applied to the antecedents of the fuzzy rules to obtain a single number that represents the result of the antecedent evaluation (i.e., rule or firing strength). The result of the antecedent evaluation is then applied to the membership function of the consequent (i.e., rule implication). Two implication methods are commonly used; clipping where the consequent membership function is sliced at the level of the level of the rule firing strength. The clipped function set loses some information, however, it is preferred because it involves less complex computations and generates an aggregated output surface that is easier to defuzzify [22]. Another method, named scaling, offers a better approach for preserving the original shape of the fuzzy set: the original membership function of the rule consequent is adjusted by multiplying all its membership degrees by the truth value of the rule antecedent.

Step 3. Aggregation of rule outputs where the membership functions of all rule consequents previously clipped or scaled are combined into a single fuzzy set. Implication is modeled by means of minimum operator, and the resulting output MFs are combined using maximum operator (i.e. aggregation).

Step 4. Defuzzification in which the aggregated fuzzy sets are converted into a single crisp output. The most popular method is the centroid technique where a point representing the center of gravity (COG) of the aggregated fuzzy set is found. In this paper, the center of gravity (COG) method is applied. The crisp value of question i is then obtained by

$$y_i = \int_x x.\mu(x)dx \Big/ \int_x \mu(x)dx \tag{9}$$

where integrals are taken over the entire range of the output and $\mu(x)$, and $\mu(x)$ is the membership degree of x. By taking the center of gravity, conflicting rules essentially are cancelled and a fair weighting is obtained. Each of the three nodes follows the above scheme. The difficulty node has two inputs, the accuracy rate and the time rate, and one output, the difficulty. The answer-cost node has two inputs, the difficulty and complexity, and one output of the answer-cost. The adjustment node has two inputs, the answer-cost and the importance, and one output of the adjustment. The adjustment vector, W, is then used to obtain the adjusted grade vector, $\widetilde{G} = [\widetilde{g}_i]$, of dimension $m \times 1$, where $\widetilde{g}_i$ is the adjusted grade of question i, and is obtained using the formula:

$$\widetilde{g}_i = (1 + w_i) \cdot g_i \tag{10}$$

It is then scaled to its total grade by using the formula:

$$\widetilde{g}_i = \widetilde{g}_i \cdot \sum_i^m g_i \Big/ \sum_i^m \widetilde{g}_i \tag{11}$$

Then we obtain the adjusted total scores of students by,

$$\widetilde{S} = A^T \cdot \widetilde{G} \tag{12}$$

The new rank of students is then obtained by sorting values of $\widetilde{S}$ in a descending order.

3 Advanced Fuzzy Grading Approaches

In this section, the 3-nodes fuzzy grading system presented in Sect. 2.3 will be implemented using other forms of fuzzy sets and fuzzy systems.

3.1 Gaussian Based Three-Nodes Fuzzy Evaluation Approach

The three nodes fuzzy evaluation system described in Sect. 2.3 is based on simple triangular-shaped MFs formed using straight lines. Triangular MFs are defined by three scalar parameters a, b and c. The parameters a and c locate the feet of the triangle MF while b locates its peak. There is no way to get its optimum values, however, they should be chosen in a manner to provide a satisfying overlap between different MFs. The simplicity of this function makes it ideal for control applications where computational power and resources are crucial [23]. However, it was noted that when theses parameters are slightly changed, different ranking orders are obtained which could impair the system's reliability.

In order to avoid losing reliability and having a robust evaluation system, it should be able to give the same ranking orders without changing students' scores and for various values of these parameters. In this connection, Gaussian MFs are proposed [17]. Gaussian MFs are suitable for problems that require continuously differentiable curves and smooth transitions between levels, whereas triangular MFs do not have. Gaussian MFs are defined by two parameters; c which locates the distance from the origin to the center of each MF and σ which determines its width. Gaussian MFs is one parameter less than that of the triangular MFs which can lead to an evaluation system with 15 less Degrees-Of-Freedom (DOF) and hence a more robust and reliable performance [23]. Gaussian MF is defined as

$$\mu_{A_i}(x) = e^{-\frac{1}{2}(x-c_i/\sigma_i)^2} \tag{13}$$

where c_i is the center (i.e., mean) and σ_i is the width (i.e., standard deviation) of the ith fuzzy set, which has by nature, infinite support. Therefore, for Gaussian MFs with wide widths it is possible to obtain a membership degree to each fuzzy set greater than 0 and hence every rule in the rule base fires. Consequently, the relationship between input and output can be described accurate enough. Here, the centers of the five Gaussian MFs are chosen to be the same as that of the triangular MFs shown in Fig. 3 (i.e. [0.1 0.3 0.5 0.7 0.9]). Gaussian MFs of the five levels for $\sigma = 0.1$ are shown in Fig. 6.

From Fig. 6 it is obvious that Gaussian MFs provide more continuous transition from one level to the other and hence provides smoother control surface from the fuzzy rules. The Gaussian based fuzzy evaluation system shows the ability to provide correct ranking order of students with equal total scores without changing the total mean scores of all students and the score of each student for $\sigma \geq 4.0$ [4],[17].

3.2 Interval T2FL Based Evaluation System

Type-1 fuzzy sets were first introduced by Zadeh in 1965 [21]. Fuzzy logic systems (FLSs) constructed based on type-1 fuzzy sets (FSs), referred to as type-1 FLSs (T1FLSs). T1FLSs have demonstrated their ability in many applications, especially for the control of complex nonlinear systems, which are difficult to model analytically [24,25]. However, researchers have shown that T1FLSs have

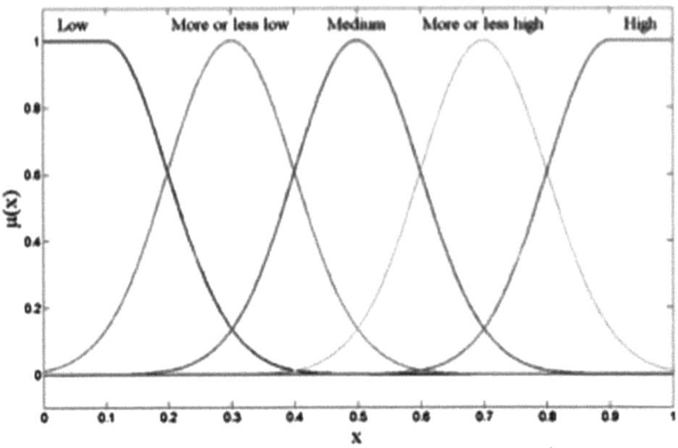

Fig. 6. Gaussian membership functions of the five levels for $\sigma = 0.1$.

difficulties in modeling and minimizing the effect of uncertainties [26]. A reason being that a type-1 FSs are certain in the sense that for each input, there is a crisp membership grade. Type-2 FSs, on the other hand, are characterized by membership grades that are themselves fuzzy.

The concept of T2FSs was first introduced by Zadeh in 1975 [27] as an extension of the concept of an ordinary type-1 fuzzy set. Such sets are fuzzy sets whose membership grades themselves are T1FSs instead of crisp numbers in T1 FS. Mendel and Liang (1999) demonstrated the first type-2 fuzzy framework where the information about the linguistic/numerical uncertainty can be incorporated [28]. They introduced the concept of concept of footprint-of-uncertainty (FOU) where the an interval type-2 membership function (MF) is characterized by an upper and lower type-1 MFs bounding the region called FOU, as it is shown in Fig. 7 for Gaussian and Triangle MFs.

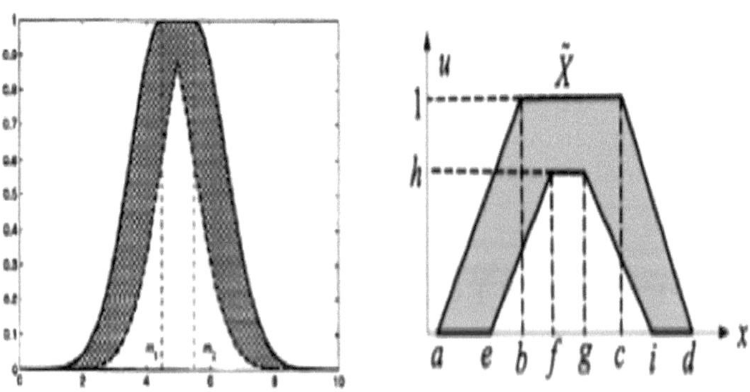

(a) T2 Gaussian MF.

(b) T2 Triangle MF.

Fig. 7. Footprint-Of-Uncertainty (FOU) of T2FS.

As it is illustrated in Fig. 8, the MFs of a type-2 fuzzy set have a footprint-of-uncertainty (FOU), which represents the uncertainties in the shape and position of type-1 FSs [29]. An interval type-2 MF can be obtained by either blurring the width, Fig. 8(a), or center of a type-1 MFs, Fig. 8(b). The FOU is bounded up by an upper MF and a lower MF, both of which are type-1 MFs. Type-2 FLSs is a FLS in which one of more of the antecedent or consequent membership functions or both are type-2 FSs. FOU of type-2 FSs provides an extra mathematical dimension and therefore is it is very useful in circumstances where it is difficult to determine an exact membership grade for FS. Therefore, the amount of uncertainty in a system could be reduced by using type-2 FLS since it offers better capabilities to handle linguistic uncertainties by modeling vagueness and unreliability of information and hence have the potential to outperform their type-1 counterpart [30,31].

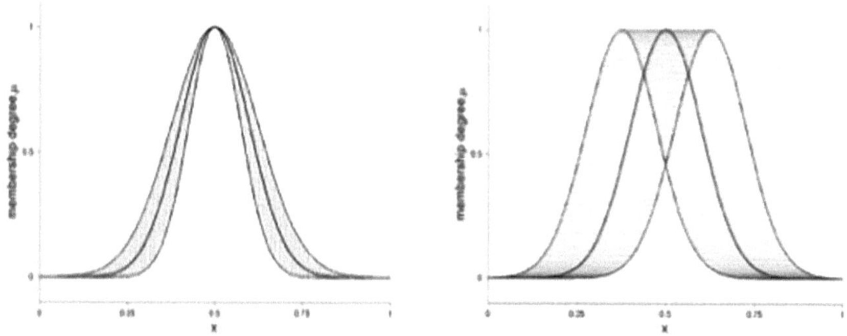

(a) Blurring the width (i.e., variance) of a type-1 MFs.

(b) Blurring the center (i.e., mean) of a type-1 MFs.

Fig. 8. Gaussian type-2 MFs.

3.3 Interval T2FL Based Evaluation System

A fuzzy logic system can be considered as T2 when at least one of the antecedents or consequents of its rule-base is T2 [28]. As the outputs of the inference engine are IT2 FSs, a type-reducer is required to convert its T2FSs into T1FSs to be defuzzified. A detailed description can be found in [32]. T2FSs are useful in such cases when it becomes difficult to determine exact membership function for a fuzzy set and hence are useful for incorporating linguistic uncertainties. Figure 9 shows the schematic diagram of an IT2 FLS. It is similar to its T1 counterpart, shown in Fig. 2, the major difference being that at least one of the FSs in the rule base is an IT2 FS. Hence, the outputs of the inference engine are IT2FSs. A type-reducer is needed to convert them into T1FSs before defuzzification can be carried out [33].

In this paper, the three-nodes fuzzy evaluation framework presented in Sect. 2.3 is implemented using triangle T2FSs shown in Fig. 7(b). Five T2 triangle MFs with different FOU values are used to represent the five levels used to

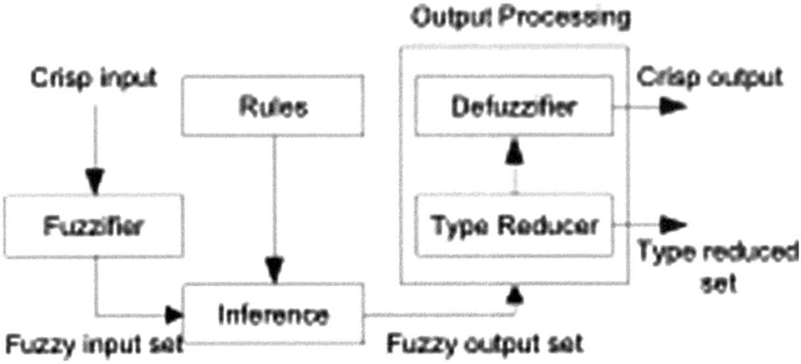

Fig. 9. Schematic diagram of IT2 FLS.

describe each variable, as it is shown in Fig. 10. The FOU (i.e., thickness of the MFs) is provided as an external input by the domain expert as an estimate of the amount of uncertainty in his/her knowledge. In this paper, FOU is chosen

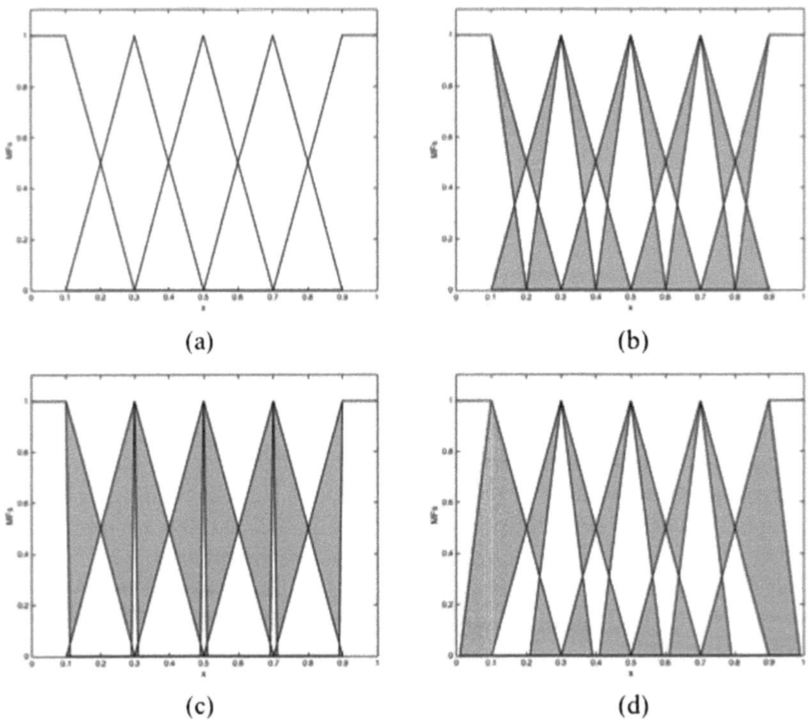

Fig. 10. FOU: (a) zero uncertainty ($FOU = 0$), (b) low uncertainty ($0 < FOU \leq 0.1$), (c) medium uncertainty ($0.1 < FOU \leq 0.2$), and (d) high uncertainty ($0.2 < FOU \leq 0.3$).

to be a number in the range of 0 to 0.3 where 0 refers to zero uncertainty, 0.1 refers to low uncertainty, 0.2 refers to medium uncertainty and 0.3 refers to high uncertainty. It is worth noting that the T2 fuzzy system will converge to its T1 counterpart when uncertainty measure is set to zero [1], as it is shown in Fig. 10(a). In this paper, it is assumed that the domain expert has a medium degree of uncertainty in his knowledge (i.e., $FOU \approx 0.2$).

3.4 Simplified Interval T2FL Based Evaluation System

In this Section, IT2 MFs with different value of FOU (i.e., zero, low, medium and high uncertainty) as it is shown in Fig. 7. The new ranking orders for different FOU values are shown in Table 3. A comparing between the ranking orders of the four types is shown in Table 3. In this section, a simplified implementation of IT2FL is introduced. A type-2 FS could be thought as a set of an infinite number of type-1 FSs, and correspondingly, the defuzzified output of type-2 FLS could be considered as an aggregation of the centroids of an infinite number of embedded type-1 FLSs [29], [34]. When the antecedent and consequent membership grades in type-2 FLS have a continuous domain, the number of embedded type-1 FLSs becomes uncountable. When membership grades are assumed to have discrete domains, each type-2 MF, for simplicity, could be represented by its upper (U) and lower (L) type-1 MFs, as shown in Fig. 11. In this case, each type-2 fuzzy rule could be rewritten in terms of all possible combinations of the upper and lower MFs, for more details please refer to [19].

For students' academic evaluation, five Type-2 Gaussian MFs with fixed mean and blurred width (i.e., uncertain variance) are used to fuzzify each input variable; *low*, *more or less low*, *medium*, *more or less high*, and *high* as it is shown in Fig. 12. The type-2 Gaussian MFs, for simplicity and ease of implementation, are decomposed into four type-1 MFs UU, UL, LU and LL to represent each

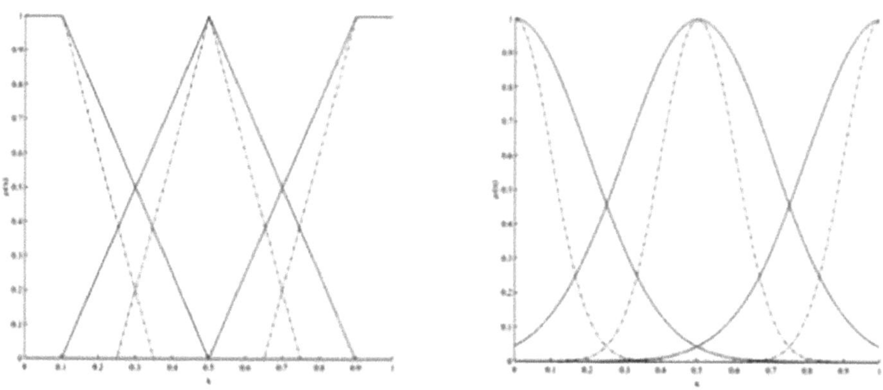

(a) Decomposed triangle T2MF. (b) Decomposed Gaussian T2MF.

Fig. 11. Simplified representation of a type-2 Mfs by its upper MF (UMF) (in sold line) and lower MF (LMF) (in dotted line) type-1 MFs.

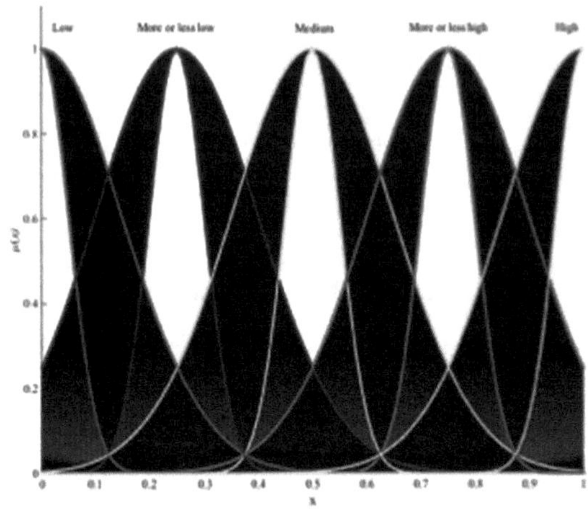

Fig. 12. Five type-2 Gaussian Mfs; *low*, *more or less low*, *medium*, *more or less high*, and *high*.

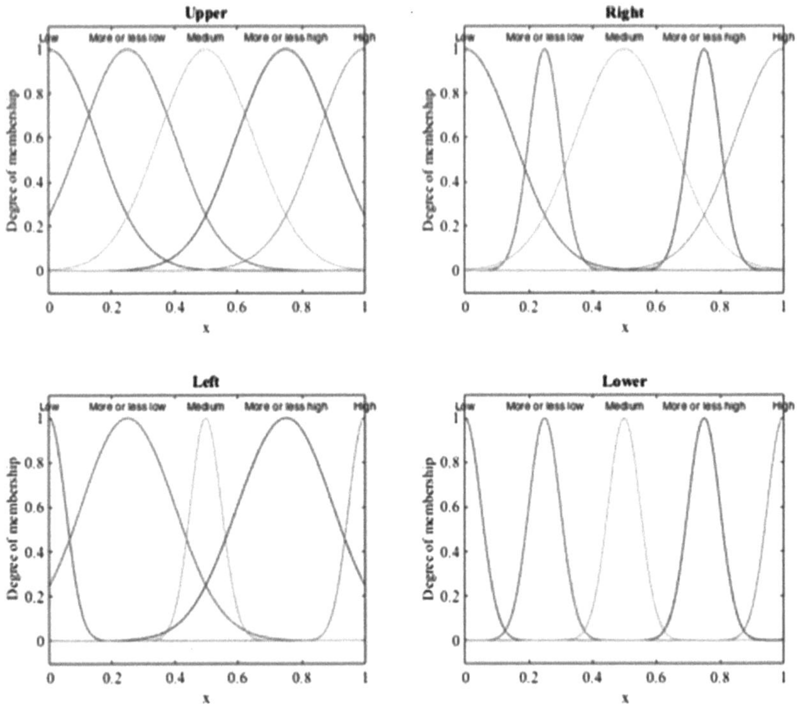

Fig. 13. Decomposition of Type-2 FS into four type-1 FSs.

intersection point, as it is shown in Fig. 13. Upper type-1 FS represents the intersection point composed of two neighbor U MFs (i.e., UU). Lower type-1 FS represents the intersection point composed of two neighbor L MFs (i.e., LL). Right type-1 FS represents the intersection point composed of two neighbors U and L MFs (i.e., UL). Left type-1 FS represents the intersection point composed of two neighbors L and U MFs (i.e., LU). The schematic diagram of the simplified implementation of Type-2 FS is shown in Fig. 13 where the output is the average of the outputs of the four type-1 FS described above. The same fuzzy rules will be used for the four type-1 FSs (Fig. 14).

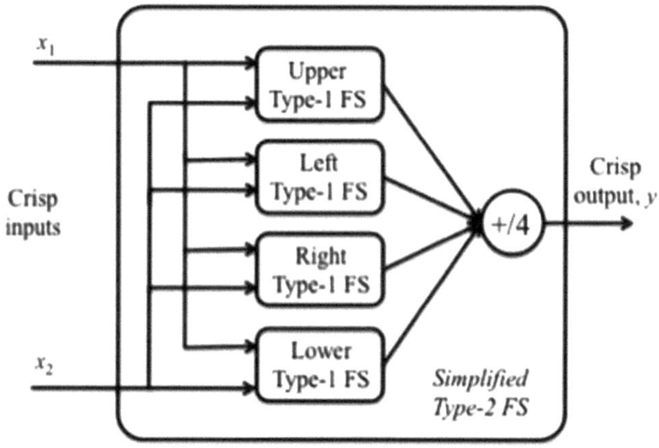

Fig. 14. Simplified implementation of Type-2 FS.

4 Results

In this section, a comparison between the different evaluation approaches presented in Sects. 2 and 3 is introduced using an example.

4.1 Example

Assume that we have n students laid to an exam of m questions where $n = 10$ and $m = 5$. The accuracy rate matrix, A, the time rate matrix, T, and the grade vector, G, are given as follows [3]:

$$A = \begin{bmatrix} 0.59 & 0.35 & 1.0 & 0.66 & 0.11 & 0.08 & 0.84 & 0.23 & 0.04 & 0.24 \\ 0.01 & 0.27 & 0.14 & 0.04 & 0.88 & 0.16 & 0.04 & 0.22 & 0.81 & 0.53 \\ 0.77 & 0.69 & 0.97 & 0.71 & 0.17 & 0.86 & 0.87 & 0.42 & 0.91 & 0.74 \\ 0.73 & 0.72 & 0.81 & 0.16 & 0.5 & 0.02 & 0.32 & 0.92 & 0.9 & 0.25 \\ 0.93 & 0.49 & 0.08 & 0.81 & 0.65 & 0.93 & 0.39 & 0.51 & 0.97 & 0.61 \end{bmatrix},$$

$$T = \begin{bmatrix} 0.7 & 0.4 & 0.1 & 1.0 & 0.7 & 0.2 & 0.7 & 0.6 & 0.4 & 0.9 \\ 1.0 & 0.0 & 0.9 & 0.3 & 1.0 & 0.3 & 0.2 & 0.8 & 0.0 & 0.3 \\ 0.0 & 0.1 & 0.0 & 0.1 & 0.9 & 1.0 & 0.2 & 0.3 & 0.1 & 0.4 \\ 0.2 & 0.1 & 0.0 & 1.0 & 1.0 & 0.3 & 0.4 & 0.8 & 0.7 & 0.5 \\ 0.0 & 0.1 & 1.0 & 1.0 & 0.6 & 1.0 & 0.8 & 0.2 & 0.8 & 0.2 \end{bmatrix}, \quad \text{and}$$

$$G^T = \begin{bmatrix} 10 & 15 & 20 & 25 & 30 \end{bmatrix}.$$

Importance and complexity of each question, I and C, are determined by the domain expert as follows:

$$I = \begin{bmatrix} 0.0 & 0.0 & 0.0 & 0.0 & 1.0 \\ 0.0 & 0.33 & 0.67 & 0.0 & 0.0 \\ 0.0 & 0.0 & 0.0 & 0.15 & 0.85 \\ 1.0 & 0.0 & 0.0 & 0.0 & 0.0 \\ 0.0 & 0.07 & 0.93 & 0.0 & 0.0 \end{bmatrix}, \quad \text{and}$$

$$C = \begin{bmatrix} 0.0 & 0.85 & 0.15 & 0.0 & 0.0 \\ 0.0 & 0.0 & 0.33 & 0.67 & 0.0 \\ 0.0 & 0.0 & 0.0 & 0.69 & 0.31 \\ 0.56 & 0.44 & 0.0 & 0.0 & 0.0 \\ 0.0 & 0.0 & 0.7 & 0.3 & 0.0 \end{bmatrix}.$$

4.2 Classical Approach

In this approach, total score for the 10 students in order can be obtained using formula 4 as follows:

$$S^T = \begin{bmatrix} 67.60 & 54.05 & 38.40 & 49.70 & 49.70 & 48.80 & 46.10 & 52.30 & 85.95 & 49.70 \end{bmatrix}.$$

Ranks of students using this approach can then be obtained by simply sorting S in a descending order to get:

$$S_9 > S_1 > S_2 > S_8 > S_4 = S_5 = S_{10} > S_6 > S_7 > S_3,$$

where $S_a > S_b$ means score of student a is higher than score of student b while $S_a = S_b$ means that their scores are equal.

4.3 Triangle MFs Based Fuzzy Approach

The process starts by averaging the accuracy rate and answer-time rate matrices A and T, respectively, for each student to get:

$$\bar{A}^T = \begin{bmatrix} 0.45 & 0.31 & 0.71 & 0.47 & 0.64 \end{bmatrix},$$

and

$$\bar{T}^T = \begin{bmatrix} 0.57 & 0.48 & 0.31 & 0.50 & 0.57 \end{bmatrix}.$$

Based on the fuzzy MFs shown in Fig. 3 we obtain the fuzzy accuracy rate matrix and the fuzzy time rate matrix as follows:

$$A_{fuzzy} = \begin{bmatrix} 0.0 & 0.25 & 0.75 & 0.0 & 0.0 \\ 0.0 & 0.95 & 0.05 & 0.0 & 0.0 \\ 0.0 & 0.0 & 0.0 & 0.95 & 0.05 \\ 0.0 & 0.15 & 0.85 & 0.0 & 0.0 \\ 0.0 & 0.0 & 0.32 & 0.68 & 0.0 \end{bmatrix}, \quad \text{and}$$

$$T_{fuzzy} = \begin{bmatrix} 0.0 & 0.0 & 0.65 & 0.35 & 0.0 \\ 0.0 & 0.1 & 0.9 & 0.0 & 0.0 \\ 0.0 & 0.95 & 0.05 & 0.0 & 0.0 \\ 0.0 & 0.0 & 1.0 & 0.0 & 0.0 \\ 0.0 & 0.0 & 0.65 & 0.35 & 0.0 \end{bmatrix}.$$

In the first node, both inputs are given by examination results, whereas in later nodes, one input will be the output of its previous node and the other by the domain expert. The output of each node can be obtained as a crisp value (i.e., defuzzified) or as fuzzy numbers (i.e., degrees of membership (MFs) of each variable in the five linguistic levels). Each node has two scale factors (SFs shown in Fig. 1). Here, we let both SFs have the same value of unity assuming equal influence of each input on the output. Each fuzzy node performs Mamdani fuzzy inference to compute its output given the inputs and the fuzzy rules (described in Tables 1 and 2) [35]. Each fuzzy node proceeds in a number of steps described in Sect. 2.3. By applying A_{fuzzy} and $T_{fuzzy}$to the first node, the difficulty vector, D, and its fuzzy counterpart, D_{fuzzy}. In the same way, the cost vector will be obtained by applying the difficulty and complexity to the second node. Finally, the adjustment vector, W, will be obtained by applying the cost and importance to the third node as follows:

$$W^T = \begin{bmatrix} 0.7 & 0.55 & 0.75 & 0.18 & 0.5 \end{bmatrix}.$$

The new scores of students S_1 to S_{10} are then obtained using Equations - to be:

$$S^T = \begin{bmatrix} 67.15 & 53.17 & 42.10 & 52.19 & 48.31 & 51.81 & 48.47 & 49.27 & 85.25 & 51.49 \end{bmatrix}.$$

The new rank of students is then obtained by sorting values of S in a descending order to be:

$$S_9 > S_1 > S_2 > S_4 > S_6 > S_{10} > S_8 > S_7 > S_5 > S_3.$$

4.4 Gaussian MFs Based Fuzzy Approach

By replacing triangle MFs, used in Sect. 4.3, which are formed simply using straight lines with Gaussian MFs with the same center points (i.e., mean) as the triangle MFs, as it is shown in Fig. 4 with stand deviation (i.e., width) $\sigma \geq 4.0$, new scores for the 10 students are obtained where the mean score is still equal to that of their original scores obtained using the classical approach:

$$S^T = \left[64.60\ 54.05\ 38.40\ 49.70\ 49.70\ 48.80\ 46.10\ 52.30\ 84.95\ 49.70\right].$$

The new rank of students is then obtained by sorting values of S in a descending

$$S_9 > S_1 > S_2 > S_8 > S_4 > S_{10} > S_5 > S_6 > S_7 > S_3$$

.

4.5 IT2 MFs Based Fuzzy Approach

In this Section, IT2 MFs with different values of FOU (i.e., zero, low, medium and high uncertainty) as it is shown in Figure 10 is used to generate new scores and new ranking orders of the students. The new ranking orders for different FOU values are shown in Table 3.

Table 3. Ranking order for different FOU values using IT2 approach.

FOU	Rank									
	1>	2>	3>	4>	5>	6>	7>	8>	9>	10
0	9	1	2	4	6	10	8	5	7	3
0.1	9	1	2	4	6	10	5	8	7	3
0.2	9	1	2	4	6	10	8	7	5	3
0.3	9	1	2	8	5	10	4	6	7	3

4.6 Simplified IT2 MFs Based Fuzzy Approach

Here, simplified IT2 MFs, presented in Sect. 3.4 with different values of FOU is used to generate new scores and hence new ranking order of students, as it is shown in Table 4. A comparing between the ranking orders of the various grading approaches is shown in Table 5.

Table 4. Ranking order for different FOU values using simplified IT2 approach.

FOU	Rank									
	1>	2>	3>	4>	5>	6>	7>	8>	9>	10
0	9	1	2	4	8	10	6	5	7	3
0.1	9	1	2	4	8	10	6	5	7	3
0.2	9	1	2	8	4	10	6	5	7	3
0.3	9	1	2	8	4	10	6	5	7	3
0.4	9	1	2	8	4	10	5	6	7	3

Table 5. Ranking order for different approaches: classical, T1T for type-1 triangle MFs, T1G for type-1 Gaussian MFs, IT2 for interval type-2 MFs, and SIT2 for simplified IT2.

Method	Rank									
	1>	2>	3>	4>	5>	6>	7>	8>	9>	10
Classical	9	1	2	8	4=	5=	10=	6	7	3
T1T	9	1	2	4	6	10	8	7	5	3
T1G ($\sigma \geq 4.0$)	9	1	2	8	4	10	5	6	7	3
IT2 ($FOU = 0.3$)	9	1	2	8	5	10	4	6	7	3
SIT2 ($FOU = 0.4$)	9	1	2	8	4	10	5	6	7	3

5 Conclusions

As it is shown in Table 5, classical assessment approach resulted in students of equal scores (i.e., S_4, S_4, and S_{10}) that make it difficult to determine a distinguished order of each student. T1 Triangular FSs overcome the problem of students of equal scores but at the same time it changed scores of other students who does not fall in that category (i.e., S_6, S_7, and S_8) which might spark questions and make students skeptic about the evaluation process. On the other hand, T1 Gaussian FSs based system influenced only that category of students with equal scores (i.e., S_4, S_4, and S_{10}) while other students of different scores are left intact.

Similarly, IT2 FSs changed only the scores and hence the rank order of students with equal scores while the others are left intact. A major difference between T2 and T1G FSs is that T2 system gave preferences to complexity of questions over importance and that is clear from the rank for student S_5 who has given a higher rank (rank#5) on account of student S_4 who has given a lower rank (rank#7). On the other side, T1G gave preferences to importance of questions over its complexity and that explains why S_4 has given higher rank (rank#5) on account of S_5 who has given a lower rank (rank#7). Simplified IT2 FSs gave identical results to T1G FSs for a $FOU = 0.4$.

The transparency and the human logic nature of fuzzy logic system make it easy to interpret and explain why certain scores have changed. The system inherently has a kind a feedback system to correct erroneous scores assigned by indifferent or inexperienced examiners. Easy of implementation of the proposed system recommended it to spread out and to be broadly used in other decisions support systems. In this paper, a collective FOU for all the fuzzy variables is used to represent a collective uncertainty in the knowledge of the domain expert. As a future work, the effect of using various FOU values for each fuzzy variable such as importance, complexity, etc. will be investigated. The presented evaluation approaches should be evaluated and validated using large data sets obtained from real exams and how much students and teachers are satisfied about it should be measured. The evaluation systems proposed in this paper have been implemented using the Fuzzy Logic Toolbox™ for building a fuzzy inference system from MathWorks™ [36].

Acknowledgements. The heading should be treated as a subsubsection heading and should not be assigned a number.

References

1. Hameed, I.A., Elhoushy, M., Zalam, B.A., Osen, O.L.: An interval type-2 fuzzy logic system for assessment of students' answer scripts under high levels of uncertainty. In: Proceedings of the 8th International Conference on Computer Supported Education (CSEDU 2016), Rome, Italy, vol. 2, pp. 40–48 (2016)
2. Boud, D.: Developing Student Autonomy in Learning, 2nd edn. Kogan Page, London (1988)
3. Saleh, I., Kim, S.-I.: A fuzzy system for evaluating students' learning achievement. Expert Syst. Appl. **36**(3), 6236–6243 (2009)
4. Hameed, I.A., Sørensen, C.G.: Fuzzy systems in education: a more reliable system for student evaluation. In: Azar, A.T. (ed.) Fuzzy Systems, INTECH, Croatia (2010). ISBN: 978-953-7619-92-3
5. Zadeh, L.A.: Towards a generalized theory of uncertainity (GTU) - an outline. Inf. Sci. **172**, 1–40 (2005)
6. Daradkeh, M., McKinnon, A., Churcher, C.: Supporting informed decision-making under uncertainty and risk through interactive visualization. Aust. Comput. Sci. Commun. **35**(5), 23–32 (2013)
7. Biswas, R.: An application of fuzzy sets in students' evaluation. Fuzzy Sets Syst. **74**(2), 187–194 (1995)
8. Echauz, J.R., Vachtsevanos, G.J.: Fuzzy grading system. IEEE Trans. Educ. **38**(2), 158–165 (1995)
9. Law, C.K.: Using fuzzy numbers in education grading system. Fuzzy Sets Syst. **83**(3), 311–323 (1996)
10. Wilson, E., Karr, C.L., Freeman, L.M.: Flexible, adaptive, automatic fuzzy-based grade assigning system. In: Proceedings of the North American Fuzzy Information Processing Society Conference, pp. 334–338 (1998)
11. Chen, S.M., Lee, C.H.: New methods for students' evaluating using fuzzy sets. Fuzzy Sets Syst. **104**(2), 209–218 (1999)
12. Ma, J., Zhou, D.: Fuzzy set approach to the assessment of student-centered learning. IEEE Trans. Educ. **43**(2), 237–241 (2000)
13. Weon, S., Kim, J.: Learning achievement evaluation strategy using fuzzy membership function. In: Proceedings of the 31st ASEE/IEEE Frontiers in Education Conference, Reno, NV (2001)
14. Wang, H.Y., Chen, S.M.: Evaluating students' answerscripts using fuzzy numbers associated with degrees of confidence. Proc. IEEE Trans. Fuzzy Syst. **16**(2), 403–415 (2008)
15. Bai, S.-M., Chen, S.-M.: Automatically constructing grade membership functions of fuzzy rules for students' evaluation. Expert Syst. Appl. **35**(3), 1408–1414 (2008)
16. Bai, S.-M., Chen, S.-M.: Evaluating students' learning achievement using fuzzy membership functions and fuzzy rules. Expert Syst. Appl. **34**, 399–410 (2008)
17. Hameed, I.A.: Using Gaussian membership functions for improving the reliability and robustness of students' evaluation systems. Expert Syst. Appl. **38**(6), 7135–7142 (2011)

18. Hameed, I.A.: A fuzzy system to automatically evaluate and improve fairness of multiple-choice questions (MCQs) based exams. In: Proceedings of the 8th International Conference on Computer Supported Education (CSEDU 2016), Rome, Italy, vol. 1, pp. 476–481 (2016)
19. Hameed, I.A.: A simplified implementation of interval type-2 fuzzy system and its application in students' academic evaluation. In: Proceedings of the IEEE World Congress on Computational Intelligence, Vancouver, Canada (2016)
20. Liang, Q., Mendel, J.M.: Interval type-2 fuzzy logic systems: theory and design. IEEE Trans. Fuzzy Syst. **8**(5), 535–550 (2000)
21. Zadeh, L.A.: Fuzzy sets. Inf. Control **8**, 80–99 (1965)
22. Iancu, I.: A mamdani type fuzzy logic controller. In: Dadios, E. (ed.) Fuzzy Logic - Controls, Concepts, Theories and Applications (2012). ISBN: 978-953-51-0396-7, InTech
23. Zhao, J., Bose, B.K.: Evaluation of membership functions for fuzzy logic controlled induction motor drive. In: 28th IEEE Annual Conference of the Industrial Electronics Society, pp. 229–234. IEEE Press, New York (2002)
24. Zadeh, L.A.: Outline of a new approach to the analysis of complex systems and decision processes. IEEE Trans. Syst. Man Cybern. **3**(1), 28–44 (1973)
25. King, P., Mamdani, E.: The application of fuzzy control to industrial process. Automatica **13**, 235–242 (1997)
26. Mendel, J.M.: Rule-based Fuzzy Logic Systems: Introduction and New Directions. Prentice-Hall, Upper Saddle River (2001)
27. Zadeh, L.A.: The concept of a linguistic variable and its application to approximate reasoning-I. Inf. Sci. **8**, 199–249 (1975)
28. Mendel, J.M., Liang, Q.: Pictorial comparison of type-1 and type-2 fuzzy logic systems. In: Proceedings of IASTED International Conference on Intelligent Systems and Control (1999)
29. Wu, D., Tan, W.W.: A simplified architecture for type-2 FLSs and its application to nonlinear control. In: Proceedings of the 2004 IEEE Conference on Cybernetics and Intelligent Systems, Singapore, pp. 485–490, (2004)
30. Karnik, N.N., Mendel, J.M.: Operations on type-2 fuzzy set. Int. J. Fuzzy Sets Syst. **122**(2), 327–348 (2001)
31. Sepulveda, R., Castillo, O., Melin, P., Rodriguez-Diaz, A., Montiel, O.: Experimental study of intelligent controllers under uncertainty using type-1 and type-2 fuzzy logic. Inf. Sci. **177**, 2023–2048 (2007)
32. Mendel, J.M.: Uncertain Rule-Based Fuzzy Logic Systems. Prentice-Hall, Upper Saddle River (2001). 07458
33. Wu, D.: Approaches for reducing the computational cost of interval type-2 fuzzy logic systems: overview and comparisons. IEEE Trans. Fuzzy Syst. **21**(1), 80–99 (2013)
34. Mendel, J.M., John, R.I.B.: Type-2 fuzzy sets made simple. IEEE Trans. Fuzzy Syst. **10**(2), 117–127 (2002)
35. Mamdani, E.M., Assilian, S.: An experiment in linguistic synthesis with a fuzzy logic controller. Int. J. Man-Mach. Stud. **7**, 1–13 (1975)
36. Fuzzy Logic Toolbox™ 2.2.7 (2016). http://www.mathworks.com/products/fuzzylogic/

Teacher Supported Peer Evaluation Through OpenAnswer: A Study of Some Factors

Maria De Marsico[1], Andrea Sterbini[1], and Marco Temperini[2(✉)]

[1] Department of Computer Science, Sapienza University, Rome, Italy
[2] Department of Computer, Control and Management Engineering, Sapienza University, Rome, Italy
marte@dis.uniroma1.it

Abstract. In the OpenAnswer system it is possible to compute grades for/to the answers to open-ended questions given to a class of students, based on the students' peer-evaluation and on the teacher's grading work, performed on a subset of the answers. Here we analyze the systems' performances, expressed as the capability to infer correct grades based on a limited amount of grading work by the teacher. In particular, considering that the performance may well depend on alternative definitions (valorization) of several aspects of the system, we show an analysis of such alternative choices, with the intention of seeing what choices might result in better system's behavior. The factors we investigate are related to the Bayesian framework underpinning OpenAnswer. In particular we tackle the different possibilities to define probability distribution of key variables, conditional probabilities tables, and methods to map our statistical variables onto usable grades. Moreover we analyze the relationship between two main variables that express knowledge possessed by the student and her/his peer-assessing skill. By exploring alternative configurations of the system's parameters we can conclude that Knowledge is in general more difficult than Assessment. The way to reach such a (not astonishing) conclusion provides also a quantitative evidence of Bloom's ranking.

Keywords: Peer assessment · Open-answer questions · Automatic grade prediction

1 Introduction

Students' learning activities are based upon cognitive and metacognitive abilities, and aim to foster them both. According to Bloom's taxonomy [3], the learners' abilities increase when passing from pure knowledge (*remembering* about a topic), through *comprehension*, *application*, *analysis*, *evaluation*, to *synthesis*. In [1] a revised version of the taxonomy is proposed, where *remember*, *understand* and *apply* lay at increasing levels, while *analyze*, *evaluate* and *create* lay at the same top level. In any case, the ability to "evaluate" is considered a high level one. It is indeed a *metacognitive* skill, ranging beyond proficiency on a topic, yet by no means excluding it. On the contrary, metacognitive activities require not only knowing but also knowing about knowing [21], and the definition of metacognition refers to higher order thinking, also entailing

G. Costagliola et al. (Eds.): CSEDU 2016, CCIS 739, pp. 442–463, 2017.
DOI: 10.1007/978-3-319-63184-4_23

the ability to exercise an active control over the cognitive processes underlying learning. Activities such as the following play a critical role in successful learning: (1) planning strategies and schedules, devised to support execution of a learning task, (2) monitoring one's own and others' comprehension of a topic, (3) checking the proceeding of a task towards completion, and (4) being aware of how to apply newly acquired concepts and rules. Therefore, besides exercising cognitive skills, also metacognitive ones should be cared for in educational planning.

Peer assessment is widely renowned as a useful exercise in order to challenge as well as to improve one's understanding of a topic, and to achieve higher *metacognitive* abilities. The framework implemented through the OpenAnswer system [29] allows for (semi-)automated grading of open answers through peer assessment, with the further goal of relieving the teacher from part of the burden of grading the complete set of answers. As a matter of fact, while dealing with open ended questions provides a much more reliable evaluation of students' proficiency with respect to, e.g., multiple-choice tests [23], they are also much more demanding for the student and for the teacher; in particular, for the teacher, they require a longer revision activity.

In OpenAnswer, during an assessment session, each student is requested to grade some (e.g., 3) of her/his peers' answers. The validity of results of peer evaluation is enforced by requiring that a subset of answers (chosen according to some relevant criterion which will be discussed in the following) is further graded by the teacher. Information provided by peers' and teacher's assessments is fed and propagated within a Bayesian Network (BN). In such network the students are modeled by their Knowledge level on the topic (K), and by the ability to evaluate peers' answers, denoted as Judgment (J). In the network, the answers of a single student have an estimated Correctness (C). Such a value can be updated by evidence propagation. When a student marks an answer by a peer, a corresponding Grade (G) is injected into the network, and propagates its effects depending on both a J of the grading student and a current estimation of C of the peer answer. Variables C and J are assumed to be conditioned by K ($C|K$ and $J|K$), therefore for each of them we have a Conditional Probability Table (CPT).

In this process, students may both understand how the grading process should work, by matching the grades they assigned with final ones (possibly by the teacher, or inferred by the system through the BN), and learn from smarter peers how to improve their results, which is a significant aspect of peer-evaluation [25]. Moreover, *opening* the system's student model to some extent, by disclosing to the students also the final values of their own K and J, can spur further metacognitive awareness.

However, a "must-have" condition for such a system to be useful, is in that it provides reliable outcomes: as to OpenAnswer, we are investigating several factors such outcomes could be dependent on.

So, in this paper we (1) present an evaluation of OpenAnswer's performance, based on the use of a collection of dataset we came to build in time; (2) provide a study about some factors of the system that we see may be influential on pedagogical qualities of the system, namely (2.1) how different tuning of aspects of the Bayesian framework can affect the system's grading performances, and (2.2) how the main elements of our student model, i.e. Knowledge (K), and assessment capability (J) can be related to each other (or, in other words, what the relation between the two corresponding macro-abilities defined in the Bloom's Taxonomy [3] is).

1.1 Research Questions

Here we anticipate some aspects of the OpenAnswer System and of its underpinning Bayesian framework, to make the research questions more readable.

A first aspect to consider, is in that the discrete variables (C, G, K, J) are expressed as probability distributions (telling how probable is each one of the allowed values). Moreover there are dependences in place between some of such variables, which are expressed in terms of Conditional Probability Tables (CPT). Additionally the K variable needs an initial Probability Distribution (PD) over the class of students in which we are using OpenAnswer. And, finally, the grades/marks computed by the system are obtained out of the value of the variable C (i.e. a probability distribution) through a "mapping" process towards, for instance, the scale A…F. Choice of different CPTs, PD, and MAPPING methods are crucial factors which the system's performances may depend on. So, in order to give a first evaluation of the system we take care of the following research questions

RQ1: Is OpenAnswer improving on a simple "pure" peer-evaluation approach?
RQ2: In relation to the possible advantages in using OpenAnswer, is the system sensitive on its factors? In particular

[PD] *[is previous knowledge about the class significant?]*
[CPT] *[do different CPTs yield different system's behaviors?]*
[MAPPING] *[are different mapping methods from P(C) to (A ... F) influential?]*

Moreover, the system (and the concept itself of peer-evaluation as a pedagogical means) relies on the relationship holding between the knowledge possessed by the student and the student's capability of making good assessments. In particular we model the conditional probabilities of J given K, C given K, and G given J and C, as Gaussian distributions, whose parameters are basically the μ (expectation) and the σ (stand. dev.).

RQ3: What value of μ for P(J|C) produces the better adherence of the systems results to correct grades?

Section 2 provides the reader with a description of currently available research work on the topics of this paper. Section 3 describes the system. In Sect. 4 we show and discuss the experimental work conducted in regard to RQ1 and RQ2. We perform a comparison between a "Pure" peer-evaluation approach and what OpenAnswer can do without the teacher intervention (i.e. OpenAnswer using only the peers assessments, that we call "none" approach); then we compare the "none" approach and the full-fledged use of OpenAnswer. Section 5 then presents the work related to RQ3. Some conclusions are finally drawn in Sect. 6.

2 Related Work

The automatic analysis of open answers is a powerful means to manage assessment in education. It is also known as *knowledge tracing* [2]. It is applied, though, in other fields, such as in the context of marketing applications, where techniques of data mining and natural language processing are used to extract customer opinions and synthesize products reputation [31]. In [15] concept mapping and *coding schemes* are used with the same goals.

In [24] the application of the above approaches to education is studied. A method for the (semi-)automatic assessment of open-answers is proposed in [4]: it relies on ontologies and semantic web technologies. An ontology models the knowledge domain related to the question(s); it also represents aspects of the overall educational process. The teacher plays a crucial role in the definition of course ontology and questions' semantic annotations, while such role is much less significant later.

In [11] open answers are examined to identify and treat students misconceptions which might hinder learning. Actually the answer is interpreted as a set of algebraic transformations to be analyzed. The treatment of the misconceptions is in the lines of an intelligent tutoring system. The approach is effective when dealing with answers mainly made of plain algebraic expressions (i.e. with no accompanying natural language involved). Management, derivation, rewriting and evaluation of expressions of a formal language can be done extensively in an automated manner [12, 13], and this characteristics of algebra is put to consequence very fruitfully in the system.

Peer-assessment is the activity in which a learner, or a group of learners, assesses the product of other learners (the peers) while engaging in a notoriously high cognitive level activity [3]. Peer-assessment can be used to pursue both *formative* and *summative* aims [30]: in the former case the aim is to allow the learner to appreciate her cognitive situation (such as level of knowledge, or lacks therein) and monitor her progress. In the latter case the focus is on evaluation, and possibly on the selection of appropriate remedial activities.

Li et al. [16] states that a relationships does exist between the quality of the peers feedback, on a learner's job, and the quality of the final project submitted by the learner. A comprehensive study of peer assessment in a prototype educational application is in [6].

The OpenAnswer system presented here relies on the evaluation of answers coming from peer-assessment, and on the student modeling organized through the use of Bayesian Networks.

Another machine learning approach to student modeling is in [7], where an application of Bayesian Network techniques is shown, aiming to support learner's modeling in the framework of an Intelligent Tutoring System (ITS). The modelling is devised to support activities relevant in an ITS: knowledge assessment, plan recognition and prediction, the last two deemed to see what intentions are behind a learner's choice, and what following choices might be, during the phase of problem solving. The work is applied to the ITS *Andes*, where the learner is supported in two kinds of tasks: problems to be solved, and exercises to be understood. Domain knowledge and Task-related knowledge (about Newtonian Physics) are encoded in Andes' Bayesian Networks: the former attains the concepts in the study field, and their possession by the learner; the latter is used to model the tasks and the related learner's solving abilities. When a task is solved, the student model is updated, for the next activity.

In OpenAnswer the peer is presented with a set of assessing criteria, to which referring during the marking; the criteria are defined by the teacher, while authoring the question, and are supposed to be adhered to by the teacher, during her grading too.

In our experience too many criteria might result cumbersome for the peers. We have not investigated, though, on this aspect (the number of criteria). In literature the specificity of "scoring criteria" has been identified as an important factor against the problem of having assessors that limit the range of their marks to a subset (typically in the high end) of the scale; in this case the problem is twofold, involving both leniency in the peers marking and an actual shrinking of the marking scale [22].

An aspect of research in peer-assessment regards the number of peer-evaluations that a job should undergo during the peer-evaluation process. In OpenAnswer this is a configurable value, set to three by default. In literature it has been found that more feedbacks on the same job make the peers suitable to perform more complex revisions on their products, ending up with a better assessment result [5].

3 The OpenAnswer System

The intended use of OpenAnswer [27–29] is to support semi-automatic grading of answers to open-ended questions (*open answers*) through peer assessment. The use of "semi" above refers mainly to the fact that also teacher's grading work, on a limited subset of the answers, is requested. From one side, the system can be used by the teacher to spur a metacognitive ability [3] in students. This in turn allows for evaluating assessment performance, and ultimately getting further information on students' understanding. From a more utilitarian side, it may also reduce the amount of teacher's grading effort, which in turn would allow to expose students to open-ended questionnaires more often.

In OpenAnswer, in order to enforce/emend the results of peer evaluation, and therefore increase the reliability of final grades, the teacher is required to assess some of the answers, whose number and identification depends on the chosen corresponding strategies that will be presented in the following. In this way the teacher's grading workload will be reduced, therefore encouraging a more frequent use of an educational strategy entailing open answer tests and peer assessment, while students will receive both the grading of their answers and be able to compare their peer grading with the correct one. As further detailed below, the system suggests to the teacher the order of answers to manually grade, according to a selection strategy chosen in advance among a number of available ones. Manual grading can stop when some pre-defined termination criterion is met. Even in this case, a number of criteria are available. After the termination criterion is met, the system automatically completes the grading task for the remaining answers using the correctness information collected so far, together with the results of the peer grading. The OpenAnswer approach relies on a simple Bayesian network model. The individual student model is represented by a Bayesian network. The variables defining the model include an assumed value for the learner's state of knowledge on the exercise topic (K), and the ability to judge (J) answers given by peers on the same topic. Actually, as it is quite natural, we assume that the value of J is conditioned by the value of K. These variables are exploited in the system state evolution and affect the way information is weighted while propagated. For each peer assessment session, the individual student networks are interconnected depending on the current sets of answers that each student receives to grade. Therefore, different sessions may entail different interconnection patterns. Each answer is characterized by its correctness (*C*), measuring the student ability to provide a correct solution, and by the grades (*G*) assigned by the peers to it. *C* is a variable depending on the student *K* value and is characterized by a conditional PD, that reduces to a single grade once the answer is manually graded by the teacher. All variables are characterized by a probability distribution (PD) of discrete values that follows the same convention of grading. In our case, depending on the datasets used as testbed, this entails 6 (from A to F) or 5 (A, B, C, D, F) values, with F = Fail.

C and *G* control evidence propagation according to the possible matching between teacher's and peer assessments. In particular, the *J* of a student is connected to the *C*s corresponding to the evaluated peer answers through the assigned grades *G*. The resulting compound network is continuously updated. Figure 1 shows an example BN fragment for a student that graded three peers.

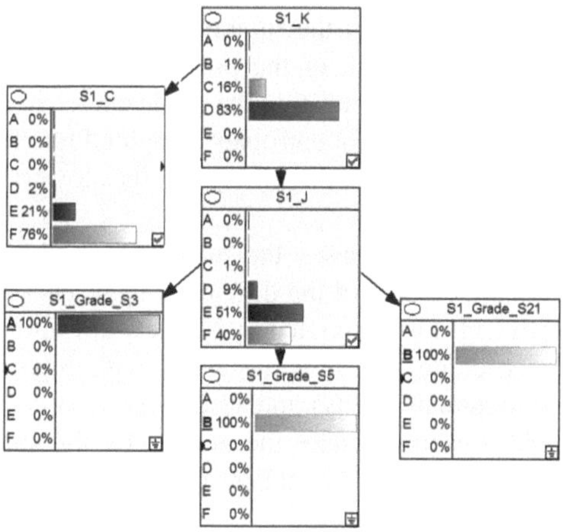

Fig. 1. An example fragment of Bayesian Network in OpenAnswer: student S1 grades the answers of students S3, S5 and S21, and notwithstanding the most probable value of D for K, presents a current most probable grade F for his/her answer.

Evidence propagation happens in two phases. The first one is only based on peer assessment grades (*G*). Afterwards, when the teacher starts grading, the grades provided affect the *C* variables of corresponding answers (they become fixed values, i.e. the conditional PD concentrates on a single value), therefore affecting *J* values of grading peers through the *G*s that they assigned to the same answers. In turn, this indirectly affects *J* and *K* variables of the student author of the answer, and indirectly the *J* and *K* values of grading peers. During the following manual grading phase, the system supports the teacher by suggesting the next "significant" answer to grade according to one of the selection criteria detailed below, and by propagating in the network the added information provided by the teacher's grade. After each evidence propagation step, the teacher grading step is iterated until a termination condition is met. In practice, the latter states that new information from additional teacher's grades would be less decisive. When the teacher stops grading after a sufficient number of answers, the information collected so far allows to automatically grade those answers that were not directly graded by the teacher. In practice, grades not directly given by the teacher are inferred according to the current probability distribution associated to the *C* values. Of course, it is necessary to devise also a suitable mapping strategy from PDs to single values to return to students.

The possible system strategies to suggest the next answer to grade are:

- *max_wrong*: the system suggests to grade the most probably incorrect answer, i.e. the one with highest probability of having *C* = *'F'*;
- max_*entropy*: the system suggests to grade the answer presenting the highest entropy (the answer the system *knows* less about, or about which has less information for inference); the entropy of an answer is the entropy of the corresponding *C* variable;
- *maxInfoGain*: the system chooses the answer that guarantees the greater *assured information variation*; the latter is the minimum variation of *total entropy* of the network that is produced by each of the possible grades that the teacher might assign to a certain answer, by propagating the grade choice in the network; the *total entropy* of the network is the sum of entropies computed for all *K, J* and *C* variables of all students in the BN; of course this strategy is the slowest one, but no real time outcome is required;
- *maxStrangeness:* the system chooses the answer with the greater *strangeness*; *strangeness* is the absolute value of the difference between *J* and *C* (after mapping their current respective PDs as computed by the network into single values); this is to capture the two peculiar cases of a student with high *C* but low *J* (good knowledge but low judgment ability) and vice versa;
- *maxTotalEntropy*: the system chooses the answer by the student with maximum *total entropy*, with *total entropy* of a student being the sum of the entropies of the associated C, J and K variables;
- *random*: the next answer to grade is chosen at random; this strategy is mostly used for testing purposes, as it should provide a comparison with totally random choices, and indirectly information on the effectiveness of chosen alternatives; it is not used in the present work;

The termination criterion can be chosen among the following:

- *none*: no answer at all is graded by the teacher, therefore this corresponds to "pure" peer assessment yet with the evidence propagation provided by OpenAnswer;
- *no_wrong*: no more ungraded answers exist which would be automatically graded as wrong (C = *'F'*) once the PD of C is mapped onto a grade;
- *no_wrong2:* for all remaining answers $P(C = \text{'F'}) \leq 1/2$;
- *no_wrong3:* for all remaining answers $P(C = \text{'F'}) \leq 1/3$;
- *no_flip(N):* the automatically computed grades remained stable in the last N correction steps.

In general, max_wrong is best associated with no_wrong<p> and max_entropy with no_flip(N), while random can be associated with both the termination criteria.

4 The Aspects of the Bayesian Framework, Investigated in the Experiments

In this section we explore different evaluation settings for OpenAnswer. First, we matched grading accuracy achievable through peer assessment, against traditional assessment (i.e. done entirely by the teacher, providing our ground truth) in different settings: (1) pure peer assessment (a traditional peer-assessment approach, with no use of OpenAnswer), (2) exclusive peer assessment done in OpenAnswer: only the peer-assessments are used to infer the final grades; no use of the teacher's grading work is done. This approach is called "none" (from *termination* = *none*), (3) "full-fledged" OpenAnswer: the peer assessment is complemented by teacher's (partial) grading, with different policies for the choice of next answer to grade and for the termination condition. Our initial goal is to evaluate the influence of strategies and termination conditions on system performance, i.e., on the quality (reliability) of assessment; so the amount of grades correctly inferred, and the rate of work requested by the teacher, are of interest.

In this context we investigated also the effect of different choices for the initial distribution of the K values (for each student) on system evaluation performances. This factor is labeled as [PD] in the research questions section. Here we could proceed along two possible alternatives, discussed in the next two paragraphs.

The first alternative entails an ex-post knowledge of the group of students: from our dataset we actually know how the learning state of the students is, about the topic of the question; so we assume that the propagation of information through the BN can be improved by such knowledge, if we come to exploit it. Of course such a course of action can be adopted only in experimental settings: we couldn't count on such information to support the system in a real application. Or could we? Actually, it is quite reasonable to think that the state of knowledge shown after an OpenAnswer session (a question) by the class (and/or its individual students) might as well be the initial state for the next session, if this is about the same topic as the former's (or a similar one); so the first alternative we are discussing might be not as idle as it could seem, and it's worth to be considered. To implement it we have two possible ways, again. The first, more relaxed, one is to assume for all students the same probability distribution for K, which is equal to the distribution obtained for the manual exercise grading (performed completely by the teacher) that is used as ground truth. In the next tables, this is reported by columns labelled as **TgrDist** (*Teacher's Grade Distribution*). The second way goes by assigning to each student a level of knowledge with probability 1, corresponding to the grade achieved (coming from teacher's grading). In the table this is given in **Tgrade** (Teacher's Grades) columns.

The second alternative entails ex-ante attempts to model students in a starting setting, where information on the students' skills on the topic is little or none. Also in this case we have two sub-choices, namely: either assuming for each student an equal probability for all K levels, reported by columns labeled as **flat** in the tables, or applying to all students a same, synthetic and "reasonable" PD for K (see Fig. 2, and cfr. columns labeled as **synthetic** in the tables).

K	
A	0,10
B	0,20
C	0,30
D	0,20
E	0,10
F	0,10

K	
A	0,15
B	0,30
C	0,30
D	0,15
E	0,10

Fig. 2. Synthetic PDs, with the initial values of K, in the cases of 6-valued and 5-valued scale.

We use the "artificial" setting - Tgrade in particular - to evaluate an upper bound for the achievable results. Once we identify the combination <strategy, termination> achieving the best results, we can observe which is the best realistic distribution for K values to adopt with this combination.

As of the [CPT] part of RQ2, we tested different CPTs expressing how the Correctness of an answer is dependent on the student's Knowledge: P($C|K$). Our starting point for this CPT was P($J|K$), so each value of $C|K = k$ has its maximum on $k - 1$. We call this CPT as **CPT1**: in Fig. 3 the two cases of 6-valued and 5-valued grading scale are shown.

C|K	A	B	C	D	E	F
A	0,20	0,09	0,01	0,01	0,01	0,01
B	0,40	0,20	0,09	0,07	0,06	0,01
C	0,20	0,40	0,20	0,12	0,10	0,01
D	0,12	0,20	0,40	0,20	0,18	0,07
E	0,07	0,09	0,20	0,40	0,25	0,20
F	0,01	0,02	0,10	0,20	0,40	0,70

C|K	A	B	C	D	F
A	0,20	0,09	0,01	0,01	0,01
B	0,40	0,20	0,09	0,07	0,01
C	0,20	0,40	0,20	0,12	0,01
D	0,17	0,26	0,55	0,40	0,12
F	0,03	0,05	0,15	0,40	0,85

Fig. 3. CPT1: for each value of $C|K = k$ has its maximum on $k - 1$. The two cases of 6-valued and 5-valued grading scale are shown.

A second CPT (CPT2) we devised for the tests is supposed to give a "reasonable" (i.e. based on a teacher's experience) distribution of C: the values of C with respect to each value $K = k$ are shown in Fig. 4.

C|K	A	B	C	D	E	F
A	0,40	0,05	0,05	0,05	0,05	0,02
B	0,30	0,40	0,05	0,05	0,05	0,03
C	0,15	0,25	0,45	0,15	0,10	0,10
D	0,10	0,15	0,20	0,45	0,15	0,15
E	0,04	0,10	0,15	0,15	0,45	0,25
F	0,01	0,05	0,10	0,15	0,20	0,45

C|K	A	B	C	D	F
A	0,40	0,05	0,05	0,05	0,02
B	0,30	0,40	0,05	0,05	0,03
C	0,15	0,25	0,45	0,15	0,10
D	0,12	0,20	0,28	0,55	0,27
F	0,03	0,10	0,17	0,20	0,58

Fig. 4. CPT2: for each value $K = k$ we devised a "reasonable" distribution for C values.

We also tested two further CPTs, concentrating the highest probability for the value c of C, given $K = k$, on $c = k$, and stating such probability $P(C = k|K = k)$ equal to 0.5. So, in CPT3 and CPT4, half conditional probability is concentrated on the same value the student achieves for K, while the remaining 0.5 is divided according to two different criteria among the other grades. And in both cases we assumed, for the value c of C corresponding to $K = k$, $c < k$ more likely than otherwise.

In CPT3 the conditional probability distributions $P(C|K = \text{'}A\text{'})$ and $P(C|K = \text{'}F\text{'})$ (first and last column), represent extreme cases, on which we set some values coming from (informal) experience. As of the other columns, we stated that out of the remaining probability (*0.5*) a lesser part (*2/5*) would go to the case of $c > k$, and the rest (*0.3*) would go for $c <= k$. Given m the number of higher (lower) grades to handle, we then computed $SLICES = \sum_{i=1}^{m} 1$, and assigned to the less probable grade $0.20 \times SLICES$, to the second less probable the grade $0.20 \times 2 \times SLICES$, and so on (respectively, $0.20 \times SLICES$, $0.20 \times 2 \times SLICES$, and so on). Figure 5 shows the resulting CPTs.

C|K	A	B	C	D	E	F
A	0,50	0,20	0,07	0,03	0,02	0,01
B	0,30	0,50	0,13	0,07	0,04	0,03
C	0,10	0,12	0,50	0,10	0,06	0,06
D	0,06	0,09	0,15	0,50	0,08	0,10
E	0,03	0,06	0,10	0,20	0,50	0,30
F	0,01	0,03	0,05	0,10	0,30	0,50

C|K	A	B	C	D	F
A	0,50	0,20	0,07	0,03	0,02
B	0,30	0,50	0,13	0,07	0,08
C	0,10	0,15	0,50	0,10	0,10
D	0,08	0,10	0,20	0,50	0,30
F	0,02	0,05	0,10	0,30	0,50

Fig. 5. CPT3: half probability is concentrated on $C = k|K = k$.

The last CPT tested (CPT4, Fig. 6) follows the rules above also for the first and last columns (K = *'A'* and K = *'F'*), except that the amount of probability which is not applicable (the probability to increase the grade for K = *'A'* or decrease it for K = *'F'*) is summed to $P(C = k|K = k)$.

C|K	A	B	C	D	E	F
A	0,70	0,20	0,07	0,03	0,02	0,01
B	0,10	0,50	0,13	0,07	0,04	0,03
C	0,08	0,12	0,50	0,10	0,06	0,04
D	0,06	0,09	0,15	0,50	0,08	0,05
E	0,04	0,06	0,10	0,20	0,50	0,07
F	0,02	0,03	0,05	0,10	0,30	0,80

C|K	A	B	C	D	F
A	0,70	0,20	0,07	0,03	0,02
B	0,12	0,50	0,13	0,07	0,04
C	0,09	0,15	0,50	0,10	0,06
D	0,06	0,10	0,20	0,50	0,08
F	0,03	0,05	0,10	0,30	0,80

Fig. 6. CPT4: same as CPT3, but for first and last columns.

Regarding the [MAPPING] part of RQ2, we evaluated different strategies to map back to a grade the value (distribution) of C for each student (except for those grades directly coming from the teacher). We call *prob2value* this mapping: it's results are reported in column PROB2VAL in tables. In particular, given the probability distribution of C, for an individual student, over the values A…F, at the end of the session, we explored the following mappings for the grade inferred by the system: (1) the grade is the center of the interval corresponding to the grade with highest probability (this solution is labelled **max1P** in tables); (2) the grade is the weighted and normalized sum of the two grades in the distribution with the highest probabilities, where weights are the achieved probabilities (label **max2P**); (3) the grade is the weighted and normalized sum of the three grades in the distribution with the highest probabilities (weights as above; label **max3P**); (4) the grade is the weighted and normalized sum of all grades in the distribution (weights are determined as above; the label is *weightedSum*-**wSum** in tables); (5) the grade is the weighted sum of the most probable values, selected among the highest until accumulating 75% of probability (label **best75%**).

4.1 Experiments

To perform the experiments we used some datasets, either developed during our research/teaching activity or borrowed from colleagues such is the case for the dataset, labeled as A2-5-4, shown in Table 1. The datasets are collections of exercises (open ended questions) on which OpenAnswer sessions were performed, each one associated to the corresponding peer assessment data and complete teacher grading. They are originated in different educational contexts (High School or University). Moreover they are ranging over different topics, met in scientific or social science courses. Table 1 reports the composition of each collection: The dataset name contains a label (such as A in A-6-1), the number of distinct values used for the grade scale (such as 6 in A-6-1), and the number of teachers involved in the grading process (such as 4 in A2-5-4). When there were more teachers involved than one, each one of them performed the complete grading of the students' answers; in particular, in this case we run a distinct simulation for each one of the teachers, using the common student's data and the individual teacher's grading.

Table 1. The composition of the datasets.

Dataset	Level	Topic	Groups	Students
A-6-1	Univ.	4 exercises on multi-level cache systems	2	7 to 15
M-6-1	Univ.	3 exercises on C programming	2	9 to 13
I-6-1	High School	1 physics exercise	2	14 and 12
A2-5-4	Univ.	1 essay on social tools	5	12

Notice that, in the presentation of the experimental data to come, we show the average results (e.g. percentages) computed on all simulations as a whole.

We first report the average performance of pure peer assessment over the different sessions in the different datasets, i.e., the accuracy of students' grading compared with the ground truth of teachers' grading. Table 2 reports the percentage of average peer grades which are correct (OK/TOTAL) or within 1 grade (IN1/TOTAL) from the teacher grade. This provides an overall average rate of correct grades of 42.72%, while if we admit a difference of ± 1 grade we get 84.16%. The overall average is weighted respect to the number of experiments in each dataset.

Before going further, we want to shortly comment on the rows labelled as "A2 avg" and "A2 median" in Table 2. We remind that in dataset A2-5-4 the students' answers were graded by 4 different teachers. In the first row of the table, the grade set of each teacher is considered as a separate experiment, and then the average is performed over the percentages obtained from such experiments. On the contrary, in "A2 avg" ("A2 median") we compute a single experiment, in which the teachers' grades are the average (the median) of the four teachers' individual grades. It is interesting to notice that in this way better performance parameters are obtained. This seems to suggest that the difference in grading criteria among different teachers has a clear influence on the evaluation of the results of peer assessment. In practice, the students' assessment is closer to the assessment carried out by an "average" or "median" teacher, so that individual episodic differences are smoothed. More investigations on the difference between grades of multiple teachers is called for.

Table 2. *Pure Peer Assessment*: OK/TOTAL states the percentage of success of peer assessment, i.e. how many times the average peer evaluation is equal to the teacher's grade. IN1/TOTAL provides a relaxed success rate, computed as the times the peer evaluation is equal to the teacher's grade or differs by at most one mark from it.

Dataset	Domain	OK/TOTAL	IN1/TOTAL
A2	5	47.13%	91.57%
A2 avg	5	58.82%	94.12%
A2 median	5	58.82%	95.59%
A	6	37.84%	67.57%
I	6	57.69%	96.15%
M	6	27.94%	72.06%
A + M + I + A2 (weighted)	6 and 5	42.72%	84.16%

In order to deal with RQ1 and RQ2, we started comparing the rates in Table 2 with what is obtained by "using OpenAnswer without the teacher", i.e. by just letting the peer grades propagate across the BN. In this case we say that *no termination condition* is adopted (*none* is the label). The results we present show the behavior of the same "percentages of success" mentioned above (OK/TPTAL and IN1/TOTAL) with respect to different combinations of the CPTs, P(K) distributions and mappings described earlier: cfr. Table 3.

The first observation is that, among the CPTs tested in our experiments, the best one is the one modeled manually by an experienced teacher (**CPT2**). This kind of primacy is maintained in the following experiments we performed, so in the rest of our presentation we will refer only to CPT2. It is interesting to notice that this CPT causes a fair behavior of the BN. When no information is provided about the class, the network is quite neutral (the results are very close to those obtained by pure peer assessment) while when some amount of knowledge about the class learning state is added (**TgrDist**) a significant improvement is obtained by the use of the BN. Of course the best result is obtained with **Tgrade**, entailing to know the exact grade in advance (as noticed, this is an upper bound). In the following, we will compare the more realistic

Table 3. Results obtained for pure peer assessment supported by BN propagation, using different CPTs, different initial settings for P(K) and different procedures to map a probability distribution onto a single vote; no teacher grading is entailed.

		TERMINATION = none (no teacher correction)											
		Average - OK/TOTAL						Average – IN1/TOTAL					
	P(K)	best75	max1P	max2P	max3P	wSUm	Incr	best75	max1P	max2P	max3P	wSum	Incr
CPT1	flat	39,01	38,62	36,96	39,72	**39,44**	−3,00	**81,44**	81,25	80,56	80,86	81,22	−2,72
	synthetic	38,79	36,56	35,51	**39,90**	39,30	−2,83	82,76	80,44	79,66	**83,25**	81,68	**−0,91**
	Tgrade	39,76	29,80	28,60	**46,23**	40,86	3,50	92,83	**94,74**	92,72	90,83	91,29	**10,58**
	TgrDist	39,60	37,34	37,35	40,72	**42,01**	−0,72	**85,81**	82,32	81,00	83,65	84,41	**1,65**
CPT2	flat	40,30	37,85	36,18	40,24	**42,12**	−0,60	81,16	81,02	80,73	84,12	**85,45**	**1,29**
	synthetic	40,68	40,34	39,56	40,40	**41,85**	−0,87	82,17	80,83	81,09	84,66	**86,04**	**1,88**
	Tgrade	64,03	**82,96**	73,83	55,04	58,28	40,23	93,72	93,26	92,48	**94,21**	93,94	**10,05**
	TgrDist	43,67	**48,44**	46,04	44,63	45,60	**5,72**	85,71	84,02	83,72	86,89	**87,05**	**2,89**
CPT3	flat	38,56	36,67	35,75	40,33	**40,87**	−1,85	80,94	81,03	81,12	83,61	**84,43**	**0,27**
	synthetic	37,90	37,22	35,76	38,15	**42,50**	−0,23	80,90	82,06	81,59	82,59	**84,19**	**0,03**
	Tgrade	70,39	**81,10**	72,24	63,07	66,51	38,38	**94,94**	94,61	94,81	95,43	94,54	**11,27**
	TgrDist	40,71	43,12	41,59	40,37	**43,32**	0,60	82,86	84,29	83,83	84,90	**85,69**	**1,53**
CPT4	flat	37,10	32,02	33,52	37,12	**39,34**	−3,38	79,92	72,38	76,32	81,41	**83,44**	**−0,72**
	synthetic	36,68	35,24	35,52	37,06	**41,09**	−1,63	79,43	77,68	78,27	82,44	**84,21**	**0,05**
	Tgrade	72,25	**81,48**	74,37	67,80	71,22	38,75	95,41	94,34	95,01	**95,90**	94,77	**11,74**
	TgrDist	39,10	42,10	39,76	39,46	**43,50**	0,78	81,61	80,28	81,24	83,64	**84,22**	**0,06**

flat (no knowledge at all on the class) and **TgrDist** (past knowledge) distributions. As a further observation, the weighted sum (**wSum**) rule to map a distribution onto a final value gives the best results in most cases even in the following experiments, therefore we will always report results obtained by this strategy.

Tables 4 and 5 present the results that we obtained for the best candidates identified from Table 3 (CPT2, wSum). The tables show the performance results associated to different combinations of *strategies* (for the suggestion to the teacher of the next answer to grade) and *termination conditions* (stating when the teacher's grades are not needed anymore and the grade inference can be performed, through a mapping procedure, on the answers not directly graded by the teacher).

As initial P(K) distributions we keep analyzing only flat and TgrDist. In these tables, the groups or rows labeled **L/TOTAL** report, for each strategy and for each termination condition, the percentage of questions manually graded by the teacher (a measure of the teacher's effort), The groups of rows labeled as **(OK + L)/TOTAL** report the total percentage of answers correctly graded (either by the teacher or by the system through peer assessment), while groups **(IN1 + L)/TOTAL** report a similar value for answers finally graded by a value that is ± 1 the correct grade. We remind that correct grades are available as ground truth for experimental evaluation.

In Table 4 it is possible to notice that inferred grades alone do not reach the accuracy of pure peer evaluation with propagation (column **none**). However, if we also consider the teacher's work, we can observe a significant improvement in accuracy, even though this is obtained at the expense of more teacher's work (see discussion). Using MaxTotalEntropy with noFlip3, we reach 80.63% (OK + L)/TOTAL and 95.32% for (IN1 + L)/TOTAL at the expense of about 68% answers manually graded. It is also possible to consider, by comparing values in the different combinations, that the earliest the system stop (e.g., noFlip1 vs. noFlip3) the lower the teacher's work but the lower the accuracy too.

Although these results may seem not brilliant, it is to be considered that Table 4 refers to a situation where we assume no knowledge about student's learning state, i.e. *P(K) = flat*: we start with an initial setting for P(K) where all values are equally probable. On the contrary, Table 5 shows that a certain amount of preliminary knowledge of the class learning achievements can improve accuracy results.

4.2 Discussion

As far as RQ1 is concerned, in the presentation of Table 3 we pointed out some factors that allow us to say that using OpenAnswer we are not wasting info with respect to the case of pure peer evaluations, and moreover we can expect further gains. In particular while using CPT2, under the flat, or, even better, the TGrDist P(K) distributions, with the *weightedSum* mapping, we get generally better results for OK/TOTAL and IN1/TOTAL than we would do with pure peer evaluation.

As of RQ2, the analysis of the results, conducted in Sect. 4.1 with Tables 4 and 5, says that by using OpenAnswer, and leveraging on the strategies and termination conditions, there is a further gain. In particular we can conclude that the system is in fact sensitive to changes in the PD, CPT, and MAPPING factors. Table 4 shows a

Table 4. OpenAnswer, with peer assessments and teacher's grades. CPT2 is used. P(K) = flat (no assumptions on class knowledge). MAPPING is P2VAL = wSum. Teacher's grading is with different combinations of strategies (*next answer to grade*), and termination conditions.

P(K) = flat	P2VAL = wSum	TERMINATION						
Data	STRATEGY	noFlip1	noFlip2	noFlip3	none	noWrong	noWrong2	noWrong3
Average - OK/TOTAL	maxEntropy	35,97%	24,85%	17,34%	42,12%	31,08%	31,59%	31,08%
	maxInfoGain	32,40%	26,24%	18,08%	42,12%	31,77%	32,27%	31,45%
	maxStrangeness	29,41%	23,23%	15,22%	42,12%	34,36%	35,08%	34,36%
	maxTotalEntropy	33,65%	25,33%	12,87%	42,12%	31,44%	32,80%	31,73%
	maxWrong	30,06%	17,96%	11,95%	42,12%	38,59%	40,40%	38,59%
	random	30,05%	22,64%	15,02%	42,12%	34,42%	37,67%	33,76%
Average - L/TOTAL	maxEntropy	18,63%	43,25%	60,44%		34,44%	30,61%	34,44%
	maxInfoGain	18,81%	33,86%	53,85%		32,56%	29,13%	32,88%
	maxStrangeness	29,01%	44,36%	61,67%		24,69%	20,03%	24,69%
	maxTotalEntropy	17,81%	37,92%	**67,76%**		31,49%	27,47%	30,60%
	maxWrong	25,58%	52,46%	66,41%		8,86%	5,02%	8,84%
	random	21,74%	44,70%	65,89%		23,41%	13,63%	24,60%
Average - OK + L/TOTAL	maxEntropy	54,60%	68,10%	77,78%	42,12%	65,52%	62,20%	65,52%
	maxInfoGain	51,22%	60,10%	71,93%	42,12%	64,33%	61,40%	64,33%
	maxStrangeness	58,43%	67,58%	76,89%	42,12%	59,04%	55,12%	59,04%
	maxTotalEntropy	51,46%	63,25%	**80,63%**	42,12%	62,92%	60,26%	62,34%
	maxWrong	55,64%	70,41%	78,36%	42,12%	47,44%	45,42%	47,43%
	random	51,79%	67,34%	80,91%	42,12%	57,83%	51,30%	58,36%
Average - IN1 + L/TOTAL	maxEntropy	88,66%	93,19%	95,10%	85,45%	94,42%	93,18%	94,42%
	maxInfoGain	89,75%	91,83%	93,83%	85,45%	93,70%	92,76%	93,70%
	maxStrangeness	88,32%	90,84%	92,84%	85,45%	92,59%	90,26%	92,59%
	maxTotalEntropy	87,78%	91,70%	**95,32%**	85,45%	93,54%	92,30%	92,95%
	maxWrong	90,60%	93,76%	95,14%	85,45%	88,56%	86,96%	88,56%
	random	88,05%	91,27%	93,91%	85,45%	92,54%	89,55%	92,29%

Table 5. Use of OpenAnswer. Everything is as in Table 4; here, yet, *P(K) = TgrDist* (we assume to know the class knowledge state as a distribution, not as single individual values).

TgrDist	wSum	TERMINATION						
Data	STRATEGY	noFlip1	noFlip2	noFlip3	none	noWrong	noWrong2	noWrong3
Average - OK/TOTAL	maxEntropy	38,76%	31,01%	21,53%	45,60%	34,41%	35,97%	34,41%
	maxInfoGain	39,03%	30,87%	23,68%	45,60%	35,53%	37,02%	35,53%
	maxStrangeness	38,63%	28,11%	21,84%	45,60%	37,91%	40,01%	37,91%
	maxTotalEntropy	40,11%	33,95%	21,28%	45,60%	34,55%	36,77%	34,55%
	maxWrong	38,06%	27,55%	20,99%	45,60%	41,77%	43,61%	42,25%
	random	35,99%	27,16%	18,31%	45,60%	38,74%	41,23%	38,74%
Average - L/TOTAL	maxEntropy	16,72%	33,24%	53,99%		33,21%	25,81%	33,21%
	maxInfoGain	15,86%	35,74%	51,83%		30,42%	22,93%	30,21%
	maxStrangeness	16,59%	38,99%	54,60%		22,46%	16,42%	22,46%
	maxTotalEntropy	15,94%	31,68%	**54,37%**		30,54%	24,09%	30,54%
	maxWrong	16,61%	39,08%	53,51%		10,55%	3,85%	8,71%
	random	16,78%	41,27%	59,94%		23,88%	13,57%	23,88%
Average – OK + L/TOTAL	maxEntropy	55,48%	64,25%	75,51%	45,60%	67,63%	61,78%	67,63%
	maxInfoGain	54,89%	66,61%	75,51%	45,60%	65,95%	59,95%	65,74%
	maxStrangeness	55,22%	67,10%	76,44%	45,60%	60,37%	56,43%	60,37%
	maxTotalEntropy	56,05%	65,63%	**75,65%**	45,60%	65,08%	60,86%	65,08%
	maxWrong	54,67%	66,63%	74,50%	45,60%	52,32%	47,46%	50,97%
	random	52,76%	68,43%	78,26%	45,60%	62,62%	54,80%	62,62%
Average – IN1 + L/TOTAL	maxEntropy	90,92%	93,29%	95,42%	87,05%	94,68%	93,19%	94,68%
	maxInfoGain	89,82%	93,09%	95,10%	87,05%	94,35%	93,39%	94,35%
	maxStrangeness	88,19%	90,32%	92,55%	87,05%	91,38%	90,16%	91,38%
	maxTotalEntropy	91,43%	93,17%	**95,98%**	87,05%	93,61%	92,70%	93,61%
	maxWrong	90,07%	93,84%	95,61%	87,05%	90,44%	88,02%	89,26%
	random	88,23%	92,97%	95,80%	87,05%	92,32%	90,07%	92,32%

difference in performance between the cases of a full-fledged use of OpenAnswer (CPT2, *weightedSum* mapping, and flat P(K) distribution) and a limited use of OpenAnswer (none): the difference is a gain, between 12 and 16 percentage points for (OK + L)/TOTAL, and between 2 and 5 points for (IN1 + L)/TOTAL. Similarly, the full-fledged use of OpenAnswer, with TgrDist P(K) distribution gains over "none" between 7 and 10 points for (OK + L)/TOTAL, and between 1 and 4 points for (IN1 + L)/TOTAL. To conclude that RQ2 is answered (with a "yes") we just have to consider the amount of teacher's work (grading) implied by the above results. We selected the above measure of gain by considering the "noflip1" column in the tables, as this is the case when the teacher's grading is shorter. So, the results associated to the flat P(K) distribution are related to an amount of teacher's work between 17% and 29% of the (TOTAL) number of answers. Not surprisingly indeed, by using TGrDist as P(K) initial distribution we get our results with less teacher's work (between 15% and 17%).

A final consideration might be dedicated to the case of the "random" strategy for selection of the next answer to grade by the teacher. Often this strategy shows better accuracy results, in terms of (OK + L)/TOTAL. Rather than a negation of the usefulness of using strategies to select the next answer, we think that this result is actually a corroboration: without a strategy, the amount of information that the next grading will pour into the system cannot be anticipated, nor decided; a consequence of this is in that the teacher will grade more answers (this strategy shows higher L/TOTAL). In other words, the better accuracy is paid with more teacher's work.

5 Relationships Between Knowledge and Assessment Capabilities

In this section we investigate another factor of OpenAnswer, that is the expression of the relationship between the two macro-abilities (cfr. the occurrence of related keywords in the Bloom's taxonomy [3]) *knowledge* (K), i.e., competence on the topic of a question, and *judgment* (J), i.e. the ability to correctly assess a peer's answer. As a "factor" in OpenAnswer this is quite foundational, and admittedly of a different nature with respect to the BN-related aspects discussed in the previous section. To study such relationship we try and model the conditional relations between J and C, P(J|C), where C is the correctness of a peer's answer (with respect to the grade stated by the teacher in our datasets). This modeling is done indirectly, as C and J express two different macro-abilities: in particular it is derived by the collaboration among

- the P(G|J,C), that is the conditional probability of G given J and C, where G is the (correctness of the) mark assigned by the peer to an answer
- and the two P(J|K) and P(C|K) already mentioned.

In our model the probabilistic dependencies of *J*, *C* and *G*, are rendered as Gaussian distributions. Such distributions are actually parametrized, with respect to their mean (μ) and standard deviation (σ). In particular, we denote by C_G the correctness value for the answer under peer evaluation (while C would be the correctness of the answer given by the peer doing the assessment), and define:

1. $P(G|J, C_G) = Gauss(C_G + \delta_G, \sigma_G * J)$
2. $P(C|K) = Gauss(K + \delta_C, \sigma_C)$
3. $P(J|K) = Gauss(K + \delta_J, \sigma_J)$

where the δ coefficients, δ_J, δ_C, and δ_G, displace the center of the Gaussian distribution from the correctness of the answer under assessment or from the Knowledge value for the peer doing the assessment, and the σ values are used to determine the standard deviation of the respective distribution. In particular, we interpret δ_G as an expression of the bias acting upon the peer assessment grade (difference between the assessment and the correct grade), while δ_C represents the additional difficulty of providing an answer against having knowledge of the question's topic, and δ_J is conceived as representing the additional difficulty of stating an assessments, with respect to just providing an answer. We will also consider the difference $\delta_J - \delta_C$, denoting the added ability to judge a peer's answer compared to answering.

The linear dependence on J of the standard deviation, in $P(G|J, C_G)$ is posited with the aim to capture different assessing capabilities; in particular we might notice that a very good assessor (J = A) is likely to give correct assessments, according to a Gaussian distribution which is quite narrow (we use 1…6 for the values of, respectively, A…F); on the contrary a poor assessor, corresponding to a wide (J = F) distribution, is likely to grade far from correct.

In this context, RQ3 seeks the better localization estimate of the value μ of $P(J|C)$ with respect to the value for Correctness (C) of the student's answers. This gives the relation between the *ability to assess* an answer to a given question, and the *success in answering correctly* to that question; that, in turn, brings to the relation between J and K, via the dependence of J from K.

To seek an answer to RQ3 we produced simulated OpenAnswer sessions, in the ways described in Sect. 4. In particular, we considered the average difference between the correct grade and the one inferred by the system, under the various conditions. We call AvgTotDV this value. Finding the parameters of the Gaussian distributions above, that get a minimal AvgTotDV is the aim of our optimization steps: *min(AvgTotDV)* is our objective function.

Notice that in the simulated sessions, the computation of the *noFlip* termination criteria requires mapping the estimated probability distribution $P(C_G)$ onto a discrete vote in the range [A–F]. To obtain this, we compute a continuous numeric grades in [0, 10], as the weighted sum of the probabilities of the different intervals. The weight of each interval is the value of its center (A = 9.75, B = 9, C = 8, D = 7, E = 6, F = 2.75). The resulting grade is then discretized back to the corresponding interval. This is done because if we just computed the difference between discretized grades and the teacher's grade, the latter being discretized as well, we could obtain only integer values. Given that both the teacher's grade and the one inferred by the system are in a continuous range, we can increase the precision of the computed difference by considering the difference between continuous values instead of discretized ones. After the first experiments we have noticed that the objective function appears to be continuous as well, and thus we have been able to reduce the parameter space explored by our optimization process, by separately optimizing the δ_J, δ_C, δ_G, and the σ_J, σ_C, σ_G, parameters as follows:

1. First we fixed $\sigma_J = 1.0$, $\sigma_C = 1.0$, $\sigma_G = 0.5$ with an educated guess and explored the parameter space of the remaining parameters over the set of values:
   - δ_J: from −2 to +2 in 0.5 increments
   - δ_C: from −2 to +2 in 0.5 increments
   - δ_G: from −2 to +2 in 0.5 increments

   This allowed us to find a suitable set of values for the following σ_J, σ_C, σ_G, optimization. So we stated $\delta_J = 1.5$, $\delta_C = -1.5$, $\delta_G = 0.5$ and searched for the best corresponding values of σ_J, σ_C, σ_G. Such values are $<\sigma_J = 1.0, \sigma_C = 0.5, \sigma_G = 0.5>$: indeed our initial educated guess was almost correct (we landed, after two rounds of optimization, on values quite close to it).

2. Then we re-optimized δ_J, δ_C, δ_G relative to the new fixed sigma parameters.

The next sub-section provides a discussion of the experience. The values resulting for δ_J, δ_C, and δ_G are shown in Fig. 7, where MIN, AVG and MAX of the AvgTotDV objective function are reported with respect to the $\delta_J - \delta_C$ and δ_G parameters.

	Delta_G																										
	MIN of AvgTotDV									AVG of AvgTotDV									MAX of AvgTotDV								
DJ-DC	2,0	1,5	1,0	0,5	0,0	-0,5	-1,0	-1,5	-2,0	2,0	1,5	1,0	0,5	0,0	-0,5	-1,0	-1,5	-2,0	2,0	1,5	1,0	0,5	0,0	-0,5	-1,0	-1,5	-2,0
4,0	2,72	2,08	1,80	0,94	0,85	0,65	0,51	0,48	0,67	3,72	3,05	2,57	2,08	1,89	1,76	2,27	2,39	2,55	4,82	4,39	3,96	3,40	3,06	3,08	4,52	4,92	5,03
3,5	2,34	1,98	1,37	0,94	0,77	0,62	0,55	0,45	0,62	3,55	2,94	2,48	2,02	1,78	1,64	1,88	2,01	2,24	4,76	4,31	3,93	3,36	3,06	3,06	4,52	4,87	4,98
3,0	2,27	1,76	1,32	0,96	0,76	0,60	0,54	0,46	0,60	3,39	2,81	2,38	1,94	1,70	1,57	1,71	1,82	2,07	4,67	4,22	3,85	3,27	3,07	3,06	4,43	4,75	4,86
2,5	1,71	1,46	0,92	0,86	0,76	0,53	0,44	0,50	0,57	3,21	2,68	2,26	1,85	1,61	1,49	1,52	1,63	1,85	4,49	4,09	3,70	3,17	3,07	3,06	3,76	4,44	4,69
2,0	1,55	1,20	0,86	0,84	0,69	0,51	0,38	0,51	0,57	2,97	2,54	2,13	1,75	1,53	1,40	1,40	1,47	1,64	4,36	3,90	3,53	3,12	3,07	3,07	3,06	4,10	4,36
1,5	1,28	1,01	0,85	0,80	0,56	0,53	0,38	0,51	0,54	2,74	2,35	1,98	1,65	1,45	1,33	1,32	1,38	1,47	4,20	3,71	3,39	3,07	3,07	3,07	3,07	3,66	4,00
1,0	0,34	0,31	0,31	0,43	0,49	0,51	0,37	0,50	0,51	2,45	2,12	1,80	1,54	1,38	1,29	1,28	1,32	1,39	4,05	3,59	3,33	3,07	3,07	3,07	3,07	3,07	3,51
0,5	0,30	0,31	0,37	0,51	0,44	0,47	0,41	0,47	0,49	2,20	1,94	1,68	1,46	1,33	1,25	1,25	1,29	1,35	3,92	3,46	3,22	3,07	3,07	3,07	3,07	3,07	3,07
0,0	0,32	0,36	0,47	0,48	0,39	0,43	0,43	0,47	0,46	2,02	1,80	1,59	1,42	1,30	1,25	1,25	1,29	1,35	3,81	3,38	3,11	3,07	3,07	3,07	3,07	3,07	3,07
-0,5	0,37	0,48	0,56	0,44	0,36	0,38	0,43	0,47	0,45	1,81	1,64	1,45	1,32	1,22	1,18	1,19	1,22	1,28	3,43	3,12	2,97	2,99	2,98	2,96	2,95	2,94	2,93
-1,0	0,45	0,55	0,50	0,41	0,33	0,34	0,40	0,42	0,44	1,62	1,48	1,33	1,22	1,16	1,13	1,16	1,20	1,26	3,21	2,93	2,88	2,88	2,85	2,82	2,80	2,77	2,75
-1,5	0,55	0,59	0,47	0,38	0,32	0,32	0,36	0,38	0,42	1,44	1,33	1,22	1,14	1,10	1,10	1,14	1,19	1,26	2,96	2,71	2,39	2,16	2,27	2,34	2,46	2,42	2,52
-2,0	0,62	0,56	0,45	0,37	0,31	0,31	0,33	0,37	0,41	1,28	1,20	1,13	1,09	**1,08**	1,10	1,16	1,21	1,28	2,74	2,46	2,16	2,20	2,28	2,30	2,35	2,47	2,50
-2,5	0,65	0,54	0,44	0,37	0,31	**0,30**	0,32	0,37	0,40	1,19	1,14	1,10	1,09	1,11	1,15	1,21	1,28	1,36	2,38	2,18	2,12	2,22	2,31	2,33	2,45	2,50	2,63
-3,0	0,65	0,68	0,62	0,49	0,50	0,56	0,60	0,64	0,71	1,14	1,13	1,13	1,15	1,19	1,23	1,29	1,36	1,46	**1,99**	2,03	2,18	2,24	2,38	2,45	2,45	2,53	2,63
-3,5	0,78	0,70	0,51	0,50	0,51	0,57	0,64	0,68	0,76	1,17	1,18	1,19	1,23	1,27	1,32	1,38	1,46	1,55	2,10	2,15	2,20	2,29	2,38	2,41	2,42	2,47	2,65
-4,0	0,72	0,72	0,71	0,65	0,68	0,73	0,80	0,86	0,97	1,27	1,28	1,32	1,35	1,40	1,46	1,52	1,58	1,66	2,12	2,17	2,24	2,31	2,42	2,43	2,44	2,54	2,69

Fig. 7. MIN (left), AVG (center) and MAX (right) of AvgTotDV (green = better, red = worse) with respect to different values of $\delta_J - \delta_C$ and δ_G over the 3 datasets A, I, M. (Color figure online)

5.1 Discussion

Our simulations assume no previous known information on the student's *K* except the *P(K)* distribution of the current assessment, which is obtained from the teacher's grades. All units in the table are in grades, i.e. 1 is the distance between two consecutive values in [A…F]. We see that the best average (AVG) values reside in the bottom part of the table. Here, $\delta_J - \delta_C$ is negative, meaning that *J* is lower than the corresponding *C* (the average minimum 1.08 is obtained at $\delta_J - \delta_C = -2$). There seems not to be a significant grade displacement as the average minimum 1.08 is obtained for $\delta_G = 0$.

By looking at the MIN (leftmost) set of columns we see that OpenAnswer could infer grades with very low error (0.3 grades) over some combination of parameters, selection strategy, termination criteria and data-set. The MAX (rightmost) columns instead show that we are able to ensure an upper bound on the average error of the grades inferred by the system: such upper bound is less than 2 grades (1.99 at $\delta_G = 2$ and $\delta_J - \delta_C = -3$), which is promising. More work is needed to improve the strategies and termination criteria and to rule out particularly bad combinations (e.g. maxEntropy/noWrong).

The most interesting result is that in all cases the best AvgTotDV values are obtained in correspondence to negative $\delta_J - \delta_C$. Such negative values mean that J is lower than the corresponding C. In other words, the student get a lower grade for J than for C, meaning that the ability required to provide a correct assessment is "harder" than that required to give the correct answer. Considering how both J and C are in relation to K, this confirms the validity of Bloom's ranking, and suggests that judgement lies at a higher cognitive level.

A side interest in this investigation is in finding how much the conditional distribution P(J|C) is spread around the average value, i.e., how much variation can be expected in the dependence between J and C. The results show that the best localization of μ for P(J|C) is below the value for C, meaning that on average the ability to judge is lower than ability to answer correctly to the question, which in turn means, again, that assessment is a "harder" task, i.e., it is at a higher cognitive level.

6 Conclusions

Admittedly the first inspiration for the work presented in this paper was the attempt to apply peer-evaluation and lighten the grading work of teachers, when they adopt the formative and summative technique of open-ended questionnaires. Our bend towards peer (possibly self) evaluation was also due to previous experiences in social-collaborative learning and related reputation systems [8–10, 26]; however, the support to the teacher's work, based on social and social-collaborative aspects, is a well-established research topic [14, 17–20]. Regarding open-ended questionnaires we have posited that an effective motivation for supporting the teacher is in that the use of this assessment method can more likely spread. Moreover, the practice of peer assessment would train the meta-cognitive abilities of students.

In particular we have shown as OpenAnswer can support the use of open-ended questionnaires and exploit the fruitful effects of peer-evaluation. It appears that it is still necessary to gain a deeper understanding of the effect obtained by the system under different configurations. We have listed the many and varied parameters of such a configuration: our continuing investigation seems to be crucial to see how such parameters my actually be more than pure mathematical elements, and be in addition the carrier for pedagogical and educational issues. Looking, for instance, to the evaluations we came to make about the Conditional Probability Tables, we saw that "manual" adjustments, driven by field experience in educational tasks, may achieve the best (possible) results (cfr. the decision to use only CPT2 in the second part of Sect. 4.1).

In addition, the results we have shown support the idea that the teacher is still crucial in maintaining the overall system's reliability. This might surely be due to a kind of implicit knowledge that is entailed in the educational process, that is difficult to formalize through automatic operational rules. As "comforting" the idea of delivering the whole assessment work to an automated process might be, we are is still far from the possibility to use a reliable, unsupervised, application (and this conclusion, in turn, may give some comfort to the teachers instead).

References

1. Anderson, L.W., Krathwohl, D.R. (eds.): A Taxonomy for Learning, Teaching, and Assessing: A Revision of Bloom's Taxonomy of Educational Objectives. Allyn and Bacon, Boston (2000)
2. Anderson, J.R., Corbett, A.T., Koedinger, K.R., Pelletier, R.: Cognitive tutors: lessons learned. J. Learn. Sci. **4**(2), 167–207 (1995)
3. Bloom, B.S., Engelhart, M.D., Furst, E.J., Hill, W.H., Krathwohl, D.R.: Taxonomy of Educational Objectives: The Classification of Educational Goals. Handbook I: Cognitive Domain. David McKay, New York (1956)
4. Castellanos-Nieves, D., Fernández-Breis, J., Valencia-García, R., Martínez-Béjar, R., Iniesta-Moreno, M.: Semantic Web Technologies for supporting learning assessment. Inf. Sciences **181**, 9 (2011)
5. Cho, K., MacArthur, C.: Student revision with peer and expert reviewing. Learn. Instr. **20**(4), 328–338 (2010)
6. Chung, H., Graf, S., Robert Lai, K.: Kinshuk: enrichment of peer assessment with agent negotiation. IEEE Trans. Learn. Technol. **4**(1), 35–46 (2011)
7. Conati, C., Gartner, A., Vanlehn, K.: Using Bayesian networks to manage uncertainty in student modeling. User Model. User-Adap. Inter. **12**, 371–417 (2002)
8. De Marsico, M., Sterbini, A., Temperini, M.: The definition of a tunneling strategy between adaptive learning and reputation-based group activities. In: Proceedings of 11th IEEE International Conference on Advanced Learning Technologies, pp. 498–500 (2011)
9. De Marsico, M., Sterbini, A., Temperini, M.: A framework to support social-collaborative personalized e-Learning. In: Kurosu, M. (ed.) HCI 2013. LNCS, vol. 8005, pp. 351–360. Springer, Heidelberg (2013). doi:10.1007/978-3-642-39262-7_40
10. De Marsico, M., Sterbini, A., Temperini, M.: A strategy to join adaptive and reputation-based social-collaborative e-learning, through the Zone of Proximal Development. Int. J. Distance Educ. Tech. (IJDET) **11**(3), 12–31 (2013)
11. El-Kechaï, N., Delozanne, É., Prévit, D., Grugeon, B., Chenevotot, F.: Evaluating the performance of a diagnosis system in school algebra. In: Leung, H., Popescu, E., Cao, Y., Lau, R.W.H., Nejdl, W. (eds.) ICWL 2011. LNCS, vol. 7048, pp. 263–272. Springer, Heidelberg (2011). doi:10.1007/978-3-642-25813-8_28
12. Formisano, A., Omodeo, E.G., Temperini, M.: Layered map reasoning: an experimental approach put to trial on sets. Electron. Notes Theor. Comput. Sci. **48**, 1–28 (2001). Elsevier Science B. V., Amsterdam
13. Formisano, A., Omodeo, E.G., Temperini, M.: Goals and benchmarks for automated map reasoning. J. Symb. Comput. **29**(2), 259–297 (2000)
14. Gasparetti, F., Limongelli, C., Sciarrone, F.: Wiki course builder: a system for retrieving and sequencing didactic materials from wikipedia. In: Proceedings of ITHET 2015 (2015)
15. Jackson, K., Trochim, W.: Concept mapping as an alternative approach for the analysis of open-ended survey responses. Organ. Res. Methods **5**, 307–336 (2002). Sage
16. Li, L.X., Liu, X., Steckelberg, A.L.: Assessor or assessee: how student learning improves by giving and receiving peer feedback. Br. J. Ed. Tech. **41**(3), 525–536 (2010)

17. Limongelli, C., Lombardi, M., Marani, A., Sciarrone, F., Temperini, M.: A recommendation module to help teachers build courses through the Moodle Learning Management System. New Rev. Hypermedia Multimed. **22**, 1–2 (2016)
18. Limongelli, C., Lombardi, M., Marani, A., Sciarrone, F.: A teacher model to speed up the process of building courses. In: Kurosu, M. (ed.) HCI 2013. LNCS, vol. 8005, pp. 434–443. Springer, Heidelberg (2013). doi:10.1007/978-3-642-39262-7_50
19. Limongelli, C., Lombardi, M., Marani, A., Sciarrone, F.: A teaching-style based social network for didactic building and sharing. In: Lane, H.C., Yacef, K., Mostow, J., Pavlik, P. (eds.) AIED 2013. LNCS, vol. 7926, pp. 774–777. Springer, Heidelberg (2013). doi:10.1007/978-3-642-39112-5_110
20. Limongelli, C., Sciarrone, F., Temperini, M.: A social network-based teacher model to support course construction. Comput. Hum. Behav. **51**, 1077–1085 (2015)
21. Metcalfe, J., Shimamura, A.P.: Metacognition: Knowing About Knowing. MIT Press, Cambridge (1994)
22. Miller, P.: The effect of scoring criteria specificity on peer and self-assessment. Assess. Eval. High. Educ. **28**(4), 383–394 (2003)
23. Palmer, K., Richardson, P.: On-line assessment and free-response input-a pedagogic and technical model for squaring the circle. In: Proceedings of 7th Computer Assisted Assessment Conference, pp. 289–300 (2003)
24. Romero, C., Ventura, S.: Educational data mining: a review of the state of the art. IEEE Trans. SMC Part C **40**(6), 601–618 (2010)
25. Sadler, P.M., Good, E.: The impact of self- and peer-grading on student learning. Educ. Assess. **11**(1), 1–31 (2006)
26. Sterbini, A., Temperini, M.: Collaborative projects and self evaluation within a social reputation-based exercise-sharing system. In: Proceedings of WI-IAT 2009, vol. 3, pp. 243–246 (2009)
27. Sterbini, A., Temperini, M.: Dealing with open-answer questions in a peer-assessment environment. In: Popescu, E., Li, Q., Klamma, R., Leung, H., Specht, M. (eds.) ICWL 2012. LNCS, vol. 7558, pp. 240–248. Springer, Heidelberg (2012). doi:10.1007/978-3-642-33642-3_26
28. Sterbini, A., Temperini, M.: Analysis of OpenAnswers via mediated peer-assessment. In: Proceedings of the International Conference on System Theory, Control and Computing, Workshop SPEL (2013)
29. Sterbini, A., Temperini, M.: OpenAnswer, a framework to support teacher's management of open answers through peer assessment. In: Proceedings of Frontiers in Education, pp. 164–170 (2013)
30. Topping, K.: Peer assessment between students in colleges and universities. Rev. Educ. Res. **68**, 249–276 (1998)
31. Yamanishi, K., Li, H.: Mining open answers in questionnaire data. IEEE Intell. Syst. **17**, 58–63 (2002)

Factors Affecting the Gaming Experience of Older Adults in Community and Senior Centres

Fan Zhang(✉), Simone Hausknecht, Robyn Schell, and David Kaufman

Faculty of Education, Simon Fraser University, Burnaby, Canada
{fza26,shauskne,rmschell,dkaufman}@sfu.ca

Abstract. This study investigated whether a Wii Bowling tournament could improve older adults' attitudes towards digital games and factors affecting their gaming experience. This study applied a two-group pre-post design. A total of 142 older adults aged 60 and over were recruited from 14 community and senior centers ($N = 81$ in the experimental group; $N = 61$ in the control group). The participants in the experimental group formed a total of 21 teams, which played against one another once a week for a period of eight weeks. The findings indicated that the Wii Bowling tournament improved older adults' attitudes towards digital games ($t = 2.53$, $p = .01$). More importantly, the authors identified six factors that contributed to the positive gaming experience of older adults in community and senior centers.

Keywords: Digital games · Older adults · Attitudes toward digital games · Gaming experience

1 Introduction

1.1 Age-Related Challenges

Older adults represent a growing proportion of the world population due to advancement of health care. The proportion of the world's population over 60 years will double from about 11% to 22% between 2000 and 2050 [1]. People are living longer as a result of better health and living conditions. However, being old is typically associated with negative connotations (e.g., frail, impaired and dependent) and comprises a number of physical and cognitive declines [2]. Impaired balance and falls can lead to injury, increased morbidity, fear of falling, loss of independence, death, and direct medical costs [3]. Cognitive decline is associated with decreased ability to perform everyday tasks required for functional independence, such as car driving and financial management [4]. What's more, many older adults face key social and psychological challenges such as loneliness, depression, and lack of social support due to living alone, lack of close family ties, lose connection with their friendship networks and reduced ability to participate in community [5]. Since these changes negatively affect older adults' quality of life [6] there are growing needs to understand and find ways to prevent or reshape age-related physical and cognitive decline and to increase older adults' social interaction.

G. Costagliola et al. (Eds.): CSEDU 2016, CCIS 739, pp. 464–475, 2017.
DOI: 10.1007/978-3-319-63184-4_24

1.2 Benefits of Playing Digital Games on Older Adults

Digital games (e.g., action, strategy, role-play, sports, and casual games) can be complex, offering flexible activities that use multiple cognitive abilities. Games that require progressively more accurate and more challenging judgments at higher speed, and the suppression of irrelevant information, can drive positive neurological changes in the brain systems that support these behaviours. Today, playing digital games has become a social activity [7]. Online games such as Massively Multiplayer Online Role-Playing Games (MMORPGs, e.g., World of Warcraft) allow thousands of players from around the world to interact with each other in the same virtual environment. With advances in virtual-reality interaction technology, somatosensory digital games that combine traditional digital games and physical activities provide older adults with alternative leisure opportunities [8]; for example, the Nintendo Wii Fit includes more than 40 activities such as yoga postures, strength training, and balance designed to engage the player in physical exercise.

These games can be played with family and friends in real-world situations. Face-to-face contacts and frequent, meaningful social interactions can happen through "interacting with other people, spending time with friends, watching others play, chatting and talking about the game, seeing other people's reactions and expressions, gloating when beating a friend, or feeling pride when they win" [9, p.11]. Engagement in social activities not only meets older adults' psychological needs for social interaction, but also keeps them physically and mentally active – the "use it or lose it" metaphor.

In addition, games are designed to be fun to play. They appeal to older adults' desires and needs for entertainment, mental fitness enhancement, competition and success, a satisfying use of time, and, in social games, a sense of belonging [10]. Digital gameplay is inherently enjoyable and motivating, a state which can be described in terms of Csikszentmihalyi's [11] flow experience. Flow describes a mental state of complete absorption, accompanied by positive feelings. Gamberini et al. [12] pointed out that digital games can provide older adults with new opportunities for leisure and entertainment, combined with training that avoids both intimidating task complexity and boredom.

Ijsselsteijn and colleagues [13] identified four potential areas for digital games to contribute to improving the quality of life for older adults: (1) relaxation and entertainment, (2) socializing, (3) sharpening the mind, and (4) more natural ways of interacting. Chen, Chiang, Liu and Chang (2012) indicated that digital games can be used as tools to encourage older adults to exercise physically and mentally, delaying the occurrence of diseases and thus improving their quality of life. There is now substantial evidence showing that playing digital games can improve older adults' physical and cognitive abilities and psychological health. Zhang and Kaufman [14] conducted a meta-analysis study to examine the physical and cognitive impacts of digital games on older adults. It was found that playing digital game is effective in improving older adults' physical balance ($g = 0.67$), balance confidence ($g = 0.46$), functional mobility ($g = 0.53$), executive function ($g = 0.76$), and processing speed ($g = 0.54$). Jung, Li, Janissa, Gladys, and Lee [15] examined the impact of playing Nintendo Wii on the psychological and physical well-being of seniors in a long-term care facility. Results showed that playing Wii yielded a positive impact on loneliness, self-esteem, and well-being among older adults, compared to a control group that played traditional board games. Allaire and colleagues' [16] study suggested that regular and occasional gamers exhibited significantly higher levels of well-being and lower levels of loneliness compared to non-gamers. Cota and Ishitani' s [17] review suggested that digital games can be classified as low-cost tools in treating diseases related to cognitive aspects and psychosocial problems without letting older adults leave their comfortable home.

1.3 Older Adults and New Technology

Czaja and Lee [18] emphasized that older adults represent an extremely diverse group and do not uniformly conform to technology averse stereotypes. Although physical and cognitive declines may hamper their ability to use technology as effectively or proficiently as younger people, older adults have been found to be willing to use technology when they are aware of the benefits such technology can offer them [19, 20]. Reviewing studies that compare older and younger adults' attitudes towards and abilities with computers, Broady, Chan and Caputi [21] found that lack of knowledge of the capabilities of modern technologies and how to use them is a major influence on older adults' avoidance of technology. Other barriers include confusion regarding usage procedures, fear of the unknown, lack of confidence, and lack of understanding of the value of products and services. Understanding technology as being personally relevant and useful, as well as overcoming the initial fears and external factors (e.g. how one is viewed and treated by others) are crucial to overcoming those barriers. Overall, Broady et al. [21] concluded that older people appear eager to accept technological advancements and exhibit attitudes that are as positive as young peoples' towards the use of computers. Mitzner et al. [22] also indicated that older and young adults did not differ very much in the actual knowledge of computers but more in their confidence.

In addition, first-hand experience can trigger older adults' interest and provide opportunities for improving attitudes towards a new technology [23, 24] and self-efficacy [25]. In addition to capabilities, attitudes and perceptions, Wagner, Hassanein and Head [26] highlighted that using technology is also influenced by environmental factors such as interactions, and context of use.

2 Research Questions

Previous study has shown that older adults are far less likely than younger people to play digital games [27]. Older gamers are playing more and more games, but only 29% of gamers are over the age of 50 [28]. In the U.S., some 61% of gamers are younger than 36-years old [29]. It is understandable that older adults play fewer digital games, as many did not grow up with computer and information technologies. However, encouraging their engagement with these new technologies could help to realize the potential of digital games to address a variety of health, social-psychological, and functional needs for older adults.

Cota and Ishitani [17] conducted a literature review to understand the main factors that motivate older adults to become interested in digital games and the genres of digital games most suitable for older adults. Factors identified as important for older adults' experience include low level of difficulty (e.g., reach the goal without spending much mental effort), clear and immediate feedback, a sense of control, and real-life scenes in the game. Social interaction has an important effect on older adults' successful aging [30] and is a strong motivator among older people for playing digital games [31]. Competition is another important factor that affects in-game enjoyment [32]. Previous research has shown that playing together in the same place, as opposed to remotely, significantly contributes to fun, challenge, and perceived competence in the game as older adults prefer co-located co-play to playing with other people online [33, 34].

Taking into account above factors, the authors designed a digital games intervention. Older adults from senior and community centres played in teams of four members formed within each participating site. A total of 21 teams were formed and played against one another in an eight-week tournament.

The research questions are:

(1) Can the digital game intervention improve older adults' attitudes towards digital games?
(2) Which factors affect the gaming experience of older adults in community and senior centres?

3 Methods

3.1 Research Design

Participants were older adults aged 60 and over. A total of 142 older adults were recruited from 14 community and senior centres, 81 were placed in the experimental group and 61 were in the control group (see Table 1). The participants in the experimental group played in teams of four members formed within each participating site. Since older adults might have appointments, commitments, or illnesses that prevented them from attending a session, only the top three scores of each game were recorded each week, even if four players attended that session. This approach allowed some flexibility when one team member was absent.

A total of 21 teams played against one another in the tournament (see Fig. 1). To avoid potential issues (e.g., social anxiety, time conflicts) that might have affected outcomes, team members, team names, availability and avatar names in the Wii Bowling game were all decided by participants. Follow-up interviews found that the teams were formed based on availability. Before the tournament, participants had one practice session, where observations and interviews showed that most participants felt tired after playing two games in succession. To sustain participants' interest to the game but not make them feel overwhelmed, the experimental group played two games in one week. A research assistant (RA) was assigned to each team. During the eight-week tournament, the RA visited the site every week, set up the game for the team, and recorded each member's score and the team's weekly score. The control group didn't play digital games during the tournament, but they were welcome to watch the gameplay of the experimental group.

Table 1. Baseline characteristics of participants and outcome measure in each group.

Variables	Control group	Experiment group	Chi-square	p
Gender (frequency, percent)			1.35	.25
Male	13(21.3%)	24(30.0%)		
Female	48(78.7%)	56(70.0%)		
Age (frequency, percent)			8.33	.14
60–69	5(8.2%)	16(20.0%)		
70–74	4(6.6%)	8(10.0%)		
75–79	8(13.1%)	16(20.0%)		
80–84	19(31.1%)	14(17.5%)		
85–89	15(24.6%)	14(17.5%)		
> = 90	10(16.4%)	12(15.0%)		
Current relationship status			3.61	.06
Married/Common law	6(10.9%)	18(24.0%)		
Single/Windowed	49(89.1%)	57(76.0%)		
Living arrangement			2.58	.11
Alone	44(83.0%)	53(70.7%)		
With someone	9(17.0%)	22(29.3%)		
Education level(frequency, percent)			.86	.93
Less than high school	4(6.6%)	4(5.1%)		
High school or equivalent	24(39.3%)	34(43.0%)		
Some college/CEGEP	14(23.0%)	18(22.8%)		
Two-year degree	7(11.5%)	6(7.6%)		
University degree	12(19.7%)	17(21.5%)		

Fig. 1. A Wii bowing team in a senior centre.

Wii Bowling offers a convenient platform for multiple players. The Wii console allows users to interact with the game via remote, using natural body movements that are recognized by motion sensors. The game action is displayed on a large screen. Wii Bowling was selected for this study because: (1) most older adults are familiar with bowling; (2) bowling and the WII are fun to play; (3) the game is relatively simple to learn and to play; and (4) bowling is a social activity that allows a group to play together. In a qualitative focus group study, Diaz-Orueta, Facal, Nap, and Ranga [35] identified digital game features of most interest to older adults: the social aspect of the experience, the challenge it presents, the combination of cognitive and physical activity, and the ability to gain specific skills. Wii Bowling is a game that offers these features.

Both the experiment and control groups completed a pre-post questionnaire. The pre-test questionnaire collected demographic data (e.g., age, gender, and education level) and data about participants' attitudes towards digital games. The post-questionnaire only measured game attitudes. Selected items from the Computer Game Attitude Scale were used to assess the level of positive attitude toward digital games [36]. Items were rated on a 5-point Likert-scale ranging from 1 (Strongly disagree) to 5 (Strongly agree). Higher scores indicated higher level of positive attitude towards the social aspects of digital game. Its reliability is .79. In addition, a weekly observation protocol was used to understand which factors affected participants gaming experience. The protocol asked questions about social interactions among team members indicated by verbal and nonverbal interaction, any technological problems and how they were resolved, and the role of coordinators.

3.2 Data Analysis

Quantitative data were analyzed using IBM SPSS Statistics V22. Demographic characteristics of the participants in each group were compared using chi-squared analysis to examine whether the two groups were equivalent at baseline. Then, independent t-test analyses were conducted to compare the difference between the two groups before and after the intervention. The weekly observation notes were imported into MaxQDA for coding. The coding process included familiarization with the content of the notes, applying open coding to the content, and analyzing codes for emergent themes [37]. Descriptive codes were assigned to summarize the basic topic of a data chunk. The codes then were compared to identify themes.

4 Results

4.1 Results of Quantitative Data Analysis

There was no statistically difference between the two groups in terms of demographic characteristics (see Table 1). However, the majority of participants were single or widowed and lived alone, which means they might be at the risk of social isolation. For game attitudes, the two groups did not statistically differ from each other in the pre-test (t = 1.51, p = .13), but the post-test showed a significant difference between the two groups (t = 2.53, p = .01). The level of game attitudes was increased from 3.72

(*SD* = .58) to 3.89 (*SD* = .70) in the experimental group, but only from 3.54 (*SD* = .66) to 3.55 (*SD* = .73) in the control group. Generally, the experimental group generally had higher levels of positive attitudes towards digital games than control group.

4.2 Results of Qualitative Data Analysis

The authors identified five themes from the qualitative data analysis: direct and in-situation teaching, encouragement, audiences, humor and easy use of Wii Bowling.

Direct and In-situation Teaching. Although team members took turns playing, they had to support and improve the game performance of each member in order to win the tournament. Gaming skills differed from one member to another. The majority of the participants had never played Wii Bowling before the tournament. Some participants could easily master the game, but some struggled with it almost every session. In addition, the game performance of older adults was affected by many factors rather than just gaming skills. For example, one participant was late for a game session; he felt nervous and forgot how to use the remote. Therefore, direct and in-situation teaching among team members was quite frequent. For example, on one occasion, D wanted to get a strike (all pins hit down in one throw) because all of the other three team members had already gotten one, leading to the following conversation:

A: Move the line over.
B: Make sure your hand is straight.
A: Get your hand straight.
C: You can do it, D.

Encouragement. Positive encouragement was a key aspect of social interactions because it contributed to building trust among team members. One player was left-handed, and her ball always ran slowly. When she didn't do very well in one throw, her teammates said, "At least, that's a fast bowl" and "It's good. At least, it's straight." On another occasion, she got many curves and couldn't make the ball run straight. When her ball ran slowly and gradually changed direction, her teammates murmured, "Come on, and come on"; "Yes, yes…" Finally, the ball hit the last pin. Everyone in the room applauded and cheered for her with "Good for you"; "You have some suspenders."

At another site, a participant's vision was so poor that she needed help to locate the button in the controller and the pins in the screen, but she did very well every week. Her teammates said: "You are remarkable. You always inspire us." On one occasion, she had technical problems and needed several tries to let the bowl go. She was disappointed, saying "I'm sorry. At least, I let it go," but her team members were kind and supportive, saying "It's fine"; "That's OK. You can't hit them all the time"; "You participated. It's fine." The positive encouragement among team members were more likely to decrease feelings of guilt, fear and anxiety.

Audiences. Audiences played important roles in supporting players and sustaining their interest and passion during the tournament. Approximately half of the players were aged 80 and over. People at this age are more likely to suffer from some age-related functional limitations [38], and thus play much less digital games compared to young older adults [39]. Many participants felt proud of themselves because they were doing something that they never thought they could do. The support from the audiences made them believe what they were doing was interesting. They felt sad and did not talk with each other very much when no audience showed up. Conversely, they were enlightened when there were audiences cheering for them. For example, at one session an audience member who sat next to a player and coached that player every week was late arriving for the game. The players were quite reserved, and didn't interact with each other as much as they had in previous weeks. However, once the audience member walked in, the four players became alive and said: "We need you, coach."

Humour. Humour was another key aspect of social interactions among team members, contributing significantly to players' enjoyment of the game. Team members would like to joke and laugh together during gameplay, as in the following conversation about a pin that didn't fall down:

A: Stupid pins.
B: Silly pins.
C: Not smart pins.
D: The nice pin is going to fall down.

Shared amusement, laughter and good feelings created a natural context for entertainment and social interaction.

Easy Use of Wii Bowling. Wii Bowling enables enactive interactions, or motor acts used in real life such as swinging arms to play bowling [40]. One advantage of enactive interaction was that players could focus on hitting the pins rather than having to learn complex mappings between in-game actions and specific button presses [41]. So, the game was easy to learn and use for older adults who have experienced physical and cognitive declines and even impairments. Some participants mentioned minor medical effects of playing Wii Bowling; one said that she was surprised that she didn't feel arm pain when swinging her arm.

5 Discussion

The themes identified from the weekly observation indicated that the majority of participants enjoyed the Wii Bowling tournament. The quantitative data analysis also indicated that the tournament was effective for improving older adults' attitudes towards digital games. However, this should not be taken for granted. Digital games are symbolic and cultural tools that provide resources (e.g., avatars, narratives, and mechanisms) for interactions. Collaborative play forms a rich social context in which the expert members can coach or mentor the less experienced members. These meaningful interactions may further facilitate enjoyable conversations and build positive relationships among the group members.

The authors identified six factors that contributed to participants' positive gaming experience. First, the tournament was engaging. Participants were excited and even danced whenever they got a strike or several strikes in a row, especially when there were audiences cheering for their good performance. Second, the competitive aspect has motivated older adults to play Wii Bowling. Many participants mentioned that they enjoyed the competition and cared about their team's position among all the teams. One participant said: "It's great to beat another team because we have two teams here (in an assisted living centre)." Nap, de Kort and IJsselsteijin [42] found that the majority of older adults have negative perceptions about multiplayer gaming. Gajadhar et al. [34] pointed that older adults' negative perceptions about playing against other human players could be caused by the fear of failure. In this study, many participants highlighted their positive experiences of competing with other teams. It is possible that the team competition could have decreased their anxiety and fear when using a new technology. Third, playing Wii Bowling together has created a natural context for participants to exchange social and emotional support, which contributed a significant part to participants' enjoyment. Encouragement from team members, jokes, and applause created a natural social context in which participants felt free to express themselves. Fourth, the positive experience of gameplay improved participants' confidence with digital games. The majority of participants were proud of themselves. They were able to master the game by the end of the eight-week tournament even though they hadn't played Wii Bowling before the tournament. During each session, participants were provided with directions for each game and individual assistance from their team members and research assistants. This on-demand support and guided participation helped them to acclimate to the game controls, alleviating potential confusion and frustration. Fifth, Wii Bowling was easy for older adults to use since it allowed participants to interact naturally with the game. The game also provided clear and positive feedback to promote players' self-confidence. Marston [42] pointed out that older adults will only invest their time in such entertainment if they can understand and see the purpose of their actions. Last but not least, coordinators from different centres played an important role in this study. They worked hard for the smooth going of this study. For example, they reminded their senior participants of this study every week.

The authors were aware of two limitations to this study. First, the participants were recruited based on their availability and interest in this study. Therefore, the results cannot be generalized to other populations, such as older adults who are not interested in Wii Bowling. Second, health condition was not one of the sample inclusion criteria. Some participants had to sit to play due to Parkinson's disease or physical impairments. We are unsure whether participants' physical health affected attitudes towards playing Wii Bowling.

6 Conclusion

The Wii Bowling tournament provided positive gaming experiences to the participants and was an effective way to improve their attitudes towards digital games. The authors also identified six factors that contributed to participants' enjoyment. The findings shed light on older adults' social interactions mediated by digital games. However, it is still unclear how the positive experiences affect their quality of life from older adults' perspectives. It is also unclear which challenges they face when participating in the collaborative play. Further studies could be conducted to investigate in more depth how to help older adults benefit from digital games. These studies can contribute to the adoption of digital games in many community and senior centres, thus enriching older adults' daily activities and enhancing their social interactions.

Acknowledgements. We gratefully acknowledge the financial support received for this study from the Age-Well National Centre of Excellence and the Social Sciences and Humanities Research Council of Canada (SSHRC).

References

1. World Health Organization (WHO): Ageing and Life Course (2015). www.who.int/ageing/en/
2. Hawkins, M.J.: College students' attitudes towards elderly persons. Educ. Gerontol. **22**(3), 271–280 (1996). doi:10.1080/0360127960220305
3. Lai, C.H., Peng, C.W., Chen, Y.L., Huang, C.P., Hsiao, Y.L., Chen, S.C.: Effects of interactive digital-game based system exercise on the balance of the elderly. Gait Posture 1–5 (2012)
4. Boot, W.R., Champion, M., Blakely, D.P., Wright, T., Souders, D.J., Chamess, N.: Video games as a means to reduce age-related cognitive decline: attitudes, compliances, and effectiveness. Front. Psychol. **4**, 1–9 (2013)
5. Singh, A., Misra, N.: Loneliness, depression and sociability in old age. Ind. Psychiatry J. **18**(1), 51–55 (2009). doi:10.4103/0972-6748.57861
6. Aison, C., Davis, G., Milner, J., Targum, E.: Appeal and Interest of Video Game Use Among the Elderly. http://www.booizzy.com/jrmilner/portfolio/harvard/gameselderly.pdf
7. Ekman, I., Chanel, G., Järvelä, S., Kivikangas, J.M., Salminen, M., Ravaja, N.: Social interaction in games measuring physiological linkage and social presence. Simul. Gaming. **43**(3), 321–338 (2012). doi:10.1177/1046878111422121
8. Chiang, I.T., Tsai, J.C., Chen, S.T.: Using Xbox 360 Kinect games on enhancing visual performance skills on institutionalized older adults with wheelchairs. In: Proceedings of Fourth IEEE International Conference on Digital Game and Intelligent Toy Enhanced Learning, DIGITEL 2012, pp. 263–267. IEEE Computer Society, Los Alamitos (2012). doi:10.1109/DIGITEL.2012.69
9. Sweetser, P., Wyeth, P.: Game flow: A model for evaluating player enjoyment in games. ACM Comput. Entertainment **3**(3), 1–24 (2005)
10. Hoppes, S., Wilcox, T., Graham, G.: Meanings of play for older adults. Phys. Occup. Ther. Geriatr. **18**(3), 57–68 (2001)
11. Csıkszentmihalyi, M.: Beyond Boredom and Anxiety: Experiencing Flow in Work and Play. Jossey-Bass, San Francisco (2000). 25th Anniversary Edition
12. Gamberini, L., Alcaniz, M., Fabregat, M., Gonzales, A.L., Grant, J., Jensen, R.B., Zemmerman, A.: Eldergames: Videogames for empowering, training and monitoring elderly cognitive capabilities. Gerontechnology **7**(2), 111 (2008). http://dx.doi.org/10.4017/gt.2008.07.02.048.00
13. IJsselsteijn, W., Nap, H.H., De Kort, Y., Poels, K: Digital game design for elderly users. In: Proceedings of the 2007 Conference on Future Play, Future Play 2007, Toronto, Canada, pp. 17–22 (2007). doi:10.1145/1328202.1328206

14. Zhang, F., Kaufman, D.: Physical and cognitive impacts of digital games on older adults: A meta-analytic review. J. Appl. Gerontol. (2015) doi:10.1177/0733464814566678. Advance online publication
15. Jung, Y., Li, K.J., Janissa, N.S., Gladys, W.L.C., Lee, K.M.: Games for a better life: effects of playing Wii games on the well-being of seniors in a long-term care facility. In: Proceedings of the Sixth Australasian Conference on Interactive Entertainment, NY, USA (2009)
16. Allaire, J.C., McLaughlin, A.C., Trujillo, A., Whitlock, L.A., LaPorte, L., Gandy, M.: Successful aging through digital games: Socioemotional differences between older adult gamers and Non-gamers. Comput. Hum. Behav. **29**(4), 1302–1306 (2013). doi:10.1016/j.chb.2013.01.014
17. Cota, T.T., Ishitani, L.: Motivation and benefits of digital games for the elderly: a systematic literature review. Revista Brasileira de Computação Aplicada. **7**(1), 2–16 (2015)
18. Czaja, S.J., Lee, C.C.: The potential influence of the Internet on the transition to older adulthood. In: Wahl, H.-W., Tesch-Romer, C., Hoff, A. (eds.) New Dynamics in Old Age: Individual Environmental and Societal Perspectives, pp. 239–252. Baywood Publishing Co. Inc., Amityville (2006)
19. Eisma, R., Dickinson, A., Goodman, J., Syme, A., Tiwari, L., Newell, A.F.: Early user involvement in the development of information technology-related products for older people. Univ. Access Inf. Soc. **3**, 131–140 (2004)
20. Heinz, M., Martin, P., Margrett, J.A., Yearns, M., Franke, W., Yang, H.I., Chang, C.K.: Perceptions of technology among older adults. J. Gerontol. Nurs. **39**(1), 42–51 (2013)
21. Broady, T., Chan, A., Caputi, P.: Comparison of older and younger adults' attitudes towards and abilities with computers: Implications for training and learning. Br. J. Edu. Technol. **41**(3), 473–485 (2010)
22. Mitzner, T.L., Boron, J.B., Fausset, C.B., Adams, A.E., Charness, N., Czaja, S.J., Dijkstra, K., Fisk, A.D., Rogers, W.A., Sharit, J.: Older adults talk technology: Technology usage and attitudes. Comput. Hum. Behav. **26**(6), 1710–1721 (2010)
23. Bandura, A.: Social cognitive theory of mass communications. In: Bryant, J., Zillman, D. (eds.) Media effects: Advances in Theory and Research, 2nd edn., pp. 121–153. Lawrence Erlbaum, Hillsdale (2001)
24. Melenhorst, A.S.: Adopting communication technology in later life: The decisive role of benefits. Doctoral dissertation. The Netherlands: Eindhoven University of Technology (2002)
25. Lagana, L., Oliver, T., Ainsworth, A., Edwards, M.: Enhancing computer self-efficacy and attitudes in multi-ethnic older adults: A randomised controlled study. Ageing Soc. **31**, 911–933 (2011)
26. Wagner, N., Hassanein, K., Head, M.: Computer use by older adults: A multi-disciplinary review. Comput. Hum. Behav. **26**(5), 870–882 (2010)
27. McKay, S.M., Maki, B.E.: Attitudes of older adults toward shooter video games: An initial study to select an acceptable game for training visual processing. Gerontechnology **9**(1), 5–17 (2010)
28. Galarneau, L.: 2014 Global Gaming Stats: Who's Playing What, and Why? (2014). http://www.bigfishgames.com/blog/2014-global-gaming-stats-whos-playing-what-and-why/
29. Entertainment Software Association: Essential facts about the computer and video game industry. Entertainment Software Association, Washington, DC. http://www.theesa.com/wp-content/uploads/2014/10/ESA_EF_2014.pdf
30. Lewis, J.: The role of the social engagement in the definition of successful ageing among alaska native elders in Bristol Bay, Alaska. Psychol. Dev. Soc. **26**(2), 263–290 (2014)

31. Rice, M., Cheong, Y.L., Ng, J., Chua, P.H., Theng, Y.L.: Co-creating games through intergenerational design workshops. In: Proceedings of the Designing Interactive Systems Conference on – DIS 2012, Newcastle, UK, pp. 368–377 (2012). doi:10.1145/2317956.2318012
32. De Schutter, B.: Never too old to play: the appeal of digital games to an older audience. Games Culture **6**(2), 155–170 (2011)
33. Gajadhar, B.J., de Kort, Y.A.W., IJsselsteijn, W.A.: Shared fun is doubled fun: player enjoyment as a function of social setting. In: Markopoulos, P., Ruyter, B., IJsselsteijn, W., Rowland, D. (eds.) Fun and Games 2008. LNCS, vol. 5294, pp. 106–117. Springer, Heidelberg (2008). doi:10.1007/978-3-540-88322-7_11
34. Gajadhar, B.J., Nap, H.H., de Kort, Y.A.W., IJsselsteijn, W.A.: Out of sight, out of mind: co-player effects on seniors' player experience. In: Proceedings of Fun and Games, Leuven, Belgium (2010)
35. Diaz-Orueta, U., Facal, D., Nap, H.H., Ranga, M.M.: What is the key for older people to show interest in playing digital learning games? initial qualitative findings from the LEAGE project on a multicultural european sample. Games Health J. **1**(2), 115–123 (2012). doi:10.1089/g4h.2011.0024
36. Jones, T., Clarke, V.A.: A computer attitude scale for secondary students. Comput. Educ. **4**(22), 315–318 (1994)
37. Schell, R., Hausknecht, S., Zhang, F., Kaufman, D.: Social benefits of playing wii bowling for older adults. Games Culture. **11**(1–2), 81–103 (2016)
38. Bouma, H.: Document and interface design for older citizens. In: Westendorp, P., Jansen, C., Punselie, R. (eds.) Interface Design & Document Design, pp. 67–80. Rodopi, Amsterdam (2000)
39. Zhang, F., Kaufman, D.: Older adults' social interactions in MMORPGs. Games Culture **11**(12), 150–169 (2016). doi:10.1177/1555412015601757. Special Issue: Games and Aging
40. Vanden Abeele, V., De Schutter, B.: Designing intergenerational play via enactive interaction, competition and acceleration. Pers. Ubiquit. Comput. **14**(5), 425–433 (2010)
41. Nap, H.H., de Kort, Y.A.W., IJsselsteijn, W.A.: Senior gamers preferences motivations and needs. Gerontechnology **8**, 247–262 (2009)
42. Marston, H.R.: Digital gaming perspectives of older adults: content vs interaction. Educ. Gerontol. **39**(3), 194–208 (2013)

The Bridge21 Model of 21st Century Learning in the Mathematics Classroom – Teachers' Perspectives

Aibhín Bray(✉)

School of Education and School of Computer Science and Statistics, Trinity Centre for Research in IT in Education, Trinity College Dublin, The University of Dublin, Dublin, Ireland
braya@tcd.ie

Abstract. Research highlights a need for a structured approach, consistent support and continuous professional development for teachers in order to facilitate the development of 21st Century pedagogies and the integration of technology, as well as to support their changing role in the classroom. This chapter describes a particular model of 21st Century teaching and learning, and explores teachers' experiences of its implementation in their classrooms. A total of 15 teachers who attended a Contextual Mathematics module on a postgraduate certificate course provided consent for their data to be used in this study. A qualitative, case study approach has been taken in order to explore the teachers' experiences of using the model of teaching and learning, as well as their perceptions of the students' experiences. A constant comparative analytic technique has been used to analyze their written reflections. Results indicate that the approach has the potential to address many of the issues associated with the integration of 21st Century teaching and learning, identified in the literature.

Keywords: 21st century learning · Post-primary education · Mathematics education · Continuous professional development

1 Introduction

It is widely accepted that there is a need to adapt our educational systems and curricula to accommodate the shift from an industrial to a knowledge-based society [1–4]. Although there is no universally recognized definition of 21st Century skills, or of the types of teaching and learning required to achieve them, there is agreement that skills relating to communication and collaboration, problem-solving and creativity, as well as technological fluency, are fundamental to the concept [3, 5]. The value of effective collaboration has been consistently prized in workplaces. However, in the knowledge-based 21st Century, jobs are increasingly accomplished by teams of people with complementary skills and expertise, and frequently require critical thinking and creative approaches [3]. The prevalence of sophisticated information and communication technologies means that citizens in modern society have the tools to filter, manage and evaluate large amounts of data. However, in order to be able to do so,

G. Costagliola et al. (Eds.): CSEDU 2016, CCIS 739, pp. 476–496, 2017.
DOI: 10.1007/978-3-319-63184-4_25

the development of competences regarding the effective use, management and evaluation of information across many different platforms is essential [5, 6].

While recognition of the benefits of such skills is not unique to the 21st Century, the capabilities and skill requirements of modern society mean that they are increasingly valued [2, 3]. The meaningful incorporation of 21st Century Learning (21CL) skills in mainstream curricula however, is not a straightforward task, and requires a change in pedagogic focus and in teaching and learning approaches [4, 7]. Less emphasis should be placed on low-level facts and rote activities, and increasing emphasis on the more complex skills that require an understanding of 'why' as well as 'how' the information and routine procedures should be used [2, 4, 5, 8].

It is generally recognized that pedagogic approaches such as Project-Based Learning, Inquiry-Based Learning, and Design-Based Learning, in combination with team-based collaboration, are most suited to support the development of 21st Century skills [4, 5, 9, 10]. The Bridge21 model of 21st Century teaching and learning is a particular approach to collaborative, technology-mediated, project-based learning. In this chapter the Bridge21 model will be discussed, and its implementation in mathematics classrooms, as a means of facilitating 21st Century Learning, will be explored through the perspectives of teachers participating in an associated continuous professional development (CPD) program.

2 Literature Review

Sufficient structure, support and scaffolding are required in order to create opportunities for learners to develop key 21CL competences within the school environment [11, 12]. However, achieving these requirements is not a trivial task. Although many teachers wish to develop teaching and learning strategies that incorporate skills associated with 21CL, they are frequently hindered by factors outside their control.

Three levels of problems associated with the integration of a 21CL approach have been identified: the overarching school system, including curriculum and assessment; a lack of resources including teacher CPD; and teachers' beliefs [5, 12]. The higher level, systemic issues, while fundamental, are not addressed in detail in this research.

Problems relating to classroom management and the redefinition of the role of the teachers from transmitter of information to facilitator of learning, have been identified as contributing to the disparity between the intended curriculum, which is generally framed to recognise the importance of 21st Century skills, and that which is actually implemented [5, 9, 12]. A fundamental shift in the beliefs and practices of policy-makers and practitioners is required [2], as teachers are expected to facilitate the acquisition of 21st Century skills among their students, often without having developed the skills themselves [3, 5]. However, in order to achieve this, educators require appropriate structure and support in order to master the necessary skills and teaching strategies, and to 'unlearn' the beliefs and assumptions on which the traditional industrial-model of classroom practice is predicated [2, 5, 8].

This has clear links with the approach to professional development described in this study.

3 Context: Postgraduate Certificate in 21st Century Teaching and Learning

One of the significant findings that emerged through the literature review, is that there is a demand for ongoing support and professional development for teachers in order to facilitate the development of 21st Century pedagogies and the integration of technology, as well as to scaffold their changing role in the classroom [3, 5, 9, 13]. This research has its foundations in a structured CPD module that has been incorporated into a larger Postgraduate Certificate (PG Cert) course in 21st Century Teaching and Learning for post-primary school teachers, coordinated by the School of Education in Trinity College Dublin [14]. This course began in September 2014 and the first cohort of teachers graduated from the programme in autumn 2015.

The initial experience for participants on each module of the PG Cert involves active participation in immersive and authentic activities, which enables them to understand the power of the Bridge21 approach at a personal level. Throughout the process, attendees are provided with the resources, practical designs and collegial support that Donnelly, McGarr, and O'Reilly [15] highlight as necessary conditions to motivate change amongst teachers.

The Contextual Mathematics module on the PG Cert requires each of the attending teachers to complete an assignment involving the creation and implementation of a math-focused, 21CL activity with one of their classes. The assignment stipulates that the activity should use the Bridge21 model of 21CL (Sect. 4) and a set of design heuristics (Sect. 5) developed for the creation of contextual, 21CL mathematics learning activities [16–19]. The written part of the assignment involves a description of the activity, highlighting the curriculum-specific, and 21st Century skills that are covered, as well as a reflection on their own, and the students' perceptions of the experience.

Participating teachers came from diverse schools, including fee-paying, disadvantaged, single-sex and co-educational. They had levels of teaching experience ranging from 3 to 19 years. In a number of cases, two or three of the teachers came from the same school, which promoted greater levels of collaboration in the design and implementation of their activities, and also strengthened the communities of practice within the schools. Out of a total of twenty-two participants on the contextual mathematics module, fifteen gave consent for their work to be included in this study. This paper provides an analysis of their work, placing particular emphasis on participants' reflections on the process of integrating 21st Century practices in their mathematics classrooms.

4 The Bridge21 Model

Bridge21 (www.bridge21.ie) is a model of collaborative, project-based, technology-mediated learning that has been developed at the author's institution [20, 21]. Initially established in 2007 as part of a computer science outreach program, the Bridge21 model has been developed in the intervening years, and is currently being trialed in a number post-primary schools as part of a process of reform of the education system in Ireland [21–23].

Bridge21 adheres to a particular model of collaboration and teamwork influenced by the World Organisation of the Scout Movement [24], which emphasises mixed-ability students working together to achieve a common goal. Use of this model encourages young people to become confident learners, improves problem-solving skills, raises personal educational horizons, and encourages peer learning [14].

Project- and inquiry-based learning forms the basis of all Bridge21 activities. This approach begins with a question or problem, rather than with presentation of established facts and rules. It is characterised by active participation of students, and promotes creative engagement with processes such as: identification of the problem or area of inquiry; critical analysis of approaches, and identification of alternatives; planning investigations, searching for information, research, justification of conjectures; and presentation of coherent arguments. Reflection is encouraged at various points throughout activities.

The pedagogic model within a Bridge21 classroom pedagogic model looks quite different to the traditional classroom. Teachers act as facilitators or mentors, scaffolding and orchestrating the learning. A sense of partnership develops in the classroom, and the teachers often become co-learners, learning with, and from their students.

Bridge21 activities are "technology-mediated", but the technology can be low-tech (white-boards, post-its etc.) or high-tech (mobile devices, software packages). However, in all cases students learn with, rather than from technology; the technology is meaningful and relevant to the particular problem; and the technology is shared to encourage collaboration.

The physical learning space is configured to support an inquiry-based, technology-mediated, and collaborative approach to learning. Furniture that can be arranged in a variety of different configurations is ideal.

The Bridge21 activity model is inspired by the concept of Design Thinking [25], and brings together many of the elements of 21CL in a structured manner, scaffolding teachers' introduction of the pedagogical approach. A Bridge21 learning experience involves a specific set of steps (Fig. 1), which can be adapted based on the content and duration of the activity, and the group of participants.

Within the context of a Bridge21-mathematics activity, this can be expanded as follows:

1. **Set-Up:** Ice breaker and team formation.
2. **Warm-up:** Mathematical divergent thinking activity; generally related to the main task.
3. **Investigate:** Presentation of the problem, explanation of the problem context, and brainstorming of possible strategies.
4. **Plan:** Group planning, assigning roles and deadlines.
5. **Create:** An iterative process, involving:
   (i) Exploration with available resources including digital technologies. This can involve working outdoors as well as in the classroom.
   (ii) Modelling and Calculation: Analysis and Synthesis of the results.

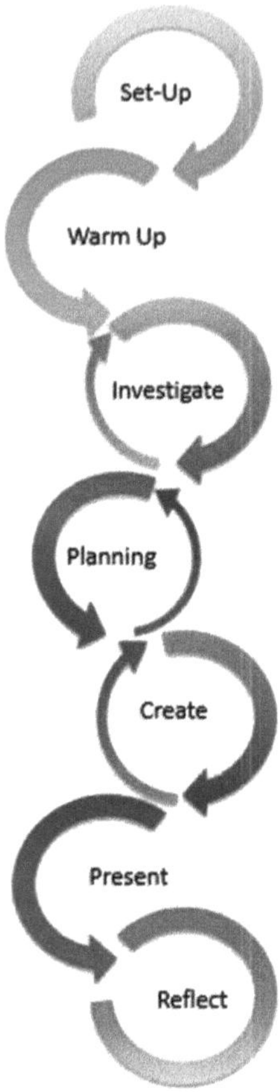

Fig. 1. Bridge21 activity model.

6. **Present:** Competition and/or Presentations of results.
7. **Reflect:** Reflection and Discussion. This usually involves a plenary session, followed by individual student reflections.

The Bridge21 approach to CPD involves teacher participation in a full cycle of the activity model prior to the collaborative development of their own activities based on this experience. The assignment constitutes the development and delivery of these activities in the classroom, along with written reflections on their own, and their students' experiences.

5 The Design Heuristics

In the Contextual Mathematics module, the use of Design Heuristics for the creation of contextual 21CL mathematics activities is encouraged. These heuristics were developed and refined by the author over the course of a three year research project.

The theoretical foundations of the Design Heuristics (described in the following subsection) were derived from an extensive literature review [17, 18, 26].

5.1 Theoretical Foundations

Research indicates that within an appropriate educational framework, the use of technology can make mathematics more practical, meaningful, and engaging [27–30]. Social constructivist pedagogies are advocated as aligning particularly well with the affordances of technology [17, 31, 32], however, activities that combine technology and socially constructivist strategies, tend not to suit the didactic teaching and short class periods that persist in many conventional classrooms [33]. Pedagogical models such as Bridge21, which are more in line with 21st Century learning, have been shown to be more appropriate [5, 34].

In terms of the mathematical pedagogy underpinning the development of the Design Heuristics, particular emphasis was placed on the Realistic Mathematics Education, or RME [35] approach to mathematics education, which, since its inception in the 1960s, has become internationally influential in curriculum design [36]. RME involves students in the development of their understanding of mathematics through the exploration and solution of problems set in contexts that engage their interest. Rather than transmitting information in a lecture-based manner, teachers scaffold the "reinvention" of the mathematics that the students are confronted with [35]. Five essential characteristics of RME have been identified:

1. "The importance of problems set in contexts that are real to the students,
2. The attention paid to the development of models,
3. The contributions of the students by means of their own productions and constructions,
4. The interactive character of the learning process, and
5. The intertwinement of learning strands" [26].

The use of context and the process of mathematization inherent in Realistic Mathematics Education have been identified as having the potential to address some of the limitations associated with the more formal and abstract traditional mathematics education, as well as sitting well with 21st Century learning paradigms [37–39].

5.2 Design Heuristics

In conjunction with the theoretical foundations stemming from the literature, an iterative process of activity design, pilot activities and in-school interventions were used to refine the Design Heuristics [16–18, 34]. The primary concepts that underpin the heuristics can be summarised as follows:

1. "Activities should follow a 21CL model such as Bridge21: they should be collaborative and team-based in accordance with a socially constructivist approach to learning.

2. They should make use of a variety of technologies (digital and traditional) suited to the task, in particular, non-specialist mobile technology such as smartphones and digital cameras that students have to hand. Emphasis should be placed on the transformative, as well as the computational, capabilities of the technology.
3. Task design should prioritise guided-discovery, involving problem-solving, investigation and sense-making, and a move from concrete to abstract concepts. Tasks should be open-ended, allowing for different trajectories and solutions; they should have a "low-floor" and "high-ceiling", such that all students will be able to engage meaningfully with the problem, with the potential for more interested/able students to push its boundaries.
4. The context of the problem, and the learning experience, should be interesting and immersive/real, adapting the environment and class routine as appropriate;
5. Presentation, competition and reflection can be used for assessment purposes" [19].

Activities designed in accordance with these heuristics, and implemented using the Bridge21 approach have been shown to be associated with increases in students' levels of engagement with mathematics, and their attitudes to using technology for its learning [19, 34].

6 Methodology and Research Questions

The research presented in this chapter is based on an exploratory case study in which teachers' experiences of the creation and implementation of mathematics activities designed in accordance with the Design Heuristics and the Bridge21 methodology are investigated. The research design consists of a single case study, with multiple embedded units, each consisting of one of the fifteen teachers' implementations of an activity in their school, and subsequent reflection on the process.

Teachers' written assignments form the basis of the data for analysis. The assignments include a description of the learning experience and an associated rationale, an explanation of the content and skills to be covered, evidence to demonstrate student learning, and a personal reflection on the experience. A constant comparative analytic technique was used to highlight the emerging themes [40].

The research aims of this exploratory case study are:

1. To explore the experiences of teachers in the creation and implementation of such activities, with particular emphasis on their perceived barriers to, and benefits of, the Bridge21 approach in the classroom.
2. To explore teachers' perceptions of their students' experiences with the activities.

The data that has been collected for this exploratory study are qualitative and come from the written reports of the teachers.

7 The Maths Learning Activities

A number of the teachers collaborated on the design of the activities, and joint implementation was allowed for participants working in the same school. A total of eleven distinct activities were created by the fifteen teachers. These activities were implemented with students across four different year groups, ranging in age from twelve to sixteen. All of the activities involved students' active and creative participation, and provided meaningful context to the mathematics. They also involved the use of a variety of technologies in a "transformative" manner, i.e., the use of technology allowed for significant task redesign, or for the creation of tasks that would not have been possible in its absence [41].

The mathematics involved in the majority of the activities was linked to data collection and representation, patterns, and linear and quadratic functions. In all instances this was reported as being the students' first experience of generating their own functions using "real" data that they had collected empirically. The teachers' brief descriptions of the activities are provided in Table 1.

Table 1. Teachers' activities.

Activity	Class	Teachers' descriptions
Heights with helium	Transition year[a] (age 15/16)	A helium balloon and digital technology were used to measure certain heights around our school. This meant dealing with two variables, height and time and being able to use the free video analysis software, Kinovea, (www.kinovea.org) to obtain these variables and a Spreadsheet to graph the data.
Functions in context: analysing trajectory.	2nd year (age 13/14)	Each team of students takes video clips of attempts to throw a ball into a basket. They then use appropriate software to analyse the trajectory of a successful shot. Using a suitable [digitally generated] graph, they compare successful and unsuccessful shots.
Distance, speed and time	3rd year (age 14/15)	Students ask themselves "how fast am I running?" Based on their introduction to the software Kinovea, and their knowledge of Microsoft Excel, they are asked to answer this question and illustrate their answers with graphs and tables.
Statistics/height/distance, speed and time	1st year (age 12/13)	Working in groups, students are tasked with comparing the speed of the shortest and tallest members of their group over a specified distance. The data collected, and analysis of their findings, will be done using Kinovea.
Egg drop challenge	Transition year (age 15/16)	Teams of students work to design a method of safely dropping an egg from a first floor window. They use smart phones, digital camera and iPads to visually record the activity. They generate data from the activity and use a video App and maths analysis software to provide mathematical evidence for their approach.
Quadratic equations, functions and algebra.	Transition year (age 15/16)	The students are asked to plot the quadratic function for the flight of their shot in a football crossbar challenge. Each group of 3–4 students works with the Tracker video analysis software (*physlets.org/tracker*) to analyse the shot that is closest to hitting the crossbar. The students use the software Kinovea and excel to plot

(*continued*)

Table 1. (*continued*)

Activity	Class	Teachers' descriptions
		the flight of their shot. The students are asked to analyse the graph produced.
Children's birthday party	2nd year (age 13/14)	Given an advertisement for a party hire company, the students use dynamic geometry software, GeoGebra, to explore different combinations of tables etc. to get the best value for money.
Speed, distance, time	Transition year (age 15/16)	The students are presented with the problem 'Who is the fastest in the class?' In their groups they must produce a method of experiment and a Microsoft excel presentation of their results.
Shoot a basket!	2nd year (age 13/14)	In groups, the students develop different ways to analyse and make 'real' quadratic functions through group work and peer learning. Students learn to select, create, and use many new forms of technology, e.g., GeoGebra and Tracker. The groups are briefly introduced to the programmes but need to decide if it will help answer the question, "What makes a successful shot successful?" As students use the programmes, they become aware of the technology available around them.
Speed\distance\time, statistics	1st year (age 12/13)	The students undertake a study to determine if the speed of the ball affects the chances of scoring goal.

[a]Transition year is a one-year school program in Irish schools, in which the focus is on personal, social, vocational and educational development, providing opportunities for students to experience diverse educational inputs in a year that is free from formal examinations.

The written reflection portion of the teachers' assignments is of particular relevance to this research, providing insight into their experiences with the implementation of contextual mathematics learning activities as well as into the barriers to, and benefits of, the Bridge21 approach.

8 Analysis of Results

Results are drawn from a qualitative analysis of the teachers' reflections and a constant comparative approach to the analysis of the data has been taken. The steps in this analysis follow the process outlined by Glaser [42] and Strauss and Corbin [40]. Constant comparison is a method of reducing qualitative data to codes emerging from within the original source, while retaining much of the richness of the original data. In this way, the results of the analysis are used to create a rich picture of the teachers' experiences, and permit the identification of any common themes or categories.

8.1 Generation of Initial Codes and Categories

The data analysis software package NVivo10 was used to facilitate the process of coding and theming. Following the analysis of the first five assignments, a total of 23 codes were identified. These fell into the two primary categories of Barriers, with five associated codes, and Benefits, with eighteen related codes. All segments of text associated with each of these codes were re-examined and compared before considering the next set of assignments. Of these, the next four assignments led to the addition of five new codes, four under the category of Benefits, and one under Barriers. At this point, the process of memoing – recording detailed notes on the thought process involved in the coding – was useful for identifying sections that could potentially benefit from re-classification (Fig. 2). In particular, codes associated with the category of Benefits appeared to have a number of emerging subcategories relating to teachers, students, the development of key skills, and so on.

27/05/2015

AH: Two new nodes added in the Benefits category. The first relates to learning, and the second to key skills. I would imagine there is some re-jigging of codes to be done...

HT: No new nodes

LS: No new nodes

MC: New node in Barriers - Teachers' beliefs
New nodes in Benefits - Ownership, Teacher as facilitator, Inquiry, Confidence

Fig. 2. Sample memo.

The six remaining assignments only led to the generation of two more codes, leading to the tentative conclusion that a reasonable level of saturation of codes may have been reached [40].

All of the data was re-examined after each session of analysis, and particularly after the addition of new codes. The purpose of this was to compare the coded text within their assigned nodes and also to identify whether they could be associated with any other codes. This process of constant evaluation and comparison has led to a rigorous association of codes and text.

8.2 Reduction of Codes

After completion of the initial development of codes and categories, the process of reducing and merging the codes, and developing sub-categories, began. This involved an examination of the codes and the coded segments in order to determine whether there was any crossover of themes.

The Barriers category had significantly fewer references than Benefits, and included student abilities, teams, technical difficulties (at individual and school level), and time constraints (Fig. 3).

(In Figs. 3, 4 and 5, *Sources* refers to the number of individual teachers whose data were categorised at the related code, while *References* relates to the overall number of coded segments of text.)

Name	Sources	References	Created On
Barriers	14	37	12/05/2015 15:28
Student abilities	3	3	12/05/2015 15:35
Teams	3	3	12/05/2015 18:25
Technical	10	16	12/05/2015 15:33
Individual Level	5	7	12/05/2015 15:33
School Level	8	9	12/05/2015 15:33
Time	11	15	12/05/2015 15:35

Fig. 3. Barriers category.

Name	Sources	References
To students	21	273
Key skills	19	107
Collaboration	14	22
Communication	10	15
Confidence	4	7
Creativity	8	10
Flexibility	5	8
Organisation	4	4
Presentation	6	6
Problem-Solving	7	9
Reflection	2	2
Technological competence	12	19

Fig. 4. Key skills category.

Name	Sources	References
Outcomes	19	89
Conceptual Understanding	11	20
Engagement	16	35
Enjoyment	13	20
Ownership	8	13
Prepared for 3rd level and w	1	1

Fig. 5. Additional beneficial outcomes

At the end of this section of the analysis, the category of Benefits had a total of 295 references, compared with only 37 in the Barriers category. At this point, a number of sub-categories were confirmed in the Benefits category. These related to benefits to the students (key skills, other out-comes, associated task attributes) and benefits to the teachers (change in beliefs, teacher as facilitator, and teacher as learner).

8.3 Analysis of Relationships

Possible relationships between codes were identified using the coding matrix facility of NVivo10. Analysis focused on the relationships between the teachers' perceptions of the task design elements that had an impact on themselves and on their students, and their perceived benefits. No associations between task attributes and barriers were identified. Table 2 provides a numerical analysis of the frequency that segments of text were co-coded with a particular aspect of task design, and a perceived benefit. The most significant elements (most frequently coded) of the task design columns and of the benefits columns have been highlighted.

Table 2. Matrix Coding of Task Design and Perceived Benefits.

Task Design v Perceived Benefits	Contextual	Cross-curricular	Hands-on	High Ceiling	Inquiry	Meaningful	Multiple Learning Styles	Open ended	Peer Learning	Student -led	sum
Ownership	1	0	0	0	0	0	1	1	2	7	12
Conceptual Understanding	5	1	0	1	1	3	0	2	2	6	21
Engagement	5	1	0	0	1	5	2	2	3	5	24
Teacher as Learner	1	1	1	0	1	1	0	0	2	4	11
Confidence	0	0	0	0	0	0	0	0	1	4	5
Communication	2	0	0	0	0	0	1	1	5	3	12
Teacher as facilitator	0	0	0	0	0	0	0	0	1	3	4
Collaboration	3	0	0	0	1	2	0	2	6	2	16
Technological competence	1	0	0	0	0	0	0	0	2	2	5
Problem-Solving	0	0	0	0	1	0	0	0	1	2	4
Flexibility	3	1	1	0	0	1	0	0	1	1	8
Creativity	0	0	0	0	0	0	0	0	1	1	2
Teacher Beliefs	0	0	0	0	1	0	0	0	0	1	2
Enjoyment	2	1	0	0	1	2	1	1	1	0	9
Organisation	1	0	0	0	0	0	1	0	0	0	2
Presentation	0	0	0	0	0	0	0	0	1	0	1
Sum	24	5	2	1	7	14	6	9	28	41	

Using the sum functionality at the end of each row and column, it is evident that student-led nature of the tasks has had the most significant impact on perceived benefits, particularly on the sense of student ownership or autonomy, on their conceptual understanding, and on engagement. The student-led approach also seems to be noteworthy in effecting a change in the role of the teacher in the classroom. Peer learning and the contextual nature of the task design seems to have had beneficial effects on the students and teachers, particularly in relation to collaboration, communication and engagement.

In terms of perceived benefits, task design appears to have had most impact on student engagement, with the tasks set in contexts that were meaningful to the students and the student-centred nature of the activities appearing to have the greatest effect.

Conceptual understanding is highlighted as the second highest co-coded perceived benefit, and this appears to be related to tasks that are set in contexts that are meaningful to the students, as well as the student-led nature of the learning.

9 Findings

The findings that have emerged through analysis of the relationships between task design and the perceived benefits of the approach serve to consolidate earlier research that identified a correlation between the Bridge21 approach to mathematics teaching and learning and increases in student engagement [19, 34]. In particular, there is an apparent link between the student-led, contextual and meaningful approach to activity design, and increased levels of student engagement, conceptual understanding, and confidence. In addition to strengthening the validity of these previously established hypotheses, a number of new findings have been identified in relation to the teachers' perceptions of the benefits that engagement with activities of this kind can engender, as well as to the barriers associated with the implementation of such tasks. These barriers and benefits will be discussed in the following sections.

9.1 Barriers

The professional development model presented in this research has addressed some of the barriers to the integration of technology and the implementation of 21st Century pedagogies highlighted in the literature review, such as a need for a structured and supportive approach [3, 5, 8, 12, 43]. However, many of the more systemic barriers remain, and were identified by the teachers. The most significant relates to time constraints and the difficulty of implementing a project-based activity in a series of individual classes of forty minutes duration. This was identified as a problem in 10 of the 15 assignments (Note: teacher initials were used to code quotations): *"Having a longer block of time would have been more productive, having to stop after 40* min *and then pick up again a day or two later was inconsistent, especially when we were running into problems" (AH).*

Technical barriers were an issue for nine of the teachers, with five identifying personal difficulties with the technology, which would be easily rectifiable on a re-run of the project: *"The camera we were using ran out of battery power during the penalty shoot outs... More cameras would need to be made available, especially if more teachers were to start working with this approach" (WMI).*

Eight teachers identified technical barriers at the school level, primarily in relation to inadequate access to the resources: *"Resourcing fully functioning laptops could be a challenge - I need to ensure that the limited number of laptops are available for at least three class periods" (IS).*

Other barriers that were identified by the teachers referred to lower than expected levels of students' technical expertise, and difficulties relating to the development of well-functioning teams.

9.2 Benefits

The benefits associated with the approach far outweigh the barriers, and have been broken down into two subcategories, which distinguish between the benefits to teachers and benefits to students.

9.2.1 Benefits to Teachers

A number of changes associated with teachers' beliefs and to their role in the classroom were identified. Two of the teachers in particular discussed the impact that teaching in this way has had on their beliefs about teaching mathematics:

> *"After trying this, my eyes have been opened to the possibilities of covering the curriculum, but by changing the setting of the learning, you can teach a lot more effectively to an audience who are stimulated and engaged." (JPF)*
> *"I found it more difficult to change my teaching style when it came to Maths. I was teaching the way I was taught, which was with very little understanding." (MC)*

It appears that the role of the teacher in the classroom was significantly affected through the implementation of these activities. The change in role from transmitter of information to facilitator of learning was not a comfortable transition for some; however, all of the teachers hailed it as a positive development, which empowered the students to take ownership of their own progress.

> *"I decided to tell the students of how this was as much of a learning curve to me as it was to them. This was because I really did feel that they would lose confidence in me if they felt that I was trying to teach them rather than facilitate them. This seemed to empower them as they felt that even though I wasn't part of their team, I was learning and teaching with them." (MC)*

In addition to the change in role from traditional teacher to facilitator, six of the teachers also identified themselves as co-learners in the classroom, both in terms of how to make activities of this kind more successful in the future, and learning about the technology with and from the students.

9.2.2 Benefits to Students

Benefits to the students have been broken down into the subcategories of 'key skills', 'other outcomes' and 'associated task attributes'. The relationships between the task attributes and the perceived benefits of the approach have been discussed in Sect. 7.3, and therefore this section will focus on the other perceived benefits of the approach to students.

The key skills subcategory is made up of the codes listed in Fig. 4. This figure highlights that the skills most commonly developed relate to collaboration and communication, technological confidence, creativity and problem-solving. The majority of students appear to have enjoyed working in teams and learning with, and from, their peers. Many of the teachers recognised the potential that technology has to facilitate a deeper conceptual understanding of the mathematics involved in the activities, as well as increasing the students' technological skills.

> *"The resounding theme of the [student] reflection was that they could really engage with one another and more importantly that they could engage more with the abstract topics of maths because of their ability to use technology in everyday maths." (DR)*

In addition to the development of key skills, a number of other beneficial outcomes (listed in Fig. 5) emerged through students' participation in the activities designed by the teachers.

An increase in student engagement, both in terms of how they felt about the subject (affective engagement) and how they behaved in the classroom (behavioural engagement) [44], was evident through the teachers' reflections. Comments such as those below, illustrate the sense of engagement and motivation experienced by students and teachers alike. These responses tally with the author's extensive student-focussed work [19, 45].

> *"All the team members were fully engaged in the activity; their pride in and ownership of their learning was clearly expressed... It's really heartening to encounter such a level of motivation and commitment." (DD)*
> *"Please let's do more of this stuff! It's brought Maths to life! I really get it now!" (Student)*
> *"This project was a thoroughly enriching experience for both the students and teachers assisting them." (DOC)*
> *"After this contextual Maths workshop, they asked for a Maths club. To me that is success!" (MC)*

There was a high level of cross-coding of segments of text coded as *engagement* and as *enjoyment*. Deeper analysis of the text coded at *enjoyment* indicated that this code is particularly closely related to affective engagement, or how the students feel about the subject. Segments coded at *enjoyment* and not at engagement relate specifically to the idea of having fun in the class, both from the point of view of the students, and the teachers:

> *"This project has highlighted one of the most enjoyable pieces of technology that I have used in my teaching career" (IB)*
> *"I feel that the students enjoyed this realistic, contextualized activity and by taking part they have taken a step forward in developing their technological skills, becoming better problem solvers and gaining attributes in working as part of a team." (AH)*
> *"The students also had fun, which they said that they thought they would never be able to say about Maths." (MC)*

An increase in students' conceptual understanding and confidence was identified in nine of the analysed assignments. This seems to be particularly closely associated with the contextual and meaningful nature of the tasks: *"I am sure that none of these students will ever forget how they deepened their understanding of quadratic functions: the next time they video a friend kicking a football or teeing off in golf they will visualise that ball moving across the Cartesian plane, describing a smooth parabola." (DD)*. In addition, the open-ended task design and the student-led approach also appears to have led to a deepening of the students' conceptual understanding of the subject: *"The open-ended nature of the activity produced a new energy in the teams:*

they were not working to find one answer (already known to me) but were engaged in a meaningful exploration of the topic" (DD).

Seven of the reports refer to an increased sense of student ownership of their work, leading to pride, engagement and motivation.

> *"Students came into their own when given the opportunity to work as a group and they seemed to grow as individuals even in the short space of time while working in groups with their peers" (DR)*
> *"Moreover, I feel that if I had taken over this aspect of the project... I would be impacting on their self-efficacy." (DF)*

Giving the responsibility for the learning to the students encouraged them to develop as individuals and as members of a group, with the attendant increase in levels of motivation and pride in their learning leading to higher levels of conceptual understanding.

> *"All the participants felt that they had created their own quadratic function and understood that it could be mathematically analysed." (DD)*

These findings provide a compellingly positive picture of the approach to the development and implementation of mathematics learning activities that combine the Bridge21 methodology and the design heuristics described in this and related research [19, 21, 46].

10 Discussion

The analysis of teachers' reflections described in this paper has provided an opportunity to examine various aspects of the participants' creation and implementation of Bridge21-style, contextual mathematics activities, thereby addressing the research aims identified in Sect. 5. In particular, analysis of the data has permitted:

- Examination of the experiences of teachers in the creation and implementation of such activities, paying particular attention to the barriers to, and benefits of, the approach.
- Exploration of the teachers' perceptions of their students' experiences with the activities.

These themes have been explored throughout this research. The discussion section examines aspects of the written assignments that reflect some of the concerns emerging from the literature review, and also presents the main limitations of the study.

10.1 Addressing the Issues

It is interesting to note that many of the problems associated with mathematics education that had been identified through the literature review, were mirrored in the reports of the teachers participating in the PGCert. The formulaic approach to text-book questions [47] was identified by one teacher as an area that the approach advocated in this research, had the potential to address.

"These problems involved being given the function, algebraically or graphically, and all the information required to answer some fairly predictable questions. There was never any redundant information either: just enough and not too much to apply the usual procedures... I considered that setting the students the task of creating their own quadratic curve would give them a real sense of ownership and a greater insight into the nature of quadratic functions." (DD)

Within the reports, there is evidence of a belief that this approach to mathematics education may go some way to address the fragmented, and de-contextualised nature that frequently pervades the presentation of the subject in schools [3, 48].

"It was useful for students to see different aspects of Maths used in one place rather than the disjointed treatment that they usually receive in a text book." (WMI)

In addition, as observed by Oldknow [49], the use of ubiquitous personal devices such a mobile phones to generate mathematical models, provided relevance, meaning and context to the mathematics for the students:

"For students, to discover that they can take their ubiquitous phone out of their pocket and create a mathematical model of an everyday event grounds Maths in the real world." (DD)

Issues surrounding teachers' beliefs and their changing role in the classroom also appear to be addressed by the structured, immersive and supportive nature of the CPD program. The pedagogical structure provided by the Bridge21 model, and the set of lesson design heuristics, present the teachers with an approach that has been empirically tested and shown to be successful. All of the participating teachers seemed to have been empowered by this, and were confident to approach their classes in a different way. The results appear to have been beneficial for both teachers and students.

"I have worked with this particular class group on two other 21st Century Teaching and Learning Assignments. Their development throughout the course of the year has been astounding. The flair with which they now competently and confidently use technology to gather and analyse information, and present their findings is very impressive. This project was a thoroughly enriching experience for both the students and teachers assisting them." (DOC)

10.2 Limitations

It is clear from this analysis that the approach to the creation and implementation of mathematics learning activities that has been developed in this research has the potential to address many of the issues highlighted in the literature. However, it is important to identify the limitations of this study.

Firstly, the sample that is used in this exploratory study consists of teachers who have opted to be a part of the research, and who are participants on a CPD course that they have chosen to attend. It is therefore a self-selecting sample and cannot be seen as representative.

Another point that needs to be highlighted is that the reflective pieces provided by the teachers were all submitted for assessment purposes. There is a possibility that the participants therefore emphasised the positive aspects of their experiences more than the negative. This is a limitation of the study to date, which future work will aim to overcome through interviews with participants and their students and non-participant observation of the classes.

Another drawback of this exploratory study is its small size. The analysis of fifteen teachers' reports is unlikely to permit the generation of any substantive theory. However, the consistency of the results, and their congruity with related research [19, 45], do allow the generation of hypotheses and research questions to follow up on the initial, very promising, findings.

11 Conclusion

In relation to the shift from an industrial to a knowledge-based economy, Green and Hannon [50] highlight that employers tend to value the 21st Century skills, such as creativity, communication, presentation skills and teamwork. As schools are at the forefront of change they should be encouraging teaching and learning practices that prepare their students for a society in which these skills are prized. Although this study requires expansion in order to fully examine the emerging themes, it appears that the pedagogic approach to mathematics education described in this chapter has the potential to address this need.

> *"As such a huge emphasis is being placed on STEM subjects/activities in schools, RME in conjunction with the B21 model helps to contextualise maths for our students, increasing their engagement and allowing them to use technology in a meaningful way." (MC)*

The Postgraduate Certificate from which the results were drawn is ongoing, and data from the 2015/2016 cohort is currently under analysis. Initial findings point towards a continuation of the predominantly positive responses from the teachers and their students.

References

1. Voogt, J., Pelgrum, H.: ICT and curriculum change. Hum. Technol. **1**(2), 157–175 (2005)
2. Dede, C.: Technological supports for acquiring 21st century skills. In: International Encyclopedia of Education, pp. 158–166 (2010)
3. Dede, C.: Comparing frameworks for 21st century skills. In: Bellanca, J., Brandt, R. (eds.) 21st Century Skills: Rethinking How Students Learn, pp. 51–76. Solution Tree Press, Bloomington (2010)
4. Fullan, M., Langworthy, M.: A Rich Seam: How New Pedagogies Find Deep Learning, vol. 100. Pearson, London (2014)
5. Voogt, J., Roblin, N.P.: A comparative analysis of international frameworks for 21st century competences: implications for national curriculum policies. J. Curriculum Stud. **44**(3), 299–321 (2012)
6. Martin, A., Grudziecki, J.: DigEuLit: concepts and tools for digital literacy development. Innov. Teach. Learn. Inf. Comput. Sci. **5**(4), 249–267 (2006)
7. Ertmer, P.A., Ottenbreit-Leftwich, A.T.: Teacher technology change: how knowledge, confidence, beliefs, and culture intersect. J. Res. Technol. Educ. **42**(3), 255–284 (2010)

8. Conneely, C., Lawlor, J., Tangney, B.: Technology, teamwork and 21st century skills in the irish classroom. In: Marshall, K. (ed.) Shaping Our Future: How the Lessons of the Past Can Shape Educational Transformation. Liffey Press, Dublin (2013)
9. Conneely, C., et al.: 21 century learning - teachers' and students' experiences and views of the bridge21 approach within mainstream education. In: Society for Information Technology & Teacher Education International Conference (SITE), pp. 5125–5132 (2013)
10. Conole, G.: New schemas for mapping pedagogies and technologies. Ariadne **56**, 2 (2008)
11. Commission of the European Communities, Improving competences for the 21st Century: An Agenda for European Cooperation on Schools (2008)
12. Euler, M., Maaß, K.: Report about the survey on inquiry-based learning and teaching in the European partner countries. In: Maaß, K., (ed.) PRIMAS (Promoting Inquiry-Based Learning in Mathematics and Science Education Across Europe), University of Education Freiburg, Freiburg (2011)
13. Maaß, K., Artigue, M.: Implementation of inquiry-based learning in day-to-day teaching: a synthesis. ZDM **45**(6), 779–795 (2013)
14. Bridge21, Postgraduate Certificate in 21st Century Teaching and Learning Course Handbook 2014/2015. Dublin, Trinity College Dublin (2014)
15. Donnelly, D., McGarr, O., O'Reilly, J.: A framework for teachers' integration of ICT into their classroom practice. Comput. Educ. **57**(2), 1469–1483 (2011)
16. Bray, A., Oldham, E., Tangney, B.: The human catapult and other stories – adventures with technology in mathematics education. In: 11th International Conference on Technology in Mathematics Teaching (ICTMT11), pp. 77–83 (2013)
17. Bray, A., Tangney, B.: Mathematics, pedagogy and technology - seeing the wood from the trees. In: 5th International Conference on Computer Supported Education (CSEDU 2013), pp. 57–63 (2013)
18. Bray, A., Tangney, B.: Barbie bungee jumping, technology and contextual learning of mathematics. In: 6th International Conference on Computer Supported Education (CSEDU 2014), vol. 3, pp. 206–213 (2014)
19. Bray, A., Tangney, B.: Enhancing student engagement through the affordances of mobile technology: a 21st century learning perspective on realistic mathematics education. Mathe. Educ. Res. J. **28**(1), 173–197 (2016)
20. Lawlor, J., Conneely, C., Tangney, B.: Towards a pragmatic model for group-based, technology-mediated, project-oriented learning–an overview of the B2C model. In: Lytras, M.D., et al. (eds.) Proceedings of the 2010 TechEduca Conference, Athens, pp. 602–609 (2010)
21. Lawlor, J., Marshall, K., Tangney, B.: Bridge21 – exploring the potential to foster intrinsic student motivation through a team-based, technology mediated learning mode. Technol. Pedagogy Educ. **25**(2), 1–20 (2015)
22. Conneely, C., Girvan, C., Tangney, B.: An exploratory case study into the adaption of the bridge21 model for 21st century learning in irish classrooms. In: Butler, D., Marshall, K., Leahy, M. (eds.) Shaping our Future: How the Lessons of the Past Can Shape Educational Transformation, pp. 348–381. Liffey Press, Dublin (2015)
23. Department of Education and Skills, A Framework for Junior Cycle. Department of Education and Skills, Dublin (2012)
24. Bénard, D.: A method of non-formal education for young people from 11 to 15. In: Handbook for Leaders of the Scout Section. World Scout Bureau, Geneva (2002)
25. Brown, T.: Design thinking. Harvard Bus. Rev. **86**(6), 84 (2008)

26. Tangney, B., Bray, A., Oldham, E.: Realistic mathematics education, mobile technology & the bridge21 model for 21st century learning - a perfect storm. In: Crompton, H., Traxler, J. (eds.) Mobile Learning and Mathematics: Foundations, Design, and Case Studies, Routledge, Oxon, UK, pp. 96–106 (2015)
27. Ainley, J., et al.: Digital technologies and mathematics education. In: Clark-Wilson, A., Oldknow, A., Sutherland, R. (eds.) JMC Report, Joint Mathematical Council of the United Kingdom, London UK (2011)
28. Drijvers, P., et al.: Integrating technology into mathematics education: theoretical perspectives. In: Hoyles, C., Lagrange, J.-B. (eds.) Mathematics Education and Technology-Rethinking the Terrain: The 17th ICMI Study, pp. 89–132. Springer, New York (2010)
29. Hoyles, C., Lagrange, J.B.: Mathematics Education and Technology: Rethinking the Terrain: The 17th ICMI Study, vol. 13. Springer, New York (2010)
30. Olive, J., et al.: Mathematical knowledge and practices resulting from access to digital technologies. In: Hoyles, C., Lagrange, J.B. (eds.) Mathematics Education and Technology - Rethinking the Terrain: The 17th ICMI Study, pp. 133–177. Springer, New York (2010)
31. Li, Q., Ma, X.: A meta-analysis of the effects of computer technology on school students' mathematics learning. Educ. Psychol. Rev. **22**(3), 215–243 (2010)
32. Patten, B., Sánchez, I.A., Tangney, B.: Designing collaborative, constructionist and contextual applications for handheld devices. Comput. Educ. **46**(3), 294–308 (2006)
33. Wijers, M., Jonker, V., Kerstens, K.: MobileMath: the phone, the game and the math. In: Proceedings of the European Conference on Game Based Learning, pp. 507–516 (2008)
34. Bray, A., Oldham, E., Tangney, B.: Technology-mediated realistic mathematics education and the Bridge21 model: a teaching experiment. In: Krainer, K., Vondrová, N. (eds.) Ninth Congress of European Research in Mathematics Education (CERME9), European Society for Research in Mathematics Education Prague, pp. 2487–2494 (2015)
35. Freudenthal, H.: Revisiting Mathematics Education: China Lectures. Mathematics Education Library, vol. 9. Springer, Dordrecht (1991). Bishop, A.J. (ed.)
36. Clements, M.A., et al.: From the few to the many: historical perspectives on who should learn mathematics. In: Clements, M.A., et al. (eds.) Third International Handbook of Mathematics Education, pp. 7–40. Springer, New York (2013)
37. Gravemeijer, K.: Developing Realistic Mathematics Education (Ontwikkelen van realistisch reken/wiskundeonderwijs). CD-Beta-Press, Utrecht (1994)
38. Noss, R., et al.: Broadening the sense of 'dynamic': a microworld to support students' mathematical generalisation. ZDM **41**(4), 493–503 (2009)
39. van den Heuvel-Panhuizen, M.: Realistic mathematics education: work in progress. common sense in mathematics education. In: The Netherlands and Taiwan Conference on Mathematics Education, pp. 1–39 (2002)
40. Strauss, A.L., Corbin, J.M.: Basics of Qualitative Research: Techniques and Procedures for Developing Grounded Theory 3e, 3rd edn. Sage Publications Inc., Thousand Oaks (2008)
41. Puentedura, R.: Transformation, Technology, and Education (2006). http://hippasus.com/resources/tte/
42. Glaser, B.G.: The constant comparative method of qualitative analysis. Soc. Probl. **12**(4), 436–445 (1965)
43. Means, B.: Technology and education change: Focus on student learning. J. Res. Technol. Educ. **42**(3), 285–307 (2010)
44. Pierce, R., Stacey, K., Barkatsas, A.: A scale for monitoring students' attitudes to learning mathematics with technology. Comput. Educ. **48**(2), 285–300 (2007)
45. Bray, A.: Collaborative, contextual, and technology-mediated mathematics learning activities: design heuristics and effects on student engagement. In: School of Computer Science & Statistics. Trinity College Dublin, The University of Dublin, Dublin (2016)

46. Bray, A.: Teachers' experiences of the integration of 21st century learning in the mathematics classroom – the Bridge21 model in action. In: 8th International Conference on Computer Supported Education (CSEDU 2016), vol. 2, pp. 219–230 (2016)
47. Boaler, J.: Encouraging the transfer of 'school' mathematics to the 'real world' through the integration of process and content, context and culture. Educ. Stud. Mathe. **25**(4), 341–373 (1993)
48. Albert, L.R., Kim, R.: Developing creativity through collaborative problem solving. J. Mathe. Educ. Teach. Coll. **4**(2), 32–38 (2013)
49. Oldknow, A.: Their world, our world—bridging the divide. Teach. Mathe. Appl. **28**(4), 180–195 (2009)
50. Green, H., Hannon, C.: Their Space. Education for a Digital Generation, in ICTlogy. Demos, London (2007)

Sharing Life Stories: Design and Evaluation of a Digital Storytelling Workshop for Older Adults

Simone Hausknecht(✉), Michelle Vanchu-Orosco, and David Kaufman

Department of Education, Simon Fraser University, Burnaby, Canada
{shauskne, mvanchuo, dkaufman}@sfu.ca

Abstract. This chapter presents the design and evaluation of a digital storytelling workshop for older adults held across multiple workshop iterations and examines the adjustments made across these iterations. Adjustments to the design were made prior to the second and the third iteration to accommodate the needs of the learners. Results from older adult participants' evaluations of three iterations of the workshop, involving seven different workshop groups, are also presented. Researchers found that the facilitation approach and socially supportive environment were important to the digital learning experience and were seen as benefits that workshop participants appreciated. Furthermore, participants reported increased digital storytelling skills and, to a lesser degree, other computer and internet skills. Additionally, participants reported enjoying the contribution of others, sharing stories with each other, and being able to learn something new. The main challenge reported by participants was the lack of sufficient time provided in the workshop.

Keywords: Digital storytelling · Older adults · Workshop evaluation · Lifelong learning

1 Introduction

The aging population is becoming increasingly disproportionate to other age demographics in many parts of the world. It is estimated that 30% of the population will be over 60 years of age by the year 2050 [1]. This has led to increased discourse on improving quality of life to live a happy and healthy lifespan. For example, the concept of 'active aging' promoted by the World Health Organization (2002) has been described as follows: "Active ageing is the process of optimizing opportunities for health, participation and security in order to enhance quality of life as people age." [2]. Improving older adults' quality of life can incorporate a vast number of aspects and can be attained in many different ways depending on the individual. It requires a holistic approach, incorporating not only physical and cognitive health, but also aspects that contribute to well-being such as creativity, social engagement, and lifelong learning [3].

Technology and communication are tools which have the opportunity to enhance the lives of older adults [4]. Increasing digital literacy may improve quality of life in a

G. Costagliola et al. (Eds.): CSEDU 2016, CCIS 739, pp. 497–512, 2017.
DOI: 10.1007/978-3-319-63184-4_26

number of ways, including increased socialization and information access [5]. Technology also offers the opportunity for creative expression and sharing capabilities. One technology activity that could be beneficial for older adults is digital storytelling. Digital storytelling could encourage older adults to share their stories, become digital producers, express creativity, and improve digital literacy. Furthermore, digital storytelling could also serve as a learning experience where participants are both diving into traditional structures of writing a story (such as the story arc) but also learning technology [6]. Thus, there is the crossover between what has been culturally available for many centuries and that which is new and adds to the art of storytelling.

Story and narrative are powerful cultural tools and are traditional ways to share knowledge. They serve as one of our main tools of identity, in that we perceive our lives as embedded in narratives and our memories are wrapped around these stories [7]. When we are able to create artefacts, either written or digital, it can be beneficial for exploring identity and self-knowledge [8]. The combination of technology and autobiographical narrative could offer many opportunities for older adults to express themselves in new and different ways.

The purpose of the current chapter is to extend our discussion on the design and evaluation of a series of digital storytelling workshops for older adults that was presented at the Computer Supported Education conference in 2016 [9]. In this chapter we outline the design of the workshop and adaptation over three iterations of workshop. Through examining the results of quantitative and qualitative evaluation data gathered from participants, we discuss perceived learning outcomes and the success of the workshop, as well as the challenges. This study contributes to both research on the use of digital storytelling and the design of workshops for older adult cohorts.

2 Background

2.1 Digital Storytelling

A digital story is a story that utilizes multimedia in its expression. Leslie Rule [10] describes it eloquently as a "modern expression of the ancient art of storytelling. Digital stories derive their power by weaving images, music, narrative and voice together, thereby giving deep dimension and vivid color to characters, situations, experiences, and insights." The process involves creating a script and incorporating the narrative, photos, videos, music, and sound together to create a short movie. There are few rules regarding what can and can't be used in creating a digital story. Furthermore, digital storytellers do not simply create their stories; they also play the role of editor and producer making many choices on style, color, pace and other design considerations. All choices and decisions are made by the story makers, creating an ambience of their own self-expression within the story presentation.

Digital storytelling arose as a new art form in the 1980's. A large part of the drive for its popularity was through the founding of the Center for Digital Storytelling (CDS) by Joe Lambert and Dana Atcheley [11]. Over the next couple of decades, the art of digital storytelling slowly gained momentum in the United States. In the early 2000s, Daniel Meadows and Cardiff University, in partnership with BBC, brought digital storytelling to England [12]. The art of digital storytelling has now spread throughout many countries and for various purposes.

Digital storytelling has not only gained popularity as an artistic expression but has been touted as a tool with a diversity of benefits. For example, digital storytelling has recently been the subject of research in education [11], to create a voice or participatory media [13], as a public historical archive [14], and as a means of creating empathy, understanding and giving voice to marginalized cultures [15].

Much of the digital storytelling research has centered around its use in education, whether K-12, higher education, or professional development. In the K-12 system, it has been praised as a tool for increasing literacy and digital literacy skills [16]. However, the learning is not just limited to the digital aspects, but also incorporates traditional story writing structures [6]. Furthermore, digital storytelling has also gained use in its ability to promote reflective practice in various fields such as pre-service teachers [17] and nursing [18].

The reflective nature of stories has been noted in other areas. Bruner [7] suggests that one cannot tell an autobiographical story without having some level of reflection. For example, Stacey and Hardy [18] report on a study where newly registered nurses were provided digital storytelling workshops to help with adjustment. They created stories on recent distressing events. Many of the participants found this to be an opportunity to reflect on difficult experiences and created time to process the event. It also provided a venue for expressing themselves openly, although that also created concern about how they would appear to others. In another phase of the study the stories were shared with final year nurses, who appreciated and recognized the authenticity of the digital storyteller's experience. The digital stories created an environment where the viewers could reflect on their own fears and empathize with the story teller. This study emphasizes the power of stories for both teller and viewer.

Other studies have also found that digital stories could be used to increase empathy and understanding of patients and disadvantaged individuals [19, 20]. The digital stories of patients have been used in nursing education to create a patient-centered approach [19]. The creation of the digital stories do not simply help the medical practitioner, but the process can be useful to patients. A study by Stenhouse, Tait, Hardy, and Sumner [20] of seven adults with early stage dementia suggested that the act of creating a digital story helped with the patient's ability to express themselves and supported a sense of identity. Furthermore, over the four-day workshop, participants became more social.

Besides medical education, there has been a cross over between using digital stories as a learning tool and a community tool through projects where students are working with disadvantaged persons to create stories [21] or the stories are used specifically to educate. For example, *Silence Speaks* gives those individuals who may have experienced human rights violations an opportunity to express themselves. In turn, these narratives are then shared globally in strategic places to promote human rights, equality and health [22].

Digital stories are a way for ordinary people to produce and share their own stories [13]. Thus, digital storytelling is a way of amplifying the voices of ordinary people [13]. In the context of older adults, it could allow for a new avenue to tell their story and archive their history. It is a way of communicating and making oneself heard, empathizing with others, and forming meaning through self-reflection.

There is limited research on older adults creating digital stories. One example, a study by Loe [23] evaluated a course on aging that involved students going to local senior communities and working with elders to produce a digital story. They were paired together, elder storyteller and student facilitator, to produce a digital life story. After completion, the digital stories were presented to the community. This study reported positive results, including building a reciprocal relationship between the pairs, a reviewing and reflection upon the future and past, and reducing ageism. This was likely due to the intergenerational nature of the study and the story process [23].

When given the chance, older adults seem to embrace the opportunity to be content producers versus simply consumers, as was seen in a study of the program Enmesh [24]. Participants could share photos and comment, tell stories and discuss with other older adults. Although not specifically a digital story in the way we are considering it here, the study emphasized the social benefit and creative expression older adults gained through sharing photos and stories.

2.2 The Older Adult Learner

Lifelong learning and cognitive engagement are valuable elements that can contribute to quality of life [25]. Jenkins and Mostafa [25] conducted a study examining data from a longitudinal study that compared participants' subjective well-being with their learning habits and found a significant relationship between high levels of reported well-being and learning. However, this only applied to informal learning that included arts groups and night classes. Older adult learning may also have an effect on community engagement and increase community well-being [26].

Older adults have different reasons for continued learning than younger adults. In many instances, learning for the older adult is a personal choice versus formal learning for a degree or work, and therefore, requires interest and relevance for the older adult. It has been found that there are two main motivations for continued learning by the older adult, interest in the content and social factors [27]. When learning new technologies, older adult learners come with pre-conceived ideas and attitudes on their self-efficacy [28]. If this negative conception is too strong it may be difficult to accept learning a new technology; however, supportive environment may help [28]. Digital literacy in itself may be important for older adults as it can increase access to information [29] and social connections [5].

The informal and social nature of learning seems to be valuable for older adults who may benefit from constructivist design considerations, such as the program being learner-centred, and learners having the opportunity for collaboration and sharing of different perspectives. Furthermore, the knowledge and learning is part of the practice of performing an activity [30]. In the current workshop design, all learning is embedded in the practice of creating a digital story.

Two other aspects specifically considered in the current design were scaffolding and planning for group sharing and knowledge construction. Participants' computer experience was expected to vary, and their zones of proximal development would also vary. The zone of proximal development is the level to which an individual can attain learning goals with the guidance of another, either a peer or facilitator, compared to what they can attain on their own, as the task may be too difficult to achieve on their own [31]. Thus, to reach certain goals, scaffolding (support for learners), such as through peers, artefacts, or facilitators, is needed. Scaffolds are supports designed to help and guide the learner towards their achievement [32]. In the current workshop design, the scaffolds had to be flexible and multiple to account for participants' different skill levels coming into the program.

Another aspect that may be valuable for educational programs is a collaborative, social environment where participants can share experiences and understanding. This allows for multiple perspectives for reflective practice and negotiating meaning [30]. Furthermore, previous studies have found that older adults find leisure activities more rewarding when they are social [27, 33]. In the current workshop design, all learning occurs within a social and sharing environment.

3 Workshop Design

The workshop design was inspired by the work of the Center for Digital Storytelling (now called StoryCenter), the Digital Storytelling Cookbook [34], creative writing and film techniques. This combined generating stories in the workshops, emotion and meaning exploration, picture and sound choices, editing, and a number of other areas. The workshop was also designed to create as many shared experiences as possible so as to create community and a social learning environment. Each participant worked on their own digital story. The social opportunities became more limited as the participants moved to the computers, where they were divided by a screen. However, a collaborative environment was still maintained.

The workshop was designed with two specific phases, story creation and digital creation.

Story Creation Phase: Since many participants had limited story writing experience, it was important that they learn how to write a narrative script. As many of the learners wanted to share their work and a piece of their lives with family and the community, learning how to create a succinct and engaging narrative was a valuable starting point. The second reason for starting without using computers in the workshop was that it facilitated a writing group environment where participants could get to know each other through sharing life narratives. This was valuable for creating a supportive, sharing, community where learners felt they could explore issues that arose.

A digital story is not composed of individual parts which are combined but is a unified piece. Therefore, it was necessary for participants to have a full story to work with, and also to understand it as a digital story script and not just a story. For the second iteration we implemented an introduction to the software, which provided understanding of the digital story process as a whole, earlier in the workshop. This helped to provide a rich understanding of the length of the story, number of pictures and other aspects that differentiate digital stories from written stories.

Digital Story Creation Phase: After the participants had a script and a storyboard, they moved to a computer lab (or brought their own laptop computers). At this point learners were more focused upon their own stories and creating a multimedia experience. There were lessons on different aspects of using the program, editing, and recording (see the following outline).

Outline of Workshop (weekly)

Week 1: Introduction to the Research Study and Digital Storytelling Workshop
Learners are introduced to the research study and to digital storytelling. They will start to think about the stories of their life.

Week 2: Intro to WeVideo, Practice Creating a Digital Story
Learners are introduced to the digital storytelling software. They are given photos, music, sound clips, a video clip, and a voice clip then shown how to upload these, and lay them out.

Week 3: Writing a Script (draft)
Learners will begin to explore the art of story writing and think about the story they may want to tell. Activities are used to help them explore story ideas and get peer feedback.

Week 4: Sharing Your Story and Editing
Learners bring their story to class and get an opportunity to share their drafts with other learners and the facilitator who provide peer feedback.

Week 5: Images and Storyboarding
Learners bring their edited script and create a storyboard, deciding on which photos go with each section.

Week 6: Voice, Sound, Music; Record the Narrative
Learners explore ideas of voice, sound and music, and start recording their stories. Learners upload images, recording, etc.... to Wevideo and start to put their digital story together.

Week 7: Record and Edit in WeVideo
Learners continue putting the pieces of their digital story together.

Week 8/9/10: Record, Edit, Final Touches, Publish.
Learners continue editing. They share their stories on the final session.

3.1 Further Design Consideration

Software Choice: During the design phase, we faced a difficult decision regarding choice of software tools. We wanted software that would be easily accessible, simple, could be accessed from multiple locations, had publishing options, and would suit our demographic and workshop setting. The software also needed to meet the different levels of computer skill and knowledge of the participants. Thus, we wanted a system that had some built in scaffolding to provide users with 'how to use the program' information readily available.

We reviewed the existing software programs that were available in the summer of 2014. We also consulted researchers and programs that had experience with digital storytelling. Of the available software programs, most were aimed at students and often used to create 'comic book' stories. After careful consideration, our top three choices were MS Photostory, PhotoStage, and WeVideo. After conducting further research we found that MS Photostory was no longer supported and Photostage required installation, so it would appear 'different' on MACs and PCs. Thus we chose a software program called WeVideo.

WeVideo was recommended by Bernard Robin (University of Houston) and is a browser-based software application that does not change, regardless of hardware used. Further, WeVideo has been adopted by StoryCentre (formerly the Center for Digital Storytelling). The program has a full range of options and tools that can be used to create digital stories, instructional videos, is online so can be accessed from any computer, and produces a digital story with good quality MPEG-4 multimedia files that can be viewed with most digital media players.

Technical Experience: We required no technical experience since we wanted to make the workshop accessible to all. As expected, the participants ranged from those who had worked with computers in their careers to those who had never used one. For this reason, a ratio of at least one facilitator to five participants was used and additional research assistants were brought in to help during the computer sessions.

Time Constraints: The initial workshops were based on two-hour sessions, occurring once a week, for eight weeks. These time constraints were due to venue requirements. In our initial design we realized this could be a limiting factor, but it was a design restriction that we could not change. However, some venues allowed the workshop to be extended to 10 weeks. Additionally, it was hoped that workshop participants would do some work at home.

Story Style: Within digital storytelling there are many different forms. Sometimes digital storytellers select a life history approach which is a retelling of a person's life. Others tell a complete short story with a beginning, middle, and end, seen more frequently in the digital stories produced by those participating in *StoryCenter's* workshops. For our workshop we chose the latter. Participants were asked to reflect on an event or moment in their lives that stood out. We also incorporated reflective journals to help develop the theme, emotions, and personal understanding of the story. While many of the stories did not take place over one incident, although some did, a specific idea or lessons learned were incorporated. For example, one participant wrote about her experiences a dancer until her body failed in later years due to arthritis. She had to learn to accept her aging body and found new ways to dance.

3.2 Implementation

The first iteration of the workshop design took place in September of 2014. For the second and third iterations, some changes were made based on feedback from participants and observations by facilitators. Two specific adjustment made to the workshop were familiarizing participants with a more comprehensive view of the process by introducing participants to the digital storytelling software earlier and having extra hours, tutorials, with facilitators outside of the workshop.

The first adjustment was to have an earlier session in the program focused on creating a digital story in the chosen software. The participants were given photos, sound, and other parts of a digital story and shown how to upload these. They were also given mini lessons in different aspects of the software (e.g., adding images and videos to the 'main track' and editing narration in the 'audio track') and encouraged to play around with the software.

From the initial feedback we also noted that participants were finding it difficult to finish their stories given the amount of time. Our first adjustment was to have a facilitator meet with individual participants outside of the workshop in one-on-one learning sessions. However, this was not sustainable so tutorial groups were formed with a set time for facilitators to work with multiple participants.

The viewing of the participants' digital stories occurred in class. Special events were also held where participants from multiple workshops (i.e., more than one workshop was held at each venue) had an opportunity to showcase their work to family, friends, and others in the community.

4 Method for Evaluation

The workshops took place in the Greater Vancouver area, Canada. The research grant is a partnership grant where the researchers worked with community organizations to host digital storytelling workshops for older adults. Participants were recruited through advertisement (e.g., newspaper, community website) with the partnership facilities. The digital storytelling workshops ran once a week for two hours, for 8–10 weeks depending upon the centre and time restrictions. Three iterations of the program consisting of 7 groups of 4–10 participants are reported here.

Participants: Participants were adults, aged 55+, who signed up for the digital storytelling workshop. A total of 40 participants, from all three initial iterations of the workshop, filled out the final evaluation forms.

Instrumentation: Participants were given an anonymous survey at the end of the workshop evaluating the program. A five-point scale was used to rate various aspects of the workshop and to rate perceptions of digital skills improvement. There were also open ended questions asking the participants what they liked best about the workshop and what could be improved.

5 Results

The quantitative questions on the evaluation forms were analysed using IBM SPSS Statistics V22, a statistical software package. For the open-ended questions, two researchers coded the data and formed categories, continuously checking on their agreement.

5.1 Workshop Evaluation

The workshop was evaluated on facilitation, process, and software used. All participants were able to use the software; however, varying levels of assistance were required. Some participants required more hands-on help from facilitators. Most of the participants completed their digital stories during the course of the workshop and were given the opportunity to share their work during the final session.

Almost two-thirds of participants found the workshop just right (see Table 1). However, 28.2% of participants found it difficult, while a few participants found it easy

Table 1. Difficulty level of workshop.

Question	Categories	Frequency (n)	Percent (%)
I found the workshop	Very Easy	0	0
	Easy	3	7.7
	Just right	24	61.5
	Difficult	11	28.2
	Very difficult	1	2.6
	Total	39	100.0

Table 2. Workshop evaluation.

Question	Categories	Frequency (n)	Percent (%)
Facilitator's ability to communicate	Very Poor	0	0
	Poor	0	0
	Fair	3	7.5
	Good	9	22.5
	Very Good	28	70
	Total	40	100.0
Facilitator's helpfulness	Very Poor	0	0
	Poor	0	0
	Fair	1	2.5
	Good	6	15
	Very Good	33	82.5
	Total	40	100.0
Process used to create digital story	Very Poor	0	0
	Poor	1	2.6
	Fair	1	2.6
	Good	16	41
	Very Good	21	53.8
	Total	39	100.0
Software used to create digital story	Very Poor	0	0
	Poor	2	4.3
	Fair	3	7.9
	Good	18	47.4
	Very Good	15	39.5
	Total	39	100.0

and one found it very difficult. Overall this is a good outcome and would suggest the workshop was accessible to most participants.

Overall most participants rated the workshop as being good or very good as can be observed in Table 2. The facilitation was rated as being very good by most participants, both in regard to communication (70%) and helpfulness (82.5%). Approximately 95% of participants felt the process used was good to very good. The software used was also rated high with close to 87% of participants rating it good to very good.

5.2 Skill Improvement

Participants were asked whether they thought their skills improved in specific digital literacies and digital storytelling skills.

Approximately two-thirds of participants reported that they improved on computer and computer software skills either slightly or moderately (see Table 3). A small percentage reported no improvement, while almost one-quarter of participants reported that their computer and computer software skills were very or extremely improved over the course of the workshop. Just over one-quarter of participants reported no improvement of their internet skills, with one-fifth reporting a slight improvement. However a large number of participants (38.5%) reported moderate improvement in their internet skills.

Table 3. Skill improvement.

Did skills improve:	Categories	Frequency (n)	Percent (%)
Using a computer	Not at all	4	10.3
	Slightly	11	28.2
	Moderately	13	33.3
	Very	7	17.9
	Extremely	4	10.3
	Total	38	100.0
Using computer software	Not at all	3	7.9
	Slightly	10	26.3
	Moderately	16	42.1
	Very	7	18.4
	Extremely	2	5.3
	Total	40	100.0
Using the internet	Not at all	11	28.2
	Slightly	8	20.5
	Moderately	15	38.5
	Very	3	7.7
	Extremely	2	5.1
	Total	40	100.0

As might be expected, the skill with the most improvement reported was digital storytelling (Table 4). All participants reported some increase, with over three-quarters reporting their skills were very or extremely improved.

Table 4. Skill creating a digital story.

Did skills improve:	Categories	Frequency (n)	Percent (%)
Creating a digital story	Not at all	0	0
	Slightly	1	2.5
	Moderately	10	25
	Very	20	50
	Extremely	9	27.5
	Total	40	100.0

5.3 Benefits and Improvements

The participants were asked open-ended questions about what they liked best and what they would improve. Answers were sorted by similarity to each other and then themes were identified.

What Participants Liked Best

Three major themes were identified from the open-ended questions regarding what participants like most about the workshop. These are sharing/interactions with others, digital story creation/learning, and facilitation.

Shared Social Experience

One major theme that emerged was the shared experience with other participants and what that brought to the program. The environment allowed for participants to give each other feedback, share stories, and socialize. This came out as an important aspect of participants' experience. Below is an example of some of the comments.

"The fellowship/moral support of fellow participants"
"Sharing the works of the other participants."
"Interaction with other participants"
"Story sharing"
"Supporting each other"

These examples of some of the comments shows the comradery and appreciation participants had of the shared learning experience.

Expression through Learning Story Creation

Some participants revealed that what they liked best was learning something new and creating their own story. As one participant wrote:

"I liked learning the software and the process of putting the pieces together."

There were also comments that showed the excitement of learning how to turn pictures into living stories as expressed by these two participants

> *"Turning still photographs into a live picture, with sound and life. And also learning to build a story"*
> *"Able to tell and express the story of a picture with emotions."*

And as one participant wrote the best aspect was *"Finding new ways to tell my story"* and another participant simply wrote that they *"learned or discovered I can write stories."*

The story creation could even be very empowering as expressed by a participant who wrote, *"The very organized and helpful approach to build an effective and powerful story - it is a process that gives one a bit more self-respect!"*

Helpful Facilitation

Another aspect that came up for many of the participants was facilitation. As outlined earlier the program involved a high level of facilitation both during the workshop, and outside the workshop when needed. This was appreciated by participants and can be observed by comments such as,

> *"Friendly, kind assistance of the mentors"*
> *"Approachable, supportive facilitators"*
> *"Got opportunity to ask questions and get assistance when I got stuck"*
> *"The facilitators teaching us something new"*

Improvements

The major theme that appeared for needing improvements was related to time, or not enough of it. These did not encompass one aspect of the program but different participants felt they needed more time on different areas, as seen by these participant comments.

> *"More editing time"*
> *"We could have had more time to do research and work more on the timeline."*
> *"A lengthier course to help people like me who are not too computer savvy to grasp the technological details"*
> *"Needed a lot more time - in developing the story and in the lab."*

The need for time was the only consistent theme identified for the improvements in the evaluation form. Other suggestions were very individual in nature and not easily paired. Time limitations as a theme mentioned by participants is understandable as it was a concern from the start. We described how we attempted to adjust for this through tutorials. Even with the extra facilitation sessions, the later groups still had time come up as something they would like more of as one person wrote "longer training".

6 Discussion

Overall participants were satisfied with the digital storytelling process and workshop. They reported gaining skills in digital storytelling which may contribute to lifelong learning. Hopefully, these new skills will encourage some of the participants to continue their exploration of digital storytelling. Furthermore, many participants also suggested that the workshop improved their digital skills. The learning of technology was embedded in the program, due to its necessity, and was an added benefit. It was the authentic practice of creating a digital story with technology in which the learning occurred.

Increasing digital literacy can be important for older adults. This project found that a program in which older adults can learn technology through creating online artefacts may be an effective way to digital literacy. Digital storytelling specifically requires learning basic computer skills, as well as internet use if the participant is planning to find pictures or music. Although using digital storytelling for digital literacy in schools has been examined in previous research [11, 16], it should not be overlooked as an interesting and fun way to increase older adults' skills and understanding.

The program included a high level of scaffolding, particularly by guidance from facilitators, since some participants needed the extra help and time to finish creating their stories. As was reported by participants, this was appreciated and was seen as one of the aspects that was most favorable. However, the sustainability of having many one-on-one sessions is not realistic in many community programs. Time limitations was one of the main factors affecting the need for extra sessions.

Although, for many, there was a high level of guidance, participants managed to create their own individual stories with the freedom to express themselves and their life narrative in new and meaningful ways. Moreover, they became digital producers and not simply consumers producing artifacts that could be distributed among family, friends, or whomever they wished. Similar to the work of Waycott [24], we found that they were eager producers of digital content and found the program rewarding as noted by the evaluation.

In regards to the level of difficulty of the program, participants mainly marked that the workshop was *just right* or *a little difficult*. This places the workshop design within most learners' zone of proximal development, yet required the program to have a fair amount of scaffolding built in. The one on one time with facilitators allowed for the wide range of different digital skill levels.

What the older participants liked best about the program seemed a strong indication of what made the learning a valuable experience for them. The opportunity for shared experience, creative expression, and helpful facilitation appeared to have made the program successful for the participants. Shared experience has come up in previous work on leisure activities and learning as being important for older adults [27]. Similar to the nurses in Stacey and Hardy [18], the older adults seemed to appreciate learning a new way to express themselves and having the opportunity to do so.

Time as a difficulty was not surprising as we had restrictions due to venue requirements. It also was due to the many dimensions that make up digital storytelling. For example, some participants felt they needed more time writing, others needed more time learning the program, others' needed more time editing. Where time was needed was individual, but more time was needed.

As time was a factor, we have slowly developed a way to increase time for participant learning. We did this through tutorials which were optional and could be held in many spaces (such as a library). The extra time and patience that the facilitators used was appreciated. Having this allowed those that started with a higher level of computer skills to move at the pace of the workshop, while others who entered with more limited skills could get the assistance they needed. One benefit with digital stories is that the narrative is often the core of the composition. The focus on story creation earlier on allowed for even the simplest of multimedia to be a powerful viewing/listening experience. Although the initial theory of the two phases worked overall, adding the one day to familiarize learners with the software, process and future expectations was valuable for preparing learners. Simply showing them digital stories and discussing it, was necessary, but having a quick initial activity helped to bring everything together.

We felt that our design was successful, but required the adjustments noted earlier in the article. It is our position that design is not a stagnant process, but one that must be evaluated, adapted and improved with each iteration. Each group will present with a unique combination of context, varied backgrounds, and other factors that may require further changes.

6.1 Limitations and Future Directions

This study was limited by the fact that it was a self-reported survey. Thus, participants claimed to have learned something, but this was not specifically tested. However, the fact that they created a digital story would suggest that they learned how to do this, but for increased digital literacy skills this is dependent on self-assessment. This could be improved by more rigorous assessment methods, but at the same time it comes back to the demographic needs. The older adults in this study were there for their own reasons and not to go into industry. Given this, a self-report that they have learned a few extra digital skills and how to create a digital story is important.

However, this may not be critical as lifelong learning is more related to feeling engaged and enjoying the experience. Furthermore, at this point the digital stories created have not been analyzed. This will be done soon may provide a more thorough understanding. The workshop also had a high level of support with a least two facilitators per group of up to 10 participants, it is difficult to determine what the success would be with less individual support provided. Another possibility is that designs could be longer or broken into two sections. Thus, participants could learn storytelling techniques and development in one workshop series, and digital storytelling in another workshop series. One area that would be interesting to follow up is in developing an intergenerational program where youth and older adults can create together. This may provide added intergenerational aspects and help with the issue of limited time. At the Computer Supported Education Conference (CSEDU) during the presentation by Hausknecht, Vanchu-Orosco, and Kaufman [9], a member in the audience (Aibhin Bray) suggested that this program could be of benefit in the school system. Presenting a lived history may help future generations empathize and understanding the challenges and experiences of previous generations.

7 Conclusions

In conclusion, this book chapter examined the design and evaluation of a series of digital storytelling workshops for older adults. Through the various iterations we were able to make adjustments and improve on the original design. This adaptive approach provided insights into older adult learning through digital storytelling. The added advantage of reported increases in digital skills was important to considering informal methods for increasing digital literacy. Two valuable approaches to the design were creating a social community and providing facilitation to adjust for different computer skills. Creating a story that was shared gave older adults an opportunity to express themselves and explore new ways to tell their life stories, creating a rewarding experience. Overall, the workshops were successful and can contribute to future designs and research.

Acknowledgements. We wish to thank the Social Sciences and Humanities Research Council of Canada (SSHRC) and the AGE-WELL Network of Centres of Excellence (NCE) for supporting this project financially.

References

1. World Health Organization: Global Health and Aging (2012). http://www.who.int/ageing/publications/global_health.pdf
2. World Health Organization (WHO): Active aging: A policy framework. CITY: World Health Organization (2002). http://whqlibdoc.who.int/hq/2002/WHO_NMH_NPH_02.8.pdf. Accessed 23 Sep 2015
3. Hanna, G.P., Noelker, L.S., Bienvenu, B.: The arts, health, and aging in America: 2005–2015. Gerontologist **55**(2), 271–277 (2015)
4. Mitzner, T.L., Boron, J.B., Fausset, C.B., Adams, A.E., Charness, N., Czaja, S.J., Sharit, J.: Older adults talk technology: technology usage and attitudes. Comput. Hum. Behav. **26**(6), 1710–1721 (2010)
5. Baecker, R., Moffatt, K., Massimi, M.: Technologies for aging gracefully. Interactions **19**(3), 32–36 (2012)
6. Czarnecki, K.: How digital storytelling builds 21st century skills. Libr. Technol. Rep. **45**(7), 15–19 (2009)
7. Bruner, J.: Life as narrative. Soc. Res. **71**, 691–710 (2004)
8. Birren, J.E., Deutchman, D.E.: Guiding Autobiography Groups for Older Adults: Exploring the Fabric of Life. JHU Press, Baltimore (1991)
9. Hausknecht, S., Vanchu-Orosco, M., Kaufman, D.: New ways to tell my story: evaluation of a digital storytelling workshop for older adults. In: Proceedings, 8th International Conference on Computer Supported Education (CSEDU 2016), Rome, Italy. SciTePress Digital Library Online, Setubal (2016)
10. Rule, L.: Digital storytelling: never has storytelling been so easy or so powerful. Knowl. Quest **38**(4), 56 (2010)
11. Robin, B.R.: Digital storytelling: A powerful technology tool for the 21st century classroom. Theory Pract. **47**(3), 220–228 (2008)
12. Meadows, D.: Digital storytelling: research-based practice in new media. Vis. Commun. **2** (2), 189–193 (2003)
13. Burgess, J.: Hearing ordinary voices: cultural studies, vernacular creativity and digital storytelling. Continuum J. Media Cult. Stud. **20**(2), 201–214 (2006)
14. Klaebe, H.G., Foth, M., Burgess, J.E., Bilandzic, M.: Digital storytelling and history lines: community engagement in a master-planned development. In: Proceedings of the 13th International Conference on Virtual Systems and Multimedia: Exchange and Experience in Space and Place, VSMM 2007. Australasian Cooperative Research Centre for Interaction Design Pty, Limited (2007)

15. Sawhney, N.: Voices beyond walls: the role of digital storytelling for empowering marginalized youth in refugee camps. In: Proceedings of the 8th International Conference on Interaction Design and Children, pp. 302–305. ACM (2009)
16. Behmer, S., Schmidt, D., Schmidt, J.: Everyone has a story to tell: Examining digital storytelling in the classroom. In: Society for Information Technology and Teacher Education International Conference, Vol. 2006(1), pp. 655–662 (2006)
17. Tendero, A.: Facing your selves: the effects of digital storytelling on teacher education. Contemp. Issues Technol. Teach. Educ. **6**(2), 174–194 (2006)
18. Stacey, G., Hardy, P.: Challenging the shock of reality through digital storytelling. Nurse Educ. Pract. **11**(2), 159–164 (2011)
19. Christiansen, A.: Storytelling and professional learning: a phenomenographic study of students' experience of patient digital stories in nurse education. Nurse Educ. Today **31**(3), 289–293 (2011)
20. Stenhouse, R., Tait, J., Hardy, P., Sumner, T.: Dangling conversations: reflections on the process of creating digital stories during a workshop with people with early-stage dementia. J. Psychiatr. Ment. Health Nurs. **20**(2), 134–141 (2013)
21. Militello, M., Guajardo, F.: Virtually speaking: How digital storytelling can facilitate organizational learning. J. Commun. Posit. Pract. **13**(2), 80–91 (2013)
22. McLellan, H.: Digital storytelling in higher education. J. Comput. High. Educ. **19**(1), 65–79 (2007)
23. Loc, M.: The digital life history project: intergenerational collaborative research. Gerontol. Geriatr. Educ. **34**(1), 26–42 (2013)
24. Waycott, J., Vetere, F., Pedell, S., Kulik, L., Ozanne, E., Gruner, A., Downs, J.: Older adults as digital content producers. In: Proceedings of the SIGCHI Conference on Human Factors in Computing Systems, pp. 39–48. ACM (2013)
25. Jenkins, A., Mostafa, T.: The effects of learning on wellbeing for older adults in England. Ageing Soc. **35**, 2053–2070 (2015)
26. Merriam, S.B., Kee, Y.: Promoting community wellbeing: the case for lifelong learning for older adults. Adult Educ. Q. **64**(2), 128–144 (2014)
27. Kim, A., Merriam, S.B.: Motivations for learning among older adults in a learning in retirement institute. Educ. Gerontol. **30**(6), 441–455 (2004)
28. Barnard, Y., Bradley, M.D., Hodgson, F., Lloyd, A.D.: Learning to use new technologies by older adults: Perceived difficulties, experimentation behaviour and usability. Comput. Hum. Behav. **29**(4), 1715–1724 (2013)
29. Gatto, S.L., Tak, S.H.: Computer, Internet, and e-mail use among older adults: Benefits and barriers. Educ. Gerontol. **34**(9), 800–811 (2008)
30. Land, S.M., Hannafin, M.J.: Student-centered learning environments: foundations, assumptions, and implications. In: Jonassen, D., Land, S. (eds.) Theoretical Foundations of Learning Environments. Routledge, London (2012)
31. Vygotzky, L.S.: Mind in Society. Harvard University Press, Cambridge (1978)
32. Hannafin, M., Land, S., Oliver, K.: Open learning environments: foundations, methods, and models. Instr. Des. Theor. Models New Paradig. Instr. Theory **2**, 115–140 (1999)
33. Mannell, R.C., Kleiber, D.A.: A Social Psychology of Leisure. Venture Publishing Inc., State College (1997)
34. Lambert, J.: Digital Storytelling Cookbook. Digital Diner Press, Berkeley (2010)

Assessing the Adoption of Virtual Learning Environments in Primary Schools: An Activity Oriented Study of Teacher's Acceptance

Elena Codreanu[1,2,3,4(✉)], Christine Michel[1,3(✉)], Marc-Eric Bobillier-Chaumon[1,2], and Olivier Vigneau[4]

[1] Université de Lyon, Lyon, France
{elena.codreanu,marc-eric.bobillier-chaumon}@univ-lyon2.fr, christine.michel@insa-lyon.fr
[2] Université Lyon2, GRePS, EA 4163, Bron, France
[3] INSA-Lyon, LIRIS, UMR5205, 69621 Villeurbanne, France
[4] WebServices pour l'Education, Paris, France
olivier.vigneau@web-education.net

Abstract. This article studies the conditions of use of a VLE (Virtual Learning Environment) by primary school teachers. It first presents a triangulated model to explore Virtual Learning Environments' adoption in primary schools. The theoretical models cover three approaches: the social acceptance, the practical acceptance and the situated acceptance. The situated acceptance of teachers is studied according to the model by using activity theory and qualitative methods (individual and collective interviews). Our study describes how teachers (8 participants) perceived the role of the VLE in the evolution of their working practices (maintaining, transforming or restricting existent practices), in their relationship with parents and in the follow-up of their students.

Keywords: VLE · Acceptance · Activity theory · Primary school · Professional practices

1 Introduction

The definition of Virtual Learning Environments differs from country to country. In UK, the VLEs were designed mainly as pedagogical and collaborative and lately there were added school management tools. In this view, a VLE is *"learner centred and facilitates the offering of active learning opportunities, including specific tutor guidance, granularity of group working by tutor and learners"* [1]. By contrast, in France, the VLEs were since the beginning designed as a unique access workspace, both for school management and for learning activities. The initially management modules (marks, absences) designed for virtual classrooms served then to design pedagogical applications and collaborative group works. In both British and French systems, VLEs aim to encourage communication and collaborative practices between the members of a school community through tools – such as blogging and a messaging service – and to foster

G. Costagliola et al. (Eds.): CSEDU 2016, CCIS 739, pp. 513–531, 2017.
DOI: 10.1007/978-3-319-63184-4_27

access to information (in regards to homework, for example) through the use of a digital planner.

The last report of OECD (Organization for Economic Co-operation and Development) mentions that technologies are not sufficient to support teaching and instructional purposes. They are simple tools in the hands of teachers and it depends on them to take good use in their activities. Yet, our society is *"not yet good enough at the kind of pedagogies that make the most of technologies (…). Adding 21st century technologies to 20th-century teaching practices will just dilute the effectiveness of teaching"* [2, p. 3]. VLEs serve to carry out diverse activities, are intended for several distinct user groups (teachers, students, parents, and staff), and can be exploited in very different contexts: in the classroom, at home or on the move. This complexity can limit the development of practices and the motivation to use it. In this article we chose to evaluate the factors involved in VLEs adoption in primary schools and to consider two processes: technology acceptance and appropriation. When they explain acceptance, the existing studies focus either on individual factors (like satisfaction, effort expectancy) or practical factors (technological features like ergonomic of the system), or, lately, contextual factors (like history and evolution of professional practices). In this article, we propose to present the main theoretical frameworks in the study of acceptance and to eventually describe a triangulated model to evaluate technology adoption. Then we present a situated study analysing the technology acceptance of teachers and the practices they develop.

2 Teachers' VLE Acceptance Studies

Some studies analyse the teachers' attitudes to and beliefs about this type of technology. In their study, Kolias et al. [3] examined attitudes and beliefs of teachers from Finland, Greece, Italy and the Netherlands after a first teaching experience with a computer learning environment in order to see if they would be able to include technology in their everyday practices. The study gives very promising conclusion about the possible use of technology, but miss of real practice and acceptance observations.

Others studies analyse the teachers practices and the problems linked with the VLE uses. Indeed, the VLEs have been mainly used in secondary education and higher education. French studies showed that certain teachers had partly integrated VLEs in their professional practices. Prieur and Steck [4] indicated that, although teachers recognized the pedagogical benefits of VLEs, they were not ready to endorse them due to poor ergonomics, and to their lack of training and proficiency in IT tools. Teachers also felt overworked and resisted the idea of extending the *"school space-time continuum"* outside of school. For their part, Poyet and Genevois [5] identified differences in culture: since VLEs are often seen as management tools for businesses, they may need to be "translated" and the meaning adapted to the context of school. One of the ways to solve this issue would be to use school-based metaphors ("notebooks", "lockers") instead of bureaucratic terms ("messaging", "agenda"). Poyet and Genevois showed how VLE tools were unfamiliar to teachers and how the latter did not fully grasp their pedagogical uses and benefits. This led to unsatisfying experimental phases in which teachers tested the tool's various functions, *"without always having a full representation of the tool's potentialities and specific limits"*. This drew teachers to prefer using personal and familiar tools (such as their own emails). Similar observations were made by Pacurar and Abbas [6] who noticed that the VLE was perceived as a communication tool (through the messaging service) and an administrative tool (assigning grades, writing down absences), but that it *"was not firmly anchored in pedagogical practices"*, especially when it came to using it during class time or to design class material. The prescribed uses did not answer the real needs felt by teachers on a daily basis. These conclusions are also given by Firmin and Genesi, [7] and Blin and Munro [8]. Bruillard [9] mentioned the complexities in deploying VLEs when a variety of people are involved: teachers, parents, students, school districts, local authorities, software publishers and the Ministry of Education. Bruillard also noticed a paradox between the Ministry's will to open schools up to parents, and the actual low amount of parental implication. Teachers are also concerned that parents may interfere in their pedagogical choices. These difficulties are further amplified by the fact that teachers who use VLEs do not get institutional recognition. Practitioners in the field have also felt disempowered since external companies were called to design the VLEs. There is also the risk of creating inequalities or even to exclude certain parents who are less equipped and trained in digital technologies. Missonier [10] developed these points based on the design and the deployment of VLE projects that were managed by local authorities and service providers. These approaches have not always been very effective, since they depend on the project manager – who may lack in transparency or carefulness – to solve disputes linked to functionalities or uses. This, in turn, leads to different protagonists within the network to decrease their commitment. Prieur and Steck [4] recommend implementing spaces for ideas *"that articulate the current practices of teachers, practices that can help foster the acquisition of skills and the potentialities of different VLE tools, in order to develop possible instrumentalisations"*. This would help to adapt prescribed uses, depending on the context.

Voulgre [11] introduced a political dimension. Teachers are generally favourable to arguments promoting the uses of VLEs: the latter are useful to catch up on classes (illness, loss of grades), to retrieve previous work or to support students with schooling difficulties. But the fact that not all children have Internet at home represents an inequality, thus preventing teachers from fully using VLEs. Such a refusal is seen as a "*type of counter-power*" against political injunctions. On the contrary, acceptance factors are linked to the respect of hierarchy, of the institution and of the law (obligation to use a VLE); other positive factors are linked to the values of solidarity and cooperation that are promoted by VLE tools.

Other studies also point out the importance of technical infrastructure: access to the computer classroom, number of computers in classrooms, Internet access, broadband speed and technical support. The school institution's management, the organisational culture and VLE implementation strategies have all a great role in technology acceptance [12–15]. Finally, lack of competences in technology, lack of confidence and lack of time were mentioned [16]. In the end, all of these studies showed that the acceptance of VLEs by teachers depended on practical considerations, as well as strategic concerns that were both professional and political.

VLE began to be deployed now in primary schools. Only a few studies explored the acceptance of VLE in these contexts. Berry [17] highlighted that primary school pupils can use VLEs and appreciate it in case of absence because they can easily get lesson content and homework. Moreover, they have more confidence to discuss mathematics problems on the VLE platform. But younger children differ greatly from students in secondary or higher education in terms of their autonomy and their use of digital media. So we are led to ask ourselves how primary school teachers take this factor into account and more generally how they include such a new tool in their professional practices: are they able to adapt or develop their practices or not and what are their reasons?

We need to evaluate how actual teaching practices can evolve in order to integrate and make profit of the existing technologies. This is why we aimed in this field study to identify the current teaching practices that constitute the core of professional activities for primary school teachers. We also wanted to identify tensions that could lead us to find ways to improve the design of VLEs and to provide recommendations for uses and services.

3 Analyzing Acceptance and Appropriation

3.1 The Models of "Social Acceptance"

These approaches focus on human factors in the process of technological acceptance. The main idea is that people's perceptions and attitudes may play a major role in this process. According to Davis [18] and his model TAM (Technology Acceptance Model), acceptance can be explained through two factors: perceived usefulness and perceived ease of use. These two perceptions influence the intentions to use the technology which, in turn, influence its acceptance. Other attitudinal factors are later added: satisfaction, performance expectancy, effort expectancy. This model is inspired by the theory of reasoned action [19] which consider that behaviour is guided from inside by people's intentions. Other authors [20] talk about internal factors (like beliefs, convictions and attitudes of users), and external factors (like support, training, technical infrastructure). Some authors support the idea that internal factors take priority in the decision to use an educational technology [21, 22] while others think that external factors are predominant [23]. When they study VLEs acceptance in particular, authors highlight the same duality. While some support the major role of technical infrastructure like access to the computer classroom, number of computers in classroom, Internet access and high speed Internet access and institution management [12–15], others admit that causes of VLEs reject are lack of confidence in technology and lack of time to train [16]. Other studies show that it is actually the connection between the internal and the external factors that matters: external factor (like institutional support, training) will subsequently shape the beliefs and attitudes toward the technologies and then the intention to use those [24].

In primary teaching, technologies are less frequent, so there are not many studies on this particular subject. Studies demonstrated the importance of self-confidence toward computer use in the development of attitudes toward technologies and indirectly in the intention to use the technologies [25–28]. Beside confidence, some authors outline the role of perceived security in the acceptance of VLEs in primary school [29]. VLEs suppose a functioning similar to that of social networks, with a unique access to content. Teachers doubt their own possibilities of control and moderation in cases of on-line bullying and interrogate about the responsibilities in case of misappropriation of the VLE by students. Also, they worry about the misuse identity by other colleagues. In primary schools, these issues are particular important, because the students are particular young and vulnerable to these forms of harassment.

Social acceptance approaches have nonetheless been subject to a number of criticisms concerning both methodological criteria and the models' foundations [30]. One criticism is that these studies have little practical relevance for the technological design and improvement of the system. In effect, these studies indicate that a system is not acceptable to the target group without giving any information about the changes and adaptations required. Added to this is the fact that the research is based on small samples that are not representative of the professional context, and use questionnaires (scale of measurement) as the sole method of evaluation. Critics claim that such a method results in a truncated, partial and rather disembodied picture of the meaning people attach to the technology. However, in educational context, we retain the effort to specify precise factors directly implied in technological acceptance: confidence in computer use, social and institutional support, technological infrastructure and children's security.

3.2 The Models of "Practical Acceptance"

This approach focuses on the technology characteristics (human factors and ergonomics) and how the tool is implemented (support, training, participatory design). The prevailing idea is that when technology is easy to use and well implemented (training is provided and end users are included in the design process, for example) the device's acceptance is enhanced. In sum, the aim is not only to design a suitable product, but also a suitable relationship to technology, and ultimately contribute to an acceptable user experience for the individual [31].

According to Nielsen [32], the two most important attributes for technology acceptance are usability and utility. Usability refers to the fact that people can easily use the functions of a system. Utility refers to the capacity of the system to help users do their tasks. In short, a technology easy to use and useful will be accepted by the users. To these two attributes, Nielsen adds others: costs of the technology, compatibility, and reliability. We have to mention that the notion of "usability" is different of that of "perceived ease of use" in the previous social model. While the first refers to the effective usability and is evaluated through user tests, the second refers to perceptions and subjective attitude toward usability and is evaluated through questionnaires. The ISO 9241 norm specify that the three dimension of usability are: effectiveness (the accuracy with which users achieve specified goals), efficiency (the effort required for users to do theirs tasks) and satisfaction: what users think about the system.

Ergonomics specialists proposed a list of criteria to evaluate the usability of computer interfaces. Bastien and Scapin [33] proposed eight criteria: guidance (means available to orient the user throughout the interface), workload (interface elements that play a role in the reduction of users' perceptual and cognitive load), explicit control (the control users have on the processing of their actions), adaptability (the system's capacity to behave according to users' needs), error management (means available to recover from errors), consistency (maintaining the interface choices in similar contexts), significance of codes (codes and names should be meaningful for users) and compatibility (match between the users characteristics and task characteristics). Concerning the last criteria, compatibility is particularly important when technologies are used by users with specific characteristics (in terms of age, customs, perceptions, skills). For instance, technologies designed to be used in primary schools, should be adapted to a public of young children, who do not master writing, reading and have limited fine motor skills. So, the interfaces should avoid using a lot of text content and complex pull-down menus; they should prefer instead images and simple menus [34, 35]. Budiu and Nielsen [36] used specific methods in order to evaluate children's behaviour on the web (think aloud, card sorting). They proposed a list of 130 recommendations for interfaces designed for children (aged 3 to 12), organised by the type of content (general interaction, navigation, images, videos etc.). Generally, they recommend to use interactive content, sound and colours, use of the metaphors and big buttons. They also advise to ensure children's control over the interface and to avoid sensory and cognitive overload.

These studies are important because they provide precious practical advising for designers. The main criticism is that they are focused on functional aspects and do not consider the intrinsic characteristics of user like emotions (pleasure, fun, amusement). Recently, studies began to consider user as a real partner in design of a technology in approaches like User Centred Design and participatory design [37, 38]. Participatory design "relies on the collective generativity of stakeholders; in other words, it uses the collective ability of stakeholders to generate or create thoughts and imaginings" [39, p. 173]. In school technologies, participatory design suppose that teachers and students can be actively involved in the design of their future tools so that these tools would better meet their needs [40–43].

This approach focuses therefore on the technology conception, on ergonomic improvements and on support to collaboration between designers and end users. In this context, ergonomic approaches intend to prescribe recommendations and guidelines for designers in terms of technological adaption to users 'needs. However, these studies remain focused on the functional aspects and on the performance of users with the system. In addition, participatory design, mostly applied in industry, is less adopted by the stakeholders in digital education. This is due, on one side, to the difficulty and high cost of putting participatory design into practice and, on the other side, to the diversity of educational contexts and high number of schools, with their own autonomy and specific organization which make technological generalization difficult.

3.3 Appropriation and Situated Acceptance Models

According to Jonsson [44], appropriation is "the gradual process by which participants successively become more proficient in using the tools" (p. 11) Unlike mastery, which entails the acquisition of a skill, appropriation, in addition to a technical skill, includes the competence to use the technology for carrying out an authentic task in a given context. As such, appropriation is thought to be strongly linked to the notion of change. Using a text editor at school changes practices very little, but being able to modify a digital text without having to copy it out can change the importance traditionally attached to writing. Bobillier-Chaumon [45] considers that the appropriation of a technological tool is a condition of its acceptance. When someone appropriates a tool, she contributes to it and is able to innovate, and therefore use the tool for previously unforeseen purposes. By making this contribution to the technology, the person can identify with it, make it her own, give it meaning and therefore accept it. Bobillier-Chaumon proposes the notion of situated acceptance, defined "as the way in which an individual – or a group or organization – perceives the issues related to these technologies (strengths, benefits, risks, opportunity) through their use in everyday situations, and reacts to them (favourably or not)." [46] What is taken into account here is the experience in a situation of interaction between users and a certain technology that already exists. In this approach, the object of study is not the perception or attitude towards technology but the practices and activities carried out as part of a real job. The advantage of this approach is that it brings into light for the first time dimensions like "history" and "context" and proposes to look for acceptance directly in daily activities of end users.

Activity theory, as detailed by Engeström, Miettinen and Punamaki [47] and Kuutti [48], provides more complete elements to quantify the context of use. Instead of referring to uses, activity theory refers to an activity system: the user (subject) has a precise objective and accomplishes it by using certain instruments (tools). He/she fits into a social community (the group of people who intervene in the activity). This community is regulated by certain operating rules (the norms and rules to respect in a given activity), and respects specific divisions of work (the ways in which roles are distributed among individuals).

Activity systems are characterized by contradictions (or internal tensions), which favour and trigger innovation; such changes contribute to further development. Therefore, activity theory appears to be useful to qualify the context as well as to define the dynamics at work when accepting and taking ownership of technology.

The teacher's activity system is summarized in Fig. 1 and relates to the educator's daily practices. These practices occur with or without instruments, since they often take the shape of direct communication in class, and can be supplemented with instruments such as the board, posters, notebooks, etc. These practices follow rules that are specific to the educational system and fit into an educational community composed of teachers, students and parents. The division of work includes the effective practices inherent to the profession and the ways in which the different tasks are distributed among the different protagonists. In terms of the education and follow-up of students, teachers and parents work together, but in different contexts. Each group's responsibility is therefore

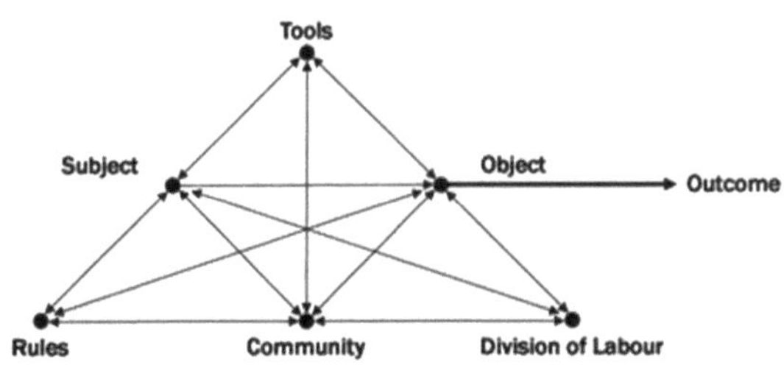

Fig. 1. Activity system [47].

well defined. With the arrival of a new technological tool, used both in class and at home, these differentiated roles and identities may come into conflict.

Furthermore, according to Rabardel and Bourmaud [49], the conditions needed to implement human-machine interactions lead to the modification of the technology's properties and, consequently, to the readjustment of human conducts. This occurs through the process known by Rabardel and Bourmaud as the instrumental genesis (a double process of instrumentation/instrumentalisation). The tool therefore does not only exist for itself or in an isolated way. It is socially embedded and fits within certain practices, habits and social communities that guide its use and transform its characteristics.

3.4 An Analytical Model of VLE Adoption in Primary Schools

We have identified three categories of approaches. The first, social acceptance, focuses on the individual perceptions and attitudes of prospective users but is not precise enough to explain the raison why users develop them; the second, practical acceptance, concentrates on the tool's ergonomic characteristics; and the third analyses users' activities and hence the interaction between the technology and actual practices. We assume that practical acceptance and situated acceptance can explain the social acceptance and that the three approaches have to be combined to analyze the development of the uses and the long term acceptance and appropriation. Consequently, we consider that acceptance is a process that can be evaluated through three sets of factors:

- Technological factors (derived from practical acceptance approaches) grouped in system quality factors (like usability) and design quality factors (participatory design),
- Activity and task factors (derived from appropriation and situated acceptance approaches) related to characteristics of professional activity like rules, prescriptions, professional practices, objectives,
- Perception factors (derived from social acceptance approaches and from appropriation and situated acceptance one's) related to individual opinions about the qualities of the technology and it's adaptation to task context (perceived ease of use, utility, satisfaction, security and confidence in VLE's use skills to design uses or solve contradictions).

In the above diagram (see Fig. 2), the single arrow indicates a one-way relationship between the two factor categories. The double arrow indicates a two-way relationship. The technological factors (quality of the product, quality of support) influence the perceptions of the tool, which in turn influence the tool's appropriation and acceptance. For their part, the activity and task factors (activity, practices, community) also influence the perception factors. The creation of technology's meaning is made during the actual use. The use trials influence significantly the level of technology acceptation and appropriation. The quality of use will build a new form of appropriation (by creating new forms of practices and innovative use) and acceptance (through the lens of new emotions and new benefits related to use). These two constructs will modify the initial perception of the technology and the users' perceptions on their technological skills. The retroactive loop describes how appropriation (seen as mastery of the tool plus innovation) is decisive for the acceptance of the tool (seen as the subjective decision to start using the technology) and vice versa.

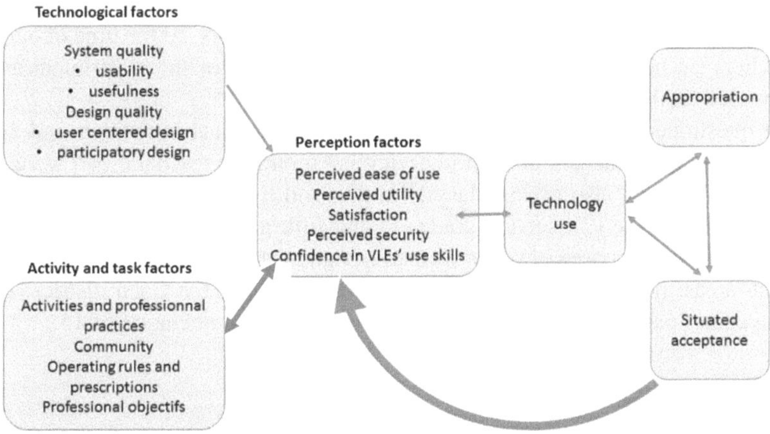

Fig. 2. Model of VLE adoption: factors involved in the acceptance and appropriation of VLEs.

It is a dynamic model that may enable the plurality of viewpoints and situations to be reconstructed. Dynamism of the model is important for explaining the principles of technology adoption through articulation of factors issued of different theoretical approaches. This model may restore a diversity of points of view and situations and the formalisation of factors' progression in context. In order to deepen this approach and qualify the criteria of each factor, we propose to use triangulated methods [50] which consists in using more than one method to study a phenomenon. In terms of methodology, we propose a triangulation consisting of qualitative methods (interviews, elicitation interviews, content analysis) and quantitative methods (questionnaires, analysis of connection logs). The next section describes a first analyse using qualitative methods.

4 Field Study Methodology

According to this model, we choose to focus the first observations on teacher perception about technological factor, activity and task factor and use to answer the questions "How primary school teachers include a new tool like VLE in their professional practices? Are they able to adapt or develop their practices or not and what are their reasons?" We propose to use the activity theory to detect VLE acceptance and non-acceptance factors according to contexts of use. The standards considered to define acceptance are linked to the ways in which the profession is practiced, to social and work constructs and to ways in which the VLE tool is used and deployed. The approach developed in this study is essentially qualitative. We aimed to collect testimonies from teachers in which they represented and perceived their experiences as they teached with and used a VLE.

4.1 Observed Context and Participants

All participants in our study were part of the Versailles and Caen school districts (situated near Paris). 6 schools were in the Versailles district and 6 were in the Caen district. They volunteered to experiment with the VLE One for 2 years. At the time of our study, 26 teachers (in both districts) had volunteered to be part of the experiment and had already used the VLE One for 3 to 6 months.

We questioned 8 teachers over the course of 4 individual interviews and 2 group interviews (with 2 teachers in each interview). Among the teachers, two were school principals who were also giving classes (in first and fifth grades). The other teachers worked in first grade (2), second grade (1) and fifth grade (3) classes. The group of participants was composed of seven women and one man. The schools were all situated in urban areas, in the Versailles school district (6) and in the Caen district (2). The average age of participants was of 46 years with a standard deviation of 15.

4.2 Description of the Tool

The VLE used in this study is entitled One. It was specifically designed for an elementary school audience, with ergonomics and interfaces that are suitable for children [35, 36]. The One interface is therefore simple, intuitive and attractive (see Fig. 3). The collaboration functions that are offered consist in a Messaging Service, a Blog and a Storage Space. One also offers customization features (My Account, My Mood), notifications (a News Feed, birthday notifications), organizational tools (Calendar) and a school website. Each user has the option of customizing his/her profile with a picture and personal information (motto, mood, information on favourite leisure activities, films, music, food). Students are by default included in their class group and have access to the content published in the group by the teacher.

Fig. 3. Interfaces for the pages « News Feed » « The Classroom » and « My Apps » in the VLE One.

When we were conducting our study, the VLE One had not yet offered services such as the Planner notebook and the Multimedia notebook.

4.3 Data Collection

Teachers participated to semi-structured interviews. These interviews lasted an hour and a half on average and tackled the following themes: the teachers' experience with TEL (Technology Enhanced Learning), the school's computer equipment, the teacher's representation of the VLE, needs related to the VLE, the VLE's usefulness, ease of use and intentions of use, difficulties of use, and the implications of the VLE for the teaching profession. Teachers could speak openly and were able to give their critical point of view on various uses, share their own representations of the tool, and give their opinion on functions that were being developed, such as the planner notebook, the digital parent-teacher notebook and the multimedia notebook. They were also welcome to recount difficulties linked to the use of the VLE, using Flanagan's critical incident technique [51]. Technological, task and perception factors considered in the model can so be described.

4.4 Analysing the Teachers' Interviews

The interviews were entirely recorded and transcribed so that they could be systematically studied [52]. We considered in our analysis the comments that associated One with daily teaching practices, operating rules (linked to the educational system), the education community (composed of teachers, students and parents) and the division of work (the ways in which tasks are shared between different groups of people). We used the sentence – a basic syntactic unit built around a verb – as the main unit to study the transcripts. Sentences were identified as in the following example: *"I showed them how to make folders (sentence 1)/, but it is hard for the students (sentence 2)"*. We also distinguished between the comments that were rather favourable (supporting initiatives) and the ones that were less favourable (difficulties in use). We proceeded to do counts and percentage calculations to rank the different factors. We determined that the users had accepted the VLE when they mentioned the successful ways in which they used it, the adjustments they made or the contradictions they encountered and overcame. Categories weren't pre-established and we retained the themes that had been mentioned at least three times.

5 Results

The analysis revealed 4 main themes (see Table 1), as well as 16 sub-factors (see Table 2): (1) factors linked to the practice of the profession (the workload, raising awareness of digital uses and habits, work recognition), (2) factors linked to pedagogical monitoring (pedagogy, health and safety, emotions and attractiveness); (3) factors linked to social and work-related organization (collaboration, communication, the reorganization of communicative practices), (4) factors linked to the tool's use and deployment (ease of use, usefulness, feedback, computer and network equipment, support and assistance). We will first present the results that stemmed from the four main factors; we will then proceed to describe the sub-factors.

Table 1. Main factor occurrences.

Factor	Number of positive comments	Number of negative comments
Profession	35 (15,56%)	90 (36%)
Pedagogical follow-up	54 (24%)	57 (22,8%)
Social organisation	88 (39,11%)	14 (5,6%)
The tool's use and deployment	48 (21,33%)	89 (35,6%)
Total	**225 (100%)**	**250 (100%)**

Table 2. Sub-factor occurrences.

Sub-factor	Number of positive comments	Number of negative comments
Factors linked to the practice of the profession		
Workload	0(0%)	72 (28,8%)
Raising awareness on digital uses	20 (8,89%)	12 (4,8%)
Work recognition	15 (6,67%)	15 (6%)
Total	**35 (15,56%)**	**90 (36%)**
Factors linked to student monitoring		
Pedagogy	20 (8,89%)	0 (0%)
Health and safety	4 (1,78%)	57 (22,8%)
Emotions and attractiveness	30 (13,3%)	0 (0%)
Total	**54 (24%)**	**57 (22,8%)**
Factors linked to social and work-related organization		
Collaboration	12 (5,33%)	0 (0%)
Communication	72 (32%)	8 (3,2%)
Reorganizing communicative practices	4 (1,78%)	6 (2,4%)
Total	**88 (39,11%)**	**14 (5,6%)**
Factors linked to the tool's use and deployment		
Ease of use	27 (12%)	24 (9,6%)
Usefulness	9 (4%)	6 (2,4%)
User feedback	4 (1,78%)	39 (15,6%)
Computer and network equipment	0 (0%)	6 (2,4%)
Support and assistance	8 (3,56%)	14 (5,6%)
Total	**48 (21,33%)**	**89 (35,6%)**

5.1 Main Factors

In Table 1, we can see that the factors linked to social organization brought about the largest number of positive comments (88), which means that the VLE played an important role in communication and collaboration practices within the school activity system. Conversely, factors linked to the teaching profession and to the use and deployment of the VLE gathered the largest number of negative comments. The deployment and use of the VLE therefore seem to raise questions linked to professional recognition and to the practice of the teaching profession. It also raises issues regarding the alignment of VLEs with school uses and habits. In the following paragraph, we present an analysis according to each sub-factor (see Table 2), thus allowing us to refine each element.

5.2 Factors Linked to the Practice of the Profession

As we can see in Table 2, the perceived workload (triggered by the use of the VLE) brought about the largest number of negative comments (72). In fact, teachers had the impression that they needed to invest additional time to master the VLE's functionalities and to imagine interesting projects to do on the platform. They also felt that using the VLE implied sustained and continuous work for new tasks that did not necessarily fit into their areas of expertise, such as: taking pictures, downloading material on the computer and then on the VLE, publishing blog posts, writing messages, and designing teaching projects that included the VLE. Since these teachers did not have a dedicated time slot to use these technologies, they had to use pedagogical time to become familiar with such tools. Teachers also felt the weight of large workloads, with the impression of having an ever increasing amount of informational solicitations. The VLE had indeed been added to a number of pre-existing educational platforms: academic e-mail, the career management platform "I-prof", online training platforms, didactic platforms and an online handbook of skills. Teachers therefore felt constantly submerged by a large amount of data which they had to manage (email addresses, different login names and passwords for each platform, various approaches and functions according to the different resources…). They also felt overwhelmed by the informational content that they had to focus on and prioritize (academic information, pedagogical information, event notifications to sort and share…). Faced with the fear of having to work twice the amount with a VLE, some teachers refused to publish their lessons on the VLE since they already did the same thing using their own automation tools: "*I already create the lesson on "paper board", so putting it up again (on the VLE)… I do not want to do that…*"

Teachers made 20 positive comments about making students more responsible when using digital tools. Teachers found that they had a part to play when training "*students to use digital tools responsibly*". On the other hand, some teachers found that parents should be in charge of raising their children's digital awareness (12 comments). These teachers' main arguments had to do with the fact that working on the students' digital responsibilities affected other teaching activities negatively. They also argued that such digital tools were massively consulted by the children at home, such as when they checked new messages. For these reasons, controlling digital tools should relate to the private sphere. This opinion was not necessarily shared by parents who believed that, on the contrary, the follow-up on digital practices should be done by the institutions that set up the tools in the first place. We can therefore see that, within the "school-home" axis, responsibilities and roles between teachers and parents may need to be redefined within the teaching program, and the division of work would need to be more efficiently coordinated (controlling and following up on uses).

Work recognition was mentioned positively 15 times. Some teachers saw the VLE as a way to highlight classroom work through the blog. Some activities, which had previously been almost invisible to parents, could now be displayed, such as sporting activities, class outings, and the work of the pupils themselves. The VLE then became a tool that could help recognize the teacher's and the students' work. But such recognition is still limited due to parents not being fully involved in the VLE project and not consulting these resources often (negative mentions).

5.3 Factors Linked to Student Monitoring

According to the teachers, the primary benefit of VLEs for students lied in the fact that VLEs helped to build a more attractive and stimulating relationship based on emotions (30 positive comments in Table 2). The VLE was a motivating tool for students and allowed them to appreciate class work. In terms of pedagogy, the VLE was seen as a benefit (20 positive comments) in the construction of verbal expression and student communication. It was also positively viewed to raise awareness and autonomy when students were working with computers. The VLE blogs were therefore often co-edited by the teachers and the students.

However, teachers also expressed many fears linked to the children's health and safety (57 negative comments versus 4 positive ones). These fears related more specifically to possible abuses (bullying, insults) or to the misuse of communication and coordination tools. Teachers have no access to the children's accounts and were therefore unable to control the content of exchanged messages. Several teachers created a fictitious student account to follow and control exchanges. This also allowed them to check the layout quality of the information and documents that they published on the VLE. We noticed that the teachers who had not used the platform in such an innovative way weren't as satisfied with the device. This example highlights the importance of offering verification and surveillance functionalities for the teachers, with parent or student views available. Another fear related to ways in which the children themselves could use the VLE in transgressive ways. It is particularly difficult for teachers to authenticate information coming from the system, as the following example shows: "*I received a parental message, I do not know if it was the older brother or the parent who sent the message…/ … so I needed to go back to the paper notepad to write a note…/… on the notepad, there's the handwriting, the signature, we can quickly tell the difference between a parent and a child*".

5.4 Factors Linked to Social and Work-Related Organization

VLEs were particularly appreciated as a tool supporting communication (72 positive comments). Certain teachers, who created blogs, mentioned these blogs in the notepads when information needed to be consulted. Teachers seemed to appreciate the positive role that the VLE played in teacher collaboration (12 mentions). Sharing resources made it easier to organize common activities and outings, and facilitated pedagogical work.

Negative comments (8) addressed the messaging service as a communication method, highlighting the fact that this service did not distinguish between in-school time and out-of-school time. Teachers mentioned the need to change the settings so that parents could only send messages outside of school time and to limit school-time messages between students. Concerning the parents, such parameters would limit the amount of last-minute intrusive messages that require additional work on the teacher's behalf during class time. Teachers have more control using the parent-teacher notepad. Providing these settings could be useful as a first step. It would reassure teachers and would give them time to set-up digital awareness activities for students and parents.

5.5 Factors Linked to the Tool's Use and Deployment

Teachers reported finding the platform user-friendly (27 positive comments). They considered the functionalities and information coherent and easily accessible through the menu and the icons. The negative comments (24) were linked to the functionalities in the VLE's Document space: teachers would have liked to share folders rather than files: *"the children receive... [the files] just like that. It is not easy for them, we have a Shared Document and everything is mixed together: music, stories. If the name of the folder is a bit vague, they will not know"*. There was also a lack of visibility as to who consulted content and who connected to the platform. By following the news feed, teachers managed to see the activity of other users (parents, students), but only if the latter had modified a certain feature, such as their avatar or their motto. But feedback could not be retrieved when users simply consulted the platform without leaving tangible traces. *"It is true that... if they do not change their mood or their motto, we do not know if they have connected or not. It would be interesting for us users to know who saw the content"*. In order to obtain such data, teachers had to do an additional task which consisted in sending a questionnaire through the parent-teacher notepad or by asking the students if their parents had connected to the platform. Such feedback was important in order to build ties with the different educational partners and to make sure that the published information had actually been seen and received. Otherwise, teachers had difficulties knowing if the system was really useful and effective.

The lack of computer infrastructure (equipment, networks...) was also seen as hampering the acceptance of VLEs (6 comments). Teachers would have liked to use the VLE in class with the students but they did not have enough computers and tablets. "*we would almost need to have computers in the class all the time to really use (VLEs) in every day teaching*". Teachers also pointed out that all students did not have equal access to VLEs: some had continuous access, while others had restricted access through their parents; some students did not have Internet access at all. Finally, teachers mentioned a lack of support and assistance. They did not feel adequately trained to use VLEs. Given the fact that this was an experimental implementation phase, not all possible means were used to support the teachers. On the long term, academic supervisors would need to get involved in training and supporting teachers.

6 Discussion and Conclusion

In this paper we presented three important models in the study of technological adoption. The three models have their origins in different fields of research. The models of "social acceptance", like TAM and UTAUT were inspired by social psychology but applied to management and marketing studies. The "practical acceptance" theories are specific to ergonomists and designers. And finally, models of "situated acceptance" are also issued from development psychology and lately applied to various fields, from change management to organization issues. The technological adoption issue is of general interest and should not be limited to one singular approach. Our objective was to resume these various models and to extract information that is salient for educational area. Factors like usability for young children, teachers' confidence in their computer use skills, teacher's perceived security toward children's use and preexistent teaching practices are example of important determinants of technology adoption in schools.

The study of teachers' acceptance done according to the model shows that, in terms of acceptance, the uses of the VLE One spurred tensions that were similar to the ones described by Prieur and Steck [4] and Voulgre [11] in secondary education. We observed contradictions between the artefact, the community and the rules as well as contradictions between the artefact and the division of work. The first type of contradiction was linked to the subverted uses of the Messaging Service or the News Feed. There was also a lack of digital access due to poor infrastructure in schools and in some homes. The second type of contradiction was due to an excessive workload and an increase in the teachers' professional responsibilities through the extension of the "school space-time continuum". We recommend that decision-makers (the Ministry, school districts) provide better information on VLE users' responsibilities. When it comes to community uses – such as the ways in which to use the messaging service or whether or not use feedback indicators – we think that such decisions can be made at a local level through discussions between the school administration, the teachers and the VLE publisher. Depending on contexts and practices, certain modes of operation may or may not be effective or acceptable.

There were fewer contradictions linked to the artefact itself. Teachers appreciated the services offered by One as well as its ergonomics; they tried to adapt the VLE to their professional practices. They did not hesitate to make requests to improve the tool. They also agreed to help train children and their parents on digital best practices. Teachers showed signs of acceptance in this area, but they still need to be given more support and assistance to maintain such uses on the long term.

To conclude, the acceptance of this VLE seems to have been overall positive since One was well designed and relatively adapted to the practices of the teachers involved. The main problems are linked to the ways in which the tool is implemented. The recommendations formulated here are meant for the Ministry of Education and school principals. Clarifications need to be made concerning the limits of the school space-time continuum and the rules of governance and communication. Such resolutions are relevant in a context in which very young children are concerned, since they are to use these platforms without having prior social digital skills.

References

1. Stiles, M.J.: Effective Learning and the Virtual Learning Environment. The Learning Development Centre, Staffordshire University, UK (2000)
2. OECD: Student, Computers and Learning. Making the Connection. PISA. OECD Publishing (2015). http://www.oecd.org/edu/students-computers-and-learning-9789264239555-en.htm
3. Kolias, V., Mamalougos, N., Vamvakoussi, X., Lakkala, M., Vosniadou, S.: Teachers' attitudes to and beliefs about web-based collaborative learning environments in the context of an international implementation. Comput. Educ. **45**(3), 295–315 (2005)
4. Prieur, M., Steck, P.: L'ENT: un levier de transformation des pratiques pédagogiques pour accompagner les apprentissages du socle commun, Colloque International INRP 2011 (2011)
5. Poyet, F., Genevois, S.: Intégration des ENT dans les pratiques enseignantes: entre ruptures et continuités. In: Rinaudo, J.-L., Poyet, F. (ed.) Environnements numériques en milieu scolaire. Quels usages et quelles pratiques?, Lyon, INRP, pp. 23–46 (2010)
6. Pacurar, E., Abbas, N.: Analyse des intentions d'usage d'un ENT chez les enseignants de lycées professionnels. In: STICEF, vol. 21 (2014). http://sticef.org
7. Firmin, M., Genesi, D.: History and implementation of classroom technology. Procedia-Soc. Behav. Sci. **93**, 1603–1617 (2013)
8. Blin, F., Munro, M.: Why hasn't technology disrupted academics' teaching practices? Understanding resistance to change through the lens of activity theory. Comput. Educ. **50**(2), 475–490 (2008)
9. Bruillard, E.: Le déploiement des ENT dans l'enseignement secondaire: entre acteurs multiples, dénis et illusions. Revue française de pédagogie, vol. 177, pp. 101–130 (2011)
10. Missonier, S.: Analyse réticulaire de projets de mise en œuvre d'une technologie de l'information: le cas des espaces numériques de travail. Ph.D. Thesis (2008)
11. Voulgre, E.: Une approche systémique des TICE dans le système scolaire français: entre finalités prescrites, ressources et usages par les enseignants. Ph.D. Thesis (2011)
12. Keller, C.: Technology acceptance in academic organisations: implementation of virtual learning environments. In: Proceeding of the 14th European Conference on Information Systems, Gothenburg (2006)
13. Keller, C.: User acceptance of virtual learning environments: a case study from three northern european universities. Commun. Assoc. Inf. Syst. 25(1), 38 (2009). http://aisel.aisnet.org/cais/vol25/iss1/38
14. Osika, E., Johnson, R., Buteau, R.: Factors influencing faculty use of technology in online instruction: A case study. Online J. Distance Learn. Adm. 12(1) (2009)
15. Babic, S.: Factors that influence academic teacher's acceptance of e-learning technology in blended learning environment. In: E-Learning-Organizational Infrastructure and Tools for Specific Areas, pp. 3–18 (2012)
16. Karasavvidis, I.: Activity theory as a conceptual framework for understanding teacher approaches to information and communication technologies. Comput. Educ. **53**(2), 436–444 (2009)
17. Berry, M.: An investigation of the effectiveness of virtual learning environment implementation in primary school. Thesis University of Leicester (2005)
18. Davis, F.D.: Perceived usefulness, perceived ease of use, and user acceptance of information technology. MIS Q. **13**, 319–340 (1989)
19. Ajzen, I.: The theory of planned behavior. Organ. Behav. Hum. Decis. Process. **50**, 179–211 (1991)

20. Blackwell, C.K., Lauricelle, A., Wartella, E., Robb, M., Schomburg, R.: Adoption and use of technology in early education: The interplay of extrinsic barriers and teachers attitudes. Comput. Educ. **69**, 310–319 (2013)
21. Pynoo, B., Devolder, P., Tondeur, J., Braak, J.V., Duyck, W., Duyck, P.: Predicting secondary school teachers' acceptance and use of a digital learning environment: A cross-sectional study. Comput. Hum. Behav. **27**, 568–575 (2011)
22. Pynoo, B., Devolder, P., Tondeur, J., Braak, J.V., Duyck, W., Sijnave, B., Duyck, P.: Teachers' acceptance and use of an educational portal. Comput. Educ. **58**, 1308–1317 (2012)
23. Ertmer, P.A.: Teacher pedagogical beliefs: the final frontier in our quest for technology information? Educ. Technol. Res. Dev. **53**(4), 25–39 (2005)
24. Inan, F., Lowther, D.: Laptops in K12 classrooms: exploring factors impacting use. Comput. Educ. **55**, 937–944 (2010)
25. Chen, J., Chang, C.: Using computers in early childhood classrooms: Teachers' attitudes, skills and practices. J. Early Child. Res. **4**(2), 169–188 (2006)
26. Faurie, I., van de Leemput, C.: Influence du Sentiment d'Efficacité informatique sur les Usages d'Internet des étudiants. L'orientation scolaire et professionnelle 36(4) (2007)
27. Giamalas, V., Nikolopulus, K.: In-service and pre-service early childhood teacher's views and intentions about ICT use in early childhood setting: A comparative study. Comput. Educ. **55**, 333–341 (2010)
28. Tsytouridou, M., Vryzas, K.: The prospect of integrating ICT into the education of young children: The views of Greek early childhood teachers. Eur. J. Teach. Educ. **27**(1), 29–45 (2004)
29. Codreanu, E., Michel, C., Bobillier-Chaumon, M.E., Vigneau, O.: Acceptation des Environnements Numériques de Travail par les Enseignants du Primaire. In: Conference Paper, EIAH 2015, 1–2 June, Agadir (2015)
30. Brangier, E., Dufresne, A., Hammes-Adele, S.: Approche symbiotique de la relation humain-technologie: perspectives pour l'ergonomie informatique. Le Travail Humain **72**(4), 333–353 (2009)
31. Barcenilla, J., Bastien, J.M.: L'acceptabilité des nouvelles technologies: quelles relations avec l'ergonomie, l'utilisabilité et l'expérience utilisateur? Le Travail Humain **72**, 311–331 (2009)
32. Nielsen, J.: Usability Engineering. Morgan Kaufman Publishers, New York (1994)
33. Bastien, J.M., Scapin, D.L.: Ergonomic Criteria for the evaluation of Human-Computer Interfaces. Institut National de recherche en Informatique et en Automatique (1993)
34. Hourcade, J.P.: Interaction Design and Children. Now Publishers Inc., Hanover (2007)
35. Lueder, R., Rice, V.J.: Ergonomics for Children: Designing Products and Places for Toddlers to Teens. Taylor & Francis, New York (2007)
36. Budiu, R., Nielsen, J.: Children (Ages 3–12) on the Web (2nd edition). NN Group (2010)
37. Carroll, J.M., Rosson, M.B.: Participatory design in community informatics. Des. Stud. **28**, 243–261 (2007)
38. Carroll, J.M.: Building educational technology partnerships through participatory design. In: Khosrow-Pour, M. (eds.) Encyclopedia on information Science and Technology, Second Edition (2008)
39. Baek, J.S., Lee, K.P.: A participatory design approach to information architecture design for children. In: CoDesign: International CoCreation in Design and the Arts 4(3), 173–191 (2008)
40. Sucupura-Furtado, M.E.: Improving the usability of interactive learning systems: the best practices of requirements engineering. In: Khosrow-Pour, M. (eds.) Encyclopedia of Information Science and Technology, Second Edition (2008)

41. Konings, K., Seidel, T., Van Merrienboer, J.: Participatory design of learning environments: integrating perspectives of student, teachers, and designers. Instr. Sci. 42(1) (2014). doi: 10.1007/s11251-013-9305-2
42. Konings, K., van Zundert, M., Bran-Gruwel, S., van Merrienboer, J.: Participatory design in secondary education: its desirability and feasibility according to teachers and students. Educ. Stud. **33**, 445–465 (2007)
43. Chin, G.: A case study in the Participatory Design of a Collaborative Science Based Learning Environment. Blacksburg, Virginia (2004)
44. Jonsson, L.E.: Appropriating Technologies in Educational Practices. Goteburg Studies in Educational sciences 215. Ph.D. Thesis (2007)
45. Bobillier-Chaumon, M.E.: Acceptation située des TIC dans et par l'activité: Premiers étayages pour une clinique de l'usage. Psychologie du Travail et des Organisations (2016, in press)
46. Bobillier-Chaumon, M.E., Dubois, M.: L'adoption des technologies en situation professionnelle: quelles articulations possibles entre acceptabilité et acceptation? Le Travail Humain **72**, 355–382 (2009)
47. Engeström, Y., Miettinen, R., Punamaki, R.L.: Perspectives on Activity Theory. Cambridge University Press, Cambridge (1999)
48. Kuutti, K.: Activity theory as a potential framework for human-computer interaction research. In: Nardi, B. (ed.) Context and Consciousness. Activity Theory and Human Computer Interaction. The MIT Press, Cambridge (1996)
49. Rabardel, P., Bourmaud, G.: From computer to instrument system: a developmental perspective. Interact. Comput. **15**(5), 665–691 (2003)
50. Denzin, N.K.: Sociological Methods. McGraw-Hill, New York (1978)
51. Flanagan, J.C.: The critical incident technique. Psychol. Bull. **51**, 327–358 (1954)
52. Bardin, L.: L'analyse de contenu. PUF, Paris (1996)

Author Index

MIX
Papier aus verantwortungsvollen Quellen
Paper from responsible sources
FSC® C105338

If you have any concerns about our products,
you can contact us on
ProductSafety@springernature.com

In case Publisher is established outside the EU,
the EU authorized representative is:
Springer Nature Customer Service Center GmbH
Europaplatz 3, 69115 Heidelberg, Germany

Printed by Libri Plureos GmbH
in Hamburg, Germany